A Charlton Standard Catalogue

ROYAL DOULTON FIGURINES

Ninth Edition

Cyngor Sir Ddinbych

WEDI TYNNU ALLAN O STOC
WITHDRAWN FROM STOCK

Denbighshire County Council

By
Jean Dale

Introduction
by
Louise Irvine

W. K. Cross
Publisher

The Charlton Press

TORONTO, ONTARIO • PALM BEACH, FLORIDA

C46 0000 0341 088

COPYRIGHT AND TRADEMARK NOTICE

Copyright © 1981-2004 Charlton International Inc. All Rights Reserved
Photographs © Charlton International Inc. 1981-2004

The terms Charlton, Charlton's, The Charlton Press and abbreviations thereof are trademarks of Charlton International Inc. and shall not be used without written consent from Charlton International Inc.

No part of this publication, except the various numbering systems, may be reproduced, stored in a retrieval system, or transmitted in any form by or by any means, digital, electronic, mechanical, photocopying, recording, or otherwise, without the prior written permission of the copyright owner.

No copyright material may be used without written permission in each instance from Charlton International Inc. Permission is hereby given for brief excerpts to be used in newspapers, magazines, periodicals and bulletins, other than in the advertising of items for sale, providing the source of the material so used is acknowledged in each instance.

ROYAL DOULTON U.K. LIMITED

Products listed or shown were manufactured by Royal Doulton U.K. Limited. This book has been produced independently and neither the author nor the publisher has any connection whatsoever with either Royal Doulton U.K. Limited or the Royal Doulton International Collectors Club. Royal Doulton is a registered trademark and is used in this book with the permission of Royal Doulton U.K. Limited. Any opinions expressed are those of the author and not necessarily endorsed by Royal Doulton U.K. Limited.

Royal Doulton figures and their images are the intellectual property of Royal Doulton U.K. Limited. All publication rights and copyrights of these images are the property of the owners.

Royal Doulton U.K. Ltd.:	The words Royal Doulton are a registered trademark of Royal Doulton U.K. Limited and are used herein to express items of collector interest. This book makes reference to various Royal Doulton figurines. The copyright of which belong to Royal Doulton U.K. Limited.

OTHER COPYRIGHTS

Disney Enterprises, Inc.:	This book makes reference to various DISNEY characters. The copyrights to these characters are owned by Disney Enterprises, Inc.
Turner Entertainment Co.:	GONE WITH THE WIND, its characters and elements are trademarks of Turner Entertainment Co & The Stephens Mitchell Trusts © 2000 Turner Entertainment

Canadian Cataloguing in Publication Data

The National Library of Canada has catal

Royal Doulton figurines (Toronto, Ont.)
    Royal Doulton figurines : a Charlton

Biennial.
8th ed.—
Continues: Charlton standard catalogue
ISSN 1706-712X
ISBN 0-88968-286-0 (9th ed.)

1. Royal Doulton figurines - Catalogs.

NK4660.C54   738.8'2'0294   C2003-901660-9

LLYFRGELLOEDD SIR DDINBYCH DENBIGHSHIRE LIBRARIES	
C4600000341088	
L B C	31/03/2004
738 . 38075	£22.95
*	RL

Printed in Canada
in the Province of Ontario

EDITORIAL

Editor	Jean Dale
Editorial Assistant	Susan Cross
Graphic Technician	Davina Rowan
Colour Technician	Marina Tsourkis
Cover Figurine	Princess Badoura, Style Two, HN 4179

ACKNOWLEDGEMENTS

The Charlton Press wished to thank those who have helped with the ninth edition of *The Charlton Standard Catalogue of Royal Doulton Figurines*.

SPECIAL THANKS

The publisher would like to thank Louise Irvine for writing the introduction to *Royal Doulton Figurines*, and for her research in connection with the Doulton Lambeth and Vellum sections. Louise Irvine is an independent writer and lecturer on Royal Doulton's history and products.

Our thanks go to the staff of Royal Doulton, who have helped with additional technical information, especially **Fiona Hawthorne**, General Manager, Director and Relationship Manager (U.K.); **Sarah Williams**, Product Manager, Royal Doulton (U.K.); **David Lovatt**, Marketing Communications Design Manager (U.K.), **Josie Hunt** and **Julie Tilestone**, Doulton & Company Doulton Direct (U.K.); **Julie Mountford**, International Collectors Club (U.K.); **Chetna Luhar**, Product Manager, Royal Doulton Collectables (U.K.); **Marion Proctor**, Marketing Manager (Canada), **Tricia A. Clemens** Brand Manager, Giftware and Collectables, (Canada); **Janet Drift**, Vice President Retail Sales (U.S.A.)

CONTRIBUTORS TO THE NINTH EDITION

The publisher would like to thank the following individuals or companies who graciously supplied photographs, date and other valuable information for the ninth edition. We offer sincere thanks to:

Nick Bevan, Swansea, U.K.**;** **Mary Dolph** of Marcus and Company, Newmarket, Ontario, Canada; **Melissa Dysart**, Precious Memories, P.E.I.; **Albert Grice**; **Jayne McEwen**, U.K.; **Ed Pascoe**, Pascoe and Company, Florida; **Paul Pound**, Precious Memories Fine China Gifts and Collectables; **Carol Stamps**; **Mrs. Wendy Tomlin**, Buckinghamshire, U.K.; **Philip Wilson**, U.K.; **Stan Worrey**, Colonial House Collectibles, Ohio, and all the past contributors who over the years have supplied so much important information that has helped establish this catalogue as the standard reference.

A SPECIAL NOTE TO COLLECTORS

We welcome and would appreciate any comments or suggestions in regard to *The Charlton Standard Catalogue of Royal Doulton Figurines*. If any errors or omissions come to your attention, please write to us, or if you would like to participate in pricing or supply previously unavailable data or information, please contact Jean Dale at (416) 488-1418 or e-mail us at chpress@charltonpress.com.

DISCLAIMER

While every care has been taken to ensure accuracy in the compilation of the data in this catalogue, the publisher cannot accept responsibility for typographical errors.

The Charlton Press

Editorial Office
P. O. Box 820, Station Willowdale B
North York, Ontario M2K 2R1 Canada
Telephone: (416) 488-1418 Fax: (416) 488-4656
Telephone: (800) 442-6042 Fax: (800) 442-1542
www.charltonpress.com
e-mail: chpress@charltonpress.com

PRICING AND THE INTERNET

Over the past thirty years we have gathered pricing information from auctions, dealer submissions, direct mail catalogues and newsletters, all contributed prices on one of two levels, wholesale or retail. We, at the Charlton Press, consider auctions basically a dealer affair, while price lists, naturally retail. To equate both prices, we needed to adjust the auction results upward, by a margin of 30% to 40%, allowing for dealer markups, before comparing and then looking for a consensus on a retail price.

The marketplace has changed, the Internet and on-line auctions are growing at such a rate that all other pricing sources we used are being completely overwhelmed by the sheer weight of the items being offered.

Below is a table to illustrate this growth. On the left under categories is a list of English brands that have produced collectables for the past hundred years. Across the top from left to right are four dates starting with January 4, 2001 and ending with December 9, 2003, below each date is the number of items offered for sale at that instant on a major Internet on-line auction.

Items for sale at a point in time from 2001 to 2003.

Category	Jan. 4th 2001	Jan. 4th 2002	Jan. 4th 2003	Dec. 9th 2003
Royal Doulton	3,500	3,700	5,700	8,200
Beswick	600	1,000	1,400	1,950
Coalport	300	525	800	1,450
Moorcroft	250	300	400	525
Royal Worcester	600	800	1,150	1,850
Wade	3,150	3,450	4,250	5,500
Total items	8,400	9,775	13,700	19,475

At that moment in time, December 9, 2003, under the Royal Doulton category 8,200 individual items were up for sale. For the six brands the total approached 19,500 items.

Comparing the totals of 8,400 for January 2001 with 19,475 for December 2003, we are witnessing a growth of more than 130% in the four year period, carrying the calculations forward to a yearly level, we first, must assume that items are added at a rate equal to the number expiring. The assumption does have flaws, for all days are not equal, due to ebb and flow of the items. However, assuming all is equal, Royal Doulton over a period of a year had 2,993,000 items listed (8,200 x 365) an extremely large number when equated to the Land Auctions that may not exceed 10% of that number for all auction catagories.

The impact the Internet will have on collectables has yet to be appreciated by collectors and dealers alike. All the old avenues such as fairs, shows, dealer stores, retail outlets, direct mail houses and auction rooms are being forced to change due to the extreme pressure of this marketing venue. Margins have come under pressure, wholesale and retail prices are starting to blend, and competition for the Collectors' budget will intensify. However, through it all one point remains, a price guide is just that, a guide, the final say is between the buyer and the seller.

HOW TO USE THIS CATALOGUE

On the pages that follow, Royal Doulton figurines are listed, illustrated, described and cross-referenced in numerical order by **HN** and **M** numbers. Their **Names** immediately follow their numbers. When two or more figures have the same name - but different physical modelling characteristics - they are listed as Style One, Style Two and so on after their names, starting with the first one issued. Such figures will also have different HN numbers. When known, the figurine's modeller or **Designer** is listed next. What then follows is the figure's **Height**, given in inches and centimeters. The actual **Colourway** of the figure is listed next. The **Dates** of issue and discontinuation are next.

The HN numbers of all **Varieties** are then listed. Varieties are minor mould changes, decorative alterations, and slight size differences due to firing. An example of a minor mould change would be The Carpet Seller HN 1464 (hand open) and HN 1464A (hand closed). Different physical modelling characteristics constitute different styles, dictating different HN numbers, and so are not varieties. If the figure is part of a **Series**, then a series name is given next.

The final listing gives the **Price**, the current market value of the figure described. The price appears in U.S. funds, then Canadian dollars and then U.K. Sterling Pounds.

Although the publisher has made every attempt to obtain and photograph all figurines and their varieties, several pieces naturally have not come before the publisher's camera. In a number of cases when the image is unobtainable, a photograph of a variety has been used in its place. The reader is cautioned then, that photographs are to be used for shape and design characteristics only. The more specific details of a figurine (i.e., Colourway) should be determined from the actual information printed below the specific figure.

INSURING YOUR FIGURINES

As with any other of your valuables, making certain figurines are protected is a very important concern. It is paramount that you display or store any porcelain items in a secure place - preferably one safely away from traffic in the home.

Your figurines are most often covered under your basic homeowner's policy and there are generally three kinds of such policies - standard, broad and comprehensive. Each has its own specific deductible and terms.

Under a general policy, your figurines are considered 'contents' and are covered for all of the perils covered under the contractual terms of your policy (fire, theft, water damage and so on).

However, since figurines are extremely delicate, breakage is treated differently by most insurance companies. There is usually an extra premium attached to insure figures against accidental breakage by or carelessness of the owner. This is sometimes referred to as 'fine arts' rider. You are advised to contact your insurance professional to get all the answers.

In order to help you protect yourself, it is critical that you take inventory of your figurines and have Colour photographs taken of all your pieces. This is the surest method of clearly establishing, for the police and your insurance company, the items lost or destroyed. It is also the easiest way to establish their replacement value in the event of a tragedy.

CONTENTS

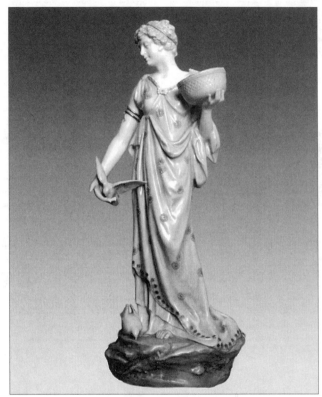

St. Mark's Birds by Charles Noke

INTRODUCTION
By Louise Irvine

THE HISTORY OF ROYAL DOULTON FIGURES

The history of Royal Doulton dates back to 1815 when John Doulton became involved in a little pottery in Lambeth on the banks of the River Thames in London. Trading as Doulton and Watts, they made general stonewares, such as ink wells and ginger beer bottles for daily use. When John's son, Henry, joined the firm in 1835 the business expanded rapidly producing chemical and industrial ceramics. The young entrepreneur also set up a new factory supplying drainpipes to service major cities around the world. The success of this sanitary ware business eventually enabled Henry Doulton to pursue more artistic interests and in 1867 he employed a young sculptor, George Tinworth, to establish an art pottery studio in Lambeth. Tinworth's monumental sculptures and decorative vases quickly focused public attention on this new venture and more artists were recruited until, by the mid 1880s, there were over 300 young men and women producing vases, figures and other ornaments for the Victorian home.

During his long career at the Lambeth studio, Tinworth modelled a wide range of figures, mainly of chubby children at play and animals in human situations. The medium he used is known as salt glaze stoneware, a high-fired clay body, literally glazed with salt. Tinworth's colleague John Broad also used this material as well as terracotta to produce royal portraits, military figures and female studies in classical style. He was a very versatile artist and his figures could range from six inches for the mantlepiece to six feet in height for the garden. He also introduced some fashionable ladies modelled in white bisque porcelain, as did fellow artist Mark Marshall.

The last modeller of note to join the Lambeth studio was Leslie Harradine who contributed a variety of stoneware figure subjects in the early 1900s, some of which were slip-cast in small editions. During the 1920s several of his Lambeth figures, including his Dickens characters, were reproduced in the famous HN collection at Doulton's other factory in Burslem, Stoke-on-Trent.

Henry Doulton invested in the Nile Street pottery at Burslem in 1877 in order to manufacture tableware and ornamental ware at the centre of the British ceramic industry. Charles Noke, an experienced modeller from the Worcester factory, was recruited in 1889 to model exhibition vases but within a few years he had also produced a range of figures. These Vellum figures, as they are now known, are very different in style from the examples sold in china shops today. They are much larger than contemporary models, some nearly 20 inches tall, and they are much less colourful. Most have an ivory body with tinted and gilded decoration by the leading studio artists and they bear a strong resemblance to the figures produced at Worcester.

Noke's first figure, introduced in 1892, was an extraordinary double-sided model depicting Mephistopheles and Marguerite from Faust, as played by the great Victorian acting duo, Henry Irving and Ellen Terry. The theatre, and these actors in particular, inspired many of Noke's early studies and his interest in the stage continued throughout his career. A selection of the early Vellum figures was shown at the Chicago exhibition of 1893 but they do not seem to have captured the public imagination, perhaps because they were very expensive. Despite their disappointing reception, Charles Noke continued to add occasional figures to the collection and by 1900 he had produced 21 free-standing figures and four wall-mounted models. Only a very limited number of each design was ever produced making them extremely hard to find today and until recently they were not well documented. However,

serious collectors are gradually recognizing the desirability of these distinctive models.

Ellen Terry as Queen Catharine, Henry Irving as Wolsey

In the opening years of the 20th century, Charles Noke was preoccupied with the development of other Doulton ranges and no new figures were produced. He did, however, experiment with smaller sizes and brighter colours for his existing designs to widen their appeal. For example, his early study of a Jester was given a suit of motley colours and it eventually became one of the most popular figures in the collection.

Noke was convinced that a revival of the 18th century Staffordshire figure tradition was desirable and feasible at the Doulton studio but he was aware that he could not achieve his goal alone. Accordingly, in 1909, he began to invite well-known independent sculptors to submit designs that they thought would be suitable for reproducing as small scale ceramic figures. By 1912 he had accumulated the nucleus of a collection and he decided to launch the new range during King George and Queen Mary's visit to the factory in 1913. The Queen was very impressed with the figures, particularly a study of a little child in a nightgown by Charles Vyse. Apparently she exclaimed "isn't he a darling" and the figure was later named **Darling** in her honour and given the first number in the collection, HN1. The 'HN' refers to Harry Nixon who was in charge of the new figure painting department, which comprised three artists in the early years. The HN numbering system is still used today and the company has issued over 4,000 numbers although they are not all new models: some are assigned to colourways of existing figures and some to animal subjects.

Between the Royal visit and the end of the decade, 80 figures were introduced and their relative popularity is recorded in some surviving production statistics for the years 1913-17. During this period 680 figures were produced, an average of three a week, and **Darling** (HN1) was by far the most popular with 148 sold, compared with 51 orders for the **Crinoline** (HN8) the first 'fair lady' figure, which was modelled by George Lambert, an Australian artist working in England. Doulton's first 'street vendor' figure **Madonna of the Square** (HN10), by London sculptor Phoebe Stabler, sold 35 in the first three years whilst there were 40 orders for **A Spook** (HN50) by the talented in-house artist Harry Tittensor. Less than a dozen copies of some subjects were produced making these amongst the rarest figures to buy today. According to the records there were only seven orders for Noke's **Pedlar Wolf** (HN7) in these early years, which explains why it is particularly elusive today along with his other bizarre subjects **Boy on a Crocodile** (HN373) and **Child on a Crab** (HN32).

Noke continued to draw upon the ideas and talents of other artists, most significantly Leslie Harradine who had worked for Doulton's factory in Lambeth from 1902-12. He left to farm with his brother in Saskatchewan, Canada, but the First World War interrupted their new life and, after fighting in Europe, Harradine eventually returned to England. When Noke heard of his return he endeavoured to persuade him to work in the Potteries but Harradine valued his new found independence too much and agreed instead to work on a freelance basis, first from his studio in Kent and then from the Channel Islands. His first figure **The Princess** (HN391) was introduced in 1920 along with **Contentment** (HN395), which was purchased by Queen Mary at the British Industries Fair that year.

For more than 30 years, Harradine sent at least one model a month to Stoke, sometimes two or three, and they ranged from stylish ladies dressed in the latest fashions, such as **The Sunshine Girl** (HN1344) or **Scotties** (HN1281), to penetrating studies of Dickens' characters. Some of his figures from the 1920s are still being made today, for example **The Balloon Man** (HN1954) of 1940. Such was the demand for Harradine's figures that the painting department was expanded to 10 artists by 1927, many of whom were transferred from painting bone china vases and dessert services following a slump in that market. Thus some of Doulton's most talented artists, including the bird painter Harry Allen and the game painter Charles Hart, introduced their considerable expertise to the decoration of Doulton figures. Many alternative colourways were produced during this decade and most involved several firings to achieve the subtle shaded effects. By the end of the decade nearly 200 new figures had been introduced, most of them the work of Leslie Harradine.

Harradine also dominated the output of the 1930s and in 1937 he introduced his most popular figure ever **Top o' the Hill** (HN1833). Many of his most successful pretty ladies were also introduced in a miniature size between 1932 and 1939, enabling collectors with limited display space to enjoy a wide range of his work. Some of the miniatures figures were mounted on ashtrays, calendars and bookends so that they could be useful as well as decorative whilst the larger ladies were incorporated in electric lamps with complimentary shades.

Harradine's 1930s lady figures, for example **Aileen** (HN1645) and **Rhythm** (HN1903), reflect the sophisticated elegance of the period with glamorous evening gowns, as worn in the Hollywood movies by Greta Garbo and others. Gone were the boyish fashions of the 1920s with their short tube-like dresses and cropped hairstyles. As the decade progressed, more famous porcelain artists joined the figure decorating department, notably the flower painter Percy Curnock, so that by 1939 there were 27 painters at work on the collection. The influence of these master painters can be seen most clearly in the faces of the 1930s fair ladies which have much more expression than the earlier models. Instead of the dark 'button' eyes of the 1920s, the iris and pupil are clearly delineated and the lips are brightly painted in one of the fashionable lipstick

shades. This more detailed approach to face painting began around 1934 and can be used as a guide to dating figures.

The Second World War limited the production of figures as luxury goods could only be made for export and, in addition, many of the experienced artists joined the armed forces. It was a time of assessment and appraisal and many of the early figures were discontinued between 1941 and 1949. Charles Noke retired in 1941 but Peggy Davies, who had been engaged as an assistant modeller before the war, decided to set up her own studio and produce figures on a contract basis for Royal Doulton. Her first, in 1946, was **Christmas Morn** (HN1992) and this was followed by **Minuet** (HN2019), a delightful study of a dancer in Regency costume. Peggy was fascinated with fashion and history and enjoyed all the research necessary to produce realistic, accurate figures. One of her most successful early collections portrayed eight illustrious ladies from English history and these are very sought after today.

From the mid 1950s Peggy worked with the new art director Jo Ledger and produced several figures in a contemporary style, mostly teenagers with ponytails and flat pumps. Her most significant piece from this era was the **Marriage of Art and Industry** (HN2261), which was designed for the Brussels exhibition of 1958. Only 12 copies of this prestigious figure were made and they were not on public sale. Peggy rapidly proved her diversity as an artist producing historical characters, fair ladies, ballerinas and other dancers, child studies and later prestige collections. More and more she dominated the collection as Harradine prepared for retirement, contributing his last figure **Dimity** (HN2169) in 1956.

Mary Nicoll's matt figures The Judge and Parisian

A new talent, Mary Nicoll, appeared on the scene in the mid 1950s. Her father had been illustrating books for the company and he effected an introduction. It soon became apparent that this young artist had tremendous potential as a character figure modeller. In 1955 she began to contribute a wide range of nautical personalities, street entertainers and historical characters, which she modelled in her Devon studio and sent to Stoke on a regular basis. During the 1950s and 1960s nearly all the figures were produced by Mary Nicoll and Peggy Davies. Although Peggy was primarily concentrating on crinoline ladies at this time, she also undertook some ambitious large scale subjects, including the **Matador and Bull** (HN2324), the **Indian Brave** (HN2376) and the **Palio** (HN2428), all of which raised the potential of the ceramic medium to its limits, so intricate and complex were her designs.

Peggy continued this prestige work in the 1970s with several extremely popular limited edition collections. **The Lady Musicians**, **Femmes Fatales** and **Dancers of the World** were produced under the supervision of the new Director of Sculpture, Eric Griffiths. He had joined the company in 1972 and his early training as a portrait painter soon became evident in his choice of famous subjects for the figures collection. Good examples are the actor Laurence Olivier and various members of the British Royal family. Eric Griffiths preferred working on a larger scale than the average 8 inch tall Doulton figure and in 1974 he introduced a collection of figures, around 12 inches tall, entitled **Haute Ensemble**. He also advocated the use of a matt finish, believing that a shiny glaze obscured some of the finer points of detail and several of Mary Nicoll's character studies were issued in the matt style.

Sadly, Mary died in 1974, but the character figure range was continued by Bill Harper, a versatile modeller with considerable experience in the ceramic industry. He has been responsible for such perennial favourites as the **Punch and Judy Man** (HN2765) and **Thanks Doc** (HN2731), which is essentially a self portrait. Amongst the other sculptors who worked for the collection during the 1970s were Robert Jefferson, Douglas Tootle, Peter Gee, Alan Maslankowski and Robert Tabbenor. Most of these artists still work for the company today.

Not surprisingly, after some 90 years of figure production Royal Doulton had a 'huge' collector following and in 1978 the first book to document the HN range, **Royal Doulton Figures**, was written by Desmond Eyles and Richard Dennis. Prior to this reference work there had been no concept of rarity on the secondary market and all the figures had sold in the region of $75 - $100. Now it was apparent that some figures were more desirable that others, depending on how attractive they were and how long they had been in production. Some models had not been found in time for illustration in the first edition of the book and the hunt was on for these elusive pieces, with prices escalating accordingly. A second edition was published in 1989, including many of the rare commissions as well as all the new models produced during the 1980s.

In response to the new collecting boom of the 1980s, Royal Doulton introduced many new series of figures appealing to different tastes and budgets. Several featured children, such as **Characters from Children's Literature** and **Childhood Days**. For those interested in royalty and history there were portraits of the current Royal family as well as historical **Queens of the Realm** and for collectors of the crinoline ladies there was the modestly priced **Vanity Fair** range of figures that were very simply decorated. A new contemporary look was achieved in 1981 with the **Images** range of stylised, symbolic sculptures in black basalt or white bone china. In 1987 the **Reflections** range of attenuated figures in fashionable pastel shades was launched.

To keep collectors abreast of all these new developments a Collectors Club was established in 1980 and many figures were commissioned exclusively for members, notably **Prized Possessions** (HN2942) by Robert Tabbenor. This piece features a lady collector consulting the figures book with her latest acquisition by her side. Another popular club commission was **Sleepy Darling** (HN2953) by Pauline Parsons, inspired by Doulton's first figure in the HN collection. Like most of the members' exclusives, it was only made for a six month period. Pauline Parsons has produced other models for the Club and is now one of the foremost modellers of the 'fair lady' figures following Peggy's retirement in 1984. Eric Griffiths also retired at the end of 1990 and a new era has begun with the appointment of Amanda Hughes Lubeck, Doulton's first female art director. It will be interesting to see what the future holds under this new direction as Royal Doulton enters its second century of figure production.

BUILDING A COLLECTION

Since the 1890s, more that 2,500 figures have been added to the range and these are now avidly collected in many parts of the world. It would be virtually impossible to acquire them all, even if space and budget allowed, but there is plenty of scope to build interesting collections, based on artist, period, style or theme.

COLLECTING LAMBETH FIGURES

Royal Doulton's famous HN series is known and appreciated all over the world, but few collectors are aware of the other types of Royal Doulton figures made at their Lambeth factory in London. They are quite different in appearance from their Burslem counterparts, being made of salt glaze stoneware or terracotta, and they are scarce in the market place as they were produced in very limited numbers.

George Tinworth, Doulton's first resident sculptor, often included human figures in practical items, such as candlesticks, menu holders and spill vases, but in the 1890s he produced an extensive collection of free-standing figures featuring boys playing musical instruments. These **Merry Musicians** have been recorded playing about 40 different instruments. They stand around 5 inches high and are executed in a plain brown stoneware body, although some have white faces. Occasionally, Tinworth produced other figurative subjects, such as the teatime group, Scandal, and a portrait of his favourite Dickens character, **Mr. Pickwick**, but these seem to have been unique pieces. A notable exception is the terracotta figure of a jester that he made for the Art Union of London in an edition of 12, around 1900.

One of the most versatile figure modellers at the Lambeth factory was **John Broad**, who was equally at home producing small studies with the aid of a magnifying glass and huge monumental commissions that required scaffolding. He particularly enjoyed working in terracotta and one of his first small-scale figures in this medium was a study of a **Thrower** in 1883. Later terracotta figures by Broad include a devotional statuette of **Our Lady** and a study of **Pomona**, the classical goddess of fruit.

Broad also modelled some delightful studies of classical maidens in salt glaze stoneware, and these were reproduced in limited numbers before and after the First World War, as denoted by their X pattern numbers. The different numbers for **Atalanta** (X7910 and X8707) and the **Bather** (X7912 and X8706) denote different types of stoneware, either plain brown or fully coloured (also known as Doultonware).

Important national events in the early 1900s, such as the Boer War, Nelson's Centenary, the death of Queen Victoria and the coronation of her son, inspired Broad to produce a number of commemorative figures, including handsome terracotta portraits of **King Edward** and **Queen Alexandra**, a faience figure of **Nelson** and imposing salt glaze stoneware studies of **Queen Victoria** and the **Boer War Soldier**.

During the First World War, Doulton developed a hard paste porcelain body for making laboratory ware, and John Broad used this new medium, with either a biscuit or glost finish, for some delicate figures of pretty ladies. His porcelain figures, particularly the portraits of the American actress **Doris Keane**, were a major influence on the HN collection in Burslem, as indeed were the pretty lady figures by **Mark Marshall**. Although Marshall is best known for his art nouveau style vases, adorned with grotesque dragons and reptiles, he dabbled occasionally in figurative sculpture, producing fashionable ladies in white glazed stoneware, accented in blue. His **Crinoline** of 1910 is almost identical to the figure of the same name (HN13) introduced a few years later in Burslem.

Marshall, Broad and Tinworth all helped train the young **Leslie Harradine** when he joined the Lambeth studio in 1902. Unlike his mentors, Harradine's special interest was modelling ornamental figures and animals and he disliked having to design vases for reproduction. Broad's **Boer War soldier** inspired him to produce a group of contemporary soldiers in salt glaze stoneware, including a **British Tommy**, a **French Legionaire**, a **North African Spahi** and a **Cossack**, whilst Marshall's pretty ladies prompted elegant figures such as **Polly Peachum**.

Most importantly, Tinworth's enthusiasm for The Pickwick Papers led Harradine to discover all the colourful characters created by Charles Dickens, and he modelled a selection of stoneware figures in time for the centenary of Dickens' birth in 1912. These were made of slip cast stoneware on square bases and were available in brown, buff or coloured Doultonware. Harradine also modelled different versions of the Dickens characters in rich brown stoneware, and these were reproduced in the HN collection (HN553-558) in 1923. He also modelled a set of miniature Dickens figures as prototypes for the HN collection and these were introduced in 1922.

Dicken's Fat Boy
Stoneware version (left), HN 555 (right)

Harradine spent little time in London after he completed his apprenticeship, preferring to work in his country studio in Hertfordshire, where he produced some powerful studies of farm workers, notably **The Harvester**, **The Peat Cutter** and The Reaper. This last character was available in three different effects, plain brown stoneware, coloured Doultonware and brighter 'toby'

colours. European peasants were also favourite subjects, and he modelled a very striking group of two Brittany peasants gossiping, a mother with her baby and some Dutch characters.

Several of Harradine's models were reproduced in white slip cast stoneware, sometimes with blue detailing, and these were allocated H pattern numbers along with his animal models and vase designs. They remained in production long after Harradine had left Doulton to emigrate to Canada. After serving in the First World War, Harradine returned to the UK and worked on a freelance basis for Charles Noke, the art director of the Burslem studio, where he became better known as the star modeller of the HN collection.

Harradine's departure from London virtually marked the end of purely ornamental figures at the Lambeth studio. Harry Simeon did some sterling work reviving the Staffordshire toby jug tradition, and little stoneware figures of Toby Philpotts and related characters were incorporated in match stands and ashtrays during the mid 1920s. At the same time, he also included models of a pixie and Pan playing his pipes in a range of bibelots or trinket trays.

Occasionally freelance artists contributed designs for reproduction at the Lambeth studio, but these are even harder to find than the work of the resident modellers. Around 1912, the successful sculptor Stanley Nicholson Babb contributed a figure of a **Lute Player**, which was issued in salt glaze stoneware in a small edition. Twenty years later, Richard Garbe, a professor at the Royal College of Art, produced several designs in conjunction with the Lambeth studio, including a salt glaze stoneware figure of a **Sea Sprite**, which was based on a bronze original.

Another twenty years elapsed before figures were made again at Lambeth, this time by Helen Walters, who worked at the studio between 1953 and 1956. Two of her salt glaze stoneware figures were exhibited at the Royal Academy, and her study of **Demeter** was purchased by Stoke City Art Gallery. It was probably the last figure model to be fired in the Lambeth kilns, as the factory closed down in 1956, thus ending another remarkable chapter in the story of Royal Doulton figures.

COLLECTING VELLUM FIGURES

In the 1890s, some twenty years before the HN collection was launched, Charles Noke was experimenting with a very different style of Doulton figures. Known as the Vellum figures, because of their parchment colour, they are very similar to the work he was doing at the Worcester factory in the 1880s.

Usually the Vellum figures are tinted with soft sheens of pink and green, but occasionally bolder on-glaze colours are used, such as scarlet or black. Gold highlights were often added and sometimes intricate printed patterns of flowers. Each figure is slightly different, thanks to the varied talents of the prestige artists who worked in Robert Allen's decorating studio. Generally the Vellum figures are much larger than the HN models, ranging from 10 to 20 inches in height, and they were made in very small editions.

In the past, collectors tended to overlook these early Noke designs as they do not come onto the market very often and information was scarce. However, there has been a new awareness of the Vellum models ever since they were catalogued in the classic reference book, Royal Doulton Figures. Their pioneering status is now fully recognised, and connoisseurs around the world appreciate the quality of Noke's early modelling and the decorative skills of Robert Allen's artists.

Most of the themes explored in the Vellum figure range preoccupied Noke throughout his modelling career. There are jesters, pierrots and other entertainers from the Victorian stage. His admiration for the acting talents of Henry Irving and Ellen Terry led to several models of them in famous roles, including **Shylock** and

Portia from "The Merchant of Venice," **Mephistopheles** and **Marguerite** from "Faust" and **Cardinal Wolsey** and **Queen Catharine** from "Henry VIII." This last pair the most popular, as they turn up most frequently today.

It would appear that **The Devil** was also based on Henry Irving's role in Faust. New discoveries are still being made in the Vellum range, notably an imposing figure of Lily Langtry as **Cleopatra**, which was not recorded in the Doulton archives. More recently **The Moorish Minstrel** has come to light as part of a candlestick.

Vellum figures of Shylock and Portia

Many of the Vellum figures also served practical purposes, either being incorporated into light fittings or flower holders. The Lady Jester, **The Sorceress** and **The Geisha** were all made with flat backs for wall mounting as vases, whilst **The Witch** was a wall mounted electric light, with the bulb at the end of her broomstick!

Charles Noke showed his first Vellum figures at the Chicago exhibition of 1893, but the reception was luke-warm. Perhaps the colouring was too bland for the taste of the times and they were very expensive. Noke continued to exhibit the figures in Paris (1900), St. Louis (1904) and Christchurch (1906), and it is likely that they continued to be made in small numbers until work on the HN collection began in 1909.

Some of the most successful Vellum models were later reissued in brighter colours as HN figures, notably The **Jester**, **Jack Point**, **Cardinal Wolsey** and **Queen Catharine**. Other Vellum designs can also be found with on-glaze enamel colours, even though they were never assigned HN numbers, for example, The **Kneeling Jester** and **The Witch**.

In all, 21 free-standing Vellum figures have been recorded in a variety of colourways, plus four wall mounted pieces. Perhaps there are even more models waiting to be discovered. Forming a complete collection would be a challenging but rewarding experience if patience and purse strings allow.

COLLECTING THE HN SERIES BY ARTIST

New collectors quickly gravitate towards a particular style of figure and often discover that they favour the work of a specific artist. In the early years the artist was acknowledged on the base of the figures and collectors could appreciate the diverse modelling skills of artists such as Charles Noke, Harry Tittensor and others. After a gap of many years, this practice was revived in 1984 when the artist's facsimile signature was incorporated into the backstamp, making identification as easy as it had been previously.

The work of each Doulton artist has a distinctive quality, even though their figures might be classified with many others as 'fair ladies' or 'character studies.' An experienced eye can quickly spot the difference between a Peggy Davies crinoline lady and one by Leslie Harradine. Similarly Mary Nicoll's nautical figures are quite distinct from Bill Harper's. Each of these artists has a wide following and the scope for collecting their work is often vast and varied, particularly in the case of Peggy Davies, who produced about 250 figures in her 40 year career with Royal Doulton.

COLLECTING BY PERIOD

It has been said of Royal Doulton figures that they are a reflection of the times in which they are made. Certainly, with many of the subjects it is possible to attribute them to a particular period, based on costume, fabric designs and hair styles. The bright young things of the 1920s, such as **Lido Lady** (HN1200) and **Angela** (HN1204) with their negligees and lounging pyjamas, are amongst the most appealing of these period figures but collections can also be formed from other decades. The glamorous style of the 1930s, inspired by the Hollywood stars, is represented in figures such as **Gloria** (HN1488) and **Clothilde** (HN1598) whilst the teenage trends of the 1950s can be seen in Faraway (HN2133) and **Sweet Sixteen** (HN2231).

For the fashion conscious, it is possible to create a cat-walk of costumes through the ages from the Medieval period to the 20th century. Some collectors focus exclusively on 18th century style costumes, as worn by **Antoinette** (HN1850) and **Kate Hardcastle** (HN1861), which were notable for their wide hooped skirts adorned with ribbons, bows and ruffles of lace. Others prefer Victorian dresses with their flounced skirts and frothy petticoats, represented by such pieces as **Spring Morning** (HN1922) and **Chloe** (HN1470). Whether it be hats (from wimples to poke bonnets), or fluttering fans, even ladies' fashionable accessories have inspired collections.

COLLECTING BY SUBJECT

Child Studies

Darling, the first figure in the HN collection, was so successful that it was soon followed by many more child studies. Consequently, there is plenty of scope to form a delightful collection, whether it includes the sort of children who were 'seen but not heard' in Victorian times, like **Monica** (HN1467) or **Lily** (HN1798), or the mischievous kids of today like **Pillow Fight** (HN2270) and **Lights Out** (HN2262). There are many popular series inspired by childhood, including Leslie Harradine's **Nursery Rhymes** figures and the **Age of Innocence** series. Many of the latest child studies incorporate animals and the special relationship young children enjoy with their pets would be an interesting theme to explore with both new and discontinued figures. As well as puppies and kittens, Doulton children also play with teddies, dolls and other toys. It would be fun to track down a representative collection, although there will be competition from serious Teddy

Bear collectors. **Sleepyhead** (HN2114), cuddling her teddy, would be a very exciting discovery whilst **Nanny** (HN2221), mending her charge's teddy, is more readily available.

Fair Ladies

There are more fair ladies than any other type of Doulton figure so it is a good idea to specialize at an early stage. Collecting by artist has already been discussed and, as well as the great names of the past, such as Leslie Harradine and Peggy Davies, there are many talented modellers to look for today. Pauline Parsons has portrayed many famous **Queens of the Realm** and Peter Gee has been inspired by the famous paintings of **Gainsborough** and **Reynolds** ladies. The latest recruits to the studio are Nada Pedley and Valerie Annand who have given us romantic interpretations of Victorian and Edwardian fashions.

Faced with this wide choice, a popular approach is to collect by colour, choosing only shades which harmonize with the furnishings of particular rooms. For example, ladies dressed in pastel shades might be suitable for a bedroom whilst richer colours might be more appropriate for the lounge or dining room. Displays could be changed to match the seasons, with all the ladies dressed in yellow and green featured in the spring and all the red outfits at Christmas time. There are many Doulton figures which celebrate the festive season, including **Noelle** (HN2179) with her ermine trimmed cloak and muff and **Santa Claus** himself (HN2725).

Figures can also be used effectively as table centres, whatever the season, or as feature displays with flower arrangements. Some of the figures are even portrayed arranging bowls of tiny hand-made flowers, whilst others carry baskets of blooms, lavish bouquets or a single red rose, so a fair ladies collection could be 'all a blooming'.

Swirling voluminous gowns have inspired many collections of dancing ladies, most of them the work of Peggy Davies who excelled at conveying movement in the folds of the fabric. Peggy's talent in this area can be seen in **Ninette** (HN2379) and **Elaine** (HN2791). **Minuet** (HN2019), one of her earliest figures (HN2019) was inspired by the stately minuet and over the years she added **Polka** (HN2156) **First Waltz** (HN2862) and the flamboyant **Gypsy Dance** (HN2230). She also studied many national dances and costumes for her **Dancers of the World** collection.

Many collectors are influenced by the names of the figures, whether it be the sentiment conveyed or the name of a loved one. In some cases it has been possible to put together a 'family' of figures representing children, grandchildren, and so on. 'Fair ladies,' of course, can form part of much wider theme collections of the types suggested below.

Character Figures

As with the fair ladies there is a huge choice of character figures from all walks of life and most collectors look for a particular artist or theme. Art director Charles Noke specialized in character modelling and many of his personal interests can be seen in his range, including literature, history and the theatre. Leslie Harradine, renowned for his beautiful lady figures, was equally at home with characters, contributing country folk, such as **Lambing Time** (HN1890), and colourful street vendors selling balloons, silks and ribbons or fruit and flowers. One such example is **The Orange Seller** (HN1325).

Mary Nicoll dominated the character collection from the mid 1950s to the 1970s and she also launched the nautical figures, which are so popular with sea lovers today. She also developed a collection of figures featuring traditional crafts and professions, for example **The Clockmaker** (HN2279) and **The Judge** (HN2443) and she celebrated the twilight years in her studies of Old Dears, notably **Family Album** (HN2321) and **Teatime** (HN2255). All these successful sub-collections have been continued in recent years by Bill Harper, who has also recently expanded the London collection of characters with **The Lifeguard** (HN2781) and **The Guardsman** (HN2784). Former Art Director Eric Griffiths portrayed many members of the British Royal family before his retirement in 1991 and he was also responsible for the **Soldiers of the Revolution** collection of military figures.

Younger modellers are also making their mark. Robert Tabbenor is producing some fine sporting characters, such as **Teeing Off** (HN3276) and Alan Maslankowski has excelled with his limited edition historical subjects, notably **Christopher Columbus** (HN3392).

Any one of these themes can form the basis of a fascinating collection, which can become even more rewarding by researching the characters behind the figures.

The World of Entertainment

Collecting Royal Doulton figures can literally be an 'entertaining' hobby as many of the stars of stage and screen have been portrayed by Doulton modellers. From the pierrots of pantomime and seaside concerts, to the great Shakespearean roles played by Henry Irving and Ellen Terry, many of the earliest figures reflect Charles Noke's fascination with the theatre. A taste for the exotic is particularly evident in his work, stemming from the fashionable oriental flavour of many operas, musicals and ballets of the time. Examples are the **Mandarin** (HN84) and the **Eastern Cobbler** (HN542).

An interesting collection could include famous stage personalities of the past, such as the American actress **Doris Keane** (HN90), and more recent stars from the silver screen such as **Groucho Marx** (HN2777) and **Charlie Chaplin** (HN2771). As well as these classic clowns of the cinema, there are also lots of circus clowns by Mary Nicoll and Bill Harper to collect. Their ancestors of mirth, the court jesters, have also been popular characters in the figures collection since the earliest days, notably **Jack Point** (HN85) and **The Wandering Minstrel** (HN1224) from Gilbert and Sullivan's famous operettas.

The ballet has been a fertile source of inspiration for Doulton modellers from the great **Pavlova** (HN487) in her most famous role as 'The Dying Swan' to aspiring young dancers practising in frilly tutus, such as **Little Ballerina** (HN3395). Like many young girls, Peggy Davies had ambitions to be a ballerina and as a result she contributed many delightful studies of dancers, including **Coppelia** (HN2115) and **Giselle** (HN2140).

Music lovers can seek out figures playing instruments, whether they be an elegant orchestra of **Lady Musicians** or a precocious violinist such as **The Young Master** (HN2872). Even street performers, such as **The Organ Grinder** (HN2173) and **The Punch and Judy Man** (HN2765), could be included in this colourful revue of the world of entertainment.

Literature

Book lovers will enjoy all of the characters from literature that have been portrayed in the figure collection over the years. Classical myths, Eastern romances, European folklore and English classics have all provided inspiration for individual figures and series. Art Director Charles Noke was a great admirer of Shakespeare and he modelled the great bard himself for the Vellum range, as well as several of his characters. The novels of Charles Dickens were an even greater influence and there are several sets of his famous characters, including the very collectable miniatures. Children's books have also been a fertile source of ideas and, as well as the obvious collection of **Characters from Children's Literature,** there have been figures based on nursery rhymes, Kate Greenaway's picture books and Victorian classics, such as Treasure Island. The figure of this name depicts a young boy poring over the pages of Stevenson's great adventure yarn and pages from the book can be enjoyed with the aid of a magnifying glass. There are many other 'readers' in the figures range, including several others with legible books and this has become a particularly popular collecting theme. A representative display might include the scholarly **Professor** (HN2281) with his nose in a book, **The Wizard** (HN2877) who is consulting his book of spells, or some of the daydreaming fair ladies who rest closed books on their laps.

History

The figures collection is like a historical pageant with famous people from all ages commemorated in clay. It is to be expected that an English company would pay homage to British national heroes and heroines such as **Florence Nightingale** (HN3144) and more recently **Winston Churchill** (HN3057), but there are also many historical personalities from other countries. It would be possible for patriotic Americans to form a 'Stars and Stripes' collection, which might include the **Soldiers of the Revolution** or the **Characters from Williamsburg** series. Canadians can look for the unusual Mountie busts of **R.C.M.P. 1973** (HN2547) and **R.C.M.P. 1873** (HN2555) or the portrait figure of **Sir John A. MacDonald** (HN2860).

Those interested in military history could seek out the rare First World War soldiers, **Digger** (HN321-2) and **Blighty** (HN323) or the **Drummer Boy** (HN2679) from the Napoleonic Wars whilst naval historians could add **Captain Cook** (HN2889) or **The Captain** (HN2260) to a general seafaring collection.

The current British royal family has proved to be a popular collection in recent years and many of the Queen's illustrious ancestors have also been portrayed as Doulton figures. **Henry VIII** (HN370, 1792 and 3350) and **King Charles I** (HN404) are good examples. As well as the reigning monarchs, there have also been portraits of their consorts, courtiers and even one of their courtesans, **Nell Gwynne** (HN1882)!

COLLECTING BY SIZE

For collectors with limited display space miniature figures are particularly appealing. The M series was launched in 1932 but there had been miniature figures in the HN range before that, notably the tiny Dickens characters which were re-numbered in line with all the new introductions. By 1949, there were 24 Dickens characters in the M series and they continued in production with minor alterations until 1981-3.

The majority of the miniature fair ladies were scaled down versions of existing figures by Leslie Harradine. Although only three to four inches tall, the detailing of the costumes and accessories is exceptional, with tiny flower baskets ¾ inch across and parasols less than an inch long. As in the standard range of the 1930s, there was also a wide range of colourways and **Polly Peachum** has been found in at least 15 different costumes. Unfortunately, rising labour costs led to the withdrawal of the miniature ladies by 1949 and, as many had only been made for about 10 years, they are very elusive for today's collector. Consequently, their prices do not match their diminutive size and they can cost as much, or more, than their standard size counterparts.

Miniature figures were revived in 1988 when the Royal Doulton International Collectors Club commissioned a tiny version of the ever popular **Top o' the Hill** (HN2126). More fair ladies followed in quick succession, with special rich colourways produced exclusively for Michael Doulton's signature collection. All have been allocated HN numbers and are reduced versions of popular figures in the current range. A selection of miniature character figures was introduced in 1989 but these were not well received. Several were quickly withdrawn so they will no doubt become hard to find in the future.

Also easily accommodated in a small display area are the figures of young girls dressed in fashions of the past. These range in size from four to six inches tall and some, such as **Dinky Do** (HN1678) and **Monica** (HN1467) were in continuous production for over 50 years testifying to the appeal of this scale and subject matter.

Today, the average Doulton fair lady stands around eight inches tall, whilst seated subjects in proportion measure around six inches. Limited editions and character figures tend to be a little larger, averaging nine inches for standing subjects. Eric Griffiths, the former director of Sculpture, favoured larger scale figures, particularly for character portraits, as he believed a better likeness could be achieved. Consequently his figure of Lord Olivier as **Richard III** (HN2881) is above average size. He also introduced the **Haute Ensemble** series of tall, slender ladies and the attenuated **Images** and **Reflections** series.

In the past, there was much more variety of scale in the collection and figures of more than 12 inches in height were not unusual. **The Welsh Girl** (HN39) and **Lady With Shawl** (HN447) are good examples. Some large scale figures from the past now form the Prestige collection and Princess Badoura (HN2081), at 20 inches in height, is the largest in the range.

COLLECTING BY SERIES

Numerous collectors subscribe to Royal Doulton's established series of figures, many of which are limited editions. In these cases the company has already chosen all the characters to fit a specific theme and has defined the limits of the collection so there are fewer decisions required than with the more general themes already discussed. This method also allows collectors to budget for forthcoming annual introductions in the more expensive limited edition series.

Some of the recently discontinued series are becoming increasingly difficult to find and it could take some time to find all 18 of the **Kate Greenaway** figures or all 24 **Dickens** miniatures. There always seems to be one or two figures in a series which are rarer than the others and prices rise accordingly. For example, **Tom Bombadil** (HN2924) is a particularly elusive model in the now desirable **Tolkien** series. Occasionally complete series come up for sale but for some collectors that spoils the fun of the chase.

MAKING DOULTON FIGURES

There are many people involved in the creation of each Royal Doulton figure, beginning with the artist who works with modelling clay to transform an image in his head, or on paper, into a three dimensional sculpture.

When the original model is complete it is taken to the mould maker, whose years of experience enable him to cut up the figure into separate parts so that a master mould, known as a block, can be produced. Complex figures are divided into many parts and a plaster of Paris mould is made from the original head, torso, arms, skirts and so on. Working moulds are made as required and care is taken to ensure that they are replaced regularly during production so that the crisp detail of the original is maintained.

Liquid clay, known as slip, is gently poured into each mould by the caster and once the body has set to the required thickness the excess slip is poured out. At this stage the parts of the figure are carefully removed from the mould and, as the clay is still very fragile, they are pieced together using slip as an adhesive.

Before the complete figure has been thoroughly dried, the seams are sponged away in a process known as fettling. The piece is then ready for its first firing. It is removed from the kiln, having shrunk to its 'biscuit' state and then, if it is a character figure, it is ready for painting. Painting takes place at this stage because pieces are coloured under-glaze to give the more rugged effect expected of these subjects.

Fair lady figures in their biscuit state are dipped into a vat of glaze and fired again before decorating begins. The dresses and accessories are painted with on-glaze colours and to achieve the rich colour effects, like the deep red, several applications of colour are needed. Each layer requires a separate firing. When the costume decoration is complete, the faces of the fair ladies are painted by the most experienced artists and a final firing ensures that the colours are permanently sealed under the glaze.

BODIES AND GLAZES

The fair lady figures are made from bone china which is a traditionally British body, composed of China clay, Cornish stone and bone ash. Most character figures are made from English Porcelain, a whiter coloured body formerly known as English Translucent China, which was pioneered by Royal Doulton chemists in 1959. Before the invention of English Porcelain, many Doulton figures were produced in an earthenware body, which is fired to a lower temperature than china and is more porous. There are slight differences in size between figures made of earthenware and those made of porcelain and colours often look different on the two bodies.

Most Royal Doulton figures have a brilliant glossy glaze. In the early 1970s, however, some matt figures were produced and this matt finish was also used for limited edition subjects as it enhanced the intricate modelling and gave a distinctive effect. A matt glazed black basalt body has been used more recently in the Images range of modern style sculptures.

There is obviously much more to a Royal Doulton figure than first meets the eye and collectors can enjoy watching the creative process during a tour of the Royal Doulton factory. For opening times and tour bookings contact: The Tours Organizer, Royal Doulton, Nile Street, Burslem, Stoke-on-Trent ST6 2AJ.

CARE AND REPAIR

A Royal Doulton figure collection can be enjoyed indefinitely as long as care is taken when handling and cleaning. When dusting in situ, a soft cosmetic brush or photographic lens brush is useful for getting into tight corners, particularly hand-modelled floral bouquets and baskets. When necessary, glazed figures should be washed in luke-warm water, using a mild liquid detergent, then rinsed thoroughly and dried naturally or buffed gently with a soft cloth. It is important that water does not get inside the figure so the hole in the bottom should be blocked up beforehand, perhaps with a cork or a rubber bung. Care should be taken not to knock figures against the tap or against each other as this may cause chips or imperceptible cracks in the glaze which could open up at a later date.

If the worst does happen, a professional restorer should be consulted as they can work 'miracles' with damaged figures. Whether it be a small chip or a shattered body, pieces can be mended so that the repair is invisible to all but the most experienced eye. It follows that when buying figures on the secondary market, it is advisable to check for restorations. The head, the arms and any projecting accessories are the most vulnerable parts, so look at these areas carefully in a good light. Repaired cracks can sometimes be detected by looking inside the figure through the hole in the bottom. There are special ultraviolet lamps which highlight some types of restoration but these are not widely used, except by professionals. Restored figures should be priced less than perfect examples, according to the amount of damage and the quality of the repair. Always enquire about the condition of a piece when buying, as a reputable dealer will stand by any guarantees they give regarding restorations.

CURRENT AND DISCONTINUED FIGURES

Figures which are produced at the Royal Doulton factories today are generally referred to as 'current' whilst models which are no longer made are variously described as 'withdrawn', 'retired' or 'discontinued'. A current figure might have been in the range for a long time and one or two have been in continuous production for over fifty years, for example **The Balloon Man.** Because this figure is still generally available today, a 1930s version is unlikely to be worth more than the current model, even though it is older and probably differs slightly in appearance, due to changes in body and paint formulations over the years. It is worth remembering, however, that originally it would have been purchased for just a few pounds or dollars.

Figures are discontinued on an annual basis in order to make way for new introductions. There is a limit to the number of models the factory can produce, or the retailer can display, so eventually some have to go. In some cases the choice is easy as it is apparent that all the collectors who want a particular model have already purchased it and world-wide sales are decreasing. Occasionally figures disappear after only a couple of years in the range and these short-lived models often become very desirable on the secondary market.

The number of figures withdrawn each year varies enormously. Sometimes it is less than 12 a year and other times, after a major reassessment of the range, there might be 50 or so. The first withdrawals took place during the Second World War and it is unlikely that more than 2,000 of each of the early models were produced. This is less than many limited editions, so it is not surprising that these pieces are amongst the most desirable figures on the secondary market today. Older figures with short production runs are obviously less likely to appear in the market-place than those that were made for many years. However, this alone does not affect the price, which will probably also be governed by aesthetic considerations and market awareness.

In 1990, the company introduced a system of marking the bases of retiring figures 'last year of issue' but this practice ceased in 1993.

LIMITED EDITIONS, PRESTIGE FIGURES AND SPECIAL EDITIONS

In 1933, discerning customers were offered a range of specially commissioned figures by Richard Garbe RA, a distinguished sculptor of the day. Inspired by his sculptures in other media, the new figures were larger than most others in the HN collection and many were embellished with gold. In order to emphasise their prestige status, it was announced that only a limited number of each model would be produced and the edition size was marked on the base. The editions ranged from 25 to 150 pieces and took several years to sell out. Not surprisingly, they are now very desirable on the secondary market. At the same time, Charles

Noke introduced a limited edition figure of **King Henry VIII**, which is more typical of Doulton's later limited editions in terms of subject matter, scale and decoration.

During the 1950s, some of the largest and most impressive figures in the range were revamped to form the basis of a Prestige collection. Three of these subjects were originally modelled by Charles Noke, **The Moor** (HN2082), **Jack Point** (HN2080), and **King Charles** (HN2084), and the first two are still produced today, although in very limited quantities to special order. The most expensive prestige figure of all, **Princess Badoura** (HN2081), was introduced in 1952. The painting and gilding on this figure take about eight weeks to complete, hence the high cost. Repeated kiln firings and complex model assembly also add to the expense of producing prestige pieces, as with the spectacular **Matador and Bull** (HN2324), which was modelled by Peggy Davies in 1964. Two more of Peggy's ambitious large scale sculptures were produced in limited editions of 500 each, **The Indian Brave** (HN2376) produced in 1967 and **The Palio** (HN2428) of 1971. However, she is better known today for her limited edition collections of **Lady Musicians** (1970-76) and **Dancers of the World** (1977-82). These highly detailed and richly decorated models were each limited to 750 pieces and were introduced at the rate of one or two each year, complete with presentation boxes and certificates of authenticity. This has become the pattern for most of the company's limited editions today, although edition sizes have grown to reflect increased demand.

Special occasions have also inspired limited editions and there are portrait figures celebrating Royal weddings, birthdays and coronation anniversaries. Expo'92 in Seville, for example prompted a limited edition colourway of **Mantilla** (HN3192) and a special edition of **Discovery** (HN3428), a reduced version of the symbolic sculpture in the British Pavilion. This piece was offered exclusively to members of the Royal Doulton International Collectors Club. The opportunity to purchase limited editions and special editions of figures is one of the benefits of joining the Club. Generally speaking, special editions are limited by the offer period, which in the case of the early Doulton Club commissions was six months. The term is also used more widely to describe special products commissioned by independent companies which are not individually numbered on their bases nor accompanied by a certificate of authenticity.

For the collector looking for something extra special, Royal Doulton limited and special editions are in great demand today and popular subjects are often quickly oversubscribed. It is important, therefore, to respond quickly to the announcements for new releases. Discontinued limited editions command premium prices in the secondary market, particularly if they are sold with their original literature and packaging and the first of a collection of six or twelve figures is usually the hardest to find.

COLOURWAYS AND VARIATIONS

From the earliest days of the figures collection, some of the most popular models have been produced in alternative colourways. The first fair lady figure, The Crinoline, was originally offered in a plain lilac dress or with a floral design. Each colourway was assigned a different HN number to distinguish the decorative treatment. Charles Noke's study of **A Jester** has been available in 12 different coloured suits as well as in Parian and Vellum finishes. Noke also experimented with different glaze effects on figures, including a lustrous red flambé, a mottled blue green Titanian, a glittering gold and a dark brown to simulate bronze. These were produced only in very limited numbers and were not given HN references.

During the 1920s, when more master painters joined the figure painting department, colour effects and patterns became more ambitious. The lady figures were dressed in all of the fashionable fabrics of the day with floral designs, polka dots, stripes, diapers and checks painted by hand. It was unusual to have a lady figure in just one colourway and in the case of **Victorian Lady**, there was a choice of 15 varied designs.

After the Second World War the collection was rationalized and alternative colourways became less common. However, the idea was revived during the 1980s, initially for special occasions such as Michael Doulton tours. A new colourway of **Wistful** (HN2472) was devised exclusively for his personal appearances in 1985. Colourways have also been commissioned by independent retailers and in some cases the name has been changed as well as the colours. For example, a variation of **Adrienne** (HN2304) was commissioned to promote Joan's Gift Shop in Scotland and was renamed **Joan** (HN3217).

Alternative colourways now appear regularly in the general range, sometimes with a new name, and it is not just fair ladies which ring the changes. Character figures have also been given a fresh new look from time to time. **The Lobster Man**, for instance, is available with two different coloured sweaters (HN2317 and HN2323).

During the 1970s, former Art Director Eric Griffiths experimented with matt glazes but these were not a commercial success and most of the models were quickly withdrawn. An exception is **The Judge** (HN2443) which was changed from a matte to a glossy finish because it was so popular.

The Carpet Seller
HN 1464 [hand open] (left), [hand close] (right)

From time to time alterations have been made to models after they have been introduced, usually to decrease the risk of damage during production or in transit. In early models of **The Carpet Seller** (HN1464) for example, the character's hand is outstretched, whereas in later models the fingers are clasped around the carpet, making them less vulnerable to breakage. The figure of **Masque** (HN2554) also had to be modified as the long metal handle of the mask was easily broken. It was removed and the hand was remodelled. Eagle eyed collectors will also notice that early models of **Autumn Breezes** (HN1911) have two feet peeping out from under the dress whilst later models have only one.

There are some keen collectors who enjoy tracking down the different model and colour variations but the majority take advantage of the wide choice of shades and patterns to co-ordinate a new purchase with an existing display.

A GUIDE TO BACKSTAMPS AND DATING

There is a wealth of information on the base of a Royal Doulton figure and some of it will help date the piece.

Most prominent is the Royal Doulton factory mark which has featured a lion standing on a crown ever since the company was awarded the Royal Warrant in 1901. Before this honour was bestowed, the mark comprised a different style of crown and the words 'Doulton Burslem England.' This early mark is found on most of the Vellum figures modelled by Charles Noke in the 1890s.

The Royal Doulton lion and crown mark has been altered slightly over the years and this can help date the figure to a specific era.

Miniature from 'HN' Series

Miniature from 'M' Series

1902-1922 Printed

1922-1927 Printed or impressed

1927-1932 Printed

1932 to the present or impressed

Printed Numeral '7', 1934

The precise year of manufacture, however, can be determined if the figure has a date code on the right side of the lion and crown symbol. A printed number 1 was used in 1928, when this dating system began. This system continued to number 27 in 1954. The year of manufacture can be easily calculated by adding the number on the figure to 1927. For example, a figure with the number 13 on it indicates that it was manufactured in 1940 (13+1927).

Registration numbers, when they are present, indicate when the design was first registered, which could be up to a year before the figure was put into production. After the Second World War, it was usual to have several registration numbers which protected the design in Royal Doulton's main export markets but this has not been required since the early 1980s. Copyright dates have also been incorporated into the backstamp since the 1940s.

RᵈNᵒ 791566

Registered Mark

H.N.2041.
COPR.:1948.
DOULTON & CO. LIMITED.
RᵈNᵒ 855287.
RᵈNᵒ 26360.
RᵈNᵒ 5772.
RᵈNᵒ 133/48.

Registered Mark With Copyright Date, 1948

 HN 2871
ROYAL DOULTON
TABLEWARE LTD 1979

Copyright Date, 1979

Collectors should note that the words 'Made in England' were added around 1920 so figures without this reference are usually very early models.

Often on miniature figures there was not enough room for the standard factory mark and so either part of it was used or just the words 'Doulton England.' Between 1932 and 1949 miniature figures were given M pattern numbers but earlier and later models have HN numbers.

Some early figures have an impressed date on the base which gives the month, year and sometimes the day, when the mould was made (not when a particular finished piece was produced). For example, 12-10-23 represents October 12th, 1923. This practice ceased during the 1930s.

Usually the design is copyrighted at least a year before production begins so, as with registration numbers, the copyright date does not necessarily indicate the year of introduction.

1983 To The Present

Between 1990 and 1993 new introductions were marked 'first year of issue' and planned withdrawals 'final year of issue,' which makes precise dating possible again for some figures.

Year Cyphers

Beginning in 1998 a cypher was added to the base of each figurine. The cypher for 1998 was an umbrella, the cypher for 1999 is the Top Hat as worn by Sir Henry Doulton and the cypher for 2000 is a fob watch containing the logo Millennium 2000.

1998 Umbrella	1999 Top Hat	2000 Fob Watch	2001 Waistcoat
2002 Boot	2003 Gloves	2004 Bottle Oven	2005 Not Available at Press Time

The HN number is particularly important as this catalogue and other reference works are designed to follow the HN sequence. Until the 1950s the HN number was written on the base by the painter so very occasionally it has been omitted. It is now incorporated in the printed backstamp along with the figure's name and copyright information. The initials stand for Harry Nixon who devised the colour schemes for the figures and recorded all the painting instructions in the pattern books. Each new decorative treatment was given an HN number, not necessarily in chronological order, and so a popular model such as Victorian Lady has several different numbers. Pattern number HN 1 was allocated to the figure Darling because of Queen Mary's interest, although it was not the first figure to be modelled.

Figures also have a model number impressed in the base but this does not normally concern collectors unless there are no other details recorded, which is sometimes the case with prototypes. Model numbers can be authenticated by referring to the shape books held in Royal Doulton's archive in Stoke-on-Trent.

Figure's Name Styles

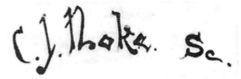

Modeller's Signature

Until around 1930 the figure's name was written by hand on the base and the modeller's name was sometimes included. This practice lapsed in the general range for over 50 years but was revived in 1984 when the modeller's facsimile signature was incorporated in the backstamp.

The painters responsible for the decoration of the figures usually initial their work on the base and in recent years the individual craftsmanship of the piece has been further emphasised by the addition of the words "Hand made and hand decorated".

Backstamps on limited edition pieces have added information about the edition size and decorative typefaces and motifs inspired by the subject are now often incorporated into the design. Special commissions, including new models, colourways and pre-releases, frequently have backstamps with details of the event being commemorated. Backstamps may also include the customer who has commissioned the piece. For example, all of the annual figures produced exclusively for Michael Doulton's tours have a special backstamp.

Although 'seconds' figures are not sold by Royal Doulton to the public, slightly faulty models can be bought by company employees at special sales and so they occasionally come on to the secondary market. They are now clearly marked with either a scored line through the backstamp or a drilled hole defacing the centre of the lion and crown symbol.

ROYAL DOULTON

INTERNATIONAL COLLECTORS CLUB

Founded in 1980 The Royal Doulton International Collectors Club provides an information service on all aspects of the company's products, past and present. A Club magazine, "Gallery," is published four times per year with information on new products and current events that will keep the collector up-to-date on the happenings in the world of Royal Doulton. Upon joining the club, each new member will receive a free gift and invitations to special events and exclusive offers throughout the year. To join the Royal Doulton Collectrors Club, please contact the club directly by writing to the address opposite or calling the appropriate number.

International Collectors Club
Sir Henry Doulton House
Forge Lane, Etruria, Stoke-on-Trent
Staffordshire, ST1 5NN, England
Telephone:
  U.K.: 8702 412696
  Overseas: +44 (0) 1782 404045
  Fax: + 44 1782 404000
  On-line at www.doulton-direct.co.uk
  E-mail: icc@royal-doulton.com

VISITOR CENTRE

Opened in the Summer of 1996, the Royal Doulton Visitor Centre houses the largest collection of Royal Doulton figurines in the world. Demonstration areas offer the collector a first hand insight on how figurines are assembled and decorated. Also at the Visitor Centre is a restaurant and a retail shop offering both best quality ware and slight seconds. Factory tours may be booked, Monday to Friday

Royal Doulton Visitor Centre
Nile Street, Burslem
Stoke-on-Trent, ST6 2AJ, England
Visitor Centre: Tel.: +44 (0) 1782 292434
                Fax: +44 (0) 1782 292424
Factory Store: Tel.: +44 (0) 1782 292451

WEBSITE AND E-MAIL ADDRESS

Websites:
  www.royal-doulton.com
  www.doulton-direct.com.au
  www.royal-doulton-brides.com

E-mail Addresses:
  Visitor Centre: visitor@royal-doulton.com
  Consumer Enquiries: enquiries@royal-doulton.com
  Museum Curator: heritage@royal-doulton.com
  Doulton-Direct: direct@royal-doulton.com

ROYAL DOULTON FACTORY SHOPS

Royal Doulton Group Factory Shop
Lawley Street, Longton
Stokoe-on-Trent, ST3 2PH, England
  Tel.: +44 (0) 1782 291237

Royal Doulton Factory Shop
Forge Lane, Etruria
Stoke-on-Trent, ST1 5NN, England
  Tel.: +44 (0) 1782 284056

Royal Doulton Factory Shop
Victoria Road, Fenton
Stoke-on-Trent, ST4 2PJ, England
  Tel.: +44 (0) 1782 291869

DOULTON CHAPTERS

Detroit Chapter
Ronald Griffin, President
629 Lynne Avenue
Ypsilanti, MI., 48198-3829

Edmonton Chapter
Mildred's Collectibles
6813 104 Street, Edmonton, AB

New England Chapter
Lee Piper, President
Meridith Nelson, Vice President
Michael Lynch, Secretary
Scott Reichenberg, Treasurer
E-mail: doingantiq@aol.com

Northern California Chapter
Edward L. Khachadourian, President
P.O. Box 214, Moraga, CA 94556-0214
Tel.: (925) 376-2221
Fax (925) 376-3581
Email: khach@pacbell.net

Northwest, Bob Haynes Chapter
Alan Matthew, President
15202 93rd Place NE, Bothell
WA 98011 Tel.: (425) 488-9604

Rochester Chapter
Judith L. Trost, President
103 Garfield Street, Rochester
NY 14611 Tel.: (716) 436-3321

Ohio Chapter
Reg Morris, President
5556 Whitehaven Avenue
North Olmstead, Ohio 44070
Tel.: (216) 779-5554

Western Pennyslvania Chapter
John Re, President
9589 Parkedge Drive, Allison Park
PA 15101
Tel.: (412) 366-0201
Fax: (412) 366-2558

THE DOULTON MARKETS

LAND AUCTIONS

AUSTRALIA

Goodman's
7 Anderson Street
Double Bay, Sydney, 2028, N.S.W., Australia
Tel.: +61 (0) 2 9327 7311; Fax: +61 (0) 2 9327 2917
Enquiries: Suzanne Brett
www.goodmans.com.au
E-mail: info@goodmans.com.au

Sotheby's
118-122 Queen Street, Woollahra
Sydney, 2025, N.S.W., Australia
Tel.: +61 (0) 2 9362 1000; Fax: +61 (0) 2 9362 1100

CANADA

Empire Auctions
Montreal
5500 Paré Street, Montreal, Quebec H4P 2M1
Tel.: (514) 737-6586; Fax: (514) 342-1352
Enquiries: Isadore Rubinfeld
E-mail: montreal@empireauctions.com

Ottawa
1380 Cyrville Road, Gloucester, ON
Tel.: (613) 748-5343; Fax: (613) 748-0354
Enquiries: Elliot Melamed
E-mail: ottawa@empireauctions.com

Toronto
165 Tycos Drive
Toronto, ON., M6B 1W6
Tel.: (416) 784-4261; Fax: (416) 784-4262
Enquiries: Michael Rogozinsky
www.empireauctions.com
E-mail: toronto@empireauctions.com

Maynard's Industries Ltd.
Arts / Antiques
415 West 2nd Avenue, Vancouver, BC, V5Y 1E3
Tel.: (604) 876-1311; Fax: (604) 876-1323
www.maynards.com
E-mail: antiques@maynards.com

Ritchie's
288 King Street East, Toronto, ON. M5A 1K4
Tel.: (416) 364-1864; Fax: (416) 364-0704
Enquiries: Caroline Kaiser
www.richies.com
E-mail: auction@ritchies.com

Waddington's
111 Bathurst Street, Toronto, ON., M5V 2R1
Tel.: (416) 504-9100; Fax: (416) 504-0033
Enquiries: Bill Kime
www.waddingtonsauctions.com
E-mail: info@waddingtonsauctions.com

UNITED KINGDOM

BBR Auctions
Elsecar Heritage Centre, Nr. Barnsley
South Yorkshire, S74 8HJ, England
Tel.: +44 (0) 1226 745156; Fax: +44 (0) 1226 351561
Enquiries: Alan Blakeman
www.bbrauctions.co.uk
E-mail: sales@bbrauctions.com

Bonhams
Bond Street:
101 New Bond Street, London. W15 1SR, England
Chelsea:
65-69 Lots Road, Chelslea, London, SW10 0RN, England
Knightsbridge
Montpelier Street, Knightsbridge, London, SW7 1HH
Tel.: +44 (0) 20 7393 3900; Fax: +44 (0) 20 7393 3905
Enquiries:
  Decorative Arts: Joy McCall
  Tel.: +44 (0) 20 7393 3942
  Contemporary Ceramics: Gareth Williams
  Tel.: +44 (0) 20 7393 3941
  Doulton Beswick Wares: Mark Oliver
  Tel.: +44 (0) 20 7468 8233
www.bonhams.com
E-mail: info@bonhams.com

Christie's
London
8 King Street, London, SW1 England
Tel.: +44 (0) 20 7839 9060; Fax: +44 (0) 20 7839 1611

South Kensington
85 Old Brompton Road, London SW7 3LD, England
Tel.: +44 (0) 20 7581 7611; Fax: +44 (0) 20 7321-3321
Enquiries: Decorative Arts
  Tel.: 44 (0) 20 7321 3237
www.christies.com; E-mail: info@christies.com

Potteries Specialist Auctions
271 Waterloo Road, Cobridge, Stoke-on-Trent
Staffordshire, ST6 3HR, England
Tel.: +44 (0) 1782 286622
Fax: +44 (0) 1782 213777
www.potteriesauctions.com
E-mail: enquiries@potteriesauctions.com

Sotheby's
London
34-35 New Bond Street, London, W1A 2AA, England
Tel.: +44 (0) 20 7293 5000; Fax: +44 (0) 20 7293 5989
Olympia
Hammersmith Road, London, W14 8UX, England
Tel.: +44 (0) 20 7293 5555; Fax: +44 (0) 20 7293 6939

Sotheby's (cont)

Sussex
Summers Place, Billingshurst, Sussex
RH14 9AF, England
Tel.: +44 (0) 1403 833500; Fax: +44 (0) 1403 833699
www.sothebys.com
E-mail: info@sothebys.com

Louis Taylor
Britannia House
10 Town Road, Hanley
Stoke-on-Trent, Staffordshire, England
Tel.: +44 (0) 1782 214111; Fax: +44 (0) 1782 215283
Enquiries: Clive Hillier

Thomson Roddick & Medcalf
60 Whitesands
Dumfries DG1 2RS
Scotland
Tel.: +44 (0) 1387 279879; Fax: +44 (0) 1387 266236
Enquiries: C. R. Graham-Campbell

Peter Wilson Auctioneers
Victoria Gallery, Market Street
Nantwich, Cheshire, CW5 5DG, England
Tel.: +44 (0) 1270 610508; Fax: +44 (0) 1270 610508
Enquiries: Peter Wilson

UNITED STATES

Christie's East
219 East 67th Street, New York, NY 10012
Tel.: +1 212 606 0400
www.christies.com

William Doyle Galleries
175 East 87th Street, New York, NY 10128
Tel.: +1 212 427 2730
Fax: +1 212 369 0892

Sotheby's Arcade Auctions
1334 York Avenue, New York, NY 10021
Tel.: +1 212 606 7000
www.sothebys.com

VIRTUAL AUCTIONS

Amazon.com ® Auctions
Main site: www.amazon.com
Plus 4 International sites

AOL.com Auctions ®
Main site: www.aol.com
Links to – E-bay.com
– U-bid.com

E-BAY ® The World's On-Line Market Place ™
Main Site: www.ebay.com
Plus 20 International sites

YAHOO! Auctions ®
Main site: www.yahoo.com
Plus 15 International auction sites

FAIRS, MARKETS AND SHOWS

AUSTRALIA

Royal Doulton and Antique Collectable Fair
Marina Hall, Civic Centre,
Hurstville, Sydney

CANADA

Christie Antique Show
Christie Conservation Park
Highway 5, Near Dundas, Ontario
Always May and September
Gadsden Promotions ltd.
P.O. Box 490, Shelburne, Ontario L0N 1S0
Tel.: (800) 667-0619
Fax: (519) 925-6498

UNITED KINGDOM

20th Century Fairs
266 Glossop Road, Sheffield S10 2HS, England
Usually in May or June
For information on times and dates:
Tel.: +44 (0) 114 275 0333; Fax: +44 (0) 114 275 4443

Doulton and Beswick Collectors Fair
National Motorcycle Museum
Meriden, Birmingham
The museum was destroyed by fire in September 2003
For information on new venue call:
Doulton and Beswick Dealers Association
Tel.: +44 (0) 181 303 3316

DGM Antiques Fairs Ltd.
Newark, the largest in the UK with usually six fairs
annually. For information on times and dates for this
and many other fairs contact:
DMG
Newark, P.O. Box 100, Newark
Nottinghamshire, NG2 1DJ
Tel.: +44 (0) 1636 702326; Fax: +44 (0) 1636 707923
www.dmgantiquefairs.com
www.antiquesdirectory.co.uk

U.K. Fairs
Doulton and Beswick Fair for Collectors
River Park Leisure Centre, Winchester
Usually held in October
For information on times and dates contact:
Enquiries U.K. Fairs; Tel.: 44 (0) 20 8500 3505
www.portia.co.uk
E-mail: ukfairs@portia.co.uk

LONDON MARKETS

Alfie's Antique Market
13-25 Church Street, London; Tuesday - Saturday
Camden Passage Market
London; Wednesday and Saturday
New Caledonia Market
Bermondsey Square, London; Friday morning
Portobello Road Market
Portobello Road, London; Saturday

UNITED STATES

Atlantique City
Atlantic City Convention Centre
Atlantic City, NJ

International Gift and Collectible Expo
Donald E. Stephens Convention Centre
Rosemont, Illinois

For information on the above two shows contact:
Krause Publications
700 East State Street, Iola, WI 54990-9990
Tel.: (877) 746-9757; Fax: (715) 445-4389
www.collectibleshow.com
E-mail: iceshow@krause.com

Doulton Convention and Sale International
Fort Lauderdale, Florida, U.S.A.
Usually February. For information on location
and dates:
Pascoe & Company
575 S.W. 22nd Ave., Miami, Florida 33135
Tel.: (305) 643-2550; Fax: (305) 643-2123
www.pascoeandcompany.com
E-mail: sales@pascoeandcompany.com

Royal Doulton Convention & Sale
Cleveland, Ohio
Usually August. For information on location
and dates:
Colonial House Productions
182 Front Street, Berea, Ohio 44308
Tel.: (866) 885-9024; Fax: (866) 854-3117
222.Colonial-House-Collectibles.com
E-mail: yworry@aol.com

FURTHER READING

Storybook Figures

Beatrix Potter Figures and Giftware, edited by Louise Irvine
Beswick Price Guide, by Harvey May
Bunnykins Collectors Book, by Louise Irvine
Cartoon Classics and Other Character Figures, by Louise Irvine
Royal Doulton Bunnykins: A Charlton Standard Catalogue by Jean Dale and Louise Irvine
Royal Doulton Bunnykins Figures, by Louise Irvine
Royal Doulton, Royal Albert, Beswick Storybook Figurines: A Charlton Standard Catalogue, by Jean Dale

Animal, Figures and Character Jugs

Beswick Animals: A Charlton Standard Catalogue by Diane and John Callow
    and Marilyn & Peter Sweet
Character Jug Collectors Handbook, by Kevin Pearson
Collecting Character and Toby Jugs, by Jocelyn Lukins
Collecting Doulton Animals, by Jocelyn Lukins
Doulton Figure Collectors Handbook, by Kevin Pearson
Doulton Flambé Animals, by Jocelyn Lukins
Royal Doulton Animals: A Charlton Standard Catalogue by Jean Dale
Royal Doulton Figures, by Desmond Eyles, Louise Irvine and Valerie Baynton
Royal Doulton Jugs: A Charlton Standard Catalogue by Jean Dale

General

Beswick Pottery: A Charlton Standard Catlaogue by Diane and John Callow
Discovering Royal Doulton, by Michael Doulton
Doulton Burslem Advertising Wares, by Jocelyn Lukins
Doulton Burslem Wares, by Desmond Eyles
Doulton for the Collector, by Jocelyn Lukins
Doulton Kingsware Flasks, by Jocelyn Lukins
Doulton Lambeth Advertising Wares, by Jocelyn Lukins
Doulton Lambeth Wares, by Desmond Eyles and Louise Irvine
Doulton Story, by Paul Atterbury and Louise Irvine
George Tinworth, by Peter Rose
Hannah Barlow, by Peter Rose
John Beswick: A World of Imagination. Catalogue reprint (1950-1996)
Limited Edition Loving Cups and Jugs, by Louise Irvine and Richard Dennis
Phillips Collectors Guide, by Catherine Braithwaite
Royal Doulton, by Jennifer Queree
Royal Doulton by Julie McKeown
Royal Doulton Series Wares, by Louise Irvine (Vols. 1-5)
Sir Henry Doulton Biography, by Edmund Gosse

Magazines and Newsletters

Beswick Quarterly (Beswick Newsletter) Contact Laura J. Rock-Smith: 10 Holmes Court, Sayville, N.Y.
    11782-2408, U.S.A. Tel./Fax (631) 589-9027

Collecting Doulton Magazine, Contact Barry Hill: Collecting Doulton, P.O. Box 310, Richmond
    Surrey TW10 7FU, England

Rabbitting On (Bunnykins Newsletter) Contact Leah Selig: 2 Harper Street, Merrylands 2160,
    New South Wales, Australia. Tel/Fax: 61 2 9637 2410 (International), 02 637 2410 (Australia)

DOULTON LAMBETH FIGURINES

JOHN BROAD

Atalanta (Headband)
Designer: John Broad
Height: 9", 23.0 cm
Colour: 1. X7910, Brown stoneware
        2. X8707, Coloured Doultonware
Issued: 1. 1912
        2. 1928

Description	U.S.$	Can. $	U.K. £
1. Brown	3,000.	3,750.	1,800.
2. Coloured	2,500.	3,500.	1,500.

Photograph not
available
at press time

Atalanta (Flowers)
Designer: John Broad
Height: 9", 23.0 cm
Colour: 1. X7910, Brown stoneware
        2. X8707, Coloured Doultonware
Issued: 1. 1912
        2. 1928

Description	U.S. $	Can. $	U.K. £
1. Brown		Extremely Rare	
2. Coloured		Extremely Rare	

Bather
Designer: John Broad
Height: 13 ½", 34.0 cm
Colour: 1. X7912, Brown stoneware
        2. X8706, Coloured Doultonware
Issued: 1. 1912
        2. 1928

Description	U.S. $	Can. $	U.K. £
1. Brown	5,000.	6,500.	3,000.
2. Coloured	5,000.	6,500.	3,000.

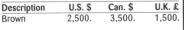

Boer War Soldier
Designer: John Broad
Height: 12 ½", 32.0 cm
Colour: Brown stoneware
Issued: 1901
Series: Soldiers

Description	U.S. $	Can. $	U.K. £
Brown	2,500.	3,500.	1,500.

Diana
Designer: John Broad
Height: 11 ½", 29.7 cm
Colour: Terracotta
Issued: c. 1880

Description	U.S. $	Can. $	U.K. £
Terracotta		Rare	

Doris Keane
(also called The Minuet)
Designer: John Broad
Height: 9", 23.0 cm
Colour: White glost porcelain
Issued: c.1918

Description	U.S. $	Can. $	U.K. £
White glost	1,500.	2,000.	800.

**Doris Keane
(also called Romance)**
Designer: John Broad
Height: 8 ¾", 22.5 cm
Colour: White biscuit porcelain
Issued: c.1918

Description	U.S. $	Can. $	U.K. £
White biscuit	1,500.	2,000.	800.

Girl Holding Vase
Designer: John Broad
Height: 13 ¼", 33 cm
Colour: X8708, Coloured Doultonware
Issued: 1928

Description	U.S. $	Can. $	U.K. £
Coloured	3,500.	4,500.	2,000.

Photograph not
available
at press time

King Edward VII
Designer: John Broad
Height: 16 ¾", 42.0 cm
Colour: Terracotta
Issued: 1901

Description	U.S. $	Can. $	U.K. £
Terracotta		Extremely Rare	

Lady in Elizabethan Dress
Designer: John Broad
Height: 8", 20.5 cm
Colour: White biscuit porcelain
Issued: c.1918

Description	U.S. $	Can. $	U.K. £
White biscuit		Rare	

Lady with Dog
Designer: John Broad
Height: 7 ½", 19.0 cm
Colour: White biscuit porcelain
Issued: c.1918

Description	U.S. $	Can. $	U.K. £
White biscuit	1,250.	1,600.	700.

Lady with Muff
Designer: John Broad
Height: 7 ¼", 18.5 cm
Colour: White biscuit porcelain
Issued: c.1918

Description	U.S. $	Can. $	U.K. £
White biscuit	1,000.	1,500.	500.

Lady with Rose

Designer: John Broad
Height: 8", 20.5 cm
Colour: White biscuit porcelain
Issued: c.1918

Description	U.S. $	Can. $	U.K. £
White biscuit	1,250.	1,600.	700.

Lady with Tall Hat

Designer: John Broad
Height: 8", 20.5 cm
Colour: White biscuit porcelain
Issued: c.1918

Description	U.S. $	Can. $	U.K. £
White biscuit	1,250.	1,600.	700.

Madame Pompadour

Designer: John Broad
Height: 8 ½", 21.5 cm
Colour: 1. X8754, Coloured Doultonware
           2. White biscuit porcelain
Issued: c.1918

Description	U.S. $	Can. $	U.K. £
1. Coloured	1,500.	2,000.	800.
2. White	1,000.	1,500.	500.

Photograph not
available
at press time

Nelson

Designer: John Broad
Height: 8", 20.5 cm
Colour: 1. X6426, Brown stoneware
           2. Green faience
Issued: 1905

Description	U.S. $	Can. $	U.K. £
1. Brown	1,500.	2,000.	800.
2. Green	1,500.	2,000.	800.

Our Lady

Designer: John Broad
Height: Unknown
Colour: Terracotta
Issued: c.1910

Description	U.S. $	Can. $	U.K. £
Terracitta		Extremely Rare	

Pomona

Designer: John Broad
Height: 14", 35.0 cm
Colour: X7911, Terracotta
Issued: 1912

Description	U.S. $	Can. $	U.K. £
Terracotta		Rare	

Photograph not
available
at press time

Queen Alexndra

Designer: John Broad
Height: 16 ½", 42.0 cm
Colour: Terracotta
Issued: 1901

Description	U.S. $	Can. $	U.K. £
Terracotta		Rare	

Queen Victoria

Designer: John Broad
Height: 11 ¾, 29.75 cm
Colour: Brown salt glaze stoneware
Issued: 1901

Description	U.S $	Can. $	U.K. £
Brown	5,000.	6,500.	3,000.

Thrower

Designer: John Broad
Height: 7", 18.0 cm
Colour: 1. Brown stoneware
2. Terracotta
Issued: 1883

Description	U.S. $	Can. $	U.K. £
1. Brown Stone		Extremely Rare	
2. Terracotta		Extremely Rare	

LESLIE HARRADINE

Amused Child Study

Model No.: H48
Designer: Leslie Harradine
Height: 6", 15.5 cm
Colour: Slip cast buff stoneware on either a
green base or a blue base
Issued: c.1912

Description	U.S. $	Can. $	U.K. £
Slip cast		Extremely Rare	

Breton Women Gossiping

Model No.: H64
Designer: Leslie Harradine
Height: 10", 25.5 cm
Colour: Black and white stoneware
Issued: c.1912

Description	U.S. $	Can. $	U.K. £
Black and white		Extremely Rare	

British Soldier

Model No.: Unknown
Designer: Leslie Harradine
Height: 9 ½", 24.0 cm
Colour: Brown stoneware
Issued: 1910
Series: Soldiers

Description	U.S. $	Can. $	U.K. £
Brown	3,000.	3,750.	1,800.

Cossack

Model No.: H78
Designer: Leslie Harradine
Height: 9 ½", 24.0 cm
Colour: Brown stoneware
Issued: c.1910
Series: Soldiers

Description	U.S. $	Can. $	U.K. £
Brown	2,000.	3,000.	1,250.

Dutch Man

Model No.: H10
Designer: Leslie Harradine
Height: 8 ½", 21.5 cm
Colour: White slip cast stoneware with blue
detailing
Issued: 1912
Varieties: Also called 'The Toiler'

Description	U.S. $	Can. $	U.K. £
White slip cast	1,000.	1,300.	500.

Dutch Woman

Model No.: H3 (X7728)
Designer: Leslie Harradine
Height: 7 ¾", 19.5 cm
Colour: White slip cast stoneware with blue
detailing
Issued: 1912

Description	U.S. $	Can. $	U.K. £
White slip cast	1,000.	1,300.	500.

Dutch Woman

Model No.:	H9		
Designer:	Leslie Harradine		
Height:	4 ½", 11.5 cm		
Colour:	White slip cast stoneware with blue or green detailing		
Issued:	1912		

Description	U.S. $	Can. $	U.K. £
White slip cast	700.	950.	400.

French Legionnaire

Model No.:	H72		
Designer:	Leslie Harradine		
Height:	9 ½", 24.0 cm		
Colour:	Brown stoneware		
Issued:	c.1910		
Series:	Soldiers		

Description	U.S. $	Can. $	U.K. £
Brown	2,500.	3,250.	1,500.

Harvester (with Scythe)

Model No.:	H66		
Designer:	Leslie Harradine		
Height:	7", 18.0 cm		
Colour:	Brown stoneware		
Issued:	c.1910		

Description	U.S. $	Can. $	U.K. £
Brown	1,200.	1,500.	725.

Hunched Figure on Pedestal

Model No.:	H45		
Designer:	Leslie Harradine		
Height:	Unknown		
Colour:	White slip cast stoneware on brown base		
Issued:	c.1910		

Description	U.S. $	Can. $	U.K. £
White slip cast	700.	950.	425.

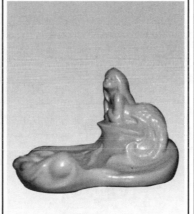

Mermaids

Model No.:	H29		
Designer:	Leslie Harradine		
Height:	7", 18.0 cm		
Colour:	White slip cast stoneware		
Issued:	1912		

Description	U.S. $	Can. $	U.K. £
White slip cast	900.	1,200.	500.

Mother and Child Standing

Model No.:	H24		
Designer:	Leslie Harradine		
Height:	8 ¾", 23.0 cm		
Colour:	1. Brown stoneware		
	2. White slip cast stoneware		
Issued:	1912		

Description	U.S. $	Can. $	U.K. £
1. Brown		Extremely Rare	
2. White slip cast		Extremely Rare	

Motherhood

Model No.:	H4 (X7729)
Designer:	Leslie Harradine
Height:	5", 12.5 cm
Colour:	White slip cast stoneware
Issued:	1912

Description	U.S. $	Can. $	U.K. £
White slip cast		Extremely Rare	

North African Spahi

Model No.:	Unknown
Designer:	Leslie Harradine
Height:	9 ½", 24.0 cm
Colour:	Brown stoneware
Issued:	c.1910
Series:	Soldiers

Description	U.S. $	Can. $	U.K. £
Brown	2,000.	3,000.	1,250.

Peasant Girl

Model No.:	H8
Designer:	Leslie Harradine
Height:	8", 21.0 cm
Colour:	White slip cast stoneware
Issued:	1912

Description	U.S. $	Can. $	U.K. £
White slip cast	800.	1,000.	475.

Peat Cutter

Model No.:	Unknown
Designer:	Leslie Harradine
Height:	7", 18.0 cm
Colour:	Brown stoneware
Issued:	c.1912

Description	U.S. $	Can. $	U.K. £
Brown	1,250.	1,600.	650.

Reaper

Model No.:	H68
Designer:	Leslie Harradine
Height:	7 ½", 19.0 cm
Colour:	1. X8666, Brown stoneware
	2. Coloured Doultonware and toby
	colours
Issued:	1. c.1912; 2. 1927

Description	U.S. $	Can. $	U.K. £
1. Brown	1,250.	1,600.	700.
2. Coloured	1,250.	1,600.	700.

Soldier

Model No.:	H78
Designer:	Leslie Harradine
Height:	9 ½", 24.0 cm
Colour:	Brown stoneware
Issued:	1910
Series:	Soldiers

Description	U.S. $	Can. $	U.K. £
Brown	2,000.	3,000.	1,250.

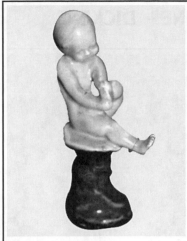

This Little Pig Child Study

Model No.: H49
Designer: Leslie Harradine
Height: 5", 13.0 cm
Colour: Slip cast buff and brown stoneware
Issued: c.1912

Description	U.S. $	Can. $	U.K. £
Slip cast buff stoneware		Extremely Rare	

Worker (with Bucket)

Model No.: Unknown
Designer: Leslie Harradine
Height: 7", 18.0 cm
Colour: Brown stoneware
Issued: c.1912

Description	U.S. $	Con. $	U.K. £
Brown stoneware		Extremely Rare	

LESLIE HARRADINE — DICKENS

Mr. Micawber
Model No.:	H20		
Designer:	Leslie Harradine		
Height:	9 ¼", 24.0 cm		
Colour:	1. Brown		
	2. Buff slip cast stoneware		
	3. Coloured Doultonware		
Issued:	1912		

Description	U.S. $	Can. $	U.K. £
Brown	1,500.	2,000.	850.
Buff slipcast	1,500.	2,000.	850.
Coloured	1,500.	2,000.	850.

Mr. Pickwick
Model No.:	H19		
Designer:	Leslie Harradine		
Height:	8 ¾", 22.0 cm		
Colour:	1. Brown		
	2. Buff slip cast stoneware		
Issued:	1912		

Description	U.S. $	Can. $	U.K. £
Brown	1,500.	2,000.	850.
Buff slipcast	1,500.	2,000.	850.

Mr. Squeers
Model No.:	Unknown		
Designer:	Leslie Harradine		
Height:	9 ¼", 23.5 cm		
Colour:	1. Brown		
	2. Buff slip cast stoneware		
Issued:	1912		

Description	U.S. $	Can. $	U.K. £
Brown	1,500.	2,000.	850.
Buff slipcast	1,500.	2,000.	850.

Pecksniff
Model No.:	H21		
Designer:	Leslie Harradine		
Height:	9", 23.0 cm		
Colour:	1. Brown		
	2. Buff slip cast stoneware		
Issued:	1912		

Description	U.S. $	Can. $	U.K. £
Brown	1,500.	2,000.	850.
Buff slip cast	1,500.	2,000.	850.

Sairey Gamp
Model No.:	Unknown		
Designer:	Leslie Harradine		
Height:	7 ½", 20.0 cm		
Colour:	1. Brown		
	2. Buff slip cast stoneware		
Issued:	1912		

Description	U.S. $	Can. $	U.K. £
Brown	1,500.	2,000.	850.
Buff slip cast	1,500.	2,000.	850.

Sam Weller
Model No.:	H23		
Designer:	Leslie Harradine		
Height:	9 ½", 24.5 cm		
Colour:	1. Brown		
	2. Buff slip cast stoneware		
Issued:	1912		

Description	U.S. $	Can. $	U.K. £
Brown	1,500.	2,000.	850.
Buff slip cast	1,500.	2,000.	850.

MARK MARSHALL

Bear Stripper
Designer: Mark Marshall
Height: 5 ½", 14.0 cm
Colour: White stoneware
Issued: c.1910

Description	U.S. $	Can. $	U.K. £
White stoneware		Extremely Rare	

Crinoline (as HN 13)
Designer: Mark Marshall
Height: 7", 18.0 cm
Colour: Matt white stoneware with blue details
Issued: 1910

Description	U.S. $	Can. $	U.K. £
Matt white stoneware	1,000.00	1,300.00	600.00

18th Century Figure with Fan
Designer: Mark Marshall
Height: 8", 20.5 cm
Colour: Matt white stoneware with blue details
Issued: c.1890

Description	U.S. $	Can. $	U.K. £
Matt white stoneware	750.00	975.00	450.00

Old Woman Figure
Designer: Mark Marshall
Height: 9 ½", 24.3 cm
Colour: Unknown
Issued: c.1900

Description	U.S. $	Can. $	U.K. £
Old Woman Figure		Extremely Rare	

CHARLES NOKE — VELLUM

Beefeater Toasting the Queen
Designer: Charles Noke
Height: 12 ¾", 32.5 cm
Colour: 1. Ivory with pink and blue tints
               2. Scarlet
Issued: 1899

Description	U.S. $	Can. $	U.K. £
1. Ivory	7,500.	10,000.	4,500.
2. Scarlet	7,500.	10,000.	4,500.

Cleopatra
Designer: Charles Noke
Height: 12", 30.5 cm
Colour: Ivory with pink and green tints
Issued: c.1892

Description	U.S. $	Can. $	U.K. £
Ivory	7,500.	10,000.	4,500.

Note: Only three pieces known.

Photograph not
available
at press time

Columbus
Designer: Charles Noke
Height: 20", 51.0 cm
Colour: 1. Gold printed pattern
               2. Ivory
               3. Parian
Issued: 1893

Description	U.S. $	Can. $	U.K. £
1. Gold		Extremely Rare	
2. Ivory		Extremely Rare	
3. Parian		Extremely Rare	

Devil
Designer: Charles Noke
Height: 20", 51.0 cm
Colour: 1. Ivory with pink and green tints
               2. Scarlet and gold
Issued: 1893

Description	U.S. $	Can. $	U.K. £
1. Ivory		Extremely Rare	
2. Scarlet		Extremely Rare	

Diana
Designer: Charles Noke
Height: 11 ½", 29.5 cm
Colour: 1. Ivory with pink and green tints
               2. Printed flowers
               3. Printed scroll pattern
Issued: 1893

Description	U.S. $	Can. $	U.K. £
1. Coloured	6,000.	7,750.	3,000.
2. Flowers	6,000.	7,750.	3,000.
3. Scroll	6,000.	7,750.	3,000.

Ellen Terry as Queen Catharine
Designer: Charles Noke
Height: 1. 12 ½", 31.0 cm
               2. 9", 23.0 cm
Colour: 1. Ivory
               2. Ivory with green and gold tints
Issued: 1893

Height	U.S. $	Can. $	U.K. £
1. 12 ½"	2,300.	3,000.	1,350.
2. 9"	1,650.	2,250.	1,000.

Henry Irving as Cardinal Wolsey

Designer: Charles Noke
Height: 1. 13", 33.0 cm
2. 9 ¼", 23.5 cm
Colour: 1. Ivory
2. Ivory with green and pink sheen
Issued: 1899

Height	U.S. $	Can. $	U.K. £
1. 13"	2,300.	3,000.	1,350.
2. 9 ¼"	1,650.	2,250.	1,000.

Photograph not available at press time

Jack Point

Designer: Charles Noke
Height: 16", 40.5 cm
Colour: Ivory
Issued: 1893

Description	U.S. $	Can. $	U.K. £
Ivory		Extremely Rare	

Jester

Designer: Charles Noke
Height: 9 ½", 23.5 cm
Colour: 1. Ivory
2. Ivory with pink and green tints
3. Parian
Issued: 1892
Varieties: Also found on lamp base

Description	U.S. $	Can. $	U.K. £
1. Ivory	5,000.	6,750.	3,000.
2. Ivory/tints	5,000.	6,750.	3,000.
3. Parian	5,000.	6,750.	3,000.

Jester (Kneeling)

Designer: Charles Noke
Height: 4 ½", 14.0 cm
Colour: Scarlet with gold, flambé
Issued: Vellum c.1900, Flambé c.1938

Description	U.S. $	Can. $	U.K. £
1. Scarlet	9,000.	12,000.	5,500.
2. Flambé	9,000.	12,000.	5,500.

Mephistopheles and Marguerite

This is a double-sided figure

Designer: Charles Noke
Height: 12 ½", 32.0 cm
Colour: 1. Deep blue with printed dragon design
2. Ivory
3. Ivory with pink and green tints
4. Purple and gold
5. Scarlet
6. Scarlet and gold
Issued: 1891

Description	U.S. $	Can. $	U.K. £
1. Blue / dragon design	5,000.	6,750.	3,000.
2. Ivory	5.000.	6,750.	3,000.
3. Ivory/ pink / green	5,000.	6,750.	3,000.
4. Purple/ gold	5,000.	6,750.	3,000.
5. Scarlet	5,000.	6,750.	3,000.
6. Scarlet / gold	5,000.	6,750.	3,000.

Mirth and Melancholy

This is a double-sided figure.
Designer: Charles Noke
Height: 16", 40.5 cm
Colour: 1. Gold printed pattern
           2. Ivory
           3. Ivory with pink and green tint
Issued: 1892

Description	U.S. $	Can. $	U.K. £
1. Gold printed pattern	8,500.	12,000.	5,000.
2. Ivory	8,500.	12,000.	5,000.
3. Ivory/pink/green	8,500.	12,000.	5,000.

Moorish Minstrel

Designer: Charles Noke
Height: Unknown
Colour: 1. Blue and grey; scarlet and blue
           2. Ivory with green and pink tints
           3. Ivory with green and pink tints, white and gold flowers
Issued: 1892
Varieties: Also found on lamp base

Description	U.S. $	Can. $	U.K. £
1. Ivory/green/pink	5,000.	6,750.	3,000.
2. Ivory/green/pink/white/gold	5,000.	6,750.	3,000.
3. Blue/grey/scarlet/blue	5,000.	6,750.	3,000.

Oh! Law

This is a double-sided figure
Designer: Charles Noke
Height: 8 ½ ", 21.5 cm
Colour: 1. Gold printed pattern
           2. Ivory
           3. Ivory with green and pink tints
Issued: 1893

Description	U.S. $	Can. $	U.K. £
1. Gold printed pattern	5,500.	7,500.	3,250.
2. Ivory	5,500.	7,500.	3,250.
3. Ivory / green / pink	5,500.	7,500.	3,250.

Pierrot

Designer: Charles Noke
Height: 6 ½", 16.5 cm
Colour: 1. Ivory with black details
           2. Ivory with green and gold details
Issued: 1899

Description	U.S. $	Can. $	U.K. £
1. Ivory / black	5,500.	7,500.	3,250.
2. Ivory / green / gold	5,500.	7,500.	3,250.

Portia

Designer:	Charles Noke
Height:	16 ¾", 42.5 cm
Colour:	1. Green and pink with flowers
	2. Green and pink with scrolls and flowers
	3. Ivory
Issued:	1893

Description	U.S.$	Can.$	U.K. £
Green/flowers	7,500.	10,000.	4,000.
Green/scrolls	7,500.	10,000.	4,000.
Ivory	7,500.	10,000.	4,000.

St. Mark's Birds

Designer:	Charles Noke
Height:	17 ½", 44.0 cm
Colour:	1. Ivory and gold
	2. Ivory with pink tints
	3. Printed flowers
Issued:	1892

Description	U.S.$	Can.$	U.K.£
Ivory/gold	7,500.	10,000.	4,000.
Ivory/pink tints	7,500.	10,000.	4,000.
Printed flowers	7,500.	10,000.	4,000.

Photograph not available at press time

Sentimental Pierrot

Designer:	Charles Noke
Height:	6", 15.0 cm
Colour:	1. Ivory
	2. Ivory with pink and green tints
Issued:	1899

Description	U.S.$	Can.$	U.K.£
Ivory	7,500.	10,000.	4,000.
Ivory/tints	7,500.	10,000.	4,000.

Shakespeare

Designer:	Charles Noke
Height:	12 ½", 31.0 cm
Colour:	1. Ivory
	2. Ivory/pink/green
Issued:	c.1899

Description	U.S.$	Can.$	U.K.£
Ivory	5,500.	7,500.	3,250.
Ivory/tints	5,500.	7,500.	3,250.

Shylock

Designer:	Charles Noke
Height:	16", 40.5 cm
Colour:	1. Brown, gold printed pattern
	2. Ivory
Issued:	1893

Description	U.S.$	Can.$	U.K.£
Brown/gold	16,500.	22,000.	10,000.
Ivory	7,500.	10,000.	4,000.

Water Carrier

Designer:	Charles Noke
Height:	20 ¾", 52.0 cm
Colour:	Ivory with pink and green tints
Issued:	1893

Description	U.S.$	Can.$	U.K.£
	Extremely Rare		

CHARLES NOKE — WALL POCKETS AND LIGHTS

Geisha Wall Pocket
Designer: Charles Noke
Height: 9 ¼", 23.5 cm
Colour: 1. Gold printed pattern
2. Ivory
3. Ivory with pink tints
Issued: 1893

Description	U.S. $	Can. $	U.K. £
1. Gold printed pattern	4,500.	5,750.	2,250.
2. Ivory	4,500.	5,750.	2,250.
3. Ivory / pink	4,500.	5,750.	2,250.

Lady Jester Wall Pocket
Designer: Charles Noke
Height: 9 ¾", 24.5 cm
Colour: 1. Ivory with green and pink tints
2. Printed floral pattern
Issued: 1892

Description	U.S. $	Can. $	U.K. £
1. Ivory / green / pink	5,000.	6,500.	3,000.
2. Printed floral pattern	5,000.	6,500.	3,000.

Sorceress Wall Pocket
Designer: Charles Noke
Height: 10 ¾, 27.5 cm
Colour: 1. Green tint with white floral pattern
2. Ivory
Issued: 1892

Description	U.S. $	Can. $	U.K. £
1. Green / white floral	5,000.	6,500.	3,000.
2. Ivory	5,000.	6,500.	3,000.

The Witch Wall Light
Designer: Charles Noke
Height: Unknown
Colour: Green and scarlet with gold floral pattern
Issued: 1897

Description	U.S. $	Can. $	U.K. £
Green / scarlet / gold		Extremely Rare	

GEORGE TINWORTH

Boy Cricketer
Designer: George Tinworth
Height: 5", 13.0 cm
Colour: 1. Brown Siliconware
          2. Coloured Doultonware
Issued: c.1890

Description	U.S. $	Can. $	U.K. £
1. Brown	3,500.	4,500.	1,750.
2. Coloured	3,500.	4,500.	1,750.

Boy Jester
Designer: George Tinworth
Height: 5", 13.0 cm
Colour: Brown stoneware
Issued: c.1890

Description	U.S. $	Can. $	U.K. £
Brown	1,750.	2,250.	850.

Boy with Melon
Designer: George Tinworth
Height: 3 ½", 9.0 cm
Colour: Brown stoneware
Issued: c.1890

Description	U.S. $	Can. $	U.K. £
Brown	1,750.	2,250.	850.

Boy with Vase
Designer: George Tinworth
Height: Unknown
Colour: Coloured Doultonware
Issued: c.1890

Description	U.S. $	Can. $	U.K. £
Coloured	3,500.	4,500.	1,750.

Drunken Husband
Designer: George Tinworth
Height: 5 ¼", 12.0 cm
Colour: Coloured Doultonware
Issued: 1881

Description	U.S. $	Can. $	U.K. £
Coloured	13,500.	18,000.	7,000.

Note: A number of variations of this figurine exist.
Mainly in the placement of the small figures.

Five Miles to London
Designer: George Tinworth
Height: 9", 23.0 cm
Colour: Coloured Doultonware
Issued: c.1885

Description	U.S. $	Can. $	U.K. £
Coloured	7,500.	9,750.	4,000.

Girl with Tambourine
Designer: George Tinworth
Height: 9", 23.0 cm
Colour: Coloured Doultonware
Issued: c.1885

Description	U.S. $	Can. $	U.K. £
Coloured	5,000.	6,500.	3,000.

Jester
Designer: George Tinworth
Height: 12 ½", 31.5 cm
Colour: Terracotta
Issued: 1900
          Produced for the Art Union in an
          edition of 12

Description	U.S. $	Can. $	U.K. £
Terracotta	7,500.	9,750.	4,000.

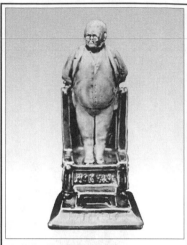

Mr. Pickwick
Designer: George Tinworth
Height: 5", 12.5 cm
Colour: Coloured Doultonware
Issued: c.1895

Description	U.S. $	Can. $	U.K. £
Coloured		Extremely Rare	

Scandal
Designer: George Tinworth
Height: 6 ¼", 16.0 cm
Colour: Coloured Doultonware
Issued: 1891

Description	U.S. $	Can. $	U.K. £
Coloured	8,000.	10,000.	4,500.

Young Carpenter
Designer: George Tinworth
Height: 5 ¼", 13.0 cm
Colour: Brown stoneware
Issued: c.1892

Description	U.S. $	Can. $	U.S.£
Coloured	2,500.	3,250.	1,500.

Note: These early Doulton Lambeth figures are all rare with limited examples known. Prices will vary widely depending on supply and demand at the time of sale. Prices listed are indications only.

The Merry Musicians

The exact number of Merry Musicians is not recorded but there are probably around a hundred different figures, playing at least forty different instruments, some of which are listed on page 20. The figures can be found with endless variations of poses, expressions, hats and instruments, many of which are very obscure. The Musicians were produced from the 1890s until the early 1900s in small numbers. Around 1910 a set was produced with white faces for the Australian agent, John Shorter. Many of the Musicians have Tinworth's monogram although some were produced entirely by assistants.

A List of Recorded Merry Musicians to Date

Bagpipes	Cymbals	Military Bass Type	Sousaphone
Banjo	Flageolet	Drum	Scottish Bagpipes
Barrel drum	Flute	Military Side	Spiral Horn
Bass Clarinet	French Horn	One Man Band	Tambourine
Bells	Harp	Organ	Trombone
Botuto	Horn	Organistrum	Trumpet
Carillon	Hurdy Gurdy	Piano	Tuba
Cello	Kettle Drum	Piccolo	Tympanum
Cittern	Lute	Positive Organ	Ukulele
Concertina	Lyre	Rebec	Viola
Conductor	Mandolin	Barrel Drum	Violin
Cornet	Marimba	Saxophone	Whistle

Pricing: The Merry Musicians can only be priced with indicating ranges. Within the series there will be rare figures, so that any demand for a scarce ro rare musician could easily double or triple the price. We also find that the more complicated the musician the higher the price. An example of this is the organ which sold at the Harriman Judd Part Two Sotheby's auction for $2,700.00 US including premium.

U.S.. $1,500.00 - $2,200.00   Can.: $2,000.00 - $3,000.00   U.K.: £900.00 - $1,300.00

Note: We would appreciate any new information, and/or photographs, of the Merry Musicians. Please refer to our editorial office address in the front of the catalogue as to where to send the information.

BAGPIPES

BOTUTO

CONCERTINA

LUTE

ORGAN

PIANO

PICCOLO

SCOTTISH BAGPIPES

SCOTTISH BAGPIPES

VIOLIN

ROYAL DOULTON FIGURINES

HN SERIES

HN 26, The Diligent Scholar

HN 1
Darling
Style One
Designer: C. Vyse
Height: 7 ¾", 19.5 cm
Issued: 1913-1928
Colour: Light grey
Varieties: HN 1319, 1371,
1372, 4140

U.S.:	$3,500.00
Can.:	$4,500.00
U.K.:	£2,000.00

HN 2
Elizabeth Fry
Designer: C. Vyse
Height: 17", 43.2 cm
Issued: 1913-1936
Colour: Light blue, green base
Varieties: HN 2A

U.S.:	$ 8,000.00
Can.:	$11,000.00
U.K.:	£ 4,750.00

HN 2A
Elizabeth Fry
Designer: C. Vyse
Height: 17", 43.2 cm
Issued: 1913-1936
Colour: Light blue, blue base
Varieties: HN 2

U.S.:	$ 8,000.00
Can.:	$11,000.00
U.K.:	£ 4,750.00

HN 3
Milking Time
Designer: P. Stabler
Height: 6 ½", 16.5 cm
Colour: Blue dress, white apron
Issued: 1913-1938
Varieties: HN 306

U.S.:	Only
Can.:	three
U.K.:	known

HN 4
Picardy Peasant (woman)
Designer: P. Stabler
Height: 9 ¼", 23.5 cm
Colour: Blue and white
Issued: 1913-1938
Varieties: HN 5, 17A, 351, 513

U.S.:	$5,000.00
Can.:	$6,500.00
U.K.:	£3,000.00

HN 5
Picardy Peasant (woman)
Designer: P. Stabler
Height: 9 ½", 24.0 cm
Colour: Grey
Issued: 1913-1938
Varieties: HN 4, 17A, 351, 513

U.S.:	
Can.:	Extremely rare
U.K.:	

HN 6
Dunce
Designer: C. J. Noke
Height: 10 ½", 26.7 cm
Colour: Light blue
Issued: 1913-1936
Varieties: HN 310, 357

U.S.:	Only
Can.:	three
U.K.:	known

HN 7
Pedlar Wolf
Designer: C. J. Noke
Height: 5 ½", 14.0 cm
Colour: Blue and black
Issued: 1913-1938
Varieties: Also known in flambé

U.S.:	Only
Can.:	two
U.K.:	known

HN 8
The Crinoline
Designer: G. Lambert
Height: 6 ¼", 15.8 cm
Colour: Lavender
Issued: 1913-1938
Varieties: HN 9, 9A, 21, 21A,
           413, 566, 628

U.S.:	$3,500.00
Can.:	$4,500.00
U.K.:	£2,100.00

HN 9
The Crinoline
Designer: G. Lambert
Height: 6 ¼", 15.8 cm
Colour: Light green,
           flowers on skirt
Issued: 1913-1938
Varieties: HN 8, 9A, 21, 21A,
           413, 566, 628

U.S.:	$3,500.00
Can.:	$4,500.00
U.K.:	£2,100.00

HN 9A
The Crinoline
Designer: G. Lambert
Height: 6 ¼", 15.8 cm
Colour: Light green,
           no flowers
Issued: 1913-1938
Varieties: HN 8, 9, 21, 21A,
           413, 566, 628

U.S.:	
Can.:	Extremely rare
U.K.:	

HN 10
Madonna of the Square
Designer: P. Stabler
Height: 7", 17.8 cm
Colour: Lavender
Issued: 1913-1936
Varieties: HN 10A, 11, 14, 27,
           326, 573, 576, 594,
           613, 764, 1968, 1969,
           2034

U.S.:	$2,500.00
Can.:	$3,250.00
U.K.:	£1,500.00

HN 10A
Madonna of the Square
Designer: P. Stabler
Height: 7", 17.8 cm
Colour: Green and blue
Issued: 1913-1936
Varieties: HN 10, 11, 14, 27,
           326, 573, 576, 594,
           613, 764, 1968,
           1969, 2034

U.S.:	
Can.:	Extremely rare
U.K.:	

HN 11
Madonna of the Square
Designer: P. Stabler
Height: 7", 17.8 cm
Colour: Grey
Issued: 1913-1936
Varieties: HN 10, 10A, 14, 27,
           326, 573, 576, 594,
           613, 764, 1968,
           1969, 2034

U.S.:	
Can.:	Extremely rare
U.K.:	

HN 12
Baby
Designer: C. J. Noke
Height: 4 ¾" 12.0 cm
Colour: Pale pink
Issued: 1913-1938

U.S.:	Only
Can.:	two
U.K.:	known

HN 13
Picardy Peasant (man)
Designer: P. Stabler
Height: 9", 22.9 cm
Colour: Blue costume
           with white cap
Issued: 1913-1938
Varieties: HN 17, 19

U.S.:	
Can.:	Extremely rare
U.K.:	

HN 14
Madonna of the Square
Designer: P. Stabler
Height: 7", 17.8 cm
Colour: Blue
Issued: 1913-1936
Varieties: HN 10, 10A, 11, 27,
           326, 573, 576, 594,
           613, 764, 1968,
           1969, 2034

U.S.:	$2,500.00
Can.:	$3,250.00
U.K.:	£1,500.00

HN 15
The Sleepy Scholar
Designer: W. White
Height: 6 ¾", 17.2 cm
Colour: Blue
Issued: 1913-1938
Varieties: HN 16, 29

U.S.:	$ 8,500.00
Can.:	$11,000.00
U.K.:	£ 5,000.00

HN 16
The Sleepy Scholar
Designer: W. White
Height: 6 ¾", 17.2 cm
Colour: Green
Issued: 1913-1938
Varieties: HN 15, 29

U.S.:	$ 8,500.00
Can.:	$11,000.00
U.K.:	£ 5,000.00

HN 17
Picardy Peasant (man)
Designer: P. Stabler
Height: 9 ½", 24.0 cm
Colour: Green
Issued: 1913-1938
Varieties: HN 13, 19,

U.S.:	
Can.:	Extremely rare
U.K.:	

HN 17A
Picardy Peasant (woman)
Designer: P. Stabler
Height: 9 ½", 24.0 cm
Colour: Green
Issued: 1913-1938
Varieties: HN 4, 5, 351, 513

U.S.:	
Can.:	Extremely rare
U.K.:	

HN 18
Pussy
Designer: F. C. Stone
Height: 7 ¾", 19.7 cm
Colour: Light blue
Issued: 1913-1938
Varieties: HN 325, 507; also
           called 'The Black Cat'

U.S.:	Only
Can.:	five
U.K.:	known

Also known with white dress.

HN 19
Picardy Peasant (man)
Designer: P. Stabler
Height: 9 ½", 24.0 cm
Colour: Green
Issued: 1913-1938
Varieties: HN 13, 17

U.S.:	
Can.:	Extremely rare
U.K.:	

HN 20
The Coquette
Designer: W. White
Height: 9 ¼", 23.5 cm
Colour: Blue
Issued: 1913-1938
Varieties: HN 20A, 37

U.S.:	$ 8,500.00
Can.:	$11,000.00
U.K.:	£ 5,000.00

HN 20A
The Coquette
Designer: W. White
Height: 9 ¼", 23.5 cm
Colour: Green
Issued: 1913-1938
Varieties: HN 20, 37

U.S.:	**$ 7,000.00**
Can.:	**$10,000.00**
U.K.:	**£ 4,000.00**

HN 21
The Crinoline
Designer: G. Lambert
Height: 6 ¼", 15.8 cm
Colour: Yellow, with rosebuds
Issued: 1913-1938
Varieties: HN 8, 9, 9A, 21A, 413,
          566, 628

U.S.:	**$3,500.00**
Can.:	**$4,500.00**
U.K.:	**£2,100.00**

HN 21A
The Crinoline
Designer: G. Lambert
Height: 6 ¼", 15.8 cm
Colour: Yellow, no rosebuds
Issued: 1913-1938
Varieties: HN 8, 9, 9A, 21, 413,
          566, 628

U.S.:	
Can.:	**Extremely rare**
U.K.:	

HN 22
The Lavender Woman
Designer: P. Stabler
Height: 8 ¼", 21.0 cm
Colour: Light blue
Issued: 1913-1936
Varieties: HN 23, 23A, 342,
          569, 744

U.S.:	**$5,500.00**
Can.:	**$7,250.00**
U.K.:	**£3,250.00**

HN 23
The Lavender Woman
Designer: P. Stabler
Height: 8 ¼", 21.0 cm
Colour: Green
Issued: 1913-1936
Varieties: HN 22, 23A, 342,
          569, 744

U.S.:	
Can.:	**Extremely rare**
U.K.:	

HN 23A
The Lavender Woman
Designer: P. Stabler
Height: 8 ¼", 21.0 cm
Colour: Blue and green
Issued: 1913-1936
Varieties: HN 22, 23, 342,
          569, 744

U.S.:	
Can.:	**Extremely rare**
U.K.:	

HN 24
Sleep
Designer: P. Stabler
Height: 8 ¼", 21.0 cm
Colour: Light green
Issued: 1913-1936
Varieties: HN 24A, 25, 25A,
          424, 692, 710

U.S.:	**$3,500.00**
Can.:	**$4,500.00**
U.K.:	**£2,000.00**

HN 24A
Sleep
Designer: P. Stabler
Height: 8 ¼", 21.0 cm
Colour: Dark blue
Issued: 1913-1936
Varieties: HN 24, 25, 25A,
          424, 692, 710

U.S.:	**$3,500.00**
Can.:	**$4,500.00**
U.K.:	**£2,000.00**

HN 25
Sleep
Designer: P. Stabler
Height: 8 ¼", 21.0 cm
Colour: Dark green
Issued: 1913-1936
Varieties: HN 24, 24A, 25A, 424, 692, 710

U.S.:	**$3,500.00**
Can.:	**$4,500.00**
U.K.:	**£2,000.00**

HN 25A
Sleep
Designer: P. Stabler
Height: 8 ¼", 21.0 cm
Colour: Dark green
Issued: 1913-1936
Varieties: HN 24, 24A, 25, 424, 692, 710

U.S.:	
Can.:	**Extremely rare**
U.K.:	

HN 26
The Diligent Scholar
Designer: W. White
Height: 7", 17.8 cm
Colour: Mottled brown and green
Issued: 1913-1936
Varieties: Also called 'The Attentive Scholar'

U.S.:	**$ 8,500.00**
Can.:	**$11,000.00**
U.K.:	**£ 5,000.00**

HN 27
Madonna of the Square
Designer: P. Stabler
Height: 7", 17.8 cm
Colour: Blue
Issued: 1913-1936
Varieties: HN 10, 10A, 11, 14, 326, 573, 576, 594, 613, 764, 1968, 1969, 2034

U.S.:	
Can.:	**Extremely rare**
U.K.:	

HN 28
Motherhood
Style One
Designer: P. Stabler
Height: 8", 20.3 cm
Colour: Light blue
Issued: 1913-1936
Varieties: HN 30, 303

U.S.:	**$ 8,000.00**
Can.:	**$10,500.00**
U.K.:	**£ 4,750.00**

HN 29
The Sleepy Scholar
Designer: W. White
Height: 6 ¾", 17.2 cm
Colour: Brown
Issued: 1913-1938
Varieties: HN 15, 16

U.S.:	**$ 8,500.00**
Can.:	**$11,000.00**
U.K.:	**£ 5,000.00**

HN 30
Motherhood
Style One
Designer: P. Stabler
Height: 8", 20.3 cm
Colour: White, blue and yellow
Issued: 1913-1936
Varieties: HN 28, 303

U.S.:	**None**
Can.:	**known**
U.K.:	**to exist**

HN 31
The Return of Persephone
Designer: C. Vyse
Height: 16", 40.6 cm
Colour: Grey and grey-blue
Issued: 1913-1938

U.S.:	**Only**
Can.:	**two**
U.K.:	**known**

HN 32
Child on Crab
Designer: C. J. Noke.
Height: 5 ¼", 13.3 cm
Colour: Pale blue, green and brown
Issued: 1913-1938
Varieties: Also known in flambé

U.S.:	**$ 8,500.00**
Can.:	**$11,000.00**
U.K.:	**£ 5,000.00**

HN 33
An Arab
Designer: C. J. Noke
Height: 16 ½", 41.9 cm
Colour: Dark blue, green
Issued: 1913-1938
Varieties: HN 343, 378; also called 'The Moor' HN 1308, 1366, 1425, 1657, 2082, 3642, 3926

U.S.:	**$5,000.00**
Can.:	**$6,500.00**
U.K.:	**£3,000.00**

HN 34
A Moorish Minstrel
Designer: C. J. Noke
Height: 13 ½", 34.3 cm
Colour: Deep purple
Issued: 1913-1938
Varieties: HN 364, 415, 797

U.S.:	**$5,000.00**
Can.:	**$6,500.00**
U.K.:	**£3,000.00**

Derived from Burslem figure produced in 1890s.

HN 35
Charley's Aunt
Style One
Designer: A. Toft
Height: 7", 17.8 cm
Colour: Black and white
Issued: 1913-1936
Varieties: HN 640

U.S.:	**$1,200.00**
Can.:	**$1,600.00**
U.K.:	**£ 700.00**

HN 36
The Sentimental Pierrot
Designer: C. J. Noke
Height: 5 ½", 14.0 cm
Colour: Grey
Issued: 1914-1936
Varieties: HN 307

U.S.:	**$ 8,500.00**
Can.:	**$11,000.00**
U.K.:	**£ 5,000.00**

HN 37
The Coquette
Designer: W. White
Height: 9 ¼", 23.5 cm
Colour: Green flowered dress
Issued: 1914-1938
Varieties: HN 20, 20A

U.S.:	**$ 8,500.00**
Can.:	**$11,000.00**
U.K.:	**£ 5,000.00**

HN 38
The Carpet Vendor
Style One
Designer: C. J. Noke
Height: 5 ½", 14.0 cm
Colour: Blue, yellow and green
Issued: 1914-1936
Varieties: HN 76, 350; also known in flambé

U.S.:	
Can.:	**Extremely rare**
U.K.:	

HN 38A
The Carpet Vendor
Style Two
Designer: C. J. Noke
Height: 6 ¼", 15.9 cm
Colour: Blue and yellow, patterned long carpet
Issued: 1914-1936
Varieties: HN 348

U.S.:	
Can.:	**Extremely rare**
U.K.:	

HN 39
Myfanwy Jones
Designer: E. W. Light
Height: 12", 30.5 cm
Colour: Red, black, purple
Issued: 1914-1936
Varieties: HN 92, 456, 514, 516,
          519, 520, 660, 668,
          669, 701, 792; also
          called 'The Welsh Girl'

U.S.:	$ 8,500.00
Can.:	$11,000.00
U.K.:	£ 5,000.00

HN 40
A Lady of the Elizabethan Period
Style One
Designer: E. W. Light
Height: 9 ½", 24.1 cm
Colour: Orange and brown
          with pattern
Issued: 1914-1938
Varieties: HN 40A, 73, 411; also
          called 'Elizabethan
          Lady' (Style One)

U.S.:	
Can.:	**Extremely rare**
U.K.:	

HN 40A
A Lady of the Elizabethan Period
Style One
Designer: E. W. Light
Height: 9 ½", 24.1 cm
Colour: Orange and brown
Issued: 1914-1938
Varieties: HN 40, 73, 411; also
          called 'Elizabethan
          Lady' (Style One)

U.S.:	
Can.:	**Extremely rare**
U.K.:	

HN 41
A Lady of the Georgian Period
Designer: E. W. Light
Height: 10 ¼", 26.0 cm
Colour: Gold and blue
Issued: 1914-1936
Varieties: HN 331, 444, 690,
          702

U.S.:	$5,000.00
Can.:	$6,500.00
U.K.:	£3,000.00

HN 42
Robert Burns
Style One
Designer: E. W. Light
Height: 14", 35.5 cm
Colour: Brown, green
          and yellow
Issued: 1914-1938

U.S.:	**Only**
Can.:	**one**
U.K.:	**known**

HN 43
A Woman of the Time of
Henry VI
Designer: E. W. Light
Height: 9 ¼", 23.5 cm
Colour: Green and yellow
Issued: 1914-1938

U.S.:	**Only**
Can.:	**three**
U.K.:	**known**

HN 44
A Lilac Shawl
Designer: C. J. Noke
Height: 8 ¾", 22.2 cm
Colour: Cream and blue
Issued: 1915-1938
Varieties: HN 44A; also called
          'In Grandma's Days'
          HN 339, 340, 388,
          442; 'The Poke Bonnet'
          HN 362, 612, 765

U.S.:	$3,500.00
Can.:	$4,500.00
U.K.:	£2,000.00

HN 44A
A Lilac Shawl
Designer: C. J. Noke
Height: 8 ¾", 22.2 cm
Colour: White and lilac
Issued: 1915-1938
Varieties: HN 44; also called
          'In Grandma's Days'
          HN 339, 340, 388,
          442; 'The Poke Bonnet'
          HN 362, 612, 765

U.S.:	$3,500.00
Can.:	$4,500.00
U.K.:	£2,000.00

HN 45
A Jester
Style One
Designer: C. J. Noke
Height: 9 ½", 24.1 cm
Colour: Black and white
Issued: 1915-1938
Varieties: HN 71, 71A, 320, 367,
          412, 426, 446, 552,
          616, 627, 1295, 1702,
          2016, 3922

U.S.: $ 8,000.00
Can.: $10,500.00
U.K.:   £ 4,750.00

HN 45A
A Jester
Style Two
Designer: C. J. Noke
Height: 10 ¼", 26.0 cm
Colour: Green and white
Issued: 1915-1938
Varieties: HN 45B, 55, 308,
          630, 1333; also known
          in black and white

U.S.: $ 8,000.00
Can.: $10,500.00
U.K.:   £ 4,750.00

HN 45B
A Jester
Style Two
Designer: C. J. Noke
Height: 10 ¼", 26.0 cm
Colour: Red and white
Issued: 1915-1938
Varieties: HN 45A, 55, 308, 630,
          1333; also known in
          black and white

U.S.: $ 8,000.00
Can.: $10,500.00
U.K.:   £ 4,750.00

HN 46
The Gainsborough Hat
Designer: H. Tittensor
Height: 8 ¾", 22.2 cm
Colour: Lavender
Issued: 1915-1936
Varieties: HN 46A, 47, 329, 352,
          383, 453, 675, 705

U.S.: $5,000.00
Can.: $6,500.00
U.K.:   £3,000.00

HN 46A
The Gainsborough Hat
Designer: H. Tittensor
Height: 8 ¾", 22.2 cm
Colour: Lavender with
          black collar
Issued: 1915-1936
Varieties: HN 46, 47, 329, 352,
          383, 453, 675, 705

U.S.:   None
Can.:   known
U.K.:   to exist

HN 47
The Gainsborough Hat
Designer: H. Tittensor
Height: 8 ¾", 22.2 cm
Colour: Green
Issued: 1915-1936
Varieties: HN 46, 46A, 329, 352,
          383, 453, 675, 705

U.S.: $5,000.00
Can.: $6,500.00
U.K.:   £3,000.00

HN 48
Lady of the Fan
Designer: E. W. Light
Height: 9 ½", 24.1 cm
Colour: Lavender
Issued: 1916-1936
Varieties: HN 52, 53, 53A,
          335, 509

U.S.:   None
Can.:   known
U.K.:   to exist

HN 48A
Lady with Rose
Designer: E. W. Light
Height: 9 ½", 24.1 cm
Colour: Cream and orange
Issued: 1916-1936
Varieties: HN 52A, 68, 304, 336,
          515, 517, 584, 624

U.S.: $4,500.00
Can.: $6,000.00
U.K.:   £2,750.00

HN 49
Under the Gooseberry Bush
Designer: C. J. Noke
Height: 3 ½", 8.9 cm
Colour: Green and brown
Issued: 1916-1938

U.S.:	**$4,000.00**
Can.:	**$5,000.00**
U.K.:	**£2,400.00**

HN 50
A Spook
Style One
Designer: H. Tittensor
Height: 7", 17.8 cm
Colour: Green robe, black cap
Issued: 1916-1936
Varieties: HN 51, 51A, 51B, 58,
           512, 625; also known
           in flambé

U.S.:	**$5,000.00**
Can.:	**$6,500.00**
U.K.:	**£3,000.00**

HN 51
A Spook
Style One
Designer: H. Tittensor
Height: 7", 17.8 cm
Colour: Green robe, red cap
Issued: 1916-1936
Varieties: HN 50, 51A, 51B, 58,
           512, 625; also known
           in flambé

U.S.:	**$5,000.00**
Can.:	**$6,500.00**
U.K.:	**£3,000.00**

HN 51A
A Spook
Style One
Designer: H. Tittensor
Height: 7", 17.8 cm
Colour: Green robe, black cap
Issued: 1916-1936
Varieties: HN 50, 51, 51B, 58,
           512, 625; also known
           in flambé

U.S.:	**$5,000.00**
Can.:	**$6,500.00**
U.K.:	**£3,000.00**

HN 51B
A Spook
Designer: H. Tittensor
Height: 7", 17.8 cm
Colour: Blue robe, red cap
Issued: 1916-1936
Varieties: HN 50, 51, 51A, 58,
           512, 625; also known
           in flambé

U.S.:	**None**
Can.:	**known**
U.K.:	**to exist**

HN 52
Lady of the Fan
Designer: E. W. Light
Height: 9 ½", 24.1 cm
Colour: Green
Issued: 1916-1936
Varieties: HN 48, 53, 53A, 335,
           509

U.S.:	**$4,500.00**
Can.:	**$6,000.00**
U.K.:	**£2,700.00**

HN 52A
Lady with Rose
Designer: E. W. Light
Height: 9 ½", 24.1 cm
Colour: Yellow
Issued: 1916-1936
Varieties: HN 48A, 68, 304, 336,
           515, 517, 584, 624

U.S.:	**None**
Can.:	**known**
U.K.:	**to exist**

HN 53
Lady of the Fan
Designer: E. W. Light
Height: 9 ½", 24.1 cm
Colour: Dark purple
Issued: 1916-1936
Varieties: HN 48, 52, 53A, 335,
           509

U.S.:	**$4,500.00**
Can.:	**$6,000.00**
U.K.:	**£2,700.00**

HN 53A
Lady of the Fan
Designer: E. W. Light
Height: 9", 22.9 cm
Colour: Green
Issued: 1916-1936
Varieties: HN 48, 52, 53,
           335, 509

U.S.:	**Only**
Can.:	**one**
U.K.:	**known**

HN 54
The Ermine Muff
Designer: C. J. Noke
Height: 8 ½", 21.6 cm
Colour: Grey coat, pale
           green dress
Issued: 1916-1938
Varieties: HN 332, 671; also
           called 'Lady Ermine'
           and 'Lady With Ermine
           Muff'

U.S.:	**$4,000.00**
Can.:	**$5,250.00**
U.K.:	**£2,500.00**

HN 55
A Jester
Style Two
Designer: C. J. Noke
Height: 10 ¼", 26.0 cm
Colour: Black and lavender
Issued: 1916-1938
Varieties: HN 45A, 45B, 308,
           630, 1333; also known
           in black and white

U.S.:	**$ 8,500.00**
Can.:	**$11,000.00**
U.K.:	**£ 5,000.00**

HN 56
The Land of Nod
First Version
Designer: H. Tittensor
Height: 9 ½", 24.1 cm
Colour: Ivory, green candlestick
Issued: 1916-1938
Varieties: HN 56A, 56B

U.S.:	**$ 9,000.00**
Can.:	**$11,750.00**
U.K.:	**£ 5,500.00**

The owl was produced as animal
figure HN 169.

HN 56A
The Land of Nod
First Version
Designer: H. Tittensor
Height: 9 ½", 24.1 cm
Colour: Light grey, green
           candlestick
Issued: 1916-1938
Varieties: HN 56, 56B

U.S.:	**$ 9,000.00**
Can.:	**$11,750.00**
U.K.:	**£ 5,500.00**

HN 56B
The Land of Nod
First Version
Designer: H. Tittensor
Height: 9 ½", 24.1 cm
Colour: Light grey, red
           candlestick
Issued: 1916-1938
Varieties: HN 56, 56A

U.S.:	**$ 9,000.00**
Can.:	**$11,750.00**
U.K.:	**£ 5,500.00**

HN 57
The Curtsey
Designer: E. W. Light
Height: 11", 27.9 cm
Colour: Orange
Issued: 1916-1936
Varieties: HN 57B, 66A, 327,
           334, 363, 371, 518,
           547, 629, 670

U.S.:	**None**
Can.:	**known**
U.K.:	**to exist**

HN 57A
The Flounced Skirt
Designer: E. W. Light
Height: 9 ¾", 24.7 cm
Colour: Orange
Issued: 1916-1938
Varieties: HN 66, 77, 78, 333;
           also called 'The Bow'

U.S.:	**None**
Can.:	**known**
U.K.:	**to exist**

HN 57B
The Curtsey
Designer: E. W. Light
Height: 11", 27.9 cm
Colour: Lavender
Issued: 1916-1936
Varieties: HN 57, 66A, 327, 334,
           363, 371, 518, 547,
           629, 670

U.S.:	$4,250.00
Can.:	$5,500.00
U.K.:	£2,500.00

HN 58
A Spook
Style One
Designer: H. Tittensor
Height: 7", 17.8 cm
Colour: Unknown
Issued: 1916 1936
Varieties: HN 50, 51, 51A, 51B,
           512, 625; also known
           in flambé

U.S.:	None
Can.:	known
U.K.:	to exist

HN 59
Upon Her Cheeks She Wept
Designer: L. Perugini
Height: 9", 22.8 cm
Colour: Grey dress
Issued: 1916-1938
Varieties: HN 511, 522

U.S.:	$ 8,500.00
Can.:	$11,000.00
U.K.:	£ 5,000.00

HN 60
Shy Anne
Designer: L. Perugini
Height: 7 ¾", 19.7 cm
Colour: Blue dress with flowers,
           blue bow in hair
Issued: 1916-1936
Varieties: HN 64, 65, 568

U.S.:	
Can.:	Extremely rare
U.K.:	

HN 61
Katharine
Style One
Designer: C. J. Noke
Height: 5 ¾", 14.6 cm
Colour: Green
Issued: 1916-1938
Varieties: HN 74, 341, 471, 615,
           793

U.S.:	$3,750.00
Can.:	$4,800.00
U.K.:	£2,250.00

HN 62
A Child's Grace
Designer: L. Perugini
Height: 9 ¼", 23.5 cm
Colour: Green and yellow coat,
           yellow dress
Issued: 1916-1938
Varieties: HN 62A, 510

U.S.:	Only
Can.:	two
U.K.:	known

HN 62A
A Child's Grace
Designer: L. Perugini
Height: 9 ¼", 23.5 cm
Colour: Green coat, yellow
           dress
Issued: 1916-1938
Varieties: HN 62, 510

U.S.:	
Can.:	Extremely rare
U.K.:	

HN 63
The Little Land
Designer: H. Tittensor
Height: 7 ½", 19.1 cm
Colour: Green and yellow
Issued: 1916-1936
Varieties: HN 67

U.S.:	$ 8,500.00
Can.:	$11,000.00
U.K.:	£ 5,000.00

HN 64
Shy Anne
Designer: L. Perugini
Height: 7 ¾", 19.7 cm
Colour: Pale blue, white bow in hair
Issued: 1916-1936
Varieties: HN 60, 65, 568

U.S.:	$ 8,000.00
Can.:	$10,500.00
U.K.:	£ 4,750.00

HN 65
Shy Anne
Designer: L. Perugini
Height: 7 ¾", 19.7 cm
Colour: Pale blue, dark blue stripe around hem of skirt, white bow in hair
Issued: 1916-1936
Varieties: HN 60, 64, 568

U.S.:	$ 8,000.00
Can.:	$10,500.00
U.K.:	£ 4,750.00

HN 66
The Flounced Skirt
Designer: E. W. Light
Height: 9 ¾", 24.7 cm
Colour: Lavender
Issued: 1916-1938
Varieties: HN 57A, 77, 78, 333; also called 'The Bow'

U.S.:	$4,250.00
Can.:	$5,500.00
U.K.:	£2,000.00

HN 66A
The Curtsey
Designer: E. W. Light
Height: 11", 27.9 cm
Colour: Lavender
Issued: 1916-1936
Varieties: HN 57, 57B, 327, 334, 363, 371, 518, 547, 629, 670

U.S.:	$4,250.00
Can.:	$5,500.00
U.K.:	£2,000.00

HN 67
The Little Land
Designer: H. Tittensor
Height: 7 ½", 19.1 cm
Colour: Lilac and yellow
Issued: 1916-1936
Varieties: HN 63

U.S.:	$ 8,500.00
Can.:	$11,000.00
U.K.:	£ 5,000.00

HN 68
Lady With Rose
Designer: E. W. Light
Height: 9 ½", 24.1 cm
Colour: Green and yellow
Issued: 1916-1936
Varieties: HN 48A, 52A, 304, 336, 515, 517, 584, 624

U.S.:	$4,500.00
Can.:	$5,800.00
U.K.:	£2,700.00

HN 69
Pretty Lady
Designer: H. Tittensor
Height: 9 ½", 24.1 cm
Colour: Blue dress with flowers
Issued: 1916-1938
Varieties: HN 70, 302, 330, 361, 384, 565, 700, 763, 783

U.S.:	None
Can.:	known
U.K.:	to exist

HN 70
Pretty Lady
Designer: H. Tittensor
Height: 9 ½", 24.1 cm
Colour: Grey
Issued: 1916-1938
Varieties: HN 69, 302, 330, 361, 384, 565, 700, 763, 783

U.S.:	$3,500.00
Can.:	$4,500.00
U.K.:	£2,100.00

HN 71
A Jester
Style One
Designer: C. J. Noke
Height: 9", 22.9 cm
Colour: Light green checks
Issued: 1917-1938
Varieties: HN 45, 71A, 320, 367,
             412, 426, 446, 552,
             616, 627, 1295, 1702,
             2016, 3922

   U.S.:   **$7,000.00**
   Can.:   **$9,000.00**
   U.K.:   **£4,000.00**

HN 71A
A Jester
Style One
Designer: C. J. Noke
Height: 9½", 24.1 cm
Colour: Dark green checks
Issued: 1917-1938
Varieties: HN 45, 71, 320, 367,
             412, 426, 446, 552,
             616, 627, 1295, 1702,
             2016, 3922

   U.S.:   **$7,000.00**
   Con.:   **$9,000.00**
   U.K.:   **£4,000.00**

HN 72
An Orange Vendor
Designer: C. J. Noke
Height: 6 ¼", 15.9 cm
Colour: Green, white and
             orange
Issued: 1917-1938
Varieties: HN 508, 521, 1966

   U.S.:   **$2,500.00**
   Can.:   **$3,250.00**
   U.K.:   **£1,500.00**

HN 73
A Lady of the Elizabethan Period
Style One
Designer: E. W. Light
Height: 9 ½", 24.1 cm
Colour: Dark turquoise
Issued: 1917-1938
Varieties: HN 40, 40A, 411; also
             called 'Elizabethan
             Lady' (Style One)

   U.S.:
   Can.:   **Extremely rare**
   U.K.:

HN 74
Katharine
Style One
Designer: C. J. Noke
Height: 5 ¾", 14.6 cm
Colour: Light blue dress with
             green spots
Issued: 1917-1938
Varieties: HN 61, 341, 471,
             615, 793

   U.S.:   **None**
   Can.:   **known**
   U.K.:   **to exist**

HN 75
Blue Beard
(With Plume on Turban)
Style One
Designer: E. W. Light
Height: 11", 27.9 cm
Colour: Light blue
Issued: 1917-1936
Varieties: HN 410

   U.S.:   **$10,000.00**
   Can.:   **$13,000.00**
   U.K.:   **£ 6,000.00**

HN 76
The Carpet Vendor
Style One
Designer: C. J. Noke
Height: 5 ½", 14.0 cm
Colour: Blue and orange
Issued: 1917-1936
Varieties: HN 38, 350; also
             known in flambé

   U.S.:   **$5,500.00**
   Can.:   **$7,000.00**
   U.K.:   **£3,250.00**

HN 77
The Flounced Skirt
Designer: E. W. Light
Height: 9 ¾", 24.7 cm
Colour: Yellow dress with
             black trim
Issued: 1917-1938
Varieties: HN 57A, 66, 78, 333;
             also called 'The Bow'

   U.S.:   **$4,250.00**
   Can.:   **$5,500.00**
   U.K.:   **£2,500.00**

HN 78
The Flounced Skirt
Designer: E. W. Light
Height: 9 ¾", 24.7 cm
Colour: Yellow dress with
          flowers
Issued: 1917-1938
Varieties: HN 57A, 66, 77, 333;
          also called 'The Bow'

U.S.:   **$4,000.00**
Can.:   **$5,250.00**
U.K.:   **£2,400.00**

HN 79
Shylock
Designer: C. J. Noke
Height: Unknown
Colour: Multicoloured robe,
          yellow sleeves
Issued: 1917-1938
Varieties: HN 317; also known
          with Titanian glaze

U.S.:   **Only**
Can.:   **one**
U.K.:   **known**

HN 80
Fisherwomen
Designer: C. J. Noke
Height: 11 ¾", 29.8 cm
Colour: Lavender, pink and
          green
Issued: 1917-1938
Varieties: HN 349, 359, 631;
          also called 'Looking for
          the Boats' and 'Waiting
          for the Boats'

U.S.:   **None**
Can.:   **known**
U.K.:   **to exist**

HN 81
A Shepherd
Style One
Designer: C. J. Noke
Height: 13 ¼", 33.6 cm
Colour: Brown
Issued: 1918-1938
Varieties: HN 617, 632

U.S.:
Can.:   **Extremely rare**
U.K.:

Earthenware

HN 82
Lady with an Ermine Muff
Designer: E. W. Light
Height: 6 ¾", 17.2 cm
Colour: Grey and cream,
          grey hat
Issued: 1918-1938
Varieties: Also called 'Afternoon
          Call' and ''Making a
          Call'

U.S.:   **$7,500.00**
Can.:   **$9,750.00**
U.K.:   **£4,500.00**

HN 83
The Lady Anne
Designer: E. W. Light
Height: 9 ½", 24.0 cm
Colour: Yellow
Issued: 1918-1938
Varieties: HN 87, 93

U.S.:   **$7,500.00**
Can.:   **$9,750.00**
U.K.:   **£4,500.00**

HN 84
A Mandarin
Style One
Designer: C. J. Noke
Height: 10 ¼", 26.0 cm
Colour: Mauve and green
Issued: 1918-1936
Varieties: HN 316, 318, 382,
          611, 746, 787, 791;
          'Chinese Mandarin'
          and 'The Mikado'

U.S.:   **None**
Can.:   **known**
U.K.:   **to exist**

HN 85
Jack Point
Designer: C. J. Noke
Height: 16 ¼", 41.2 cm
Colour: Red checks,
          green base
Issued: 1918-1938
Varieties: HN 91, 99, 2080,
          3920, 3925

U.S.:   **None**
Can.:   **known**
U.K.:   **to exist**

HN 86
Out For a Walk
Designer: E. W. Light
Height: 10", 25.4 cm
Colour: Grey, white and black
Issued: 1918-1936
Varieties: HN 443, 748

U.S.:	**$6,000.00**
Can.:	**$7,750.00**
U.K.:	**£3,500.00**

HN 87
The Lady Anne
Designer: E. W. Light
Height: 9 ½", 24.0 cm
Colour: Green
Issued: 1918-1938
Varieties: HN 83, 93

U.S.:	**$7,500.00**
Can.:	**$9,750.00**
U.K.:	**£4,500.00**

HN 88
Spooks
Designer: C. J. Noke
Height: 7 ¼", 18.4 cm
Colour: Green robes, black caps
Issued: 1918-1936
Varieties: HN 89, 372; also called 'Double Spook'

U.S.:	**$7,000.00**
Can.:	**$9,000.00**
U.K.:	**£4,000.00**

HN 89
Spooks
Designer: C. J. Noke
Height: 7 ¼", 18.4 cm
Colour: Green robes, red caps
Issued: 1918-1936
Varieties: IIN 88, 372; also called 'Double Spook'

U.S.:	**$7,000.00**
Can.:	**$9,000.00**
U.K.:	**£4,000.00**

HN 90
Doris Keene as Cavallini
Style One
Designer: C. J. Noke
Height: 11", 27.9 cm
Colour: Dark green
Issued: 1918-1936
Varieties: HN 467

U.S.:	**$4,000.00**
Can.:	**$5,250.00**
U.K.:	**£2,400.00**

HN 91
Jack Point
Designer: C. J. Noke
Height: 16 ¼", 41.2 cm
Colour: Green and black checked suit
Issued: 1918-1938
Varieties: HN 85, 99, 2080, 3920, 3925

U.S.:	**$7,000.00**
Can.:	**$9,000.00**
U.K.:	**£4,250.00**

HN 92
Myfanwy Jones
Designer: E. W. Light
Height: 12", 30.5 cm
Colour: White
Issued: 1918-1936
Varieties: HN 39, 456, 514, 516, 519, 520, 660, 668, 669, 701, 792; also called 'The Welsh Girl'

U.S.:	**Only**
Can.:	**two**
U.K.:	**known**

HN 93
The Lady Anne
Designer: E. W. Light
Height: 9 ½", 24.0 cm
Colour: Blue
Issued: 1918-1938
Varieties: HN 83, 87

U.S.:	**$7,500.00**
Can.:	**$9,750.00**
U.K.:	**£4,500.00**

HN 94
The Young Knight
Designer: C. J. Noke
Height: 9 ½", 24.1 cm
Colour: Purple, green and black
Issued: 1918-1936

U.S.:	**Only**
Can.:	**one**
U.K.:	**known**

HN 95
Europa and the Bull
Style One
Designer: E. W. Light
Height: 9 ¾", 24.7 cm
Colour: Lavender with browns
Issued: 1918-1936

U.S.:	**$ 9,500.00**
Can.:	**$12,250.00**
U.K.:	**£ 5,700.00**

HN 96
Doris Keene as Cavallini
Style Two
Designer: C. J. Noke
Height: 10 ¾", 27.8 cm
Colour: Black and white
Issued: 1918-1936
Varieties: HN 345; also called
           'Romance' (Style One)

U.S.:	**$5,000.00**
Can.:	**$6,500.00**
U.K.:	**£3,000.00**

HN 97
The Mermaid
Designer: H. Tittensor
Height: 7", 17.8 cm
Colour: Green and cream
Issued: 1918-1936
Varieties: HN 300

U.S.:	**$1,500.00**
Can.:	**$2,000.00**
U.K.:	**£ 900.00**

HN 98
Guy Fawkes
Style One
Designer: C. J. Noke
Height: 10 ½", 26.7 cm
Colour: Red cloak, black hat
           and robes
Issued: 1918-1949
Varieties: HN 347, 445; also
           known in Sung

U.S.:	**$3,000.00**
Can.:	**$4,000.00**
U.K.:	**£1,750.00**

HN 99
Jack Point
Designer: C. J. Noke
Height: 16 ¼", 41.2 cm
Colour: Purple and green
Issued   1918-1938
Varieties: HN 85, 91, 2080,
           3920, 3925

U.S.:	**$6,000.00**
Can.:	**$7,750.00**
U.K.:	**£3,500.00**

HN 100 - 299 Animal, Bird figures,
except HN 174, 177 and 230, not
issued.

HN 300
The Mermaid
Designer: H. Tittensor
Height: 7", 17.8 cm
Colour: Green and cream,
           red berries in hair
Issued: 1918-1936
Varieties: HN 97

U.S.:	**Only**
Can.:	**two**
U.K.:	**known**

HN 301
Moorish Piper Minstrel
Designer: C. J. Noke
Height: 13 ½", 34.3 cm
Colour: Purple
Issued: 1918-1938
Varieties: HN 328, 416

U.S.:	**$4,500.00**
Can.:	**$5,750.00**
U.K.:	**£2,700.00**

HN 302
Pretty Lady
Designer: H. Tittensor
Height: 9 ½", 24.1 cm
Colour: Green and lavender
Issued: 1918-1938
Varieties: HN 69, 70, 330, 361,
           384, 565, 700, 763,
           783

U.S.:	**$3,250.00**
Can.:	**$4,250.00**
U.K.:	**£2,000.00**

HN 303
Motherhood
Style One
Designer: P. Stabler
Height: 8", 20.3 cm
Colour: White dress with black
Issued: 1918-1936
Varieties: HN 28, 30

U.S.:	**None**
Can.:	**known**
U.K.:	**to exist**

HN 304
Lady with Rose
Designer: E. W. Light
Height: 9 ½", 24.1 cm
Colour: Patterned lavender
           dress
Issued: 1918-1936
Varieties: HN 48A, 52A, 68, 336,
           515, 517, 584, 624

U.S.:	**Only**
Can.:	**one**
U.K.:	**known**

HN 305
A Scribe
Designer: C. J. Noke
Height: 6", 15.2 cm
Colour: Green, blue and orange
Issued: 1918-1936
Varieties: HN 324, 1235

U.S.:	**$2,750.00**
Can.:	**$3,575.00**
U.K.:	**£1,650.00**

HN 306
Milking Time
Designer: P. Stabler
Height: 6 ½", 16.5 cm
Colour: Light blue dress with
           black
Issued: 1913-1938
Varieties: HN 3

U.S.:	
Can.:	**Extremely rare**
U.K.:	

HN 307
The Sentimental Pierrot
Designer: C. J. Noke
Height: 5 ½", 14.0 cm
Colour: Black, white
Issued: 1918-1936
Varieties: HN 36

U.S.:	**$ 9,000.00**
Can.:	**$11,750.00**
U.K.:	**£ 5,500.00**

HN 308
A Jester
Style Two
Designer: C. J. Noke
Height: 10 ¼", 26.0 cm
Colour: Black and lavender
Issued: 1918-1938
Varieties: HN 45A, 45B, 55, 630;
           also known in black
           and white

U.S.:	**Only**
Can.:	**two**
U.K.:	**known**

HN 309
An Elizabethan Lady
Style Two
Designer: E. W. Light
Height: 9 ½", 24.1 cm
Colour: Dark green-blue,
           green and black
Issued: 1918-1938
Varieties: Also called 'A Lady of
           the Elizabethan Period'
           (Style Two)

U.S.:	**$5,000.00**
Can.:	**$6,500.00**
U.K.:	**£3,000.00**

HN 310
Dunce
Designer: C. J. Noke
Height: 10 ½", 26.7 cm
Colour: Black and white
          with green base
Issued: 1918-1936
Varieties: HN 6, 357

U.S.:   **None**
Can.:   **known**
U.K.:   **to exist**

HN 311
Dancing Figure
Designer: Unknown
Height: 17 ¾", 45.0 cm
Colour: Pink
Issued: 1918-1938

U.S.:   **Only**
Can.:   **two**
U.K.:   **known**

HN 312
Spring
Style One
Designer: Unknown
Height: 7 ½", 19.1 cm
Colour: Yellow
Issued: 1918-1938
Varieties: HN 472
Series: The Seasons
          (Series One)

U.S.:   **$2,500.00**
Can.:   **$3,250.00**
U.K.:   **£1,500.00**

HN 313
Summer
Style One
Designer: Unknown
Height: 7 ½", 19.1 cm
Colour: Pale green
Issued: 1918-1938
Varieties: HN 473
Series: The Seasons
          (Series One)

U.S.:   **$2,500.00**
Can.:   **$3,250.00**
U.K.:   **£1,500.00**

HN 314
Autumn
Style One
Designer: Unknown
Height: 7 ½", 19.1 cm
Colour: Lavender
Issued: 1918-1938
Varieties: HN 474
Series: The Seasons
          (Series One)

U.S.:   **$2,500.00**
Can.:   **$3,250.00**
U.K.:   **£1,500.00**

HN 315
Winter
Style One
Designer: Unknown
Height: 7 ½", 19.1 cm
Colour: Pale green
Issued: 1918-1938
Varieties: HN 475
Series: The Seasons
          (Series One)

U.S.:   **$2,500.00**
Can.:   **$3,250.00**
U.K.:   **£1,500.00**

HN 316
A Mandarin
Style One
Designer: C. J. Noke
Height: 10 ¼", 26.0 cm
Colour: Black and yellow
Issued: 1918-1936
Varieties: HN 84, 318, 382, 611,
          746, 787, 791; also
          called 'Chinese
          Mandarin' and 'The
          Mikado'

U.S.:   **$ 8,000.00**
Can.:   **$11,000.00**
U.K.:   **£ 5,000.00**

HN 317
Shylock
Designer: C. J. Noke
Height: Unknown
Colour: Brown and green
Issued: 1918-1938
Varieties: HN 79; also known
          with Titanian glaze

U.S.:
Can.:   **Extremely rare**
U.K.:

HN 318
A Mandarin
Style One
Designer: C. J. Noke
Height: 10 ¼", 26.0 cm
Colour: Gold
Issued: 1918-1936
Varieties: HN 84, 316, 382, 611, 746, 787, 791; also called 'Chinese Mandarin' and 'The Mikado'

U.S.: $ 8,000.00
Can.: $11,000.00
U.K.: £ 5,000.00

HN 319
A Gnome
Designer: H. Tittensor
Height: 6 ¼", 15.9 cm
Colour: Light blue
Issued: 1918-1938
Varieties: HN 380, 381; also known in flambé

U.S.:
Can.: **Extremely rare**
U.K.:

Note: A Titanian 4 ½" model is known to exist.

HN 320
A Jester
Style One
Designer: C. J. Noke
Height: 10", 25.4 cm
Colour: Green and black
Issued: 1918-1938
Varieties: HN 45, 71, 71A, 367, 412, 426, 446, 552, 616, 627, 1295, 1702, 2016, 3922

U.S.: $ 8,500.00
Can.: $11,000.00
U.K.: £ 5,000.00

HN 321
Digger (New Zealand)
Designer: E. W. Light
Height: 11 ¼", 28.5 cm
Colour: Mottled green
Issued: 1918-1938

U.S.: $3,000.00
Can.: $4,000.00
U.K.: £2,000.00

HN 322
Digger (Australian)
Designer: E. W. Light
Height: 11 ¼", 28.5 cm
Colour: Brown
Issued: 1918-1938
Varieties: HN 353

U.S.: $3,000.00
Can.: $4,000.00
U.K.: £2,000.00

HN 323
Blighty
Designer: E. W. Light
Height: 11 ¼", 28.5 cm
Colour: Green
Issued: 1918-1938
Varieties: Khaki version

U.S.: $3,000.00
Can.: $4,000.00
U.K.: £2,000.00

HN 324
A Scribe
Designer: C. J. Noke
Height: 6", 15.2 cm
Colour: Brown, green and orange
Issued: 1918-1938
Varieties: HN 305, 1235

U.S.: $2,500.00
Can.: $3,250.00
U.K.: £1,500.00

HN 325
Pussy
Designer: F. C. Stone
Height: 7 ½", 19.1 cm
Colour: White patterned dress with black
Issued: 1918-1938
Varieties: HN 18, 507; also called 'The Black Cat'

U.S.: **Only**
Can.: **one**
U.K.: **known**

HN 326
Madonna of the Square
Designer: P. Stabler
Height: 7", 17.8 cm
Colour: Grey
Issued: 1918-1936
Varieties: HN 10, 10A, 11, 14, 27, 573, 576, 594, 613, 764, 1968, 1969, 2034

U.S.: $2,250.00
Can.: $3,000.00
U.K.: £1,300.00

HN 327
The Curtsey
Designer: E. W. Light
Height: 11", 27.9 cm
Colour: Blue
Issued: 1918-1936
Varieties: HN 57, 57B, 66A, 334, 363, 371, 518, 547, 629 670

U.S.: $4,000.00
Can.: $5,000.00
U.K.: £2,400.00

HN 328
Moorish Piper Minstrel
Designer: C. J. Noke
Height: 13 ½", 34.3 cm
Colour: Green and brown stripes
Issued: 1918-1938
Varieties: HN 301, 416

U.S.: None
Can.: known
U.K.: to exist

HN 329
The Gainsborough Hat
Designer: H. Tittensor
Height: 8 ¾", 22.2 cm
Colour: Patterned blue dress
Issued: 1918-1936
Varieties: HN 46, 46A, 47, 352, 383, 453, 675, 705

U.S.: None
Can.: known
U.K.: to exist

HN 330
Pretty Lady
Designer: H. Tittensor
Height: 9 ½", 24.1 cm
Colour: Patterned blue dress
Issued: 1918-1938
Varieties: HN 69, 70, 302, 361, 384, 565, 700, 763, 783

U.S.: None
Can.: known
U.K.: to exist

HN 331
A Lady of the
Georgian Period
Designer: E. W. Light
Height: 10 ¼", 26.0 cm
Colour: Mottled green overskirt, yellow underskirt
Issued: 1918-1936
Varieties: HN 41, 444, 690, 702

U.S.: $5,000.00
Can.: $6,500.00
U.K.: £3,000.00

HN 332
The Ermine Muff
Designer: C. J. Noke
Height: 8 ½", 21.6 cm
Colour: Red coat, green and yellow skirt
Issued: 1918-1938
Varieties: HN 54, 671; also called 'Lady Ermine' and 'Lady with Ermine Muff'

U.S.: Only
Can.: one
U.K.: known

HN 333
The Flounced Skirt
Designer: E. W. Light
Height: 9 ¾", 24.7 cm
Colour: Mottled green and blue
Issued: 1918-1938
Varieties: HN 57A, 66, 77, 78; also called 'The Bow'

U.S.: $4,000.00
Can.: $5,000.00
U.K.: £2,400.00

HN 334
The Curtsey
Designer: E. W. Light
Height: 11", 27.9 cm
Colour: Purple
Issued: 1918-1936
Varieties: HN 57, 57B, 66A, 327, 363, 371, 518, 547, 629, 670

U.S.: $4,000.00
Can.: $5,000.00
U.K.: £2,400.00

HN 335
Lady of the Fan
Designer: E. W. Light
Height: 9 ½", 24.1 cm
Colour: Blue
Issued: 1919-1936
Varieties: HN 48, 52, 53, 53A, 509

U.S.: $4,500.00
Can.: $6,000.00
U.K.: £2,700.00

HN 336
Lady with Rose
Designer: E. W. Light
Height: 9 ½", 24.1 cm
Colour: Multicoloured
Issued: 1919-1936
Varieties: HN 48A, 52A, 68, 304, 515, 517, 584, 624

U.S.: None
Can.: known
U.K.: to exist

HN 337
The Parson's Daughter
Designer: H. Tittensor
Height: 10", 25.4 cm
Colour: Lavender dress with brown flowers
Issued: 1919-1938
Varieties: HN 338, 441, 564, 790, 1242, 1356, 2018

U.S.: $2,750.00
Can.: $3,600.00
U.K.: £1,600.00

HN 338
The Parson's Daughter
Designer: H. Tittensor
Height: 10", 25.4 cm
Colour: Green and red
Issued: 1919-1938
Varieties: HN 337, 441, 564, 790, 1242, 1356, 2018

U.S.: $2,750.00
Can.: $3,600.00
U.K.: £1,600.00

HN 339
In Grandma's Days
Designer: C. J. Noke
Height: 8 ¾", 22.2 cm
Colour: Green and yellow
Issued: 1919-1938
Varieties: HN 340, 388, 442; also called 'A Lilac Shawl' HN 44, 44A; 'The Poke Bonnet' HN 362, 612, 765;

U.S.: $4,000.00
Can.: $5,000.00
U.K.: £2,400.00

HN 340
In Grandma's Days
Designer: C. J. Noke
Height: 8 ¾", 22.2 cm
Colour: Yellow and lavender
Issued: 1919-1938
Varieties: HN 339, 388, 442; also called 'A Lilac Shawl' HN 44, 44A; 'The Poke Bonnet' HN 362, 612, 765

U.S.: $4,000.00
Can.: $5,000.00
U.K.: £2,400.00

HN 341
Katharine
Style One
Designer: C. J. Noke
Height: 5 ¾", 14.6 cm
Colour: Red
Issued: 1919-1938
Varieties: HN 61, 74, 471, 615, 793

U.S.: $3,500.00
Can.: $4,500.00
U.K.: £2,000.00

HN 342
The Lavender Woman
Designer: P. Stabler
Height: 8 ¼", 21.0 cm
Colour: Multicoloured dress, lavender shawl
Issued: 1919-1938
Varieties: HN 22, 23, 23A, 569, 744

U.S.:	$5,500.00
Can.:	$7,250.00
U.K.:	£3,250.00

HN 343
An Arab
Designer: C. J. Noke
Height: 16 ½", 41.9 cm
Colour: Yellow and purple
Issued: 1919-1938
Varieties: HN 33, 378; also called 'The Moor' HN 1308, 1366, 1425, 1657, 2082, 3642, 3926

U.S.:	None
Can.:	known
U.K.:	to exist

HN 344
Henry Irving as Cardinal Wolsey
Designer: C. J. Noke
Height: 13 ¼", 33.7 cm
Colour: Red
Issued: 1919-1949

U.S.:	$5,000.00
Can.:	$6,500.00
U.K.:	£3,000.00

HN 345
Doris Keene as Cavallini
Style Two
Designer: C. J. Noke
Height: 10 ½", 26.6 cm
Colour: Black and white, dark collar and striped muff
Issued: 1919-1949
Varieties: HN 96; Also called 'Romance' (Style One)

U.S.:	$5,000.00
Can.:	$6,500.00
U.K.:	£3,000.00

HN 346
Tony Weller
Style One
Designer: C. J. Noke
Height: 10 ½", 26.7 cm
Colour: Green, blue and brown
Issued: 1919-1938
Varieties: HN 368, 684

U.S.:	None
Can.:	known
U.K.:	to exist

HN 347
Guy Fawkes
Style One
Designer: C. J. Noke
Height: 10 ½", 26.7 cm
Colour: Brown cloak
Issued: 1919-1938
Varieties: HN 98, 445; also known in Sung

U.S.:	
Can.:	Extremely rare
U.K.:	

HN 348
The Carpet Vendor
Style Two
Designer: C. J. Noke
Height: 6 ¼", 15.9 cm
Colour: Turquoise, long patterned carpet
Issued: 1919-1936
Varieties: HN 38A

U.S.:	One
Can.:	known
U.K.:	to exist

HN 349
Fisherwomen
Designer: C. J. Noke
Height: 11 ¾", 29.8 cm
Colour: Lavender, yellow and green
Issued: 1919-1938
Varieties: HN 80, 359, 631; also called 'Looking for the Boats' and 'Waiting for the Boats'

U.S.:	None
Can.:	known
U.K.:	to exist

HN 350
The Carpet Vendor
Style One
Designer: C. J. Noke
Height: 5 ½", 14.0 cm
Colour: Blue and mottled green
Issued: 1919-1936
Varieties: HN 38, 76; also known in flambé

U.S.: $5,500.00
Can.: $7,000.00
U.K.: £3,250.00

HN 351
Picardy Peasant (woman)
Designer: P. Stabler
Height: 9 ½", 24.0 cm
Colour: Blue striped skirt, spotted hat
Issued: 1919-1938
Varieties: HN 4, 5, 17A, 513

U.S.: $7,500.00
Can.: $9,500.00
U.K.: £4,500.00

HN 352
The Gainsborough Hat
Designer: H. Tittensor
Height: 8 ¾", 22.2 cm
Colour: Yellow dress, purple hat
Issued: 1919-1936
Varieties: HN 46, 46A, 47, 329, 383, 453, 675, 705

U.S.: None
Can.: known
U.K.: to exist

HN 353
Digger (Australian)
Designer: E. W. Light
Height: 11 ¼", 28.5 cm
Colour: Brown
Issued: 1919-1938
Varieties: HN 322

U.S.:
Can.: Extremely rare
U.K.:

HN 354
A Geisha
Style One
Designer: H. Tittensor
Height: 10 ¾", 27.3 cm
Colour: Yellow, pink, blue
Issued: 1919-1938
Varieties: HN 376, 376A, 387, 634, 741, 779, 1321, 1322; also called 'The Japanese Lady'

U.S.: $ 7,500.00
Can.: $10,000.00
U.K.: £ 4,500.00

HN 355
Dolly
Style One
Designer: C. J. Noke
Height: 7 ¼", 18.4 cm
Colour: Blue
Issued: 1919-1938

U.S.: $ 8,500.00
Can.: $11,000.00
U.K.: £ 5,000.00

HN 356
Sir Thomas Lovell
Designer: C. J. Noke
Height: 7 ¾", 19.7 cm
Colour: Brown and green
Issued: 1919-1936

U.S.: $6,500.00
Can.: $8,500.00
U.K.: £3,750.00

HN 357
Dunce
Designer: C. J. Noke
Height: 10 ½", 26.7 cm
Colour: Light brown
Issued: 1919-1936
Varieties: HN 6, 310

U.S.:
Can.: Extremely rare
U.K.:

HN 358
An Old King
Designer: C. J. Noke
Height: 9 ¾", 24.7 cm
Colour: Green and purple
Issued: 1919-1938
Varieties: HN 623, 1801, 2134

U.S.:	**None**
Can.:	**known**
U.K.:	**to exist**

HN 359
Fisherwomen
Designer: C. J. Noke
Height: 11 ¾", 29.8 cm
Colour: Lavender, red
          and green
Issued: 1919-1938
Varieties: HN 80, 349, 631; also
          called 'Looking for the
          Boats' and 'Waiting for
          the Boats'

U.S.:	
Can.:	**Extremely rare**
U.K.:	

HN 360 not issued.

HN 361
Pretty Lady
Designer: H. Tittensor
Height: 9 ½", 24.1 cm
Colour: Turquoise
Issued: 1919-1938
Varieties: HN 69, 70, 302, 330,
          384, 565, 700, 763,
          783

U.S.:	**$3,250.00**
Can.:	**$4,250.00**
U.K.:	**£2,000.00**

HN 362
The Poke Bonnet
Designer: C. J. Noke
Height: 8 ¾", 22.2 cm
Colour: Green, yellow, red
Issued: 1919-1938
Varieties: HN 612, 765; 'A Lilac
          Shawl' HN 44, 44A;
          'In Grandma's Days'
          HN 339, 340, 388, 442

U.S.:	**$4,000.00**
Can.:	**$5,250.00**
U.K.:	**£2,400.00**

HN 363
The Curtsey
Designer: E. W. Light
Height: 11", 27.9 cm
Colour: Lavender and peach
Issued: 1919-1936
Varieties: HN 57, 57B, 66A, 327,
          334, 371, 518, 547,
          629, 670

U.S.:	**None**
Can.:	**known**
U.K.:	**to exist**

HN 364
A Moorish Minstrel
Designer: C. J. Noke
Height: 13 ½", 34.3 cm
Colour: Blue, green and orange
Issued: 1920-1938
Varieties: HN 34, 415, 797

U.S.:	**$5,000.00**
Can.:	**$6,500.00**
U.K.:	**£3,000.00**

HN 365
Double Jester
Designer: C. J. Noke
Height: Unknown
Colour: Brown, green and
          purple
Issued: 1920-1938

U.S.:	**Only**
Can.:	**two**
U.K.:	**known**

HN 366
A Mandarin
Style Two
Designer: C. J. Noke
Height: 8 ¼" 21.0 cm
Colour: Yellow and blue
Issued: 1920-1938
Varieties: HN 455, 641

U.S.:	**Only**
Can.:	**one**
U.K.:	**known**

HN 367
A Jester
Style One
Designer: C. J. Noke
Height: 10", 25.4 cm
Colour: Green and red
Issued: 1920-1938
Varieties: HN 45, 71, 71A, 320,
                  412, 426, 446, 552,
                  616, 627, 1295, 1702,
                  2016, 3922

  U.S.: $ 8,500.00
  Can.: $11,000.00
  U.K.:   £ 5,000.00

HN 368
Tony Weller
Style One
Designer: C. J. Noke
Height: 10 ½", 26.7 cm
Colour: Green and brown
Issued: 1920-1938
Varieties: HN 346, 684

  U.S.: $2,500.00
  Can.: $3,250.00
  U.K.:   £1,500.00

Photograph
Not
Available

HN 369
Cavalier
Style One
Designer: Unknown
Height: Unknown
Colour: Turquoise
Issued: 1920-1936

  U.S.:   None
  Can.:   known
  U.K.:   to exist

Photograph
Not
Available

HN 370
Henry VIII
Style One
Designer: C. J. Noke
Height: Unknown
Colour: Brown, green and
                  purple
Issued: 1920-1938
Varieties: HN 673

  U.S.:   Only
  Can.:   one
  U.K.:   known

HN 371
The Curtsey
Designer: E. W. Light
Height: 11", 27.9 gm
Colour: Yellow
Issued: 1920-1936
Varieties: HN 57, 57B, 66A, 327,
                  334, 363, 518, 547,
                  629, 670

  U.S.:   None
  Can.:   known
  U.K.:   to exist

HN 372
Spooks
Designer: C. J. Noke
Height: 7 ¼", 18.4 cm
Colour: Brown
Issued: 1920-1936
Varieties: HN 88, 89; also called
                  'Double Spook'

  U.S.: $7,000.00
  Can.: $9,000.00
  U.K.:   £4,250.00

HN 373
Boy on Crocodile
Designer: C. J. Noke
Height: 5", 12.7 cm
Length: 14 ½, 36.8 cm
Colour: Green-brown
Issued: 1920-1936
Varieties: Also known in flambé

  U.S.:   Only
  Can.:   two
  U.K.:   known

Photograph
Not
Available

HN 374
Lady and Blackamoor
Style One
Designer: H. Tittensor
Height: Unknown
Colour: Blue and green
Issued: 1920-1936

  U.S.:   Only
  Can.:   one
  U.K.:   known

HN 375
Lady and Blackamoor
Style Two
Designer: H. Tittensor
Height: 7 ¼", 18.4 cm
Colour: Purple and yellow
Issued: 1920-1936
Varieties: HN 377, 470

U.S.:	Only
Can.:	one
U.K.:	known

HN 376
A Geisha
Style One
Designer: H. Tittensor
Height: 10 ¾", 27.3 cm
Colour: Lilac and yellow
Issued: 1920-1936
Varieties: HN 354, 376A, 387, 634, 741, 779, 1321, 1322; also called 'The Japanese Lady'

U.S.:	$ 8,000.00
Can:	$10,000.00
U.K.:	£ 4,750.00

HN 376A
A Geisha
Style One
Designer: H. Tittensor
Height: 10 ¾", 27.3 cm
Colour: Blue
Issued: 1920-1936
Varieties: HN 354, 376, 387, 634, 741, 779, 1321, 1322; also called 'The Japanese Lady'

U.S.:	$ 8,000.00
Can.:	$10,000.00
U.K.:	£ 4,750.00

HN 377
Lady and Blackamoor
Style Two
Designer: H. Tittensor
Height: 7 ¼", 18.4 cm
Colour: Pink and green
Issued: 1920-1936
Varieties: HN 375, 470

U.S.:	None
Can.:	known
U.K.:	to exist

HN 378
An Arab
Designer: C. J. Noke
Height: 16 ½", 41.9 cm
Colour: Green, brown and yellow
Issued: 1920-1938
Varieties: HN 33, 343; also called 'The Moor' HN 1308, 1366, 1425, 1657, 2082, 3642, 3926

U.S.:	$5,000.00
Can.:	$6,500.00
U.K.:	£3,000.00

HN 379
Ellen Terry as Queen Catharine
Designer: C. J. Noke
Height: 12 ½", 31.7 cm
Colour: Purple and blue
Issued: 1920-1949

U.S.:	$4,500.00
Can.:	$6,000.00
U.K.:	£2,700.00

HN 380
A Gnome
Designer: H. Tittensor
Height: 6 ¼", 15.9 cm
Colour: Purple
Issued: 1920-1938
Varieties: HN 319, 381; also known in flambé

U.S.:	None
Can.:	known
U.K.:	to exist

Note: A Titanian 4 ½" model is known to exist.

HN 381
A Gnome
Designer: H. Tittensor
Height: 6 ¼", 15.9 cm
Colour: Green
Issued: 1920-1938
Varieties: HN 319, 380; also known in flambé

U.S.:	Only
Can.:	one
U.K.:	known

Note: A Titanian 4 ½" model is known to exist.

HN 382
A Mandarin
Style One
Designer: C. J. Noke
Height: 10 ¼", 26.0 cm
Colour: Green
Issued: 1920-1936
Varieties: HN 84, 316, 318, 611, 746, 787, 791; also called 'Chinese Mandarin' and 'The Mikado'

U.S.:	$ 8,000.00
Can.:	$11,000.00
U.K.:	£ 5,000.00

HN 383
The Gainsborough Hat
Designer: H. Tittensor
Height: 8 ¾", 22.2 cm
Colour: Green stripes
Issued: 1920-1936
Varieties: HN 46, 46A, 47, 329, 352, 453, 675, 705

U.S.:	None
Can.:	known
U.K.:	to exist

HN 384
Pretty Lady
Designer: H. Tittensor
Height: 9 ½", 24.1 cm
Colour: Red
Issued: 1920-1938
Varieties: HN 69, 70, 302, 330, 361, 565, 700, 763, 783

U.S.:	$3,500.00
Can.:	$4,500.00
U.K.:	£2,000.00

HN 385
St. George
Style One
Designer: S. Thorogood
Height: 16", 40.6 cm
Colour: Grey, purple and gold
Issued: 1920-1938
Varieties: HN 386, 1800, 2067

U.S.:	$7,500.00
Can.:	$9,750.00
U.K.:	£4,500.00

HN 386
St. George
Style One
Designer: S. Thorogood
Height: 16", 40.6 cm
Colour: Blue and white
Issued: 1920-1938
Varieties: HN 385, 1800, 2067

U.S.:	$7,500.00
Can.:	$9,750.00
U.K.:	£4,500.00

HN 387
A Geisha
Style One
Designer: H. Tittensor
Height: 10 ¾", 27.3 cm
Colour: Blue and yellow
Issued: 1920-1936
Varieties: HN 354, 376, 376A, 634, 741, 779, 1321, 1322; also called 'The Japanese Lady'

U.S.:	$ 7,500.00
Can.:	$10,000.00
U.K.:	£ 4,500.00

HN 388
In Grandma's Days
Designer: C. J. Noke
Height: 8 ¾", 22.2 cm
Colour: Blue
Issued: 1920-1938
Varieties: HN 339, 340, 442; also called 'A Lilac Shawl' HN 44, 44A; 'The Poke Bonnet' HN 362, 612, 765

U.S.:	None
Can.:	known
U.K.:	to exist

HN 389
Dolly
Style Two
Designer: H. Tittensor
Height: 11", 27.9 cm
Colour: Pink dress, blonde hair
Issued: 1920-1938
Varieties: HN 390; also called 'The Little Mother' (Style One) HN 469

U.S.:	Only
Can.:	two
U.K.:	known

HN 390
Dolly
Style Two
Designer: H. Tittensor
Height: 11", 27.9 cm
Colour: Pink dress, brown hair
Issued: 1920-1938
Varieties: HN 389; also called
'The Little Mother'
(Style One) HN 469

U.S.:	Only
Can.:	one
U.K.:	known

HN 391
The Princess
Designer: L. Harradine
Height: 9 ¼", 23.5 cm
Colour: Green and purple
Issued: 1920-1936
Varieties: HN 392, 420, 430, 431, 633

U.S.:	Only
Can.:	one
U.K.:	known

HN 392
The Princess
Designer: L. Harradine
Height: 9 ¼", 23.5 cm
Colour: Multicoloured
Issued: 1920-1936
Varieties: HN 391, 420, 430, 431, 633

U.S.:	Only
Can.:	one
U.K.:	known

Photograph
Not
Available

HN 393
The Necklace
Designer: G. Lambert
Height: 9", 22.9 cm
Colour: Yellow, green and
purple
Issued: 1920-1936
Varieties: HN 394

U.S.:	Only
Can.:	one
U.K.:	known

Photograph
Not
Available

HN 394
The Necklace
Designer: G. Lambert
Height: 9", 22.9 cm
Colour: Green and yellow
Issued: 1920-1936
Varieties: HN 393

U.S.:	
Can.:	Extremely rare
U.K.:	

HN 395
Contentment
Designer: L. Harradine
Height: 7 ¼", 18.4 cm
Colour: Yellow and lilac
Issued: 1920-1938
Varieties: HN 396, 421, 468, 572, 685, 686, 1323

U.S.:	$4,000.00
Can.:	$5,250.00
U.K.:	£2,400.00

HN 396
Contentment
Designer: L. Harradine
Height: 7 ¼", 18.4 cm
Colour: Blue, yellow and pink
Issued: 1920-1938
Varieties: HN 395, 421, 468, 572, 685, 686, 1323

U.S.:	$4,000.00
Can.:	$5,250.00
U.K.:	£2,400.00

HN 397
Puff and Powder
Designer: L. Harradine
Height: 6 ½", 16.5 cm
Colour: Yellow skirt, brown
bodice
Issued: 1920-1936
Varieties: HN 398, 400, 432, 433

U.S.:	$5,500.00
Can.:	$7,500.00
U.K.:	£3,300.00

HN 398
Puff and Powder
Designer: L. Harradine
Height: 6 ½", 16.5 cm
Colour: Lavender
Issued: 1920-1936
Varieties: HN 397, 400, 432, 433

U.S.:	None
Can.:	known
U.K.:	to exist

HN 399
Japanese Fan
Designer: H. Tittensor
Height: 4 ¾", 12.1 cm
Colour: Dark blue and yellow
Issued: 1920-1936
Varieties: HN 405, 439, 440; also known in flambé

U.S.:	$5,000.00
Can.:	$6,500.00
U.K.:	£3,000.00

Unpainted model Illustrated.

HN 400
Puff and Powder
Designer: L. Harradine
Height: 6 ½", 16.5 cm
Colour: Green, blue and yellow
Issued: 1920-1936
Varieties: HN 397, 398, 432, 433

U.S.:	None
Can.:	known
U.K.:	to exist

Photograph
Not
Available

HN 401
Marie
Style One
Designer: L. Harradine
Height: 7", 17.8 cm
Colour: Pink, cream and blue
Issued: 1920-1938
Varieties: HN 434, 502, 504, 505, 506

U.S.:	
Can.:	Extremely rare
U.K.ı	

HN 402
Betty
Style One
Designer: L. Harradine
Height: 7 ½", 19.1 cm
Colour: Pink and black
Issued: 1920-1938
Varieties: HN 403, 435, 438, 477, 478

U.S.:	
Can.:	Extremely rare
U.K.:	

Unpainted model illustrated.

HN 403
Betty
Style One
Designer: L. Harradine
Height: 7 ½", 19.1 cm
Colour: Green, blue and yellow
Issued: 1920-1938
Varieties: HN 402, 435, 438, 477, 478

U.S.:	
Can.:	Extremely rare
U.K.:	

Unpainted model Illustrated.

HN 404
King Charles
Designer: C. J. Noke and H. Tittensor
Height: 16 ¾", 42.5 cm
Colour: Black, pink base
Issued: 1920-1951
Varieties: HN 2084, 3459

U.S.:	$4,500.00
Can.:	$6,000.00
U.K.:	£2,700.00

HN 405
Japanese Fan
Designer: H. Tittensor
Height: 5", 12.7 cm
Colour: Light yellow
Issued: 1920-1936
Varieties: HN 399, 439, 440; also known in flambé

U.S.:	None
Can.:	known
U.K.:	to exist

Unpainted model illustrated.

HN 406
The Bouquet
Designer: G. Lambert
Height: 9", 22.9 cm
Colour: Yellow and blue
Issued: 1920-1936
Varieties: HN 414, 422, 428,
           429, 567, 794; also
           called 'The Nosegay'
U.S.: $5,500.00
Can.: $7,250.00
U.K.:   £3,250.00

HN 407
Omar Khayyam and the Beloved
Designer: C. J. Noke
Height: 10", 25.4 cm
Colour: Unknown
Issued: 1920-1936
Varieties: HN 419, 459, 598
U.S.:   **Only**
Can.:   **one**
U.K.:   **known**

HN 408
Omar Khayyam
Style One
Designer: C. J. Noke
Height: 6", 15.2 cm
Colour: Blue, green and brown
Issued: 1920-1938
Varieties: HN 409
U.S.:   **Only**
Can.:   **one**
U.K.:   **known**

HN 409
Omar Khayyam
Style One
Designer: C. J. Noke
Height: 6", 15.2 cm
Colour: Black and yellow
Issued: 1920-1938
Varieties: HN 408
U.S.:   **Only**
Can.:   **one**
U.K.:   **known**

HN 410
Blue Beard
(Without plume on turban)
Style One
Designer: E. W. Light
Height: 11", 27.9 cm
Colour: Green and blue
Issued: 1920-1936
Varieties: HN 75
U.S.: $10,000.00
Can.: $13,000.00
U.K.:   £ 6,000.00

HN 411
A Lady of the Elizabethan Period
Style One
Designer: E. W. Light
Height: 9 ¾", 24.7 cm
Colour: Purple
Issued: 1920-1938
Varieties: HN 40, 40A, 73; also
           called 'Elizabethan Lady'
U.S.: $4,500.00
Can.: $6,000.00
U.K.:   £2,700.00

HN 412
A Jester
Style One
Designer: C. J. Noke
Height: 10", 25.4 cm
Colour: Green and red
Issued: 1920-1938
Varieties: HN 45, 71, 71A, 320,
           367, 426, 446, 552,
           616, 627, 1295, 1702,
           2016, 3922
U.S.:
Can.:   **Extremely rare**
U.K.:

HN 413
The Crinoline
Designer: G. Lambert
Height: 6 ¼" 15.8 cm
Colour: Light blue and lemon
Issued: 1920-1938
Varieties: HN 8, 9, 9A, 21, 21A,
           566, 628
U.S.: $3,500.00
Can.: $4,500.00
U.K.:   £2,100.00

HN 414
The Bouquet
Designer: G. Lambert
Height: 9", 22.9 cm
Colour: Pink and yellow
Issued   1920-1936
Varieties: HN 406, 422, 428, 429,
          567, 794; also called
          'The Nosegay'

U.S.:   None
Can.:   known
U.K.:   to exist

HN 415
A Moorish Minstrel
Designer: C. J. Noke
Height: 13 ½", 34.3 cm
Colour: Green and yellow
Issued: 1920-1938
Varieties: HN 34, 364, 797

U.S.:   **$5,000.00**
Can.:   **$6,500.00**
U.K.:   **£3,000.00**

HN 416
Moorish Piper Minstrel
Designer: C. J. Noke
Height: 13 ½", 34.3 cm
Colour: Green and yellow
          stripes
Issued: 1920-1938
Varieties: HN 301, 328

U.S.:   None
Can.:   known
U.K.:   to exist

HN 417
One of the Forty
Style One
Designer: H. Tittensor
Height: 8 ¼", 21.0 cm
Colour: Green and blue
Issued: 1920-1936
Varieties: HN 490, 495, 501, 528,
          648, 677, 1351, 1352

U.S.:   None
Can.:   known
U.K.:   to exist

HN 418
One of the Forty
Style Two
Designer: H. Tittensor
Height: 7 ¼", 18.4 cm
Colour: Striped green robes
Issued: 1920-1936
Varieties: HN 494, 498, 647, 666,
          704, 1353

U.S.:   None
Can.:   known
U.K.:   to exist

HN 419
Omar Khayyam and the Beloved
Designer: C. J. Noke
Height: 10", 25.4 cm
Colour: Green and blue
Issued: 1920-1936
Varieties: HN 407, 459, 598

U.S.:   Only
Can.:   two
U.K.:   known

HN 420
The Princess
Designer: L. Harradine
Height: 9 ¼", 23.5 cm
Colour: Pink and green striped
          skirt, blue cape
Issued: 1920-1936
Varieties: HN 391, 392, 430, 431,
          633

U.S.:   Only
Can.:   one
U.K.:   known

HN 421
Contentment
Designer: L. Harradine
Height: 7 ¼", 18.4 cm
Colour: Light green
Issued: 1920-1938
Varieties: HN 395, 396, 468,
          572, 685, 686, 1323

U.S.:   **$4,000.00**
Can.:   **$5,250.00**
U.K.:   **£2,400.00**

HN 422
The Bouquet
Designer: G. Lambert
Height: 9", 22.9 cm
Colour: Yellow and pink
Issued: 1920-1936
Varieties: HN 406, 414, 428,
           429, 567, 794; also
           called 'The Nosegay'

U.S.:   **None**
Can.:   **known**
U.K.:   **to exist**

HN 423
One of the Forty
Style Three
Designer: H. Tittensor
Height: 3", 7.6 cm
Colour: Varied
Issued: 1921-1936

U.S.:	**$1,500.00**
Can.:	**$2,000.00**
U.K.:	**£ 900.00**

HN 423A
One of the Forty
Style Four
Designer: H. Tittensor
Height: 2 ¾", 6.9 cm
Colour: Varied
Issued: 1921-1936

U.S.:	**$1,500.00**
Can.:	**$2,000.00**
U.K.:	**£ 900.00**

HN 423B
One of the Forty
Style Five
Designer: H. Tittensor
Height: 2 ¾", 6.9 cm
Colour: Varied
Issued: 1921-1936

U.S.:	**$1,500.00**
Can.:	**$2,000.00**
U.K.:	**£ 900.00**

HN 423C
One of the Forty
Style Six
Designer: H. Tittensor
Height: 2 ¾", 6.9 cm
Colour: Varied
Issued: 1921-1936

U.S.:	**$1,500.00**
Can.:	**$2,000.00**
U.K.:	**£ 900.00**

HN 423D
One of the Forty
Style Seven
Designer: H. Tittensor
Height: 2 ¾", 6.9 cm
Colour: Varied
Issued: 1921-1936

U.S.:	**$1,500.00**
Can.:	**$2,000.00**
U.K.:	**£ 900.00**

Also known in all-white.

HN 423E
One of the Forty
Style Eight
Designer: H. Tittensor
Height: 2 ¾", 6.9 cm
Colour: Varied
Issued: 1921-1936

U.S.:	**$1,500.00**
Can.:	**$2,000.00**
U.K.:	**£ 900.00**

HN 423F
One of the Forty
Style Nine
Designer: H. Tittensor
Height: 2 ¾", 6.9 cm
Colour: Olive green and yellow
Issued: 1921-1938

U.S.:	**$1,500.00**
Can.:	**$2,000.00**
U.K.:	**£ 900.00**

Photograph
Not
Available

HN 424
Sleep
Designer: P. Stabler
Height: 6", 15.2 cm
Colour: Blue
Issued: 1921-1936
Varieties: HN 24, 24A, 25, 25A,
692, 710

U.S.: $3,250.00
Can.: $4,250.00
U.K.: £1,950.00

HN 425
The Goosegirl
Style One
Designer: L. Harradine
Height: 8", 20.3 cm
Colour: Blue
Issued: 1921-1936
Varieties: HN 436, 437, 448, 559,
560

U.S.: None
Can.: known
U.K.: to exist

HN 426
A Jester
Style One
Designer: C. J. Noke
Height: 10", 25.4 cm
Colour: Pink and black
Issued: 1921-1938
Varieties: HN 45, 71, 71A, 320,
367, 412, 446, 552,
616, 627, 1295, 1702,
2016, 3922

U.S.: $ 8,500.00
Can.: $11,000.00
U.K.: £ 5,000.00

HN 427
One of the Forty
Style Ten
Designer: H. Tittensor
Height: Unknown
Colour: Green
Issued: 1921-1936

U.S.:
Can.: **Extremely rare**
U.K.:

HN 428
The Bouquet
Designer: G. Lambert
Height: 9", 22.9 cm
Colour: Blue and green
Issued: 1921-1936
Varieties: HN 406, 414, 422, 429,
567, 794; also called
'The Nosegay'

U.S.: $6,000.00
Can.: $7,750.00
U.K.: £3,500.00

HN 429
The Bouquet
Designer: G. Lambert
Height: 9", 22.9 cm
Colour: Green and red
Issued: 1921-1936
Varieties: HN 406, 414, 422, 428,
567, 794; also called
'The Nosegay'

U.S.: $6,000.00
Can.: $7,750.00
U.K.: £3,500.00

HN 430
The Princess
Designer: L. Harradine
Height: 9 ¼", 23.5 cm
Colour: Green
Issued: 1921-1936
Varieties: HN 391, 392, 402, 431,
633

U.S.: Only
Can.: one
U.K.: known

HN 431
The Princess
Designer: L. Harradine
Height: 9 ¼", 23.5 cm
Colour: Yellow and white
Issued: 1921-1936
Varieties: HN 391, 392, 420, 430,
633

U.S.: Only
Can.: one
U.K.: known

HN 432
Puff and Powder
Designer: L. Harradine
Height: 6 ½", 16.5 cm
Colour: Lavender and orange
Issued: 1921-1936
Varieties: HN 397, 398, 400, 433

U.S.:	None
Can.:	known
U.K.:	to exist

HN 433
Puff and Powder
Designer: L. Harradine
Height: 6 ½", 16.5 cm
Colour: Lilac and green
Issued: 1921-1936
Varieties: HN 397, 398, 400, 432

U.S.:	$5,500.00
Can.:	$7,500.00
U.K.:	£3,250.00

Photograph
Not
Available

HN 434
Marie
Style One
Designer: L. Harradine
Height: 7", 17.8 cm
Colour: Yellow and orange
Issued: 1921-1938
Varieties: HN 401, 502, 504, 505, 506

U.S.:	None
Can.:	known
U.K.:	to exist

HN 435
Betty
Style One
Designer: L. Harradine
Height: 7 ½", 19.1 cm
Colour: Blue and yellow
Issued: 1921-1938
Varieties: HN 402, 403, 438, 477, 478

U.S.:	None
Can.:	known
U.K.:	to exist

Unpainted model illustrated.

HN 436
The Goosegirl
Style One
Designer: L. Harradine
Height: 8", 20.3 cm
Colour: Green and blue
Issued: 1921-1936
Varieties: HN 425, 437, 448, 559, 560

U.S.:	$6,000.00
Can.:	$7,750.00
U.K.:	£3,500.00

HN 437
The Goosegirl
Style One
Designer: L. Harradine
Height: 8", 20.3 cm
Colour: Brown and blue
Issued: 1921-1936
Varieties: HN 425, 436, 448, 559, 560

U.S.:	$6,000.00
Can.:	$7,750.00
U.K.:	£3,500.00

HN 438
Betty
Style One
Designer: L. Harradine
Height: 7 ½", 19.1 cm
Colour: Blue and cream
Issued: 1921-1938
Varieties: HN 402, 403, 435, 477, 478

U.S.:	Only
Can.:	one
U.K.:	known

Unpainted model illustrated.

HN 439
Japanese Fan
Designer: H. Tittensor
Height: 4 ¾", 12.1 cm
Colour: Blue with green spots
Issued: 1921-1936
Varieties: HN 399, 405, 440; also known in flambé

U.S.:	None
Can.:	known
U.K.:	to exist

Unpainted model illustrated.

HN 440
Japanese Fan
Designer: H. Tittensor
Height: 4 ¾", 12.1 cm
Colour: Cream and orange
Issued: 1921-1936
Varieties: HN 399, 405, 439; also known in flambé

U.S.:	$5,000.00
Can.:	$6,500.00
U.K.:	£3,000.00

Unpainted model illustrated.

HN 441
The Parson's Daughter
Designer: H. Tittensor
Height: 10", 25.4 cm
Colour: Yellow and orange
Issued: 1921-1938
Varieties: HN 337, 338, 564, 790, 1242, 1356, 2018

U.S.:	$2,750.00
Can.:	$3,600.00
U.K.:	£1,650.00

HN 442
In Grandma's Days
Designer: C. J. Noke
Height: 8 ¾", 22.2 cm
Colour: White and green
Issued: 1921-1938
Varieties: HN 339, 340, 388; also called 'A Lilac Shawl' HN 44, 44A; 'The Poke Bonnet' HN 362, 612, 765

U.S.:	None
Can.:	known
U.K.:	to exist

HN 443
Out For a Walk
Designer: E. W. Light
Height: 10", 25.4 cm
Colour: Brown check
Issued: 1921-1936
Varieties: HN 86, 748

U.S.:	None
Can.:	known
U.K.:	to exist

HN 444
A Lady of the Georgian Period
Designer: E. W. Light
Height: 10 ¼", 26.0 cm
Colour: Blue-green spotted dress
Issued: 1921-1936
Varieties: HN 41, 331, 690, 702

U.S.:	None
Can.:	known
U.K.:	to exist

HN 445
Guy Fawkes
Style One
Designer: C. J. Noke
Height: 10 ½", 26.7 cm
Colour: Green cloak
Issued: 1921-1938
Varieties: HN 98, 347; also known in Sung

U.S.:	
Can.:	Extremely rare
U.K.:	

HN 446
A Jester
Style One
Designer: C. J. Noke
Height: 10", 25.4 cm
Colour: Black, green, blue
Issued: 1921-1938
Varieties: HN 45, 71, 71A, 320, 367, 412, 426, 552, 616, 627, 1295, 1702, 2016, 3922

U.S.:	$ 8,000.00
Can.:	$10,500.00
U.K.:	£ 4,750.00

HN 447
Lady with Shawl
Designer: L. Harradine
Height: 13 ¼", 33.7 cm
Colour: Green and cream striped dress
Issued: 1921-1936
Varieties: HN 458, 626, 678, 679

U.S.:	$7,500.00
Can.:	$9,750.00
U.K.:	£4,500.00

HN 448
The Goosegirl
Style One
Designer: L. Harradine
Height: 8", 20.3 cm
Colour: Blue
Issued: 1921-1936
Varieties: HN 425, 436, 437,
           559, 560

U.S.:	None
Can.:	known
U.K.:	to exist

HN 449
Fruit Gathering
Designer: L. Harradine
Height: 7 ¾", 19.7 cm
Colour: Blue
Issued: 1921-1936
Varieties: HN 476, 503, 561,
           562, 706, 707

U.S.:	None
Can.:	known
U.K.:	to exist

Photograph
Not
Available

HN 450
Chu Chin Chow
Style One
Designer: C. J. Noke
Height: 6 ½", 16.5 cm
Colour: Red coat and green cap
Issued: 1921-1936
Varieties: HN 460, 461

U.S.:	
Can.:	Extremely rare
U.K.:	

HN 451
An Old Man
Designer: Unknown
Height: 3", 7.5 cm
Colour: Blue, green and red
Issued: 1921-1938

U.S.:	Only
Can.:	Two
U.K.:	known

HN 452 not issued.

HN 453
The Gainsborough Hat
Designer: H. Tittensor
Height: 8 ¾", 22.2 cm
Colour: Red, blue and green
Issued: 1921-1936
Varieties: HN 46, 46A, 47, 329,
           352, 383, 675, 705

U.S.:	None
Can.:	known
U.K.:	to exist

HN 454
The Smiling Buddha
Designer: C. J. Noke
Height: 6 ¼", 15.9 cm
Colour: Green-blue
Issued: 1921-1936
Varieties: Also known in
           flambé and Sung

U.S.:	$6,500.00
Can.:	$8,500.00
U.K.:	£4,000.00

HN 455
A Mandarin
Style Two
Designer: C. J. Noke
Height: 8 ¼", 21.0 cm
Colour: Green
Issued: 1921-1938
Varieties: HN 366, 641

U.S.:	None
Can.:	known
U.K.:	to exist

HN 456
Myfanwy Jones
Designer: E. W. Light
Height: 12", 30.5 cm
Colour: Green and brown
Issued: 1921-1936
Varieties: HN 39, 92, 514, 516,
           519, 520, 660, 668,
           669, 701, 792; also
           called 'The Welsh Girl'

U.S:	$ 8,500.00
Can.:	$11,000.00
U.K.:	£ 5,000.00

HN Series

HN 66
The Flounced Skirt
1916-1938

HN 71
A Jester, Style One
1917-1938

HN 82
Lady with an Ermine Muff
1918-1938

HN 97
The Mermaid
1918-1936

HN 362
The Poke Bonnet
1919-1938

HN 406
The Bouquet
1920-1936

HN Series

HN 464
Captain MacHeath
1921-1949

HN 562
Fruit Gathering
1923-1936

HN 581
The Perfect Pair
1923-1938

HN 715
The Proposal (woman)
1925-1940

HN 725
The Proposal (man)
1925-1938

HN Series

HN 723
Mephisto
1925-1938

HN 752
London Cry, Turnips and Carrots
1925-1938

HN 1211
Quality Street
1926-1936

HN 798
Tete-a-Tete, Style One
1926-1938

HN 780
Harlequinade
1926-1940

HN 1220
Lido Lady, First Version
1927-1936

HN Series

HN 1265
Lady Fayre
1928-1938

HN 1267
Carmen, Style One
1928-1938

HN 1269
Scotch Girl
1928-1938

HN 1274
Harlequinade Masked
1928-1938

HN 1289
Midinette, Style One
1928-1938

HN 1294
Spanish Lady
1928-1940

HN Series

HN 1334
Tulips
1929-1936

HN 1359
Two-A-Penny
1929-1938

HN 1397
Gretchen
1930-1940

HN 1398
Derrick
1930-1940

HN 1407
The Winner
1930-1938

HN 1439
Colombine, Style One
1930-1940

HN Series

HN 1444
Pauline, Style One
1931-1940

HN 1455
Molly Malone
1931-1937

HN 1464A
The Carpet Seller (Hand Closed)
Style One, Unknown-1969

HN 1465
Lady Clare
1931-1937

HN 1486
Phyllis, Style One
1931-1949

HN 1598
Clothilde
1933-1949

HN 1605
The Emir
1933-1949

HN Series

HN 1476
Chloe, Style One
1931-1938

HN 1587
Fleurette
1933-1949

HN 1632
A Gentlewoman
1934-1949

HN 1670A
Gillian, Style One
Unknown

HN 1714
Millicent
1935-1949

HN 1745
The Rustic Swain
1935-1949

HN Series

HN 1818
Miranda, Style One
1937-1949

HN 1820
Reflections
1937-1938

HN 1832
Granny
1937-1949

HN 1837
Mariquita
1938-1949

HN 1881
The Lambeth Walk
1938-1949

HN 1885
Nadine, Style One
1938-1949

HN 1940
Toinette
1940-1949

HN 457
Crouching Nude
Designer: Unknown
Height: 5 ½", 14.0 cm
Colour: Cream, green base
Issued: 1921-1936

U.S.:	**$5,000.00**
Can.:	**$6,500.00**
U.K.:	**£3,000.00**

HN 458
Lady with Shawl
Designer: L. Harradine
Height: 13 ¼", 33.7 cm
Colour: Pink
Issued: 1921-1936
Varieties: HN 447, 626, 678,
           679

U.S.:	**None**
Can.:	**known**
U.K.:	**to exist**

HN 459
Omar Khayyam and the Beloved
Designer: C. J. Noke
Height: 10", 25.4 cm
Colour: Multicoloured
Issued: 1921-1936
Varieties: HN 407, 419, 598

U.S.:	
Can.:	**Extremely rare**
U.K.:	

Photograph
Not
Available

HN 460
Chu Chow Chin
Style One
Designer: C. J. Noke
Height: 6 ½", 16.5 cm
Colour: Blue and green
Issued: 1921-1936
Varieties: HN 450, 461

U.S.:	**Only**
Can.:	**one**
U.K.:	**known**

Photograph
Not
Available

HN 461
Chu Chow Chin
Style One
Designer: C. J. Noke
Height: 6 ½", 16.5 cm
Colour: Red
Issued: 1921-1936
Varieties: HN 450, 460

U.S.:	**Only**
Can.:	**one**
U.K.:	**known**

HN 462
Motherhood
Style Two
Designer: Unknown
Height: 9 ¼", 23.5 cm
Colour: Green and white
Issued: 1921-1938
Varieties: HN 570, 703, 743

U.S.:	**$ 8,500.00**
Can.:	**$11,000.00**
U.K.:	**£ 5,000.00**

HN 463
Polly Peachum
Style One
Designer: L. Harradine
Height: 6 ¼", 15.9 cm
Colour: Pale blue
Issued: 1921-1949
Varieties: HN 465, 550, 589,
           614, 680, 693
Series: Beggar's Opera

U.S.:	**$1,350.00**
Can.:	**$1,750.00**
U.K.:	**£ 800.00**

HN 464
Captain MacHeath
Designer: L. Harradine
Height: 7", 17.8 cm
Colour: Red, yellow and black
Issued: 1921-1949
Varieties: HN 590, 1256
Series: Beggar's Opera

U.S.:	**$1,500.00**
Can.:	**$1,950.00**
U.K.:	**£ 900.00**

HN 465
Polly Peachum
Style One
Designer: L. Harradine
Height: 6 ¼", 15.9 cm
Colour: Red
Issued: 1921-1949
Varieties: HN 463, 550, 589,
           614, 680, 693
Series: Beggar's Opera
U.S.:   **$1,500.00**
Can.:   **$1,950.00**
U.K.:   **£ 900.00**

HN 466
Tulips
Designer: Unknown
Height: 9 ½", 24.1 cm
Colour: Green
Issued: 1921-1936
Varieties: HN 488, 672, 747,
           1334
U.S.:   **None**
Can.:   **known**
U.K.:   **to exist**

HN 467
Doris Keene as Cavallini
Style One
Designer: C. J. Noke
Height: 11", 27.9 cm
Colour: Dark green with gold
           jewellery
Issued: 1921-1936
Varieties: HN 90
U.S.:
Can.:   **Extremely rare**
U.K.:

HN 468
Contentment
Designer: L. Harradine
Height: 7 ¼", 18.4 cm
Colour: Green spotted dress
Issued: 1921-1938
Varieties: HN 395, 396, 421, 572,
           685, 686, 1323
U.S.:   **$4,500.00**
Can.:   **$6,000.00**
U.K.:   **£2,750.00**

HN 469
Little Mother
Style One
Designer: H. Tittensor
Height: 11", 27.9 cm
Colour: White
Issued: 1921-1938
Varieties: Also called 'Dolly'
           (Style Two) HN 389,
           390
U.S.:   **Only**
Can.:   **one**
U.K.:   **known**

HN 470
Lady and Blackamoor
Style Two
Designer: H. Tittensor
Height: 7 ¼", 18.4 cm
Colour: Green patterned dress
           lilac bodice; boy with
           red turban and blue
           coat
Issued: 1921-1936
Varieties: HN 375, 377
U.S.:   **Only**
Can.:   **one**
U.K.:   **known**

HN 471
Katharine
Style One
Designer: C. J. Noke
Height: 5 ¾", 14.6 cm
Colour: Patterned green dress
Issued: 1921-1938
Varieties: HN 61, 74, 341, 615,
           793
U.S.:   **$3,500.00**
Can.:   **$4,500.00**
U.K.:   **£2,000.00**

HN 472
Spring
Style One
Designer: Unknown
Colour: Patterned lavender
           robe
Height: 7 ½", 19.1 cm
Issued: 1921-1938
Varieties: HN 312
Series: The Seasons
           (Series One)
U.S.:   **$2,500.00**
Can.:   **$3,250.00**
U.K.:   **£1,500.00**

HN 473
Summer
Style One
Designer: Unknown
Height: 7 ½", 19.1 cm
Colour: Patterned light green
          robes
Issued: 1921-1938
Varieties: HN 313
Series: The Seasons
          (Series One)

U.S.:	None
Can.:	known
U.K.:	to exist

HN 474
Autumn
Style One
Designer: Unknown
Height: 7 ½", 19.1 cm
Colour: Patterned pink robes
Issued: 1921-1938
Varieties: HN 314
Series: The Seasons
          (Series One)

U.S.:	None
Can.:	known
U.K.:	to exist

HN 475
Winter
Style One
Designer: Unknown
Height: 7 ½", 19.1 cm
Colour: Patterned pale green
          robes
Issued: 1921-1938
Varieties: HN 315
Series: The Seasons
          (Series One)

U.S.:	None
Can.:	known
U.K.:	to exist

HN 476
Fruit Gathering
Designer: L. Harradine
Height: 8" 20.3 cm
Colour: Lavender and yellow
Issued: 1921-1936
Varieties: HN 449, 503, 561,
          562, 706, 707

U.S.:	$4,500.00
Can.:	$6,000.00
U.K.:	£2,750.00

HN 477
Betty
Style One
Designer: L. Harradine
Height: 7 ½", 19.1 cm
Colour: Green
Issued: 1921-1938
Varieties: HN 402, 403, 435,
          438, 478

U.S.:	Only
Can.:	one
U.K.:	known

Unpainted model illustrated.

HN 478
Betty
Style One
Designer: L. Harradine
Height: 7 ½", 19.1 cm
Colour: White
Issued: 1921-1938
Varieties: HN 402, 403, 435,
          438, 477

U.S.:	
Can.:	Extremely rare
U.K.:	

Unpainted model illustrated.

HN 479
The Balloon Seller
Style One
Designer: L. Harradine
Height: 9", 22.9 cm
Colour: Dark blue and lavender
Issued: 1921-1938
Varieties: HN 486, 548, 583,
          697; also called 'The
          Balloon Woman'

U.S.:	$4,500.00
Can.:	$6,000.00
U.K.:	£2,750.00

HN 480
One of the Forty
Style Eleven
Designer: H. Tittensor
Height: 7", 17.8 cm
Colour: Brown, yellow and blue
Issued: 1921-1938
Varieties: HN 493, 497, 499,
          664, 714

U.S.:	$6,000.00
Can.:	$7,750.00
U.K.:	£3,500.00

HN 481
One of the Forty
Style Twelve
Designer: H. Tittensor
Height: Unknown
Colour: Dark colour
Issued: 1921-1936
Varieties: HN 483, 491, 646,
          667, 712, 1336, 1350;
          also known in flambé

U.S.:	None
Can.:	known
U.K.:	to exist

Photograph
Not
Available

HN 482
One of the Forty
Style Thirteen
Designer: H. Tittensor
Height: 6", 15.2 cm
Colour: White
Issued: 1921-1938
Varieties: HN 484, 492, 645,
          663, 713

U.S.:	None
Can.:	known
U.K.:	to exist

HN 483
One of the Forty
Style Twelve
Designer: H. Tittensor
Height: Unknown
Colour: Brown and green
Issued: 1921-1938
Varieties: HN 481, 491, 646, 667,
          712, 1336, 1350; also
          known in flambé

U.S.:	None
Can.:	known
U.K.:	to exist

Photograph
Not
Available

HN 484
One of the Forty
Style Thirteen
Designer: H. Tittensor
Height: 6", 15.2 cm
Colour: Green
Issued: 1921-1938
Varieties: HN 482, 492, 645,
          663, 713

U.S.:	None
Can.:	known
U.K.:	to exist

Photograph
Not
Available

HN 485
Lucy Lockett
Style One
Designer: L. Harradine
Height: 6", 15.2 cm
Colour: Green
Issued: 1921-1949
Series: Beggar's Opera

U.S.:	$2,500.00
Can.:	$3,750.00
U.K.:	£1,500.00

HN 486
The Balloon Seller
Style One
Designer: L. Harradine
Height: 9", 22.9 cm
Colour: Blue dress, no hat
Issued: 1921-1938
Varieties: HN 479, 548, 583, 697;
          also called 'The Balloon
          Woman'

U.S.:	None
Can.:	known
U.K.:	to exist

HN 487
Pavlova
Designer: C. J. Noke
Height: 4 ¼", 10.8 cm
Colour: White, black base
Issued: 1921-1938
Varieties: HN 676; also called
          'Swan Song'

U.S.:	Only
Can.:	two
U.K.:	known

HN 488
Tulips
Designer: Unknown
Height: 9 ½", 24.1 cm
Colour: Cream
Issued: 1921-1936
Varieties: HN 466, 672, 747,
          1334

U.S.:	None
Can.:	known
U.K.:	to exist

HN 489
Polly Peachum
Style Two
Designer: L. Harradine
Height: 4 ¼", 10.8 cm
Colour: Turquoise
Issued: 1921-1938
Varieties: HN 549, 620, 694,
            734
Series: Beggar's Opera

U.S.:	**$1,250.00**
Can.:	**$1,550.00**
U.K.:	**£ 700.00**

HN 490
One of the Forty
Style One
Dsigner: H. Tittensor
Height: 8 ¼", 21.0 cm
Colour: Blue and brown
Issued: 1921-1938
Varieties: HN 417, 495, 501, 528,
           648, 677, 1351, 1352

U.S.:	**None**
Can.:	**known**
U.K.:	**to exist**

HN 491
One of the Forty
Style Twelve
Designer: H. Tittensor
Height: Unknown
Colour: Green and white
Issued: 1921-1936
Varieties: HN 481, 483, 646,
           667, 712, 1336, 1350;
           also known in flambé

U.S.:	**None**
Can.:	**known**
U.K.:	**to exist**

Photograph
Not
Available

HN 492
One of the Forty
Style Thirteen
Designer: H. Tittensor
Height: 6", 15.2 cm
Colour: Yellow and white
Issued: 1921-1938
Varieties: HN 482, 484, 645,
           663, 713

U.S.:	**None**
Can.:	**known**
U.K.:	**to exist**

HN 493
One of the Forty
Style Eleven
Designer: H. Tittensor
Height: 6 ¾", 17.1 cm
Colour: Blue and black
Issued: 1921-1938
Varieties: HN 480, 497, 499,
           664, 714

U.S.:	**None**
Can.:	**known**
U.K.:	**to exist**

HN 494
One of the Forty
Style Two
Designer: H. Tittensor
Height: 7 ¼", 18.4 cm
Colour: Cream and blue
Issued: 1921-1936
Varieties: HN 418, 498, 647, 666,
           704, 1353

U.S.:	**None**
Can.:	**known**
U.K.:	**to exist**

HN 495
One of the Forty
Style One
Designer: H. Tittensor
Height: 8 ¼", 21.0 cm
Colour: Brown and blue
Issued: 1921-1938
Varieties: HN 417, 490, 501, 528,
           648, 677, 1351, 1352

U.S.:	**None**
Can.:	**known**
U.K.:	**to exist**

Photograph
Not
Available

HN 496
One of the Forty
Style Fourteen
Designer: H. Tittensor
Height: 7 ¾", 19.6 cm
Colour: Orange and yellow
           checks
Issued: 1921-1938
Varieties: HN 500, 649, 665,
           1354

U.S.:	**None**
Can.:	**known**
U.K.:	**to exist**

HN 497
One of the Forty
Style Eleven
Designer: H. Tittensor
Height: 6 ¾", 17.1 cm
Colour: Brown and green
Issued: 1921-1938
Varieties: HN 480, 493, 499,
           664, 714

U.S.:	
Can.:	**Extremely rare**
U.K.:	

HN 498
One of the Forty
Style Two
Designer: H. Tittensor
Height: 7 ¼", 18.4 cm
Colour: Dark colours
Issued: 1921-1936
Varieties: HN 418, 494, 647, 666,
           704, 1353

U.S.:	**None**
Can.:	**known**
U.K.:	**to exist**

HN 499
One of the Forty
Style Eleven
Designer: H. Tittensor
Height: 6 ¾", 17.1 cm
Colour: Cream and green
Issued: 1921-1938
Varieties: HN 480, 493, 497, 664,
           714

U.S.:	**None**
Can.:	**known**
U.K.:	**to exist**

Photograph
Not
Available

HN 500
One of the Forty
Style Fourteen
Designer: H. Tittensor
Height: 7 ¾", 19.6 cm
Colour: Orange checks and
           red turban
Issued: 1921-1938
Varieties: HN 496, 649, 665, 1354

U.S.:	**None**
Can.:	**known**
U.K.:	**to exist**

HN 501
One of the Forty
Style One
Designer: H. Tittensor
Height: 8 ¼", 21.0 cm
Colour: Green stripes
Issued: 1921-1938
Varieties: HN 417, 490, 495, 528,
           648, 677, 1351, 1352

U.S.:	**None**
Can.:	**known**
U.K.:	**to exist**

Photograph
Not
Available

HN 502
Marie
Style One
Designer: L. Harradine
Height: 7", 17.8 cm
Colour: White, red and blue
Issued: 1921-1938
Varieties: HN 401, 434, 504, 505,
           506

U.S.:	**None**
Can.:	**known**
U.K.:	**to exist**

HN 503
Fruit Gathering
Designer: L. Harradine
Height: 7 ¾", 19.7 cm
Colour: Brown and blue
Issued: 1921-1936
Varieties: HN 449, 476, 561, 562,
           706, 707

U.S.:	**$4,500.00**
Can.:	**$6,000.00**
U.K.:	**£2,750.00**

Photograph
Not
Available

HN 504
Marie
Style One
Designer: L. Harradine
Height: 7", 17.8 cm
Colour: Green, blue and red
Issued: 1921-1938
Varieties: HN 401, 434, 502, 505,
           506

U.S.:	**None**
Can.:	**known**
U.K.:	**to exist**

Photograph
Not
Available

HN 505
Marie
Style One
Designer: L. Harradine
Height: 7", 17.8 cm
Colour: Blue bodice, green
           and lavender skirt
Issued: 1921-1938
Varieties: HN 401, 434, 502, 504,
           506

U.S.:   **None**
Can.:   **known**
U.K.:   **to exist**

Photograph
Not
Available

HN 506
Marie
Style One
Designer: L. Harradine
Height: 7", 17.8 cm
Colour: Blue and green bodice,
           lavender skirt
Issued: 1921-1938
Varieties: HN 401, 434, 502, 504,
           505

U.S.:   **None**
Can.:   **known**
U.K.:   **to exist**

HN 507
Pussy
Designer: F. C. Stone
Height: 7 ½", 19.1 cm
Colour: Spotted blue dress
Issued: 1921-1938
Varieties: HN 18, 325; also
           called 'The Black Cat'

U.S.:   **None**
Can.:   **known**
U.K.:   **to exist**

HN 508
An Orange Vendor
Designer: C. J. Noke
Height: 6 ¼", 15.9 cm
Colour: Red, cream and orange
Issued: 1921-1938
Varieties: HN 72, 521, 1966

U.S.:   **$3,500.00**
Can.:   **$4,500.00**
U.K.:   **£2,000.00**

HN 509
Lady of the Fan
Designer: E. W. Light
Height: 9 ½", 24.1 cm
Colour: Green and lavender
Issued: 1921-1936
Varieties: HN 48, 52, 53, 53A,
           335

U.S.:   **None**
Can.:   **known**
U.K.:   **to exist**

HN 510
A Child's Grace
Designer: L. Perugini
Height: 9 ¼", 23.5 cm
Colour: Green and yellow
Issued: 1921-1938
Varieties: HN 62, 62A

U.S.:   **None**
Can.:   **known**
U.K.:   **to exist**

HN 511
Upon Her Cheeks She Wept
Designer: L. Perugini
Height: 9", 22.8 cm
Colour: Lavender
Issued: 1921-1938
Varieties: HN 59, 522

U.S.:   **None**
Can.:   **known**
U.K.:   **to exist**

HN 512
A Spook
Style Two
Designer: H. Tittensor
Height: 7", 17.8 cm
Colour: Purple
Issued: 1921-1936
Varieties: HN 50, 51, 51A, 51B,
           58, 625; also known in
           flambé

U.S.:
Can.:   **Extremely rare**
U.K.:

HN 513
Picardy Peasant (woman)
Designer: P. Stabler
Height: 9 ½", 24.0 cm
Colour: Blue
Issued: 1921-1938
Varieties: HN 4, 5, 17A, 351

U.S.:   **None**
Can.:   **known**
U.K.:   **to exist**

HN 514
Myfanwy Jones
Designer: E. W. Light
Height: 12", 30.5 cm
Colour: Green and red
Issued: 1921-1936
Varieties: HN 39, 92, 456, 516,
           519, 520, 660, 668,
           669, 701, 792; also
           called 'The Welsh Girl'

U.S.:   **None**
Can.:   **known**
U.K.:   **to exist**

HN 515
Lady with Rose
Designer: E. W. Light
Height: 9 ½", 24.1 cm
Colour: Lavender, green
Issued: 1921-1936
Varieties: HN 48A, 52A, 68, 304,
           336, 517, 584, 624

U.S.:   **None**
Can.:   **known**
U.K.:   **to exist**

HN 516
Myfanwy Jones
Designer: E. W. Light
Height: 12", 30.5 cm
Colour: Black and lavender
Issued: 1921-1936
Varieties: HN 39, 92, 456, 514,
           519, 520, 660, 668,
           669, 701, 792; also
           called 'The Welsh Girl'

U.S.:   **None**
Can.:   **known**
U.K.:   **to exist**

HN 517
Lady with Rose
Designer: E. W. Light
Height: 9 ½", 24.1 cm
Colour: Lavender with orange
           spots
Issued: 1921-1936
Varieties: HN 48A, 52A, 68, 304,
           336, 515, 584, 624

U.S.:   **None**
Can.:   **known**
U.K.:   **to exist**

HN 518
The Curtsey
Designer: E. W. Light
Height: 11", 27.9 cm
Colour: Lavender
Issued: 1921-1936
Varieties: HN 57, 57B, 66A, 327,
           334, 363, 371, 547,
           629, 670

U.S.:   **None**
Can.:   **known**
U.K.:   **to exist**

HN 519
Myfanwy Jones
Designer: E. W. Light
Height: 12", 30.5 cm
Colour: Blue and lavender
Issued: 1921-1936
Varieties: HN 39, 92, 456, 514,
           516, 520, 660, 668,
           669, 701, 792; also
           called 'The Welsh Girl'

U.S.:   **None**
Can.:   **known**
U.K.:   **to exist**

HN 520
Myfanwy Jones
Designer: E. W. Light
Height: 12", 30.5 cm
Colour: Black and lavender
Issued: 1921-1936
Varieties: HN 39, 92, 456, 514,
           516, 519, 660, 668,
           669, 701, 792; also
           called 'The Welsh Girl'

U.S.:   **None**
Can.:   **known**
U.K.:   **to exist**

HN 521
An Orange Vendor
Designer: C. J. Noke
Height: 6 ¼", 15.9 cm
Colour: Pale blue, black and purple
Issued: 1921-1938
Varieties: HN 72, 508, 1966

U.S.:	None
Can.:	known
U.K.:	to exist

HN 522
Upon Her Cheeks She Wept
Designer: L. Perugini
Height: 9", 22.8 cm
Colour: Lavender
Issued: 1921-1938
Varieties: HN 59, 511

U.S.:	None
Can.:	known
U.K.:	to exist

HN 523
Sentinel
Designer: Unknown
Height: 17 ½", 44.4 cm
Colour: Red, blue and black
Issued: 1921-1938

U.S.:	Only
Can.:	three
U.K.:	known

HN 524
Lucy Lockett
Style Two
Designer: L. Harradine
Height: 6", 15.2 cm
Colour: Orange
Issued: 1921-1949
Varieties: Earthenware and China
Series: Beggar's Opera

U.S.:	$ 950.00
Can.:	$1,250.00
U.K.:	£ 575.00

HN 525
The Flower Seller's Children
Designer: L. Harradine
Height: 8 ¼", 21.0 cm
Colour: Green and blue
Issued: 1921-1949
Varieties: HN 551, 1206, 1342, 1406

U.S.:	None
Can.:	known
U.K.:	to exist

HN 526
The Beggar
Style One
Designer: L. Harradine
Height: 6 ½", 16.5 cm
Colour: Green and blue
Issued: 1921-1949
Varieties: HN 591
Series: Beggar's Opera

U.S.:	$1,300.00
Can.:	$1,700.00
U.K.:	£ 775.00

HN 527
The Highwayman
Designer: L. Harradine
Height: 6 ½", 16.5 cm
Colour: Green and red
Issued: 1921-1949
Varieties: HN 592, 1257
Series: Beggar's Opera

U.S.:	$1,200.00
Can.:	$1,500.00
U.K.:	£ 700.00

HN 528
One of the Forty
Style One
Designer: H. Tittensor
Height: 8 ¼", 21.0 cm
Colour: Brown
Issued: 1921-1938
Varieties: HN 417, 490, 495, 501, 648, 677, 1351, 1352

U.S.:	None
Can.:	known
U.K.:	to exist

HN 529
Mr. Pickwick
Style One
Designer: L. Harradine
Height: 3 ¾", 9.5 cm
Colour: Black and tan
Issued: 1922-1932
Varieties: M41
Series: Dickens (Series One)

  U.S.:   **$125.00**
  Can.:   **$160.00**
  U.K.:   **£ 75.00**

HN 530
Fat Boy
Style One
Designer: L. Harradine
Height: 3 ½", 8.9 cm
Colour: Blue and white
Issued: 1922-1932
Varieties: M44
Series: Dickens (Series One)

  U.S.:   **$125.00**
  Can.:   **$160.00**
  U.K.:   **£ 75.00**

HN 531
Sam Weller
Designer: L. Harradine
Height: 4", 10.1 cm
Colour: Yellow and brown
Issued: 1922-1932
Varieties: M48
Series: Dickens (Series One)

  U.S.:   **$125.00**
  Can.:   **$160.00**
  U.K.:   **£ 75.00**

HN 532
Mr. Micawber
Style One
Designer: L. Harradine
Height: 3 ½", 8.9 cm
Colour: Tan and black
Issued: 1922-1932
Varieties: M42
Series: Dickens (Series One)

  U.S.:   **$125.00**
  Can.:   **$160.00**
  U.K.:   **£ 75.00**

HN 533
Sairey Gamp
Style One
Designer: L. Harradine
Height: 4", 10.1 cm
Colour: Light and dark green
Issued: 1922-1932
Varieties: M46
Series: Dickens (Series One)

  U.S.:   **$125.00**
  Can.:   **$160.00**
  U.K.:   **£ 75.00**

HN 534
Fagin
Style One
Designer: L. Harradine
Height: 4", 10.1 cm
Colour: Dark brown
Issued: 1922-1932
Varieties: M49
Series: Dickens (Series One)

  U.S.:   **$125.00**
  Can.:   **$160.00**
  U.K.:   **£ 75.00**

HN 535
Pecksniff
Style One
Designer: L. Harradine
Height: 3 ¾", 9.5 cm
Colour: Brown
Issued: 1922-1932
Varieties: M43
Series: Dickens (Series One)

  U.S.:   **$125.00**
  Can.:   **$160.00**
  U.K.:   **£ 75.00**

HN 536
Stiggins
Designer: L. Harradine
Height: 3 ¾", 9.5 cm
Colour: Black
Issued: 1922-1932
Varieties: M50
Series: Dickens (Series One)

  U.S.:   **$125.00**
  Can.:   **$160.00**
  U.K.:   **£ 75.00**

HN 537
Bill Sykes
Designer: L. Harradine
Height: 3 ¾", 9.5 cm
Colour: Black and brown
Issued: 1922-1932
Varieties: M54
Series: Dickens (Series One)

U.S.:	**$125.00**
Can.:	**$160.00**
U.K.:	**£ 75.00**

HN 538
Buz Fuz
Designer: L. Harradine
Height: 3 ¾", 9.5 cm
Colour: Black and brown
Issued: 1922-1932
Varieties: M53
Series: Dickens (Series One)

U.S.:	**$125.00**
Can.:	**$160.00**
U.K.:	**£ 75.00**

HN 539
Tiny Tim
Designer: L. Harradine
Height: 3 ½", 8.9 cm
Colour: Black, brown and blue
Issued: 1922-1932
Varieties: M56
Series: Dickens (Series One)

U.S.:	**$125.00**
Can.:	**$160.00**
U.K.:	**£ 75.00**

HN 540
Little Nell
Designer: L. Harradine
Height: 4", 10.1 cm
Colour: Pink
Issued: 1922-1932
Varieties: M51
Series: Dickens (Series One)

U.S.:	**$125.00**
Can.:	**$160.00**
U.K.:	**£ 75.00**

HN 541
Alfred Jingle
Designer: L. Harradine
Height: 3 ¾", 9.5 cm
Colour: Brown and black
Issued: 1922-1932
Varieties: M52
Series: Dickens (Series One)

U.S.:	**$125.00**
Can.:	**$160.00**
U.K.:	**£ 75.00**

HN 542
The Cobbler
Style One
Designer: C. J. Noke
Height: 7 ½", 19.1 cm
Colour: Green and brown
Issued: 1922-1939
Varieties: HN 543, 682

U.S.:	**$1,750.00**
Can.:	**$2,250.00**
U.K.:	**£ 975.00**

HN 543
The Cobbler
Style One
Designer: C. J. Noke
Height: 7 ½", 19.1 cm
Colour: Green and brown
Issued: 1922-1938
Varieties: HN 542, 682

U.S.:	**Only**
Can.:	**two**
U.K.:	**known**

HN 544
Tony Weller
Style Two
Designer: L. Harradine
Height: 3 ½", 8.9 cm
Colour: Green and yellow
Issued: 1922-1932
Varieties: M47
Series: Dickens (Series One)

U.S.:	**$125.00**
Can.:	**$160.00**
U.K.:	**£ 75.00**

HN 545
Uriah Heep
Style One
Designer: L. Harradine
Height: 4", 10.1 cm
Colour: Black
Issued: 1922-1932
Varieties: M45
Series: Dickens (Series One)
U.S.:   **$125.00**
Can.:   **$160.00**
U.K.:   **£ 75.00**

HN 546
Artful Dodger
Designer: L. Harradine
Height: 3 ¾", 9.5 cm
Colour: Black and brown
Issued: 1922-1932
Varieties: M55
Series: Dickens (Series One)
U.S.:   **$125.00**
Can.:   **$160.00**
U.K.:   **£ 75.00**

HN 547
The Curtsey
Designer: E. W. Light
Height: 11", 27.9 cm
Colour: Blue, green
           and yellow
Issued: 1922-1936
Varieties: HN 57, 57B, 66A, 327,
           334, 363, 371, 518,
           629, 670
U.S.:
Can.:   **Extremely rare**
U.K.:

HN 548
The Balloon Seller
Style One
Designer: L. Harradine
Height: 9", 22.9 cm
Colour: Blue and black
Issued: 1922-1938
Varieties: HN 479, 486, 583, 697;
           also called 'The
           Balloon Woman'
U.S.:
Can.:   **Extremely rare**
U.K.:

HN 549
Polly Peachum
Style Two
Designer: L. Harradine
Height: 4 ¼", 10.8 cm
Colour: Rose pink
Issued: 1922-1949
Varieties: HN 489, 620, 694,
           734
Series: Beggar's Opera
U.S.:   **$ 850.00**
Can.:   **$1,100.00**
U.K.:   **£ 500.00**

HN 550
Polly Peachum
Style One
Designer: L. Harradine
Height: 6 ½", 16.5 cm
Colour: Rose pink
Issued: 1922-1949
Varieties: HN 463, 465, 589, 614,
           680, 693
Series: Beggar's Opera
U.S.:   **$1,200.00**
Can.:   **$1,550.00**
U.K.:   **£ 700.00**

HN 551
The Flower Seller's Children
Designer: L. Harradine
Height: 8 ¼", 21.0 cm
Colour: Blue, orange and
           yellow
Issued: 1922-1949
Varieties: HN 525, 1206, 1342,
           1406
U.S.:   **None**
Can.:   **known**
U.K.:   **to exist**

HN 552
A Jester
Style One
Designer: C. J. Noke
Height: 10", 25.4 cm
Colour: Black and red
Issued: 1922-1938
Varieties: HN 45, 71, 71A, 320,
           367, 412, 426, 446,
           616, 627, 1295, 1702,
           2016, 3922
U.S.:   **$ 8,500.00**
Can.:   **$11,000.00**
U.K.:   **£ 5,000.00**

HN 553
Pecksniff
Style Two
Designer: L. Harradine
Height: 7", 17.8 cm
Colour: Black and brown
Issued: 1923-1939
Varieties: HN 1891
Series: Dickens (Series Two)

U.S.:	$ 800.00
Can.:	$1,000.00
U.K.:	£ 475.00

HN 554
Uriah Heep
Style Two
Designer: L. Harradine
Height: 7 ¼", 18.4 cm
Colour: Black
Issued: 1923-1939
Varieties: HN 1892
Series: Dickens (Series Two)

U.S.:	$ 800.00
Can.:	$1,000.00
U.K.:	£ 475.00

HN 555
Fat Boy
Style Two
Designer: L. Harradine
Height: 7", 17.8 cm
Colour: Blue and cream
Issued: 1923-1939
Varieties: HN 1893
Series: Dickens (Series Two)

U.S.:	$ 800.00
Can.:	$1,000.00
U.K.:	£ 475.00

HN 556
Mr. Pickwick
Style Two
Designer: L. Harradine
Height: 7", 17.8 cm
Colour: Blue, yellow and tan
Issued: 1923-1939
Varieties: HN 1894
Series: Dickens (Series Two)

U.S.:	$ 800.00
Can.:	$1,000.00
U.K.:	£ 475.00

HN 557
Mr. Micawber
Style Two
Designer: L. Harradine
Height: 7", 17.8 cm
Colour: Brown, black and tan
Issued: 1923-1939
Varieties: HN 1895
Series: Dickens (Series Two)

U.S.:	$ 800.00
Can.:	$1,000.00
U.K.:	£ 475.00

HN 558
Sairey Gamp
Style Two
Designer: L. Harradine
Height: 7", 17.8 cm
Colour: Black
Issued: 1923-1939
Varieties: HN 1896
Series: Dickens (Series Two)

U.S.:	$1,000.00
Can.:	$1,300.00
U.K.:	£ 600.00

HN 559
The Goosegirl
Style One
Designer: L. Harradine
Height: 8", 20.3 cm
Colour: Pink
Issued: 1923-1936
Varieties: HN 425, 436, 437, 448, 560

U.S.:	$6,000.00
Can.:	$7,750.00
U.K.:	£3,500.00

Earthenware

NOTE ON PRICING

As with all price guides, prices listed in this catalogue are suggested retail values. This is not a fixed price catalogue and figurines will be offered for sale at higher, lower, or catalogue prices, depending upon the supply-demand factors of the market place.

When our first edition was published in 1981 the Royal Doulton market was divided into three or four different geographical areas and pricing was based on each individual area.

In 2004 this is all changing, the global market place is coming to collectables. Our prices, while based on many different avenues that offer figurines for sale, are slowly turning into foreign exchange transactions between the former market areas. For now the collector is able to shop globally.

HN 560
The Goosegirl
Style One
Designer: L. Harradine
Height: 8", 20.3 cm
Colour: Pink and white
Issued: 1923-1936
Varieties: HN 425, 436,
           437, 448, 559

U.S.:	
Can.:	Extremely rare
U.K.:	

HN 561
Fruit Gathering
Designer: L. Harradine
Height: 7 ¾", 19.7 cm
Colour: Green, white and pink
Issued: 1923-1936
Varieties: HN 449, 476, 503, 562,
           706, 707

U.S.:	None
Can.:	known
U.K.:	to exist

HN 562
Fruit Gathering
Designer: L. Harradine
Height: 7 ¾", 19.7 cm
Colour: Pink, white and green
Issued: 1923-1936
Varieties: HN 449, 476, 503, 561,
           706, 707

U.S.:	$4,500.00
Can.:	$6,000.00
U.K.:	£2,750.00

HN 563
Man in Tudor Costume
Designer: Unknown
Height: 3 ¾", 9.5 cm
Colour: Orange striped tunic,
           black cloak
Issued: 1923-1938

U.S.:	$5,000.00
Can.:	$6,500.00
U.K.:	£3,000.00

HN 564
The Parson's Daughter
Designer: H. Tittensor
Height: 9 ½", 24.1 cm
Colour: Red, yellow and green
Issued: 1923-1949
Varieties: HN 337, 338, 441, 790,
           1242, 1356, 2018

U.S.:	$650.00
Can.:	$850.00
U.K.:	£400.00

HN 565
Pretty Lady
Designer: H. Tittensor
Height: 10", 25.4 cm
Colour: Yellow and green
Issued: 1923-1938
Varieties: HN 69, 70, 302, 330,
           361, 384, 700, 763,
           783; appears in two
           colours, yellow and
           orange

U.S.:	$2,750.00
Can.:	$3,600.00
U.K.:	£1,650.00

HN 566
The Crinoline
Designer: G. Lambert
Height: 6 ¼", 15.8 cm
Colour: Cream and green
Issued: 1923-1938
Varieties: HN 8, 9, 9A, 21, 21A,
           413, 628

U.S.:	$3,500.00
Can.:	$4,500.00
U.K.:	£2,000.00

HN 567
The Bouquet
Designer: G. Lambert
Height: 9 ½", 24.1 cm
Colour: Pink dress, beige
           patterned shawl
Issued: 1923-1936
Varieties: HN 406, 414, 422,
           428, 429, 794; also
           called 'The Nosegay'

U.S.:	$5,000.00
Can.:	$6,500.00
U.K.:	£3,000.00

HN 568
Shy Anne
Designer: L. Perugini
Height: 7 ½", 19.1 cm
Colour: Green dress with black
spots
Issued: 1923-1936
Varieties: HN 60, 64, 65

U.S.:	$7,500.00
Can.:	$9,750.00
U.K.:	£4,500.00

Earthenware and China

HN 569
The Lavender Woman
Designer: P. Stabler
Height: 8 ¼", 21.0 cm
Colour: Lavender
Issued: 1924-1936
Varieties: HN 22, 23, 23A, 342,
744

U.S.:	$5,500.00
Can.:	$7,250.00
U.K.:	£3,250.00

HN 570
Motherhood
Style Two
Designer: Unknown
Height: 9 ¼", 23.5 cm
Colour: Pink and green
Issued: 1923-1938
Varieties: HN 462, 703, 743

U.S.:	$ 8,500.00
Can.:	$11,000.00
U.K.:	£ 5,000.00

HN 571
Falstaff
Style One
Designer: C. J. Noke
Height: 7", 17.8 cm
Colour: Brown and green
Issued: 1923-1938
Varieties: HN 575, 608, 609,
619, 638, 1216, 1606

U.S.:	$3,500.00
Can.:	$4,500.00
U.K.:	£2,000.00

HN 572
Contentment
Designer: L. Harradine
Height: 7 ¼", 18.4 cm
Colour: Cream and orange
Issued: 1923-1938
Varieties: HN 395, 396, 421,
468, 685, 686, 1323

U.S.:	$3,500.00
Can.:	$4,500.00
U.K.:	£1,750.00

HN 573
Madonna of the Square
Designer: P. Stabler
Height: 7", 17.8 cm
Colour: Orange
Issued: 1923-1936
Varieties: HN 10, 10A, 11, 14,
27, 326, 576, 594,
613, 764, 1968, 1969,
2034

U.S.:	None
Can.:	known
U.K.:	to exist

HN 574 not issued.

HN 575
Falstaff
Style One
Designer: C. J. Noke
Height: 7", 17.8 cm
Colour: Brown and yellow
Issued: 1923-1938
Varieties: HN 571, 608, 609,
619, 638, 1216, 1606

U.S.:	$3,500.00
Can.:	$4,500.00
U.K.:	£1,750.00

HN 576
Madonna of the Square
Designer: P. Stabler
Height: 7", 17.8 cm
Colour: Green and black
Issued: 1923-1936
Varieties: HN 10, 10A, 11, 14, 27,
326, 573, 594, 613,
764, 1968, 1969,
2034

U.S.:	$2,750.00
Can.:	$3,600.00
U.K.:	£1,650.00

HN 577
The Chelsea Pair (woman)
Designer: L. Harradine
Height: 6", 15.2 cm
Colour: White dress, blue
         flowers
Issued: 1923-1938
Varieties: HN 578

U.S.:	**$1,000.00**
Can.:	**$1,300.00**
U.K.:	**£ 600.00**

HN 578
The Chelsea Pair (woman)
Designer: L. Harradine
Height: 6", 15.2 cm
Colour: White dress, yellow
         flowers
Issued: 1923-1938
Varieties: HN 577

U.S.:	**$1,000.00**
Can.:	**$1,300.00**
U.K.:	**£ 600.00**

HN 579
The Chelsea Pair (man)
Designer: L. Harradine
Height: 6", 15.2 cm
Colour: Red and black, yellow
         flowers
Issued: 1923-1938
Varieties: HN 580

U.S.:	**$1,000.00**
Can.:	**$1,300.00**
U.K.:	**£ 600.00**

HN 580
The Chelsea Pair (man)
Designer: L. Harradine
Height: 6", 15.2 cm
Colour: Red and black, blue
         flowers
Issued: 1923-1938
Varieties: HN 579

U.S.:	**$1,000.00**
Can.:	**$1,300.00**
U.K.:	**£ 600.00**

HN 581
The Perfect Pair
Designer: L. Harradine
Height: 6 ¾", 17.2 cm
Colour: Pink and red
Issued: 1923-1938

U.S.:	**$1,500.00**
Can.:	**$1,950.00**
U.K.:	**£ 900.00**

HN 582
Grossmith's 'Tsang Ihang'
Perfume of Thibet
Designer: Unknown
Height: 11 ½", 29.2 cm
Colour: Yellow, black and blue
Issued: 1923-Unknown

U.S.:	**$1,300.00**
Can.:	**$1,700.00**
U.K.:	**£ 800.00**

Earthenware

HN 583
The Balloon Seller
Style One
Designer: L. Harradine
Height: 9", 22.9 cm
Colour: Green and cream
Issued: 1923-1949
Varieties: HN 479, 486, 548,
           697; also called 'The
           Balloon Woman'

U.S.:	**$1,500.00**
Can.:	**$1,950.00**
U.K.:	**£ 900.00**

HN 584
Lady with Rose
Designer: E.W. Light
Height: 9 ½", 24.1 cm
Colour: Green and pink
Issued: 1923-1936
Varieties: HN 48A, 52A, 68, 304,
           336, 515, 517, 624

U.S.:	**None**
Can.:	**known**
U.K.:	**to exist**

HN 585
Harlequinade
Designer: L. Harradine
Height: 6 ½", 16.5 cm
Colour: Purple, black and green
Issued: 1923-1940
Varieties: HN 635, 711, 780

U.S.:	$6,000.00
Can.:	$7,750.00
U.K.:	£3,500.00

HN 586
Boy with Turban
Designer: L. Harradine
Height: 3 ¾", 9.5 cm
Colour: Blue and green
Issued: 1923-1936
Varieties: HN 587, 661, 662, 1210, 1212, 1213, 1214, 1225

U.S.:	$1,850.00
Can.:	$2,500.00
U.K.:	£1,100.00

HN 587
Boy with Turban
Designer: L. Harradine
Height: 3 ¾", 9.5 cm
Colour: Green, red and blue
Issued: 1923-1936
Varieties: HN 586, 661, 662, 1210, 1212, 1213, 1214, 1225

U.S.:	$1,850.00
Can.:	$2,500.00
U.K.:	£1,100.00

HN 588
Spring
Style Two
Designer: L. Harradine
Height: 6 ¼", 15.9 cm
Colour: Pink or yellow dress
Issued: 1923-1938

U.S.:	
Can.:	Extremely rare
U.K.:	

HN 589
Polly Peachum
Style One
Designer: L. Harradine
Height: 6 ½", 16.5 cm
Colour: Pink and yellow
Issued: 1924-1949
Varieties: HN 463, 465, 550, 614, 680, 693
Series: Beggar's Opera

U.S.:	
Can.:	Extremely rare
U.K.:	

HN 590
Captain MacHeath
Designer: L. Harradine
Height: 7", 17.8 cm
Colour: Red, black and yellow
Issued: 1924-1949
Varieties: HN 464, 1256
Series: Beggar's Opera

U.S.:	$1,500.00
Can.:	$1,950.00
U.K.:	£ 900.00

HN 591
The Beggar
Style One
Designer: L. Harradine
Height: 6 ¾", 17.2 cm
Colour: Green and blue
Issued: 1924-1949
Varieties: HN 526
Series: Beggar's Opera

U.S.:	$1,200.00
Can.:	$1,575.00
U.K.:	£ 725.00

Earthenware

HN 592
The Highwayman
Designer: L. Harradine
Height: 6 ½", 16.5 cm
Colour: Green and red
Issued: 1924-1949
Varieties: HN 527, 1257
Series: Beggar's Opera

U.S.:	$1,200.00
Can.:	$1,575.00
U.K.:	£ 725.00

HN 593
Nude on Rock
Designer: Unknown
Height: 6 ¾", 17.1 cm
Colour: Blue
Issued: 1924-1938

U.S.:	Only
Can.:	one
U.K.:	known

HN 594
Madonna of the Square
Designer: P. Stabler
Height: 7", 17.8 cm
Colour: Green and brown
Issued: 1924-1936
Varieties: HN 10, 10A, 11, 14, 27,
           326, 573, 576, 613,
           764, 1968, 1969,
           2034

U.S.:	None
Can.:	known
U.K.:	to exist

HN 595
Grief
Designer: C. J. Noke
Height: 1 ¾", 4.5 cm
Colour: Blue
Issued: 1924-1938

U.S.:	$3,000.00
Can.:	$4,000.00
U.K.:	£1,750.00

Photograph
Not
Available

HN 596
Despair
Designer: C. J. Noke
Height: 4 ¾", 9.5 cm
Colour: Mottled blue
Issued: Unknown
Varieties: Also known in flambé

U.S.:	Only
Can.:	one
U.K.:	known

HN 597
The Bather
Style One, First Version
Designer: L. Harradine
Height: 7 ¾", 19.7 cm
Colour: Grey
Issued: 1924-1938
Varieties: HN 687, 781, 782,
           1238, 1708

U.S.:	$4,750.00
Can.:	$6,000.00
U.K.:	£2,750.00

HN 598
Omar Khayyam and the Beloved
Designer: C. J. Noke
Height: 10", 25.4 cm
Colour: Green, pink and blue
Issued: 1924-1936
Varieties: HN 407, 419, 459

U.S.:	None
Can.:	known
U.K.:	to exist

HN 599
Masquerade (man)
Style One
Designer: L. Harradine
Height: 6 ¾", 17.2 cm
Colour: Red
Issued: 1924-1936
Varieties: HN 636, 683

U.S.:	$1,500.00
Can.:	$1,950.00
U.K.:	£ 900.00

HN 600
Masquerade (woman)
Style One
Designer: L. Harradine
Height: 6 ¾", 17.2 cm
Colour: Pink
Issued: 1924-1949
Varieties: HN 637, 674

U.S.:	$1,500.00
Can.:	$1,950.00
U.K.:	£ 900.00

Photograph
Not
Available

HN 601
A Mandarin
Style Three
Designer: C. J. Noke
Height: 10", 25.4 cm
Colour: Red
Issued: 1924-1938

U.S.:	$ 8,000.00
Can.:	$12,000.00
U.K.:	£ 5,000.00

HN 602 not issued.

HN 603A
A Child Study
Style One
Designer: L. Harradine
Height: 4 ¾", 12.0 cm
Colour: White, primroses
           around base
Issued: 1924-1938
Varieties: HN 603B, 1441; also
           known in flambé

U.S.:	$1,250.00
Can.:	$1,600.00
U.K.:	£ 750.00

HN 603B
A Child Study
Style One
Designer: L. Harradine
Height: 4 ¾", 12.0 cm
Colour: White, kingcups
           around base
Issued: 1924-1938
Varieties: HN 603A, 1441; also
           known in flambé

U.S.:	$1,250.00
Can.:	$1,600.00
U.K.:	£ 750.00

HN 604A
A Child Study
Style Two
Designer: L. Harradine
Height: 5 ½", 14.0 cm
Colour: White, primroses
           around base
Issued: 1924-1938
Varieties: HN 604B, 1442, 1443

U.S.:	$1,250.00
Can.:	$1,600.00
U.K.:	£ 750.00

HN 604B
A Child Study
Style Two
Designer: L. Harradine
Height: 5 ½", 14.0 cm
Colour: White, kingcups
           around base
Issued: 1924-1938
Varieties: HN 604A, 1442, 1443

U.S.:	$1,250.00
Can.:	$1,600.00
U.K.:	£ 750.00

HN 605A
A Child Study
Style Three
Designer: L. Harradine
Height: Unknown
Colour: White, primroses
           around base
Issued: 1924-1938
Varieties: HN 605B

U.S.:	$1,250.00
Can.:	$1,600.00
U.K.:	£ 750.00

HN 605B
A Child Study
Style Three
Designer: L. Harradine
Height: Unknown
Colour: White, kingcups
           around base
Issued: 1924-1938
Varieties: HN 605A

U.S.:	$1,250.00
Can.:	$1,600.00
U.K.:	£ 750.00

HN 606A
Female Study
Designer: L. Harradine
Height: 5", 12.7 cm
Colour: White, primroses
           around base
Issued: 1924-1936
Varieties: HN 606B; also known
           in flambé

U.S.:	$1,250.00
Can.:	$1,600.00
U.K.:	£ 750.00

HN 606B
Female Study
Designer: L. Harradine
Height: 5", 12.7 cm
Colour: White, kingcups
around base
Issued: 1924-1936
Varieties: HN 606A; also known
in flambé

U.S.:	**$1,250.00**
Can.:	**$1,600.00**
U.K.:	**£ 750.00**

HN 607 not issued.

HN 608
Falstaff
Style One
Designer: C. J. Noke
Height: 7", 17.8 cm
Colour: Red
Issued: 1924-1938
Varieties: HN 571, 575, 609,
619, 638, 1216, 1606

U.S.:	**None**
Can.:	**known**
U.K.:	**to exist**

HN 609
Falstaff
Style One
Designer: C. J. Noke
Height: 7", 17.8 cm
Colour: Green
Issued: 1924-1938
Varieties: HN 571, 575, 608,
619, 638, 1216, 1606

U.S.:	**None**
Can.:	**known**
U.K.:	**to exist**

HN 610
Henry Lytton as Jack Point
Designer: C. J. Noke
Height: 6 ½", 16.5 cm
Colour: Blue, black and brown
Issued: 1924-1949

U.S.:	**$1,600.00**
Can.:	**$2,000.00**
U.K.:	**£ 950.00**

HN 611
A Mandarin
Style One
Designer: C. J. Noke
Height: 10 ¼", 26.0 cm
Colour: Gold and yellow
Issued: 1924-1936
Varieties: HN 84, 316, 318, 382,
746, 787, 791; also
called 'Chinese
Mandarin' and
'The Mikado'

U.S.:	**$ 8,500.00**
Can.:	**$11,000.00**
U.K.:	**£ 5,000.00**

HN 612
The Poke Bonnet
Designer: C. J. Noke
Height: 9 ½", 24.1 cm
Colour: Yellow and green
Issued: 1924-1938
Varieties: HN 362, 765; 'A Lilac
Shawl' HN 44, 44A; 'In
Grandma's Days'
HN 339, 340, 388,
442

U.S.:	**$3,500.00**
Can.:	**$4,500.00**
U.K.:	**£2,000.00**

HN 613
Madonna of the Square
Designer: P. Stabler
Height: 7", 17.8 cm
Colour: Pink and orange
Issued: 1924-1936
Varieties: HN 10, 10A, 11, 14, 27,
326, 573, 576, 594,
764, 1968, 1969,
2034

U.S.:	**$2,750.00**
Can.:	**$3,500.00**
U.K.:	**£1,650.00**

HN 614
Polly Peachum
Style One
Designer: L. Harradine
Height: 6 ½", 16.5 cm
Colour: Pale pink and blue
Issued: 1924-1949
Varieties: HN 463, 465, 550, 589,
680, 693
Series: Beggar's Opera

U.S.:	**$1,500.00**
Can.:	**$1,950.00**
U.K.:	**£ 900.00**

HN 615
Katharine
Designer: C. J. Noke
Height: 5 ¾", 14.6 cm
Colour: Red with green spots
Issued: 1924-1938
Varieties: HN 61, 74, 341, 471, 793

U.S.:	**$3,500.00**
Can.:	**$4,500.00**
U.K.:	**£2,000.00**

HN 616
A Jester
Style One
Designer: C. J. Noke
Height: 10", 25.4 cm
Colour: Black and white
Issued: 1924-1938
Varieties: HN 45, 71, 71A, 320, 367, 412, 426, 446, 552, 627, 1295, 1702, 2016, 3922

U.S.:	**None**
Can.:	**known**
U.K.:	**to exist**

HN 617
A Shepherd
Style One
Designer: C. J. Noke
Height: 13 ¼", 33.6 cm
Colour: Dark blue
Issued: 1924-1938
Varieties: HN 81, 632

U.S.:	
Can.:	**Extremely rare**
U.K.:	

China

HN 618
Falstaff
Style Two
Designer: C. J. Noke
Height: 7", 17.8 cm
Colour: Black, red and green
Issued: 1924-1938
Varieties: HN 2054

U.S.:	
Can.:	**Extremely rare**
U.K.:	

HN 619
Falstaff
Style One
Designer: C. J. Noke
Height: 7", 17.8 cm
Colour: Brown, green and yellow
Issued: 1924-1938
Varieties: HN 571, 575, 608, 609, 638, 1216, 1606

U.S.:	
Can.:	**Extremely rare**
U.K.:	

HN 620
Polly Peachum
Style Two
Designer: L. Harradine
Height: 4 ¼", 10.8 cm
Colour: Pink
Issued: 1924-1938
Varieties: HN 489, 549, 694, 734
Series: Beggar's Opera

U.S.:	**$1,250.00**
Can.:	**$1,600.00**
U.K.:	**£ 750.00**

HN 621
Pan on Rock
Designer: Unknown
Height: 5 ¼", 13.3 cm
Colour: Cream, green base
Issued: 1924-1936
Varieties: HN 622

U.S.:	
Can.:	**Extremely rare**
U.K.:	

HN 622
Pan on Rock
Designer: Unknown
Height: 5 ¼", 13.3 cm
Colour: Cream, black base
Issued: 1924-1938
Varieties: HN 621

U.S.:	
Can.:	**Extremely rare**
U.K.:	

HN 623
An Old King
Designer: C. J. Noke
Height: 9 ¾", 24.7 cm
Colour: Grey, red and green
Issued: 1924-1938
Varieties: HN 358, 1801, 2134

U.S.:	None
Can.:	known
U.K.:	to exist

HN 624
Lady with Rose
Designer: E. W Light
Height: 9 ½", 24.1 cm
Colour: Turquoise
Issued: 1924-1936
Varieties: HN 48A, 52A, 68, 304, 336, 515, 517, 584

U.S.:	None
Can.:	known
U.K.:	to exist

HN 625
A Spook
Style One
Designer: H. Tittensor
Height: 7", 17.8 cm
Colour: Yellow
Issued: 1924-1936
Varieties: HN 50, 51, 51A, 51B, 58, 512; also known in flambé

U.S.:	$5,500.00
Can.:	$7,000.00
U.K.:	£3,300.00

HN 626
Lady with Shawl
Designer: L. Harradine
Height: 13 ¼", 33.6 cm
Colour: Yellow and white
Issued: 1924-1936
Varieties: HN 447, 458, 678, 679

U.S.:	None
Can.:	known
U.K.:	to exist

HN 627
A Jester
Style One
Designer: C. J. Noke
Height: 10", 25.4 cm
Colour: Brown checks
Issued: 1924-1938
Varieties: HN 45, 71, 71A, 320, 367, 412, 426, 446, 552, 616, 1295, 1702, 2016, 3922

U.S.:	$ 8,500.00
Can.:	$11,000.00
U.K.:	£ 5,000.00

HN 628
The Crinoline
Designer: G. Lambert
Height: 6 ¼", 15.8 cm
Colour: Yellow and blue
Issued: 1924-1938
Varieties: HN 8, 9, 9A, 21, 21A, 413, 566

U.S.:	None
Can.:	known
U.K.:	to exist

HN 629
The Curtsey
Designer: E. W. Light
Height: 11", 27.9 cm
Colour: Green and black
Issued: 1924-1936
Varieties: HN 57, 57B, 66A, 327, 334, 363, 371, 518, 547, 670

U.S.:	None
Can.:	known
U.K.:	to exist

HN 630
A Jester
Style Two
Designer: C. J. Noke
Height: 10 ¼", 26.0 cm
Colour: Brown
Issued: 1924-1938
Varieties: HN 45A, 45B, 55, 308, 1333; also known in black and white

U.S.:	$ 8,500.00
Can.:	$11,000.00
U.K.:	£ 5,000.00

HN 631
Fisherwomen
Designer: C. J. Noke
Height: 11 ¾", 29.8 cm
Colour: Mauve and green
Issued: 1924-1938
Varieties: HN 80, 349, 359; also
called 'Looking for the
Boats' and 'Waiting
For The Boats'

U.S.:
Can.: **Extremely rare**
U.K.:

HN 632
A Shepherd
Style One
Designer: C. J. Noke
Height: 13 ¼", 33.6 cm
Colour: Blue and white
Issued: 1924-1938
Varieties: HN 81, 617

U.S.:	**None**
Can.:	**known**
U.K.:	**to exist**

China

HN 633
The Princess
Designer: L. Harradine
Height: 9 ¼", 23.5 cm
Colour: Black and white
Issued: 1924-1936
Varieties: HN 391, 392, 420, 430,
431

U.S.:	**None**
Can.:	**known**
U.K.:	**to exist**

HN 634
A Geisha
Style One
Designer: H. Tittensor
Height: 10 ¾", 27.3 cm
Colour: Black and white
Issued: 1924-1936
Varieties: HN 354, 376, 376A, 387,
741, 779, 1321, 1322;
also called 'The
Japanese Lady'

U.S.:	**$ 7,500.00**
Can.:	**$10,000.00**
U.K.:	**£ 4,500.00**

HN 635
Harlequinade
Designer: L. Harradine
Height: 6 ½", 16.5 cm
Colour: Gold
Issued: 1924-1940
Varieties: HN 585, 711, 780

U.S.:	**$6,000.00**
Can.:	**$8,000.00**
U.K.:	**£3,750.00**

HN 636
Masquerade (man)
Style One
Designer: L. Harradine
Height: 6 ¾", 17.2 cm
Colour: Gold
Issued: 1924-1936
Varieties: HN 599, 683

U.S.:	**$1,500.00**
Can.:	**$1,950.00**
U.K.:	**£ 900.00**

HN 637
Masquerade (woman)
Style One
Designer: L. Harradine
Height: 6 ¾", 17.2 cm
Colour: Gold
Issued: 1924-1938
Varieties: HN 600, 674

U.S.:	**$1,500.00**
Can.:	**$1,950.00**
U.K.:	**£ 900.00**

HN 638
Falstaff
Style One
Designer: C. J. Noke
Height: 7", 17.8 cm
Colour: Red and cream
Issued: 1924-1938
Varieties: HN 571, 575, 608,
609, 619, 1216, 1606

U.S.:
Can.: **Extremely Rare**
U.K.:

HN 639
Elsie Maynard
Style One
Designer: C. J. Noke
Height: 7", 17.8 cm
Colour: Mauve and pink
Issued: 1924-1949

U.S.:	**$1,750.00**
Can.:	**$2,275.00**
U.K.:	**£1,000.00**

HN 640
Charley's Aunt
Style One
Designer: A. Taft
Height: 7", 17.8 cm
Colour: Green and lavender
Issued: 1924-1936
Varieties: HN 35

U.S.:	**$2,500.00**
Can.:	**$3,250.00**
U.K.:	**£1,500.00**

HN 641
A Mandarin
Style Two
Designer: C. J. Noke
Height: 8 ¼", 21.0 cm
Colour: Yellow and blue
Issued: 1924-1938
Varieties: HN 366, 455

U.S.:	**Only**
Can.:	**two**
U.K.:	**known**

HN 642
Pierrette
Style One
Designer: L. Harradine
Height: 7 ¼", 18.4 cm
Colour: Red
Issued: 1924-1938
Varieties: HN 643, 644, 691,
           721, 731, 732, 784

U.S.:	**$4,750.00**
Can.:	**$6,000.00**
U.K.:	**£2,750.00**

HN 643
Pierrette
Style One
Designer: L. Harradine
Height: 7 ¼", 18.4 cm
Colour: Red, black and white
Issued: 1924-1938
Varieties: HN 642, 644, 691,
           721, 731, 732, 784

U.S.:	**$4,500.00**
Can.:	**$6,000.00**
U.K.:	**£2,750.00**

HN 644
Pierrette
Style One
Designer: L. Harradine
Height: 7 ¼", 18.4 cm
Colour: White and black
Issued: 1924-1938
Varieties: HN 642, 643, 691,
           721, 731, 732, 784

U.S.:	**$4,000.00**
Can.:	**$6,000.00**
U.K.:	**£2,750.00**

Photograph
Not
Available

HN 645
One of the Forty
Style Thirteen
Designer: H. Tittensor
Height: 6", 15.2 cm
Colour: Blue, black and white
Issued: 1924-1938
Varieties: HN 482, 484, 492,
           663, 713

U.S.:	**None**
Can.:	**known**
U.K.:	**to exist**

HN 646
One of the Forty
Style Twelve
Designer: H. Tittensor
Height: Unknown
Colour: Cream, blue and black
Issued: 1924-1936
Varieties: HN 481, 483, 491,
           667, 712, 1336, 1350;
           also known in flambé

U.S.:	
Can.:	**Extremely rare**
U.K.:	

Photograph
Not
Available

HN 647
One of the Forty
Style Two
Designer: H. Tittensor
Height: 7 ¼", 18.4 cm
Colour: Blue, black and white
Issued: 1924-1936
Varieties: HN 418, 494, 498, 666, 704, 1353

U.S.:	None
Can.:	known
U.K.:	to exist

HN 648
One of the Forty
Style One
Designer: H. Tittensor
Height: 8 ¼", 21.0 cm
Colour: Blue, black and white
Issued: 1924-1938
Varieties: HN 417, 490, 495, 501, 528, 677, 1351, 1352

U.S.:	None
Can.:	known
U.K.:	to exist

HN 649
One of the Forty
Style Fourteen
Designer: H. Tittensor
Height: 7 ¾", 19.7 cm
Colour: Blue, black and white
Issued: 1924-1938
Varieties: HN 496, 500, 665, 1354

U.S.:	None
Can.:	known
U.K.:	to exist

HN 650
Crinoline Lady
Designer: Unknown
Height: 3", 7.6 cm
Colour: Green and white
Issued: 1924-1938
Varieties: HN 651, 652, 653, 654, 655

U.S.:	$3,250.00
Can.:	$4,250.00
U.K.:	£1,950.00

HN 651
Crinoline Lady
Designer: Unknown
Height: 3", 7.6 cm
Colour: Orange and white
Issued: 1924-1938
Varieties: HN 650, 652, 653, 654, 655

U.S.:	$3,250.00
Can.:	$4,250.00
U.K.:	£1,950.00

HN 652
Crinoline Lady
Designer: Unknown
Height: 3", 7.6 cm
Colour: Purple
Issued: 1924-1938
Varieties: HN 650, 651, 653, 654, 655

U.S.:	$3,250.00
Can.:	$4,250.00
U.K.:	£1,950.00

HN 653
Crinoline Lady
Designer: Unknown
Height: 3", 7.6 cm
Colour: Black and white
Issued: 1924-1938
Varieties: HN 650, 651, 652, 654, 655

U.S.:	$3,250.00
Can.:	$4,250.00
U.K.:	£1,950.00

HN 654
Crinoline Lady
Designer: Unknown
Height: 3", 7.6 cm
Colour: Red and purple
Issued: 1924-1938
Varieties: HN 650, 651, 652, 653, 655

U.S.:	$3,250.00
Can.:	$4,250.00
U.K.:	£1,950.00

HN 655
Crinoline Lady
Designer: Unknown
Height: 3", 7.6 cm
Colour: Blue and black
Issued: 1924-1938
Varieties: HN 650, 651, 652, 653,
            654

U.S.:	**$3,250.00**
Can.:	**$4,250.00**
U.K.:	**£1,950.00**

HN 656
The Mask
Style One
Designer: L. Harradine
Height: 6 ¾", 17.2 cm
Colour: Blue and purple
Issued: 1924-1938
Varieties: HN 657, 729, 733, 785,
            1271

U.S.:	**$5,000.00**
Can.:	**$6,500.00**
U.K.:	**£3,000.00**

HN 657
The Mask
Style One
Designer: L. Harradine
Height: 6 ¾", 17.2 cm
Colour: Black and white
Issued: 1924-1938
Varieties: HN 656, 729, 733, 785,
            1271

U.S.:	**$5,000.00**
Can.:	**$6,500.00**
U.K.:	**£3,000.00**

HN 658
Mam'selle
Designer: L. Harradine
Height: 7", 17.8 cm
Colour: Black and white
Issued: 1924-1938
Varieties: HN 659, 724, 786

U.S.:	**$5,500.00**
Can.:	**$7,250.00**
U.K.:	**£3,250.00**

HN 659
Mam'selle
Designer: L. Harradine
Height: 7", 17.8 cm
Colour: Dark blue
Issued: 1924-1938
Varieties: HN 658, 724, 786

U.S.:	**$5,500.00**
Can.:	**$7,250.00**
U.K.:	**£3,250.00**

HN 660
Myfanwy Jones
Designer: E. W. Light
Height: 12", 30.5 cm
Colour: White and blue
Issued: 1924-1936
Varieties: HN 39, 92, 456,514,
            516, 519, 520, 668,
            669, 701, 792; also
            called 'The Welsh Girl'

U.S.:	
Can.:	**Extremely rare**
U.K.:	

HN 661
Boy with Turban
Designer: L. Harradine
Height: 3 ¾", 9.5 cm
Colour: Blue
Issued: 1924-1936
Varieties: HN 586, 587, 662,
            1210, 1212, 1213,
            1214, 1225

U.S.:	**$1,850.00**
Can.:	**$2,500.00**
U.K.:	**£1,100.00**

HN 662
Boy with Turban
Designer: L. Harradine
Height: 3 ¾", 9.5 cm
Colour: Black and white
Issued: 1924-1936
Varieties: HN 586, 587, 661,
            1210, 1212, 1213,
            1214, 1225

U.S.:	**$1,850.00**
Can.:	**$2,500.00**
U.K.:	**£1,100.00**

HN 663
One of the Forty
Style Thirteen
Designer: H. Tittensor
Height: 6", 15.2 cm
Colour: Yellow
Issued: 1924-1938
Varieties: HN 482, 484, 492, 645,
           713,

U.S.:	
Can.:	**Extremely rare**
U.K.:	

HN 664
One of the Forty
Style Eleven
Designer: H. Tittensor
Height: 7 ¾", 19.7 cm
Colour: Yellow, green and
           black
Issued: 1924-1938
Varieties: HN 480, 493, 497, 499,
           714

U.S.:	**$4,500.00**
Can.:	**$6,000.00**
U.K.:	**£2,700.00**

HN 665
One of the Forty
Style Fourteen
Designer: H. Tittensor
Height: 7 ¾", 19.7 cm
Colour: Yellow
Issued: 1924-1938
Varieties: HN 496, 500, 649,
           1354

U.S.:	
Can.:	**Extremely rare**
U.K.:	

HN 666
One of the Forty
Style Two
Designer: H. Tittensor
Height: 7 ¼", 18.4 cm
Colour: Yellow
Issued: 1924-1936
Varieties: HN 418, 494, 498,
           647, 704, 1353

U.S.:	
Can.:	**Extremely rare**
U.K.:	

HN 667
One of the Forty
Style Twelve
Designer: H. Tittensor
Height: Unknown
Colour: Yellow and black
Issued: 1924-1936
Varieties: HN 481, 483, 491, 646,
           712, 1336, 1350; also
           known in flambé

U.S.:	
Can.:	**Extremely rare**
U.K.:	

HN 668
Myfanwy Jones
Designer: E. W. Light
Height: 12", 30.5 cm
Colour: Yellow and pink
Issued: 1924-1936
Varieties: HN 39, 92, 456, 514,
           516, 519, 520, 660,
           669, 701, 792; also
           called 'The Welsh Girl'

U.S.:	**$ 8,500.00**
Can.:	**$11,000.00**
U.K.:	**£ 5,000.00**

HN 669
Myfanwy Jones
Designer: E. W. Light
Height: 8 ½", 21.5 cm
Colour: Yellow and green
Issued: 1924-1936
Varieties: HN 39, 92, 456, 514,
           516, 519, 520, 660,
           668, 701, 792; also
           called 'The Welsh Girl'

U.S.:	**$ 8,500.00**
Can.:	**$11,000.00**
U.K.:	**£ 5,000.00**

HN 670
The Curtsey
Designer: E. W. Light
Height: 11", 27.9 cm
Colour: Pink and yellow
Issued: 1924-1936
Varieties: HN 57, 57B, 66A, 327,
           334, 363, 371, 518,
           547, 629

U.S.:	**$4,000.00**
Can.:	**$5,250.00**
U.K.:	**£2,400.00**

HN 671
The Ermine Muff
Designer: C. J. Noke
Height: 8 ½", 21.6 cm
Colour: Green and yellow
Issued: 1924-1938
Varieties: HN 54, 332; also called
           'Lady Ermine' and 'Lady
           with the Ermine Muff'

U.S.:   **None**
Can.:   **known**
U.K.:   **to exist**

HN 672
Tulips
Designer: Unknown
Height: 9 ½" 24.1 cm
Colour: Green and blue
Issued: 1924-1936
Varieties: HN 466, 488, 747,
           1334

U.S.:   **$5,000.00**
Can.:   **$6,500.00**
U.K.:   **£3,000.00**

Earthenware

Photograph
Not
Available

HN 673
Henry VIII
Style One
Designer: C. J. Noke
Height: Unknown
Colour: Brown and lavender
Issued: 1924-1938
Varieties: HN 370

U.S.:   **None**
Can.:   **known**
U.K.:   **to exist**

HN 674
Masquerade (woman)
Style One
Designer: L. Harradine
Height: 6 ¾", 17.2 cm
Colour: Orange and yellow
Issued: 1924-1938
Varieties: HN 600, 637

U.S.:   **$1,750.00**
Can.:   **$2,250.00**
U.K.:   **£1,000.00**

HN 675
The Gainsborough Hat
Designer: H. Tittensor
Height: 8 ¾", 22.2 cm
Colour: Cream
Issued: 1924-1936
Varieties: HN 46, 46A, 47, 329,
           352, 383, 453, 705

U.S.:   **$5,000.00**
Can.:   **$6,500.00**
U.K.:   **£3,000.00**

HN 676
Pavlova
Designer: C. J. Noke
Height: 4 ¼", 10.8 cm
Colour: White and blue tutu,
           black base
Issued: 1924-1938
Varieties: HN 487; also called
           'Swan Song'

U.S.:
Can.:   **Extremely rare**
U.K.:

HN 677
One of the Forty
Style One
Designer: H. Tittensor
Height: 8 ¼", 21.0 cm
Colour: Orange, yellow and red
Issued: 1924-1938
Varieties: HN 417, 490, 495, 501,
           528, 648, 1351, 1352

U.S.:
Can.:   **Extremely rare**
U.K.:

HN 678
Lady with Shawl
Designer: L. Harradine
Height: 13 ¼", 33.7 cm
Colour: Black, yellow and white
Issued: 1924-1936
Varieties: HN 447, 458, 626,
           679

U.S.:   **$7,500.00**
Can.:   **$9,750.00**
U.K.:   **£4,500.00**

HN 679
Lady with Shawl
Designer: L. Harradine
Height: 13 ¼", 33.7 cm
Colour: Black, yellow, blue
           and white
Issued: 1924-1936
Varieties: HN 447, 458, 626,
           678

U.S.:	**None**
Can.:	**known**
U.K.:	**to exist**

HN 680
Polly Peachum
Style One
Designer: L. Harradine
Height: 6 ½", 16.5 cm
Colour: White
Issued: 1924-1949
Varieties: HN 463, 465, 550, 589,
           614, 693
Series: Beggar's Opera

U.S.:	**None**
Can.:	**known**
U.K.:	**to exist**

HN 681
The Cobbler
Style Two
Designer: C. J. Noke
Height: 8 ½", 21.6 cm
Colour: Green and red
Issued: 1924-1938
Varieties: HN 1251, 1283

U.S.:	**None**
Can.:	**known**
U.K.:	**to exist**

HN 682
The Cobbler
Style One
Designer: C. J. Noke
Height: 7 ½", 19.1 cm
Colour: Red and green
Issued: 1924-1938
Varieties: HN 542, 543

U.S.:	**None**
Can.:	**known**
U.K.:	**to exist**

HN 683
Masquerade (man)
Style One
Designer: L. Harradine
Height: 7 ¼", 18.4 cm
Colour: Green
Issued: 1924-1936
Varieties: HN 599, 636

U.S.:	**$1,500.00**
Can.:	**$1,950.00**
U.K.:	**£ 900.00**

HN 684
Tony Weller
Style One
Designer: C. J. Noke
Height: 10 ¼", 26.0 cm
Colour: Green and brown
Issued: 1924-1938
Varieties: HN 346, 368

U.S.:	**$2,250.00**
Can.:	**$3,000.00**
U.K.:	**£1,350.00**

HN 685
Contentment
Designer: L. Harradine
Height: 7 ¼", 18.4 cm
Colour: Black and white
Issued: 1924-1938
Varieties: HN 395, 396, 421,
           468, 572, 686, 1323

U.S.:	**Only**
Can.:	**one**
U.K.:	**known**

HN 686
Contentment
Designer: L. Harradine
Height: 7 ¼", 18.4 cm
Colour: Black and white
Issued: 1924-1938
Varieties: HN 395, 396, 421,
           468, 572, 685, 1323

U.S.:	**None**
Can.:	**known**
U.K.:	**to exist**

Earthenware

HN 687
The Bather
Style One, First Version
Designer: L. Harradine
Height: 7 ¾", 19.7 cm
Colour: Blue
Issued: 1924-1949
Varieties: HN 597, 781, 782,
           1238, 1708

U.S.:	**$2,500.00**
Can.:	**$3,250.00**
U.K.:	**£1,500.00**

HN 688
A Yeoman of the Guard
Designer: L. Harradine
Height: 5 ¾", 14.6 cm
Colour: Red, gold and brown
Issued: 1924-1938
Varieties: HN 2122

U.S.:	**$1,250.00**
Can.:	**$1,600.00**
U.K.:	**£ 750.00**

HN 689
A Chelsea Pensioner
Designer: L. Harradine
Height: 5 ¾", 14.6 cm
Colour: Red
Issued: 1924-1938

U.S.:	**$3,000.00**
Can.:	**$4,000.00**
U.K.:	**£1,750.00**

Also produced as a miniature
figurine, but without an M number.

HN 690
A Lady of the Georgian Period
Designer: E. W. Light
Height: 10 ¼", 26.0 cm
Colour: Pink, white and
           yellow overdress
Issued: 1925-1936
Varieties: HN 41, 331, 444, 702

U.S.:	**None**
Can.:	**known**
U.K.:	**to exist**

HN 691
Pierrette
Style One
Designer: L. Harradine
Height: 7 ¼", 18.4 cm
Colour: Gold
Issued: 1925-1938
Varieties: HN 642, 643, 644,
           721, 731, 732, 784

U.S.:	**$5,000.00**
Can.:	**$6,500.00**
U.K.:	**£3,000.00**

HN 692
Sleep
Designer: P. Stabler
Height: 6", 15.2 cm
Colour: Gold
Issued: 1925-1936
Varieties: HN 24, 24A, 25, 25A,
           424, 710

U.S.:	**$3,250.00**
Can.:	**$4,250.00**
U.K.:	**£1,950.00**

HN 693
Polly Peachum
Style One
Designer: L. Harradine
Height: 6 ½", 16.5 cm
Colour: Pink and green
Issued: 1925-1949
Varieties: HN 463, 465, 550, 589,
           614, 680
Series: Beggar's Opera

U.S.:	**$1,500.00**
Can.:	**$1,950.00**
U.K.:	**£ 900.00**

HN 694
Polly Peachum
Style Two
Designer: L. Harradine
Height: 4 ¼", 10.8 cm
Colour: Pink and green
Issued: 1925-1949
Varieties: HN 489, 549, 620,
           734
Series: Beggar's Opera

U.S.:	**$1,500.00**
Can.:	**$1,950.00**
U.K.:	**£ 900.00**

HN 695
Lucy Lockett
Style Three
Designer: L. Harradine
Height: 6", 15.2 cm
Colour: Orange
Issued: 1925-1949
Varieties: HN 696
Series: Beggar's Opera

U.S.:	$1,500.00
Can.:	$2,000.00
U.K.:	£ 900.00

HN 696
Lucy Lockett
Style Three
Designer: L. Harradine
Height: 6", 15.2 cm
Colour: Pale blue
Issued: 1925-1949
Varieties: HN 695
Series: Beggar's Opera

U.S.:	None
Can.:	known
U.K.:	to exist

HN 697
The Balloon Seller
Style One
Designer: L. Harradine
Height: 9", 22.9 cm
Colour: Red and blue
Issued: 1925-1938
Varieties: HN 479, 486, 548, 583; also called 'The Balloon Woman'

U.S.:	None
Can.:	known
U.K.:	to exist

HN 698
Polly Peachum
Style Three
Designer: L. Harradine
Height: 2 ¼", 5.7 cm
Colour: Rose pink
Issued: 1925 1949
Varieties: HN 699, 757, 758, 759, 760, 761, 762, M21, M22, M23
Series: Beggar's Opera

U.S.:	$1,500.00
Can.:	$2,000.00
U.K.:	£ 900.00

HN 699
Polly Peachum
Style Three
Designer: L. Harradine
Height: 2 ¼", 5.7 cm
Colour: Pale blue
Issued: 1925-1949
Varieties: HN 698, 757, 758, 759, 760, 761, 762, M21, M22, M23
Series: Beggar's Opera

U.S.:	$1,500.00
Can.:	$2,000.00
U.K.:	£ 900.00

HN 700
Pretty Lady
Designer: H. Tittensor
Height: 9 ½", 24.1 cm
Colour: Yellow and green
Issued: 1925-1938
Varieties: HN 69, 70, 302, 330, 361, 384, 565, 763, 783

U.S.:	$3,250.00
Can.:	$4,500.00
U.K.:	£2,000.00

HN 701
Myfanwy Jones
Designer: E. W. Light
Height: 12", 30.5 cm
Colour: Multicoloured
Issued: 1925-1936
Varieties: HN 39, 92, 456, 514, 516, 519, 520, 660, 668, 669, 792; also called 'The Welsh Girl'

U.S.:	None
Can.:	known
U.K.:	to exist

HN 702
A Lady of the Georgian Period
Designer: E. W. Light
Height: 10 ¼", 26.0 cm
Colour: Pink and green
Issued: 1925-1936
Varieties: HN 41, 331, 444, 690

U.S.:	None
Can.:	known
U.K.:	to exist

HN 703
Motherhood
Style Two
Designer: Unknown
Height:　9 ¼" 23.5 cm
Colour:　Purple, black and red
Issued:　1925-1938
Varieties: HN 462, 570, 743

U.S.:	**None**
Can.:	**known**
U.K.:	**to exist**

HN 704
One of the Forty
Style Two
Designer: H. Tittensor
Height:　7 ¼", 18.4 cm
Colour:　Red
Issued:　1925-1936
Varieties: HN 418, 494, 498, 647,
　　　　　666, 1353

U.S.:	**None**
Can.:	**known**
U.K.:	**to exist**

HN 705
The Gainsborough Hat
Designer: H. Tittensor
Height:　9", 22.9 cm
Colour:　Blue
Issued:　1925-1936
Varieties: HN 46, 46A, 47, 329,
　　　　　352, 383, 453, 675

U.S.:	**$5,000.00**
Can.:	**$6,500.00**
U.K.:	**£3,000.00**

Earthenware

HN 706
Fruit Gathering
Designer: L. Harradine
Height:　7 ¼", 18.4 cm
Colour:　Purple and yellow
Issued:　1925-1936
Varieties: HN 449, 476, 503, 561,
　　　　　562, 707

U.S.:	
Can.:	**Extremely rare**
U.K.:	

HN 707
Fruit Gathering
Designer: L. Harradine
Height:　7 ¼", 18.4 cm
Colour:　Red
Issued:　1925-1936
Varieties: HN 449, 476, 503,
　　　　　561, 562, 706

U.S.:	**$4,500.00**
Can.:	**$6,000.00**
U.K.:	**£2,750.00**

Earthenware

HN 708
Shepherdess
Style One
Designer: L. Harradine
Height:　3 ½", 8.8 cm
Colour:　Red, yellow and pink
Issued:　1925-1938
Varieties: M18, M20

U.S.:	**$3,500.00**
Can.:	**$4,500.00**
U.K.:	**£2,000.00**

HN 709
Shepherd
Style Two
Designer: L. Harradine
Height:　3 ½", 8.8 cm
Colour:　Green, red and black
Issued:　1925-1938
Varieties: M17, M19

U.S.:	**$3,500.00**
Can.:	**$4,500.00**
U.K.:	**£2,000.00**

HN 710
Sleep
Designer: P. Stabler
Height:　6", 15.2 cm
Colour:　Blue
Issued:　1925-1936
Varieties: HN 24, 24A, 25, 25A,
　　　　　424, 692

U.S.:	**$3,500.00**
Can.:	**$4,500.00**
U.K.:	**£2,000.00**

HN 711
Harlequinade
Designer: L. Harradine
Height: 7", 17.8 cm
Colour: White and black
Issued: 1925-1940
Varieties: HN 585, 635, 780

U.S.:	**$6,000.00**
Can.:	**$8,000.00**
U.K.:	**£3,750.00**

HN 712
One of the Forty
Style Twelve
Designer: H. Tittensor
Height: Unknown
Colour: Red and black
Issued: 1925-1936
Varieties: HN 481, 483, 491, 646, 667, 1336, 1350; also known in flambé

U.S.:	
Con.:	**Extremely rare**
U.K.:	

Photograph
Not
Available

HN 713
One of the Forty
Style Thirteen
Designer: H. Tittensor
Height: 6", 15.2 cm
Colour: Red
Issued: 1925-1938
Varieties: HN 482, 484, 492, 645, 663

U.S.:	**None**
Can.:	**known**
U.K.:	**to exist**

HN 714
One of the Forty
Style Eleven
Designer: H. Tittensor
Height: 6 ¾", 17.2 cm
Colour: Red and blue
Issued: 1925-1938
Varieties: HN 480, 493, 497, 499, 664

U.S.:	**$4,500.00**
Can.:	**$6,000.00**
U.K.:	**£2,750.00**

HN 715
Proposal (woman)
Designer: L. Harradine
Height: 5 ¾", 14.6 cm
Colour: Burgundy and black
Issued: 1925-1940
Varieties: HN 716, 788

U.S.:	**$2,500.00**
Can.:	**$3,250.00**
U.K.:	**£1,500.00**

HN 716
Proposal (woman)
Designer: L. Harradine
Height: 5 ¾", 14.6 cm
Colour: White and black
Issued: 1925-1940
Varieties: HN 715, 788

U.S.:	**$3,750.00**
Can.:	**$5,000.00**
U.K.:	**£2,250.00**

HN 717
Lady Clown
Designer: L. Harradine
Height: 7 ½", 19.1 cm
Colour: White, red and black
Issued: 1925-1938
Varieties: HN 718, 738, 770; also called 'Clownette' HN 1263

U.S.:	**$ 8,500.00**
Can.:	**$11,000.00**
U.K.:	**£ 5,000.00**

HN 718
Lady Clown
Designer: L. Harradine
Height: 7 ½", 19.1 cm
Colour: White, red and black
Issued: 1925-1938
Varieties: HN 717, 738, 770; also called 'Clownette' HN1263

U.S.:	**One**
Can.:	**known**
U.K.:	**to exist**

HN 719
Butterfly
Designer: L. Harradine
Height: 6 ½", 16.5 cm
Colour: Pink, yellow and black
Issued: 1925-1940
Varieties: HN 720, 730, 1203;
also called 'Butterfly
Woman' HN 1456

U.S.:	**$5,000.00**
Can.:	**$6,500.00**
U.K.:	**£3,000.00**

HN 720
Butterfly
Designer: L. Harradine
Height: 6 ½", 16.5 cm
Colour: Orange, white and
black
Issued: 1925-1940
Varieties: HN 719, 730, 1203;
also called 'Butterfly
Woman' HN 1456

U.S.:	**$5,000.00**
Can.:	**$6,500.00**
U.K.:	**£3,000.00**

HN 721
Pierrette
Style One
Designer: L. Harradine
Height: 7 ¼", 18.4 cm
Colour: Black and white
Issued: 1925-1938
Varieties: HN 642, 643, 644,
691, 731, 732, 784

U.S.:	**$5,000.00**
Can.:	**$6,500.00**
U.K.:	**£3,000.00**

HN 722
Mephisto
Designer: L. Harradine
Height: 6 ½", 16.5 cm
Colour: Black and red
Issued: 1925-1938
Varieties: HN 723

U.S.:	**$7,000.00**
Can.:	**$9,000.00**
U.K.:	**£4,250.00**

HN 723
Mephisto
Designer: L. Harradine
Height: 6 ½", 16.5 cm
Colour: Red and black
Issued: 1925-1938
Varieties: HN 722

U.S.:	**$7,000.00**
Can.:	**$9,000.00**
U.K.:	**£4,250.00**

HN 724
Mam'selle
Designer: L. Harradine
Height: 7", 17.8 cm
Colour: White, red and yellow
Issued: 1925-1938
Varieties: HN 658, 659, 786

U.S.:	**$6,000.00**
Can.:	**$7,750.00**
U.K.:	**£3,600.00**

HN 725
The Proposal (man)
Designer: Unknown
Height: 5 ½", 14.0 cm
Colour: Red and black
Issued: 1925-1938
Varieties: HN 1209

U.S.:	**$4,000.00**
Can.:	**$5,250.00**
U.K.:	**£2,250.00**

HN 726
A Victorian Lady
Style One
Designer: L. Harradine
Height: 7 ½", 19.1 cm
Colour: Purple and yellow
Issued: 1925-1938
Varieties: HN 727, 728, 736,
739, 740, 742, 745,
1208, 1258, 1276,
1277, 1345, 1452,
1529

U.S.:	**$1,500.00**
Can.:	**$1,950.00**
U.K.:	**£ 900.00**

HN 727
A Victorian Lady
Style One
Designer: L. Harradine
Height: 7 ½", 19.1 cm
Colour: Pink and green
Issued: 1925-1938
Varieties: HN 726, 728, 736, 739,
          740, 742, 745, 1208,
          1258, 1276, 1277,
          1345, 1452, 1529

U.S.: $ 850.00
Can.: $1,100.00
U.K.:   £   500.00

HN 728
A Victorian Lady
Style One
Designer: L. Harradine
Height: 7 ¾", 19.7 cm
Colour: Pink and purple
Issued: 1925-1952
Varieties: HN 726, 727, 736, 739,
          740, 742, 745, 1208,
          1258, 1276, 1277,
          1345, 1452, 1529

U.S.: $750.00
Can.: $975.00
U.K.:   £450.00

HN 729
The Mask
Style One
Designer: L. Harradine
Height: 6 ¾", 17.2 cm
Colour: Red and black
Issued: 1925-1938
Varieties: HN 656, 657, 733,
          785, 1271

U.S.: $5,000.00
Can.: $6,600.00
U.K.:   £3,000.00

HN 730
Butterfly
Designer: L. Harradine
Height: 6 ½", 16.5 cm
Colour: Yellow , blue
          and black
Issued: 1925-1940
Varieties: HN 719, 720, 1203;
          also called 'Butterfly
          Woman' HN 1456

U.S.: $5,000.00
Can.: $6,500.00
U.K.:   £3,000.00

HN 731
Pierrette
Style One
Designer: L. Harradine
Height: 7 ¼", 18.4 cm
Colour: Black and white
Issued: 1925-1938
Varieties: HN 642, 643, 644,
          691, 721, 732, 784

U.S.: $5,000.00
Can.: $6,500.00
U.K.:   £3,000.00

HN 732
Pierrette
Style One
Designer: L. Harradine
Height: 7 ¼", 18.4 cm
Colour: Black and white
Issued: 1925-1938
Varieties: HN 642, 643, 644,
          691, 721, 731, 784

U.S.: $5,000.00
Can.: $6,500.00
U.K.:   £3,000.00

HN 733
The Mask
Style One
Designer: L. Harradine
Height: 6 ¾", 17.2 cm
Colour: White and black
Issued: 1925-1938
Varieties: HN 656, 657, 729,
          785, 1271

U.S.: $5,000.00
Can.: $6,500.00
U.K.:   £3,000.00

HN 734
Polly Peachum
Style Two
Designer: L. Harradine
Height: 4 ¼", 10.8 cm
Colour: Black and white
Issued: 1925-1949
Varieties: HN 489, 549, 620,
          694
Series: Beggar's Opera

U.S.: $2,500.00
Can.: $3,250.00
U.K.:   £1,500.00

HN 735
Shepherdess
Style Two
Designer:　L. Harradine
Height:　　7", 17.8 cm
Colour:　　Blue and black
Issued:　　1925-1938
Varieties:　HN 750; also called
　　　　　　'Milkmaid' (Style One)

U.S.:	**$4,000.00**
Can.:	**$5,250.00**
U.K.:	**£2,500.00**

HN 736
A Victorian Lady
Style One
Designer:　L. Harradine
Height:　　7 ¾", 19.7 cm
Colour:　　Pink and purple
Issued:　　1925-1938
Varieties:　HN 726, 727, 728, 739,
　　　　　　740, 742, 745, 1208,
　　　　　　1258, 1276, 1277,
　　　　　　1345, 1452, 1529

U.S.:	**$ 850.00**
Can.:	**$1,100.00**
U.K.:	**£ 500.00**

HN 737 not issued.

HN 738
Lady Clown
Designer:　L. Harradine
Height:　　7 ½", 19.1 cm
Colour:　　Black, white and red
Issued:　　1925-1938
Varieties:　HN 717, 718, 770;
　　　　　　also called 'Clownette'
　　　　　　HN 1263

U.S.:	**None**
Can.:	**known**
U.K.:	**to exist**

HN 739
A Victorian Lady
Style One
Designer:　L. Harradine
Height:　　7 ¾", 19.7 cm
Colour:　　Red, blue, yellow
Issued:　　1925-1938
Varieties:　HN 726, 727, 728, 736,
　　　　　　740, 742, 745, 1208,
　　　　　　1258, 1276, 1277,
　　　　　　1345, 1452, 1529

U.S.:	**$1,650.00**
Can.:	**$2,250.00**
U.K.:	**£ 975.00**

HN 740
A Victorian Lady
Style One
Designer:　L. Harradine
Height:　　7 ¾", 19.7 cm
Colour:　　Pink
Issued:　　1925-1938
Varieties:　HN 726, 727, 728, 736,
　　　　　　739, 742, 745, 1208,
　　　　　　1258, 1276, 1277,
　　　　　　1345, 1452, 1529

U.S.:	**$1,500.00**
Can.:	**$1,950.00**
U.K.:	**£ 900.00**

HN 741
A Geisha
Style One
Designer:　H. Tittensor
Height:　　10 ¾", 27.3 cm
Colour:　　Multicoloured
Issued:　　1925-1936
Varieties:　HN 354, 376, 376A,
　　　　　　387, 634, 779, 1321,
　　　　　　1322; also called 'The
　　　　　　Japanese Lady'

U.S.:	**None**
Can.:	**known**
U.K.:	**to exist**

HN 742
A Victorian Lady
Style One
Designer:　L. Harradine
Height:　　7 ¾", 19.7 cm
Colour:　　Black and white
Issued:　　1925-1938
Varieties:　HN 726, 727, 728, 736,
　　　　　　739, 740, 745, 1208,
　　　　　　1258, 1276, 1277,
　　　　　　1345, 1452, 1529

U.S.:	**$1,650.00**
Can.:	**$2,250.00**
U.K.:	**£ 975.00**

HN 743
Motherhood
Style Two
Designer:　Unknown
Height:　　9 ¼", 23.5 cm
Colour:　　Blue and yellow
Issued:　　1925-1938
Varieties:　HN 462, 570, 703

U.S.:	**None**
Can.:	**known**
U.K.:	**to exist**

HN 744
The Lavender Woman
Designer: P. Stabler
Height: 8 ¼", 21.0 cm
Colour: Blue
Issued: 1925-1936
Varieties: HN 22, 23, 23A, 342, 569

U.S.:	$5,500.00
Can.:	$7,250.00
U.K.:	£3,250.00

HN 745
A Victorian Lady
Style One
Designer: L. Harradine
Height: 7 ¾", 19.7 cm
Colour: Pink and green
Issued: 1925-1938
Varieties: HN 726, 727, 728, 736, 739, 740, 742, 1208, 1258, 1276, 1277, 1345, 1452, 1529

U.S.:	$ 1,500.00
Can.:	$ 1,950.00
U.K.:	£ 900.00

HN 746
A Mandarin
Style One
Designer: C. J. Noke
Height: 10 ¼", 26.0 cm
Colour: Yellow, black and lilac
Issued: 1925-1936
Varieties: HN 84, 316, 318, 382, 611, 787, 791; 'Chinese Mandarin' and 'The Mikado'

U.S.:	$ 8,500.00
Can.:	$11,000.00
U.K.:	£ 5,000.00

HN 747
Tulips
Designer: Unknown
Height: 9 ½", 24.1 cm
Colour: Blue and green
Issued: 1925-1936
Varieties: HN 466, 488, 672, 1334

U.S.:	$5,000.00
Can.:	$6,500.00
U.K.:	£2,250.00

HN 748
Out For a Walk
Designer: E. W. Light
Height: 10", 25.4 cm
Colour: Green, red and white
Issued: 1925-1936
Varieties: HN 86, 443

U.S.:	$6,500.00
Can.:	$9,000.00
U.K.:	£4,000.00

HN 749
London Cry, Strawberries
Designer: L. Harradine
Height: 6 ¾", 17.2 cm
Colour: Red and cream
Issued: 1925-1936
Varieties: HN 772

U.S.:	$3,650.00
Can.:	$4,750.00
U.K.:	£2,200.00

HN 750
Shepherdess
Style Two
Designer: L. Harradine
Height: 7", 17.8 cm
Colour: Pink and yellow
Issued: 1925-1938
Varieties: HN 735; also called 'Milkmaid' (Style One)

U.S.:	$4,000.00
Can.:	$5,250.00
U.K.:	£2,400.00

HN 751
Shepherd
Style Three
Designer: L. Harradine
Height: 7", 17.8 cm
Colour: Green, black, red and white
Issued: 1925-1938

U.S.:	$4,000.00
Can.:	$5,250.00
U.K.:	£2,400.00

HN 752
London Cry,
Turnips and Carrots
Designer: L. Harradine
Height: 6 ¾", 17.2 cm
Colour: Purple, red, black
          and green
Issued: 1925-1938
Varieties: HN 771
  U.S.:   **$3,650.00**
  Can.:   **$4,750.00**
  U.K.:   **£2,200.00**

HN 753
The Dandy
Designer: L. Harradine
Height: 6 ¾", 17.2 cm
Colour: Red, white, black
          and green
Issued: 1925-1936
  U.S.:   **$2,750.00**
  Can.:   **$3,600.00**
  U.K.:   **£1,650.00**

HN 754
The Belle
Style One
Designer: L. Harradine
Height: 6 ½", 16.5 cm
Colour: Multicoloured
Issued: 1925-1938
Varieties: HN 776
  U.S.:   **$2,500.00**
  Can.:   **$3,250.00**
  U.K.:   **£1,500.00**

HN 755
Mephistopheles
and Marguerite
Designer: C. J. Noke
Height: 7 ¾", 19.7 cm
Colour: Orange and purple
Issued: 1925-1949
Varieties: HN 775
  U.S.:   **$3,750.00**
  Can.:   **$5,000.00**
  U.K.:   **£2,250.00**

HN 756
The Modern Piper
Designer: L. Harradine
Height: 8 ½", 21.6 cm
Colour: Lavender and green
Issued: 1925-1940
  U.S.:   **$5,500.00**
  Can.:   **$7,500.00**
  U.K.:   **£3,300.00**

HN 757
Polly Peachum
Style Three
Designer: L. Harradine
Height: 2 ¼", 5.7 cm
Colour: Red
Issued: 1925-1949
Varieties: HN 698, 699, 758, 759,
           760, 761, 762; M21,
           M22, M23
Series: Beggar's Opera
  U.S.:   **$1,600.00**
  Can.:   **$2,100.00**
  U.K.:   **£ 950.00**

HN 758
Polly Peachum
Style Three
Designer: L. Harradine
Height: 2 ¼", 5.7 cm
Colour: Pink and orange
Issued: 1925-1949
Varieties: HN 698, 699, 757,
           759, 760, 761, 762;
           M21, M22, M23
Series: Beggar's Opera
  U.S.:   **$1,600.00**
  Can.:   **$2,100.00**
  U.K.:   **£ 950.00**

HN 759
Polly Peachum
Style Three
Designer: L. Harradine
Height: 2 ¼", 5.7 cm
Colour: Yellow, white and black
Issued: 1925-1949
Varieties: HN 698, 699, 757,
           758, 760, 761, 762;
           M21, M22, M23
Series: Beggar's Opera
  U.S.:   **$1,600.00**
  Can.:   **$2,100.00**
  U.K.:   **£ 950.00**

HN 760
Polly Peachum
Style Three
Designer: L. Harradine
Height: 2 ¼", 5.7 cm
Colour: Multicoloured
Issued: 1925-1949
Varieties: HN 698, 699, 757, 758, 759, 761, 762; M21, M22, M23
Series: Beggar's Opera

U.S.:	$1,750.00
Can.:	$2,275.00
U.K.:	£1,000.00

HN 761
Polly Peachum
Style Three
Designer: L. Harradine
Height: 2 ¼", 5.7 cm
Colour: Blue and purple
Issued: 1925-1949
Varieties: HN 698, 699, 757, 758, 759, 760, 762 M21, M22, M23
Series: Beggar's Opera

U.S.:	$1,600.00
Can.:	$2,100.00
U.K.:	£ 950.00

HN 762
Polly Peachum
Style Three
Designer: L. Harradine
Height: 2 ¼", 5.7 cm
Colour: Red and white
Issued: 1925-1949
Varieties: HN 698, 699, 757, 758, 759, 760, 761; M21, M22, M23
Series: Beggar's Opera

U.S.:	$1,600.00
Can.:	$2,100.00
U.K.:	£ 950.00

HN 763
Pretty Lady
Designer: H. Tittensor
Height: 9 ½", 24.1 cm
Colour: Orange, white and green
Issued: 1925-1938
Varieties: HN 69, 70, 302, 330, 361, 384, 565, 700, 783

U.S.:	None
Can.:	known
U.K.:	to exist

HN 764
Madonna of the Square
Designer: P. Stabler
Height: 7", 17.8 cm
Colour: Blue, purple and yellow
Issued: 1925-1936
Varieties: HN 10, 10A, 11, 14, 27, 326, 573, 576, 594, 613, 1968, 1969, 2034

U.S.:	
Can.:	Extremely rare
U.K.:	

HN 765
The Poke Bonnet
Designer: C. J. Noke
Height: 8 ¾", 22.2 cm
Colour: Green, blue, purple
Issued: 1925-1938
Varieties: HN 362, 612; also called 'A Lilac Shawl' HN 44, 44A; and 'In Grandma's Days' HN 339, 340, 388, 442

U.S.:	None
Can.:	known
U.K.:	to exist

HN 766
Irish Colleen
Designer: L. Harradine
Height: 6 ½", 16.5 cm
Colour: Red, black, white and grey
Issued: 1925-1936
Varieties: HN 767

U.S.:	$6,000.00
Can.:	$8,000.00
U.K.:	£3,600.00

NOTE ON CONDITION

Prices on the secondary market for Royal Doulton Figures, particularly the early HN numbers, have risen considerably over the years. As values rise, the condition and quality of these figurines takes on an increasingly important role.

The prices listed in *The Charlton Standard Catalogue of Royal Doulton Figurines* are for figures in mint condition. Naturally, repaired or restored figures, no matter how professionally done, will sell at a discount. However the early figures, due to their rarity, may experience smaller discounts.

On Condition: For figures to command catalogue prices they must be in mint condition. This simply means that a figure will have no chips, scratches, hairline cracks, crazing, blemishes, or repairs. Any of which will remove the figure from the mint category.

On Quality: Some figures are better moulded, assembled and painted than others. High quality figures may command a premium over listed catalogue prices.

HN 767
Irish Colleen
Designer: L. Harradine
Height: 6 ½", 16.5 cm
Colour: Black, red and green
Issued: 1925-1936
Varieties: HN 766

U.S.:	**$6,000.00**
Can.:	**$8,000.00**
U.K.:	**£3,600.00**

HN 768
Harlequinade Masked
Designer: L. Harradine
Height: 6 ½", 16.5 cm
Colour: Black, red and green
Issued: 1925-1938
Varieties: HN 769, 1274, 1304

U.S.:	
Can.:	**Extremely rare**
U.K.:	

HN 769
Harlequinade Masked
Designer: L. Harradine
Height: 6 ½", 16.5 cm
Colour: Blue, red and yellow
Issued: 1925-1938
Varieties: HN 768, 1274, 1304

U.S.:	**$6,000.00**
Can.:	**$8,000.00**
U.K.:	**£3,600.00**

HN 770
Lady Clown
Designer: L. Harradine
Height: 7 ½", 19.1 cm
Colour: White and green
Issued: 1925-1938
Varieties: HN 717, 718, 738;
also called 'Clownette'
HN 1263

U.S.:	**$ 8,500.00**
Can.:	**$11,000.00**
U.K.:	**£ 5,000.00**

HN 771
London Cry,
Turnips and Carrots
Designer: L. Harradine
Height: 6 ¾", 17.2 cm
Colour: Lavender, cream
and brown
Issued: 1925-1938
Varieties: HN 752

U.S.:	**$3,650.00**
Can.:	**$4,750.00**
U.K.:	**£2,200.00**

HN 772
London Cry, Strawberries
Designer: L. Harradine
Height: 6 ¾", 17.2 cm
Colour: Lavender and cream
Issued: 1925-1936
Varieties: HN 749

U.S.:	**$3,650.00**
Can.:	**$4,750.00**
U.K.:	**£2,200.00**

HN 773
The Bather
Style Two
Designer: L. Harradine
Height: 7 ½", 19.1 cm
Colour: Red, purple and black
Issued: 1925-1938
Varieties: HN 774, 1227

U.S.:	**$5,250.00**
Can.:	**$6,750.00**
U.K.:	**£3,200.00**

HN 774
The Bather
Style Two
Designer: L. Harradine
Height: 7 ¾", 19.7 cm
Colour: Blue and red
Issued: 1925-1938
Varieties: HN 773, 1227

U.S.:	**$5,250.00**
Can.:	**$6,750.00**
U.K.:	**£3,200.00**

HN 775
Mephistopheles
and Marguerite
Designer: C. J. Noke
Height: 7 ¾", 19.7 cm
Colour: Orange and cream
Issued: 1925-1949
Varieties: HN 755

U.S.:	$3,000.00
Can.:	$4,000.00
U.K.:	£1,750.00

HN 776
The Belle
Style One
Designer: L. Harradine
Height: 6 ½", 16.5 cm
Colour: Unknown
Issued: 1925-1938
Varieties: HN 754

U.S.:	
Can.:	**Extremely rare**
U.K.:	

HN 777
Bo-Peep
Style One
Designer: L. Harradine
Height: 6 ¾", 17.2 cm
Colour: Dark blue
Issued: 1926-1936
Varieties: HN 1202, 1327, 1328

U.S.:	$5,000.00
Can.:	$6,500.00
U.K.:	£3,000.00

HN 778
Captain
Style One
Designer: L. Harradine
Height: 7", 17.8 cm
Colour: Red and white
Issued: 1926-1936

U.S.:	$4,000.00
Can.:	$5,250.00
U.K.:	£2,400.00

HN 779
Geisha
Style One
Designer: H. Tittensor
Height: 10 ¾", 27.3 cm
Colour: Red and purple
Issued: 1926-1936
Varieties: HN 354, 376, 376A,
            387, 634, 741, 1321,
            1322; also called
            'The Japanese Lady'

U.S.:	$ 8,000.00
Can.:	$10,500.00
U.K.:	£ 4,750.00

HN 780
Harlequinade
Designer: L. Harradine
Height: 6 ½", 16.5 cm
Colour: Pink, blue and brown
Issued: 1926-1940
Varieties: HN 585, 635, 711

U.S.:	$6,000.00
Can.:	$8,000.00
U.K.:	£3,600.00

HN 781
The Bather
Style One, First Version
Designer: L. Harradine
Height: 7 ¾", 19.7 cm
Colour: Blue and green
Issued: 1926-1938
Varieties: HN 597, 687, 782,
            1238, 1708

U.S.:	
Can.:	**Extremely rare**
U.K.:	

HN 782
The Bather
Style One, First Version
Designer: L. Harradine
Height: 7 ¾", 19.7 cm
Colour: Purple and black
Issued: 1926-1938
Varieties: HN 597, 687, 781,
            1238, 1708

U.S.:	
Can.:	**Extremely rare**
U.K.:	

HN 783
Pretty Lady
Designer: H. Tittensor
Height: 9 ½", 24.1 cm
Colour: Blue
Issued: 1926-1938
Varieties: HN 69, 70, 302, 330,
           361, 384, 565, 700, 763

U.S.:	**$3,500.00**
Can.:	**$4,500.00**
U.K.:	**£2,000.00**

HN 784
Pierrette
Style One
Designer: L. Harradine
Height: 7 ¼", 18.4 cm
Colour: Pink and black
Issued: 1926-1938
Varieties: HN 642, 643, 644,
           691, 721, 731, 732

U.S.:	**$4,500.00**
Can.:	**$6,000.00**
U.K.:	**£2,750.00**

HN 785
The Mask
Style One
Designer: L. Harradine
Height: 6 ¾", 17.2 cm
Colour: Blue, black and pink
Issued: 1926-1938
Varieties: HN 656, 657, 729,
           733, 1271

U.S.:	**$5,000.00**
Can.:	**$6,500.00**
U.K.:	**£3,000.00**

HN 786
Mam'selle
Designer: L. Harradine
Height: 7", 17.8 cm
Colour: Pink and black
Issued: 1926-1938
Varieties: HN 658, 659, 724

U.S.:	**$6,000.00**
Can.:	**$8,000.00**
U.K.:	**£3,500.00**

HN 787
A Mandarin
Style One
Designer: C. J. Noke
Height: 10 ¼", 26.0 cm
Colour: Pink and orange
Issued: 1926-1936
Varieties: HN 84, 316, 318, 382,
           611, 746, 791; also
           called 'Chinese
           Mandarin' and 'The
           Mikado'

U.S.:	
Can.:	**Extremely rare**
U.K.:	

HN 788
Proposal (woman)
Designer: L. Harradine
Height: 5 ¾", 14.6 cm
Colour: Pink
Issued: 1926-1940
Varieties: HN 715, 716

U.S.:	
Can.:	**Extremely rare**
U.K.:	

HN 789
The Flower Seller
Designer: L. Harradine
Height: 8 ¾", 22.2 cm
Colour: Green, cream
           and white
Issued: 1926-1938

U.S.:	**$2,250.00**
Can.:	**$3,000.00**
U.K.:	**£1,350.00**

Earthenware

HN 790
The Parson's Daughter
Designer: H. Tittensor
Height: 10", 25.4 cm
Colour: Multicoloured
Issued: 1926-1938
Varieties: HN 337, 338, 441,
           564, 1242, 1356,
           2018

U.S.:	**$3,000.00**
Can.:	**$4,000.00**
U.K.:	**£1,750.00**

HN 791
A Mandarin
Style One
Designer: C. J. Noke
Height: 10 ¼", 26.0 cm
Colour: Black and purple
Issued: 1926-1936
Varieties: HN 84, 316, 318, 382,
611, 746, 787; also
called 'Chinese
Mandarin' and 'The
Mikado'

U.S.:	$ 8,500.00
Can.:	$11,000.00
U.K.:	£ 5,000.00

HN 792
Myfanwy Jones
Designer: E. W. Light
Height: 12", 30.5 cm
Colour: Pink and blue
Issued: 1926-1936
Varieties: HN 39, 92, 456, 514,
516, 519, 520, 660,
668, 669, 701; also
called 'The Welsh Girl'

U.S.:	
Can.:	Extremely rare
U.K.:	

HN 793
Katharine
Style One
Designer: C. J. Noke
Height: 5 ¾", 14.6 cm
Colour: Lavender and green
Issued: 1926-1938
Varieties: HN 61, 74, 341, 471,
615

U.S.:	$3,500.00
Can.:	$4,500.00
U.K.:	£2,000.00

HN 794
The Bouquet
Designer: G. Lambert
Height: 9", 22.9 cm
Colour: Blue, red and green
Issued: 1926-1936
Varieties: HN 406, 414, 422,
428, 429, 567; also
called 'The Nosegay'

U.S.:	
Can.:	Extremely rare
U.K.:	

HN 795
Pierrette
Style Two
Designer: L. Harradine
Height: 3 ½", 8.9 cm
Colour: Pink
Issued: 1926-1938
Varieties: HN 796

U.S.:	
Can.:	Extremely rare
U.K.:	

HN 796
Pierrette
Style Two
Designer: L. Harradine
Height: 3 ½", 8.9 cm
Colour: White and silver
Issued: 1926-1938
Varieties: HN 795

U.S.:	
Can.:	Extremely rare
U.K.:	

HN 797
Moorish Minstrel
Designer: C. J. Noke
Height: 13 ½", 34.3 cm
Colour: Purple
Issued: 1926-1949
Varieties: HN 34, 364, 415

U.S.:	$5,000.00
Can.:	$6,500.00
U.K.:	£3,000.00

HN 798
Tete-a-Tete
Style One
Designer: L. Harradine
Height: 5 ¾", 14.6 cm
Colour: Pink and red
Issued: 1926-1938
Varieties: HN 799

U.S.:	$4,000.00
Can.:	$5,250.00
U.K.:	£2,400.00

HN 799
Tete-a-Tete
Style One
Designer: L. Harradine
Height: 5 ¾", 14.6 cm
Colour: Blue and red
Issued: 1926-1940
Varieties: HN 798

  U.S.:   **$4,000.00**
  Can.:   **$5,250.00**
  U.K.:   **£2,400.00**

HN 800 - 1200 Animal and Bird
figures, except HN 816, 817, 830,
887, 959, 1006, 1060, 1061, 1122,
1123, 1124, 1200 not issued.

HN 1201
Hunts Lady
Designer: L. Harradine
Height: 8 ¼", 21.0 cm
Colour: Grey and cream
Issued: 1926-1938

  U.S.:   **$4,500.00**
  Can.:   **$6,000.00**
  U.K.:   **£2,750.00**

HN 1202
Bo-Peep
Style One
Designer: L. Harradine
Height: 6 ¾", 17.2 cm
Colour: Purple, green and pink
Issued: 1926-1936
Varieties: HN 777, 1327, 1328

  U.S.:
  Can.:   **Extremely rare**
  U.K.:

HN 1203
Butterfly
Designer: L. Harradine
Height: 6 ½", 16.5 cm
Colour: Black and gold
Issued: 1926-1940
Varieties: HN 719, 720, 730;
           also called 'Butterfly
           Woman' HN 1456

  U.S.:
  Can.:   **Extremely rare**
  U.K.:

HN 1204
Angela
Style One
Designer: L. Harradine
Height: 7 ¼", 18.4 cm
Colour: Purple and pink
Issued: 1926-1940
Varieties: HN 1303; also called
           'Fanny'
  U.S.:   **$3,500.00**
  Can.:   **$4,500.00**
  U.K.:   **£2,000.00**

HN 1205
Miss 1926
Designer: L. Harradine
Height: 7 ¼", 18.4 cm
Colour: Black and white
Issued: 1926-1938
Varieties: HN 1207

  U.S.:   **$7,500.00**
  Can.:   **$9,750.00**
  U.K.:   **£4,500.00**

HN 1206
The Flower Seller's Children
Designer: L. Harradine
Height: 8 ¼", 21.0 cm
Colour: Blue and purple
Issued: 1926-1949
Varieties: HN 525, 551, 1342,
           1406
  U.S.:   **$3,000.00**
  Can.:   **$4,000.00**
  U.K.:   **£1,800.00**

HN 1207
Miss 1926
Designer: L. Harradine
Height: 7 ¼", 18.4 cm
Colour: Black
Issued: Unknown
Varieties: HN 1205

  U.S.:
  Can.:   **Extremely rare**
  U.K.:

HN 1208
A Victoria Lady
Style One
Designer: L. Harradine
Height: 7 ¾", 19.7 cm
Colour: Green and purple
Issued: 1926-1938
Varieties: HN 726, 727, 728,
736, 739, 740, 742,
745, 1258, 1276,
1277, 1345, 1452,
1529

U.S.: $1,500.00
Can.: $2,000.00
U.K.: £ 900.00

HN 1209
The Proposal (Man)
Designer: Unknown
Height: 5 ½", 14.0 cm
Colour: Blue and pink
Issued: 1926-1938
Varieties: HN 725

U.S.: $4,000.00
Can.: $5,250.00
U.K.: £2,400.00

HN 1210
Boy with Turban
Designer: L. Harradine
Height: 3 ¾", 9.5 cm
Colour: Orange, black and
white
Issued: 1926-1936
Varieties: HN 586, 587, 661, 662,
1212, 1213, 1214,
1225

U.S.: $1,850.00
Can.: $2,500.00
U.K.: £1,100.00

HN 1211
Quality Street
Designer: Unknown
Height: 7 ¼", 18.4 cm
Colour: Red
Issued: 1926-1936
Varieties: HN 1211A

U.S.: $2,250.00
Can.: $3,000.00
U.K.: £1,350.00

HN 1211A
Quality Street
Designer: Unknown
Height: 7 ¼", 18.4 cm
Colour: Lavender
Issued: 1926-1936
Varieties: HN 1211

U.S.: $3,000.00
Can.: $4,000.00
U.K.: £1,750.00

HN 1212
Boy with Turban
Designer: L. Harradine
Height: 3 ¾", 9.5 cm
Colour: Purple and green
Issued: 1926-1936
Varieties: HN 586, 587, 661, 662,
1210, 1213, 1214, 1225

U.S.: $1,850.00
Can.: $2,500.00
U.K.: £1,100.00

HN 1213
Boy with Turban
Designer: L. Harradine
Height: 3 ¾", 9.5 cm
Colour: White and black
Issued: 1926-1936
Varieties: HN 586, 587, 661, 662,
1210, 1212, 1214, 1225

U.S.: $1,850.00
Can.: $2,500.00
U.K.: £1,100.00

HN 1214
Boy with Turban
Designer: L. Harradine
Height: 3 ½", 8.9 cm
Colour: Black, white
and green
Issued: 1926-1936
Varieties: HN 586, 587, 661, 662,
1210, 1212, 1213, 1225

U.S.: $1,850.00
Can.: $2,500.00
U.K.: £1,100.00

HN 1215
The Pied Piper
Style One
Designer: L. Harradine
Height: 8 ¼", 21.0 cm
Colour: Red, black and yellow
Issued: 1926-1938
Varieties: HN 2102

U.S.:   **$3,500.00**
Can.:   **$4,500.00**
U.K.:   **£2,000.00**

HN 1216
Falstaff
Style One
Designer: C. J. Noke
Height: 7", 17.8 cm
Colour: Multicoloured
Issued: 1926-1949
Varieties: HN 571, 575, 608,
          609, 619, 638, 1606

U.S.:   **$3,000.00**
Can.:   **$4,000.00**
U.K.:   **£1,800.00**

HN 1217
The Prince of Wales
Designer: L. Harradine
Height: 7 ½", 19.1 cm
Colour: Red and white
Issued: 1926-1938

U.S.:   **$2,500.00**
Can.:   **$3,250.00**
U.K.:   **£1,500.00**

HN 1218
A Spook
Style Two
Designer: H. Tittensor
Height: 3", 7.6 cm
Colour: Multicoloured
Issued: 1926-1936
Varieties: Colourway: Red
          cloak, black cap

U.S.:   **$3,600.00**
Can.:   **$4,700.00**
U.K.:   **£2,200.00**

HN 1219
Negligée
Designer: L. Harradine
Height: 5", 12.7 cm
Colour: Bluish-yellow, blue
          hair band
Issued: 1927-1936
Varieties: HN 1228, 1272, 1273,
          1454

U.S.:   **$3,500.00**
Can.:   **$4,500.00**
U.K.:   **£2,000.00**

HN 1220
Lido Lady
First Version
Designer: L. Harradine
Height: 6 ¾", 17.2 cm
Colour: Pink
Issued: 1927-1936
Varieties: HN 1229

U.S.:   **$2,750.00**
Can.:   **$3,750.00**
U.K.:   **£1,650.00**

HN 1221
Lady Jester
Style One
Designer: L. Harradine
Height: 7", 17.8 cm
Colour: Multicoloured
Issued: 1927-1938
Varieties: HN 1222, 1332

U.S.:   **$4,750.00**
Can.:   **$6,500.00**
U.K.:   **£2,850.00**

HN 1222
Lady Jester
Style One
Designer: L. Harradine
Height: 7", 17.8 cm
Colour: Black and white
Issued: 1927-1938
Varieties: HN 1221, 1332

U.S.:   **$4,750.00**
Can.:   **$6,500.00**
U.K.:   **£2,850.00**

HN 1223
A Geisha
Style Two
Designer: C. J. Noke
Height: 6 ¾", 17.2 cm
Colour: Black and orange
Issued: 1927-1938
Varieties: HN 1234, 1292, 1310

U.S.:	$2,750.00
Con.:	$3,750.00
U.K.:	£1,650.00

HN 1224
The Wandering Minstrel
Designer: L. Harradine
Height: 7", 17.8 cm
Colour: Purple and red
Issued: 1927-1936

U.S.:	$4,500.00
Can.:	$6,000.00
U.K.:	£2,700.00

HN 1225
Boy with Turban
Designer: L. Harradine
Height: 3 ¾", 9.5 cm
Colour: Yellow and blue
Issued: 1927-1936
Varieties: HN 586, 587, 661, 662,
           1210, 1212, 1213, 1214

U.S.:	$2,000.00
Can.:	$2,600.00
U.K.:	£1,200.00

HN 1226
The Huntsman
Style One
Designer: L. Harradine
Height: 8 ¾", 22.2 cm
Colour: Red and white
Issued: 1927-1938

U.S.:	$4,500.00
Can.:	$6,000.00
U.K.:	£2,700.00

HN 1227
The Bather
Style Two
Designer: L. Harradine
Height: 7 ½", 19.1 cm
Colour: Pink and black
Issued: 1927-1938
Varieties: HN 773, 774

U.S.:	$6,000.00
Can.:	$7,750.00
U.K.:	£3,600.00

HN 1228
Negligée
Designer: L. Harradine
Height: 5", 12.7 cm
Colour: Bluish-yellow, red
           hair band
Issued: 1927-1936
Varieties: HN 1219, 1272,
           1273, 1454

U.S.:	$3,500.00
Can.:	$4,500.00
U.K.:	£2,000.00

HN 1229
Lido Lady
First Version
Designer: L. Harradine
Height: 6 ¾", 17.2 cm
Colour: Blue
Issued: 1927-1936
Varieties: HN 1220

U.S.:	$5,000.00
Can.:	$6,500.00
U.K.:	£3,000.00

HN 1230
Baba
Designer: L. Harradine
Height: 3 ¼", 8.3 cm
Colour: Blue, yellow and purple
Issued: 1927-1938
Varieties: HN 1243, 1244, 1245,
           1246, 1247, 1248

U.S.:	$2,000.00
Can.:	$2,600.00
U.K.:	£1,200.00

HN 1231
Cassim
Style One
Designer: L. Harradine
Height: 3", 7.6 cm
Colour: Blue, yellow and
          turquoise
Issued: 1927-1938
Varieties: HN 1232

  U.S.: $2,000.00
  Can.: $2,600.00
  U.K.:   £1,200.00

HN 1232
Cassim
Style One
Designer: L. Harradine
Height: 3", 7.6 cm
Colour: Orange and black
Issued: 1927-1938
Varieties: HN 1231

  U.S.: $1,850.00
  Can.: $2,500.00
  U.K.:   £1,100.00

HN 1233
Susanna
Designer: L. Harradine
Height: 6", 15.2 cm
Colour: Pink
Issued: 1927-1936
Varieties: HN 1288, 1299

  U.S.: $3,000.00
  Can.: $4,000.00
  U.K.:   £1,800.00

HN 1234
A Geisha
Style Two
Designer: C. J. Noke
Height: 6 ¾", 17.2 cm
Colour: Green and red
Issued: 1927-1938
Varieties: HN 1223, 1292, 1310

  U.S.: $2,500.00
  Can.: $3,250.00
  U.K.:   £1,500.00

HN 1235
A Scribe
Designer: C. J. Noke
Height: 6", 15.2 cm
Colour: Brown, blue and
          orange
Issued: 1927-1938
Varieties: HN 305, 324

  U.S.: $2,750.00
  Can.: $3,750.00
  U.K.:   £1,650.00

HN 1236
Tete-a-Tete
Style Two
Designer: C. J. Noke
Height: 3", 7.6 cm
Colour: Purple and red
Issued: 1927-1938
Varieties: HN 1237

  U.S.: $4,500.00
  Can.: $6,000.00
  U.K.:   £2,700.00

HN 1237
Tete-a-Tete
Style Two
Designer: C. J. Noke
Height: 3", 7.6 cm
Colour: Pink
Issued: 1927-1938
Varieties: HN 1236

  U.S.: $4,500.00
  Can.: $6,000.00
  U.K.:   £2,700.00

HN 1238
The Bather
Style One, First Version
Designer: L. Harradine
Height: 7 ¾", 19.7 cm
Colour: Red and black
Issued: 1927-1938
Varieties: HN 597, 687, 781,
           782, 1708

  U.S.: $4,000.00
  Can.: $5,250.00
  U.K.:   £2,400.00

HN 1239 - 1241 not issued.

HN 1242
The Parson's Daughter
Designer: H. Tittesnor
Height: 10", 25.4 cm
Colour: Lavender and yellow
Issued: 1927-1938
Varieties: HN 337, 338, 441, 564, 790, 1356, 2018

U.S.:	$2,750.00
Can.:	$3,750.00
U.K.:	£1,650.00

HN 1243
Baba
Designer: L. Harradine
Height: 3 ¼", 8.3 cm
Colour: Orange
Issued: 1927-1938
Varieties: HN 1230, 1244,1245, 1246, 1247, 1248

U.S.:	$1,850.00
Can.:	$2,500.00
U.K.:	£1,100.00

HN 1244
Baba
Designer: L. Harradine
Height: 3 ¼", 8.3 cm
Colour: Yellow and green
Issued: 1927-1938
Varieties: HN 1230, 1243,1245, 1246, 1247, 1248

U.S.:	$2,000.00
Can.:	$2,500.00
U.K.:	£1,200.00

HN 1245
Baba
Designer: L. Harradine
Height: 3 ¼", 8.3 cm
Colour: White and black
Issued: 1927-1938
Varieties: HN 1230, 1243, 1244, 1246, 1247, 1248

U.S.:	$2,000.00
Can.:	$2,500.00
U.K.:	£1,200.00

HN 1246
Baba
Designer: L. Harradine
Height: 3 ¼", 8.3 cm
Colour: Green
Issued: 1927-1938
Varieties: HN 1230, 1243,1244, 1245, 1247, 1248

U.S.:	$2,000.00
Can.:	$2,500.00
U.K.:	£1,200.00

HN 1247
Baba
Designer: L. Harradine
Height: 3 ¼", 8.3 cm
Colour: Black, white and orange
Issued: 1927-1938
Varieties: HN 1230, 1243, 1244, 1245, 1246, 1248

U.S.:	$2,000.00
Can.:	$2,500.00
U.K.:	£1,200.00

HN 1248
Baba
Designer: L. Harradine
Height: 3 ¼", 8.3 cm
Colour: Green and orange
Issued: 1927-1938
Varieties: HN 1230, 1243, 1244, 1245, 1246, 1247

U.S.:	$2,000.00
Can.:	$2,500.00
U.K.:	£1,200.00

HN 1249
Circe
Designer: L. Harradine
Height: 7 ¾", 19.7 cm
Colour: Green, orange and pink
Issued: 1927-1936
Varieties: HN 1250, 1254, 1255

U.S.:	$4,750.00
Can.:	$6,500.00
U.K.:	£2,850.00

HN 1250
Circe
Designer: L. Harradine
Height: 7 ½", 19.1 cm
Colour: Orange and black
Issued: 1927-1936
Varieties: HN 1249, 1254, 1255

U.S.:	**$4,750.00**
Can.:	**$6,500.00**
U.K.:	**£2,850.00**

HN 1251
The Cobbler
Style Two
Designer: C. J. Noke
Height: 8 ½", 21.6 cm
Colour: Black and red
Issued: 1927-1938
Varieties: HN 681, 1283

U.S.:	**$2,750.00**
Can.:	**$3,750.00**
U.K.:	**£1,650.00**

HN 1252
Kathleen
Style One
Designer: L. Harradine
Height: 7 ¾", 19.7 cm
Colour: Lavender, pink and purple
Issued: 1927-1938
Varieties: HN 1253, 1275, 1279, 1291, 1357, 1512

U.S.:	**$1,400.00**
Can.:	**$2,000.00**
U.K.:	**£　850.00**

HN 1253
Kathleen
Style One
Designer: L. Harradine
Height: 7 ½", 19.1 cm
Colour: Red and purple
Issued: 1927-1938
Varieties: HN 1252, 1275, 1279, 1291, 1357, 1512

U.S.:	**$1,400.00**
Can.:	**$2,000.00**
U.K.:	**£　850.00**

HN 1254
Circe
Designer: L. Harradine
Height: 7 ½", 19.1 cm
Colour: Orange and red
Issued: 1927-1936
Varieties: HN 1249, 1250, 1255

U.S.:	
Can.:	**Extremely rare**
U.K.:	

HN 1255
Circe
Designer: L. Harradine
Height: 7 ½", 19.1 cm
Colour: Blue
Issued: 1927-1938
Varieties: HN 1249, 1250, 1254

U.S.:	
Can.:	**Extremely rare**
U.K.:	

HN 1256
Captain MacHeath
Designer: L. Harradine
Height: 7", 17.8 cm
Colour: Red, yellow and black
Issued: 1927-1949
Varieties: HN 464, 590
Series: Beggar's Opera

U.S.:	**$1,500.00**
Can.:	**$2,000.00**
U.K.:	**£　900.00**

Earthenware

HN 1257
Highwayman
Designer: L. Harradine
Height: 6 ½", 16.5 cm
Colour: Green and red
Issued: 1927-1949
Varieties: HN 527, 592
Series: Beggar's Opera

U.S.:	**$1,200.00**
Can.:	**$1,500.00**
U.K.:	**£　725.00**

Earthenware

HN 1258
A Victorian Lady
Style One
Designer: L. Harradine
Height: 7 ¾", 19.7 cm
Colour: Purple and blue
Issued: 1927-1938
Varieties: HN 726, 727, 728, 736,
            739, 740, 742, 745,
            1208, 1276,1277,
            1345, 1452, 1529

U.S.:	$1,400.00
Can.:	$1,850.00
U.K.:	£ 850.00

HN 1259
The Alchemist
Designer: L. Harradine
Height: 11 ½", 29.2 cm
Colour: Green and red
Issued: 1927-1938
Varieties: HN 1282

U.S.:	$3,000.00
Can.:	$4,000.00
U.K.:	£1,800.00

HN 1260
Carnival
Designer: L. Harradine
Height: 8 ¼", 21.0 cm
Colour: Red, black and purple
Issued: 1927-1936
Varieties: HN 1278

U.S.:	$6,500.00
Can.:	$9,000.00
U.K.:	£4,000.00

HN 1261
Sea Sprite
Style One
Designer: L. Harradine
Height: 5", 12.7 cm
Colour: Red, purple and black
Issued: 1927-1938

U.S.:	$1,500.00
Can.:	$1,950.00
U.K.:	£ 900.00

HN 1262
Spanish Lady
Designer: L. Harradine
Height: 8 ½", 21.6 cm
Colour: Black with red flowers
Issued: 1927-1940
Varieties: HN 1290, 1293, 1294,
            1309

U.S.:	$2,250.00
Can.:	$2,900.00
U.K.:	£1,350.00

HN 1263
Clownette
Designer: L. Harradine
Height: 7 ¼", 18.4 cm
Colour: Mottled purple
Issued: 1927-1938
Varieties: Also called 'Lady
            Clown' HN 717, 718,
            738, 770

U.S.:	$ 8,500.00
Can.:	$11,000.00
U.K.:	£ 5,000.00

HN 1264
Judge and Jury
Designer: J. G. Hughes
Height: 6", 15.2 cm
Colour: Red and white
Issued: 1927-1938

U.S.:	
Can.:	Extremely rare
U.K.:	

HN 1265
Lady Fayre
Designer: L. Harradine
Height: 5 ¼", 13.3 cm
Colour: Lavender and red
Issued: 1928-1938
Varieties: HN 1557

U.S.:	$1,400.00
Can.:	$1,750.00
U.K.:	£ 800.00

HN 1266
Ko-Ko
Style One
Designer: L. Harradine
Height: 5", 12.7 cm
Colour: Black, white and yellow
Issued: 1928-1936
Varieties: HN 1286

U.S.:	$2,200.00
Can.:	$3,000.00
U.K.:	£1,300.00

HN 1267
Carmen
Style One
Designer: L. Harradine
Height: 7", 17.8 cm
Colour: Red and black
Issued: 1928-1938
Varieties: HN 1300

U.S.:	$2,000.00
Can.:	$2,750.00
U.K.:	£1,200.00

HN 1268
Yum-Yum
Style One
Designer: L. Harradine
Height: 5", 12.7 cm
Colour: Pink and cream
Issued: 1928-1936
Varieties: HN 1287

U.S.:	$2,200.00
Can.:	$3,000.00
U.K.:	£1,300.00

HN 1269
Scotch Girl
Designer: L. Harradine
Height: 7 ½", 19.1 cm
Colour: Red and green
Issued: 1928-1938

U.S.:	$4,500.00
Can.:	$6,000.00
U.K.:	£2,700.00

HN 1270
The Swimmer
First Version
Designer: L. Harradine
Height: 7 ¼", 18.4 cm
Colour: Multicoloured
Issued: 1928-1938
Varieties: HN 1326, 1329

U.S.:	$4,750.00
Can.:	$6,750.00
U.K.:	£3,000.00

HN 1271
The Mask
Style One
Designer: L. Harradine
Height: 6 ¾", 17.2 cm
Colour: Black, blue and red
Issued: 1928-1938
Varieties: HN 656, 657, 729, 733, 785

U.S.:	$5,000.00
Can.:	$6,750.00
U.K.:	£3,000.00

HN 1272
Negligée
Designer: L. Harradine
Height: 5", 12.7 cm
Colour: Red and black
Issued: 1928-1936
Varieties: HN 1219, 1228, 1273, 1454

U.S.:	$3,250.00
Can.:	$4,500.00
U.K.:	£2,000.00

HN 1273
Negligée
Designer: L. Harradine
Height: 5", 12.7 cm
Colour: White and pink
Issued: 1928-1936
Varieties: HN 1219, 1228, 1272, 1454

U.S.:	$3,250.00
Can.:	$4,500.00
U.K.:	£2,000.00

HN 1274
Harlequinade Masked
Designer: L. Harradine
Height: 6 ½", 16.5 cm
Colour: Orange and black
Issued: 1928-1938
Varieties: HN 768, 769, 1304

U.S.:	$6,000.00
Can.:	$7,500.00
U.K.:	£3,500.00

HN 1275
Kathleen
Style One
Designer: L. Harradine
Height: 7 ½", 19.1 cm
Colour: Pink and black
Issued: 1928-1938
Varieties: HN 1252, 1253, 1279, 1291, 1357, 1512

U.S.:	
Can.:	**Extremely rare**
U.K.:	

HN 1276
A Victorian Lady
Style One
Designer: L. Harradine
Height: 7 ½", 19.1 cm
Colour: Purple, red, yellow
Issued: 1928-1938
Varieties: HN 726, 727, 728, 736, 739, 740, 742, 745, 1208, 1258, 1277, 1345, 1452, 1529

U.S.:	$1,650.00
Can.:	$2,250.00
U.K.:	£ 975.00

HN 1277
A Victorian Lady
Style One
Designer: L. Harradine
Height: 7 ¾", 19.7 cm
Colour: Red, yellow, blue
Issued: 1928-1938
Varieties: HN 726, 727, 728, 736, 739, 740, 742, 745, 1208, 1258, 1276, 1345, 1452, 1529

U.S.:	$1,650.00
Can.:	$2,250.00
U.K.:	£ 975.00

HN 1278
Carnival
Designer: L. Harradine
Height: 8 ½", 21.6 cm
Colour: Blue, orange and purple
Issued: 1928-1936
Varieties: HN 1260

U.S.:	$7,500.00
Can.:	$9,500.00
U.K.:	£4,500.00

HN 1279
Kathleen
Style One
Designer: L. Harradine
Height: 7 ¾", 19.7 cm
Colour: Red
Issued: 1928-1938
Varieties: HN 1252, 1253, 1275, 1291, 1357, 1512

U.S.:	$1,400.00
Can.:	$2,000.00
U.K.:	£ 850.00

HN 1280
Blue Bird
Designer: L. Harradine
Height: 4 ¾", 12.0 cm
Colour: Pink base
Issued: 1928-1938

U.S.:	$1,650.00
Can.:	$2,250.00
U.K.:	£ 975.00

HN 1281
Scotties
Designer: L. Harradine
Height: 5 ½", 14.0 cm
Colour: Red and black
Issued: 1928-1936
Varieties: HN 1349

U.S.:	$3,000.00
Can.:	$4,500.00
U.K.:	£1,750.00

HN 1282
The Alchemist
Designer: L. Harradine
Height: 11 ¼", 28.5 cm
Colour: Purple and red
Issued: 1928-1938
Varieties: HN 1259

U.S.:	**$3,000.00**
Can.:	**$4,000.00**
U.K.:	**£1,800.00**

Earthenware

HN 1283
The Cobbler
Style Two
Designer: C. J. Noke
Height: 8 ½", 21.6 cm
Colour: Light green
Issued: 1928-1949
Varieties: HN 681, 1251

U.S.:	**$1,500.00**
Can.:	**$1,950.00**
U.K.:	**£ 900.00**

HN 1284
Lady Jester
Style Two
Designer: L. Harradine
Height: 4 ¼", 10.8 cm
Colour: Purple and red
Issued: 1928-1938
Varieties: HN 1285

U.S.:	**$4,000.00**
Can.:	**$5,000.00**
U.K.:	**£2,400.00**

HN 1285
Lady Jester
Style Two
Designer: L. Harradine
Height: 4 ¼", 10.8 cm
Colour: Red, pink and blue
Issued: 1928-1938
Varieties: HN 1284

U.S.:	**$4,000.00**
Can.:	**$5,000.00**
U.K.:	**£2,400.00**

HN 1286
Ko-Ko
Style One
Designer: L. Harradine
Height: 5", 12.7 cm
Colour: Red and purple
Issued: 1938-1949
Varieties: HN 1266

U.S.:	**$2,000.00**
Can.:	**$2,600.00**
U.K.:	**£1,200.00**

HN 1287
Yum-Yum
Style One
Designer: L. Harradine
Height: 5", 12.7 cm
Colour: Purple and cream
Issued: 1928-1936
Varieties: HN 1268

U.S.:	**$2,000.00**
Can.:	**$2,600.00**
U.K.:	**£1,200.00**

HN 1288
Susanna
Designer: L. Harradine
Height: 6", 15.2 cm
Colour: Red
Issued: 1928-1936
Varieties: HN 1233, 1299

U.S.:	**$3,000.00**
Can.:	**$4,000.00**
U.K.:	**£1,800.00**

HN 1289
Midinette
Style One
Designer: L. Harradine
Height: 9", 22.9 cm
Colour: Purple and pink
Issued: 1928-1938
Varieties: HN 1306

U.S.:	**$6,000.00**
Can.:	**$7,750.00**
U.K.:	**£3,500.00**

HN 1290
Spanish Lady
Designer: L. Harradine
Height: 8 ¼", 21.0 cm
Colour: Lavender, yellow and black
Issued: 1928-1940
Varieties: HN 1262, 1293, 1294, 1309

U.S.:	$2,000.00
Can.:	$2,600.00
U.K.:	£1,200.00

HN 1291
Kathleen
Style One
Designer: L. Harradine
Height: 7 ½", 19.1 cm
Colour: Red and yellow
Issued: 1928-1938
Varieties: HN 1252, 1253, 1275, 1279, 1357, 1512

U.S.:	$1,500.00
Can.:	$2,000.00
U.K.:	£ 900.00

HN 1292
A Geisha
Style Two
Designer: C. J. Noke
Height: 6 ¾", 17.2 cm
Colour: Pink and lavender
Issued: 1928-1938
Varieties: HN 1223, 1234, 1310

U.S.:	$2,250.00
Can.:	$3,000.00
U.K.:	£1,350.00

HN 1293
Spanish Lady
Designer: L. Harradine
Height: 8 ¼", 21.0 cm
Colour: Black with yellow flowers
Issued: 1928-1940
Varieties: HN 1262, 1290, 1294, 1309

U.S.:	$2,250.00
Can.:	$3,000.00
U.K.:	£1,350.00

HN 1294
Spanish Lady
Designer: L. Harradine
Height: 8 ¼", 21.0 cm
Colour: Red and black
Issued: 1928-1940
Varieties: HN 1262, 1290, 1293, 1309

U.S.:	$1,750.00
Can.:	$2,250.00
U.K.:	£1,000.00

HN 1295
A Jester
Style One
Designer: C. J. Noke
Height: 10", 25.4 cm
Colour: Brown and purple
Issued: 1928-1949
Varieties: HN 45, 71, 71A, 320, 367, 412, 426, 446, 552, 616, 627, 1702, 2016, 3922

U.S.:	$2,250.00
Can.:	$3,000.00
U.K.:	£1,350.00

HN 1296
Columbine
Style One
Designer: L. Harradine
Height: 6", 15.2 cm
Colour: Orange and lavender
Issued: 1928-1940
Varieties: HN 1297, 1439

U.S.:	$2,000.00
Can.:	$2,750.00
U.K.:	£1,200.00

HN 1297
Columbine
Style One
Designer: L. Harradine
Height: 6", 15.2 cm
Colour: Pink and purple
Issued: 1928-1940
Varieties: HN 1296, 1439

U.S.:	$2,000.00
Can.:	$2,750.00
U.K.:	£1,200.00

HN 1298
Sweet and Twenty
Style One
Designer: L. Harradine
Height: 5 ¾", 14.6 cm
Colour: Red and blue-green
Issued: 1928-1969
Varieties: HN 1360, 1437, 1438,
           1549, 1563, 1649

U.S.:   **$450.00**
Can.:   **$600.00**
U.K.:   **£275.00**

HN 1299
Susanna
Designer: L. Harradine
Height: 6", 15.2 cm
Colour: Black, red and blue
Issued: 1928-1936
Varieties: HN 1233, 1288

U.S.:   **$3,000.00**
Can.:   **$4,000.00**
U.K.:   **£1,800.00**

HN 1300
Carmen
Style One
Designer: L. Harradine
Height: 7", 17.8 cm
Colour: Pale blue-lavender
Issued: 1928-1938
Varieties: HN 1267

U.S.:   **$5,000.00**
Can.:   **$6,500.00**
U.K.:   **£3,000.00**

HN 1301
Young Mother with Child
Designer: Unknown
Height: 14 ½", 37.0 cm
Colour: Green and red
Issued: 1928-1938

U.S.:   **Only**
Can.:   **one**
U.K.:   **known**

HN 1302
The Gleaner
Designer: Unknown
Height: 14 ½", 36.2 cm
Colour: Red and cream
Issued: 1928-1936

U.S.:   **Only**
Can.:   **one**
U.K.:   **known**

HN 1303
Angela
Style One
Designer: L. Harradine
Height: 7 ¼", 18.4 cm
Colour: Blue
Issued: 1928-1940
Varieties: HN 1204; also called
           'Fanny'

U.S.:   **$6,000.00**
Can.:   **$7,750.00**
U.K.:   **£3,500.00**

HN 1304
Harlequinade Masked
Designer: L. Harradine
Height: 6 ½", 16.5 cm
Colour: Mottled blue
Issued: 1928-1938
Varieties: HN 768, 769, 1274

U.S.:   **$6,000.00**
Can.:   **$7,750.00**
U.K.:   **£3,500.00**

HN 1305
Siesta
Designer: L. Harradine
Height: 4 ¾", 12.0 cm
Colour: Red
Issued: 1928-1940

U.S.:   **$6,000.00**
Can.:   **$8,000.00**
U.K.:   **£3,500.00**

HN 1306
Midinette
Style One
Designer: L. Harradine
Height: 9", 22.9 cm
Colour: Red and green
Issued: 1928-1938
Varieties: HN 1289

U.S.:	**$6,000.00**
Can.:	**$7,750.00**
U.K.:	**£3,500.00**

HN 1307
An Irishman
Designer: H. Fenton
Height: 6 ¾", 17.2 cm
Colour: Green coat with
           brown striped trousers
Issued: 1928-1938

U.S.:	**$5,000.00**
Can.:	**$6,500.00**
U.K.:	**£3,000.00**

HN 1308
The Moor
Designer: C. J. Noke
Height: 16 ½", 41.9 cm
Colour: Blue and mottled red
Issued: 1929-1938
Varieties: HN 1366, 1425, 1657,
           2082, 3642, 3926;
           also called 'An Arab'
           HN 33, 343, 378

U.S.:	**$4,500.00**
Can.:	**$6,000.00**
U.K.:	**£2,700.00**

HN 1309
Spanish Lady
Designer: L. Harradine
Height: 8 ¼", 21.0 cm
Colour: Black and
           multicoloured
Issued: 1929-1940
Varieties: HN 1262, 1290, 1293,
           1294

U.S.:	**$3,000.00**
Can.:	**$4,000.00**
U.K.:	**£1,750.00**

HN 1310
A Geisha
Style Two
Designer: C. J. Noke
Height: 6 ¾", 17.2 cm
Colour: Green
Issued: 1929-1938
Varieties: HN 1223, 1234, 1292

U.S.:	**$2,250.00**
Can.:	**$3,000.00**
U.K.:	**£1,350.00**

Photograph
Not
Available

HN 1311
Cassim
Style Two
Designer: L. Harradine
Height: 3 ¾", 9.5 cm
Colour: Unknown
Issued: 1929-1938
Varieties: HN 1312

U.S.:	
Can.:	**Very Rare**
U.K.:	

Photograph
Not
Available

HN 1312
Cassim
Style Two
Designer: L. Harradine
Height: 3 ¾", 9.5 cm
Colour: Unknown
Issued: 1929-1938
Varieties: HN 1311

U.S.:	
Can.:	**Very Rare**
U.K.:	

HN 1313
Sonny
Designer: L. Harradine
Height: 3 ½", 8.9 cm
Colour: Pink
Issued: 1929-1938
Varieties: HN 1314

U.S.:	**$1,600.00**
Can.:	**$2,250.00**
U.K.:	**£1,000.00**

HN 1314
Sonny
Designer: L. Harradine
Height: 3 ½", 8.9 cm
Colour: Blue
Issued: 1929-1938
Varieties: HN 1313

U.S.:	$1,600.00
Can.:	$2,250.00
U.K.:	£1,000.00

HN 1315
Old Balloon Seller
Style One
Designer: L. Harradine
Height: 7 ½", 19.1 cm
Colour: Green, purple and
           white
Issued: 1929-1998
Varieties: HN 3737

U.S.:	$250.00
Can.:	$350.00
U.K.:	£150.00

Earthenware and china

Photograph
Not
Available

HN 1316
Toys
Designer: L. Harradine
Height: Unknown
Colour: Green, red and yellow
Issued: 1929-1938

U.S.:	
Can.:	**Extremely rare**
U.K.:	

HN 1317
The Snake Charmer
Designer: Unknown
Height: 4", 10.1 cm
Colour: Green and black
Issued: 1929-1938

U.S.:	$2,500.00
Can.:	$3,750.00
U.K.:	£1,500.00

HN 1318
Sweet Anne
Style One
Designer: L. Harradine
Height: 7 ½", 19.1 cm
Colour: Blue and green
Issued: 1929-1949
Varieties: HN 1330, 1331, 1453,
           1496, 1631, 1701

U.S.:	$350.00
Can.:	$450.00
U.K.:	£200.00

HN 1319
Darling
Style One
Designer: C. Vyse
Height: 7 ½", 19.1 cm
Colour: White, black base
Issued: 1929-1959
Varieties: HN 1, 1371, 1372,
           4140

U.S.:	$250.00
Can.:	$350.00
U.K.:	£150.00

HN 1320
Rosamund
Style One
Designer: L. Harradine
Height: 7 ¼", 18.4 cm
Colour: Lavender
Issued: 1929-1937

U.S.:	$3,750.00
Can.:	$5,000.00
U.K.:	£2,250.00

HN 1321
A Geisha
Style One
Designer: H. Tittensor
Height: 10 ¾", 27.3 cm
Colour: Green
Issued: 1929-1936
Varieties: HN 354, 376, 376A,
           387, 634, 741, 779,
           1322; also called
           'The Japanese Lady'

U.S.:	
Can.:	**Extremely rare**
U.K.:	

HN 1322
A Geisha
Style One
Designer: H. Tittensor
Height: 10 ¾", 27.3 cm
Colour: Pink and blue
Issued: 1929-1936
Varieties: HN 354, 376, 376A
387, 634, 741, 779,
1321; Also called
'The Japanese Lady'

U.S.:
Can.: **Extremely rare**
U.K.:

HN 1323
Contentment
Designer: L. Harradine
Height: 7 ¼", 18.4 cm
Colour: Red and blue
Issued: 1929-1938
Varieties: HN 395, 396, 421,
468, 572, 685, 686

U.S.: **$3,000.00**
Can.: **$4,000.00**
U.K.: **£1,750.00**

HN 1324
Fairy
Style One
Designer: L. Harradine
Height: 6 ½", 16.5 cm
Colour: Multicoloured
Issued: 1929-1938

U.S.: **$2,750.00**
Can.: **$3,750.00**
U.K.: **£1,650.00**

HN 1325
The Orange Seller
Designer: L. Harradine
Height: 7", 17.8 cm
Colour: Green and lavender
Issued: 1929-1940

U.S.: **$2,000.00**
Can.: **$2,600.00**
U.K.: **£1,200.00**

HN 1326
The Swimmer
First Version
Designer: L. Harradine
Height: 7 ½", 19.1 cm
Colour: Pink and purple
Issued: 1929-1938
Varieties: HN 1270, 1329

U.S.: **$5,000.00**
Can.: **$6,750.00**
U.K.: **£3,000.00**

HN 1327
Bo-Peep
Style One
Designer: L. Harradine
Height: 6 ¾", 17.2 cm
Colour: Multicoloured
Issued: 1929-1936
Varieties: HN 777, 1202, 1328

U.S.: **$4,500.00**
Can.: **$6,000.00**
U.K.: **£2,750.00**

HN 1328
Bo-Peep
Style One
Designer: L. Harradine
Height: 6 ¾", 17.2 cm
Colour: Purple and cream
Issued: 1929-1936
Varieties: HN 777, 1202, 1327

U.S.: **$4,500.00**
Can.: **$6,000.00**
U.K.: **£2,750.00**

HN 1329
The Swimmer
First Version
Designer: L. Harradine
Height: 7 ½", 19.1 cm
Colour: Pink
Issued: 1929-1938
Varieties: HN 1270, 1326

U.S.: **$5,000.00**
Can.: **$6,750.00**
U.K.: **£3,000.00**

HN 1330
Sweet Anne
Style One
Designer: L. Harradine
Height: 7 ¼", 18.4 cm
Colour: Blue, pink-yellow
Issued: 1929-1949
Varieties: HN 1318, 1331, 1453,
           1496, 1631, 1701

U.S.:	$500.00
Can.:	$675.00
U.K.:	£300.00

HN 1331
Sweet Anne
Style One
Designer: L. Harradine
Height: 7 ¼", 18.4 cm
Colour: Red, blue-yellow
Issued: 1929-1949
Varieties: HN 1318, 1330, 1453,
           1496, 1631, 1701

U.S.:	$500.00
Can.:	$675.00
U.K.:	£300.00

HN 1332
Lady Jester
Style One
Designer: L. Harradine
Height: 7", 17.8 cm
Colour: Red, blue and black
Issued: 1929-1938
Varieties: HN 1221, 1222

U.S.:	$5,000.00
Can.:	$6,500.00
U.K.:	£3,000.00

HN 1333
A Jester
Style Two
Designer: C. J. Noke
Height: 10 ¼", 26.0 cm
Colour: Blue, yellow and black
Issued: 1929-1949
Varieties: HN 45A, 45B, 55, 308,
           630; also known in
           black and white

U.S.:	$ 8,500.00
Can.:	$11,000.00
U.K.:	£ 5,000.00

HN 1334
Tulips
Designer: Unknown
Height: 9 ½", 24.1 cm
Colour: Lavender and pink
Issued: 1929-1936
Varieties: HN 466, 488, 672,
           747

U.S.:	$3,500.00
Can.:	$4,500.00
U.K.:	£2,000.00

HN 1335
Folly
Designer: L. Harradine
Height: 9", 22.9 cm
Colour: Lavender with orange
           and yellow balloons
Issued: 1929-1938
Varieties: HN 1750

U.S.:	$3,500.00
Can.:	$4,500.00
U.K.:	£2,000.00

China

HN 1336
One of the Forty
Style Eleven
Designer: H. Tittensor
Height: Unknown
Colour: Red, orange and blue
Issued: 1929-1938
Varieties: HN 481, 483, 491, 646,
           667, 712, 1350; also
           known in flambé

U.S.:	$6,000.00
Can.:	$7,750.00
U.K.:	£3,600.00

HN 1337
Priscilla
Style One
Designer: L. Harradine
Height: 8", 20.3 cm
Colour: Lavender and yellow
Issued: 1929-1938
Varieties: HN 1340, 1495, 1501,
           1559

U.S.:	$1,300.00
Can.:	$1,700.00
U.K.:	£ 775.00

HN 1338
The Courtier
Designer: L. Harradine
Height: 4 ½", 11.4 cm
Colour: Red and white
Issued: 1929-1938

U.S.:	**$4,500.00**
Can.:	**$6,750.00**
U.K.:	**£2,700.00**

HN 1339
Covent Garden
Style One
Designer: L. Harradine
Height: 9", 22.9 cm
Colour: Green and lavender
Issued: 1929-1938

U.S.:	**$3,500.00**
Can.:	**$4,500.00**
U.K.:	**£2,000.00**

HN 1340
Priscilla
Style One
Designer: L. Harradine
Height: 8", 20.3 cm
Colour: Red and purple
Issued: 1929-1949
Varieties: HN 1337, 1495, 1501,
          1559

U.S.:	**$650.00**
Can.:	**$850.00**
U.K.:	**£400.00**

HN 1341
Marietta
Designer: L. Harradine
Height: 8", 20.3 cm
Colour: Red and black
Issued: 1929-1940
Varieties: HN 1446, 1699

U.S.:	**$2,000.00**
Can.:	**$2,750.00**
U.K.:	**£1,200.00**

HN 1342
The Flower Seller's Children
Designer: L. Harradine
Height: 8", 20.3 cm
Colour: Purple, red and yellow
Issued: 1929-1993
Varieties: HN 525, 551, 1206,
          1406

U.S.:	**$ 650.00**
Can.:	**$1,000.00**
U.K.:	**£ 400.00**

HN 1343
Dulcinea
Designer: L. Harradine
Height: 5 ½", 14.0 cm
Colour: Red, black, green
          and blue
Issued: 1929-1936
Varieties: HN 1419

U.S.:	**$4,500.00**
Can.:	**$7,250.00**
U.K.:	**£2,750.00**

HN 1344
Sunshine Girl
First Version
Designer: L. Harradine
Height: 5", 12.7 cm
Colour: Green, black and red
Issued: 1929-1938
Varieties: HN 1348

U.S.:	**$ 7,500.00**
Can.:	**$10,000.00**
U.K.:	**£ 5,000.00**

HN 1345
A Victorian Lady
Style One
Designer: L. Harradine
Height: 7 ¾", 19.7 cm
Colour: Green and purple
Issued: 1929-1949
Varieties: HN 726, 727, 728,
          736, 739, 740, 742,
          745, 1208, 1258, 1276,
          1277, 1452, 1529

U.S.:	**$750.00**
Can.:	**$975.00**
U.K.:	**£450.00**

HN 1346
Iona
Designer: L. Harradine
Height: 7 ½", 19.1 cm
Colour: Green, black and
lavender
Issued: 1929-1938

U.S.:	**$6,000.00**
Can.:	**$8,000.00**
U.K.:	**£3,500.00**

HN 1347
Moira
Designer: L. Harradine
Height: 6 ½", 16.5 cm
Colour: Lavender, pink and
green
Issued: 1929-1938

U.S.:	**$6,000.00**
Can.:	**$8,000.00**
U.K.:	**£3,500.00**

HN 1348
Sunshine Girl
First Version
Designer: L. Harradine
Height: 5", 12.7 cm
Colour: Black and orange
Issued: 1929-1937
Varieties: HN 1344

U.S.:	**$ 7,500.00**
Can.:	**$10,000.00**
U.K.:	**£ 5,000.00**

HN 1349
Scotties
Designer: L. Harradine
Height: 5 ¼", 13.3 cm
Colour: Blue
Issued: 1929-1936
Varieties: HN 1281

U.S.:	**$5,000.00**
Can.:	**$7,500.00**
U.K.:	**£3,000.00**

HN 1350
One of the Forty
Style Twelve
Designer: H. Tittensor
Height: Unknown
Colour: Multicoloured
Issued: 1929-1949
Varieties: HN 481, 483, 491,
646, 667, 712, 1336,
also known in flambé

U.S.:	**None**
Can.:	**known**
U.K.:	**to exist**

HN 1351
One of the Forty
Style One
Designer: H. Tittensor
Height: 8 ¼", 21.0 cm
Colour: Mottled red
and purple
Issued: 1929-1949
Varieties: HN 417, 490, 495, 501,
528, 648, 677, 1352

U.S.:	**$6,000.00**
Can.:	**$7,750.00**
U.K.:	**£3,500.00**

HN 1352
One of the Forty
Style One
Designer: H. Tittensor
Height: 8 ¼", 21.0 cm
Colour: Multicoloured
Issued: 1929-1949
Varieties: HN 417, 490, 495, 501,
528, 648, 677, 1351

U.S.:	**$6,000.00**
Can.:	**$7,750.00**
U.K.:	**£3,500.00**

HN 1353
One of the Forty
Style Two
Designer: H. Tittensor
Height: 7 ¼", 18.4 cm
Colour: Orange and purple
Issued: 1929-1936
Varieties: HN 418, 494, 498,
647, 666, 704

U.S.:	**$6,000.00**
Can.:	**$7,750.00**
U.K.:	**£3,500.00**

Photograph
Not
Available

HN 1354
One of the Forty
Style Fourteen
Designer: H. Tittensor
Height: 7 ¾", 19.7 cm
Colour: Multicoloured
Issued: 1929-1949
Varieties: HN 496, 500, 649,
                 665

U.S.:	$6,000.00
Can.:	$7,750.00
U.K.:	£3,500.00

HN 1355
The Mendicant
Designer: L. Harradine
Height: 8 ¼", 21.0 cm
Colour: Brown
Issued: 1929-1938
Varieties: HN 1365 (minor
                 glaze difference)

U.S.:	$350.00
Con.:	$475.00
U.K.:	£200.00

Earthenware

HN 1356
The Parson's Daughter
Designer: H. Tittensor
Height: 9 ¼", 23.5 cm
Colour: Multicoloured
Issued: 1929-1938
Varieties: HN 337, 338, 441,
                 564, 790, 1242, 2018

U.S.:	$1,400.00
Can.:	$1,850.00
U.K.:	£ 850.00

HN 1357
Kathleen
Style One
Designer: L. Harradine
Height: 7 ½", 19.1 cm
Colour: Pink and lavender
Issued: 1929-1938
Varieties: HN 1252, 1253, 1275,
                 1279, 1291, 1512

U.S.:	$1,400.00
Can.:	$2,000.00
U.K.:	£ 850.00

HN 1358
Rosina
Designer: L. Harradine
Height: 5 ¾", 14.6 cm
Colour: Red
Issued: 1929-1937
Varieties: HN 1364, 1556

U.S.:	$1,750.00
Can.:	$2,250.00
U.K.:	£1,000.00

HN 1359
Two-A-Penny
Designer: L. Harradine
Height: 8 ¼", 21.0 cm
Colour: Red and green
Issued: 1929-1938

U.S.:	$7,000.00
Can.:	$9,000.00
U.K.:	£4,000.00

Earthenware

HN 1360
Sweet and Twenty
Style One
Designer: L. Harradine
Height: 6", 15.2 cm
Colour: Blue and green
Issued: 1929-1938
Varieties: HN 1298, 1437, 1438,
                 1549, 1563, 1649

U.S.:	$1,200.00
Can.:	$1,575.00
U.K.:	£ 700.00

NOTE ON PRICING

As with all price guides, prices listed in this catalogue are suggested retail values. This is not a fixed price catalogue and figurines will be offered for sale at higher, lower, or catalogue prices, depending upon the supply-demand factors of the market place.

When our first edition was published in 1981 the Royal Doulton market was divided into three or four different geographical areas and pricing was based on each individual area.

In 2004 this is all changing, the global market place is coming to collectables. Our prices, while based on many different avenues that offer figurines for sale, are slowly turning into foreign exchange transactions between the former market areas. For now the collector is able to shop globally.

HN 1361
Mask Seller
Designer: L. Harradine
Height: 8 ½", 21.6 cm
Colour: Black, white and red
Issued: 1929-1938
Varieties: HN 2103

U.S.:	$3,000.00
Can.:	$4,000.00
U.K.:	£1,800.00

HN 1362
Pantalettes
Style One
Designer: L. Harradine
Height: 7 ¾", 19.7 cm
Colour: Green and blue
Issued: 1929-1942
Varieties: HN 1412, 1507, 1709

U.S.:	$650.00
Can.:	$900.00
U.K.:	£400.00

HN 1363
Doreen
Designer: L. Harradine
Height: 5 ¼", 13.3 cm
Colour: Red
Issued: 1929-1940
Varieties: HN 1389, 1390

U.S.:	$2,000.00
Can.:	$2,500.00
U.K.:	£1,200.00

HN 1364
Rosina
Designer: L. Harradine
Height: 5 ¼", 13.3 cm
Colour: Purple and red
Issued: 1929-1937
Varieties: HN 1358, 1556

U.S.:	$1,750.00
Can.:	$2,250.00
U.K.:	£1,100.00

HN 1365
The Mendicant
Designer: L. Harradine
Height: 8 ¼", 21.0 cm
Colour: Brown
Issued: 1929-1969
Varieties: HN 1355 (minor
           glaze differences)

U.S.:	$350.00
Can.:	$475.00
U.K.:	£200.00

HN 1366
The Moor
Designer: C. J. Noke
Height: 16 ½", 41.9 cm
Colour: Multicoloured
Issued: 1930-1949
Varieties: HN 1308, 1425, 1657,
           2082, 3642, 3926;
           also called 'An Arab'
           HN 33, 343, 378

U.S.:	$4,500.00
Can.:	$6,000.00
U.K.:	£2,700.00

Photograph
Not
Available

HN 1367
Kitty
Style One
Designer: Unknown
Height: 4", 10.1 cm
Colour: White, yellow
           and purple
Issued: 1930-1938

U.S.:	
Can.:	**Extremely rare**
U.K.:	

HN 1368
Rose
Style One
Designer: L. Harradine
Height: 4 ½", 11.4 cm
Colour: Pink
Issued: 1930-1995
Varieties: HN 1387, 1416, 1506,
           1654, 2123

U.S.:	$100.00
Can.:	$135.00
U.K.:	£ 50.00

Earthenware

Photograph
Not
Available

HN 1369
Boy on Pig
Designer: C. J. Noke
Height: 4", 10.1 cm
Colour: Green and brown
Issued: 1930-1938
Varieties: Also known in flambé

   U.S.:
   Can.:   **Extremely rare**
   U.K.:

HN 1370
Marie
Style Two
Designer: L. Harradine
Height: 4 ¾", 12.0 cm
Colour: Purple
Issued: 1930-1988
Varieties: HN 1388, 1417, 1489,
            1531, 1635, 1655

   U.S.: $150.00
   Can.: $200.00
   U.K.:   £ 90.00

HN 1371
Darling
Style One
Designer: C. Vyse
Height: 7 ½", 19.1 cm
Colour: Green
Issued: 1930-1938
Varieties: HN 1, 1319, 1372,
            4140

   U.S.: $1,650.00
   Can.: $2,750.00
   U.K.:   £ 975.00

HN 1372
Darling
Style One
Designer: C. Vyse
Height: 7 ¾", 19.7 cm
Colour: Pink, black base
Issued: 1930-1938
Varieties: HN 1, 1319, 1371,
            4140

   U.S.: $1,650.00
   Can.: $2,750.00
   U.K.:   £ 975.00

HN 1373
Sweet Lavender
Designer: L. Harradine
Height: 9", 22.8 cm
Colour: Green, red and black
Issued: 1930-1949
Varieties: Also called 'Any Old
            Lavender'

   U.S.: $1,250.00
   Can.: $1,650.00
   U.K.:   £ 750.00

HN 1374
Fairy
Style Two
Designer: L. Harradine
Height: 4", 10.1 cm
Colour: Yellow flowers
Issued: 1930-1938
Varieties: HN 1380, 1532

   U.S.: $3,250.00
   Can.: $4,500.00
   U.K.:   £2,000.00

HN 1375
Fairy
Style Three
Designer: L. Harradine
Height: 3", 7.6 cm
Colour: Yellow flowers
Issued: 1930-1938
Varieties: HN 1395, 1533

   U.S.: $3,250.00
   Can.: $4,500.00
   U.K.:   £2,000.00

HN 1376
Fairy
Style Four
Designer: L. Harradine
Height: 2 ½", 6.3 cm
Colour: Yellow flowers
Issued: 1930-1938
Varieties: HN 1536

   U.S.: $1,650.00
   Can.: $2,250.00
   U.K.:   £1,000.00

Earthenware

Photograph
Not
Available

HN 1377
Fairy
Style Five
Designer: L. Harradine
Height: 1 ½", 3.8 cm
Colour: Lavender and yellow
Issued: 1930-1938
U.S.:
Can.:   **Extremely Rare**
U.K.:

HN 1378
Fairy
Style Six
Designer: L. Harradine
Height: 2 ½", 6.3 cm
Colour: Orange flowers
Issued: 1930-1938
Varieties: HN 1396, 1535
U.S.:   **$1,750.00**
Can.:   **$2,250.00**
U.K.:   **£1,000.00**

HN 1379
Fairy
Style Seven
Designer: L. Harradine
Height: 2 ½", 6.3 cm
Colour: Blue flowers
Issued: 1930-1938
Varieties: HN 1394, 1534
U.S.:   **$1,750.00**
Can.:   **$2,250.00**
U.K.:   **£1,000.00**

HN 1380
Fairy
Style Two
Designer: L. Harradine
Height: 4", 10.1 cm
Colour: Multicoloured
Issued: 1930-1938
Varieties: HN 1374, 1532
U.S.:   **$3,250.00**
Can.:   **$4,500.00**
U.K.:   **£2.000.00**

HN 1381 - 1386 not issued.

HN 1387
Rose
Style One
Designer: L. Harradine
Height: 4 ½", 11.4 cm
Colour: Blue, pink and orange
Issued: 1930-1938
Varieties: HN 1368, 1416, 1506,
            1654, 2123
U.S.:   **$325.00**
Can.:   **$475.00**
U.K.:   **£200.00**

HN 1388
Marie
Style Two
Designer: L. Harradine
Height: 4 ½", 11.4 cm
Colour: Pink
Issued: 1930-1938
Varieties: HN 1370, 1417, 1489,
            1531, 1635, 1655
U.S.:   **$325.00**
Can.:   **$475.00**
U.K.:   **£200.00**

HN 1389
Doreen
Designer: L. Harradine
Height: 5 ¼", 13.3 cm
Colour: Green
Issued: 1930-1940
Varieties: HN 1363, 1390
U.S.:   **$2,000.00**
Can.:   **$2,500.00**
U.K.:   **£1,200.00**

HN 1390
Doreen
Designer: L. Harradine
Height: 5 ¾", 14.6 cm
Colour: Lavender
Issued: 1929-1940
Varieties: HN 1363, 1389
U.S.:   **$2,000.00**
Can.:   **$2,500.00**
U.K.:   **£1,200.00**

HN 1391
Pierrette
Style Three
Designer: L. Harradine
Height: 8 ½", 21.6 cm
Colour: Red
Issued: 1930-1938
Varieties: HN 1749

U.S.:	**$3,250.00**
Can.:	**$4,500.00**
U.K.:	**£2,000.00**

Earthenware

HN 1392
Paisley Shawl
Style One
Designer: L. Harradine
Height: 8 ¼", 21.0 cm
Colour: Red shawl, flowered
         cream dress
Issued: 1930-1949
Varieties: HN 1460, 1707,
         1739, 1987

U.S.:	**$550.00**
Can.:	**$700.00**
U.K.:	**£325.00**

HN 1393
Fairy
Style Eight
Designer: L. Harradine
Height: 2 ½", 6.3 cm
Colour: Yellow flowers
Issued: 1930-1938

U.S.:	**$1,650.00**
Can.:	**$2,250.00**
U.K.:	**£1,000.00**

HN 1394
Fairy
Style Seven
Designer: L. Harradine
Height: 2 ½", 6.3 cm
Colour: Yellow flowers
Issued: 1930-1938
Varieties: HN 1379, 1534

U.S.:	**$1,750.00**
Can.:	**$2,250.00**
U.K.:	**£1,000.00**

HN 1395
Fairy
Style Three
Designer: L. Harradine
Height: 3", 7.6 cm
Colour: Blue flowers
Issued: 1930-1938
Varieties: HN 1375, 1533

U.S.:	**$3,250.00**
Can.:	**$4,500.00**
U.K.:	**£2,000.00**

HN 1396
Fairy
Style Six
Designer: L. Harradine
Height: 2 ½", 6.3 cm
Colour: Blue flowers
Issued: 1930-1938
Varieties: HN 1378, 1535

U.S.:	**$1,750.00**
Can.:	**$2,250.00**
U.K.:	**£1,000.00**

HN 1397
Gretchen
Designer: L. Harradine
Height: 7 ¾", 19.7 cm
Colour: Blue and white
Issued: 1930-1940
Varieties: HN 1562

U.S.:	**$1,250.00**
Can.:	**$1,600.00**
U.K.:	**£ 750.00**

HN 1398
Derrick
Designer: L. Harradine
Height: 8", 20.3 cm
Colour: Blue and white
Issued: 1930-1940

U.S.:	**$1,250.00**
Can.:	**$1,600.00**
U.K.:	**£ 750.00**

HN 1399
The Young Widow
Designer: L. Harradine
Height: 8", 20.3 cm
Colour: Purple
Issued: 1930-1930
Varieties: Also called 'Little
           Mother' (Style Two)
           HN 1418, 1641
U.S.:   **$5,000.00**
Can.:   **$6,750.00**
U.K.:   **£3,000.00**

HN 1400
The Windmill Lady
Designer: L. Harradine
Height: 8 ½", 21.6 cm
Colour: Green, yellow and
           orange
Issued: 1930-1937
U.S.:   **$7,500.00**
Can.:   **$9,750.00**
U.K.:   **£4,500.00**

HN 1401
Chorus Girl
Designer: L. Harradine
Height: 8 ½", 21.6 cm
Colour: Red and orange
Issued: 1930-1936
U.S.:   **$4,000.00**
Can.:   **$5,250.00**
U.K.:   **£2,500.00**

HN 1402
Miss Demure
Designer: L. Harradine
Height: 7 ½", 19.1 cm
Colour: Lavender and pink
Issued: 1930-1975
Varieties: HN 1440, 1463, 1499,
           1560
U.S.:   **$325.00**
Can.:   **$475.00**
U.K.:   **£200.00**

HN 1403 not issued.

HN 1404
Betty
Style Two
Designer: L. Harradine
Height: 4 ½", 11.4 cm
Colour: Lavender
Issued: 1930-1936
Varieties: HN 1405, 1435, 1436
U.S.:   **$4,000.00**
Can.:   **$5,250.00**
U.K.:   **£2,400.00**

HN 1405
Betty
Style Two
Designer: L. Harradine
Height: 4 ½", 11.4 cm
Colour: Green
Issued: 1930-1936
Varieties: HN 1404, 1435, 1436
U.S.:   **$4,000.00**
Can.:   **$5,250.00**
U.K.:   **£2,400.00**

HN 1406
The Flower Seller's Children
Designer: L. Harradine
Height: 8 ¼", 21.0 cm
Colour: Yellow and blue
Issued: 1930-1938
Varieties: HN 525, 551, 1206,
           1342
U.S.:   **$3,000.00**
Can.:   **$4,000.00**
U.K.:   **£1,750.00**

HN 1407
The Winner
Designer: Unknown
Height: 6 ¾", 17.2 cm
Colour: Red, blue and grey
Issued: 1930-1938
U.S.:
Can.:   **Very rare**
U.K.:

HN 1408
John Peel
Designer: Unknown
Height: 9 ½", 24.1 cm
Colour: Red and brown
Issued: 1930-1937
Varieties: Also called
            'The Huntsman'
            (Style Two) HN 1815

U.S.: $5,500.00
Can.: $7,500.00
U.K.:   £3,500.00

HN 1409
Hunting Squire
Designer: Unknown
Height: 9 ¾", 24.7 cm
Colour: Red and grey
Issued: 1930-1938
Varieties: Also called
            'The Squire' HN 1814

U.S.: $5,500.00
Can.: $7,500.00
U.K.:   £3,500.00

HN 1410
Abdullah
Designer: L. Harradine
Height: 5 ¾", 14.6 cm
Colour: Blue, lavender
            and green
Issued: 1930-1937
Varieties: HN 2104

U.S.: $2,500.00
Can.: $3,250.00
U.K.:   £1,500.00

HN 1411
Charley's Aunt
Style Two
Designer: H. Fenton
Height: 8", 20.3 cm
Colour: Black
Issued: 1930-1938
Varieties: HN 1554

U.S.: $2,000.00
Can.: $2,500.00
U.K.:   £1,200.00

HN 1412
Pantalettes
Style One
Designer: L. Harradine
Height: 7 ¾", 19.7 cm
Colour: Blue and pink
Issued: 1930-1949
Varieties: HN 1362, 1507, 1709

U.S.: $750.00
Can.: $975.00
U.K.:   £450.00

HN 1413
Margery
Designer: L. Harradine
Height: 11", 27.9 cm
Colour: Maroon and purple
Issued: 1930-1949

U.S.: $750.00
Can.: $975.00
U.K.:   £450.00

Earthenware

HN 1414
Patricia
Style One
Designer: L. Harradine
Height: 8 ½", 21.6 cm
Colour: Yellow and green
Issued: 1930-1949
Varieties: HN 1431, 1462, 1567

U.S.: $1,250.00
Can.: $1,650.00
U.K.:   £ 750.00

HN 1415 not issued.

HN 1416
Rose
Style One
Designer: L. Harradine
Height: 4 ½", 11.4 cm
Colour: Lavender
Issued: 1930-1949
Varieties: HN 1368, 1387, 1506,
            1654, 2123

U.S.: $325.00
Can.: $475.00
U.K.:   £200.00

HN 1417
Marie
Style Two
Designer: L. Harradine
Height: 4 ¾", 12.0 cm
Colour: Rose-pink
Issued: 1930-1949
Varieties: HN 1370, 1388, 1489,
           1531, 1635, 1655

U.S.:   **$325.00**
Can.:   **$475.00**
U.K.:   **£200.00**

HN 1418
The Little Mother
Style Two
Designer: L. Harradine
Height: 8", 20.3 cm
Colour: Purple
Issued: 1930-1938
Varieties: HN 1641; also called
           'Young Widow'
           HN 1399

U.S.:   **$6,000.00**
Can.:   **$7,750.00**
U.K.:   **£3,500.00**

HN 1419
Dulcinea
Designer: L. Harradine
Height: 5 ½", 14.0 cm
Colour: Red
Issued: 1930-1938
Varieties: HN 1343

U.S.:   **$4,500.00**
Can.:   **$6,000.00**
U.K.:   **£2,750.00**

HN 1420
Phyllis
Style One
Designer: L. Harradine
Height: 9", 22.9 cm
Colour: Purple and green
Issued: 1930-1949
Varieties: HN 1430, 1486, 1698

U.S.:   **$1,250.00**
Can.:   **$1,650.00**
U.K.:   **£ 750.00**

HN 1421
Barbara
Style One
Designer: L. Harradine
Height: 7 ¾", 19.7 cm
Colour: Cream and lavender
Issued: 1930-1937
Varieties: HN 1432, 1461

U.S.:   **$2,000.00**
Can.:   **$2,750.00**
U.K.:   **£1,200.00**

HN 1422
Joan
Style One
Designer: L. Harradine
Height: 5 ½", 14.0 cm
Colour: Blue
Issued: 1930-1949
Varieties: HN 2023 (minor
           glaze difference)

U.S.:   **$500.00**
Can.:   **$675.00**
U.K.:   **£300.00**

HN 1423
Babette
Designer: L. Harradine
Height: 5", 12.7 cm
Colour: Yellow, green and red
Issued: 1930-1938
Varieties: HN 1424

U.S.:   **$2,250.00**
Can.:   **$3,000.00**
U.K.:   **£1,350.00**

HN 1424
Babette
Designer: L. Harradine
Height: 5", 12.7 cm
Colour: Blue
Issued: 1930-1938
Varieties: HN 1423

U.S.:   **$2,000.00**
Can.:   **$2,750.00**
U.K.:   **£1,200.00**

HN 1425
The Moor
Designer: C. J. Noke
Height: 16 ½", 41.9 cm
Colour: Multicoloured
Issued: 1930-1949
Varieties: HN 1308, 1366, 1657,
           2082, 3642, 3926;
           also called 'An Arab'
           HN 33, 343, 378

U.S.:	**$4,500.00**
Can.:	**$6,000.00**
U.K.:	**£2,700.00**

HN 1426
The Gossips
Designer: L. Harradine
Height: 5 ¾", 14.6 cm
Colour: Turquoise and pink
Issued: 1930-1949
Varieties: HN 1429, 2025

U.S.:	**$2,250.00**
Can.:	**$3,000.00**
U.K.:	**£1,350.00**

HN 1427
Darby
Designer: L. Harradine
Height: 5 ½", 14.0 cm
Colour: Pink and blue
Issued: 1930-1949
Varieties: HN 2024 (minor
           glaze difference)

U.S.:	**$500.00**
Can.:	**$675.00**
U.K.:	**£300.00**

HN 1428
Calumet
Designer: C. J. Noke
Height: 6", 15.2 cm
Colour: Brown, blue
           and yellow
Issued: 1930-1949
Varieties: HN 1689, 2068

U.S.:	**$1,650.00**
Can.:	**$2,200.00**
U.K.:	**£1,000.00**

HN 1429
The Gossips
Designer: L. Harradine
Height: 5 ¾", 14.6 cm
Colour: Red and cream
Issued: 1930-1949
Varieties: HN 1426, 2025

U.S.:	**$1,500.00**
Can.:	**$1,950.00**
U.K.:	**£ 900.00**

HN 1430
Phyllis
Style One
Designer: L. Harradine
Height: 9", 22.9 cm
Colour: Blue and pink
Issued: 1930-1938
Varieties: HN 1420, 1486, 1698

U.S.:	**$2,000.00**
Can.:	**$2,500.00**
U.K.:	**£1,200.00**

HN 1431
Patricia
Style One
Designer: L. Harradine
Height: 8 ½", 21.6 cm
Colour: Lavender
Issued: 1930-1949
Varieties: HN 1414, 1462, 1567

U.S.:	**$1,500.00**
Can.:	**$1,950.00**
U.K.:	**£ 900.00**

HN 1432
Barbara
Style One
Designer: L. Harradine
Height: 7 ¾", 19.7 cm
Colour: Lavender
Issued: 1930-1937
Varieties: HN 1421, 1461

U.S.:	**$2,000.00**
Can.:	**$2,750.00**
U.K.:	**£1,200.00**

HN 1433
The Little Bridesmaid
Style One
Designer: L. Harradine
Height: 5 ¼", 13.3 cm
Colour: Lavender and pink
Issued: 1930-1951
Varieties: HN 1434, 1530

U.S.:	$250.00
Can.:	$375.00
U.K.:	£150.00

HN 1434
The Little Bridesmaid
Style One
Designer: L. Harradine
Height: 5", 12.7 cm
Colour: Yellow-green
Issued: 1930-1949
Varieties: HN 1433, 1530

U.S.:	$400.00
Can.:	$550.00
U.K.:	£250.00

HN 1435
Betty
Style Two
Designer: L. Harradine
Height: 4 ½", 11.4 cm
Colour: Multicoloured
Issued: 1930-1936
Varieties: HN 1404, 1405, 1436

U.S.:	$4,250.00
Can.:	$5,500.00
U.K.:	£2,500.00

HN 1436
Betty
Style Two
Designer: L. Harradine
Height: 4 ½", 11.4 cm
Colour: Green
Issued: 1930-1936
Varieties: HN 1404, 1405, 1435

U.S.:	$4,250.00
Can.:	$5,500.00
U.K.:	£2,500.00

HN 1437
Sweet and Twenty
Style One
Designer: L. Harradine
Height: 6", 15.2 cm
Colour: Red
Issued: 1930-1938
Varieties: HN 1298, 1360, 1438,
          1549, 1563, 1649

U.S.:	$1,500.00
Can.:	$1,950.00
U.K.:	£ 900.00

HN 1438
Sweet and Twenty
Style One
Designer: L. Harradine
Height: 6", 15.2 cm
Colour: Multicoloured
Issued: 1930-1938
Varieties: HN 1298, 1360, 1437,
          1549, 1563, 1649

U.S.:	$1,500.00
Can.:	$1,950.00
U.K.:	£ 900.00

HN 1439
Columbine
Style One
Designer: L. Harradine
Height: 6", 15.2 cm
Colour: Mottled lavender
          and cream
Issued: 1930-1940
Varieties: HN 1296, 1297

U.S.:	$2,000.00
Can.:	$2,750.00
U.K.:	£1,200.00

HN 1440
Miss Demure
Designer: L. Harradine
Height: 7", 17.8 cm
Colour: Blue
Issued: 1930-1949
Varieties: HN 1402, 1463,
          1499, 1560

U.S.:	$1,100.00
Can.:	$1,500.00
U.K.:	£ 650.00

HN 1441
Child Study
Style One
Designer: L. Harradine
Height: 5", 12.7 cm
Colour: Cream, green
flowered base
Issued: 1931-1938
Varieties: HN 603A, 603B; also
known in flambé

U.S.: $1,500.00
Can.: $1,950.00
U.K.: £ 900.00

HN 1442
Child Study
Style Two
Designer: L. Harradine
Height: 6 ¼", 15.9 cm
Colour: Cream, green
flowered base
Issued: 1931-1938
Varieties: HN 604A, 604B, 1443

U.S.: $1,500.00
Can.: $1,950.00
U.K.: £ 900.00

HN 1443
Child Study
Style Two
Designer: L. Harradine
Height: 5", 12.7 cm
Colour: Cream, green
flowered base
Issued: 1931-1938
Varieties: HN 604A, 604B, 1442

U.S.: $1,500.00
Can.: $1,950.00
U.K.: £ 900.00

HN 1444
Pauline
Style One
Designer: L. Harradine
Height: 6", 15.2 cm
Colour: Blue
Issued: 1931-1940

U.S.: $750.00
Can.: $975.00
U.K.: £450.00

HN 1445
Biddy
Designer: L. Harradine
Height: 5 ½", 14.0 cm
Colour: Yellow-green
Issued: 1931-1937
Varieties: HN 1500, 1513

U.S.: $500.00
Can.: $675.00
U.K.: £300.00

HN 1446
Marietta
Designer: L. Harradine
Height: 8", 20.3 cm
Colour: Green and lavender
Issued: 1931-1940
Varieties: HN 1341, 1699

U.S.: $2,250.00
Can.: $3,000.00
U.K.: £1,350.00

HN 1447
Marigold
Designer: L. Harradine
Height: 6", 15.2 cm
Colour: Lavender
Issued: 1931-1949
Varieties: HN 1451, 1555

U.S.: $750.00
Can.: $975.00
U.K.: £450.00

HN 1448
Rita
Designer: L. Harradine
Height: 7", 17.8 cm
Colour: Red dress with
green shawl
Issued: 1931-1938
Varieties: HN 1450

U.S.: $1,750.00
Can.: $2,250.00
U.K.: £1,000.00

HN 1449
The Little Mistress
Designer: L. Harradine
Height: 5 ¾", 14.6 cm
Colour: Green and blue
Issued: 1931-1949

U.S.: $ 850.00
Can.: $1,100.00
U.K.:   £ 500.00

HN 1450
Rita
Designer: L. Harradine
Height: 7", 17.8 cm
Colour: Blue dress with
          red shawl
Issued: 1931-1938
Varieties: HN 1448

U.S.: $1,700.00
Can.: $2,250.00
U.K.:   £1,000.00

HN 1451
Marigold
Designer: L. Harradine
Height: 6", 15.2 cm
Colour: Yellow
Issued: 1931-1938
Varieties: HN 1447, 1555

U.S.: $1,250.00
Can.: $1,600.00
U.K.:   £ 750.00

HN 1452
A Victorian Lady
Style one
Designer: L. Harradine
Height: 7 ¾", 19.7 cm
Colour: Green
Issued: 1931-1949
Varieties: HN 726, 727, 728,
          736, 739, 740, 742,
          745, 1208, 1258,
          1276, 1277, 1345,
          1529

U.S.: $ 850.00
Can.: $1,100.00
U.K.:   £ 500.00

HN 1453
Sweet Anne
Style One
Designer: L. Harradine
Height: 7", 17.8 cm
Colour: Green
Issued: 1931-1949
Varieties: HN 1318, 1330, 1331,
          1496, 1631, 1701

U.S.: $ 850.00
Can.: $1,100.00
U.K.:   £ 500.00

HN 1454
Negligée
Designer: L. Harradine
Height: 5", 12.7 cm
Colour: Pink
Issued: 1931-1936
Varieties: HN 1219, 1228,
          1272, 1273

U.S.: $3,250.00
Can.: $4,500.00
U.K.:   £2,000.00

HN 1455
Molly Malone
Designer: L. Harradine
Height: 7", 17.8 cm
Colour: Red and brown
Issued: 1931-1937

U.S.: $6,000.00
Can.: $8,000.00
U.K.:   £3,600.00

HN 1456
The Butterfly Woman
Designer: L. Harradine
Height: 6 ½", 16.5 cm
Colour: Lavender and green
Issued: 1931-1940
Varieties: Also called 'Butterfly'
          HN 719, 720, 730,
          1203

U.S.: $4,500.00
Can.: $6,000.00
U.K.:   £2,700.00

HN 1457
All-A-Blooming
Designer: L. Harradine
Height: 6 ½", 16.5 cm
Colour: Blue
Issued: 1931-1938
Varieties: HN 1466

U.S.:	**$3,000.00**
Can.:	**$4,000.00**
U.K.:	**£1,800.00**

HN 1458
Monica
Style One
Designer: L. Harradine
Height: 4", 10.1 cm
Colour: Flowered cream dress
Issued: 1931-1949
Varieties: HN 1459, 1467, 3617

U.S.:	**$600.00**
Can.:	**$800.00**
U.K.:	**£350.00**

HN 1459
Monica
Style One
Designer: L. Harradine
Height: 4", 10.1 cm
Colour: Lavender
Issued: 1931-1949
Varieties: HN 1458, 1467, 3617

U.S.:	**$600.00**
Can.:	**$800.00**
U.K.:	**£350.00**

HN 1460
Paisley Shawl
Style One
Designer: L. Harradine
Height: 8 ¼", 21.0 cm
Colour: Green
Issued: 1931-1949
Varieties: HN 1392, 1707, 1739, 1987

U.S.:	**$ 900.00**
Can.:	**$1,250.00**
U.K.:	**£ 550.00**

HN 1461
Barbara
Style One
Designer: L. Harradine
Height: 7 ¾", 19.7 cm
Colour: Green
Issued: 1931-1937
Varieties: HN 1421, 1432

U.S.:	**$2,000.00**
Can.:	**$2,750.00**
U.K.:	**£1,200.00**

HN 1462
Patricia
Style One
Designer: L. Harradine
Height: 8", 20.3 cm
Colour: Green
Issued: 1931-1938
Varieties: HN 1414, 1431, 1567

U.S.:	**$1,500.00**
Can.:	**$1,950.00**
U.K.:	**£ 900.00**

HN 1463
Miss Demure
Designer: L. Harradine
Height: 7", 17.8 cm
Colour: Green
Issued: 1931-1949
Varieties: HN 1402, 1440, 1499, 1560

U.S.:	**$1,250.00**
Can.:	**$1,650.00**
U.K.:	**£ 750.00**

HN 1464
The Carpet Seller
(Hand Open)
Style One
Designer: L. Harradine
Height: 9 ¼", 23.5 cm
Colour: Green and orange
Issued: 1929-Unknown
Varieties: HN 1464A (hand closed)

U.S.:	**$1,000.00**
Can.:	**$1,300.00**
U.K.:	**£ 600.00**

Earthenware

HN 1464A
The Carpet Seller
(Hand Closed)
Style One
Designer: L. Harradine
Height: 9", 22.9 cm
Colour: Green and orange
Issued: Unknown-1969
Varieties: HN 1464 (hand open)

U.S.:	**$350.00**
Can.:	**$450.00**
U.K.:	**£225.00**

Porcelain

HN 1465
Lady Clare
Designer: L. Harradine
Height: 7 ¾", 19.7 cm
Colour: Red
Issued: 1931-1937

U.S.:	**$1,400.00**
Can.:	**$1,850.00**
U.K.:	**£ 850.00**

HN 1466
All-A-Blooming
Designer: L. Harradine
Height: 6 ½", 16.5 cm
Colour: Purple, green and red
Issued: 1931-1938
Varieties: HN 1457

U.S.:	**$3,000.00**
Can.:	**$4,000.00**
U.K.:	**£1,750.00**

HN 1467
Monica
Style One
Designer: L. Harradine
Height: 4", 10.1 cm
Colour: Flowered purple dress
Issued: 1931-1995
Varieties: HN 1458, 1459, 3617

U.S.:	**$175.00**
Can.:	**$225.00**
U.K.:	**£100.00**

HN 1468
Pamela
Style One
Designer: L. Harradine
Height: 7 ½", 19.1 cm
Colour: Blue
Issued: 1931-1937
Varieties: HN 1469, 1564

U.S.:	**$2,000.00**
Can.:	**$2,500.00**
U.K.:	**£1,200.00**

HN 1469
Pamela
Style One
Designer: L. Harradine
Height: 7 ½", 19.1 cm
Colour: Yellow
Issued: 1931-1937
Varieties: HN 1468, 1564

U.S.:	**$2,000.00**
Can.:	**$2,500.00**
U.K.:	**£1,200.00**

HN 1470
Chloe
Style One
Designer: L. Harradine
Height: 5 ½", 14.0 cm
Colour: Yellow and purple
Issued: 1931-1949
Varieties: HN 1476, 1479,
           1498, 1765, 1956

U.S.:	**$ 800.00**
Can.:	**$1,100.00**
U.K.:	**£ 475.00**

HN 1471
Annette
Style One
Designer: L. Harradine
Height: 6 ¼", 15.9 cm
Colour: Blue and white
Issued: 1931-1938
Varieties: HN 1472, 1550

U.S.:	**$ 850.00**
Can.:	**$1,150.00**
U.K.:	**£ 500.00**

HN 1472
Annette
Style One
Designer: L. Harradine
Height: 6", 15.2 cm
Colour: Green
Issued: 1931-1949
Varieties: HN 1471, 1550

U.S.:	$ 850.00
Can.:	$1,150.00
U.K.:	£ 500.00

HN 1473
Dreamland
Designer: L. Harradine
Height: 4 ¾", 12.0 cm
Colour: Lavender
Issued: 1931-1937
Varieties: HN 1481

U.S.:	$6,000.00
Can.:	$8,000.00
U.K.:	£3,600.00

HN 1474
In the Stocks
Style One
Designer: L. Harradine
Height: 5", 12.7 cm
Colour: Red and brown
Issued: 1931-1938
Varieties: HN 1475; also called 'Love in the Stocks' and 'Love Locked In'

U.S.:	$4,000.00
Can.:	$5,250.00
U.K.:	£2,400.00

HN 1475
In the Stocks
Style One
Designer: L. Harradine
Height: 5 ¼", 13.3 cm
Colour: Green
Issued: 1931-1937
Varieties: HN 1474; also called 'Love in the Stocks' and 'Love Locked In'

U.S.:	$4,000.00
Can.:	$5,250.00
U.K.:	£2,400.00

HN 1476
Chloe
Style One
Designer: L. Harradine
Height: 5 ½", 14.0 cm
Colour: Blue
Issued: 1931-1938
Varieties: HN 1470, 1479, 1498, 1765, 1956

U.S.:	$450.00
Can.:	$600.00
U.K.:	£275.00

HN 1477 not issued.

HN 1478
Sylvia
Designer: L. Harradine
Height: 10 ½", 26.7 cm
Colour: Orange and blue
Issued: 1931-1938

U.S.:	$1,100.00
Can.:	$1,500.00
U.K.:	£ 650.00

Earthenware

HN 1479
Chloe
Style One
Designer: L. Harradine
Height: 5 ½", 14.0 cm
Colour: Lavender
Issued: 1931-1949
Varieties: HN 1470, 1476, 1498, 1765, 1956

U.S.:	$1,000.00
Can.:	$1,300.00
U.K.:	£ 600.00

HN 1480
Newhaven Fishwife
Designer: H. Fenton
Height: 7 ¾", 19.7 cm
Colour: Red, white and black
Issued: 1931-1937

U.S.:	$6,500.00
Can.:	$8,500.00
U.K.:	£4,000.00

HN 1481
Dreamland
Designer: L. Harradine
Height: 4 ¾", 12.0 cm
Colour: Orange and purple
Issued: 1931-1937
Varieties: HN 1473

U.S.:	**$6,000.00**
Can.:	**$8,000.00**
U.K.:	**£3,500.00**

HN 1482
Pearly Boy
Style One
Designer: L. Harradine
Height: 5 ½", 14.0 cm
Colour: Brown suit, red vest
Issued: 1931-1949
Varieties: HN 1547

U.S.:	**$400.00**
Can.:	**$525.00**
U.K.:	**£225.00**

HN 1483
Pearly Girl
Style One
Designer: L. Harradine
Height: 5 ½", 14.0 cm
Colour: Orange and brown
Issued: 1931-1949
Varieties: HN 1548

U.S.:	**$400.00**
Can.:	**$525.00**
U.K.:	**£225.00**

HN 1484
Jennifer
Style One
Designer: L. Harradine
Height: 6 ½", 16.5 cm
Colour: Yellow flowers on
             cream dress
Issued: 1931-1949

U.S.:	**$1,100.00**
Can.:	**$1,500.00**
U.K.:	**£ 650.00**

HN 1485
Greta
Designer: L. Harradine
Height: 5 ½", 14.0 cm
Colour: Lavender
Issued: 1931-1953

U.S.:	**$500.00**
Can.:	**$650.00**
U.K.:	**£300.00**

HN 1486
Phyllis
Style One
Designer: L. Harradine
Height: 9", 22.9 cm
Colour: Blue and pink
Issued: 1931-1949
Varieties: HN 1420, 1430, 1698

U.S.:	**$1,600.00**
Can.:	**$2,250.00**
U.K.:	**£ 750.00**

HN 1487
Suzette
Designer: L. Harradine
Height: 7 ½", 19.1 cm
Colour: Flowered pink dress
Issued: 1931-1950
Varieties: HN 1577, 1585,
             1696, 2026

U.S.:	**$700.00**
Can.:	**$900.00**
U.K.:	**£375.00**

HN 1488
Gloria
Style One
Designer: L. Harradine
Height: 7 ¼", 18.4 cm
Colour: Green-blue
Issued: 1932-1938
Varieties: HN 1700

U.S.:	**$3,600.00**
Can.:	**$4,500.00**
U.K.:	**£1,800.00**

HN 1489
Marie
Style Two
Designer: L. Harradine
Height: 4 ½", 11.4 cm
Colour: Pale green
Issued: 1932-1949
Varieties: HN 1370, 1388, 1417,
           1531, 1635, 1655

U.S.: $350.00
Can.: $475.00
U.K.:   £200.00

HN 1490
Dorcas
Designer: L. Harradine
Height: 7", 17.8 cm
Colour: Light blue
Issued: 1932-1938
Varieties: HN 1491, 1558

U.S.: $1,000.00
Can.: $1,300.00
U.K.:   £ 600.00

HN 1491
Dorcas
Designer: L. Harradine
Height: 6 ¾", 17.2 cm
Colour: Pale green and
           lavender
Issued: 1932-1938
Varieties: HN 1490, 1558

U.S.: $1,000.00
Can.: $1,300.00
U.K.:   £ 600.00

HN 1492
Old Lavender Seller
Designer: L. Harradine
Height: 6", 15.2 cm
Colour: Green and orange
Issued: 1932-1949
Varieties: HN 1571

U.S.: $1,600.00
Can.: $2,250.00
U.K.:   £ 950.00

Earthenware

HN 1493
The Potter
Designer: C. J. Noke
Height: 7", 17.8 cm
Colour: Brown
Issued: 1932 -1992
Varieties: HN 1518, 1522

U.S.: $450.00
Can.: $600.00
U.K.:   £270.00

HN 1494
Gwendolen
Designer: L. Harradine
Height: 6", 15.2 cm
Colour: Green and pink
Issued: 1932-1940
Varieties: HN 1503, 1570

U.S.: $2,000.00
Can.: $3,000.00
U.K.:   £1,250.00

HN 1495
Priscilla
Style One
Designer: L. Harradine
Height: 8", 20.3 cm
Colour: Blue
Issued: 1932-1949
Varieties: HN 1337, 1340,
           1501, 1559

U.S.: $1,350.00
Can.: $1,850.00
U.K.:   £ 800.00

HN 1496
Sweet Anne
Style One
Designer: L. Harradine
Height: 7", 17.8 cm
Colour: Purple
Issued: 1932-1967
Varieties: HN 1318, 1330, 1331,
           1453, 1631, 1701

U.S.: $325.00
Can.: $450.00
U.K.:   £200.00

HN 1497
Rosamund
Style Two
Designer: L. Harradine
Height: 8 ½", 21.6 cm
Colour: Red
Issued: 1932-1938
Varieties: HN 1551
U.S.: $3,500.00
Can.: $4,500.00
U.K.: £2,000.00

HN 1498
Chloe
Style One
Designer: L. Harradine
Height: 6", 15.2 cm
Colour: Peach-yellow
Issued: 1932-1938
Varieties: HN 1470, 1476,
1479, 1765, 1956
U.S.: $1,000.00
Can.: $1,300.00
U.K.: £ 600.00

HN 1499
Miss Demure
Designer: L. Harradine
Height: 7", 17.8 cm
Colour: Pink and yellow
Issued: 1932-1938
Varieties: HN 1402, 1440,
1463, 1560
U.S.: $1,100.00
Can.: $1,500.00
U.K.: £ 650.00

HN 1500
Biddy
Designer: L. Harradine
Height: 5 ½", 14.0 cm
Colour: Yellow
Issued: 1932-1937
Varieties: HN 1445, 1513
U.S.: $ 800.00
Can.: $1,000.00
U.K.: £ 500.00

HN 1501
Priscilla
Style One
Designer: L. Harradine
Height: 8", 20.3 cm
Colour: Orange
Issued: 1932-1938
Varieties: HN 1337, 1340,
1495, 1559
U.S.: $1,350.00
Can.: $1,850.00
U.K.: £ 800.00

HN 1502
Lucy Ann
Designer: L. Harradine
Height: 5 ¼", 13.3 cm
Colour: Lavender
Issued: 1932-1951
Varieties: HN 1565
U.S.: $450.00
Can.: $600.00
U.K.: £270.00

HN 1503
Gwendolen
Designer: L. Harradine
Height: 6", 15.2 cm
Colour: Orange and yellow
Issued: 1932-1949
Varieties: HN 1494, 1570
U.S.: $2,000.00
Can.: $2,750.00
U.K.: £1,250.00

HN 1504
Sweet Maid
Style One
Designer: L. Harradine
Height: 8", 20.3 cm
Colour: Lavender and blue
Issued: 1932-1936
Varieties: HN 1505
U.S.: $2,250.00
Can.: $3,000.00
U.K.: £1,350.00

HN 1505
Sweet Maid
Style One
Designer: L. Harradine
Height: 8", 20.3 cm
Colour: Red and green
Issued: 1932-1936
Varieties: HN 1504

U.S.:	$2,250.00
Can.:	$3,000.00
U.K.:	£1,250.00

HN 1506
Rose
Style One
Designer: L. Harradine
Height: 4 ½", 11.4 cm
Colour: Yellow
Issued: 1932-1938
Varieties: IIN 1368, 1387, 1416, 1654, 2123

U.S.:	$350.00
Can.:	$475.00
U.K.:	£200.00

HN 1507
Pantalettes
Style One
Designer: L. Harradine
Height: 7 ¾", 19.7 cm
Colour: Yellow
Issued: 1932-1949
Varieties: HN 1362, 1412, 1709

U.S.:	$1,400.00
Can.:	$1,875.00
U.K.:	£ 850.00

HN 1508
Helen
Style One
Designer: L. Harradine
Height: 8", 20.3 cm
Colour: Flowered green dress
Issued: 1932-1938
Varieties: HN 1509, 1572

U.S.:	$2,250.00
Can.:	$3,000.00
U.K.:	£1,350.00

HN 1509
Helen
Style One
Designer: L. Harradine
Height: 8", 20.3 cm
Colour: Flowered blue-yellow dress
Issued: 1932-1938
Varieties: HN 1508, 1572

U.S.:	$2,250.00
Can.:	$3,000.00
U.K.:	£1,350.00

HN 1510
Constance
Style One
Designer: L. Harradine
Height: 6 ¾", 17.1 cm
Colour: Yellow-purple
Issued: 1932-1936
Varieties: HN 1511

U.S.:	$2,250.00
Can.:	$3,000.00
U.K.:	£1,350.00

HN 1511
Constance
Style One
Designer: L. Harradine
Height: 6 ¾", 17.1 cm
Colour: Lavender
Issued: 1932-1936
Varieties: HN 1510

U.S.:	$2,250.00
Can.:	$3,000.00
U.K.:	£1,350.00

HN 1512
Kathleen
Style One
Designer: L. Harradine
Height: 7 ½", 19.1 cm
Colour: Lavender and blue
Issued: 1932-1938
Varieties: HN 1252, 1253, 1275, 1279, 1291, 1357

U.S.:	$1,400.00
Can.:	$2,000.00
U.K.:	£ 850.00

HN 1513
Biddy
Designer: L. Harradine
Height: 5 ½", 14.0 cm
Colour: Pink dress with
          mauve shawl
Issued: 1932-1937
Varieties: HN 1445, 1500

U.S.:   **$300.00**
Can.:   **$400.00**
U.K.:   **£200.00**

HN 1514
Dolly Vardon
Designer: L. Harradine
Height: 8 ½", 21.6 cm
Colour: Multicoloured
Issued: 1932-1938
Varieties: HN 1515

U.S.:   **$2,250.00**
Can.:   **$3,000.00**
U.K.:   **£1,350.00**

HN 1515
Dolly Vardon
Designer: L. Harradine
Height: 8 ½", 21.6 cm
Colour: Red and lavender
Issued: 1932-1949
Varieties: HN 1514

U.S.:   **$2,000.00**
Can.:   **$2,750.00**
U.K.:   **£1,200.00**

HN 1516
Cicely
Designer: L. Harradine
Height: 5 ¾", 14.6 cm
Colour: Purple and red
Issued: 1932-1949

U.S.:   **$2,000.00**
Can.:   **$2,750.00**
U.K.:   **£1,200.00**

HN 1517
Veronica
Style One
Designer: L. Harradine
Height: 8", 20.3 cm
Colour: Red-cream
Issued: 1932-1951
Varieties: HN 1519, 1650, 1943

U.S.:   **$500.00**
Can.:   **$675.00**
U.K.:   **£300.00**

HN 1518
The Potter
Designer: C. J. Noke
Height: 6 ¾", 17.2 cm
Colour: Green
Issued: 1932-1949
Varieties: HN 1493, 1522

U.S.:   **$2,000.00**
Can.:   **$2,750.00**
U.K.:   **£1,200.00**

HN 1519
Veronica
Style One
Designer: L. Harradine
Height: 8", 20.3 cm
Colour: Blue-cream
Issued: 1932-1938
Varieties: HN 1517, 1650, 1943

U.S.:   **$1,000.00**
Can.:   **$1,350.00**
U.K.:   **£ 600.00**

HN 1520
Eugene
Designer: L. Harradine
Height: 5 ¾", 14.6 cm
Colour: Green and pink
Issued: 1932-1936
Varieties: HN 1521

U.S.:   **$2,250.00**
Can.:   **$3,000.00**
U.K.:   **£1,350.00**

HN 1521
Eugene
Designer: L. Harradine
Height: 5", 12.7 cm
Colour: Orange, yellow and white
Issued: 1932-1936
Varieties: HN 1520

U.S.:	**$2,250.00**
Can.:	**$3,000.00**
U.K.:	**£1,350.00**

HN 1522
The Potter
Designer: L. Harradine
Height: 6 ¾", 17.2 cm
Colour: Green and purple
Issued: 1932-1949
Varieties: HN 1493, 1518

U.S.:	**$1,900.00**
Can.:	**$2,500.00**
U.K.:	**£1,150.00**

HN 1523
Lisette
Designer: L. Harradine
Height: 5 ¼", 13.3 cm
Colour: Yellow and red
Issued: 1932-1936
Varieties: HN 1524, 1684

U.S.:	**$2,500.00**
Can.:	**$3,250.00**
U.K.:	**£1,500.00**

HN 1524
Lisette
Designer: L. Harradine
Height: 5 ¼", 13.3 cm
Colour: Blue, pink and yellow
Issued: 1932-1936
Varieties: HN 1523, 1684

U.S.:	**$2,500.00**
Can.:	**$3,250.00**
U.K.:	**£1,500.00**

HN 1525
Clarissa
Style One
Designer: L. Harradine
Height: 10", 25.4 cm
Colour: Green and red
Issued: 1932-1938
Varieties: HN 1687

U.S.:	**$1,200.00**
Can.:	**$1,550.00**
U.K.:	**£ 725.00**

Earthenware

HN 1526
Anthea
Designer: L. Harradine
Height: 6 ½", 16.5 cm
Colour: Green and blue
Issued: 1932-1940
Varieties: HN 1527, 1669

U.S.:	**$2,000.00**
Can.:	**$2,600.00**
U.K.:	**£1,200.00**

HN 1527
Anthea
Designer: L. Harradine
Height: 6 ½", 16.5 cm
Colour: Lavender
Issued: 1932-1940
Varieties: HN 1526, 1669

U.S.:	**$2,000.00**
Can.:	**$2,600.00**
U.K.:	**£1,200.00**

HN 1528
Bluebeard
Style Two
Designer: L. Harradine
Height: 11 ½", 29.2 cm
Colour: Red and purple
Issued: 1932-1949
Varieties: HN 2105

U.S.:	**$1,500.00**
Can.:	**$1,950.00**
U.K.:	**£ 900.00**

Earthenware

HN 1529
A Victorian Lady
Style One
Designer: L. Harradine
Height: 7 ¾", 19.7 cm
Colour: Green and orange
Issued: 1932-1938
Varieties: HN 726, 727, 728,
  736, 739, 740, 742,
  745, 1208, 1258, 1276,
  1277, 1345, 1452

U.S.:	**$1,000.00**
Can.:	**$1,300.00**
U.K.:	**£ 600.00**

HN 1530
The Little Bridesmaid
Style One
Designer: L. Harradine
Height: 5", 12.7 cm
Colour: Yellow and green
Issued: 1932-1938
Varieties: HN 1433, 1434

U.S.:	**$750.00**
Can.:	**$975.00**
U.K.:	**£450.00**

HN 1531
Marie
Style Two
Designer: L. Harradine
Height: 4 ½", 11.4 cm
Colour: Yellow-green
Issued: 1932-1938
Varieties: HN 1370, 1388, 1417,
  1489, 1635, 1655

U.S.:	**$400.00**
Can.:	**$525.00**
U.K.:	**£250.00**

HN 1532
Fairy
Style Two
Designer: L. Harradine
Height: 4", 10.1 cm
Colour: Multicoloured
Issued: 1932-1938
Varieties: HN 1374, 1380

U.S.:	**$3,250.00**
Can.:	**$4,500.00**
U.K.:	**£2,000.00**

HN 1533
Fairy
Style Three
Designer: L. Harradine
Height: 3", 7.6 cm
Colour: Multicoloured
Issued: 1932-1938
Varieties: HN 1375, 1395

U.S.:	**$3,250.00**
Can.:	**$4,500.00**
U.K.:	**£2,000.00**

HN 1534
Fairy
Style Seven
Designer: L. Harradine
Height: 2 ½", 6.3 cm
Colour: Yellow flowers
Issued: 1932-1938
Varieties: HN 1379, 1394

U.S.:	**$1,800.00**
Can.:	**$2,500.00**
U.K.:	**£1,100.00**

HN 1535
Fairy
Style Six
Designer: L. Harradine
Height: 2 ½", 6.3 cm
Colour: Yellow and blue
  flowers
Issued: 1932-1938
Varieties: HN 1378, 1396

U.S.:	**$1,800.00**
Can.:	**$2,500.00**
U.K.:	**£1,100.00**

HN 1536
Fairy
Style Four
Designer: L. Harradine
Height: 2 ½", 6.3 cm
Colour: Yellow and blue
  flowers
Issued: 1932-1938
Varieties: HN 1376

U.S.:	**$1,650.00**
Can.:	**$2,250.00**
U.K.:	**£1,000.00**

HN 1537
Janet
Style One
Designer: L. Harradine
Height: 6 ¼", 15.9 cm
Colour: Red
Issued: 1932-1995
Varieties: HN 1538, 1652, 1737

U.S.:	**$225.00**
Can.:	**$300.00**
U.K.:	**£125.00**

HN 1538
Janet
Style One
Designer: L. Harradine
Height: 6 ¼", 15.9 cm
Colour: Purple
Issued: 1932-1949
Varieties: HN 1537, 1652, 1737

U.S.:	**$1,000.00**
Can.:	**$1,300.00**
U.K.:	**£ 600.00**

HN 1539
A Saucy Nymph
Designer: L. Harradine
Height: 4 ½", 11.4 cm
Colour: Green base
Issued: 1933-1949
Varieties: Also with pearl glaze

U.S.:	**$750.00**
Can.:	**$950.00**
U.K.:	**£450.00**

HN 1540
'Little Child So Rare and Sweet'
Style One
Designer: L. Harradine
Height: 5", 12.7 cm
Colour: Green base
Issued: 1933-1949

U.S.:	**$1,200.00**
Can.:	**$1,550.00**
U.K.:	**£ 725.00**

HN 1541
'Happy Joy, Baby Boy'
Designer: L. Harradine
Height: 6 ¼", 15.9 cm
Colour: Green base
Issued: 1933-1949

U.S.:	**$1,500.00**
Can.:	**$1,950.00**
U.K.:	**£ 900.00**

HN 1542
'Little Child So Rare and Sweet'
Style Two
Designer: L. Harradine
Height: 5", 12.7 cm
Colour: Blue base
Issued: 1933-1949

U.S.:	**$1,250.00**
Can.:	**$1,600.00**
U.K.:	**£ 750.00**

HN 1543
'Dancing Eyes and Sunny Hair'
Style One
Designer: L. Harradine
Height: 5", 12.7 cm
Colour: Blue base
Issued: 1933-1949

U.S.:	**$1,250.00**
Can.:	**$1,600.00**
U.K.:	**£ 750.00**

HN 1544
'Do You Wonder Where Fairies Are That Folk Declare Have Vanished'
First Version
Designer: L. Harradine
Height: 5", 12.7 cm
Colour: Lavender with
         yellow base
Issued: 1933-1949

U.S.:	**$1,600.00**
Can.:	**$2,000.00**
U.K.:	**£ 950.00**

HN 1545
'Called Love, A Little Boy, Almost Naked, Wanton, Blind, Cruel Now, and Then as Kind'
Designer: L. Harradine
Height: 3 ½", 8.9 cm
Colour: Tan base
Issued: 1933-1949

U.S.:	**$1,600.00**
Can.:	**$2,000.00**
U.K.:	**£ 950.00**

HN 1546
'Here A Little Child I Stand'
First Version
Designer: L. Harradine
Height: 6 ¼", 15.9 cm
Colour: Lavender with
           green base
Issued: 1933-1949

U.S.:	**$1,500.00**
Can.:	**$1,950.00**
U.K.:	**£ 900.00**

HN 1547
Pearly Boy
Style One
Designer: L. Harradine
Height: 5 ½", 14.0 cm
Colour: Green and purple
Issued: 1933-1949
Varieties: HN 1482

U.S.:	**$ 850.00**
Can.:	**$1,100.00**
U.K.:	**£ 500.00**

HN 1548
Pearly Girl
Style One
Designer: L. Harradine
Height: 5 ½", 14.0 cm
Colour: Green and purple
Issued: 1933-1949
Varieties: HN 1483

U.S.:	**$ 850.00**
Can.:	**$1,100.00**
U.K.:	**£ 500.00**

HN 1549
Sweet and Twenty
Style One
Designer: L. Harradine
Height: 6", 15.2 cm
Colour: Multicoloured
Issued: 1933-1949
Varieties: HN 1298, 1360, 1437,
           1438, 1563, 1649

U.S.:	**$1,250.00**
Can.:	**$1,600.00**
U.K.:	**£ 750.00**

HN 1550
Annette
Style One
Designer: L. Harradine
Height: 6 ¼", 15.9 cm
Colour: Red and green
Issued: 1933-1949
Varieties: HN 1471, 1472

U.S.:	**$ 800.00**
Can.:	**$1,000.00**
U.K.:	**£ 475.00**

HN 1551
Rosamund
Style Two
Designer: L. Harradine
Height: 8 ½", 21.6 cm
Colour: Blue
Issued: 1933-1938
Varieties: HN 1497

U.S.:	**$4,750.00**
Can.:	**$6,000.00**
U.K.:	**£2,750.00**

HN 1552
Pinkie
Designer: L. Harradine
Height: 5", 12.7 cm
Colour: Pink
Issued: 1933-1938
Varieties: HN 1553

U.S.:	**$2,000.00**
Can.:	**$2,500.00**
U.K.:	**£1,200.00**

HN 1553
Pinkie
Designer: L. Harradine
Height: 5", 12.7 cm
Colour: Yellow and blue
Issued: 1933-1938
Varieties: HN 1552

U.S.:	$2,000.00
Can.:	$2,500.00
U.K.:	£1,300.00

HN 1554
Charley's Aunt
Style Two
Designer: H. Fenton
Height: 7 ½", 19.1 cm
Colour: Purple
Issued: 1933-1938
Varieties: HN 1411

U.S.:	$2,250.00
Can.:	$3,000.00
U.K.:	£1,350.00

HN 1555
Marigold
Designer: L. Harradine
Height: 6", 15.2 cm
Colour: Pink and blue
Issued: 1933-1949
Varieties: HN 1447, 1451

U.S.:	$ 950.00
Can.:	$1,200.00
U.K.:	£ 575.00

HN 1556
Rosina
Designer: L. Harradine
Height: 5 ¾", 14.6 cm
Colour: Lavender
Issued: 1933-1937
Varieties: HN 1358, 1364

U.S.:	$1,800.00
Can.:	$2,350.00
U.K.:	£1,050.00

HN 1557
Lady Fayre
Designer: L. Harradine
Height: 5 ¾", 14.6 cm
Colour: Purple
Issued: 1933-1938
Varieties: HN 1265

U.S.:	$2,750.00
Can.:	$3,500.00
U.K.:	£1,650.00

HN 1558
Dorcas
Designer: L. Harradine
Height: 6 ¾", 17.2 cm
Colour: Purple
Issued: 1933-1952
Varieties: HN 1490, 1491

U.S.:	$450.00
Can.:	$700.00
U.K.:	£275.00

HN 1559
Priscilla
Style One
Designer: L. Harradine
Height: 8", 20.3 cm
Colour: Purple
Issued: 1933-1949
Varieties: HN 1337, 1340, 1495, 1501

U.S.:	$1,500.00
Can.:	$1,950.00
U.K.:	£ 900.00

HN 1560
Miss Demure
Designer: L. Harradine
Height: 7", 17.8 cm
Colour: Blue dress with red shawl
Issued: 1933-1949
Varieties: HN 1402, 1440, 1463, 1499

U.S.:	$1,200.00
Can.:	$1,500.00
U.K.:	£ 725.00

HN 1561
Willy-Won't He
Designer: L. Harradine
Height: 6", 15.2 cm
Colour: Blue, pink and white
Issued: 1933-1949
Varieties: HN 1584, 2150

U.S.:	**$1,850.00**
Can.:	**$2,500.00**
U.K.:	**£1,100.00**

HN 1562
Gretchen
Designer: L. Harradine
Height: 7 ¾", 19.7 cm
Colour: Purple and white
Issued: 1933-1940
Varieties: HN 1397

U.S.:	**$1,650.00**
Can.:	**$2,250.00**
U.K.:	**£ 995.00**

HN 1563
Sweet and Twenty
Style One
Designer: L. Harradine
Height: 6", 15.2 cm
Colour: Black and light pink
Issued: 1933-1938
Varieties: HN 1298, 1360, 1437,
          1438, 1549, 1649

U.S.:	**$1,500.00**
Can.:	**$1,950.00**
U.K.:	**£ 900.00**

HN 1564
Pamela
Style One
Designer: L. Harradine
Height: 8", 20.3 cm
Colour: Pink
Issued: 1933-1937
Varieties: HN 1468, 1469

U.S.:	**$2,000.00**
Can.:	**$2,500.00**
U.K.:	**£1,200.00**

HN 1565
Lucy Ann
Designer: L. Harradine
Height: 5 ¼", 13.3 cm
Colour: Light green
Issued: 1933-1938
Varieties: HN 1502

U.S.:	**$ 900.00**
Can.:	**$1,200.00**
U.K.:	**£ 550.00**

HN 1566
Estelle
Designer: L. Harradine
Height: 8", 20.3 cm
Colour: Lavender
Issued: 1933-1940
Varieties: HN 1802

U.S.:	**$2,250.00**
Can.:	**$3,000.00**
U.K.:	**£1,350.00**

HN 1567
Patricia
Style One
Designer: L. Harradine
Height: 8 ½", 21.6 cm
Colour: Red
Issued: 1933-1949
Varieties: HN 1414, 1431, 1462

U.S.:	**$2,250.00**
Can.:	**$3,000.00**
U.K.:	**£1,350.00**

HN 1568
Charmian
Designer: L. Harradine
Height: 6 ½", 16.5 cm
Colour: Red and cream
Issued: 1933-1940
Varieties: HN 1569, 1651

U.S.:	**$1,700.00**
Can.:	**$2,250.00**
U.K.:	**£1,000.00**

HN 1569
Charmian
Designer: L. Harradine
Height: 6 ½", 16.5 cm
Colour: Cream and lavender
Issued: 1933-1940
Varieties: HN 1568, 1651

U.S.:	**$1,700.00**
Can.:	**$2,250.00**
U.K.:	**£1,000.00**

HN 1570
Gwendolen
Designer: L. Harradine
Height: 6", 15.2 cm
Colour: Rose-pink
Issued: 1933-1949
Varieties: HN 1494, 1503

U.S.:	**$2,000.00**
Can.:	**$3,000.00**
U.K.:	**£1,250.00**

HN 1571
Old Lavender Seller
Designer: L. Harradine
Height: 6 ½", 16.5 cm
Colour: Orange and black
Issued: 1933-1949
Varieties: HN 1492

U.S.:	**$1,650.00**
Can.:	**$2,250.00**
U.K.:	**£1,000.00**

HN 1572
Helen
Style One
Designer: L. Harradine
Height: 8", 20.3 cm
Colour: Red
Issued: 1933-1938
Varieties: HN 1508, 1509

U.S.:	**$2,250.00**
Can.:	**$3,000.00**
U.K.:	**£1,350.00**

HN 1573
Rhoda
Designer: L. Harradine
Height: 10 ¼", 26.7 cm
Colour: Green and orange
Issued: 1933-1940
Varieties: HN 1574, 1688

U.S.:	**$1,000.00**
Can.:	**$1,500.00**
U.K.:	**£ 600.00**

Earthenware

HN 1574
Rhoda
Designer: L. Harradine
Height: 10 ¼", 26.7 cm
Colour: Burgundy and orange
Issued: 1933-1940
Varieties: HN 1573, 1688

U.S.:	**$1,000.00**
Can.:	**$1,350.00**
U.K.:	**£ 600.00**

Earthenware

HN 1575
Daisy
Style One
Designer: L. Harradine
Height: 3 ¾", 9.5 cm
Colour: Blue dress with flowers
Issued: 1933-1949
Varieties: HN 1961

U.S.:	**$750.00**
Can.:	**$975.00**
U.K.:	**£450.00**

HN 1576
Tildy
Designer: L. Harradine
Height: 5", 12.7 cm
Colour: Red and pink-cream
Issued: 1933-1939
Varieties: HN 1859

U.S.:	**$2,000.00**
Can.:	**$2,500.00**
U.K.:	**£1,200.00**

HN 1577
Suzette
Designer: L. Harradine
Height: 7 ½", 19.1 cm
Colour: Flowered lavender
           dress
Issued: 1933-1949
Varieties: HN 1487, 1585,
           1696, 2026

U.S.: $1,250.00
Can.: $1,600.00
U.K.:   £ 750.00

HN 1578
The Hinged Parasol
Designer: L. Harradine
Height: 6 ½", 16.5 cm
Colour: Red and yellow
           dress with spots
Issued: 1933-1949
Varieties: HN 1579

U.S.: $1,800.00
Can.: $2,350.00
U.K.:   £1,075.00

HN 1579
The Hinged Parasol
Designer: L. Harradine
Height: 6 ½", 16.5 cm
Colour: Red and purple
Issued: 1933-1949
Varieties: HN 1578

U.S.: $1,800.00
Can.: $2,350.00
U.K.:   £1,075.00

HN 1580
Rosebud
Style One
Designer: L. Harradine
Height: 3", 7.6 cm
Colour: Pink
Issued: 1933-1938
Varieties: HN 1581

U.S.: $1,400.00
Can.: $1,850.00
U.K.:   £ 850.00

HN 1581
Rosebud
Style One
Designer: L. Harradine
Height: 3", 7.6 cm
Colour: Blue dress with flowers
Issued: 1933-1938
Varieties: HN 1580

U.S.: $1,400.00
Can.: $1,850.00
U.K.:   £ 850.00

HN 1582
Marion
Designer: L. Harradine
Height: 6 ½", 16.5 cm
Colour: Purple
Issued: 1933-1940
Varieties: HN 1583

U.S.: $2,750.00
Can.: $3,600.00
U.K.:   £1,650.00

HN 1583
Marion
Designer: L. Harradine
Height: 6 ½", 16.5 cm
Colour: Blue dress,
           patterned shawl
Issued: 1933-1940
Varieties: HN 1582

U.S.: $2,750.00
Can.: $3,600.00
U.K.:   £1,650.00

HN 1584
Willy-Won't He
Designer: L. Harradine
Height: 6", 15.2 cm
Colour: Red, green,
           blue and white
Issued: 1933-1949
Varieties: HN 1561, 2150
           (minor glaze difference)

U.S.: $700.00
Can.: $900.00
U.K.:   £425.00

HN 1585
Suzette
Designer: L. Harradine
Height: 7 ½", 19.1 cm
Colour: Green and yellow
Issued: 1933-1938
Varieties: HN 1487, 1577, 1696, 2026

U.S.:	**$1,200.00**
Can.:	**$1,500.00**
U.K.:	**£ 700.00**

HN 1586
Camille
Style One
Designer: L. Harradine
Height: 6 ½", 16.5 cm
Colour: Red and pink
Issued: 1933-1949
Varieties: HN 1648, 1736

U.S.:	**$1,800.00**
Can.:	**$2,350.00**
U.K.:	**£1,075.00**

HN 1587
Fleurette
Designr: L. Harradine
Height: 6 ½", 16.5 cm
Colour: Red and pink
Issued: 1933-1949

U.S.:	**$1,000.00**
Can.:	**$1,300.00**
U.K.:	**£ 600.00**

HN 1588
The Bride
Style One
Designer: L. Harradine
Height: 8 ¾", 22.2 cm
Colour: Cream
Issued: 1933-1938
Varieties: HN 1600, 1762, 1841

U.S.:	**$2,000.00**
Can.:	**$2,500.00**
U.K.:	**£1,700.00**

HN 1589
Sweet and Twenty
Style Two
Designer: L. Harradine
Height: 3 ½", 8.9 cm
Colour: Red dress, pale green sofa
Issued: 1933-1949
Varieties: HN 1610

U.S.:	**$650.00**
Can.:	**$850.00**
U.K.:	**£395.00**

HN 1590 - 1597 Wall Masks.

HN 1598
Clothilde
Designer: L. Harradine
Height: 7 ¼", 18.4 cm
Colour: Yellow and red
Issued: 1933-1949
Varieties: HN 1599

U.S.:	**$1,500.00**
Can.:	**$1,950.00**
U.K.:	**£ 900.00**

HN 1599
Clothilde
Designer: L. Harradine
Height: 7 ¼", 18.4 cm
Colour: Purple and red
Issued: 1933-1949
Varieties: HN 1598

U.S.:	**$1,500.00**
Can.:	**$1,950.00**
U.K.:	**£ 900.00**

HN 1600
The Bride
Style One
Designer: L. Harradine
Height: 8 ¾", 22.2 cm
Colour: Pale pink
Issued: 1933-1949
Varieties: HN 1588, 1762, 1841

U.S.:	**$2,000.00**
Can.:	**$2,500.00**
U.K.:	**£1,200.00**

HN 1601 - 1603 Wall Masks.

HN 1604
The Emir
Designer: C. J. Noke
Height: 7 ½", 19.1 cm
Colour: Yellow and red
Issued: 1933-1949
Varieties: HN 1605; also called
           'Ibrahim' HN 2095

   U.S.:   **$1,500.00**
   Can.:   **$1,950.00**
   U.K.:   **£ 900.00**

Pattern design on scarf may vary.

HN 1605
The Emir
Designer: C. J. Noke
Height: 7 ¼", 18.4 cm
Colour: Yellow and purple
Issued: 1933-1949
Varieties: HN 1604; also called
           'Ibrahim' HN 2095

   U.S.:   **$1,500.00**
   Can.:   **$1,950.00**
   U.K.:   **£ 900.00**

Pattern design on scarf may vary.

HN 1606
Falstaff
Style One
Designer: C. J. Noke
Height: 7", 17.8 cm
Colour: Red and brown
Issued: 1933-1949
Varieties: HN 571, 575, 608,
           609, 619, 638, 1216

   U.S.:   **$3,250.00**
   Can.:   **$4,500.00**
   U.K.:   **£1,950.00**

HN 1607
Cerise
Designer: L. Harradine
Height: 5 ¼", 13.3 cm
Colour: Lavender dress
           with flowers
Issued: 1933-1949

   U.S.:   **$750.00**
   Can.:   **$975.00**
   U.K.:   **£450.00**

HN 1608 - 1609 Wall Masks.

HN 1610
Sweet and Twenty
Style Two
Designer: L. Harradine
Height: 3 ½", 8.9 cm
Colour: Red dress, green sofa
Issued: 1933-1938
Varieties: HN 1589

   U.S.:   **$ 800.00**
   Can.:   **$1,000.00**
   U.K.:   **£ 475.00**

HN 1611 - 1616 Bookends.

HN 1617
Primroses
Designer: L. Harradine
Height: 6 ½", 16.5 cm
Colour: Purple, red, white
           and yellow
Issued: 1934-1949

   U.S.:   **$1,650.00**
   Can.:   **$2,250.00**
   U.K.:   **£ 995.00**

Earthenware

HN 1618
Maisie
Designer: L. Harradine
Height: 6 ¼", 15.9 cm
Colour: Yellow and blue
Issued: 1934-1949
Varieties: HN 1619

   U.S.:   **$ 950.00**
   Can.:   **$1,250.00**
   U.K.:   **£ 575.00**

HN 1619
Maisie
Designer: L. Harradine
Height: 6 ¼", 15.9 cm
Colour: Red and pink
Issued: 1934-1949
Varieties: HN 1618

   U.S.:   **$750.00**
   Can.:   **$975.00**
   U.K.:   **£450.00**

HN 1620
Rosabell
Designer: L. Harradine
Height: 6 ¾", 17.1 cm
Colour: Red and green
Issued: 1934-1940

U.S.:	**$1,800.00**
Can.:	**$2,500.00**
U.K.:	**£1,050.00**

HN 1621
Irene
Designer: L. Harradine
Height: 6 ½", 16.5 cm
Colour: Yellow
Issued: 1934-1951
Varieties: HN 1697, 1952

U.S.:	**$700.00**
Can.:	**$900.00**
U.K.:	**£425.00**

HN 1622
Evelyn
Designer: L. Harradine
Height: 6 ¼", 15.9 cm
Colour: Red and cream
Issued: 1934-1940
Varieties: HN 1637

U.S.:	**$2,000.00**
Can.:	**$2,500.00**
U.K.:	**£1,200.00**

HN 1623 - 1625 Bookends.

HN 1626
Bonnie Lassie
Designer: L. Harradine
Height: 5 ¼", 13.3 cm
Colour: Red
Issued: 1934-1953

U.S.:	**$ 900.00**
Can.:	**$1,200.00**
U.K.:	**£ 550.00**

HN 1627
Curly Knob
Designer: L. Harradine
Height: 6", 15.2 cm
Colour: Blue and red
Issued: 1934-1949

U.S.:	**$1,500.00**
Can.:	**$2,000.00**
U.K.:	**£ 900.00**

HN 1628
Margot
Designer: L. Harradine
Height: 5 ½", 14.0 cm
Colour: Blue and yellow
Issued: 1934-1940
Varieties: HN 1636, 1653

U.S.:	**$1,800.00**
Can.:	**$2,500.00**
U.K.:	**£1,000.00**

HN 1629
Grizel
Designer: L. Harradine
Height: 6 ¾", 17.2 cm
Colour: Red and cream
Issued: 1934-1938

U.S.:	**$3,000.00**
Can.:	**$4,000.00**
U.K.:	**£1,750.00**

HN 1630 Wall Mask.

HN 1631
Sweet Anne
Style One
Designer: L. Harradine
Height: 7", 17.8 cm
Colour: Green, red, pink
and yellow
Issued: 1934-1938
Varieties: HN 1318, 1330, 1331,
1453, 1496, 1701

U.S.:	**$1,400.00**
Can.:	**$1,850.00**
U.K.:	**£ 825.00**

HN 1632
A Gentlewoman
Designer: L. Harradine
Height: 7 ½", 19.1 cm
Colour: Lavender dress,
           green hat
Issued: 1934-1949

U.S.:	**$1,350.00**
Can.:	**$1,750.00**
U.K.:	**£ 800.00**

HN 1633
Clemency
Designer: L. Harradine
Height: 7", 17.8 cm
Colour: Lavender jacket,
           cream flowered dress
Issued: 1934-1938
Varieties: HN 1634, 1643

U.S.:	**$2,000.00**
Can.:	**$2,600.00**
U.K.:	**£1,200.00**

HN 1634
Clemency
Designer: L. Harradine
Height: 7", 17.8 cm
Colour: Green and orange
           patterned jacket,
           green dress
Issued: 1934-1949
Varieties: HN 1633, 1643

U.S.:	**$1,700.00**
Can.:	**$2,250.00**
U.K.:	**£1,000.00**

HN 1635
Marie
Style Two
Designer: L. Harradine
Height: 4 ¾", 12.0 cm
Colour: Blue, pink and
           white, pink flowers
Issued: 1934-1949
Varieties: HN 1370, 1388, 1417,
           1489, 1531, 1655

U.S.:	**$400.00**
Can.:	**$525.00**
U.K.:	**£225.00**

HN 1636
Margot
Designer: L. Harradine
Height: 5 ¾", 14.6 cm
Colour: Red, pink and yellow
Issued: 1934-1940
Varieties: HN 1628, 1653

U.S.:	**$2,000.00**
Can.:	**$2,600.00**
U.K.:	**£1,200.00**

HN 1637
Evelyn
Designer: L. Harradine
Height: 6", 15.2 cm
Colour: Blue and cream
Issued: 1934-1940
Varieties: HN 1622

U.S.:	**$2,000.00**
Can.:	**$2,600.00**
U.K.:	**£1,200.00**

HN 1638
Ladybird
Designer: L. Harradine
Height: 7 ¾", 19.7 cm
Colour: Pink
Issued: 1934-1949
Varieties: HN 1640

U.S.:	**$3,250.00**
Can.:	**$4,500.00**
U.K.:	**£2,000.00**

HN 1639
Dainty May
Style One
Designer: L. Harradine
Height: 6", 15.2 cm
Colour: Red and green
Issued: 1934-1949
Varieties: HN 1656

U.S.:	**$700.00**
Can.:	**$900.00**
U.K.:	**£425.00**

HN 1640
Ladybird
Designer: L. Harradine
Height: 7 ¾", 19.7 cm
Colour: Blue
Issued: 1934-1938
Varieties: HN 1638

U.S.:	**$4,500.00**
Can.:	**$6,000.00**
U.K.:	**£2,700.00**

HN 1641
The Little Mother
Style Two
Designer: L. Harradine
Height: 8", 20.3 cm
Colour: Red, green, white
and purple
Issued: 1934-1949
Varieties: HN 1418; also called
'Young Widow'
HN 1399

U.S.:	**$5,000.00**
Can.:	**$6,750.00**
U.K.:	**£3,000.00**

HN 1642
Granny's Shawl
Designer: L. Harradine
Height: 5 ¾", 14.6 cm
Colour: Cream dress,
red shawl
Issued: 1934-1949
Varieties: HN 1647

U.S.:	**$750.00**
Can.:	**$975.00**
U.K.:	**£450.00**

HN 1643
Clemency
Designer: L. Harradine
Height: 7", 17.8 cm
Colour: Red jacket, white
and green dress
Issued: 1934-1938
Varieties: HN 1633, 1634

U.S.:	**$2,000.00**
Can.:	**$2,600.00**
U.K.:	**£1,200.00**

HN 1644
Herminia
Designer: L. Harradine
Height: 6 ½", 16.5 cm
Colour: Flowered cream dress
Issued: 1934-1938
Varieties: HN 1646, 1704

U.S.:	**$2,250.00**
Can.:	**$3,000.00**
U.K.:	**£1,350.00**

HN 1645
Aileen
Designer: L. Harradine
Height: 6", 15.2 cm
Colour: Green dress,
flowered shawl
Issued: 1934-1938
Varieties: HN 1664, 1803

U.S.:	**$2,250.00**
Can.:	**$3,000.00**
U.K.:	**£1,350.00**

HN 1646
Herminia
Designer: L. Harradine
Height: 6 ½", 16.5 cm
Colour: Red dress with
cream stripe
Issued: 1934-1938
Varieties: HN 1644, 1704

U.S.:	**$2,250.00**
Can.:	**$3,000.00**
U.K.:	**£1,350.00**

HN 1647
Granny's Shawl
Designer: L. Harradine
Height: 5 ¾", 14.6 cm
Colour: Cream dress
with blue shawl
Issued: 1934-1949
Varieties: HN 1642

U.S.:	**$ 950.00**
Can.:	**$1,250.00**
U.K.:	**£ 575.00**

HN 1648
Camille
Style One
Designer: L. Harradine
Height: 6 ½", 16.5 cm
Colour: Pale green
          flowered dress
Issued: 1934-1949
Varieties: HN 1586, 1736

  U.S.:   **$2,250.00**
  Can.:   **$3,000.00**
  U.K.:   **£1,350.00**

HN 1649
Sweet and Twenty
Style One
Designer: L. Harradine
Height: 6", 15.2 cm
Colour: Green and cream
          dress, brown sofa
Issued: 1934-1936
Varieties: HN 1298, 1360, 1437,
          1438, 1549, 1563

  U.S.:   **$1,400.00**
  Can.:   **$1,850.00**
  U.K.:   **£   850.00**

HN 1650
Veronica
Style One
Designer: L. Harradine
Height: 8", 20.3 cm
Colour: Green and pink
Issued: 1934-1949
Varieties: HN 1517, 1519, 1943

  U.S.:   **$1,500.00**
  Can.:   **$2,000.00**
  U.K.:   **£   900.00**

HN 1651
Charmian
Designer: L. Harradine
Height: 6 ½", 16.5 cm
Colour: Red and green
Issued: 1934-1940
Varieties: HN 1568, 1569

  U.S.:   **$1,900.00**
  Can.:   **$2,500.00**
  U.K.:   **£1,100.00**

HN 1652
Janet
Style One
Designer: L. Harradine
Height: 6 ½", 16.5 cm
Colour: Red with pink
          flowered skirt
Issued: 1934-1949
Varieties: HN 1537, 1538, 1737

  U.S.:   **$1,850.00**
  Can.:   **$2,500.00**
  U.K.:   **£1,100.00**

HN 1653
Margot
Designer: L. Harradine
Height: 5 ¾", 14.6 cm
Colour: White and red
Issued: 1934-1940
Varieties: HN 1628, 1636

  U.S.:   **$2,000.00**
  Can.:   **$2,500.00**
  U.K.:   **£1,200.00**

HN 1654
Rose
Style One
Designer: L. Harradine
Height: 4 ½", 11.4 cm
Colour: Green and cream
Issued: 1934-1938
Varieties: HN 1368, 1387, 1416,
          1506, 2123

  U.S.:   **$375.00**
  Can.:   **$475.00**
  U.K.:   **£225.00**

HN 1655
Marie
Style Two
Designer: L. Harradine
Height: 4 ½", 11.4 cm
Colour: Pink and white
Issued: 1934-1938
Varieties: HN 1370, 1388, 1417,
          1489, 1531, 1635

  U.S.:   **$375.00**
  Can.:   **$475.00**
  U.K.:   **£225.00**

HN 1656
Dainty May
Style One
Designer: L. Harradine
Height: 6", 15.2 cm
Colour: Lavender
Issued: 1934-1949
Varieties: HN 1639

U.S.:	$ 850.00
Can.:	$1,100.00
U.K.:	£ 500.00

HN 1657
The Moor
Designer: C. J. Noke
Height: 16 ½", 41.9 cm
Colour: Red and black
Issued: 1934-1949
Varieties: HN 1308, 1366, 1425,
           2082, 3642, 3926;
           also called 'An Arab'
           HN 33, 343, 378

U.S.:	$4,500.00
Can.:	$6,000.00
U.K.:	£2,700.00

HN 1658 - 1661 Wall Masks.

HN 1662
Delicia
Designer: L. Harradine
Height: 5 ¾", 14.6 cm
Colour: Pink and lavender
Issued: 1934-1938
Varieties: HN 1663, 1681

U.S.:	$1,900.00
Can.:	$2,500.00
U.K.:	£1,150.00

HN 1663
Delicia
Designer: L. Harradine
Height: 5 ¾", 14.6 cm
Colour: Lavender, pink
           and green
Issued: 1934-1938
Varieties: HN 1662, 1681

U.S.:	$1,900.00
Can.:	$2,500.00
U.K.:	£1,150.00

HN 1664
Aileen
Designer: L. Harradine
Height: 6", 15.2 cm
Colour: Pink dress,
           patterned shawl
Issued: 1934-1938
Varieties: HN 1645, 1803

U.S.:	$2,250.00
Can.:	$3,000.00
U.K.:	£1,350.00

HN 1665
Miss Winsome
Designer: L. Harradine
Height: 6 ¾", 17.2 cm
Colour: Lavender dress,
           patterned shawl
Issued: 1934-1949
Varieties: HN 1666

U.S.:	$1,500.00
Can.:	$2,000.00
U.K.:	£ 900.00

HN 1666
Miss Winsome
Designer: L. Harradine
Height: 6 ¾", 17.2 cm
Colour: Green dress,
           patterned shawl
Issued: 1934-1938
Varieties: HN 1665

U.S.:	$1,650.00
Can.:	$2,250.00
U.K.:	£ 975.00

NOTE ON PRICING

As with all price guides, prices listed in this catalogue are suggested retail values. This is not a fixed price catalogue and figurines will be offered for sale at higher, lower, or catalogue prices, depending upon the supply-demand factors of the market place.

When our first edition was published in 1981 the Royal Doulton market was divided into three or four different geographical areas and pricing was based on each individual area.

In 2004 this is all changing, the global market place is coming to collectables. Our prices, while based on many different avenues that offer figurines for sale, are slowly turning into foreign exchange transactions between the former market areas. For now the collector is able to shop globally.

HN 1667
Blossom
Designer: L. Harradine
Height: 6 ¾", 17.2 cm
Colour: Orange and blue
Issued: 1934-1949

U.S.:	**$3,000.00**
Can.:	**$4,000.00**
U.K.:	**£1,750.00**

HN 1668
Sibell
Designer: L. Harradine
Height: 6 ½", 16.5 cm
Colour: Red and green
Issued: 1934-1949
Varieties: HN 1695, 1735

U.S.:	**$1,750.00**
Can.:	**$2,250.00**
U.K.:	**£1,000.00**

HN 1669
Anthea
Designer: L. Harradine
Height: 6 ½", 16.5 cm
Colour: Pink dress,
green shawl
Issued: 1934-1940
Varieties: HN 1526, 1527

U.S.:	**$2,000.00**
Can.:	**$2,500.00**
U.K.:	**£1,200.00**

HN 1670
Gillian
Style One
Designer: L. Harradine
Height: 7 ¾", 19.7 cm
Colour: Pink
Issued: 1934-1949
Varieties: HN 1670A

U.S.:	**$1,750.00**
Can.:	**$2,250.00**
U.K.:	**£1,000.00**

HN 1670A
Gillian
Style One
Designer: L. Harradine
Height: 7 ¾", 19.7 cm
Colour: Green jacket, white
flowered skirt
Issued: Unknown
Varieties: HN 1670

U.S.:	**$2,000.00**
Can.:	**$2,250.00**
U.K.:	**£1,200.00**

HN 1671 - 1676 Wall Masks.

HN 1677
Tinkle Bell
Designer: L. Harradine
Height: 4 ¾", 12.0 cm
Colour: Pink
Issued: 1935-1988

U.S.:	**$125.00**
Can.:	**$175.00**
U.K.:	**£ 75.00**

HN 1678
Dinky Doo
Designer: L. Harradine
Height: 4 ¾", 12.0 cm
Colour: Lavender
Issued: 1934-1996
Varieties: HN 2120, 3618

U.S.:	**$125.00**
Can.:	**$175.00**
U.K.:	**£ 75.00**

HN 1679
Babie
Designer: L. Harradine
Height: 4 ¾", 12.0 cm
Colour: Green
Issued: 1935-1992
Varieties: HN 1842, 2121

U.S.:	**$125.00**
Can.:	**$175.00**
U.K.:	**£ 75.00**

HN 1680
Tootles
Designer: L. Harradine
Height: 4 ¾", 12.0 cm
Colour: Pink
Issued: 1935-1975

U.S.:	$125.00
Can.:	$175.00
U.K.:	£ 75.00

HN 1681
Delicia
Designer: L. Harradine
Height: 5 ¾", 14.6 cm
Colour: Green and purple
Issued: 1935-1938
Varieties: HN 1662, 1663

U.S.:	$1,900.00
Can.:	$2,500.00
U.K.:	£1,100.00

HN 1682
Teresa
Style One
Designer: L. Harradine
Height: 5 ¾", 14.6 cm
Colour: Red and brown
Issued: 1935-1949
Varieties: HN 1683

U.S.:	$3,000.00
Can.:	$4,000.00
U.K.:	£1,750.00

HN 1683
Teresa
Style One
Designer: L. Harradine
Height: 5 ¾", 14.6 cm
Colour: Light blue and brown
Issued: 1935-1938
Varieties: HN 1682

U.S.:	$4,000.00
Can.:	$5,500.00
U.K.:	£2,400.00

HN 1684
Lisette
Designer: L. Harradine
Height: 5 ¼", 13.3 cm
Colour: Rose-pink dress, green trim
Issued: 1935-1936
Varieties: HN 1523, 1524

U.S.:	$3,000.00
Can.:	$3,750.00
U.K.:	£1,500.00

HN 1685
Cynthia
Style One
Designer: L. Harradine
Height: 5 ¾", 14.6 cm
Colour: Pink and turquoise
Issued: 1935-1949
Varieties: HN 1686, 1686A

U.S.:	$1,800.00
Can.:	$2,350.00
U.K.:	£1,050.00

HN 1686
Cynthia
Style One
Designer: L. Harradine
Height: 5 ¾", 14.6 cm
Colour: Blue and red
Issued: 1935-1949
Varieties: HN 1685, 1686A

U.S.:	$1,800.00
Can.:	$2,350.00
U.K.:	£1,050.00

HN 1686A
Cynthia
Style One
Designer: L. Harradine
Height: 5 ¾", 14.6 cm
Colour: Red and purple
Issued: 1935-1949
Varieties: HN 1685, 1686

U.S.:	$1,800.00
Can.:	$2,350.00
U.K.:	£1,050.00

HN 1687
Clarissa
Style One
Designer: L. Harradine
Height: 9 ¾", 24.8 cm
Colour: Blue, green and orange
Issued: 1935-1949
Varieties: HN 1525

U.S.:	**$1,200.00**
Can.:	**$1,500.00**
U.K.:	**£ 725.00**

Earthenware

HN 1688
Rhoda
Designer: L. Harradine
Height: 10 ¼, 26.7 cm
Colour: Orange and red
Issued: 1935-1940
Varieties: HN 1573, 1574

U.S.:	**$1,100.00**
Can.:	**$1,450.00**
U.K.:	**£ 650.00**

Earthenware

HN 1689
Calumet
Designer: C. J. Noke
Height: 6 ½", 16.5 cm
Colour: Green and brown
Issued: 1935-1949
Varieties: HN 1428, 2068

U.S.:	**$1,600.00**
Can.:	**$2,100.00**
U.K.:	**£ 850.00**

Earthenware

HN 1690
June
Style One
Designer: L. Harradine
Height: 7 ¼", 18.4 cm
Colour: Pale green and pink
Issued: 1935-1949
Varieties: HN 1691, 1947, 2027

U.S.:	**$1,400.00**
Can.:	**$1,800.00**
U.K.:	**£ 850.00**

HN 1691
June
Style One
Designer: L. Harradine
Height: 7 ¼", 18.4 cm
Colour: Yellow and pink
Issued: 1935-1949
Varieties: HN 1690, 1947, 2027

U.S.:	**$ 900.00**
Can.:	**$1,175.00**
U.K.:	**£ 550.00**

HN 1692
Sonia
Designer: L. Harradine
Height: 6 ¼", 15.9 cm
Colour: Pink, white and green
Issued: 1935-1949
Varieties: HN 1738

U.S.:	**$1,800.00**
Can.:	**$2,500.00**
U.K.:	**£1,050.00**

HN 1693
Virginia
Designer: L. Harradine
Height: 7 ½", 19.1 cm
Colour: Yellow and red
Issued: 1935-1949
Varieties: HN 1694

U.S.:	**$2,000.00**
Can.:	**$2,500.00**
U.K.:	**£1,200.00**

HN 1694
Virginia
Designer: L. Harradine
Height: 7 ½", 19.1 cm
Colour: Green
Issued: 1935-1949
Varieties: HN 1693

U.S.:	**$2,000.00**
Can.:	**$2,500.00**
U.K.:	**£1,200.00**

HN 1695
Sibell
Designer: L. Harradine
Height: 6 ½", 16.5 cm
Colour: Green and orange
Issued: 1935-1949
Varieties: HN 1668, 1735

U.S.:	$1,500.00
Can.:	$1,950.00
U.K.:	£ 900.00

HN 1696
Suzette
Designer: L. Harradine
Height: 7 ½", 19.1 cm
Colour: Flowered green dress
Issued: 1935-1949
Varieties: HN 1487, 1577, 1585, 2026

U.S.:	$1,200.00
Can.:	$1,500.00
U.K.:	£ 725.00

HN 1697
Irene
Designer: L. Harradine
Height: 7", 17.8 cm
Colour: Pink
Issued: 1935-1949
Varieties: HN 1621, 1952

U.S.:	$1,500.00
Can.:	$1,950.00
U.K.:	£ 900.00

HN 1698
Phyllis
Style One
Designer: L. Harradine
Height: 9", 22.9 cm
Colour: Green
Issued: 1935-1949
Varieties: HN 1420, 1430, 1486

U.S.:	$1,650.00
Can.:	$2,250.00
U.K.:	£ 975.00

HN 1699
Marietta
Designer: L. Harradine
Height: 8", 20.3 cm
Colour: Green and red
Issued: 1935-1940
Varieties: HN 1341, 1446

U.S.:	$3,250.00
Can.:	$4,500.00
U.K.:	£1,950.00

HN 1700
Gloria
Style One
Designer: L. Harradine
Height: 7", 17.8 cm
Colour: Green and black
Issued: 1935-1938
Varieties: HN 1488

U.S.:	$4,000.00
Can.:	$5,250.00
U.K.:	£2,400.00

HN 1701
Sweet Anne
Style One
Designer: L. Harradine
Height: 7", 17.8 cm
Colour: Pink and blue
Issued: 1935-1938
Varieties: HN 1318, 1330, 1331, 1453, 1496, 1631

U.S.:	$1,350.00
Can.:	$1,750.00
U.K.:	£ 800.00

HN 1702
A Jester
Style One
Designer: C. J. Noke
Height: 10", 25.4 cm
Colour: Brown and mauve
Issued: 1935-1949
Varieties: HN 45, 71, 71A, 320, 367, 412, 426, 446, 552, 616, 627, 1295, 2016, 3922

U.S.:	$ 900.00
Can.:	$1,200.00
U.K.:	£ 525.00

HN 1703
Charley's Aunt
Style Three
Designer: A. Toft
Height: 6", 15.2 cm
Colour: Lilac and white, no base
Issued: 1935-1938

U.S.:	**$2,250.00**
Can.:	**$3,000.00**
U.K.:	**£1,350.00**

HN 1704
Herminia
Designer: L. Harradine
Height: 6 ¾", 17.2 cm
Colour: Red
Issued: 1935-1938
Varieties: HN 1644, 1646

U.S.:	**$2,250.00**
Can.:	**$3,000.00**
U.K.:	**£1,350.00**

HN 1705
The Cobbler
Style Three
Designer: C. J. Noke
Height: 8", 20.3 cm
Colour: Purple and blue
Issued: 1935-1949
Varieties: HN 1706

U.S.:	**$1,400.00**
Can.:	**$1,800.00**
U.K.:	**£ 825.00**

Earthenware

HN 1706
The Cobbler
Style Three
Designer: C. J. Noke
Height: 8 ¼", 21.0 cm
Colour: Green and brown
Issued: 1935-1969
Varieties: HN 1705

U.S.:	**$400.00**
Can.:	**$525.00**
U.K.:	**£250.00**

Earthenware

HN 1707
Paisley Shawl
Style One
Designer: L. Harradine
Height: 8 ¼", 21.0 cm
Colour: Purple
Issued: 1935-1949
Varieties: HN 1392, 1460,
           1739, 1987

U.S.:	**$1,200.00**
Can.:	**$1,500.00**
U.K.:	**£ 700.00**

HN 1708
The Bather
Style One, First Version
Designer: L. Harradine
Height: 7 ¾", 19.7 cm
Colour: Black, red and
           turquoise
Issued: 1935-1938
Varieties: HN 597, 687, 781,
           782, 1238

U.S.:	**$5,500.00**
Can.:	**$7,500.00**
U.K.:	**£3,500.00**

HN 1709
Pantalettes
Style One
Designer: L. Harradine
Height: 8", 20.3 cm
Colour: Red
Issued: 1935-1938
Varieties: HN 1362, 1412, 1507

U.S.:	**$1,800.00**
Can.:	**$2,350.00**
U.K.:	**£1,000.00**

HN 1710
Camilla
Style One
Designer: L. Harradine
Height: 7", 17.8 cm
Colour: Red and yellow
Issued: 1935-1949
Varieties: HN 1711

U.S.:	**$2,250.00**
Can.:	**$3,000.00**
U.K.:	**£1,350.00**

HN 1711
Camilla
Style One
Designer: L. Harradine
Height: 7", 17.8 cm
Colour: Green and yellow
Issued: 1935-1949
Varieties: HN 1710

U.S.:	$2,250.00
Can.:	$3,000.00
U.K.:	£1,350.00

HN 1712
Daffy Down Dilly
Designer: L. Harradine
Height: 7 ¾", 19.7 cm
Colour: Green
Issued: 1935-1975
Varieties: HN 1713

U.S.:	$475.00
Can.:	$675.00
U.K.:	£285.00

HN 1713
Daffy Down Dilly
Designer: L. Harradine
Height: 8 ¼", 21.0 cm
Colour: Turquoise
Issued: 1935-1949
Varieties: HN 1712

U.S.:	$1,500.00
Can.:	$1,950.00
U.K.:	£ 900.00

HN 1714
Millicent
Designer: L. Harradine
Height: 8", 20.3 cm
Colour: Red
Issued: 1935-1949
Varieties: HN 1715, 1860

U.S.:	$2,000.00
Can.:	$2,600.00
U.K.:	£1,200.00

HN 1715
Millicent
Designer: L. Harradine
Height: 8", 20.3 cm
Colour: Lavender
Issued: 1935-1949
Varieties: HN 1714, 1860

U.S.:	$2,500.00
Can.:	$3,250.00
U.K.:	£1,500.00

HN 1716
Diana
Style One
Designer: L. Harradine
Height: 5 ¾", 14.6 cm
Colour: Pink and blue
Issued: 1935-1949
Varieties: HN 1717, 1986

U.S.:	$ 800.00
Can.:	$1,100.00
U.K.:	£ 500.00

HN 1717
Diana
Style One
Designer: L. Harradine
Height: 5 ¾", 14.6 cm
Colour: Turquoise
Issued: 1935-1949
Varieties: HN 1716, 1986

U.S.:	$550.00
Can.:	$875.00
U.K.:	£325.00

HN 1718
Kate Hardcastle
Designer: L. Harradine
Height: 8", 20.3 cm
Colour: Pink and green
Issued: 1935-1949
Varieties: HN 1719, 1734,
1861, 1919, 2028

U.S.:	$1,400.00
Can.:	$1,800.00
U.K.:	£ 825.00

HN 1719
Kate Hardcastle
Designer: L. Harradine
Height: 8", 20.3 cm
Colour: Red and green
Issued: 1935-1949
Varieties: HN 1718, 1734,
           1861, 1919, 2028

U.S.:	**$1,400.00**
Can.:	**$1,800.00**
U.K.:	**£ 825.00**

HN 1720
Frangçon
Designer: L. Harradine
Height: 7 ½", 19.1 cm
Colour: Lavender dress with
           orange and red flowers
Issued: 1935-1949
Varieties: HN 1721

U.S.:	**$3,000.00**
Can.:	**$4,000.00**
U.K.:	**£1,750.00**

HN 1721
Frangçon
Designer: L. Harradine
Height: 7 ¼", 18.4 cm
Colour: Green
Issued: 1935-1949
Varieties: HN 1720

U.S.:	**$2,250.00**
Can.:	**$3,000.00**
U.K.:	**£1,350.00**

HN 1722
The Coming of Spring
Designer: L. Harradine
Height: 12 ½", 31.7 cm
Colour: Yellow-pink
Issued: 1935-1949
Varieties: HN 1723

U.S.:	**$4,000.00**
Can.:	**$5,000.00**
U.K.:	**£2,400.00**

HN 1723
The Coming of Spring
Designer: L. Harradine
Height: 12 ½", 31.7 cm
Colour: Pale green
Issued: 1935-1949
Varieties: HN 1722

U.S.:	**$4,000.00**
Can.:	**$5,000.00**
U.K.:	**£2,400.00**

HN 1724
Ruby
Style One
Designer: L. Harradine
Height: 5 ¼", 13.3 cm
Colour: Red
Issued: 1935-1949
Varieties: HN 1725

U.S.:	**$750.00**
Can.:	**$975.00**
U.K.:	**£450.00**

HN 1725
Ruby
Style One
Designer: L. Harradine
Height: 5 ¼", 13.3 cm
Colour: Blue
Issued: 1935-1949
Varieties: HN 1724

U.S.:	**$1,000.00**
Can.:	**$1,300.00**
U.K.:	**£ 600.00**

HN 1726
Celia
Designer: L. Harradine
Height: 11 ½", 29.2 cm
Colour: Pale lavender
Issued: 1935-1949
Varieties: HN 1727

U.S.:	**$3,000.00**
Can.:	**$3,750.00**
U.K.:	**£1,750.00**

HN 1727
Celia
Designer: L. Harradine
Height: 11 ½", 29.2 cm
Colour: Pale green
Issued: 1935-1949
Varieties: HN 1726

U.S.:	$2,000.00
Can.:	$2,500.00
U.K.:	£1,200.00

HN 1728
The New Bonnet
Designer: L. Harradine
Height: 7", 17.8 cm
Colour: Pink
Issued: 1935-1949
Varieties: HN 1957

U.S.:	$1,350.00
Can.:	$2,000.00
U.K.:	£ 800.00

HN 1729
Vera
First Version
Designer: L. Harradine
Height: 4 ¼", 10.8 cm
Colour: Pink
Issued: 1935-1940
Varieties: HN 1730

U.S.:	$1,350.00
Can.:	$1,850.00
U.K.:	£ 800.00

HN 1730
Vera
First Version
Designer: L. Harradine
Height: 4 ¼", 10.8 cm
Colour: Green
Issued: 1935-1938
Varieties: HN 1729

U.S.:	$1,350.00
Can.:	$1,850.00
U.K.:	£ 800.00

HN 1731
Daydreams
Designer: L. Harradine
Height: 5 ¾", 14.6 cm
Colour: Pale pink, blue trim
Issued: 1935-1996
Varieties: HN 1732, 1944

U.S.:	$325.00
Can.:	$450.00
U.K.:	£195.00

HN 1732
Daydreams
Designer: L. Harradine
Height: 5 ½", 14.0 cm
Colour: Pink, rose-pink trim
Issued: 1935-1949
Varieties: HN 1731, 1944

U.S.:	$1,000.00
Can.:	$1,500.00
U.K.:	£ 600.00

HN 1733 Wall Mask.

HN 1734
Kate Hardcastle
Designer: L. Harradine
Height: 8 ¼", 21.0 cm
Colour: Green and white
Issued: 1935-1949
Varieties: HN 1718, 1719,
1861, 1919, 2028

U.S.:	$2,250.00
Can.:	$3,000.00
U.K.:	£1,350.00

HN 1735
Sibell
Designer: L. Harradine
Height: 6 ½", 16.5 cm
Colour: White and blue
Issued: 1935-1949
Varieties: HN 1668, 1695

U.S.:	$1,650.00
Can.:	$2,250.00
U.K.:	£ 995.00

HN 1736
Camille
Style One
Designer: L. Harradine
Height: 6 ½", 16.5 cm
Colour: Pink and cream
Issued: 1935-1949
Varieties: HN 1586, 1648

U.S.:	**$2,500.00**
Can.:	**$3,500.00**
U.K.:	**£1,500.00**

HN 1737
Janet
Style One
Designer: L. Harradine
Height: 6 ¼", 15.9 cm
Colour: Green
Issued: 1935-1949
Varieties: HN 1537, 1538, 1652

U.S.:	**$ 900.00**
Can.:	**$1,175.00**
U.K.:	**£ 525.00**

HN 1738
Sonia
Designer: L. Harradine
Height: 6 ½", 16.5 cm
Colour: Green
Issued: 1935-1949
Varieties: HN 1692

U.S.:	**$1,750.00**
Can.:	**$2,500.00**
U.K.:	**£1,000.00**

HN 1739
Paisley Shawl
Style One
Designer: L. Harradine
Height: 8 ¼", 21.0 cm
Colour: Green and red
Issued: 1935-1949
Varieties: HN 1392, 1460,
           1707, 1987

U.S.:	**$1,150.00**
Can.:	**$1,500.00**
U.K.:	**£ 675.00**

HN 1740
Gladys
First Verson
Designer: L. Harradine
Height: 5 ¼", 13.3 cm
Colour: Green
Issued: 1935-1949
Varieties: HN 1741

U.S.:	**$1,350.00**
Can.:	**$1,850.00**
U.K.:	**£ 800.00**

HN 1741
Gladys
First Version
Designer: L. Harradine
Height: 5", 12.7 cm
Colour: Pink
Issued: 1935-1938
Varieties: HN 1740

U.S.:	**$1,350.00**
Can.:	**$1,850.00**
U.K.:	**£ 800.00**

HN 1742
Sir Walter Raleigh
Designer: L. Harradine
Height: 10 ½", 26.7 cm
Colour: Green, purple
           and orange
Issued: 1935-1949
Varieties: HN 1751, 2015

U.S.:	**$5,000.00**
Can.:	**$6,750.00**
U.K.:	**£3,000.00**

HN 1743
Mirabel
Style One
Designer: L. Harradine
Height: 7 ¾", 19.7 cm
Colour: Pale blue
Issued: 1935-1949
Varieties: HN 1744

U.S.:	**$1,750.00**
Can.:	**$2,250.00**
U.K.:	**£1,000.00**

HN 1744
Mirabel
Style One
Designer: L. Harradine
Height: 7 ¾", 19.7 cm
Colour: Pink
Issued: 1935-1949
Varieties: HN 1743

U.S.:	**$1,750.00**
Can.:	**$2,250.00**
U.K.:	**£1,000.00**

HN 1745
The Rustic Swain
Designer: L. Harradine
Height: 5 ¼", 13.3 cm
Colour: Green, white
           and brown
Issued: 1935-1949
Varieties: HN 1746

U.S.:	**$3,000.00**
Can.:	**$4,000.00**
U.K.:	**£1,750.00**

HN 1746
The Rustic Swain
Designer: L. Harradine
Height: 5 ¼", 13.3 cm
Colour: Green, blue and pink
Issued: 1935-1949
Varieties: HN 1745

U.S.:	**$3,000.00**
Can.:	**$4,000.00**
U.K.:	**£1,750.00**

HN 1747
Afternoon Tea
Designer: P. Railston
Height: 5 ¾", 14.6 cm
Colour: Pink and blue
Issued: 1935-1982
Varieties: HN 1748

U.S.:	**$650.00**
Can.:	**$850.00**
U.K.:	**£395.00**

HN 1748
Afternoon Tea
Designer: P. Railston
Height: 5 ¼", 13.3 cm
Colour: Green
Issued: 1935-1949
Varieties: HN 1747

U.S.:	**$2,500.00**
Can.:	**$3,500.00**
U.K.:	**£1,500.00**

HN 1749
Pierrette
Style Three
Designer: L. Harradine
Height: 8 ½", 21.6 cm
Colour: Purple
Issued: 1936-1949
Varieties: HN 1391

U.S.:	**$3,250.00**
Can.:	**$4,500.00**
U.K.:	**£2,000.00**

Earthenware

HN 1750
Folly
Designer: L. Harradine
Height: 9 ½", 24.1 cm
Colour: Black-purple
Issued: 1936-1949
Varieties: HN 1335

U.S.:	**$3,500.00**
Can.:	**$4,500.00**
U.K.:	**£2,000.00**

Earthenware

HN 1751
Sir Walter Raleigh
Designer: L. Harradine
Height: 11 ½", 29.2 cm
Colour: Orange and purple
Issued: 1936-1949
Varieties: HN 1742, 2015

U.S.:	**$1,800.00**
Can.:	**$2,250.00**
U.K.:	**£1,000.00**

Earthenware

HN 1752
Regency
Designer: L. Harradine
Height: 8", 20.3 cm
Colour: Lavender and green
Issued: 1936-1949

U.S.:	$1,800.00
Can.:	$2,250.00
U.K.:	£1,000.00

HN 1753
Eleanore
Designer: L. Harradine
Height: 7", 17.8 cm
Colour: Blue, green and pink
Issued: 1936-1949
Varieties: HN 1754

U.S.:	$2,500.00
Can.:	$3,250.00
U.K.:	£1,500.00

HN 1754
Eleanore
Designer: L. Harradine
Height: 7", 17.8 cm
Colour: Orange and cream
Issued: 1936-1949
Varieties: HN 1753

U.S.:	$2,500.00
Can.:	$3,250.00
U.K.:	£1,500.00

HN 1755
The Court Shoemaker
Designer: L. Harradine
Height: 6 ¾", 17.2 cm
Colour: Purple, brown and green
Issued: 1936-1949

U.S.:	$3,500.00
Can.:	$4,500.00
U.K.:	£2,000.00

HN 1756
Lizana
Designer: L. Harradine
Height: 8 ½", 21.6 cm
Colour: Green, pink and purple
Issued: 1936-1949
Varieties: HN 1761

U.S.:	$1,500.00
Can.:	$1,950.00
U.K.:	£ 900.00

HN 1757
Romany Sue
Designer: L. Harradine
Height: 9 ¼", 23.5 cm
Colour: Green and red
Issued: 1936-1949
Varieties: HN 1758

U.S.:	$2,250.00
Can.:	$3,000.00
U.K.:	£1,350.00

HN 1758
Romany Sue
Designer: L. Harradine
Height: 9 ½", 24.1 cm
Colour: Lavender
Issued: 1936-1949
Varieties: HN 1757

U.S.:	$2,250.00
Can.:	$3,000.00
U.K.:	£1,350.00

HN 1759
The Orange Lady
Designer: L. Harradine
Height: 8 ¾", 22.2 cm
Colour: Pink
Issued: 1936-1975
Varieties: HN 1953

U.S.:	$375.00
Can.:	$500.00
U.K.:	£225.00

1. Earlier pieces have holes in the oranges
2. Earthenware

HN 1760
4 O'Clock
Designer: L. Harradine
Height: 6", 15.2 cm
Colour: Lavender
Issued: 1936-1949

U.S.:	**$2,000.00**
Can.:	**$2,600.00**
U.K.:	**£1,200.00**

HN 1761
Lizana
Designer: L. Harradine
Height: 8 ½", 21.6 cm
Colour: Green
Issued: 1936-1938
Varieties: HN 1756

U.S.:	**$1,500.00**
Can.:	**$2,000.00**
U.K.:	**£ 900.00**

HN 1762
The Bride
Style One
Designer: L. Harradine
Height: 8 ¾", 22.2 cm
Colour: Cream
Issued: 1936-1949
Varieties: HN 1588, 1600, 1841

U.S.:	**$2,000.00**
Can.:	**$2,600.00**
U.K.:	**£1,200.00**

HN 1763
Windflower
Style One
Designer: L. Harradine
Height: 7 ¼", 18.4 cm
Colour: Pink
Issued: 1936-1949
Varieties: HN 1764, 2029

U.S.:	**$750.00**
Can.:	**$975.00**
U.K.:	**£450.00**

HN 1764
Windflower
Style One
Designer: L. Harradine
Height: 7 ¼", 18.4 cm
Colour: Blue
Issued: 1936-1949
Varieties: HN 1763, 2029

U.S.:	**$1,200.00**
Can.:	**$1,600.00**
U.K.:	**£ 700.00**

HN 1765
Chloe
Style One
Designer: L. Harradine
Height: 6", 15.2 cm
Colour: Blue
Issued: 1936-1950
Varieties: HN 1470, 1476, 1479, 1498, 1956

U.S.:	**$450.00**
Can.:	**$600.00**
U.K.:	**£275.00**

HN 1766
Nana
Designer: L. Harradine
Height: 4 ¾", 12.0 cm
Colour: Pink
Issued: 1936-1949
Varieties: HN 1767

U.S.:	**$575.00**
Can.:	**$750.00**
U.K.:	**£325.00**

HN 1767
Nana
Designer: L. Harradine
Height: 4 ¾", 12.0 cm
Colour: Lavender
Issued: 1936-1949
Varieties: HN 1766

U.S.:	**$575.00**
Can.:	**$750.00**
U.K.:	**£325.00**

HN 1768
Ivy
Designer: L. Harradine
Height: 4 ¾", 12.0 cm
Colour: Purple
Issued: 1936-1979
Varieties: HN 1769

U.S.:	**$150.00**
Can.:	**$225.00**
U.K.:	**£100.00**

HN 1769
Ivy
Designer: L. Harradine
Height: 4 ¾", 12.0 cm
Colour: Unknown
Issued: 1936-1938
Varieties: HN 1768

U.S.:	
Can.:	**Very Rare**
U.K.:	

HN 1770
Maureen
Style One
Designer: L. Harradine
Height: 7 ½", 19.1 cm
Colour: Pink
Issued: 1936-1959
Varieties: HN 1771

U.S.:	**$525.00**
Can.:	**$700.00**
U.K.:	**£325.00**

HN 1771
Maureen
Style One
Designer: L. Harradine
Height: 7 ½", 19.1 cm
Colour: Lavender
Issued: 1936-1949
Varieties: HN 1770

U.S.:	**$1,600.00**
Can.:	**$2,250.00**
U.K.:	**£ 950.00**

HN 1772
Delight
Designer: L. Harradine
Height: 7", 17.8 cm
Colour: Red
Issued: 1936-1967
Varieties: HN 1773

U.S.:	**$325.00**
Can.:	**$450.00**
U.K.:	**£200.00**

HN 1773
Delight
Designer: L. Harradine
Height: 6 ¾", 17.2 cm
Colour: Turquoise
Issued: 1936-1949
Varieties: HN 1772

U.S.:	**$1,000.00**
Can.:	**$1,400.00**
U.K.:	**£ 600.00**

HN 1774
Spring (Matte)
Style Three
Designer: R. Garbe
Height: 21", 53.3 cm
Colour: Ivory
Issued: 1933 in a limited
           edition of 100
Varieties: HN 1827

U.S.:	**Only**
Can.:	**five**
U.K.:	**known**

HN 1775
Salome (Matte)
Style One
Designer: R. Garbe
Height: 8", 20.3 cm
Colour: Ivory
Issued: 1933 in a limited
           edition of 100
Varieties: HN 1828

U.S.:	**Only**
Can.:	**two**
U.K.:	**known**

HN 1776
West Wind (Matte)
Designer: R. Garbe
Height: 14 ½", 36.8 cm
Colour: Ivory
Issued: 1933 in a limited
edition of 25
Varieties: HN 1826

U.S.:	Only
Can.:	three
U.K.:	known

Photograph
Not
Available

HN 1777
Spirit of the Wind (Matte)
Designer: R. Garbe
Height: Unknown
Colour: Ivory
Issued: 1933 in a limited
edition of 50
Varieties: HN 1825

U.S.:	Only
Can.:	one
U.K.:	known

HN 1778
Beethoven (Matte)
Designer: R. Garbe
Height: 22", 55.8 cm
Colour: Ivory
Issued: 1933 in a limited
edition of 25

U.S.:	Only
Can.:	three
U.K.:	known

Photograph
Not
Available

HN 1779
Macaw (Matte)
Designer: R. Garbe
Height: 14 ½", 35.6 cm
Colour: Ivory
Issued: 1933-1949
Varieties: HN 1829

U.S.:	Only
Can.:	one
U.K.:	known

HN 1780
Lady of the Snows
Designer: R. Garbe
Height: Unknown
Colour: Unknown
Issued: 1933 in a limited
edition of 50
Varieties: HN 1830

U.S.:	Only
Can.:	one
U.K.:	known

HN 1781 - 1786 Wall Masks,
HN 1787 - 1790 Not issued.

HN 1791
Old Balloon Seller and Bulldog
Designer: L. Harradine
Height: 7", 17.8 cm
Colour: Green, red and white
Issued: 1932-1938
Varieties: HN 1912

U.S.:	Only
Can.:	one
U.K.:	known

HN 1792
Henry VIII
Style Two
Designer: C. J. Noke
Height: 11 ½", 29.2 cm
Colour: Multicoloured
Issued: 1933 in a limited
edition of 200

U.S.:	$ 8,000.00
Can.:	$10,500.00
U.K.:	£ 4,750.00

HN 1793
This Little Pig
Designer: L. Harradine
Height: 4", 10.1 cm
Colour: Red
Issued: 1936-1995
Varieties: HN 1794, 2125

U.S.:	$150.00
Can.:	$200.00
U.K.:	£ 90.00

HN 1794
This Little Pig
Designer: L. Harradine
Height: 4", 10.1 cm
Colour: Blue
Issued: 1936-1949
Varieties: HN 1793, 2125

U.S.:	**$1,000.00**
Can.:	**$1,300.00**
U.K.:	**£ 600.00**

HN 1795
M'Lady's Maid
Designer: L. Harradine
Height: 9", 22.9 cm
Colour: Red
Issued: 1936-1949
Varieties: HN 1822

U.S.:	**$6,000.00**
Can.:	**$7,750.00**
U.K.:	**£3,500.00**

HN 1796
Hazel
Style One
Designer: L. Harradine
Height: 5 ¼", 13.3 cm
Colour: Green and red
Issued: 1936-1949
Varieties: HN 1797

U.S.:	**$ 950.00**
Can.:	**$1,200.00**
U.K.:	**£ 550.00**

HN 1797
Hazel
Style One
Designer: L. Harradine
Height: 5 ¼", 13.3 cm
Colour: Pink and blue
Issued: 1936-1949
Varieties: HN 1796

U.S.:	**$ 950.00**
Can.:	**$1,200.00**
U.K.:	**£ 550.00**

HN 1798
Lily
Style One
Designer: L. Harradine
Height: 5", 12.7 cm
Colour: Pink
Issued: 1936-1971
Varieties: HN 1799

U.S.:	**$200.00**
Can.:	**$300.00**
U.K.:	**£125.00**

HN 1799
Lily
Style One
Designer: L. Harradine
Height: 5", 12.7 cm
Colour: Green and blue
Issued: 1936-1949
Varieties: HN 1798

U.S.:	**$650.00**
Can.:	**$900.00**
U.K.:	**£375.00**

HN 1800
St. George
Style One
Designer: S. Thorogood
Height: 16", 40.6 cm
Colour: Purple, green
          and grey
Issued: 1934-1950
Varieties: HN 385, 386, 2067

U.S.:	**$4,500.00**
Can.:	**$6,000.00**
U.K.:	**£2,700.00**

Earthenware

HN 1801
An Old King
Designer: C. J. Noke
Height: 9 ¾", 24.7 cm
Colour: Unknown
Issued: 1937-1954
Varieties: HN 358, 623, 2134

U.S.:	
Can.:	**Extremely rare**
U.K.:	

HN 1802
Estelle
Designer: L. Harradine
Height: 8", 20.3 cm
Colour: Pink
Issued: 1937-1940
Varieties: HN 1566

U.S.:	$2,250.00
Can.:	$3,000.00
U.K.:	£1,350.00

HN 1803
Aileen
Designer: L. Harradine
Height: 6", 15.2 cm
Colour: Cream dress
with blue shawl
Issued: 1937-1949
Varieties: HN 1645, 1664

U.S.:	$3,000.00
Can.:	$4,000.00
U.K.:	£1,750.00

HN 1804
Granny
Designer: L. Harradine
Height: 7", 17.8 cm
Colour: Grey, purple
and brown
Issued: 1937-1949
Varieties: HN 1832

U.S.:	$5,000.00
Can.:	$6,500.00
U.K.:	£3,000.00

HN 1805
To Bed
Designer: L. Harradine
Height: 6", 15.2 cm
Colour: Green
Issued: 1937-1959
Varieties: HN 1806

U.S.:	$300.00
Can.:	$400.00
U.K.:	£175.00

HN 1806
To Bed
Designer: L. Harradine
Height: 6", 15.2 cm
Colour: Lavender
Issued: 1937-1949
Varieties: HN 1805

U.S.:	$750.00
Can.:	$975.00
U.K.:	£450.00

HN 1807
Spring Flowers
Designer: L. Harradine
Height: 7 ¼", 18.4 cm
Colour: Green and blue
Issued: 1937-1959
Varieties: HN 1945

U.S.:	$675.00
Can.:	$900.00
U.K.:	£400.00

HN 1808
Cissie
Designer: L. Harradine
Height: 5", 12.7 cm
Colour: Green
Issued: 1937-1951
Varieties: HN 1809

U.S.:	$700.00
Can.:	$900.00
U.K.:	£400.00

HN 1809
Cissie
Designer: L. Harradine
Height: 5", 12.7 cm
Colour: Pink
Issued: 1937-1993
Varieties: HN 1808

U.S.:	$150.00
Can.:	$225.00
U.K.:	£ 90.00

HN 1810
Bo-Peep
Style Two
Designer: L. Harradine
Height: 5", 12.7 cm
Colour: Blue
Issued: 1937-1949
Varieties: HN 1811

U.S.:	$700.00
Can.:	$950.00
U.K.:	£400.00

HN 1811
Bo-Peep
Style Two
Designer: L. Harradine
Height: 5", 12.7 cm
Colour: Pink
Issued: 1937-1995
Varieties: HN 1810

U.S.:	$150.00
Can.:	$225.00
U.K.:	£ 90.00

HN 1812
Forget-Me-Not
Style One
Designer: L. Harradine
Height: 6", 15.2 cm
Colour: Pink and green
Issued: 1937-1949
Varieties: HN 1813

U.S.:	$1,650.00
Can.:	$2,250.00
U.K.:	£ 995.00

HN 1813
Forget-Me-Not
Style One
Designer: L. Harradine
Height: 6", 15.2 cm
Colour: Red and blue
Issued: 1937-1949
Varieties: HN 1812

U.S.:	$1,250.00
Can.:	$2,000.00
U.K.:	£ 750.00

HN 1814
The Squire
Designer: Unknown
Height: 9 ¾", 24.7 cm
Colour: Red and grey
Issued: 1937-1949
Varieties: Also called ' Hunting Squire' HN 1409

U.S.:	$5,500.00
Can.:	$7,500.00
U.K.:	£3,500.00

Earthenware

HN 1815
The Huntsman
Style Two
Designer: Unknown
Height: 9 ½", 24.1 cm
Colour: Red and brown
Issued: 1937-1949
Varieties: Also called 'John Peel' HN 1408

U.S.:	$5,500.00
Can.:	$7,500.00
U.K.:	£3,500.00

Earthenware
HN 1816 - 1817 Wall Masks.

HN 1818
Miranda
Style One
Designer: L. Harradine
Height: 8 ½", 21.6 cm
Colour: Red and blue
Issued: 1937-1949
Varieties: HN 1819

U.S.:	$3,250.00
Can.:	$4,500.00
U.K.:	£1,950.00

HN 1819
Miranda
Style One
Designer: L. Harradine
Height: 8 ½", 21.6 cm
Colour: Green
Issued: 1937-1949
Varieties: HN 1818

U.S.:	$3,250.00
Can.:	$4,500.00
U.K.:	£1,950.00

HN 1820
Reflections
Designer: L. Harradine
Height: 5", 12.7 cm
Colour: Red and green
Issued: 1937-1938
Varieties: HN 1821, 1847, 1848

U.S.:	**$4,500.00**
Can.:	**$6,000.00**
U.K.:	**£2,700.00**

HN 1821
Reflections
Designer: L. Harradine
Height: 5", 12.7 cm
Colour: Green and red
Issued: 1937-1938
Varieties: HN 1820, 1847, 1848

U.S.:	**$4,500.00**
Can.:	**$6,000.00**
U.K.:	**£2,700.00**

HN 1822
M'Lady's Maid
Designer: L. Harradine
Height: 9", 22.9 cm
Colour: Multicoloured
Issued: 1937-1949
Varieties: HN 1795

U.S.:	**$6,000.00**
Can.:	**$7,750.00**
U.K.:	**£3,500.00**

HN 1823 - 1824 Wall Masks.

Photograph
Not
Available

HN 1825
Spirit of the Wind
Designer: R. Garbe
Height: Unknown
Colour: Green and ivory
Issued: 1937-1949
Varieties: HN 1777

U.S.:	**Only**
Can.:	**four**
U.K.:	**known**

HN 1826
West Wind
Designer: R. Garbe
Height: 14 ½", 36.8 cm
Colour: Antique ivory
Issued: 1937-1949
Varieties: HN 1776

U.S.:	**Only**
Can.:	**two**
U.K.:	**known**

HN 1827
Spring
Style Three
Designer: R. Garbe
Height: 21", 53.3 cm
Colour: Green and ivory
Issued: 1937-1949
Varieties: HN 1774

U.S.:	**Only**
Can.:	**four**
U.K.:	**known**

HN 1828
Salome
Style One
Designer: R. Garbe
Height: 8", 20.3 cm
Colour: Pale blue
Issued: 1937-1949
Varieties: HN 1775

U.S.:	**Only**
Can.:	**two**
U.K.:	**known**

Photograph
Not
Available

HN 1829
Macaw
Designer: R. Garbe
Height: 14 ½", 35.6 cm
Colour: Antique ivory
Issued: 1933-1949
Varieties: HN 1779

U.S.:	**Only**
Can.:	**two**
U.K.:	**known**

HN 1830
Lady of the Snows
Designer: R. Garbe
Height: Unknown
Colour: Antique ivory
Issued: 1937-1949
Varieties: HN 1780

U.S.:	Only
Can.:	two
U.K.:	known

Photograph
Not
Available

HN 1831
The Cloud
Designer: R. Garbe
Height: 23", 58.4 cm
Colour: Ivory and gold
Issued: 1937-1949

U.S.:	Only
Can.:	two
U.K.:	known

HN 1832
Granny
Designer: L. Harradine
Height: 6 ¾", 17.1 cm
Colour: Red and yellow
Issued: 1937-1949
Varieties: HN 1804

U.S.:	$4,500.00
Can.:	$6,000.00
U.K.:	£2,700.00

HN 1833
Top o' the Hill
Style One
Designer: L. Harradine
Height: 7", 17.8 cm
Colour: Green and blue
Issued: 1937-1971
Varieties: HN 1834, 1849,
          2127, 3735A

U.S.:	$350.00
Can.:	$450.00
U.K.:	£200.00

HN 1834
Top o' the Hill
Style One
Designer: L. Harradine
Height: 7", 17.8 cm
Colour: Red
Issued: 1937 to the present
Varieties: HN 1833, 1849,
          2127, 3735A

U.S.:	$410.00
Can.:	$570.00
U.K.:	£160.00

HN 1835
Verena
Designer: L. Harradine
Height: 8 ¼", 21.0 cm
Colour: Green and peach
Issued: 1938-1949
Varieties: HN 1854

U.S.:	$2,250.00
Can.:	$3,000.00
U.K.:	£1,350.00

HN 1836
Vanessa
Style One
Designer: L. Harradine
Height: 7 ½", 19.1 cm
Colour: Green and blue
Issued: 1938-1949
Varieties: HN 1838

U.S.:	$1,850.00
Can.:	$2,500.00
U.K.:	£1,100.00

HN 1837
Mariquita
Designer: L. Harradine
Height: 8", 20.3 cm
Colour: Red and purple
Issued: 1938-1949

U.S.:	$4,000.00
Can.:	$5,500.00
U.K.:	£2,500.00

HN 1838
Vanessa
Style One
Designer: L. Harradine
Height: 7 ½", 19.1 cm
Colour: Pink and green
Issued: 1938-1949
Varieties: HN 1836

U.S.:	$1,850.00
Can.:	$2,500.00
U.K.:	£1,100.00

HN 1839
Christine
Style One
Designer: L. Harradine
Height: 7 ¾", 19.6 cm
Colour: Lavender and blue
Issued: 1938-1949
Varieties: HN 1840

U.S.:	$1,650.00
Can.:	$2,250.00
U.K.:	£ 995.00

HN 1840
Christine
Style One
Designer: L. Harradine
Height: 7 ¾", 19.6 cm
Colour: Pink and blue
Issued: 1938-1949
Varieties: HN 1839

U.S.:	$1,650.00
Can.:	$2,250.00
U.K.:	£ 995.00

HN 1841
The Bride
Style One
Designer: L. Harradine
Height: 9 ½", 24.1 cm
Colour: Blue
Issued: 1938-1949
Varieties: HN 1588, 1600, 1762

U.S.:	$2,000.00
Can.:	$2,750.00
U.K.:	£1,250.00

HN 1842
Babie
Designer: L. Harradine
Height: 4 ¾", 12.0 cm
Colour: Rose and green
Issued: 1938-1949
Varieties: HN 1679, 2121

U.S.:	$400.00
Can.:	$550.00
U.K.:	£235.00

HN 1843
Biddy Penny Farthing
Designer: L. Harradine
Height: 9", 22.9 cm
Colour: Green and lavender
Issued: 1938 to the present

U.S.:	$360.00
Can.:	$550.00
U.K.:	£165.00

Earthenware and china

HN 1844
Odds and Ends
Designer: L. Harradine
Height: 7 ¾", 19.6 cm
Colour: Orange and green
Issued: 1938-1949

U.S.:	$3,750.00
Can.:	$5,250.00
U.K.:	£2,250.00

Earthenware

NOTE ON PRICING

Prices on the secondary market for Royal Doulton Figures, particularly the early HN numbers, have risen considerably over the years. As values rise, the condition and quality of these figurines takes on an increasingly important role.

The prices listed in *The Charlton Standard Catalogue of Royal Doulton Figurines* are for figures in mint condition.

Naturally, repaired or restored figures, no matter how professionally done, will sell at a discount. However the early figures, due to their rarity, may experience smaller discounts.

On Condition: For figures to command catalogue prices they must be in mint condition. This simply means that a figure will have no chips, scratches, hairline cracks, crazing, blemishes, or repairs. Any of which will remove the figure from the mint category.

On Quality: Some figures are better moulded, assembled or painted than others. High quality figures may command a premium over listed catalogue prices.

HN 1845
Modena
Designer: L. Harradine
Height: 7 ¼", 18.4 cm
Colour: Blue and pink
Issued: 1938-1949
Varieties: HN 1846

U.S.:	$3,250.00
Can.:	$4,500.00
U.K.:	£1,950.00

HN 1846
Modena
Designer: L. Harradine
Height: 7 ¼", 18.4 cm
Colour: Red and green
Issued: 1938-1949
Varieties: HN 1845

U.S.:	$3,250.00
Can.:	$4,500.00
U.K.:	£1,950.00

HN 1847
Reflections
Designer: L. Harradine
Height: 4 ½", 11.4 cm
Colour: Red and green
Issued: 1938-1949
Varieties: HN 1820, 1821, 1848

U.S.:	$3,000.00
Can.:	$4,000.00
U.K.:	£1,750.00

HN 1848
Reflections
Designer: L. Harradine
Height: 5", 12.7 cm
Colour: Green, blue and pink
Issued: 1938-1949
Varieties: HN 1820, 1821, 1847

U.S.:	$3,250.00
Can.:	$4,500.00
U.K.:	£1,950.00

HN 1849
Top o' the Hill
Style One
Designer: L. Harradine
Height: 7 ¼", 18.4 cm
Colour: Pink
Issued: 1938-1975
Varieties: HN 1833, 1834, 2127,
           3735A

U.S.:	$300.00
Can.:	$400.00
U.K.:	£175.00

HN 1850
Antoinette
Style One
Designer: L. Harradine
Height: 8 ¼", 21.0 cm
Colour: Red and pink
Issued: 1938-1949
Varieties: HN 1851

U.S.:	$2,750.00
Can.:	$3,750.00
U.K.:	£1,650.00

HN 1851
Antoinette
Style One
Designer: L. Harradine
Height: 8 ¼", 21.0 cm
Colour: Blue and lavender
Issued: 1938-1949
Varieties: HN 1850

U.S.:	$2,750.00
Can.:	$3,750.00
U.K.:	£1,650.00

HN 1852
The Mirror
Designer: L. Harradine
Height: 7 ½", 18.4 cm
Colour: Pink
Issued: 1938-1949
Varieties: HN 1853

U.S.:	$4,500.00
Can.:	$6,000.00
U.K.:	£2,700.00

HN 1853
The Mirror
Designer: L. Harradine
Height: 7 ½", 18.4 cm
Colour: Blue
Issued: 1938-1949
Varieties: HN 1852

U.S.:	$4,500.00
Can.:	$6,000.00
U.K.:	£2,700.00

HN 1854
Verena
Designer: L. Harradine
Height: 8 ¼", 21.0 cm
Colour: Blue and pink
Issued: 1938-1949
Varieties: HN 1835

U.S.:	$3,000.00
Can.:	$4,000.00
U.K.:	£1,750.00

HN 1855
Memories
Designer: L. Harradine
Height: 6", 15.2 cm
Colour: Green and red
Issued: 1938-1949
Varieties: HN 1856, 1857, 2030

U.S.:	$1,000.00
Can.:	$1,300.00
U.K.:	£ 600.00

HN 1856
Memories
Designer: L. Harradine
Height: 6", 15.2 cm
Colour: Blue and white
Issued: 1938-1949
Varieties: HN 1855, 1857, 2030

U.S.:	$1,400.00
Can.:	$1,800.00
U.K.:	£ 825.00

HN 1857
Memories
Designer: L. Harradine
Height: 6", 15.2 cm
Colour: Red and lavender
Issued: 1938-1949
Varieties: HN 1855, 1856, 2030

U.S.:	$1,400.00
Can.:	$1,800.00
U.K.:	£ 825.00

HN 1858
Dawn
(With head-dress)
Style One
Designer: L. Harradine
Height: 10", 25.4 cm
Colour: Green
Issued: 1938-Unknown
Varieties: HN 1858A

U.S.:	$3,250.00
Can.:	$4,250.00
U.K.:	£1,950.00

HN 1858A
Dawn
(Without head-dress)
Style One
Designer: L. Harradine
Height: 9 ¾", 24.7 cm
Colour: Green
Issued: Unknown-1949
Varieties: HN 1858

U.S.:	$2,250.00
Can.:	$3,000.00
U.K.:	£1,350.00

HN 1859
Tildy
Designer: L. Harradine
Height: 5 ½", 14.0 cm
Colour: Red and green
Issued: 1934-1939
Varieties: HN 1576

U.S.:	$2,000.00
Can.:	$2,500.00
U.K.:	£1,200.00

HN 1860
Millicent
Designer: L. Harradine
Height: 8", 20.3 cm
Colour: Red and blue
Issued: 1938-1949
Varieties: HN 1714, 1715

U.S.:	**$2,000.00**
Can.:	**$2,750.00**
U.K.:	**£1,200.00**

HN 1861
Kate Hardcastle
Designer: L. Harradine
Height: 8", 20.3 cm
Colour: Red and blue
Issued: 1938-1949
Varieties: HN 1718, 1719,
             1734, 1919, 2028

U.S.:	**$2,250.00**
Can.:	**$3,500.00**
U.K.:	**£1,350.00**

HN 1862
Jasmine
Style One
Designer: L. Harradine
Height: 7 ¼", 18.4 cm
Colour: Green, blue
             and orange
Issued: 1938-1949
Varieties: HN 1863, 1876

U.S.:	**$2,250.00**
Can.:	**$3,500.00**
U.K.:	**£1,350.00**

HN 1863
Jasmine
Style One
Designer: L. Harradine
Height: 7 ½", 19.1 cm
Colour: Blue and green
Issued: 1938-1949
Varieties: HN 1862, 1876

U.S.:	**$2,250.00**
Can.:	**$3,500.00**
U.K.:	**£1,350.00**

HN 1864
Sweet and Fair
Designer: L. Harradine
Height: 7 ½", 19.1 cm
Colour: Pink
Issued: 1938-1949
Varieties: HN 1865

U.S.:	**$3,250.00**
Can.:	**$4,500.00**
U.K.:	**£1,950.00**

HN 1865
Sweet and Fair
Designer: L. Harradine
Height: 7 ¼", 18.4 cm
Colour: Green
Issued: 1938-1949
Varieties: HN 1864

U.S.:	**$3,250.00**
Can.:	**$4,500.00**
U.K.:	**£1,950.00**

HN 1866
Wedding Morn
Style One
Designer: L. Harradine
Height: 10 ½", 26.7 cm
Colour: Cream
Issued: 1938-1949
Varieties: HN 1867

U.S.:	**$4,000.00**
Can.:	**$5,500.00**
U.K.:	**£2,400.00**

HN 1867
Wedding Morn
Style One
Designer: L. Harradine
Height: 10 ½", 26.7 cm
Colour: Red and cream
Issued: 1938-1949
Varieties: HN 1866

U.S.:	**$4,000.00**
Can.:	**$5,500.00**
U.K.:	**£2,400.00**

Period Figures in English History

HN 2005
Henrietta Maria, Style One
1948-1953

HN 2006
The Lady Anne Nevill
1948-1953

HN 2007
Mrs. Fitzherbert
1948-1953

HN 2008
Philippa of Hainault,
Style One, 1948-1953

HN 2009
Eleanor of Provence
1948-1953

HN 2010
The Young Miss Nightingale
1948-1953

HN 2011
Matilda
1948-1953

HN 2012
Margaret of Anjou, Style One
1948-1953

Nursery Rhymes
Series One

HN 2044
Mary, Mary
1949-1973

HN 2045
She Loves Me Not
1949-1962

HN 2046
He Loves Me
1949-1962

HN 2047
Once Upon a Time
1949-1955

HN 2048
Mary Had a Little Lamb
1949-1988

HN 2049
Curly Locks
1949-1953

HN 2050
Wee Willie Winkie, Style One
1949-1953

HN 2060
Jack
1950-1971

Nursery Rhymes
Series One

HN 2061
Jill
1950-1971

HN 2062
Little Boy Blue, Style One
1950-1973

HN 2063
Little Jack Horner, Style One
1950-1953

HN 2064
My Pretty Maid
1950-1954

Figures of Williamsburg

HN 2154
A Child from Williamsburg
1964-1983

HN 2183
Boy from Williamsburg
1969-1983

HN 2208
Silversmith of Williamsburg
1960-1983

Figures of Williamsburg

HN 2209
Hostess of Williamsburg
1960-1983

HN 2227
Gentleman from Williamsburg
1960-1983

HN 2228
Lady from Williamsburg
1960-1983

HN 2233
Royal Governor's Cook
1960-1983

HN 2239
Wigmaker of Williamsburg
1960-1983

HN 2240
Blacksmith of Williamsburg
1960-1983

Sea Characters

HN 2248
Tall Story
1968-1975

HN 2254
Shore Leave
1965-1979

HN 2260
The Captain, Style Two
1965-1982

HN 2317
The Lobster Man
1964-1994

HN 2442
Sailor's Holiday
1972-1979

HN 2455
The Seafarer (matte)
1972-1976

Sea Characters

HN 2499
Helmsman
1974-1986

HN 2729
Song of the Sea
1982 Canada, 1983 Worldwide-1991

HN 2733
Officer of the Line
1982 Canada, 1983 Worldwide-1986

Middle Earth

HN 2911
Gandalf
1980-1984

HN 2912
Frodo
1980-1984

HN 2913
Gollum
1980-1984

HN 2914
Bilbo
1980-1984

Middle Earth

HN 2915
Galadriel
1981-1984

HN 2916
Aragorn
1981-1984

HN 2917
Legolas
1981-1984

HN 2918
Boromir
1981-1984

HN 2922
Gimli
1981-1984

HN 2923
Barliman Butterbur
1982-1984

HN 2924
Tom Bombadil
1982-1984

HN 2925
Samwise
1982-1984

Haute Ensemble

HN 2542
Boudoir
1974-1979

HN 2543A
Eliza (Painted flowers)
Style One
1974-1979

HN 2544
A la Mode
1974-1979

HN 2545
Carmen, Style Two
1974-1979

HN 2712
Mantilla
1974-1979

HN 1868
Serena
Designer: L. Harradine
Height: 11", 27.9 cm
Colour: Red, pink and blue
Issued: 1938-1949
U.S.: $1,650.00
Can.: $2,250.00
U.K.:   £ 975.00

Earthenware

HN 1869
Dryad of the Pines
Designer: R. Garbe
Height: 23", 58.4 cm
Colour: Ivory and gold
Issued: 1938-1949
U.S.:
Can.:   Extremely rare
U.K.:

HN 1870
Little Lady Make Believe
Designer: L. Harradine
Height: 6 ¼", 15.9 cm
Colour: Red and blue
Issued: 1938-1949
U.S.: $ 850.00
Can.: $1,100.00
U.K.:   £ 500.00

HN 1871
Annabella
Designer: L. Harradine
Height: 5 ¼", 13.3 cm
Colour: Pink and green
Issued: 1938-1949
Varieties: HN 1872, 1875
U.S.: $1,500.00
Can.: $2,000.00
U.K.:   £ 900.00

HN 1872
Annabella
Designer: L. Harradine
Height: 5 ¼", 13.3 cm
Colour: Green and blue
Issued: 1938-1949
Varieties: HN 1871, 1875
U.S.: $1,500.00
Can.: $2,000.00
U.K.:   £ 900.00

HN 1873
Granny's Heritage
Designer: L. Harradine
Height: 6 ¾", 17.2 cm
Colour: Pink, blue and grey
Issued: 1938-1949
Varieties: HN 1874, 2031
U.S.: $1,350.00
Can.: $1,750.00
U.K.:   £ 800.00

HN 1874
Granny's Heritage
Designer: L. Harradine
Height: 6 ¼", 15.9 cm
Colour: Blue and green
Issued: 1938-1949
Varieties: HN 1873, 2031
U.S.: $1,600.00
Can.: $2,250.00
U.K.:   £ 950.00

HN 1875
Annabella
Designer: L. Harradine
Height: 4 ¾", 12.0 cm
Colour: Red
Issued: 1938-1949
Varieties: HN 1871, 1872
U.S.: $1,500.00
Can.: $2,000.00
U.K.:   £ 900.00

HN 1876
Jasmine
Style One
Designer: L. Harradine
Height: 7 ½", 19.1 cm
Colour: Green and blue
Issued: 1938-1949
Varieties: HN 1862, 1863

U.S.:	$2,250.00
Can.:	$3,500.00
U.K.:	£1,350.00

HN 1877
Jean
Style One
Designer: L. Harradine
Height: 7 ½", 19.0 cm
Colour: Pink and purple
Issued: 1938-1949
Varieties: HN 1878, 2032

U.S.:	$ 950.00
Can.:	$1,250.00
U.K.:	£ 550.00

HN 1878
Jean
Style One
Designer: L. Harradine
Height: 7 ½", 19.0 cm
Colour: Green and red
Issued: 1938-1949
Varieties: HN 1877, 2032

U.S.:	$700.00
Can.:	$900.00
U.K.:	£425.00

HN 1879
Bon Jour
Designer: L. Harradine
Height: 6 ¾", 17.2 cm
Colour: Green
Issued: 1938-1949
Varieties: HN 1888

U.S.:	$2,000.00
Can.:	$2,750.00
U.K.:	£1,250.00

HN 1880
The Lambeth Walk
Designer: L. Harradine
Height: 10", 25.4 cm
Colour: Blue
Issued: 1938-1949
Varieties: HN 1881

U.S.:	$4,000.00
Can.:	$5,250.00
U.K.:	£2,400.00

HN 1881
The Lambeth Walk
Designer: L. Harradine
Height: 10", 25.4 cm
Colour: Pink
Issued: 1938-1949
Varieties: HN 1880

U.S.:	$4,000.00
Can.:	$5,250.00
U.K.:	£2,400.00

HN 1882
Nell Gwynn
Designer: L. Harradine
Height: 6 ¾", 17.2 cm
Colour: Blue and pink
Issued: 1938-1949
Varieties: HN 1887

U.S.:	$2,250.00
Can.:	$3,500.00
U.K.:	£1,350.00

HN 1883
Prudence
Designer: L. Harradine
Height: 6 ¾", 17.2 cm
Colour: Blue
Issued: 1938-1949
Varieties: HN 1884

U.S.:	$1,400.00
Can.:	$1,800.00
U.K.:	£ 825.00

HN 1884
Prudence
Designer: L. Harradine
Height: 6 ¾", 17.2 cm
Colour: Pink
Issued: 1938-1949
Varieties: HN 1883

U.S.:	**$1,400.00**
Can.:	**$1,800.00**
U.K.:	**£ 825.00**

HN 1885
Nadine
Style One
Designer: L. Harradine
Height: 7 ¾", 19.7 cm
Colour: Turquoise
Issued: 1938-1949
Varieties: HN 1886

U.S.:	**$1,750.00**
Can.:	**$2,250.00**
U.K.:	**£1,000.00**

HN 1886
Nadine
Style One
Designer: L. Harradine
Height: 7 ¾", 19.7 cm
Colour: Pink
Issued: 1938-1949
Varieties: HN 1885

U.S.:	**$1,750.00**
Can.:	**$2,250.00**
U.K.:	**£1,000.00**

HN 1887
Nell Gwynn
Designer: L. Harradine
Height: 6 ¾", 17.2 cm
Colour: Green and pink
Issued: 1938-1949
Varieties: HN 1882

U.S.:	**$2,250.00**
Can.:	**$3,000.00**
U.K.:	**£1,350.00**

HN 1888
Bon Jour
Designer: L. Harradine
Height: 6 ¾", 17.2 cm
Colour: Red
Issued: 1938-1949
Varieties: HN 1879

U.S.:	**$2,000.00**
Can.:	**$2,750.00**
U.K.:	**£1,250.00**

HN 1889
Goody Two Shoes
Style One
Designer: L. Harradine
Height: 4 ¾", 12.0 cm
Colour: Green and purple
Issued: 1938-1949
Varieties: HN 1905, 2037

U.S.:	**$ 750.00**
Can.:	**$1,000.00**
U.K.:	**£ 450.00**

HN 1890
Lambing Time
Style One
Designer: W. M. Chance
Height: 9 ¼", 23.5 cm
Colour: Light brown
Issued: 1938-1981

U.S.:	**$300.00**
Can.:	**$400.00**
U.K.:	**£175.00**

Earthenware

HN 1891
Pecksniff
Style Two
Designer: L. Harradine
Height: 7", 17.8 cm
Colour: Black and brown
Issued: 1938-1952
Varieties: HN 553
Series: Dickens (Series Two)

U.S.:	**$625.00**
Can.:	**$800.00**
U.K.:	**£375.00**

HN 1892
Uriah Heep
Style Two
Designer: L. Harradine
Height: 7", 17.8 cm
Colour: Black
Issued: 1938-1952
Varieties: HN 554
Series: Dickens (Series Two)

U.S.:	$625.00
Can.:	$800.00
U.K.:	£375.00

HN 1893
Fat Boy
Style Two
Designer: L. Harradine
Height: 7", 17.8 cm
Colour: Blue and cream
Issued: 1938-1952
Varieties: HN 555
Series: Dickens (Series Two)

U.S.:	$625.00
Can.:	$800.00
U.K.:	£375.00

HN 1894
Mr Pickwick
Style Two
Designer: L. Harradine
Height: 7", 17.8 cm
Colour: Blue, tan and cream
Issued: 1938-1952
Varieties: HN 556
Series: Dickens (Series Two)

U.S.:	$625.00
Can.:	$800.00
U.K.:	£375.00

Earthenware and porcelain

HN 1895
Mr Micawber
Style Two
Designer: L. Harradine
Height: 7", 17.8 cm
Colour: Brown, black
           and tan
Issued: 1938-1952
Varieties: HN 557
Series: Dickens (Series Two)

U.S.:	$625.00
Can.:	$800.00
U.K.:	£375.00

HN 1896
Sairey Gamp
Style Two
Designer: L. Harradine
Height: 7", 17.8 cm
Colour: Green
Issued: 1938-1952
Varieties: HN 558
Series: Dickens (Series Two)

U.S.:	$750.00
Can.:	$975.00
U.K.:	£450.00

HN 1897
Miss Fortune
Designer: L. Harradine
Height: 6", 15.2 cm
Colour: Pink and blue
Issued: 1938-1949
Varieties: HN 1898

U.S.:	$1,200.00
Can.:	$1,600.00
U.K.:	£ 700.00

HN 1898
Miss Fortune
Designer: L. Harradine
Height: 5 ¾", 14.6 cm
Colour: Blue
Issued: 1938-1949
Varieties: HN 1897

U.S.:	$1,600.00
Can.:	$2,250.00
U.K.:	£ 950.00

HN 1899
Midsummer Noon
Designer: L. Harradine
Height: 4 ¾", 12.0 cm
Colour: Pink
Issued: 1939-1949
Varieties: HN 1900, 2033

U.S.:	$1,100.00
Can.:	$1,400.00
U.K.:	£ 650.00

HN 1900
Midsummer Noon
Designer: L. Harradine
Height: 4 ¾", 12.0 cm
Colour: Blue
Issued: 1939-1949
Varieties: HN 1899, 2033

U.S.:	**$3,000.00**
Can.:	**$4,000.00**
U.K.:	**£1,750.00**

HN 1901
Penelope
Designer: L. Harradine
Height: 7", 17.8 cm
Colour: Red
Issued: 1939-1975
Varieties: HN 1902

U.S.:	**$500.00**
Can.:	**$650.00**
U.K.:	**£300.00**

HN 1902
Penelope
Designer: L. Harradine
Height: 7", 17.8 cm
Colour: Lavender and green
Issued: 1939-1949
Varieties: HN 1901

U.S.:	**$2,250.00**
Can.:	**$3,000.00**
U.K.:	**£1,350.00**

HN 1903
Rhythm
Designer: L. Harradine
Height: 6 ¾", 17.2 cm
Colour: Pink
Issued: 1939-1949
Varieties: HN 1904

U.S.:	**$4,250.00**
Can.:	**$5,500.00**
U.K.:	**£2,500.00**

HN 1904
Rhythm
Designer: L. Harradine
Height: 6 ¾", 17.2 cm
Colour: Blue
Issued: 1939-1949
Varieties: HN 1903

U.S.:	**$5,000.00**
Can.:	**$6,500.00**
U.K.:	**£3,000.00**

HN 1905
Goody Two Shoes
Style One
Designer: L. Harradine
Height: 4 ¾", 12.0 cm
Colour: Red and pink
Issued: 1939-1949
Varieties: HN 1889, 2037

U.S.:	**$300.00**
Can.:	**$400.00**
U.K.:	**£175.00**

HN 1906
Lydia
Style One
Designer: L. Harradine
Height: 4 ¼", 10.8 cm
Colour: Orange and pink
Issued: 1939-1949
Varieties: HN 1907, 1908

U.S.:	**$750.00**
Can.:	**$975.00**
U.K.:	**£450.00**

HN 1907
Lydia
Style One
Designer: L. Harradine
Height: 4 ¾", 12.0 cm
Colour: Green
Issued: 1939-1949
Varieties: HN 1906, 1908

U.S.:	**$750.00**
Can.:	**$975.00**
U.K.:	**£450.00**

HN 1908
Lydia
Style One
Designer: L. Harradine
Height: 4 ¾", 12.0 cm
Colour: Red
Issued: 1939-1995
Varieties: HN 1906, 1907

U.S.:	**$200.00**
Can.:	**$250.00**
U.K.:	**£110.00**

HN 1909
Honey
Designer: L. Harradine
Height: 7", 17.8 cm
Colour: Pink
Issued: 1939-1949
Varieties: HN 1910, 1963

U.S.:	**$700.00**
Can.:	**$900.00**
U.K.:	**£400.00**

HN 1910
Honey
Designer: L. Harradine
Height: 6 ¾", 17.2 cm
Colour: Blue
Issued: 1939-1949
Varieties: HN 1909, 1963

U.S.:	**$1,400.00**
Can.:	**$1,800.00**
U.K.:	**£ 825.00**

HN 1911
Autumn Breezes
Style One
Designer: L. Harradine
Height: 7 ½", 19.1 cm
Colour: Green and pink
Issued: 1939-1976
Varieties: HN 1913, 1934, 2131, 2147, 3736

U.S.:	**$275.00**
Can.:	**$350.00**
U.K.:	**£175.00**

HN 1912
Old Balloon Seller and Bulldog
Designer: L. Harradine
Height: 7", 17.8 cm
Colour: Unknown
Issued: 1939-1949
Varieties: HN 1791

U.S.:	**Only**
Can.:	**one**
U.K.:	**known**

HN 1913
Autumn Breezes
Style One
Designer: L. Harradine
Height: 7 ½", 19.1 cm
Colour: Green and blue
Issued: 1939-1971
Varieties: HN 1911, 1934, 2131, 2147, 3736

U.S.:	**$275.00**
Can.:	**$350.00**
U.K.:	**£175.00**

HN 1914
Paisley Shawl
Style Three
Designer: L. Harradine
Height: 6 ½", 16.5 cm
Colour: Green and red
Issued: 1939-1949
Varieties: HN 1988

U.S.:	**$400.00**
Can.:	**$525.00**
U.K.:	**£250.00**

HN 1915
Veronica
Style Three
Designer: L. Harradine
Height: 5 ¾", 14.6 cm
Colour: Red and cream
Issued: 1939-1949

U.S.:	**$500.00**
Can.:	**$650.00**
U.K.:	**£300.00**

HN 1916
Janet
Style Three
Designer: L. Harradine
Height: 5 ¼", 13.3 cm
Colour: Pink and blue
Issued: 1939-1949
Varieties: HN 1964

U.S.:	**$350.00**
Can.:	**$450.00**
U.K.:	**£200.00**

HN 1917
Meryll
Designer: L. Harradine
Height: 6 ¾", 17.2 cm
Colour: Red and green
Issued: 1939-1940
Varieties: Also called 'Toinette'
              HN 1940

U.S.:	**$4,250.00**
Can.:	**$5,500.00**
U.K.:	**£2,600.00**

HN 1918
Sweet Suzy
Designer: L. Harradine
Height: 6 ½", 16.5 cm
Colour: Pink and green
Issued: 1939-1949

U.S.:	**$1,600.00**
Can.:	**$2,000.00**
U.K.:	**£ 950.00**

HN 1919
Kate Hardcastle
Designer: L. Harradine
Height: 8 ¼", 21.0 cm
Colour: Red and green
Issued: 1939-1949
Varieties: HN 1718, 1719, 1734,
              1861, 2028

U.S.:	**$2,300.00**
Can.:	**$3,000.00**
U.K.:	**£1,350.00**

HN 1920
Windflower
Style Two
Designer: L. Harradine
Height: 11", 27.9 cm
Colour: Multicoloured
Issued: 1939-1949
Varieties: HN 1939

U.S.:	**$4,000.00**
Can.:	**$5,250.00**
U.K.:	**£2,400.00**

HN 1921
Roseanna
Designer: L. Harradine
Height: 8", 20.3 cm
Colour: Green
Issued: 1940-1949
Varieties: HN 1926

U.S.:	**$2,500.00**
Can.:	**$3,250.00**
U.K.:	**£1,500.00**

HN 1922
Spring Morning
Style One
Designer: L. Harradine
Height: 7 ½", 19.1 cm
Colour: Pink and blue
Issued: 1940-1973
Varieties: HN 1923

U.S.:	**$325.00**
Can.:	**$425.00**
U.K.:	**£195.00**

HN 1923
Spring Morning
Style One
Designer: L. Harradine
Height: 7 ½", 19.1 cm
Colour: Green and cream
Issued: 1940-1949
Varieties: HN 1922

U.S.:	**$1,100.00**
Can.:	**$1,500.00**
U.K.:	**£ 675.00**

HN 1924
Fiona
Style One
Designer: L. Harradine
Height: 5 ¾", 14.6 cm
Colour: Pink and lavender
Issued: 1940-1949
Varieties: HN 1925, 1933

U.S.:	**$1,500.00**
Can.:	**$2,000.00**
U.K.:	**£ 900.00**

HN 1925
Fiona
Style One
Designer: L. Harradine
Height: 5 ¾", 14.6 cm
Colour: Blue
Issued: 1940-1949
Varieties: HN 1924, 1933

U.S.:	**$1,500.00**
Can.:	**$2,000.00**
U.K.:	**£ 900.00**

HN 1926
Roseanna
Designer: L. Harradine
Height: 8", 20.3 cm
Colour: Pink
Issued: 1940-1959
Varieties: HN 1921

U.S.:	**$650.00**
Can.:	**$850.00**
U.K.:	**£375.00**

HN 1927
The Awakening
Style One
Designer: L. Harradine
Height: 10 ¼", 26.0 cm
Colour: Pale pink
Issued: 1940-1949

U.S.:	**$4,500.00**
Can.:	**$6,000.00**
U.K.:	**£2,700.00**

HN 1928
Marguerite
Designer: L. Harradine
Height: 8", 20.3 cm
Colour: Pink
Issued: 1940-1959
Varieties: HN 1929, 1930, 1946

U.S.:	**$650.00**
Can.:	**$850.00**
U.K.:	**£375.00**

HN 1929
Marguerite
Designer: L. Harradine
Height: 8", 20.3 cm
Colour: Pale pink and yellow
Issued: 1940-1949
Varieties: HN 1928, 1930, 1946

U.S.:	**$2,500.00**
Can.:	**$3,250.00**
U.K.:	**£1,500.00**

HN 1930
Marguerite
Designer: L. Harradine
Height: 8", 20.3 cm
Colour: Blue and purple
Issued: 1940-1949
Varieties: HN 1928, 1929, 1946

U.S.:	**$2,000.00**
Can.:	**$2,500.00**
U.K.:	**£1,200.00**

HN 1931
Meriel
Designer: L. Harradine
Height: 7 ¼", 18.4 cm
Colour: Pink
Issued: 1940-1949
Varieties: HN 1932

U.S.:	**$3,000.00**
Can.:	**$4,000.00**
U.K.:	**£1,750.00**

HN 1932
Meriel
Designer: L. Harradine
Height: 7 ¼", 18.4 cm
Colour: Green
Issued: 1940-1949
Varieties: HN 1931

 U.S.: **$3,000.00**
 Can.: **$4,000.00**
 U.K.: **£1,750.00**

HN 1933
Fiona
Style One
Designer: L. Harradine
Height: 5 ¾", 14.6 cm
Colour: Multicoloured
Issued: 1940-1949
Varieties: HN 1924, 1925

 U.S.: **$1,750.00**
 Can.: **$2,250.00**
 U.K.: **£1,000.00**

HN 1934
Autumn Breezes
Style One
Designer: L. Harradine
Height: 7 ½", 19.1 cm
Colour: Red
Issued: 1940-1997
Varieties: HN 1911, 1913, 2131,
    2147, 3736

 U.S.: **$275.00**
 Can.: **$375.00**
 U.K.: **£150.00**

HN 1935
Sweeting
Designer: L. Harradine
Height: 6", 15.2 cm
Colour: Pink
Issued: 1940-1973
Varieties: HN 1938

 U.S.: **$175.00**
 Can.: **$225.00**
 U.K.: **£100.00**

HN 1936
Miss Muffet
Designer: L. Harradine
Height: 5 ½", 14.0 cm
Colour: Red
Issued: 1940-1967
Varieties: HN 1937

 U.S.: **$250.00**
 Can.: **$325.00**
 U.K.: **£150.00**

HN 1937
Miss Muffet
Designer: L. Harradine
Height: 5 ½", 14.0 cm
Colour: Green
Issued: 1940-1952
Varieties: HN 1936

 U.S.: **$450.00**
 Can.: **$600.00**
 U.K.: **£270.00**

HN 1938
Sweeting
Designer: L. Harradine
Height: 6", 15.2 cm
Colour: Purple and red
Issued: 1940-1949
Varieties: HN 1935

 U.S.: **$600.00**
 Can.: **$800.00**
 U.K.: **£350.00**

HN 1939
Windflower
Style Two
Designer: L. Harradine
Height: 11", 27.9 cm
Colour: Pink
Issued: 1940-1949
Varieties: HN 1920

 U.S.: **$4,000.00**
 Can.: **$5,250.00**
 U.K.: **£2,400.00**

HN 1940
Toinette
Designer: L. Harradine
Height: 6 ¾", 17.1 cm
Colour: Red
Issued: 1940-1949
Varieties: Also called 'Meryll'
           HN 1917

U.S.:	**$3,000.00**
Can.:	**$4,000.00**
U.K.:	**£1,750.00**

HN 1941
Peggy
Designer: L. Harradine
Height: 5", 12.7 cm
Colour: Red and white
Issued: 1940-1949
Varieties: HN 2038 (minor
           glaze difference)

U.S.:	**$250.00**
Can.:	**$325.00**
U.K.:	**£150.00**

HN 1942
Pyjams
Designer: L. Harradine
Height: 5 ¼", 13.3 cm
Colour: Pink
Issued: 1940-1949

U.S.:	**$1,500.00**
Can.:	**$2,000.00**
U.K.:	**£ 900.00**

HN 1943
Veronica
Style One
Designer: L. Harradine
Height: 8", 20.3 cm
Colour: Red dress and blue hat
Issued: 1940-1949
Varieties: HN 1517, 1519, 1650

U.S.:	**$1,650.00**
Can.:	**$2,250.00**
U.K.:	**£1,000.00**

HN 1944
Daydreams
Designer: L. Harradine
Height: 5 ½", 14.0 cm
Colour: Red
Issued: 1940-1949
Varieties: HN 1731, 1732

U.S.:	**$1,400.00**
Can.:	**$1,850.00**
U.K.:	**£ 850.00**

HN 1945
Spring Flowers
Designer: L. Harradine
Height: 7 ¼", 18.4 cm
Colour: Red and green
Issued: 1940-1949
Varieties: HN 1807

U.S.:	**$2,000.00**
Can.:	**$2,750.00**
U.K.:	**£1,200.00**

HN 1946
Marguerite
Designer: L. Harradine
Height: 8", 20.3 cm
Colour: Pink
Issued: 1940-1949
Varieties: HN 1928, 1929, 1930

U.S.:	**$2,500.00**
Can.:	**$3,250.00**
U.K.:	**£1,500.00**

HN 1947
June
Style One
Designer: L. Harradine
Height: 7 ¼", 18.4 cm
Colour: Red
Issued: 1940-1949
Varieties: HN 1690, 1691, 2027

U.S.:	**$1,650.00**
Can.:	**$2,250.00**
U.K.:	**£1,000.00**

HN 1948
Lady Charmian
Designer: L. Harradine
Height: 8", 20.3 cm
Colour: Green dress with
          red shawl
Issued: 1940-1973
Varieties: HN 1949

U.S.:	$325.00
Can.:	$425.00
U.K.:	£200.00

HN 1949
Lady Charmian
Designer: L. Harradine
Height: 8", 20.3 cm
Colour: Red dress with
          green shawl
Issued: 1940-1975
Varieties: HN 1948

U.S.:	$350.00
Can.:	$450.00
U.K.:	£200.00

HN 1950
Claribel
Designer: L. Harradine
Height: 4 ¾", 12.0 cm
Colour: Purple and pink
Issued: 1940-1949
Varieties: HN 1951

U.S.:	$650.00
Can.:	$900.00
U.K.:	£400.00

HN 1951
Claribel
Designer: L. Harradine
Height: 4 ¾", 12.0 cm
Colour: Red
Issued: 1940-1949
Varieties: HN 1950

U.S.:	$650.00
Can.:	$900.00
U.K.:	£400.00

HN 1952
Irene
Designer: L. Harradine
Height: 6 ¾", 17.2 cm
Colour: Blue and purple
Issued: 1940-1950
Varieties: HN 1621, 1697

U.S.:	$1,650.00
Can.:	$2,250.00
U.K.:	£1,000.00

HN 1953
Orange Lady
Designer: L. Harradine
Height: 8 ½", 21.6 cm
Colour: Light green dress,
          dark green shawl
Issued: 1940-1975
Varieties: HN 1759

U.S.:	$325.00
Can.:	$425.00
U.K.:	£200.00

HN 1954
The Balloon Man
Designer: L. Harradine
Height: 7 ¼", 18.4 cm
Colour: Black and grey
Issued: 1940 to the present

U.S.:	$360.00
Can.:	$550.00
U.K.:	£165.00

HN 1955
Lavinia
Designer: L. Harradine
Height: 5", 12.7 cm
Colour: Red
Issued: 1940-1979

U.S.:	$175.00
Can.:	$225.00
U.K.:	£100.00

Earthenware and China

HN 1956
Chloe
Style One
Designer: L. Harradine
Height: 6", 15.2 cm
Colour: Red and green
Issued: 1940-1949
Varieties: HN 1470, 1476, 1479, 1498, 1765

U.S.:	$1,100.00
Can.:	$1,500.00
U.K.:	£ 650.00

HN 1957
The New Bonnet
Designer: L. Harradine
Height: 7", 17.8 cm
Colour: Red
Issued: 1940-1949
Varieties: HN 1728

U.S.:	$2,000.00
Can.:	$2,500.00
U.K.:	£1,200.00

HN 1958
Lady April
Designer: L. Harradine
Height: 7", 17.8 cm
Colour: Red and purple
Issued: 1940-1959
Varieties: HN 1965

U.S.:	$525.00
Can.:	$675.00
U.K.:	£325.00

HN 1959
The Choice
Designer: L. Harradine
Height: 7 ¼", 18.4 cm
Colour: Red
Issued: 1941-1949
Varieties: HN 1960

U.S.:	$3,000.00
Can.:	$4,000.00
U.K.:	£1,750.00

HN 1960
The Choice
Designer: L. Harradine
Height: 7 ¼", 18.4 cm
Colour: Purple
Issued: 1941-1949
Varieties: HN 1959

U.S.:	$3,000.00
Can.:	$4,000.00
U.K.:	£1,750.00

HN 1961
Daisy
Style One
Designer: L. Harradine
Height: 3 ½", 8.9 cm
Colour: Pink
Issued: 1941-1949
Varieties: HN 1575

U.S.:	$ 900.00
Can.:	$1,200.00
U.K.:	£ 525.00

HN 1962
Genevieve
Designer: L. Harradine
Height: 7", 17.8 cm
Colour: Red
Issued: 1941-1975

U.S.:	$450.00
Can.:	$575.00
U.K.:	£275.00

HN 1963
Honey
Designer: L. Harradine
Height: 6 ¾", 17.2 cm
Colour: Red and blue
Issued: 1941-1949
Varieties: HN 1909, 1910

U.S.:	$1,500.00
Can.:	$2,000.00
U.K.:	£ 900.00

HN 1964
Janet
Style Three
Designer: L. Harradine
Height: 5", 12.7 cm
Colour: Pink
Issued: 1941-1949
Varieties: HN 1916

U.S.:	$ 850.00
Can.:	$1,100.00
U.K.:	£ 500.00

HN 1965
Lady April
Designer: L. Harradine
Height: 7", 17.8 cm
Colour: Green and pink
Issued: 1941-1949
Varieties: HN 1958

U.S.:	$1,200.00
Can.:	$1,600.00
U.K.:	£ 725.00

HN 1966
An Orange Vendor
Designer: C. J. Noke
Height: 6 ¼", 15.9 cm
Colour: Purple
Issued: 1941-1949
Varieties: HN 72, 508, 521

U.S.:	$1,400.00
Can.:	$1,800.00
U.K.:	£ 850.00

Earthenware

HN 1967
Lady Betty
Designer: L. Harradine
Height: 6 ½", 16.5 cm
Colour: Red
Issued: 1941-1951

U.S.:	$650.00
Can.:	$850.00
U.K.:	£400.00

HN 1968
Madonna of the Square
Designer: P. Stabler
Height: 7", 17.8 cm
Colour: Pale green
Issued: 1941-1949
Varieties: HN 10, 10A, 11, 14, 27, 326, 573, 576, 594, 613, 764, 1969, 2034

U.S.:	$2,250.00
Can.:	$3,000.00
U.K.:	£1,250.00

HN 1969
Madonna of the Square
Designer: P. Stabler
Height: 7", 17.8 cm
Colour: Lavender
Issued: 1941-1949
Varieties: HN 10, 10A, 11, 14, 27, 326, 573, 576, 594, 613, 764, 1968, 2034

U.S.:	$2,250.00
Can.:	$3,000.00
U.K.:	£1,250.00

HN 1970
Milady
Designer: L. Harradine
Height: 6 ½", 16.5 cm
Colour: Pink
Issued: 1941-1949

U.S.:	$1,900.00
Can.:	$2,500.00
U.K.:	£1,150.00

HN 1971
Springtime
Style One
Designer: L. Harradine
Height: 6", 15.2 cm
Colour: Pink and blue
Issued: 1941-1949

U.S.:	$1,650.00
Can.:	$2,250.00
U.K.:	£1,000.00

HN 1972
Regency Beau
Designer: H. Fenton
Height: 8", 20.3 cm
Colour: Green and pink
Issued: 1941-1949

U.S.:	**$2,000.00**
Can.:	**$2,750.00**
U.K.:	**£1,200.00**

HN 1973
The Corinthian
Designer: H. Fenton
Height: 7 ¾", 19.7 cm
Colour: Green, red and cream
Issued: 1941-1949

U.S.:	**$2,000.00**
Can.:	**$2,750.00**
U.K.:	**£1,200.00**

HN 1974
Forty Winks
Designer: H. Fenton
Height: 6 ¾", 17.2 cm
Colour: Green and tan
Issued: 1945-1973

U.S.:	**$325.00**
Can.:	**$425.00**
U.K.:	**£200.00**

HN 1975
The Shepherd
Style Four
Designer: H. Fenton
Height: 8 ½", 21.6 cm
Colour: Light brown
Issued: 1945-1975

U.S.:	**$300.00**
Can.:	**$400.00**
U.K.:	**£175.00**

HN 1976
Easter Day
Designer: L. Harradine
Height: 7 ¼", 18.4 cm
Colour: White, lilac and green
Issued: 1945-1951
Varieties: HN 2039

U.S.:	**$ 850.00**
Can.:	**$1,100.00**
U.K.:	**£ 500.00**

HN 1977
Her Ladyship
Designer: L. Harradine
Height: 7 ¼", 18.4 cm
Colour: Red and cream
Issued: 1945-1959

U.S.:	**$550.00**
Can.:	**$700.00**
U.K.:	**£325.00**

HN 1978
Bedtime
Style One
Designer: L. Harradine
Height: 5 ¾", 14.6 cm
Colour: White, black base
Issued: 1945-1997
Varieties: HN 2219

U.S.:	**$100.00**
Can.:	**$150.00**
U.K.:	**£ 60.00**

HN 1979
Gollywog
Designer: L. Harradine
Height: 5 ¼", 13.3 cm
Colour: Patterned white
           dungarees
Issued: 1945-1959
Varieties: HN 2040

U.S.:	**$1,350.00**
Can.:	**$1,750.00**
U.K.:	**£ 800.00**

HN 1980
Gwynneth
Designer: L. Harradine
Height: 7", 17.8 cm
Colour: Red
Issued: 1945-1952

U.S.: **$550.00**
Can.: **$725.00**
U.K.: **£325.00**

HN 1981
The Ermine Coat
Designer: L. Harradine
Height: 6 ¾", 17.2 cm
Colour: White and red
Issued: 1945-1967

U.S.: **$450.00**
Can.: **$600.00**
U.K.: **£275.00**

HN 1982
Sabbath Morn
Designer: L. Harradine
Height: 7 ¼", 18.4 cm
Colour: Red
Issued: 1945-1959

U.S.: **$400.00**
Can.: **$525.00**
U.K.: **£225.00**

HN 1983
Rosebud
Style Two
Designer: L. Harradine
Height: 7 ½", 19.1 cm
Colour: Pink and red
Issued: 1945-1952

U.S.: **$650.00**
Can.: **$850.00**
U.K.: **£400.00**

HN 1984
The Patchwork Quilt
Designer: L. Harradine
Height: 6", 15.2 cm
Colour: Multicoloured
Issued: 1945-1959

U.S.: **$500.00**
Can.: **$650.00**
U.K.: **£300.00**

HN 1985
Darling
Style Two
Designer: C. Vyse
Height: 5 ¼", 13.3 cm
Colour: White, black base
Issued: 1944-1997
Varieties: HN 3613

U.S.: **$100.00**
Can.: **$150.00**
U.K.: **£ 60.00**

HN 1986
Diana
Style One
Designer: L. Harradine
Height: 5 ¾", 14.6 cm
Colour: Red
Issued: 1946-1975
Varieties: HN 1716, 1717

U.S.: **$250.00**
Can.: **$325.00**
U.K.: **£150.00**

HN 1987
Paisley Shawl
Style One
Designer: L. Harradine
Height: 8 ¼", 21.0 cm
Colour: Red and cream
Issued: 1946-1959
Varieties: HN 1392, 1460, 1707, 1739

U.S.: **$500.00**
Can.: **$650.00**
U.K.: **£300.00**

HN 1988
Paisley Shawl
Style Three
Designer: L. Harradine
Height: 6 ¼", 15.9 cm
Colour: Red and pink
Issued: 1946-1975
Varieties: HN 1914

  U.S.:   **$250.00**
  Can.:   **$325.00**
  U.K.:   **£150.00**

HN 1989
Margaret
Style One
Designer: L. Harradine
Height: 7 ¼", 18.4 cm
Colour: Red and green
Issued: 1947-1959

  U.S.:   **$550.00**
  Can.:   **$700.00**
  U.K.:   **£325.00**

HN 1990
Mary Jane
Designer: L. Harradine
Height: 7 ½", 19.1 cm
Colour: Flowered pink dress
Issued: 1947-1952

  U.S.:   **$650.00**
  Can.:   **$850.00**
  U.K.:   **£400.00**

HN 1991
Market Day
Designer: L. Harradine
Height: 7 ¼", 18.4 cm
Colour: Blue, pink and white
Issued: 1947-1955
Varieties: Also called 'A Country
           Lass' HN 1991A

  U.S.:   **$400.00**
  Can.:   **$525.00**
  U.K.:   **£225.00**

HN 1991A
A Country Lass
Designer: L. Harradine
Height: 7 ¼", 18.4 cm
Colour: Blue, brown and white
Issued: 1975-1981
Varieties: Also called 'Market
           Day' HN 1991

  U.S.:   **$250.00**
  Can.:   **$325.00**
  U.K.:   **£150.00**

HN 1992
Christmas Morn
Style One
Designer: M. Davies
Height: 7", 17.8 cm
Colour: Red and white
Issued: 1947-1996

  U.S.:   **$275.00**
  Can.:   **$350.00**
  U.K.:   **£150.00**

HN 1993
Griselda
Designer: L. Harradine
Height: 5 ¾", 14.6 cm
Colour: Lavender and cream
Issued: 1947-1953

  U.S.:   **$625.00**
  Can.:   **$800.00**
  U.K.:   **£375.00**

HN 1994
Karen
Style One
Designer: L. Harradine
Height: 8", 20.3 cm
Colour: Red
Issued: 1947-1955

  U.S.:   **$750.00**
  Can.:   **$975.00**
  U.K.:   **£450.00**

HN 1995
Olivia
Style One
Designer: L. Harradine
Height: 7 ½", 19.1 cm
Colour: Red and green
Issued: 1947-1951

U.S.:	**$ 850.00**
Can.:	**$1,100.00**
U.K.:	**£ 500.00**

HN 1996
Prue
Designer: L. Harradine
Height: 6 ¾", 17.2 cm
Colour: Red, white and black
Issued: 1947-1955

U.S.:	**$600.00**
Can.:	**$775.00**
U.K.:	**£350.00**

HN 1997
Belle o' the Ball
Designer: R. Asplin
Height: 6", 15.2 cm
Colour: Red and white
Issued: 1947-1979

U.S.:	**$500.00**
Can.:	**$650.00**
U.K.:	**£300.00**

HN 1998
Collinette
Designer: L. Harradine
Height: 7 ¼", 18.4 cm
Colour: Turquoise and cream
Issued: 1947-1949
Varieties: HN 1999

U.S.:	**$ 800.00**
Can.:	**$1,000.00**
U.K.:	**£ 475.00**

HN 1999
Collinette
Designer: L. Harradine
Height: 7 ¼", 18.4 cm
Colour: Red and cream
Issued: 1947-1949
Varieties: HN 1998

U.S.:	**$ 800.00**
Can.:	**$1,000.00**
U.K.:	**£ 475.00**

HN 2000
Jacqueline
Style One
Designer: L. Harradine
Height: 7 ¼", 18.4 cm
Colour: Lavender
Issued: 1947-1951
Varieties: HN 2001

U.S.:	**$725.00**
Can.:	**$950.00**
U.K.:	**£425.00**

HN 2001
Jacqueline
Style One
Designer: L. Harradine
Height: 7 ¼", 18.4 cm
Colour: Pink
Issued: 1947-1951
Varieties: HN 2000

U.S.:	**$725.00**
Can.:	**$950.00**
U.K.:	**£425.00**

HN 2002
Bess
Designer: L. Harradine
Height: 7 ¼", 18.4 cm
Colour: Red cloak, flowered
           cream dress
Issued: 1947-1969
Varieties: HN 2003

U.S.:	**$475.00**
Can.:	**$600.00**
U.K.:	**£275.00**

HN 2003
Bess
Designer: L. Harradine
Height: 7 ¼", 18.4 cm
Colour: Pink dress, purple
          cloak
Issued: 1947-1950
Varieties: HN 2002

U.S.:	$ 875.00
Can.:	$1,150.00
U.K.:	£ 525.00

HN 2004
A'Courting
Designer: L. Harradine
Height: 7 ¼", 18.4 cm
Colour: Red, black and grey
Issued: 1947-1953

U.S.:	$700.00
Can.:	$900.00
U.K.:	£425.00

HN 2005
Henrietta Maria
Style One
Designer: M. Davies
Height: 9 ½", 24.1 cm
Colour: Yellow and red
Issued: 1948-1953
Series: Period Figures in
          English History

U.S.:	$ 900.00
Can.:	$1,150.00
U.K.:	£ 525.00

HN 2006
The Lady Anne Nevill
Designer: M. Davies
Height: 9 ¾", 24.7 cm
Colour: Purple and white
Issued: 1948-1953
Series: Period Figures in
          English History

U.S.:	$1,100.00
Can.:	$1,400.00
U.K.:	£ 650.00

HN 2007
Mrs. Fitzherbert
Designer: M. Davies
Height: 9 ¼", 23.5 cm
Colour: Yellow and cream
Issued: 1948-1953
Series: Period Figures in
          English History

U.S.:	$ 900.00
Can.:	$1,150.00
U.K.:	£ 525.00

HN 2008
Philippa of Hainault
Style One
Designer: M. Davies
Height: 9 ¾", 24.7 cm
Colour: Blue, brown and red
Issued: 1948-1953
Series: Period Figures in
          English History

U.S.:	$ 900.00
Can.:	$1,150.00
U.K.:	£ 525.00

HN 2009
Eleanor of Provence
Designer: M. Davies
Height: 9 ½", 24.1 cm
Colour: Purple and red
Issued: 1948-1953
Series: Period Figures in
          English History

U.S.:	$ 900.00
Can.:	$1,150.00
U.K.:	£ 525.00

HN 2010
The Young
Miss Nightingale
Designer: M. Davies
Height: 9 ¼", 23.5 cm
Colour: Red and green
Issued: 1948-1953
Series: Period Figures in
          English History

U.S.:	$1,100.00
Can.:	$1,400.00
U.K.:	£ 650.00

HN 2011
Matilda
Designer: M. Davies
Height: 9 ¼", 23.5 cm
Colour: Red and purple
Issued: 1948-1953
Series: Period Figures in
English History

U.S.: $ 900.00
Can.: $1,150.00
U.K.: £ 525.00

HN 2012
Margaret of Anjou
Style One
Designer: M. Davies
Height: 9 ¼", 23.5 cm
Colour: Green and yellow
Issued: 1948-1953
Series: Period Figures in
English History

U.S.: $1,000.00
Can.: $1,300.00
U.K.: £ 600.00

HN 2013
Angelina
Designer: L. Harradine
Height: 6 ¾", 17.1 cm
Colour: Red
Issued: 1948-1951

U.S.: $1,800.00
Can.: $2,750.00
U.K.: £1,050.00

HN 2014
Jane
Style One
Designer: L. Harradine
Height: 6 ¼", 15.9 cm
Colour: Red and pink
Issued: 1948-1951

U.S.: $2,000.00
Can.: $2,750.00
U.K.: £1,200.00

HN 2015
Sir Walter Raleigh
Designer: L. Harradine
Height: 11 ½", 29.2 cm
Colour: Orange and purple
Issued: 1948-1955
Varieties: HN 1742, 1751

U.S.: $1,000.00
Can.: $1,300.00
U.K.: £ 600.00

Earthenware

HN 2016
A Jester
Style One
Designer: C. J. Noke
Height: 10", 25.4 cm
Colour: Brown and mauve
Issued: 1949-1997
Varieties: HN 45, 71, 71A, 320,
367, 412, 426, 446,
552, 616, 627, 1295,
1702, 3922

U.S.: $350.00
Can.: $450.00
U.K.: £200.00

HN 2017
Silks and Ribbons
Designer: L. Harradine
Height: 6", 15.2 cm
Colour: Green, red and white
Issued: 1949-2001

U.S.: $325.00
Can.: $425.00
U.K.: £175.00

NOTES ON PRICING

Prices on the secondary market for Royal Doulton Figures, particularly the early HN numbers, have risen considerably over the years. As values rise, the condition and quality of these figurines takes on an increasingly important role.

The prices listed in *The Charlton Standard Catalogue of Royal Doulton Figurines* are for figures in mint condition.

Naturally, repaired or restored figures, no matter how professionally done, will sell at a discount. However the early figures, due to their rarity, may experience smaller discounts.

On Condition: For figures to command catalogue prices they must be in mint condition. This simply means that a figure will have no chips, scratches, hairline cracks, crazing, blemishes, or repairs. Any of which will remove the figure from the mint category.

On Quality: Some figures are better moulded, assembled or painted than others. High quality figures may command a premium over listed catalogue prices.

HN 2018
The Parson's Daughter
Designer: H. Tittensor
Height: 9 ¾", 24.7 cm
Colour: Multicoloured
Issued: 1949-1953
Varieties: HN 337, 338, 441,
           564, 790, 1242, 1356

U.S.:	**$1,000.00**
Can.:	**$1,300.00**
U.K.:	**£ 600.00**

HN 2019
Minuet
Designer: M. Davies
Height: 7 ¼", 18.4 cm
Colour: Patterned white dress
Issued: 1949-1971
Varieties: HN 2066

U.S.:	**$350.00**
Can.:	**$475.00**
U.K.:	**£225.00**

HN 2020
Deidre
Designer: L. Harradine
Height: 7", 17.8 cm
Colour: Blue and pink
Issued: 1949-1955

U.S.:	**$650.00**
Can.:	**$900.00**
U.K.:	**£400.00**

HN 2021
Blithe Morning
Designer: L. Harradine
Height: 7 ¼", 18.4 cm
Colour: Mauve and pink
Issued: 1949-1971
Varieties: HN 2065

U.S.:	**$300.00**
Can.:	**$400.00**
U.K.:	**£175.00**

HN 2022
Janice
Style One
Designer: M. Davies
Height: 7 ¼", 18.4 cm
Colour: Green and cream
Issued: 1949-1955
Varieties: HN 2165

U.S.:	**$650.00**
Can.:	**$900.00**
U.K.:	**£400.00**

HN 2023
Joan
Style One
Designer: L. Harradine
Height: 5 ¾", 14.6 cm
Colour: Blue
Issued: 1949-1959
Varieties: HN 1422 (minor
           glaze difference)

U.S.:	**$350.00**
Can.:	**$475.00**
U.K.:	**£200.00**

HN 2024
Darby
Designer: L. Harradine
Height: 5 ¾", 14.6 cm
Colour: Pink and blue
Issued: 1949-1959
Varieties: HN 1427 (minor
           glaze difference)

U.S.:	**$350.00**
Can.:	**$475.00**
U.K.:	**£200.00**

HN 2025
Gossips
Designer: L. Harradine
Height: 5 ½", 14.0 cm
Colour: Red and cream
Issued: 1949-1967
Varieties: HN 1426, 1429

U.S.:	**$700.00**
Can.:	**$900.00**
U.K.:	**£425.00**

HN 2026
Suzette
Designer: L. Harradine
Height: 7 ¼", 18.4 cm
Colour: Flowered pink dress
Issued: 1949-1959
Varieties: HN 1487, 1577,
           1585, 1696

U.S.:	$550.00
Can.:	$750.00
U.K.:	£325.00

HN 2027
June
Style One
Designer: L. Harradine
Height: 7 ¼", 18.4 cm
Colour: Yellow and pink
Issued: 1949-1952
Varieties: HN 1690, 1691, 1947

U.S.:	$ 800.00
Can.:	$1,000.00
U.K.:	£ 475.00

HN 2028
Kate Hardcastle
Designer: L. Harradine
Height: 7 ¾", 19.7 cm
Colour: Green and red
Issued: 1949-1952
Varieties: HN 1718, 1719,
           1734, 1861, 1919

U.S.:	$ 800.00
Can.:	$1,000.00
U.K.:	£ 475.00

HN 2029
Windflower
Style One
Designer: L. Harradine
Height: 7 ¼", 18.4 cm
Colour: Pink
Issued: 1949-1952
Varieties: HN 1763, 1764

U.S.:	$ 850.00
Can.:	$1,150.00
U.K.:	£ 500.00

HN 2030
Memories
Designer: L. Harradine
Height: 6", 15.2 cm
Colour: Pink and green
Issued: 1949-1959
Varieties: HN 1855, 1856, 1857

U.S.:	$700.00
Can.:	$900.00
U.K.:	£425.00

HN 2031
Granny's Heritage
Designer: L. Harradine
Height: 6 ¾", 17.2 cm
Colour: Lavender and green
Issued: 1949-1969
Varieties: HN 1873, 1874

U.S.:	$ 800.00
Can.:	$1,000.00
U.K.:	£ 500.00

HN 2032
Jean
Style One
Designer: L. Harradine
Height: 7 ½", 19.1 cm
Colour: Green and red
Issued: 1949-1959
Varieties: HN 1877, 1878

U.S.:	$450.00
Can.:	$575.00
U.K.:	£275.00

HN 2033
Midsummer Noon
Designer: L. Harradine
Height: 4 ¾", 12.0 cm
Colour: Pink
Issued: 1949-1955
Varieties: HN 1899, 1900

U.S.:	$ 950.00
Can.:	$1,250.00
U.K.:	£ 575.00

HN 2034
Madonna of the Square
Designer: P. Stabler
Height: 7", 17.8 cm
Colour: Pale green
Issued: 1949-1951
Varieties: HN 10, 10A, 11, 14,
           27, 326, 573, 576,
           594, 613, 764,1968,
           1969

U.S.:	**$1,000.00**
Can.:	**$1,350.00**
U.K.:	**£ 600.00**

HN 2035
Pearly Boy
Style Two
Designer: L. Harradine
Height: 5 ¼", 13.3 cm
Colour: Reddish-brown
Issued: 1949-1959

U.S.:	**$300.00**
Can.:	**$375.00**
U.K.:	**£175.00**

HN 2036
Pearly Girl
Style Two
Designer: L. Harradine
Height: 5 ¼", 13.3 cm
Colour: Reddish-brown
Issued: 1949-1959

U.S.:	**$300.00**
Can.:	**$375.00**
U.K.:	**£175.00**

HN 2037
Goody Two Shoes
Style One
Designer: L. Harradine
Height: 5", 12.7 cm
Colour: Red and pink
Issued: 1949-1989
Varieties: HN 1889, 1905

U.S.:	**$150.00**
Can.:	**$200.00**
U.K.:	**£100.00**

HN 2038
Peggy
Designer: L. Harradine
Height: 5", 12.7 cm
Colour: Red and white
Issued: 1949-1979
Varieties: HN 1941 (minor
           glaze difference)

U.S.:	**$175.00**
Can.:	**$225.00**
U.K.:	**£100.00**

HN 2039
Easter Day
Designer: L. Harradine
Height: 7 ¼", 18.4 cm
Colour: Multicoloured
Issued: 1949-1969
Varieties: HN 1976

U.S.:	**$550.00**
Can.:	**$750.00**
U.K.:	**£325.00**

HN 2040
Gollywog
Designer: L. Harradine
Height: 5 ¼", 13.3 cm
Colour: Blue dungarees
Issued: 1949-1959
Varieties: HN 1979

U.S.:	**$550.00**
Can.:	**$750.00**
U.K.:	**£325.00**

HN 2041
The Broken Lance
Designer: M. Davies
Height: 8 ¾", 22.2 cm
Colour: Blue, red and yellow
Issued: 1949-1975

U.S.:	**$ 750.00**
Can.:	**$1,000.00**
U.K.:	**£ 450.00**

HN 2042
Owd Willum
Designer: L. Harradine
Height: 6 ¾", 17.2 cm
Colour: Green and brown
Issued: 1949-1973

U.S.:	$350.00
Can.:	$475.00
U.K.:	£225.00

'Harradine' incised on figurine

HN 2043
The Poacher
Designer: L. Harradine
Height: 6", 15.2 cm
Colour: Black and brown
Issued: 1949-1959

U.S.:	$425.00
Can.:	$550.00
U.K.:	£250.00

HN 2044
Mary, Mary
Designer: L. Harradine
Height: 5", 12.7 cm
Colour: Pink
Issued: 1949-1973
Series: Nursery Rhymes
            (Series One)

U.S.:	$300.00
Can.:	$400.00
U.K.:	£175.00

HN 2045
She Loves Me Not
Designer: L. Harradine
Height: 5 ½", 14.0 cm
Colour: Blue
Issued: 1949-1962
Series: Nursery Rhymes
            (Series One)

U.S.:	$300.00
Can.:	$400.00
U.K.:	£175.00

HN 2046
He Loves Me
Designer: L. Harradine
Height: 5 ½", 14.0 cm
Colour: Flowered pink dress
Issued: 1949-1962
Series: Nursery Rhymes
            (Series One)

U.S.:	$300.00
Can.:	$400.00
U.K.:	£175.00

HN 2047
Once Upon a Time
Designer: L. Harradine
Height: 4 ¼", 10.8 cm
Colour: Pink dress with
            white spots
Issued: 1949-1955
Series: Nursery Rhymes
            (Series One)

U.S.:	$625.00
Can.:	$900.00
U.K.:	£400.00

HN 2048
Mary Had a Little Lamb
Designer: M. Davies
Height: 3 ½", 8.9 cm
Colour: Lavender
Issued: 1949-1988
Series: Nursery Rhymes
            (Series One)

U.S.:	$225.00
Can.:	$300.00
U.K.:	£125.00

HN 2049
Curly Locks
Designer: M. Davies
Height: 4 ½", 11.4 cm
Colour: Pink flowered dress
Issued: 1949-1953
Series: Nursery Rhymes
            (Series One)

U.S.:	$625.00
Can.:	$900.00
U.K.:	£400.00

HN 2050
Wee Willie Winkie
Style One
Designer: M. Davies
Height: 5 ¼", 13.3 cm
Colour: Blue
Issued: 1949-1953
Series: Nursery Rhymes
          (Series One)

  U.S.:   **$450.00**
  Can.:   **$600.00**
  U.K.:   **£275.00**

HN 2051
St. George
Style Two
Designer: M. Davies
Height: 7 ½", 19.1 cm
Colour: Green and white
Issued: 1950-1985

  U.S.:   **$600.00**
  Can.:   **$850.00**
  U.K.:   **£350.00**

HN 2052
Grandma
Designer: L. Harradine
Height: 6 ¾", 17.2 cm
Colour: Blue shawl with
          red and cream dress
Issued: 1950-1959
Varieties: HN 2052A

  U.S.:   **$475.00**
  Can.:   **$625.00**
  U.K.:   **£325.00**

Earthenware

HN 2052A
Grandma
Designer: L. Harradine
Height: 6 ¾", 17.2 cm
Colour: Brown shawl with
          red and cream dress
Issued: Unknown
Varieties: HN 2052

  U.S.:   **$475.00**
  Can.:   **$625.00**
  U.K.:   **£325.00**

Earthenware

HN 2053
The Gaffer
Designer: L. Harradine
Height: 7 ¾", 19.7 cm
Colour: Green and brown
Issued: 1950-1959

  U.S.:   **$475.00**
  Can.:   **$625.00**
  U.K.:   **£325.00**

Earthenware

HN 2054
Falstaff
Style Two
Designer: C. J. Noke
Height: 7", 17.8 cm
Colour: Brown
Issued: 1950-1992
Varieties: HN 618

  U.S.:   **$200.00**
  Can.:   **$250.00**
  U.K.:   **£125.00**

Earthenware and China

HN 2055
The Leisure Hour
Designer: M. Davies
Height: 7", 17.8 cm
Colour: Green, yellow
          and brown
Issued: 1950-1965

  U.S.:   **$600.00**
  Can.:   **$775.00**
  U.K.:   **£350.00**

HN 2056
Susan
Style One
Designer: L. Harradine
Height: 7", 17.8 cm
Colour: Lavender dress
          with flowered apron
Issued: 1950-1959

  U.S.:   **$575.00**
  Can.:   **$750.00**
  U.K.:   **£350.00**

HN 2057
The Jersey Milkmaid
Designer: L. Harradine
Height: 6 ½", 16.5 cm
Colour: Blue, white and red
Issued: 1950-1959
Varieties: Also called 'The
           Milkmaid' (Style Two)
           HN 2057A

U.S.:	$300.00
Can.:	$400.00
U.K.:	£175.00

HN 2057A
The Milkmaid
Style Two
Designer: L. Harradine
Height: 6 ½", 16.5 cm
Colour: Green, white
           and brown
Issued: 1975-1981
Varieties: Also called 'The
           Jersey Milkmaid'
           HN 2057

U.S.:	$200.00
Can.:	$275.00
U.K.:	£125.00

HN 2058
Hermione
Designer: M. Davies
Height: 7 ¾", 19.7 cm
Colour: Cream and lavender
Issued: 1950-1952

U.S.:	$2,350.00
Can.:	$3,250.00
U.K.:	£1,500.00

HN 2059
The Bedtime Story
Designer: L. Harradine
Height: 4 ¾", 12.0 cm
Colour: Pink, white, yellow
           and blue
Issued: 1950-1996

U.S.:	$425.00
Can.:	$550.00
U.K.:	£250.00

HN 2060
Jack
Designer: L. Harradine
Height: 5 ½", 14.0 cm
Colour: Green, white
           and black
Issued: 1950-1971
Series: Nursery Rhymes
           (Series One)

U.S.:	$275.00
Can.:	$350.00
U.K.:	£175.00

HN 2061
Jill
Designer: L. Harradine
Height: 5 ½", 14.0 cm
Colour: Pink and white
Issued: 1950-1971
Series: Nursery Rhymes
           (Series One)

U.S.:	$275.00
Can.:	$350.00
U.K.:	£175.00

HN 2062
Little Boy Blue
Style One
Designer: L. Harradine
Height: 5 ½", 14.0 cm
Colour: Blue
Issued: 1950-1973
Series: Nursery Rhymes
           (Series One)

U.S.:	$250.00
Can.:	$325.00
U.K.:	£150.00

HN 2063
Little Jack Horner
Style One
Designer: L. Harradine
Height: 4 ½", 11.4 cm
Colour: Red and white
Issued: 1950-1953
Series: Nursery Rhymes
           (Series One)

U.S.:	$ 800.00
Can.:	$1,100.00
U.K.:	£ 500.00

HN 2064
My Pretty Maid
Designer: L. Harradine
Height: 5 ½", 14.0 cm
Colour: Turquoise
Issued: 1950-1954
Series: Nursery Rhymes
           (Series One)

U.S.:	$650.00
Can.:	$850.00
U.K.:	£400.00

HN 2065
Blithe Morning
Designer: L. Harradine
Height: 7 ¼", 18.4 cm
Colour: Red
Issued: 1950-1973
Varieties: HN 2021

U.S.:	$350.00
Can.:	$450.00
U.K.:	£200.00

HN 2066
Minuet
Designer: M. Davies
Height: 7 ¼", 18.4 cm
Colour: Red
Issued: 1950-1955
Varieties: HN 2019

U.S.:	$1,850.00
Can.:	$2,500.00
U.K.:	£1,100.00

HN 2067
St. George
Style One
Designer: S. Thorogood
Height: 15 ¾", 40.0 cm
Colour: Multicoloured
Issued: 1950-1979
Varieties: HN 385, 386, 1800;
           fair and dark hair

U.S.:	$3,250.00
Can.:	$4,250.00
U.K.:	£1,950.00

HN 2068
Calumet
Designer: C. J. Noke
Height: 6 ¼", 15.9 cm
Colour: Green and brown
Issued: 1950-1953
Varieties: HN 1428, 1689

U.S.:	$1,000.00
Can.:	$1,300.00
U.K.:	£ 600.00

Earthenware

HN 2069
Farmer's Wife
Style One
Designer: L. Harradine
Height: 9", 22.9 cm
Colour: Red, green and brown
Issued: 1951-1955

U.S.:	$ 850.00
Can.:	$1,100.00
U.K.:	£ 500.00

Earthenware

HN 2070
Bridget
Designer: L. Harradine
Height: 7 ¾", 19.7 cm
Colour: Green, brown
           and lavender
Issued: 1951-1973

U.S.:	$400.00
Can.:	$525.00
U.K.:	£240.00

Earthenware

HN 2071
Bernice
Designer: M. Davies
Height: 7 ¾", 19.7 cm
Colour: Pink and red
Issued: 1951-1953

U.S.:	$1,850.00
Can.:	$2,500.00
U.K.:	£1,110.00

HN 2072
The Rocking Horse
Designer: L. Harradine
Height: 7", 17.8 cm
Colour: Red, white, blue and yellow
Issued: 1951-1953

U.S.:	$4,500.00
Can.:	$6,000.00
U.K.:	£2,700.00

HN 2073
Vivienne
Designer: L. Harradine
Height: 7 ¾", 19.7 cm
Colour: Red
Issued: 1951-1967

U.S.:	$400.00
Can.:	$525.00
U.K.:	£240.00

HN 2074
Marianne
Style One
Designer: L. Harradine
Height: 7 ¼", 18.4 cm
Colour: Red
Issued: 1951-1953

U.S.:	$1,800.00
Can.:	$2,500.00
U.K.:	£1,100.00

HN 2075
French Peasant
Designer: L. Harradine
Height: 9 ¼", 23.5 cm
Colour: Brown and green
Issued: 1951-1955

U.S.:	$700.00
Can.:	$900.00
U.K.:	£425.00

Earthenware

HN 2076
Promenade
Style One
Designer: M. Davies
Height: 8", 20.3 cm
Colour: Blue and orange
Issued: 1951-1953

U.S.:	$3,250.00
Can.:	$4,500.00
U.K.:	£2,000.00

HN 2077
Rowena
Designer: L. Harradine
Height: 7 ¼", 18.4 cm
Colour: Red and green
Issued: 1951-1955

U.S.:	$ 900.00
Can.:	$1,175.00
U.K.:	£ 550.00

HN 2078
Elfreda
Designer: L. Harradine
Height: 7 ¼", 18.4 cm
Colour: Red and purple
Issued: 1951-1955

U.S.:	$1,200.00
Can.:	$1,600.00
U.K.:	£ 725.00

HN 2079
Damaris
Designer: M. Davies
Height: 7 ¼", 18.4 cm
Colour: Green, white and purple
Issued: 1951-1952

U.S.:	$2,500.00
Can.:	$3,750.00
U.K.:	£1,500.00

HN 2080
Jack Point
Designer: C. J. Noke
Height: 16", 40.6 cm
Colour: Purple, green
           and lavender
Issued: 1952 to the present
Varieties: HN 85, 91, 99, 3920,
           3925
Series: Prestige
   U.S.:   **N/I**
   Can.:   **$4,300.00**
   U.K.:   **£2,600.00**

HN 2081
Princess Badoura
Style One
Designer: H. Tittensor,
           H. E. Stanton and
           F. Van Allen Phillips
Height: 20", 50.8 cm
Colour: Multicoloured
Issued: 1952 to the present
Varieties: HN 3921
Series: Prestige
   U.S.:   **$36,400.00**
   Can.:   **$43,000.00**
   U.K.:   **£17,000.00**

HN 2082
The Moor
Designer: C. J. Noke
Height: 16 ¼", 41.2 cm
Colour: Red and black
Issued: 1952 to the present
Varieties: HN 1308, 1366, 1425,
           1657, 3642, 3926;
           also called 'An Arab'
           HN 33, 343, 378
Series: Prestige
   U.S.:   **N/I**
   Can.:   **$3,700.00**
   U.K.:   **£2,100.00**

HN 2083 not issued.

HN 2084
King Charles
Designer: C. J. Noke and
           H. Tittensor
Height: 16", 40.6 cm
Colour: Black with yellow base
Issued: 1952-1992
Varieties: HN 404, 3459
   U.S.:   **$2,000.00**
   Can.:   **$2,500.00**
   U.K.:   **£1,200.00**

HN 2085
Spring
Style Four
Designer: M. Davies
Height: 7 ¾", 19.6 cm
Colour: Lavender and cream
Issued: 1952-1959
Series: The Seasons
           (Series Two)
   U.S.:   **$550.00**
   Can.:   **$725.00**
   U.K.:   **£325.00**

HN 2086
Summer
Style Two
Designer: M. Davies
Height: 7 ¼", 18.4 cm
Colour: Red flowered dress
Issued: 1952-1959
Series: The Seasons
           (Series Two)
   U.S.:   **$550.00**
   Can.:   **$725.00**
   U.K.:   **£325.00**

HN 2087
Autumn
Style Two
Designer: M. Davies
Height: 7 ¼", 18.4 cm
Colour: Red and lavender
Issued: 1952-1959
Series: The Seasons
           (Series Two)
   U.S.:   **$550.00**
   Can.:   **$725.00**
   U.K.:   **£325.00**

HN 2088
Winter
Style Two
Designer: M. Davies
Height: 6 ¼", 15.9 cm
Colour: Lavender, green
           and red
Issued: 1952-1959
Series: The Seasons
           (Series Two)
   U.S.:   **$550.00**
   Can.:   **$725.00**
   U.K.:   **£325.00**

HN 2089
Judith
Style One
Designer: L. Harradine
Height: 7", 17.8 cm
Colour: Red and blue
Issued: 1952-1959

U.S.:	$475.00
Can.:	$625.00
U.K.:	£300.00

HN 2090
Midinette
Style Two
Designer: L. Harradine
Height: 7 ¼", 18.4 cm
Colour: Blue
Issued: 1952-1965

U.S.:	$400.00
Can.:	$525.00
U.K.:	£250.00

HN 2091
Rosemary
Style One
Designer: L. Harradine
Height: 7", 17.8 cm
Colour: Red and blue
Issued: 1952-1959

U.S.:	$700.00
Can.:	$925.00
U.K.:	£425.00

HN 2092
Sweet Maid
Style Two
Designer: L. Harradine
Height: 7", 17.8 cm
Colour: Lavender
Issued: 1952-1955

U.S.:	$600.00
Can.:	$775.00
U.K.:	£350.00

HN 2093
Georgiana
Designer: M. Davies
Height: 8 ¼", 21.0 cm
Colour: Orange and blue
Issued: 1952-1955

U.S.:	$2,250.00
Can.:	$3,250.00
U.K.:	£1,500.00

HN 2094
Uncle Ned
Designer: H. Fenton
Height: 6 ¾", 17.2 cm
Colour: Brown
Issued: 1952-1965

U.S.:	$475.00
Can.:	$625.00
U.K.:	£275.00

Earthenware

HN 2095
Ibrahim
Designer: C. J. Noke
Height: 7 ¾", 19.7 cm
Colour: Brown and yellow
Issued: 1952-1955
Varieties: Also called 'The
Emir' HN 1604, 1605

U.S.:	$650.00
Can.:	$900.00
U.K.:	£400.00

Earthenware

HN 2096
Fat Boy
Style Three
Designer: L. Harradine
Height: 7 ¼", 18.4 cm
Colour: Blue and cream
Issued: 1952-1967
Series: Dickens (Series Three)

U.S.:	$450.00
Can.:	$575.00
U.K.:	£270.00

Earthenware

HN 2097
Mr. Micawber
Style Three
Designer: L. Harradine
Height: 7 ½", 19.1 cm
Colour: Black and brown
Issued: 1952-1967
Series: Dickens (Series Three)

U.S.:	**$450.00**
Can.:	**$575.00**
U.K.:	**£270.00**

Earthenware

HN 2098
Pecksniff
Style Three
Designer: L. Harradine
Height: 7 ¼", 18.4 cm
Colour: Black and brown
Issued: 1952-1967
Series: Dickens (Series Three)

U.S.:	**$450.00**
Can.:	**$575.00**
U.K.:	**£270.00**

Earthenware

HN 2099
Mr. Pickwick
Style Three
Designer: L. Harradine
Height: 7 ½", 19.1 cm
Colour: Blue and brown
Issued: 1952-1967
Series: Dickens (Series Three)

U.S.:	**$450.00**
Can.:	**$575.00**
U.K.:	**£270.00**

Earthenware

HN 2100
Sairey Gamp
Style Three
Designer: L. Harradine
Height: 7 ¼", 18.4 cm
Colour: Green
Issued: 1952-1967
Series: Dickens (Series Three)

U.S.:	**$600.00**
Can.:	**$575.00**
U.K.:	**£270.00**

Earthenware

HN 2101
Uriah Heep
Style Three
Designer: L. Harradine
Height: 7 ½", 19.1 cm
Colour: Black
Issued: 1952-1967
Series: Dickens (Series Three)

U.S.:	**$450.00**
Can.:	**$575.00**
U.K.:	**£270.00**

Earthenware

HN 2102
Pied Piper
Style One
Designer: L. Harradine
Height: 8 ¾", 22.2 cm
Colour: Black, red and yellow
Issued: 1953-1976
Varieties: HN 1215

U.S.:	**$375.00**
Can.:	**$500.00**
U.K.:	**£225.00**

HN 2103
Mask Seller
Designer: L. Harradine
Height: 8 ½", 21.6 cm
Colour: Green and yellow
Issued: 1953-1995
Varieties: HN 1361

U.S.:	**$375.00**
Can.:	**$500.00**
U.K.:	**£225.00**

Earthenware

HN 2104
Abdullah
Designer: L. Harradine
Height: 6", 15.2 cm
Colour: Multicoloured
Issued: 1953-1962
Varieties: HN 1410

U.S.:	**$600.00**
Can.:	**$825.00**
U.K.:	**£350.00**

HN 2105
Bluebeard
Style Two
Designer: L. Harradine
Height: 11", 27.9 cm
Colour: Purple, green
           and brown
Issued: 1953-1992
Varieties: HN 1528

U.S.:	**$550.00**
Can.:	**$725.00**
U.K.:	**£325.00**

HN 2106
Linda
Style One
Designer: L. Harradine
Height: 4 ¾", 12.0 cm
Colour: Red
Issued: 1953-1976

U.S.:	**$250.00**
Can.:	**$325.00**
U.K.:	**£150.00**

HN 2107
Valerie
Style One
Designer: M. Davies
Height: 4 ¾", 12.0 cm
Colour: Red, pink and white
Issued: 1953-1995
Varieties: HN 3620

U.S.:	**$150.00**
Can.:	**$200.00**
U.K.:	**£ 90.00**

HN 2108
Baby Bunting
Designer: M. Davies
Height: 5 ¼", 13.3 cm
Colour: Brown and cream
Issued: 1953-1959

U.S.:	**$475.00**
Can.:	**$625.00**
U.K.:	**£275.00**

HN 2109
Wendy
Designer: L. Harradine
Height: 5", 12.7 cm
Colour: Blue
Issued: 1953-1995

U.S.:	**$100.00**
Can.:	**$150.00**
U.K.:	**£ 60.00**

HN 2110
Christmas Time
Designer: M. Davies
Height: 6 ½", 16.5 cm
Colour: Red with white frills
Issued: 1953-1967

U.S.:	**$525.00**
Can.:	**$700.00**
U.K.:	**£325.00**

HN 2111
Betsy
Designer: L. Harradine
Height: 7", 17.8 cm
Colour: Lavender dress,
           flowered apron
Issued: 1953-1959

U.S.:	**$525.00**
Can.:	**$700.00**
U.K.:	**£325.00**

HN 2112
Carolyn
Style One
Designer: L. Harradine
Height: 7", 17.8 cm
Colour: White and green
           flowered dress
Issued: 1953-1965

U.S.:	**$475.00**
Can.:	**$625.00**
U.K.:	**£275.00**

HN 2113
Maytime
Designer: L. Harradine
Height: 7", 17.8 cm
Colour: Pink dress with
          blue scarf
Issued: 1953-1967
  U.S.: **$400.00**
  Can.: **$525.00**
  U.K.: **£240.00**

HN 2114
Sleepyhead
Style One
Designer: M. Davies
Height: 5", 12.7 cm
Colour: Orange, blue
          and white
Issued: 1953-1955
  U.S.: **$3,500.00**
  Can.: **$4,500.00**
  U.K.: **£2,100.00**

HN 2115
Coppelia
Designer: M. Davies
Height: 7 ¼", 18.4 cm
Colour: Blue, red and white
Issued: 1953-1959
  U.S.: **$ 900.00**
  Can.: **$1,200.00**
  U.K.: **£ 525.00**

HN 2116
Ballerina
Style One
Designer: M. Davies
Height: 7 ¼", 18.4 cm
Colour: Lavender
Issued: 1953-1973
  U.S.: **$425.00**
  Can.: **$550.00**
  U.K.: **£225.00**

HN 2117
The Skater
Style One
Designer: M. Davies
Height: 7 ¼", 18.4 cm
Colour: Red, white and brown
Issued: 1953-1971
  U.S.: **$525.00**
  Can.: **$700.00**
  U.K.: **£325.00**

HN 2118
Good King Wenceslas
Style One
Designer: M. Davies
Height: 8 ½", 21.6 cm
Colour: Brown and purple
Issued: 1953-1976
  U.S.: **$425.00**
  Can.: **$550.00**
  U.K.: **£250.00**

Earthenware

HN 2119
Town Crier
Style One
Designer: M. Davies
Height: 8 ½", 21.6 cm
Colour: Purple, green
          and yellow
Issued: 1953-1976
  U.S.: **$375.00**
  Can.: **$500.00**
  U.K.: **£225.00**

Earthenware

HN 2120
Dinky Doo
Designer: L. Harradine
Height: 4 ¾", 12.0 cm
Colour: Red
Issued: 1983-1996
Varieties: HN 1678, 3618
  U.S.: **$125.00**
  Can.: **$160.00**
  U.K.: **£ 75.00**

HN 2121
Babie
Designer: L. Harradine
Height: 4 ¾", 12.0 cm
Colour: Pink
Issued: 1983-1992
Varieties: HN 1679, 1842

U.S.:	$125.00
Can.:	$175.00
U.K.:	£ 80.00

HN 2122
Yeoman of the Guard
Designer: L. Harradine
Height: 5 ¾", 14.6 cm
Colour: Red, gold and brown
Issued: 1954-1959
Varieties: HN 688

U.S.:	$1,000.00
Can.:	$1,500.00
U.K.:	£ 600.00

HN 2123
Rose
Style One
Designer: L. Harradine
Height: 4 ½", 11.4 cm
Colour: Lavender
Issued: 1983-1995
Varieties: HN 1368, 1387, 1416, 1506, 1654

U.S.:	$125.00
Can.:	$165.00
U.K.:	£ 80.00

HN 2124 not issued.

HN 2125
This Little Pig
Designer: L. Harradine
Height: 4", 10.1 cm
Colour: White
Issued: 1984-1995
Varieties: HN 1793, 1794

U.S.:	$125.00
Can.:	$175.00
U.K.:	£ 75.00

HN 2126
Top o' The Hill
Style Two
Designer: L. Harradine
Remodeller: P. Gee
Height: 4", 10.1 cm
Colour: Green and mauve
Issued: 1988-1988
Varieties: HN 3499
Series: 1. Miniatures
2. R.D.I.C.C.

U.S.:	$175.00
Can.:	$225.00
U.K.:	£125.00

HN 2127
Top o' The Hill
Style One
Designer: L. Harradine
Height: 7", 17.8 cm
Colour: Gold
Issued: 1988-1988
Varieties: HN 1833, 1834, 1849, 3735A

U.S.:	$500.00
Can.:	$650.00
U.K.:	£300.00

Commissioned for Australian
Bicentenary.

HN 2128
River Boy
Designer: M. Davies
Height: 4", 10.1 cm
Colour: Blue and green
Issued: 1962-1975

U.S.:	$250.00
Can.:	$350.00
U.K.:	£150.00

HN 2129
The Old Balloon Seller
Style Two
Designer: L. Harradine
Remodeller: W. K. Harper
Height: 3 ½", 8.9 cm
Colour: Green and white
Issued: 1989-1991
Series: Miniatures

U.S.:	$275.00
Can.:	$350.00
U.K.:	£165.00

HN 2130
The Balloon Seller
Style Two
Designer: L. Harradine
Remodeller: R. Tabbenor
Height: 3 ¾", 8.9 cm
Colour: Green and cream
Issued: 1989-1991
Series: Miniatures
- **U.S.:**   **$275.00**
- **Can.:**   **$350.00**
- **U.K.:**   **£165.00**

HN 2131
Autumn Breezes
Style One
Designer: L. Harradine
Height: 7 ½", 19.1 cm
Colour: Orange, yellow
            and black
Issued: 1990-1994
Varieties: HN 1911, 1913,
            1934, 2147, 3736
- **U.S.:**   **$400.00**
- **Can.:**   **$525.00**
- **U.K.:**   **£240.00**

HN 2132
The Suitor
Designer: M. Davies
Height: 7 ¼", 18.4 cm
Colour: Green, yellow and blue
Issued: 1962-1971
- **U.S.:**   **$550.00**
- **Can.:**   **$700.00**
- **U.K.:**   **£325.00**

HN 2133
Faraway
Designer: M. Davies
Height: 2 ½", 6.3 cm
Colour: Blue and white
Issued: 1958-1962
Series: Teenagers
- **U.S.:**   **$500.00**
- **Can.:**   **$700.00**
- **U.K.:**   **£300.00**

HN 2134
An Old King
Designer: C. J. Noke
Height: 10 ¾", 27.3 cm
Colour: Purple, red, green
           and brown
Issued: 1954-1992
Varieties: HN 358, 623, 1801
- **U.S.:**   **$650.00**
- **Can.:**   **$850.00**
- **U.K.:**   **£375.00**

HN 2135
Gay Morning
Designer: M. Davies
Height: 7", 17.8 cm
Colour: Pink
Issued: 1954-1967
- **U.S.:**   **$400.00**
- **Can.:**   **$550.00**
- **U.K.:**   **£240.00**

HN 2136
Delphine
Designer: M. Davies
Height: 7 ¼", 18.4 cm
Colour: Blue and lavender
Issued: 1954-1967
- **U.S.:**   **$450.00**
- **Can.:**   **$600.00**
- **U.K.:**   **£275.00**

HN 2137
Lilac Time
Designer: M. Davies
Height: 7 ¼", 18.4 cm
Colour: Red
Issued: 1954-1969
- **U.S.:**   **$450.00**
- **Can.:**   **$600.00**
- **U.K.:**   **£275.00**

HN 2138
La Sylphide
Designer: M. Davies
Height: 7", 17.8 cm
Colour: White and blue
Issued: 1954-1965

U.S.: **$600.00**
Can.: **$775.00**
U.K.: **£350.00**

HN 2139
Giselle
Designer: M. Davies
Height: 6", 15.2 cm
Colour: Blue and white
Issued: 1954-1969

U.S.: **$525.00**
Can.: **$700.00**
U.K.: **£325.00**

HN 2140
Giselle, The Forest Glade
Designer: M. Davies
Height: 7", 17.8 cm
Colour: White and blue
Issued: 1954-1965

U.S.: **$550.00**
Can.: **$725.00**
U.K.: **£325.00**

HN 2141
Choir Boy
Designer: M. Davies
Height: 4 ¾", 12.0 cm
Colour: White and red
Issued: 1954-1975

U.S.: **$175.00**
Can.: **$225.00**
U.K.: **£100.00**

HN 2142
Rag Doll
Designer: M. Davies
Height: 4 ¾", 12.0 cm
Colour: White, blue and red
Issued: 1954-1986

U.S.: **$175.00**
Can.: **$225.00**
U.K.: **£100.00**

HN 2143
Friar Tuck
Designer: M. Davies
Height: 7 ½", 19.1 cm
Colour: Brown
Issued: 1954-1965

U.S.: **$600.00**
Can.: **$775.00**
U.K.: **£350.00**

Earthenware

HN 2144
The Jovial Monk
Designer: M. Davies
Height: 7 ¾", 19.7 cm
Colour: Brown
Issued: 1954-1976

U.S.: **$325.00**
Can.: **$425.00**
U.K.: **£200.00**

Earthenware

HN 2145
Wardrobe Mistress
Designer: M. Davies
Height: 5 ¾", 14.6 cm
Colour: Green, red, white
and blue
Issued: 1954-1967

U.S.: **$675.00**
Can.: **$900.00**
U.K.: **£400.00**

Earthenware

HN 2146
The Tinsmith
Designer: M. Nicoll
Height: 6 ½", 16.5 cm
Colour: Green and brown
Issued: 1962-1967

U.S.: **$600.00**
Can.: **$825.00**
U.K.: **£350.00**

HN 2147
Autumn Breezes
Style One
Designer: L. Harradine
Height: 7 ½", 19.1 cm
Colour: Black and white
Issued: 1955-1971
Varieties: HN 1911, 1913, 1934, 2131, 3736

U.S.: **$425.00**
Can.: **$550.00**
U.K.: **£250.00**

HN 2148
The Bridesmaid
Style Three
Designer: M. Davies
Height: 5 ½", 14.0 cm
Colour: Yellow
Issued: 1955-1959

U.S.: **$275.00**
Can.: **$375.00**
U.K.: **£175.00**

HN 2149
Love Letter
Style One
Designer: M. Davies
Height: 5 ½", 14.0 cm
Colour: Pink and blue
Issued: 1958-1976

U.S.: **$550.00**
Can.: **$725.00**
U.K.: **£325.00**

HN 2150
Willy-Won't He
Designer: L. Harradine
Height: 5 ½", 14.0 cm
Colour: Red, green, blue and white
Issued: 1955-1959
Varieties: HN 1561, 1584 (minor glaze differences)

U.S.: **$600.00**
Can.: **$825.00**
U.K.: **£350.00**

HN 2151
Mother's Help
Designer: M. Davies
Height: 5", 12.7 cm
Colour: Black and white
Issued: 1962-1969

U.S.: **$300.00**
Can.: **$400.00**
U.K.: **£175.00**

HN 2152
Adrienne
Designer: M. Davies
Height: 7 ½", 19.1 cm
Colour: Purple
Issued: 1964-1976
Varieties: HN 2304; also called 'Fiona' (Style Four) HN 3748; 'Joan' (Style Two) HN 3217

U.S.: **$225.00**
Can.: **$300.00**
U.K.: **£125.00**

HN 2153
The One That Got Away
Designer: M. Davies
Height: 6 ¼", 15.9 cm
Colour: Brown
Issued: 1955-1959

U.S.: **$550.00**
Can.: **$725.00**
U.K.: **£325.00**

HN 2154
A Child From Williamsburg
Designer: M. Davies
Height: 5 ½", 14.0 cm
Colour: Blue
Issued: 1964-1983
Series: Figures of Williamsburg

U.S.:	**$225.00**
Can.:	**$300.00**
U.K.:	**£125.00**

HN 2155 not issued.

HN 2156
The Polka
Designer: M. Davies
Height: 7 ½", 19.1 cm
Colour: Pink
Issued: 1955-1969

U.S.:	**$400.00**
Can.:	**$525.00**
U.K.:	**£225.00**

HN 2157
A Gypsy Dance
Style One
Designer: M. Davies
Height: 7", 17.8 cm
Colour: Lavender
Issued: 1955-1957

U.S.:	**$1,350.00**
Can.:	**$1,750.00**
U.K.:	**£ 800.00**

HN 2158
Alice
Style One
Designer: M. Davies
Height: 5", 12.7 cm
Colour: Blue
Issued: 1960-1981

U.S.:	**$250.00**
Can.:	**$325.00**
U.K.:	**£150.00**

HN 2159
Fortune Teller
Designer: L. Harradine
Height: 6 ½", 16.5 cm
Colour: Green and brown
Issued: 1955-1967

U.S.:	**$600.00**
Can.:	**$800.00**
U.K.:	**£375.00**

Earthenware

HN 2160
The Apple Maid
Designer: L. Harradine
Height: 6 ½", 16.5 cm
Colour: Blue, black
and white
Issued: 1957-1962

U.S.:	**$500.00**
Can.:	**$675.00**
U.K.:	**£275.00**

HN 2161
The Hornpipe
Designer: M. Nicoll
Height: 9 ¼", 23.5 cm
Colour: Blue and white
Issued: 1955-1962

U.S.:	**$1,100.00**
Can.:	**$1,500.00**
U.K.:	**£ 650.00**

Earthenware

HN 2162
The Foaming Quart
Designer: M. Davies
Height: 6", 15.2 cm
Colour: Brown
Issued: 1955-1992

U.S.:	**$200.00**
Can.:	**$275.00**
U.K.:	**£125.00**

HN 2163
In The Stocks
Style Two
Designer: M. Nicoll
Height: 5 ¾", 14.6 cm
Colour: Red, brown and black
Issued: 1955-1959
U.S.:   **$1,100.00**
Can.:   **$1,500.00**
U.K.:   £ **650.00**

HN 2164 not issued.

HN 2165
Janice
Style One
Designer: M. Davies
Height: 7 ¼", 18.4 cm
Colour: Black and pale blue
Issued: 1955-1965
Varieties: HN 2022
U.S.:   **$550.00**
Can.:   **$750.00**
U.K.:   **£325.00**

HN 2166
The Bride
Style Two
Designer: M. Davies
Height: 8", 20.3 cm
Colour: Pink
Issued: 1956-1976
U.S.:   **$250.00**
Can.:   **$375.00**
U.K.:   **£150.00**

HN 2167
Home Again
Designer: M. Davies
Height: 3 ¼", 8.3 cm
Colour: Red and white
Issued: 1956-1995
U.S.:   **$200.00**
Can.:   **$250.00**
U.K.:   **£120.00**

HN 2168
Esmeralda
Designer: M. Davies
Height: 5 ½", 14.0 cm
Colour: Yellow and red
Issued: 1956-1959
U.S.:   **$500.00**
Can.:   **$650.00**
U.K.:   **£300.00**

HN 2169
Dimity
Designer: L. Harradine
Height: 5 ¾", 14.6 cm
Colour: Green, lavender
          and cream
Issued: 1956-1959
U.S.:   **$500.00**
Can.:   **$650.00**
U.K.:   **£300.00**

HN 2170
Invitation
Designer: M. Davies
Height: 5 ½", 14.0 cm
Colour: Pink
Issued: 1956-1975
U.S.:   **$200.00**
Can.:   **$250.00**
U.K.:   **£125.00**

HN 2171
The Fiddler
Designer: M. Nicoll
Height: 8 ¾", 22.2 cm
Colour: Green, cream and red
Issued: 1956-1962
U.S.:   **$1,400.00**
Can.:   **$2,000.00**
U.K.:   £ **850.00**

Earthenware

HN 2172
Jolly Sailor
Designer: M. Nicoll
Height: 6 ½", 16.5 cm
Colour: Black, brown,
         blue and white
Issued: 1956-1965
  U.S.: **$1,100.00**
  Can.: **$1,500.00**
  U.K.: **£   650.00**

Earthenware

HN 2173
The Organ Grinder
Designer: M. Nicoll
Height: 8 ¾", 22.2 cm
Colour: Green, cream
         and brown
Issued: 1956-1965
  U.S.: **$1,400.00**
  Can.: **$2,000.00**
  U.K.: **£   850.00**

Earthenware

HN 2174
The Tailor
Designer: M. Nicoll
Height: 5", 12.7 cm
Colour: Blue, cream
         and orange
Issued: 1956-1959
  U.S.: **$1,100.00**
  Can.: **$1,500.00**
  U.K.: **£   650.00**

Earthenware

HN 2175
The Beggar
Style Two
Designer: L. Harradine
Height: 6 ¾", 17.2 cm
Colour: Green
Issued: 1956-1962
Series: Beggar's Opera
  U.S.: **$600.00**
  Can.: **$825.00**
  U.K.: **£400.00**

Earthenware

HN 2176
Autumn Breezes
Style Two
Designer: L. Harradine
Remodeller: D. Frith
Height: 3 ½", 8.9 cm
Colour: Red
Issued: 1991-1995
Varieties: HN 2180
Series: Miniatures
  U.S.: **$200.00**
  Can.: **$250.00**
  U.K.: **£120.00**

HN 2177
My Teddy
Designer: M. Davies
Height: 3 ¼", 8.3 cm
Colour: Turquoise and brown
Issued: 1962-1967
  U.S.: **$650.00**
  Can.: **$850.00**
  U.K.: **£395.00**

HN 2178
Enchantment
Designer: M. Davies
Height: 7 ½", 19.1 cm
Colour: Blue
Issued: 1957-1982
  U.S.: **$225.00**
  Can.: **$300.00**
  U.K.: **£135.00**

HN 2179
Noelle
Designer: M. Davies
Height: 6 ¾", 17.2 cm
Colour: Orange, white
         and black
Issued: 1957-1967
  U.S.: **$600.00**
  Can.: **$800.00**
  U.K.: **£350.00**

HN 2180
Autumn Breezes
Style Two
Designer: L. Harradine
Remodeller: D. Frith
Height: 3 ½", 8.9 cm
Colour: Red, lavender,
             gold trim
Issued: 1991-1995
Varieties: HN 2176
Series: 1. Miniatures
             2. Signature

U.S.:	**$225.00**
Can.:	**$325.00**
U.K.:	**£150.00**

HN 2181
Summer's Day
Style One
Designer: M. Davies
Height: 5 ¾", 14.6 cm
Colour: White
Issued: 1957-1962

U.S.:	**$375.00**
Can.:	**$475.00**
U.K.:	**£225.00**

HN 2182 not issued.

HN 2183
Boy from Williamsburg
Designer: M. Davies
Height: 5 ½", 14.0 cm
Colour: Blue and pink
Issued: 1969-1983
Series: Figures of Williamsburg

U.S.:	**$250.00**
Can.:	**$350.00**
U.K.:	**£150.00**

HN 2184
Sunday Morning
Designer: M. Davies
Height: 7 ½", 19.1 cm
Colour: Red and brown
Issued: 1963-1969

U.S.:	**$475.00**
Can.:	**$625.00**
U.K.:	**£275.00**

HN 2185
Columbine
Style Two
Designer: M. Davies
Height: 7", 17.8 cm
Colour: Pink
Issued: 1957-1969
Series: Teenagers

U.S.:	**$300.00**
Can.:	**$425.00**
U.K.:	**£175.00**

HN 2186
Harlequin
Style One
Designer: M. Davies
Height: 7 ¼", 18.4 cm
Colour: Blue
Issued: 1957-1969
Series: Teenagers

U.S.:	**$300.00**
Can.:	**$425.00**
U.K.:	**£175.00**

HN 2187 - 2190 not issued.

HN 2191
Sea Sprite
Style Two
Designer: M. Davies
Height: 7", 17.8 cm
Colour: Pink and blue
Issued: 1958-1962
Series: Teenagers

U.S.:	**$500.00**
Can.:	**$675.00**
U.K.:	**£300.00**

HN 2192
Wood Nymph
Designer: M. Davies
Height: 7 ¼", 18.4 cm
Colour: Blue and white
Issued: 1958-1962
Series: Teenagers

U.S.:	**$475.00**
Can.:	**$675.00**
U.K.:	**£300.00**

HN 2193
Fair Lady
Style One
Designer: M. Davies
Height: 7 ¼", 18.4 cm
Colour: Green
Issued: 1963-1996
Varieties: HN 2832, 2835; also
called 'Kay' HN 3340

U.S.: $225.00
Can.: $300.00
U.K.: £125.00

HN 2194 - 2195 not issued.

HN 2196
The Bridesmaid
Style Four
Designer: M. Davies
Height: 5 ¼", 13.3 cm
Colour: Pale blue
Issued: 1960-1976

U.S.: $150.00
Can.: $225.00
U.K.: £ 90.00

HN 2197 - 2201 not issued.

HN 2202
Melody
Style One
Designer: M. Davies
Height: 6 ¼", 15.9 cm
Colour: Blue and peach
Issued: 1957-1962
Series: Teenagers

U.S.: $475.00
Can.: $675.00
U.K.: £300.00

HN 2203
Teenager
Designer: M. Davies
Height: 7 ¼", 18.4 cm
Colour: Orange and white
Issued: 1957-1962
Series: Teenagers

U.S.: $475.00
Can.: $675.00
U.K.: £300.00

Also known in Flambé. Sold for
£1,035., Phillips, London May 2001.

HN 2204
Long John Silver
Style One
Designer: M. Nicoll
Height: 9", 22.9 cm
Colour: Green, black and white
Issued: 1957-1965

U.S.: $650.00
Can.: $850.00
U.K.: £400.00

Earthenware

HN 2205
Master Sweep
Designer: M. Nicoll
Height: 8 ½", 21.6 cm
Colour: Green, black
and brown
Issued: 1957-1962

U.S.: $1,000.00
Can.: $1,350.00
U.K.: £ 600.00

Earthenware

HN 2206
Sunday Best
Style One
Designer: M. Davies
Height: 7 ½", 19.1 cm
Colour: Yellow
Issued: 1979-1984
Varieties: HN 2698

U.S.: $250.00
Can.: $375.00
U.K.: £150.00

HN 2207
Stayed at Home
Designer: M. Davies
Height: 5", 12.7 cm
Colour: Green and white
Issued: 1958-1969

U.S.: $275.00
Can.: $375.00
U.K.: £165.00

HN 2208
Silversmith of Williamsburg
Designer: M. Davies
Height: 6 ¼", 15.9 cm
Colour: Blue, white and brown
Issued: 1960-1983
Series: Figures of Williamsburg

U.S.:	**$275.00**
Can.:	**$400.00**
U.K.:	**£175.00**

HN 2209
Hostess of Williamsburg
Designer: M. Davies
Height: 7 ¼", 18.4 cm
Colour: Pink
Issued: 1960-1983
Series: Figures of Williamsburg

U.S.:	**$300.00**
Can.:	**$400.00**
U.K.:	**£175.00**

HN 2210
Debutante
Style One
Designer: M. Davies
Height: 5", 12.7 cm
Colour: Blue
Issued: 1963-1967

U.S.:	**$350.00**
Can.:	**$475.00**
U.K.:	**£200.00**

HN 2211
Fair Maiden
Designer: M. Davies
Height: 5 ¼", 13.3 cm
Colour: Green
Issued: 1967-1994
Varieties: HN 2434

U.S.:	**$150.00**
Can.:	**$200.00**
U.K.:	**£ 90.00**

HN 2212
Rendezvous
Designer: M. Davies
Height: 7 ¼", 18.4 cm
Colour: Red and white
Issued: 1962-1971

U.S.:	**$500.00**
Can.:	**$650.00**
U.K.:	**£300.00**

HN 2213
Contemplation
Designer: M. Davies
Height: 12", 30.5 cm
Colour: White
Issued: 1982-1986
Varieties: HN 2241
Series: Images

U.S.:	**$175.00**
Can.:	**$250.00**
U.K.:	**£125.00**

HN 2214
Bunny
Designer: M. Davies
Height: 5", 12.7 cm
Colour: Turquoise
Issued: 1960-1975

U.S.:	**$250.00**
Can.:	**$350.00**
U.K.:	**£150.00**

HN 2215
Sweet April
Designer: M. Davies
Height: 7 ¼", 18.4 cm
Colour: Pink
Issued: 1965-1967

U.S.:	**$475.00**
Can.:	**$625.00**
U.K.:	**£275.00**

HN 2216
Pirouette
Designer: M. Davies
Height: 5 ¾", 14.6 cm
Colour: Pale blue
Issued: 1959-1967

U.S.:	$250.00
Can.:	$325.00
U.K.:	£150.00

HN 2217
Old King Cole
Designer: M. Davies
Height: 6 ½", 16.5 cm
Colour: Brown, yellow
 and white
Issued: 1963-1967

U.S.:	$700.00
Can.:	$975.00
U.K.:	£450.00

HN 2218
Cookie
Designer: M. Davies
Height: 4 ¾", 12.0 cm
Colour: Pink and white
Issued: 1958-1975

U.S.:	$225.00
Can.:	$300.00
U.K.:	£135.00

HN 2219
Bedtime
Style One
Designer: L. Harradine
Height: 5 ½", 14.0 cm
Colour: Pink
Issued: 1992
Varieties: HN 1978
Comm.by: Peter Jones China

U.S.:	$125.00
Can.:	$175.00
U.K.:	£ 75.00

HN 2220
Winsome
Designer: M. Davies
Height: 8", 20.3 cm
Colour: Red
Issued: 1960-1985

U.S.:	$200.00
Can.:	$300.00
U.K.:	£120.00

HN 2221
Nanny
Designer: M. Nicoll
Height: 6", 15.2 cm
Colour: Blue and white
Issued: 1958-1991

U.S.:	$375.00
Can.:	$500.00
U.K.:	£225.00

Earthenware

HN 2222
Camellia
Designer: M. Davies
Height: 7 ¾", 19.7 cm
Colour: Pink
Issued: 1960-1971

U.S.:	$275.00
Can.:	$425.00
U.K.:	£175.00

HN 2223
Schoolmarm
Designer: M. Davies
Height: 6 ¾", 17.2 cm
Colour: Purple, grey
 and brown
Issued: 1958-1981

U.S.:	$375.00
Can.:	$525.00
U.K.:	£225.00

HN 2224
Make Believe
Designer: M. Nicoll
Height: 5 ¾", 14.6 cm
Colour: White
Issued: 1984-1988
Varieties: HN 2225

U.S.:	**$175.00**
Can.:	**$225.00**
U.K.:	**£100.00**

HN 2225
Make Believe
Designer: M. Nicoll
Height: 5 ¾", 14.6 cm
Colour: Blue
Issued: 1962-1988
Varieties: HN 2224

U.S.:	**$225.00**
Can.:	**$300.00**
U.K.:	**£135.00**

HN 2226
The Cellist
Designer: M. Nicoll
Height: 8", 20.3 cm
Colour: Black and brown
Issued: 1960-1967

U.S.:	**$600.00**
Can.:	**$775.00**
U.K.:	**£360.00**

HN 2227
Gentleman from Williamsburg
Designer: M. Davies
Height: 6 ¼", 15.9 cm
Colour: Green and white
Issued: 1960-1983
Series: Figures of Williamsburg

U.S.:	**$275.00**
Can.:	**$375.00**
U.K.:	**£175.00**

HN 2228
Lady from Williamsburg
Designer: M. Davies
Height: 6", 15.2 cm
Colour: Green
Issued: 1960-1983
Series: Figures of Williamsburg

U.S.:	**$275.00**
Can.:	**$375.00**
U.K.:	**£175.00**

HN 2229
Southern Belle
Style One
Designer: M. Davies
Height: 7 ½", 19.1 cm
Colour: Red and cream
Issued: 1958-1997
Varieties: HN 2425

U.S.:	**$275.00**
Can.:	**$375.00**
U.K.:	**£150.00**

HN 2230
A Gypsy Dance
Style Two
Designer: M. Davies
Height: 7", 17.8 cm
Colour: Lavender
Issued: 1959-1971

U.S.:	**$375.00**
Can.:	**$500.00**
U.K.:	**£225.00**

HN 2231
Sweet Sixteen
Style One
Designer: M. Davies
Height: 7 ¼", 18.4 cm
Colour: Blue and white
Issued: 1958-1965
Series: Teenagers

U.S.:	**$475.00**
Can.:	**$675.00**
U.K.:	**£300.00**

HN 2232 not issued.

HN 2233
Royal Governor's Cook
Designer: M. Davies
Height: 6", 15.2 cm
Colour: Dark blue, white
           and brown
Issued: 1960-1983
Series: Figures of Williamsburg

U.S.:	**$650.00**
Can.:	**$850.00**
U.K.:	**£395.00**

HN 2234
Michele
Designer: M. Davies
Height: 7", 17.8 cm
Colour: Green
Issued: 1967-1993
Varieties: Also called 'Autumn
           Attraction' HN 3612

U.S.:	**$225.00**
Can.:	**$300.00**
U.K.:	**£125.00**

HN 2235
Dancing Years
Designer: M. Davies
Height: 6 ¾", 17.2 cm
Colour: Lavender
Issued: 1965-1971

U.S.:	**$425.00**
Can.:	**$675.00**
U.K.:	**£250.00**

HN 2236
Affection
Designer: M. Davies
Height: 4 ½", 11.4 cm
Colour: Purple
Issued: 1962-1994

U.S.:	**$175.00**
Can.:	**$225.00**
U.K.:	**£ 95.00**

HN 2237
Celeste
Style One
Designer: M. Davies
Colour: Pale blue
Height: 6 ¾", 17.2 cm
Issued: 1959-1971

U.S.:	**$275.00**
Can.:	**$375.00**
U.K.:	**£165.00**

HN 2238
My Pet
Designer: M. Davies
Height: 2 ¾", 7.0 cm
Colour: Blue and white
Issued: 1962-1975

U.S.:	**$250.00**
Can.:	**$375.00**
U.K.:	**£175.00**

HN 2239
Wigmaker of Williamsburg
Designer: M. Davies
Height: 7 ½", 19.1 cm
Colour: White and brown
Issued: 1960-1983
Series: Figures of Williamsburg

U.S.:	**$275.00**
Can.:	**$375.00**
U.K.:	**£175.00**

HN 2240
Blacksmith of Willliamsburg
Designer: M. Davies
Height: 6 ¾", 17.2 cm
Colour: Grey and white
Issued: 1960-1983
Series: Figures of Williamsburg

U.S.:	**$300.00**
Can.:	**$400.00**
U.K.:	**£200.00**

HN 2241
Contemplation
Designer: M. Davies
Height: 12", 30.5 cm
Colour: Black
Issued: 1982-1986
Varieties: HN 2213
Series: Images

U.S.:	**$175.00**
Can.:	**$250.00**
U.K.:	**£125.00**

HN 2242
First Steps
Style One
Designer: M. Davies
Height: 6 ½", 16.5 cm
Colour: Blue and yellow
Issued: 1959-1965

U.S.:	**$600.00**
Can.:	**$825.00**
U.K.:	**£350.00**

HN 2243
Treasure Island
Designer: M. Davies
Height: 4 ¾", 12.0 cm
Colour: Blue and yellow
Issued: 1962-1975

U.S.:	**$250.00**
Can.:	**$375.00**
U.K.:	**£150.00**

HN 2244
Newsboy
Designer: M. Nicoll
Height: 8 ½", 21.6 cm
Colour: Green, brown and blue
Issued: 1959-1965
Varieties: Limited edition of 250 for Evening Sentinel

U.S.:	**$650.00**
Can.:	**$900.00**
U.K.:	**£400.00**

HN 2245
The Basket Weaver
Designer: M. Nicoll
Height: 5 ¾", 14.6 cm
Colour: Pale blue and yellow
Issued: 1959-1962

U.S.:	**$600.00**
Can.:	**$800.00**
U.K.:	**£375.00**

HN 2246
Cradle Song
Designer: M. Davies
Height: 5 ½", 14.0 cm
Colour: Green and brown
Issued: 1959-1962

U.S.:	**$600.00**
Can.:	**$800.00**
U.K.:	**£375.00**

HN 2247
Omar Khayyam
Style Two
Designer: M. Nicoll
Height: 6 ¼", 15.9 cm
Colour: Brown
Issued: 1965-1983

U.S.:	**$250.00**
Can.:	**$375.00**
U.K.:	**£150.00**

Earthenware

HN 2248
Tall Story
Designer: M. Nicoll
Height: 6 ½", 16.5 cm
Colour: Blue and grey
Issued: 1968-1975
Series: Sea Characters

U.S.:	**$425.00**
Can.:	**$550.00**
U.K.:	**£250.00**

HN 2249
The Favourite
Designer: M. Nicoll
Height: 7 ¾", 19.7 cm
Colour: Blue and white
Issued: 1960-1990

U.S.:	**$275.00**
Can.:	**$375.00**
U.K.:	**£165.00**

HN 2250
The Toymaker
Designer: M. Nicoll
Height: 6", 15.2 cm
Colour: Brown and red
Issued: 1959-1973

U.S.:	**$600.00**
Can.:	**$800.00**
U.K.:	**£350.00**

HN 2251
Masquerade
Style Two
Designer: M. Davies
Height: 8 ½", 21.6 cm
Colour: Blue and white
Issued: 1960-1965
Varieties: HN 2259

U.S.:	**$375.00**
Can.:	**$525.00**
U.K.:	**£225.00**

HN 2252
The Joker
Style Two
Designer: M. Nicoll
Height: 8 ½", 21.6 cm
Colour: White
Issued: 1990-1992
Series: Clowns

U.S.:	**$350.00**
Can.:	**$450.00**
U.K.:	**£200.00**

HN 2253
The Puppetmaker
Designer: M. Nicoll
Height: 8", 20.3 cm
Colour: Green, brown and red
Issued: 1962-1973

U.S.:	**$625.00**
Can.:	**$825.00**
U.K.:	**£375.00**

HN 2254
Shore Leave
Designer: M. Nicoll
Height: 7 ½", 19.1 cm
Colour: Black
Issued: 1965-1979
Series: Sea Characters

U.S.:	**$350.00**
Can.:	**$450.00**
U.K.:	**£200.00**

HN 2255
Teatime
Designer: M. Nicoll
Height: 7 ¼", 18.4 cm
Colour: Brown
Issued: 1972-1995

U.S.:	**$275.00**
Can.:	**$375.00**
U.K.:	**£165.00**

HN 2256
Twilight
Designer: M. Nicoll
Height: 5", 12.7 cm
Colour: Green and black
Issued: 1971-1976

U.S.:	**$350.00**
Can.:	**$450.00**
U.K.:	**£200.00**

HN 2257
Sea Harvest
Designer: M. Nicoll
Height: 7 ½", 19.1 cm
Colour: Blue and brown
Issued: 1969-1976
Series: Sea Characters

U.S.:	**$400.00**
Can.:	**$525.00**
U.K.:	**£240.00**

HN 2258
A Good Catch
Designer: M. Nicoll
Height: 7 ¼", 18.4 cm
Colour: Green and grey
Issued: 1966-1986
Series: Sea Characters

U.S.:	**$300.00**
Can.:	**$400.00**
U.K.:	**£175.00**

HN 2259
Masquerade
Style Two
Designer: M. Davies
Height: 8 ½", 21.6 cm
Colour: Red and cream
Issued: 1960-1965
Varieties: HN 2251

U.S.:	**$375.00**
Can.:	**$525.00**
U.K.:	**£225.00**

HN 2260
The Captain
Style Two
Designer: M. Nicoll
Height: 9 ½", 24.1 cm
Colour: Black and white
Issued: 1965-1982
Series: Sea Characters

U.S.:	**$450.00**
Can.:	**$575.00**
U.K.:	**£270.00**

HN 2261
Marriage of Art and Industry
Designer: M. Davies
Height: 19", 48.3 cm
Colour: Green
Issued: 1958 in a limited
edition of 12

U.S.:	
Can.:	**Very Rare**
U.K.:	

HN 2262
Lights Out
Style One
Designer: M. Davies
Height: 5", 12.7 cm
Colour: Blue trousers with
yellow spotted shirt
Issued: 1965-1969

U.S.:	**$350.00**
Can.:	**$450.00**
U.K.:	**£200.00**

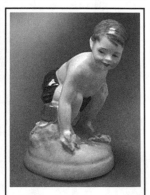

HN 2263
Seashore
Designer: M. Davies
Height: 3 ½", 8.9 cm
Colour: Yellow, red and cream
Issued: 1961-1965

U.S.:	**$425.00**
Can.:	**$600.00**
U.K.:	**£250.00**

HN 2264
Elegance
Designer: M. Davies
Height: 7 ¼", 18.4 cm
Colour: Green
Issued: 1961-1985

U.S.:	**$225.00**
Can.:	**$300.00**
U.K.:	**£135.00**

HN 2265
Sara
Style One
Designer: M. Davies
Height: 7 ½", 19.1 cm
Colour: Red and white
Issued: 1981-2000
Varieties HN 3308

U.S.: **$325.00**
Can.: **$450.00**
U.K.: **£195.00**

HN 2266
Ballad Seller
Designer: M. Davies
Height: 7 ½", 19.1 cm
Colour: Pink
Issued: 1968-1973

U.S.: **$350.00**
Can.: **$475.00**
U.K.: **£225.00**

HN 2267
Rhapsody
Designer: M. Davies
Height: 6 ¾", 17.2 cm
Colour: Green
Issued: 1961-1973

U.S.: **$275.00**
Can.: **$375.00**
U.K.: **£150.00**

HN 2268
Daphne
Designer: M. Davies
Height: 8 ¼", 21.0 cm
Colour: Pink
Issued: 1963-1975

U.S.: **$275.00**
Can.: **$400.00**
U.K.: **£165.00**

HN 2269
Leading Lady
Designer: M. Davies
Height: 7 ¾", 19.7 cm
Colour: Blue and yellow
Issued: 1965-1976

U.S.: **$250.00**
Can.: **$375.00**
U.K.: **£150.00**

HN 2270
Pillow Fight
Designer: M. Davies
Height: 5", 12.7 cm
Colour: Patterned pink
        nightdress
Issued: 1965-1969

U.S.: **$350.00**
Can.: **$475.00**
U.K.: **£225.00**

HN 2271
Melanie
Designer: M. Davies
Height: 7 ¾", 19.7 cm
Colour: Blue
Issued: 1965-1981

U.S.: **$250.00**
Can.: **$375.00**
U.K.: **£150.00**

HN 2272
Repose
Designer: M. Davies
Height: 5 ¼", 13.3 cm
Colour: Pink and green
Issued: 1972-1979

U.S.: **$350.00**
Can.: **$450.00**
U.K.: **£200.00**

HN 2273
Denise
Style Two
Designer: M. Davies
Height: 7", 17.8 cm
Colour: Red
Issued: 1964-1971

U.S.:	**$400.00**
Can.:	**$525.00**
U.K.:	**£250.00**

HN 2274
Golden Days
Designer: M. Davies
Height: 3 ¾", 9.5 cm
Colour: Yellow, white and blue
Issued: 1964-1973

U.S.:	**$275.00**
Can.:	**$375.00**
U.K.:	**£165.00**

HN 2275
Sandra
Designer: M. Davies
Height: 7 ¾", 19.7 cm
Colour: Gold
Issued: 1969-1997
Varieties: HN 2401; also
            called 'Annette'
            (Style Two) HN 3495

U.S.:	**$275.00**
Can.:	**$375.00**
U.K.:	**£165.00**

HN 2276
Heart to Heart
Designer: M. Davies
Height: 5 ½", 14.0 cm
Colour: Lavender, green
            and yellow
Issued: 1961-1971

U.S.:	**$650.00**
Can.:	**$850.00**
U.K.:	**£375.00**

HN 2277
Slapdash
Designer: M.Nicoll
Height: 10", 25.4 cm
Colour: Green, white and blue
Issued: 1990-1994
Series: Clowns

U.S.:	**$375.00**
Can.:	**$500.00**
U.K.:	**£225.00**

HN 2278
Judith
Style Two
Designer: M. Nicoll
Height: 6 ¾", 17.2 cm
Colour: Yellow
Issued: 1986 N.America
            1987 Worldwide-1989
Varieties: HN 2313

U.S.:	**$325.00**
Can.:	**$450.00**
U.K.:	**£200.00**

HN 2279
The Clockmaker
Designer: M. Nicoll
Height: 7", 17.8 cm
Colour: Green and brown
Issued: 1961-1975

U.S.:	**$425.00**
Can.:	**$550.00**
U.K.:	**£275.00**

HN 2280
The Mayor
Designer: M. Nicoll
Height: 8 ¼", 21.0 cm
Colour: Red and white
Issued: 1963-1971
Varieties: Also known in 7 ½",
            19.1 cm

U.S.:	**$475.00**
Can.:	**$625.00**
U.K.:	**£300.00**

HN 2281
The Professor
Designer: M. Nicoll
Height: 7 ¼", 18.4 cm
Colour: Brown and black
Issued: 1965-1981

U.S.:	$250.00
Can.:	$325.00
U.K.:	£175.00

HN 2282
The Coachman
Designer: M. Nicoll
Height: 7 ¼", 18.4 cm
Colour: Purple, grey and blue
Issued: 1963-1971

U.S.:	$600.00
Can.:	$850.00
U.K.:	£350.00

HN 2283
Dreamweaver (matte)
Designer: M. Nicoll
Height: 8 ¼", 21.0 cm
Colour: Blue, grey and brown
Issued: 1972-1976

U.S.:	$275.00
Can.:	$375.00
U.K.:	£165.00

HN 2284
The Craftsman
Designer: M. Nicoll
Height: 6", 15.2 cm
Colour: Blue, tan and brown
Issued: 1961-1965

U.S.:	$ 800.00
Can.:	$1,100.00
U.K.:	£ 475.00

HN 2285 - 2286 not issued.

HN 2287
Symphony
Designer: D.B. Lovegrove
Height: 5 ¼", 13.3 cm
Colour: Brown
Issued: 1961-1965

U.S.:	$300.00
Can.:	$450.00
U.K.:	£200.00

HN 2288 - 2303 not issued.

HN 2304
Adrienne
Designer: M. Davies
Height: 7 ½", 19.1 cm
Colour: Blue
Issued: 1964-1991
Varieties: HN 2152, also called
'Fiona' (Style Four)
HN 3748; 'Joan'
(Style Two) HN 3217

U.S.:	$225.00
Can.:	$300.00
U.K.:	£135.00

HN 2305
Dulcie
Designer: M. Davies
Height: 7 ¼", 18.4 cm
Colour: Blue
Issued: 1981-1984

U.S.:	$300.00
Can.:	$450.00
U.K.:	£200.00

HN 2306
Reverie
Designer: M. Davies
Height: 6 ½", 16.5 cm
Colour: Peach
Issued: 1964-1981

U.S.:	$375.00
Can.:	$475.00
U.K.:	£225.00

HN 2307
Coralie
Designer: M. Davies
Height: 7 ¼", 18.4 cm
Colour: Yellow
Issued: 1964-1988

U.S.:	**$200.00**
Can.:	**$250.00**
U.K.:	**£110.00**

HN 2308
Picnic
Designer: M. Davies
Height: 3 ¾", 9.5 cm
Colour: Yellow
Issued: 1965-1988

U.S.:	**$200.00**
Can.:	**$250.00**
U.K.:	**£110.00**

HN 2309
Buttercup
Style One
Designer: M. Davies
Height: 7", 17.8 cm
Colour: Green dress with
           yellow sleeves
Issued: 1964-1997
Varieties: HN 2399

U.S.:	**$225.00**
Can.:	**$300.00**
U.K.:	**£135.00**

HN 2310
Lisa (matte)
Style One
Designer: M. Davies
Height: 7 ¼", 18.4 cm
Colour: Blue and white
Issued: 1969-1982
Varieties: HN 2394, 3265

U.S.:	**$225.00**
Can.:	**$325.00**
U.K.:	**£135.00**

HN 2311
Lorna
Designer: M. Davies
Height: 8 ¼", 21.0 cm
Colour: Green dress,
           yellow shawl
Issued: 1965-1985

U.S.:	**$225.00**
Can.:	**$325.00**
U.K.:	**£135.00**

HN 2312
Soiree
Designer: M. Davies
Height: 7 ½", 19.1 cm
Colour: Green and cream
Issued: 1967-1984

U.S.:	**$200.00**
Can.:	**$250.00**
U.K.:	**£120.00**

HN 2313
Judith
Style Two
Designer: M. Nicholl
Height: 6 ¼", 15.9 cm
Colour: Red and cream
Issued: 1988 in a limited
           edition of 1,000
Varieties: HN 2278

U.S.:	**$350.00**
Can.:	**$450.00**
U.K.:	**£200.00**

HN 2314
Old Mother Hubbard
Designer: M. Nicholl
Height: 8", 20.3 cm
Colour: Green and white
Issued: 1964-1975

U.S.:	**$500.00**
Can.:	**$650.00**
U.K.:	**£300.00**

HN 2315
Last Waltz
Designer: M. Nicoll
Height: 7 ¾", 19.7 cm
Colour: Yellow and white
Issued: 1967-1993
Varieties: HN 2316

U.S.:	$200.00
Can.:	$275.00
U.K.:	£120.00

HN 2316
Last Waltz
Designer: M. Nicoll
Height: 7 ¾", 19.7 cm
Colour: Pink and cream
Issued: 1987 in a limited
edition of 2,000
Varieties: HN 2315
Series: M. Doulton Events

U.S.:	$350.00
Can.:	$450.00
U.K.:	£210.00

HN 2317
The Lobster Man
Designer: M. Nicoll
Height: 7 ¼", 18.4 cm
Colour: Blue, grey and brown
Issued: 1964-1994
Varieties: HN 2323
Series: Sea Characters

U.S.:	$250.00
Can.:	$375.00
U.K.:	£150.00

HN 2318
Grace
Style One
Designer: M. Nicoll
Height: 7 ¾", 19.7 cm
Colour: Green
Issued: 1966-1981

U.S.:	$300.00
Can.:	$450.00
U.K.:	£175.00

HN 2319
The Bachelor
Designer: M. Nicoll
Height: 7", 17.8 cm
Colour: Green and brown
Issued: 1964-1975

U.S.:	$425.00
Can.:	$600.00
U.K.:	£250.00

HN 2320
Tuppence a Bag
Designer: M. Nicoll
Height: 5 ½", 14.0 cm
Colour: Blue and green
Issued: 1968-1995

U.S.:	$250.00
Can.:	$325.00
U.K.:	£150.00

HN 2321
Family Album
Designer: M. Nicholl
Height: 6 ¼", 15.9 cm
Colour: Lavender and green
Issued: 1966-1973

U.S.:	$600.00
Can.:	$775.00
U.K.:	£350.00

NOTE ON PRICING

As with all price guides, prices listed in this catalogue are suggested retail values. This is not a fixed price catalogue and figurines will be offered for sale at higher, lower, or catalogue prices, depending upon the supply-demand factors of the market place.

When our first edition was published in 1981 the Royal Doulton market was divided into three or four different geographical areas and pricing was based on each individual area.

In 2004 this is all changing, the global market place is coming to collectables. Our prices, while based on many different avenues that offer figurines for sale, are slowly turning into foreign exchange transactions between the former market areas. For now the collector is able to shop globally.

HN 2322
The Cup of Tea
Designer: M. Nicoll
Height: 7", 17.8 cm
Colour: Dark blue and grey
Issued: 1964-1983

U.S.:	**$275.00**
Can.:	**$375.00**
U.K.:	**£175.00**

HN 2323
The Lobster Man
Designer: M. Nicoll
Height: 7 ¼", 18.4 cm
Colour: Cream, blue, gold
           and grey
Issued: 1987-1995
Varieties: HN 2317
Series: Sea Characters

U.S.:	**$500.00**
Can.:	**$650.00**
U.K.:	**£300.00**

HN 2324
Matador and Bull
Style One
Designer: M. Davies
Height: 16", 40.6 cm
Colour: Black and yellow
Issued: 1964 to the present
Series: Prestige

U.S.:	**$27,845.00**
Can.:	**$32,700.00**
U.K.:	**£11,900.00**

HN 2325
The Master
Designer: M. Davies
Height: 6 ¼", 15.9 cm
Colour: Green and brown
Issued: 1967-1992

U.S.:	**$275.00**
Can.:	**$375.00**
U.K.:	**£160.00**

HN 2326
Antoinette
Style Two
Designer: M. Davies
Height: 6 ¼", 15.9 cm
Colour: White, white rose
Issued: 1967-1979
Varieties: Also called 'My Love'
           HN 2339

U.S.:	**$225.00**
Can.:	**$325.00**
U.K.:	**£135.00**

HN 2327
Katrina
Style One
Designer: M. Davies
Height: 7 ½", 19.1 cm
Colour: Red
Issued: 1965-1969

U.S.:	**$425.00**
Can.:	**$600.00**
U.K.:	**£250.00**

HN 2328
Queen of Sheba
Designer: M. Davies
Height: 9", 22.9 cm
Colour: Purple and brown
           with green base
Issued: 1982 in a limited
           edition of 750
Series: Les Femmes Fatales

U.S.:	**$1,350.00**
Can.:	**$1,750.00**
U.K.:	**£ 800.00**

HN 2329
Lynne
Style One
Designer: M. Davies
Height: 7", 17.8 cm
Colour: Green
Issued: 1971-1996
Varieties: HN 3740; also called
           'Kathy' (Style Two)
           HN 3305

U.S.:	**$250.00**
Can.:	**$325.00**
U.K.:	**£150.00**

HN 2330
Meditation
Designer: M. Davies
Height: 5 ¾", 14.6 cm
Colour: Peach and cream
Issued: 1971-1983

U.S.:	**$350.00**
Can.:	**$450.00**
U.K.:	**£210.00**

HN 2331
Cello
Style One
Designer: M. Davies
Height: 6", 15.2 cm
Colour: Yellow and brown
Issued: 1970 in a limited
edition of 750
Series: Lady Musicians

U.S.:	**$1,600.00**
Can.:	**$2,250.00**
U.K.:	**£1,000.00**

HN 2332
Monte Carlo
Designer: M. Davies
Height: 8 ¼", 21.0 cm
Colour: Green
Issued: 1982 in a limited
edition of 1,500
Series: Sweet and Twenties

U.S.:	**$500.00**
Can.:	**$675.00**
U.K.:	**£300.00**

HN 2333
Jacqueline
Style Two
Designer: M. Davies
Height: 7 ½", 19.1 cm
Colour: Purple
Issued: 1982 Canada,
1983 Worldwide -1991

U.S.:	**$250.00**
Can.:	**$325.00**
U.K.:	**£150.00**

HN 2334
Fragrance
Style One
Designer: M. Davies
Height: 7 ¼", 18.4 cm
Colour: Blue
Issued: 1966-1995
Varieties: HN 3311

U.S.:	**$225.00**
Can.:	**$325.00**
U.K.:	**£135.00**

HN 2335
Hilary
Designer: M. Davies
Height: 7 ¼", 18.4 cm
Colour: Blue
Issued: 1967-1981

U.S.:	**$225.00**
Can.:	**$325.00**
U.K.:	**£135.00**

HN 2336
Alison
Designer: M. Davies
Height: 7 ½", 19.1 cm
Colour: Blue and white
Issued: 1966-1992
Varieties: HN 3264

U.S.:	**$225.00**
Can.:	**$325.00**
U.K.:	**£135.00**

HN 2337
Loretta
Designer: M. Davies
Height: 7 ¾", 19.7 cm
Colour: Purple dress,
yellow shawl
Issued: 1966-1981

U.S.:	**$225.00**
Can.:	**$325.00**
U.K.:	**£135.00**

HN 2338
Penny
Designer: M. Davies
Height: 4 ¾", 12.0 cm
Colour: Green and white
Issued: 1968-1995
Varieties: HN 2424

U.S.:	**$100.00**
Can.:	**$150.00**
U.K.:	**£ 60.00**

HN 2339
My Love
Style One
Designer: M. Davies
Height: 6 ¼", 15.9 cm
Colour: White, red rose
Issued: 1969-1996
Varieties: Also called 'Antoinette'
(Style Two) HN 2326

U.S.:	**$275.00**
Can.:	**$375.00**
U.K.:	**£165.00**

HN 2340
Belle
Style Two
Designer: M. Davies
Height: 4 ½", 11.4 cm
Colour: Green
Issued: 1968-1988

U.S.:	**$100.00**
Can.:	**$150.00**
U.K.:	**£ 60.00**

HN 2341
Cherie
Designer: M. Davies
Height: 5 ½", 14.0 cm
Colour: Blue
Issued: 1966-1992

U.S.:	**$125.00**
Can.:	**$175.00**
U.K.:	**£ 85.00**

HN 2342
Lucrezia Borgia
Designer: M. Davies
Height: 8", 20.3 cm
Colour: Yellow
Issued: 1985 in a limited
edition of 750
Series: Les Femmes Fatales

U.S.:	**$1,350.00**
Can.:	**$1,750.00**
U.K.:	**£ 800.00**

HN 2343
Premiere
(Hand holds cloak)
Designer: M. Davies
Height: 7 ½", 19.1 cm
Colour: Green
Issued: 1969-Unknown
Varieties: HN 2343A

U.S.:	**$350.00**
Can.:	**$450.00**
U.K.:	**£200.00**

HN 2343A
Premiere
(Hand rests on cloak)
Designer: M. Davies
Height: 7 ½", 19.1 cm
Colour: Green
Issued: Unknown-1979
Varieties: HN 2343

U.S.:	**$250.00**
Can.:	**$325.00**
U.K.:	**£150.00**

HN 2344
Deauville
Designer: M. Davies
Height: 8 ¼", 21.0 cm
Colour: Yellow and white
Issued: 1982 in a limited
edition of 1,500
Series: Sweet and Twenties

U.S.:	**$500.00**
Can.:	**$675.00**
U.K.:	**£300.00**

HN 2345
Clarissa
Style Two
Designer: M. Davies
Height: 7 ½", 19.1 cm
Colour: Green
Issued: 1968-1981

  U.S.:   **$225.00**
  Can.:   **$300.00**
  U.K.:   **£135.00**

HN 2346
Kathy
Style One
Designer: M. Davies
Height: 4 ¾", 12.0 cm
Colour: Cream flowered dress
Issued: 1981-1987
Series: Kate Greenaway

  U.S.:   **$275.00**
  Can.:   **$350.00**
  U.K.:   **£165.00**

HN 2347
Nina (matte)
Designer: M. Davies
Height: 7 ½", 19.1 cm
Colour: Blue
Issued: 1969-1976

  U.S.:   **$200.00**
  Can.:   **$250.00**
  U.K.:   **£120.00**

HN 2348
Geraldine (matte)
Designer: M. Davies
Height: 7 ¼", 18.4 cm
Colour: Green
Issued: 1972-1976

  U.S.:   **$200.00**
  Can.:   **$250.00**
  U.K.:   **£120.00**

HN 2349
Flora
Designer: M. Nicoll
Height: 7 ¾", 19.7 cm
Colour: Brown and white
Issued: 1966-1973

  U.S.:   **$500.00**
  Can.:   **$650.00**
  U.K.:   **£300.00**

HN 2352
A Stitch in Time
Designer: M. Nicoll
Height: 6 ¼", 15.9 cm
Colour: Purple, brown
        and turquoise
Issued: 1966-1981

  U.S.:   **$275.00**
  Can.:   **$375.00**
  U.K.:   **£175.00**

HN 2356
Ascot
Style One
Designer: M. Nicoll
Height: 5 ¾", 14.6 cm
Colour: Green dress with
        yellow shawl
Issued: 1968-1995

  U.S.:   **$250.00**
  Can.:   **$325.00**
  U.K.:   **£150.00**

HN 2359
The Detective
Designer: M. Nicoll
Height: 9 ¼", 23.5 cm
Colour: Brown
Issued: 1977-1983

  U.S.:   **$400.00**
  Can.:   **$550.00**
  U.K.:   **£240.00**

HN 2350 - 2351 not issued.   HN 2353 - 2355 not issued.   HN 2357 - 2358 not issued.   HN 2360 not issued.

HN 2361
The Laird
(Small base)
Designer: M. Nicoll
Height: 8", 20.3 cm
Colour: Green and brown
Issued: 1969-Unknown
Varieties: HN 2361A (Large base)

U.S.:	$350.00
Can.:	$475.00
U.K.:	£200.00

HN 2361A
The Laird
(Large base)
Designer: M. Nicoll
Height: 8", 20.3 cm
Colour: Green and brown
Issued: Unknown-2001
Varieties: HN 2361 (Small base)

U.S.:	$325.00
Can.:	$450.00
U.K.:	£190.00

HN 2362
The Wayfarer
Designer: M. Nicoll
Height: 5 ½", 14.0 cm
Colour: Green, grey
and brown
Issued: 1970-1976

U.S.:	$275.00
Can.:	$375.00
U.K.:	£175.00

HN 2363 - 2367 not issued.

HN 2368
Fleur
Designer: J. Bromley
Height: 7 ¼", 18.4 cm
Colour: Green
Issued: 1968-1995
Varieties: HN 2369; also called
'Flower of Love'
HN 2460, 3970

U.S.:	$225.00
Can.:	$300.00
U.K.:	£135.00

HN 2369
Fleur
Designer: J. Bromley
Height: 7 ¼", 18.4 cm
Colour: Orange and blue
Issued: 1983-1986
Varieties: HN 2368; also called
'Flower of Love'
HN 2460, 3970

U.S.:	$325.00
Can.:	$450.00
U.K.:	£200.00

HN 2370
Sir Edward
Designer: J. Bromley
Height: 11", 27.9 cm
Colour: Red and grey
Issued: 1979 in a limited
edition of 500
Series: Age of Chivalry

U.S.:	$650.00
Can.:	$850.00
U.K.:	£350.00

HN 2371
Sir Ralph
Designer: J. Bromley
Height: 10 ¾", 27.3 cm
Colour: Turquoise and grey
Issued: 1979 in a limited
edition of 500
Series: Age of Chivalry

U.S.:	$650.00
Can.:	$850.00
U.K.:	£350.00

HN 2372
Sir Thomas
Designer: J. Bromley
Height: 11", 27.9 cm
Colour: Black
Issued: 1979 in a limited
edition of 500
Series: Age of Chivalry

U.S.:	$650.00
Can.:	$850.00
U.K.:	£350.00

HN 2373
Joanne
Style One
Designer: J. Bromley
Height: 5 ¼", 13.3 cm
Colour: White
Issued: 1982-1988
Series: Vanity Fair Ladies

U.S.:	$300.00
Can.:	$450.00
U.K.:	£200.00

HN 2374
Mary
Style One
Designer: J. Bromley
Height: 7 ¾", 19.7 cm
Colour: White
Issued: 1984-1986
Series: Vanity Fair Ladies

U.S.:	$300.00
Can.:	$450.00
U.K.:	£200.00

HN 2375
The Viking (matte)
Designer: J. Bromley
Height: 8 ¾", 22.2 cm
Colour: Blue and brown
Issued: 1973-1976

U.S.:	$300.00
Can.:	$450.00
U.K.:	£200.00

HN 2376
Indian Brave
Designer: M. Davies
Height: 16", 40.6 cm
Colour: Multicoloured
Issued: 1967 in a limited
         edition of 500

U.S.:	$5,000.00
Can.:	$6,500.00
U.K.:	£3,000.00

HN 2377
Georgina
Style One
Designer: M. Davies
Height: 5 ¾", 14.6 cm
Colour: Red and yellow
Issued: 1981-1986
Series: Kate Greenaway

U.S.:	$275.00
Can.:	$350.00
U.K.:	£165.00

HN 2378
Simone
Designer: M. Davies
Height: 7 ¼", 18.4 cm
Colour: Green
Issued: 1971-1981

U.S.:	$200.00
Can.:	$275.00
U.K.:	£120.00

HN 2379
Ninette
Style One
Designer: M. Davies
Height: 7 ½", 19.1 cm
Colour: Yellow and cream
Issued: 1971-1997
Varieties: HN 3417; also called
           'Olivia' (Style Two)
           HN 3339

U.S.:	$250.00
Can.:	$325.00
U.K.:	£150.00

HN 2380
Sweet Dreams
Style One
Designer: M. Davies
Height: 5", 12.7 cm
Colour: Multicoloured
Issued: 1971-1990

U.S.:	$250.00
Can.:	$325.00
U.K.:	£150.00

HN 2381
Kirsty
Style One
Designer: M. Davies
Height: 7 ½", 19.1 cm
Colour: Orange
Issued: 1971-1996
Varieties: Also called 'Janette'
            HN 3415

U.S.:	**$250.00**
Can.:	**$325.00**
U.K.:	**£150.00**

HN 2382
Secret Thoughts
Style One
Designer: M. Davies
Height: 6 ¼", 15.9 cm
Colour: Green
Issued: 1971-1988

U.S.:	**$275.00**
Can.:	**$375.00**
U.K.:	**£165.00**

HN 2383
Breton Dancer
Designer: M. Davies
Height: 8 ½", 21.6 cm
Colour: Blue and white
Issued: 1981 in a limited
            edition of 750
Series: Dancers of the World

U.S.:	**$ 900.00**
Can.:	**$1,250.00**
U.K.:	**£ 550.00**

HN 2384
West Indian Dancer
Designer: M. Davies
Height: 8 ¾", 22.2 cm
Colour: Yellow and white
Issued: 1981 in a limited
            edition of 750
Series: Dancers of the World

U.S.:	**$ 900.00**
Can.:	**$1,250.00**
U.K.:	**£ 550.00**

HN 2385
Debbie
Designer: M. Davies
Height: 5 ½", 14.0 cm
Colour: Blue and white
Issued: 1969-1982
Varieties: HN 2400; 'Lavender
            Rose' HN 3481;
            'Memory Lane'
            HN 3746; 'Moonlight
            Rose' HN 3483; 'Old
            Country Roses' (Style
            One) HN 3482;
            'Tranquillity' HN 3747

U.S.:	**$150.00**
Can.:	**$200.00**
U.K.:	**£ 95.00**

HN 2386
HRH Prince Philip
Duke of Edinburgh
Designer: M. Davies
Height: 8 ¼", 21.0 cm
Colour: Black and gold
Issued: 1981 in a limited
            edition of 1500

U.S.:	**$450.00**
Can.:	**$575.00**
U.K.:	**£250.00**

HN 2387
Helen of Troy
Style One
Designer: M. Davies
Height: 9 ¼", 23.5 cm
Colour: Green and pink
Issued: 1981 in a limited
            edition of 750
Series: Les Femmes Fatales

U.S.:	**$1,350.00**
Can.:	**$1,800.00**
U.K.:	**£ 800.00**

HN 2388
Karen
Style Two
Designer: M. Davies
Height: 8", 20.3 cm
Colour: Red and white
Issued: 1982-1999

U.S.:	**$400.00**
Can.:	**$550.00**
U.K.:	**£230.00**

HN 2389
Angela
Style Two
Designer: M. Davies
Height: 7 ½", 19.1 cm
Colour: White
Issued: 1983-1986
Series   Vanity Fair Ladies

U.S.:   **$225.00**
Can.:   **$300.00**
U.K.:   **£135.00**

HN 2390
Spinning
Designer: M. Davies
Height: 7 ¼", 18.4 cm
Colour: Yellow, pink, blue
           and white
Issued: 1984 in a limited
           edition of 750
Series: Gentle Arts

U.S.:   **$1,600.00**
Can.:   **$2,250.00**
U.K.:   **£ 950.00**

HN 2391
T'zu-hsi, Empress Dowager
Designer: M. Davies
Height: 8", 20.3 cm
Colour: Red, white and blue
Issued: 1983 in a limited
           edition of 750
Series: Les Femmes Fatales

U.S.:   **$1,350.00**
Can.:   **$1,750.00**
U.K.:   **£ 800.00**

HN 2392
Jennifer
Style Two
Designer: M. Davies
Height: 7", 17.8 cm
Colour: Blue
Issued: 1982-1992

U.S.:   **$350.00**
Can.:   **$500.00**
U.K.:   **£220.00**

HN 2393
Rosalind
Designer: M. Davies
Height: 5 ½", 14.0 cm
Colour: Blue
Issued: 1970-1975

U.S.:   **$275.00**
Can.:   **$375.00**
U.K.:   **£165.00**

HN 2394
Lisa
Style One
Designer: M. Davies
Height: 7 ¼", 18.4 cm
Colour: Purple-yellow
Issued: 1983-1990
Varieties: HN 2310, 3265

U.S.:   **$225.00**
Can.:   **$325.00**
U.K.:   **£125.00**

HN 2395
Catherine
Style One
Designer: M. Davies
Height: 7 ½", 19.1 cm
Colour: Red and yellow
Issued: 1983-1984
Series: Ladies of Covent
           Garden
Comm.by: Amex

U.S.:   **$525.00**
Can.:   **$750.00**
U.K.:   **£325.00**

HN 2396
Wistful
Style One
Designer: M. Davies
Height: 6 ½", 16.5 cm
Colour: Peach and cream
Issued: 1979-1990
Varieties: HN 2472

U.S.:   **$300.00**
Can.:   **$400.00**
U.K.:   **£175.00**

HN 2397
Margaret
Style Two
Designer: M. Davies
Height: 7 ½", 19.1 cm
Colour: White dress,
blue sash
Issued: 1982-1999
Varieties: HN 3496; 'Adele'
HN 2480; 'Camille'
(Style Two) HN 3171
Series: Vanity Fair Ladies

U.S.:	**$225.00**
Can.:	**$325.00**
U.K.:	**£125.00**

HN 2398
Alexandra
Style One
Designer: M. Davies
Height: 7 ¾", 19.7 cm
Colour: Patterned green
dress, yellow cape
Issued: 1970-1976

U.S.:	**$275.00**
Can.:	**$375.00**
U.K.:	**£165.00**

HN 2399
Buttercup
Style One
Designer: M. Davies
Height: 7", 17.8 cm
Colour: Red dress with
yellow sleeves
Issued: 1983-1997
Varieties: HN 2309

U.S.:	**$275.00**
Can.:	**$375.00**
U.K.:	**£165.00**

HN 2400
Debbie
Designer: M. Davies
Height: 5 ½", 14.0 cm
Colour: Peach
Issued: 1983-1995
Varieties: HN 2385; 'Lavender
Rose' HN 3481;
'Memory Lane',
HN 3746; 'Moonlight
Rose' HN 3483;
'Old Country Roses'
(Style One) HN 3482;
'Tranquillity' HN 3747

U.S.:	**$150.00**
Can.:	**$190.00**
U.K.:	**£ 90.00**

HN 2401
Sandra
Designer: M. Davies
Height: 7 ¾", 19.7 cm
Colour: Green
Issued: 1983-1992
Varieties: HN 2275; Also
called 'Annette'
(Style Two) HN 3495

U.S.:	**$275.00**
Can.:	**$400.00**
U.K.:	**£175.00**

HN 2402 - 2407 not issued.

HN 2408
A Penny's Worth
Designer: M. Nicoll
Height: 7", 17.8 cm
Colour: Pale blue, yellow
and white
Issued: 1986-1990

U.S.:	**$250.00**
Can.:	**$325.00**
U.K.:	**£150.00**

HN 2409 not issued.

HN 2410
Lesley
Designer: M. Nicoll
Height: 8", 20.3 cm
Colour: Orange and yellow
Issued: 1986-1990

U.S.:	**$275.00**
Can.:	**$400.00**
U.K.:	**£175.00**

HN 2411 - 2416 not issued.

HN 2417
The Boatman 'Skylark'
Designer: M. Nicoll
Height: 6 ½", 16.5 cm
Colour: Yellow
Issued: 1971-1987
Varieties: HN 2417A
Series: Sea Characters

U.S.:	**$300.00**
Can.:	**$400.00**
U.K.:	**£175.00**

HN 2417A
The Boatman 'Pilot'
Designer: M. Nicoll
Height: 6 ½", 16.5 cm
Colour: Yellow
Issued: 1971-1987
Varieties: HN 2417
Series: Sea Characters
Comm.by: Pilot Insurance

U.S.:
Can.: Rare
U.K.:

HN 2418
Country Love
Designer: J. Bromley
Height: 8", 20.3 cm
Colour: Pink flowered dress
Issued: 1990 in a limited
edition of 12,500
Comm.by: Lawleys By Post

U.S.: $450.00
Can.: $600.00
U.K.: £275.00

HN 2419
The Goose Girl
Style Two
Designer: J. Bromley
Height: 8", 20.3 cm
Colour: Blue and white
Issued: 1990 in a limited
edition of 12,500
Comm.by: Lawleys By Post

U.S.: $450.00
Can.: $600.00
U.K.: £275.00

HN 2420
The Shepherdess
Style Four
Designer: J. Bromley
Height: 9", 22.9 cm
Colour: Peach, blue and white
Issued: 1991 in a limited
edition of 12,500
Comm.by: Lawleys By Post

U.S.: $450.00
Can.: $600.00
U.K.: £275.00

HN 2421
Charlotte
Style One
Designer: J. Bromley
Height: 6 ½", 16.5 cm
Colour: Purple
Issued: 1972-1986
Varieties: HN 2423

U.S.: $275.00
Can.: $375.00
U.K.: £165.00

HN 2422
Francine
(Birds tail up)
Designer: J. Bromley
Height: 5", 12.7 cm
Colour: Green and white
Issued: 1972-Unknown
Varieties: HN 2422A (Birds tail
moulded to hand)

U.S.: $175.00
Can.: $225.00
U.K.: £100.00

HN 2422A
Francine
(Birds tail moulded to hand)
Designer: J. Bromley
Height: 5", 12.7 cm
Colour: Green and white
Issued: Unknown-1981
Varieties: HN 2422 (Birds tail up)

U.S.: $125.00
Can.: $160.00
U.K.: £ 75.00

HN 2423
Charlotte
Style One
Designer: J. Bromley
Height: 6 ½", 16.5 cm
Colour: Pale blue and pink
Issued: 1986-1992
Varieties: HN 2421

U.S.: $275.00
Can.: $375.00
U.K.: £165.00

HN 2424
Penny
Designer: M. Davies
Height: 4 ¾", 12.0 cm
Colour: Yellow and white
Issued: 1983-1992
Varieties: HN 2338

U.S.:	**$125.00**
Can.:	**$160.00**
U.K.:	**£ 75.00**

Also known with yellow underskirt.

HN 2425
Southern Belle
Style One
Designer: M. Davies
Height: 7 ½", 19.1 cm
Colour: Pale blue and pink
Issued: 1983-1994
Varieties: HN 2229

U.S.:	**$250.00**
Can.:	**$325.00**
U.K.:	**£150.00**

HN 2426
Tranquility
Designer: M. Davies
Height: 12", 30.5 cm
Colour: Black
Issued: 1981-1986
Varieties: HN 2469
Series: Images

U.S.:	**$175.00**
Can.:	**$250.00**
U.K.:	**£125.00**

HN 2427
Virginals
Designer: M. Davies
Height: 6 ¼", 15.9 cm
Colour: Green, gold
          and brown
Issued: 1971 in a limited
          edition of 750
Series: Lady Musicians

U.S.:	**$1,750.00**
Can.:	**$2,500.00**
U.K.:	**£1,200.00**

HN 2428
The Palio
Designer: M. Davies
Height: 17 ½", 44.5 cm
Colour: Blue, yellow
          and brown
Issued: 1971 in a limited
          edition of 500

U.S.:	**$ 9,000.00**
Can.:	**$12,000.00**
U.K.:	**£ 5,250.00**

HN 2429
Elyse
Designer: M. Davies
Height: 5 ¾", 14.6 cm
Colour: Blue
Issued: 1972-1995
Varieties: HN 2474, 4131

U.S.:	**$250.00**
Can.:	**$325.00**
U.K.:	**£150.00**

HN 2430
Romance
Style Two
Designer: M. Davies
Height: 5 ¼", 13.3 cm
Colour: Gold and green
Issued: 1972-1981

U.S.:	**$250.00**
Can.:	**$325.00**
U.K.:	**£150.00**

HN 2431
Lute
Designer: M. Davies
Height: 6 ¼", 15.9 cm
Colour: Blue, white and brown
Issued: 1972 in a limited
          edition of 750
Series: Lady Musicians

U.S.:	**$1,100.00**
Can.:	**$1,400.00**
U.K.:	**£ 650.00**

HN 2432
Violin
Designer: M. Davies
Height: 6 ¼", 15.9 cm
Colour: Brown and gold
Issued: 1972 in a limited
           edition of 750
Series: Lady Musicians
   U.S.: $1,100.00
   Can.: $1,400.00
   U.K.:   £ 650.00

HN 2433
Peace
Designer: M. Davies
Height: 8", 20.3 cm
Colour: Black
Issued: 1981-1997
Varieties: HN 2470
Series: Images
   U.S.: $150.00
   Can.: $200.00
   U.K.:   £ 90.00

Flambé model known.

HN 2434
Fair Maiden
Designer: M. Davies
Height: 5 ¼", 13.3 cm
Colour: Red and white
Issued: 1983-1994
Varieties: HN 2211
   U.S.: $150.00
   Can.: $195.00
   U.K.:   £ 90.00

HN 2435
Queen of the Ice
Designer: M. Davies
Height: 8", 20.3 cm
Colour: Cream
Issued: 1983-1986
Series: Enchantment
   U.S.: $250.00
   Can.: $325.00
   U.K.:   £150.00

HN 2436
Scottish Highland Dancer
Designer: M. Davies
Height: 9 ½", 24.1 cm
Colour: Red, black and white
Issued: 1978 in a limited
           edition of 750
Series: Dancers of the World
   U.S.: $1,600.00
   Can.: $2,250.00
   U.K.:   £1,000.00

HN 2437
Queen of the Dawn
Designer: M. Davies
Height: 8 ½", 21.6 cm
Colour: Cream
Issued: 1983-1986
Series: Enchantment
   U.S.: $250.00
   Can.: $325.00
   U.K.:   £150.00

HN 2438
Sonata
Designer: M. Davies
Height: 6 ½", 16.5 cm
Colour: Cream
Issued: 1983-1985
Series: Enchantment
   U.S.: $250.00
   Can.: $325.00
   U.K.:   £150.00

HN 2439
Philippine Dancer
Designer: M. Davies
Height: 9 ½", 24.1 cm
Colour: Green and cream
Issued: 1978 in a limited
           edition of 750
Series: Dancers of the World
   U.S.: $ 900.00
   Can.: $1,175.00
   U.K.:   £ 500.00

HN 2440
Cynthia
Style Two
Designer: M. Davies
Height: 7 ¼", 18.4 cm
Colour: Green and yellow
Issued: 1984-1992

U.S.:	**$350.00**
Can.:	**$475.00**
U.K.:	**£200.00**

HN 2441
Pauline
Style Two
Designer: M. Davies
Height: 5", 12.7 cm
Colour: Peach
Issued: 1983 Canada,
           1984 Worldwide-1989

U.S.:	**$400.00**
Can.:	**$525.00**
U.K.:	**£200.00**

HN 2442
Sailor's Holiday
Designer: M. Nicoll
Height: 6 ¼", 15.9 cm
Colour: Gold, brown and white
Issued: 1972-1979
Series: Sea Characters

U.S.:	**$425.00**
Can.:	**$550.00**
U.K.:	**£250.00**

HN 2443
The Judge (matte)
Style One
Designer: M. Nicoll
Height: 6 ½", 16.5 cm
Colour: Red and white
Issued: 1972-1976
Varieties: HN 2443A (gloss)

U.S.:	**$275.00**
Can.:	**$350.00**
U.K.:	**£175.00**

HN 2443A
The Judge (gloss)
Style One
Designer: M. Nicoll
Height: 6 ½", 16.5 cm
Colour: Red and white
Issued: 1976-1992
Varieties: HN 2443 (matte)

U.S.:	**$250.00**
Can.:	**$325.00**
U.K.:	**£150.00**

HN 2444
Bon Appetit (matte)
Designer: M. Nicoll
Height: 6", 15.2 cm
Colour: Grey and brown
Issued: 1972-1976

U.S.:	**$225.00**
Can.:	**$300.00**
U.K.:	**£135.00**

HN 2445
Parisian (matte)
Designer: M. Nicoll
Height: 8", 20.3 cm
Colour: Blue and grey
Issued: 1972-1975

U.S.:	**$225.00**
Can.:	**$300.00**
U.K.:	**£135.00**

HN 2446
Thanksgiving (matte)
Designer: M. Nicoll
Height: 8", 20.3 cm
Colour: Blue, pink and grey
Issued: 1972-1976

U.S.:	**$250.00**
Can.:	**$350.00**
U.K.:	**£150.00**

HN 2447 - 2454 not issued.

HN 2455
The Seafarer (matte)
Designer: M. Nicoll
Height: 8 ½", 21.6 cm
Colour: Gold, blue and grey
Issued: 1972-1976
Series: Sea Characters

U.S.: **$325.00**
Can.: **$450.00**
U.K.: **£200.00**

HN 2456 - 2459 not issued.

HN 2460
Flower of Love
Designer: John Bromley
Height: 7 ½", 19.1 cm
Colour: White and yellow
Issued: 1991 Canada
         1992 Worldwide-1997
Varieties: HN 3970; also called
         'Fleur' HN 2368, 2369
Series: Vanity Fair Ladies

U.S.: **$225.00**
Can.: **$325.00**
U.K.: **£150.00**

HN 2461
Janine
Designer: J. Bromley
Height: 7 ½", 19.1 cm
Colour: Turquoise and white
Issued: 1971-1995

U.S.: **$250.00**
Can.: **$325.00**
U.K.: **£150.00**

HN 2462 not issued.

HN 2463
Olga
Designer: J. Bromley
Height: 8 ¼", 21.0 cm
Colour: Turquoise and gold
Issued: 1972-1975

U.S.: **$275.00**
Can.: **$350.00**
U.K.: **£150.00**

HN 2464 not issued.

HN 2465
Elizabeth
Style Two
Designer: J. Bromley
Height: 8 ½", 21.6 cm
Colour: Blue
Issued: 1990-1998

U.S.: **$350.00**
Can.: **$500.00**
U.K.: **£200.00**

HN 2466
Eve
Designer: M. Davies
Height: 9 ¼", 23.5 cm
Colour: Green and brown
Issued: 1984 in a limited
         edition of 750
Series: Les Femmes Fatales

U.S.: **$1,350.00**
Can.: **$1,750.00**
U.K.: **£ 775.00**

HN 2467
Melissa
Style One
Designer: M. Davies
Height: 6 ¾", 17.2 cm
Colour: Purple and cream
Issued: 1981-1994

U.S.: **$250.00**
Can.: **$325.00**
U.K.: **£150.00**

HN 2468
Diana
Style Two
Designer: M. Davies
Height: 8", 20.3 cm
Colour: Flowered white dress
Issued: 1986 N. America,
         1987 Worldwide-1999
Varieties: HN 3266

U.S.: **$225.00**
Can.: **$300.00**
U.K.: **£135.00**

HN 2469
Tranquility
Designer: M. Davies
Height: 12", 30.5 cm
Colour: White
Issued: 1981-1986
Varieties: HN 2426
Series: Images

U.S.:	**$175.00**
Can.:	**$250.00**
U.K.:	**£125.00**

HN 2470
Peace
Designer: M. Davies
Height: 8", 20.3 cm
Colour: White
Issued: 1981-2000
Varieties: HN 2433
Series: Images

U.S.:	**$125.00**
Can.:	**$200.00**
U.K.:	**£ 85.00**

Flambé model known.

HN 2471
Victoria
Style One
Designer: M. Davies
Height: 6 ½", 16.5 cm
Colour: Patterned pink dress
Issued: 1973-2000
Varieties: HN 3416

U.S.:	**$325.00**
Can.:	**$450.00**
U.K.:	**£195.00**

HN 2472
Wistful
Style One
Designer: M. Davies
Height: 6 ½", 16.5 cm
Colour: Blue and white
Issued: 1985-1985
Varieties: HN 2396
Series: M. Doulton Events

U.S.:	**$325.00**
Can.:	**$450.00**
U.K.:	**£200.00**

HN 2473
At Ease
Designer: M. Davies
Height: 6", 15.2 cm
Colour: Yellow
Issued: 1973-1979

U.S.:	**$325.00**
Can.:	**$450.00**
U.K.:	**£200.00**

HN 2474
Elyse
Designer: M. Davies
Height: 5 ¾", 14.6 cm
Colour: Patterned green dress
Issued: 1986 N. America,
1987 Worldwide-1999
Varieties: HN 2429, 4131

U.S.:	**$400.00**
Can.:	**$550.00**
U.K.:	**£250.00**

HN 2475
Vanity
Designer: M. Davies
Height: 5 ¼", 13.3 cm
Colour: Red
Issued: 1973-1992

U.S.:	**$150.00**
Can.:	**$225.00**
U.K.:	**£100.00**

HN 2476
Mandy
Designer: M. Davies
Height: 4 ½", 11.4 cm
Colour: White
Issued: 1982-1992

U.S.:	**$100.00**
Can.:	**$135.00**
U.K.:	**£ 60.00**

HN 2477
Denise
Style Three
Designer: M. Davies
Height: 7 ½", 19.1 cm
Colour: White
Issued: 1987-1996
Varieties: Also called 'Summer Rose' (Style Two) HN 3309
Series: Vanity Fair Ladies

U.S.: $175.00
Can.: $225.00
U.K.: £100.00

HN 2478
Kelly
Style One
Designer: M. Davies
Height: 7 ½", 19.1 cm
Colour: White with blue flowers
Issued: 1985-1992
Varieties: HN 3222

U.S.: $225.00
Can.: $300.00
U.K.: £135.00

HN 2479
Pamela
Style Two
Designer: M. Davies
Height: 7", 17.8 cm
Colour: White
Issued: 1986-1994
Varieties: HN 3223
Series: Vanity Fair Ladies

U.S.: $200.00
Can.: $250.00
U.K.: £120.00

HN 2480
Adele
Designer: M. Davies
Height: 8", 20.3 cm
Colour: Flowered white dress
Issued: 1987-1992
Varieties: Also called 'Camille' (Style Two) HN 3171; 'Margaret' (Style Two) HN 2397, 3496

U.S.: $225.00
Can.: $300.00
U.K.: £135.00

HN 2481
Maureen
Style Three
Designer: M. Davies
Height: 7 ½", 19.1 cm
Colour: White dress, purple flowers
Issued: 1987-1992
Varieties: Also called 'Tina' HN 3494
Series: Vanity Fair Ladies

U.S.: $225.00
Can.: $300.00
U.K.: £135.00

HN 2482
Harp
Designer: M. Davies
Height: 8 ¾", 22.2 cm
Colour: Purple, green and gold
Issued: 1973 in a limited edition of 750
Series: Lady Musicians

U.S.: $1,800.00
Can.: $2,500.00
U.K.: £1,100.00

HN 2483
Flute
Designer: M. Davies
Height: 6", 15.2 cm
Colour: Red and white
Issued: 1973 in a limited edition of 750
Series: Lady Musicians

U.S.: $1,100.00
Can.: $1,400.00
U.K.: £ 650.00

HN 2484
Past Glory
Designer: M. Nicoll
Height: 7 ½", 19.1 cm
Colour: Red and black
Issued: 1973-1979

U.S.: $400.00
Can.: $525.00
U.K.: £250.00

HN 2485
Lunchtime
Designer: M. Nicoll
Height: 8", 20.3 cm
Colour: Brown
Issued: 1973-1981

U.S.: **$300.00**
Can.: **$400.00**
U.K.: **£185.00**

HN 2486 not issued.

HN 2487
Beachcomber (matte)
Designer: M. Nicoll
Height: 6 ½", 15.9 cm
Colour: Purple and grey
Issued: 1973-1976

U.S.: **$250.00**
Can.: **$325.00**
U.K.: **£150.00**

HN 2488 - 2491 not issued.

HN 2492
Huntsman
Style Three
Designer: M. Nicoll
Height: 7 ½", 19.1 cm
Colour: Grey and cream
Issued: 1974-1979

U.S.: **$350.00**
Can.: **$450.00**
U.K.: **£200.00**

HN 2493 not issued.

HN 2494
Old Meg (matte)
Designer: M. Nicoll
Height: 8 ¼", 21.0 cm
Colour: Blue and grey
Issued: 1974-1976

U.S.: **$250.00**
Can.: **$325.00**
U.K.: **£150.00**

HN 2495 - 2498 not issued.

HN 2499
Helmsman
Designer: M. Nicoll
Height: 9", 22.9 cm
Colour: Brown
Issued: 1974-1986
Series: Sea Characters

U.S.: **$400.00**
Can.: **$525.00**
U.K.: **£250.00**

HN 2500 - 2501 Animal figures.

HN 2502
Queen Elizabeth II
Style One
Designer: M. Davies
Height: 7 ¾", 19.7 cm
Colour: Pale blue
Issued: 1973 in a limited
edition of 750

U.S.: **$1,750.00**
Can.: **$2,500.00**
U.K.: **£1,000.00**

HN 2503 - 2519 Animal figures.

HN 2520
The Farmer's Boy
Designer: W. M. Chance
Height: 8 ½", 21.6 cm
Colour: White, brown
and green
Issued: 1938-1960

U.S.: **$2,000.00**
Can.: **$2,500.00**
U.K.: **£1,200.00**

HN 2521
Dapple Grey
Designer: W. M. Chance
Height: 7 ¼", 18.4 cm
Colour: White, red and brown
Issued: 1938-1960

U.S.: **$3,500.00**
Can.: **$4,500.00**
U.K.: **£2,000.00**

HN 2522 - 2541 Animal and Bird
figures.

HN 2542
Boudoir
Designer: E. J. Griffiths
Height: 12 ¼", 31.1 cm
Colour: Pale blue
Issued: 1974-1979
Series: Haute Ensemble

U.S.: **$375.00**
Can.: **$550.00**
U.K.: **£250.00**

HN 2543
Eliza
(Handmade flowers)
Style One
Designer: E. J. Griffiths
Height: 11 ¾", 29.8 cm
Colour: Gold
Issued: 1974-1979
Varieties: HN 2543A
Series: Haute Ensemble

U.S.: **$275.00**
Can.: **$400.00**
U.K.: **£175.00**

HN 2543A
Eliza
(Painted flowers)
Style One
Designer: E. J. Griffiths
Height: 11 ¾", 29.8 cm
Colour: Gold
Issued: 1974-1979
Varieties: HN 2543
Series: Haute Ensemble

U.S.: **$225.00**
Can.: **$350.00**
U.K.: **£150.00**

HN 2544
A la Mode
Designer: E. J. Griffiths
Height: 12 ¼", 31.1 cm
Colour: Green
Issued: 1974-1979
Series: Haute Ensemble

U.S.: **$275.00**
Can.: **$400.00**
U.K.: **£175.00**

HN 2545
Carmen
Style Two
Designer: E. J. Griffiths
Height: 11 ½", 29.2 cm
Colour: Blue
Issued: 1974-1979
Series: Haute Ensemble

U.S.: **$300.00**
Can.: **$450.00**
U.K.: **£200.00**

HN 2546
Buddies (matte)
Style One
Designer: E. J. Griffiths
Height: 6", 15.2 cm
Colour: Blue and brown
Issued: 1973-1976

U.S.: **$250.00**
Can.: **$350.00**
U.K.: **£150.00**

HN 2547
R.C.M.P. 1973
Designer: D. V. Tootle
Height: 8", 20.3 cm
Colour: Red
Issued: 1973 in a limited
edition of 1,500

U.S.: **$750.00**
Can.: **$975.00**
U.K.: **£450.00**

HN 2548 - 2553 Bird figures.

HN 2554
Masque
(Hand holds wand of mask)
Designer: D. V. Tootle
Height: 8 ½", 21.6 cm
Colour: Blue
Issued: 1973-1975
Varieties: HN 2554A

U.S.: **$400.00**
Can.: **$600.00**
U.K.: **£250.00**

HN 2554A
Masque
(Hand holds mask to face)
Designer: D. V. Tootle
Height: 8 ½", 21.6 cm
Colour: Blue
Issued: 1975-1982
Varieties: HN 2554

U.S.:	**$275.00**
Can.:	**$350.00**
U.K.:	**£150.00**

HN 2555
R.C.M.P. 1873
Designer: D. V. Tootle
Height: 8 ¼", 21.0 cm
Colour: Red
Issued: 1973 in a limited
          edition of 1,500

U.S.:	**$750.00**
Can.:	**$975.00**
U.K.:	**£450.00**

HN 2556 - 2670 Animal and Bird
figures, except HN 2627 not issued.

HN 2671
Good Morning (matte)
Designer: M. Nicoll
Height: 8", 20.3 cm
Colour: Blue, pink and brown
Issued: 1974-1976

U.S.:	**$275.00**
Can.:	**$375.00**
U.K.:	**£175.00**

HN 2672 - 2676 not issued.

HN 2677
Taking Things Easy
Designer: M. Nicoll
Height: 6 ¾", 17.2 cm
Colour: Blue, white and brown
Issued: 1975-1987
Varieties: HN 2680

U.S.:	**$300.00**
Can.:	**$400.00**
U.K.:	**£175.00**

HN 2678
The Carpenter
Designer: M. Nicoll
Height: 8", 20.3 cm
Colour: Blue, white and brown
Issued: 1986-1992

U.S.:	**$450.00**
Can.:	**$600.00**
U.K.:	**£275.00**

HN 2679
Drummer Boy
Designer: M. Nicoll
Height: 8 ½", 21.6 cm
Colour: Multicoloured
Issued: 1976-1981

U.S.:	**$500.00**
Can.:	**$650.00**
U.K.:	**£350.00**

HN 2680
Taking Things Easy
Designer: M. Nicoll
Height: 6 ¾", 17.2 cm
Colour: Cream and blue
Issued: 1987-1996
Varieties: HN 2677

U.S.:	**$300.00**
Can.:	**$400.00**
U.K.:	**£175.00**

HN 2681 - 2682 not issued.

HN 2683
Stop Press
Designer: M. Nicoll
Height: 7 ½", 19.1 cm
Colour: Brown, blue and white
Issued: 1977-1981

U.S.:	**$250.00**
Can.:	**$350.00**
U.K.:	**£175.00**

HN 2684 - 2692 not issued.

HN 2693
October
Style One
Designer: M. Davies
Height: 7 ¾", 19.5 cm
Colour: White with blue dress,
cosmos flowers
Issued: 1987-1987
Varieties: Also called 'Gillian'
(Style Three) HN 3742
Series: Figure of the Month

U.S.:	**$200.00**
Can.:	**$275.00**
U.K.:	**£125.00**

HN 2694
Fiona
Style Two
Designer: M. Davies
Height: 7 ½", 19.1 cm
Colour: Red and white
Issued: 1974-1981

U.S.:	**$225.00**
Can.:	**$300.00**
U.K.:	**£125.00**

HN 2695
November
Style One
Designer: M. Davies
Height: 7 ¾", 19.7 cm
Colour: White with pink dress,
chrysanthemum
flowers
Issued: 1987-1987
Varieties: Also called 'Gillian'
(Style Three) HN 3742
Series: Figure of the Month

U.S.:	**$200.00**
Can.:	**$275.00**
U.K.:	**£125.00**

HN 2696
December
Style One
Designer: M. Davies
Height: 7 ¾", 19.7 cm
Colour: White with green dress,
Christmas rose flowers
Issued: 1987-1987
Varieties: Also called 'Gillian'
(Style Three) HN 3742
Series: Figure of the Month

U.S.:	**$200.00**
Can.:	**$275.00**
U.K.:	**£125.00**

HN 2697
January
Style One
Designer: M. Davies
Height: 7 ¾", 19.7 cm
Colour: White with green dress,
snowdrop flowers
Issued: 1987-1987
Varieties: Also called 'Gillian'
(Style Three) HN 3742
Series: Figure of the Month

U.S.:	**$200.00**
Can.:	**$275.00**
U.K.:	**£125.00**

HN 2698
Sunday Best
Style One
Designer: M. Davies
Height: 7 ½", 19.1 cm
Colour: Pink and white
Issued: 1985-1995
Varieties: HN 2206

U.S.:	**$225.00**
Can.:	**$300.00**
U.K.:	**£135.00**

HN 2699
Cymbals
Designer: M. Davies
Height: 7 ½", 19.1 cm
Colour: Green and gold
Issued: 1974 in a limited
edition of 750
Series: Lady Musicians

U.S.:	**$ 900.00**
Can.:	**$1,175.00**
U.K.:	**£ 550.00**

HN 2700
Chitarrone
Designer: M. Davies
Height: 7 ½", 19.1 cm
Colour: Blue
Issued: 1974 in a limited
edition of 750
Series: Lady Musicians

U.S.:	**$1,000.00**
Can.:	**$1,500.00**
U.K.:	**£ 600.00**

HN 2701
Deborah
Style One
Designer: M. Davies
Height: 7 ¾", 19.7 cm
Colour: Green and white
Issued: 1983-1984
Series: Ladies of Covent
                 Garden
Comm.by: Amex

U.S.:	**$525.00**
Can.:	**$750.00**
U.K.:	**£325.00**

HN 2702
Shirley
Designer: M. Davies
Height: 7 ¼", 18.4 cm
Colour: White dress with
                 pink flowers
Issued: 1985-1997

U.S.:	**$250.00**
Can.:	**$350.00**
U.K.:	**£150.00**

HN 2703
February
Style One
Designer: M. Davies
Height: 7 ¾", 19.7 cm
Colour: White with purple
                 dress, violet flowers
Issued: 1987-1987
Varieties: Also called 'Gillian'
                 (Style Three) HN 3742
Series: Figure of the Month

U.S.:	**$200.00**
Can.:	**$275.00**
U.K.:	**£125.00**

HN 2704
Pensive Moments
Designer: M. Davies
Height: 5", 12.7 cm
Colour: Blue
Issued: 1975-1981

U.S.:	**$300.00**
Can.:	**$400.00**
U.K.:	**£175.00**

HN 2705
Julia
Style One
Designer: M. Davies
Height: 7 ½", 19.1 cm
Colour: Gold
Issued: 1975-1990
Varieties: HN 2706

U.S.:	**$225.00**
Can.:	**$300.00**
U.K.:	**£135.00**

HN 2706
Julia
Style One
Designer: M. Davies
Height: 7 ½", 19.1 cm
Colour: Pink and green
Issued: 1985-1993
Varieties: HN 2705

U.S.:	**$225.00**
Can.:	**$350.00**
U.K.:	**£150.00**

HN 2707
March
Style One
Designer: M. Davies
Height: 7 ¾", 19.7 cm
Colour: White and green dress,
                 anemone flowers
Issued: 1987-1987
Varieties: Also called 'Gillian'
                 (Style Three) HN 3742
Series: Figure of the Month

U.S.:	**$200.00**
Can.:	**$275.00**
U.K.:	**£125.00**

HN 2708
April
Style One
Designer: M. Davies
Height: 7 ¾", 19.7 cm
Colour: White and tan dress,
                 sweet pea flowers
Issued: 1987-1987
Varieties: Also called 'Gillian'
                 (Style Three) HN 3742
Series: Figure of the Month

U.S.:	**$200.00**
Can.:	**$275.00**
U.K.:	**£125.00**

HN 2709
Regal Lady
Designer: M. Davies
Height: 7 ½", 19.1 cm
Colour: Turquoise and cream
Issued: 1975-1983

U.S.:	**$250.00**
Can.:	**$375.00**
U.K.:	**£150.00**

HN 2710
Jean
Style Two
Designer: M. Davies
Height: 5 ¾", 14.6 cm
Colour: White
Issued: 1983-1986
Series: Vanity Fair Ladies

U.S.:	**$250.00**
Can.:	**$350.00**
U.K.:	**£150.00**

HN 2711
May
Style Two
Designer: M. Davies
Height: 7 ¾", 19.7 cm
Colour: White and green dress, lily of the valley flowers
Issued: 1987-1987
Varieties: Also called 'Gillian' (Style Three) HN 3742
Series: Figure of the Month

U.S.:	**$200.00**
Can.:	**$275.00**
U.K.:	**£125.00**

HN 2712
Mantilla
Designer: E. J. Griffiths
Height: 11 ½", 29.2 cm
Colour: Red, black and white
Issued: 1974-1979
Varieties: HN 3192
Series: Haute Ensemble

U.S.:	**$400.00**
Can.:	**$600.00**
U.K.:	**£275.00**

HN 2713
Tenderness
Designer: E. J. Griffiths
Height: 12", 30.5 cm
Colour: White
Issued: 1982-1997
Varieties: HN 2714
Series: Images

U.S.:	**$150.00**
Can.:	**$225.00**
U.K.:	**£ 90.00**

HN 2714
Tenderness
Designer: E. J. Griffiths
Height: 12", 30.5 cm
Colour: Black
Issued: 1982-1992
Varieties: HN 2713
Series: Images

U.S.:	**$175.00**
Can.:	**$275.00**
U.K.:	**£110.00**

HN 2715
Patricia
Style Three
Designer: M. Davies
Height: 7 ½", 19.1 cm
Colour: White
Issued: 1982-1985
Series: Vanity Fair Ladies

U.S.:	**$275.00**
Can.:	**$400.00**
U.K.:	**£175.00**

HN 2716
Cavalier
Style Two
Designer: E. J. Griffiths
Height: 9 ¾", 24.7 cm
Colour: Brown and green
Issued: 1976-1982

U.S.:	**$275.00**
Can.:	**$350.00**
U.K.:	**£165.00**

Flambé pilot piece known

HN 2717
Private, 2nd South Carolina Regiment, 1781
Designer: E. J. Griffiths
Height: 11 ½", 29.2 cm
Colour: Blue and cream
Issued: 1975 in a limited edition of 350
Series: Soldiers of the Revolution

U.S.:	**$1,500.00**
Can.:	**$2,250.00**
U.K.:	**£ 950.00**

HN 2718
Lady Pamela
Designer: D. V. Tootle
Height: 8", 20.3 cm
Colour: Purple
Issued: 1974-1981

U.S.:	**$250.00**
Can.:	**$325.00**
U.K.:	**£150.00**

HN 2719
Laurianne
Designer: D. V. Tootle
Height: 6 ¼", 15.9 cm
Colour: Dark blue and white
Issued: 1974-1979

U.S.:	**$250.00**
Can.:	**$350.00**
U.K.:	**£150.00**

HN 2720
Family
Designer: E. J. Griffiths
Height: 12", 30.5 cm
Colour: White
Issued: 1981-2002
Varieties: HN 2721
Series: Images

U.S.:	**$200.00**
Can.:	**$275.00**
U.K.:	**£120.00**

HN 2721
Family
Designer: E. J. Griffiths
Height: 12", 30.5 cm
Colour: Black
Issued: 1981-1992
Varieties: HN 2720
Series: Images

U.S.:	**$250.00**
Can.:	**$325.00**
U.K.:	**£150.00**

HN 2722
Veneta
Designer: W. K. Harper
Height: 8", 20.3 cm
Colour: Green and white
Issued: 1974-1981

U.S.:	**$225.00**
Can.:	**$300.00**
U.K.:	**£135.00**

HN 2723
Grand Manner
Designer: W. K. Harper
Height: 7 ¾", 19.7 cm
Colour: Lavender-yellow
Issued: 1975-1981

U.S.:	**$250.00**
Can.:	**$300.00**
U.K.:	**£150.00**

HN 2724
Clarinda
Designer: W. K. Harper
Height: 8 ½", 21.6 cm
Colour: Blue and white
Issued: 1975-1981

U.S.:	**$250.00**
Can.:	**$300.00**
U.K.:	**£150.00**

HN 2725
Santa Claus
Style One
Designer: W. K. Harper
Height: 9 ¾", 24.7 cm
Colour: Red and white
Issued: 1982-1993

U.S.:	$450.00
Can.:	$600.00
U.K.:	£275.00

HN 2726
Centurian
Designer: W. K. Harper
Height: 9 ¼", 23.5 cm
Colour: Grey and purple
Issued: 1982-1984

U.S.:	$300.00
Can.:	$400.00
U.K.:	£175.00

HN 2727
Little Miss Muffet
Designer: W. K. Harper
Height: 6 ¼", 15.9 cm
Colour: White and pink
Issued: 1984-1987
Series: Nursery Rhymes
(Series Two)

U.S.:	$200.00
Can.:	$250.00
U.K.:	£120.00

HN 2728
Rest Awhile
Designer: W. K. Harper
Height: 8", 20.3 cm
Colour: Blue, white and purple
Issued: 1981-1984

U.S.:	$275.00
Can.:	$375.00
U.K.:	£175.00

HN 2729
Song of the Sea
Designer: W. K. Harper
Height: 7 ¼", 18.4 cm
Colour: Blue and grey
Issued: 1982 Canada,
1983 Worldwide -1991
Series: Sea Characters

U.S.:	$450.00
Can.:	$600.00
U.K.:	£275.00

HN 2730 not issued.

HN 2731
Thanks Doc
Designer: W. K. Harper
Height: 8 ¾", 22.2 cm
Colour: White and brown
Issued: 1975-1990

U.S.:	$350.00
Can.:	$450.00
U.K.:	£200.00

HN 2732
Thank You
Style One
Designer: W. K. Harper
Height: 8 ¼", 21.0 cm
Colour: White, brown and blue
Issued: 1982 Canada,
1983 Worldwide-1986

U.S.:	$300.00
Can.:	$400.00
U.K.:	£185.00

HN 2733
Officer of the Line
Designer: W. K. Harper
Height: 9", 22.9 cm
Colour: Red and yellow
Issued: 1982 Canada,
1983 Worldwide-1986
Series: Sea Characters

U.S.:	$475.00
Can.:	$600.00
U.K.:	£275.00

HN 2734
Sweet Seventeen
Designer: D. V. Tootle
Height: 7 ½", 19.1 cm
Colour: White with gold trim
Issued: 1975-1993

U.S.:	**$275.00**
Can.:	**$400.00**
U.K.:	**£165.00**

HN 2735
Young Love
Designer: D. V. Tootle
Height: 10", 25.4 cm
Colour: Cream, green,
           blue and brown
Issued: 1975-1990

U.S.:	**$650.00**
Can.:	**$900.00**
U.K.:	**£400.00**

HN 2736
Tracy
Designer: D. V. Tootle
Height: 7 ½", 19.1 cm
Colour: White
Issued: 1983-1994
Varieties: HN 3291
Series: Vanity Fair Ladies

U.S.:	**$225.00**
Can.:	**$300.00**
U.K.:	**£125.00**

HN 2737
Harlequin
Style Two
Designer: D. V. Tootle
Height: 12 ½", 31.7 cm
Colour: Multicoloured
Issued: 1982 to the present
Varieties: HN 3287, 4058
Series: Prestige

U.S.:	**N/I**
Can.:	**$2,900.00**
U.K.:	**£1,900.00**

HN 2738
Columbine
Style Three
Designer: D. V. Tootle
Height: 12 ½", 31.7 cm
Colour: Flowered pink
           and blue dress
Issued: 1982 to the present
Varieties: HN 3288, 4059
Series: Prestige

U.S.:	**N/I**
Can.:	**$2,900.00**
U.K.:	**£1,900.00**

HN 2739
Ann
Style One
Designer: D. V. Tootle
Height: 7 ¾", 19.7 cm
Colour: White
Issued: 1983-1985
Series: Vanity Fair Ladies

U.S.:	**$250.00**
Can.:	**$375.00**
U.K.:	**£150.00**

HN 2740
Becky
Style One
Designer: D. V. Tootle
Height: 8", 20.3 cm
Colour: Green, yellow
           and cream
Issued: 1987-1992

U.S.:	**$275.00**
Can.:	**$375.00**
U.K.:	**£165.00**

HN 2741
Sally
Style One
Designer: D. V. Tootle
Height: 5 ½", 14.0 cm
Colour: Red and lavender
Issued: 1987-1991

U.S.:	**$225.00**
Can.:	**$300.00**
U.K.:	**£135.00**

HN 2742
Sheila
Designer: D. V. Tootle
Height: 8 ¼", 21.0 cm
Colour: Pale blue flowered dress
Issued: 1983 Canada, 1984 Worldwide -1991

U.S.: **$225.00**
Can.: **$300.00**
U.K.: **£135.00**

HN 2743
Meg
Designer: D. V. Tootle
Height: 8", 20.3 cm
Colour: Lavender and yellow
Issued: 1987-1991

U.S.: **$250.00**
Can.: **$325.00**
U.K.: **£150.00**

HN 2744
Modesty
Designer: D. V. Tootle
Height: 8 ½", 21.6 cm
Colour: White
Issued: 1987-1991

U.S.: **$250.00**
Can.: **$325.00**
U.K.: **£150.00**

HN 2745
Florence
Designer: D. V. Tootle
Height: 8", 20.3 cm
Colour: Purple
Issued: 1987-1992

U.S.: **$325.00**
Can.: **$475.00**
U.K.: **£200.00**

HN 2746
May
Style One
Designer: D. V. Tootle
Height: 8", 20.3 cm
Colour: Blue, red and green
Issued: 1987-1992
Varieties: HN 3251

U.S.: **$275.00**
Can.: **$375.00**
U.K.: **£175.00**

HN 2747
First Love
Designer: D. V. Tootle
Height: 13", 33.0 cm
Colour: White
Issued: 1987-1997
Series: Images

U.S.: **$175.00**
Can.: **$250.00**
U.K.: **£100.00**

HN 2748
Wedding Day
Designer: D. V. Tootle
Height: 12 ½", 31.7 cm
Colour: White
Issued: 1987-2003
Series: Images

U.S.: **$250.00**
Can.: **$600.00**
U.K.: **£185.00**

HN 2749
Lizzie
Designer: D. V. Tootle
Height: 8 ¼", 21.0 cm
Colour: Green, white and red
Issued: 1988-1991

U.S.: **$225.00**
Can.: **$300.00**
U.K.: **£135.00**

HN 2750
Wedding Vows
Style One
Designer: D. V. Tootle
Height: 8", 20.3 cm
Colour: White
Issued: 1988-1992
  U.S.:   **$250.00**
  Can.:   **$375.00**
  U.K.:   **£150.00**

HN 2751
Encore
Style One
Designer: D. V. Tootle
Height: 10", 25.4 cm
Colour: Lavender, white
           and blue
Issued: 1988-1989
Series: Reflections
  U.S.:   **$250.00**
  Can.:   **$375.00**
  U.K.:   **£150.00**

HN 2752
Major, 3ʳᵈ New Jersey Regiment,
1776
Designer: E. J. Griffiths
Height: 10", 25.4 cm
Colour: Blue and brown
Issued: 1975 in a limited
           edition of 350
Series: Soldiers of the
           Revolution
  U.S.:   **$2,000.00**
  Can.:   **$3,000.00**
  U.K.:   **£1,250.00**

HN 2753
Serenade
Designer: E. J. Griffiths
Height: 9", 22.9 cm
Colour: Cream
Issued: 1983-1985
Series: Enchantment
  U.S.:   **$200.00**
  Can.:   **$275.00**
  U.K.:   **£125.00**

HN 2754
Private, 3ʳᵈ North Carolina
Regiment, 1778
Designer: E. J. Griffiths
Height: 11", 27.9 cm
Colour: Tan
Issued: 1976 in a limited
           edition of 350
Series: Soldiers of the
           Revolution
  U.S.:   **$1,400.00**
  Can.:   **$1,800.00**
  U.K.:   **£ 850.00**

HN 2755
Captain, 2ⁿᵈ New York
Regiment, 1775
Designer: E. J. Griffiths
Height: 10", 25.4 cm
Colour: Brown
Issued: 1976 in a limited
           edition of 350
Series: Soldiers of the
           Revolution
  U.S.:   **$1,400.00**
  Can.:   **$1,800.00**
  U.K.:   **£ 850.00**

HN 2756
Musicale
Designer: E. J. Griffiths
Height: 9", 22.9 cm
Colour: Cream
Issued: 1983-1985
Series: Enchantment
  U.S.:   **$200.00**
  Can.:   **$275.00**
  U.K.:   **£125.00**

HN 2757
Lyric
Designer: E. J. Griffiths
Height: 6 ¼", 15.9 cm
Colour: Cream
Issued: 1983-1985
Series: Enchantment
  U.S.:   **$175.00**
  Can.:   **$250.00**
  U.K.:   **£125.00**

HN 2758
Linda
Style Two
Designer: E. J. Griffiths
Height: 7 ¾", 19.7 cm
Colour: White with pink trim
Issued: 1984-1988
Series: Vanity Fair Ladies

U.S.:	**$225.00**
Can.:	**$325.00**
U.K.:	**£150.00**

HN 2759
Private, Rhode Island Regiment, 1781
Designer: E. J. Griffiths
Height: 11 ¾", 29.8 cm
Colour: Grey
Issued: 1977 in a limited edition of 350
Series: Soldiers of the Revolution

U.S.:	**$1,500.00**
Con.:	**$2,250.00**
U.K.:	**£1,000.00**

HN 2760
Private, Massachusetts Regiment, 1778
Designer: E. J. Griffiths
Height: 12 ½", 31.7 cm
Colour: Blue and tan
Issued: 1977 in a limited edition of 350
Series: Soldiers of the Revolution

U.S.:	**$1,400.00**
Can.:	**$1,800.00**
U.K.:	**£ 850.00**

HN 2761
Private, Delaware Regiment, 1776
Designer: E. J. Griffiths
Height: 12", 30.5 cm
Colour: Blue and tan
Issued: 1977 in a limited edition of 350
Series: Soldiers of the Revolution

U.S.:	**$1,400.00**
Can.:	**$1,800.00**
U.K.:	**£ 850.00**

HN 2762
Lovers
Designer: D. V. Tootle
Height: 12", 30.5 cm
Colour: White
Issued: 1981-1997
Varieties: HN 2763
Series: Images

U.S.:	**$200.00**
Can.:	**$250.00**
U.K.:	**£120.00**

Also known in flambé.

HN 2763
Lovers
Designer: D. V. Tootle
Height: 12", 30.5 cm
Colour: Black
Issued: 1981-1992
Varieties: HN 2762
Series: Images

U.S.:	**$300.00**
Can.:	**$450.00**
U.K.:	**£200.00**

Also known in flambé.

HN 2764
The Lifeboat Man
Designer: W. K. Harper
Height: 9 ¼", 23.5 cm
Colour: Yellow
Issued: 1987-1991
Series: Sea Characters

U.S.:	**$400.00**
Can.:	**$525.00**
U.K.:	**£240.00**

HN 2765
Punch and Judy Man
Designer: W. K. Harper
Height: 9", 22.9 cm
Colour: Green and yellow
Issued: 1981-1990

U.S.:	**$450.00**
Can.:	**$600.00**
U.K.:	**£270.00**

HN 2766
Autumn Glory
Designer: W. K. Harper
Height: 11 ¾", 29.9 cm
Colour: Blue-grey and tan
Issued: 1988 in a limited
edition of 1,000
Series: Reflections
Comm.by: Home Shopping
Network, Florida

U.S.:	**$325.00**
Can.:	**$450.00**
U.K.:	**£200.00**

HN 2767
Pearly Boy
Style Three
Designer: W. K. Harper
Height: 7 ½", 19.1 cm
Colour: Black, white and blue
Issued: 1988
Varieties: HN 2767A
Comm.by: Guild of Specialist
China and Glass
Retailers

U.S.:	**$250.00**
Can.:	**$325.00**
U.K.:	**£150.00**

HN 2767A
Pearly Boy
Style Three
Designer: W. K. Harper
Height: 7 ½", 19.1 cm
Colour: Black, white and blue
Issued: 1989-1992
Varieties: HN 2767

U.S.:	**$250.00**
Can.:	**$325.00**
U.K.:	**£150.00**

HN 2768
Pretty Polly
Designer: W. K. Harper
Height: 6", 15.2 cm
Colour: Pink and white
Issued: 1984-1986

U.S.:	**$250.00**
Can.:	**$325.00**
U.K.:	**£150.00**

HN 2769
Pearly Girl
Style Three
Designer: W. K. Harper
Height: 7 ½", 19.1 cm
Colour: Black, white and blue
Issued: 1988
Varieties: HN 2769A
Comm.by: Guild of Specialist
China and Glass
Retailers

U.S.:	**$250.00**
Can.:	**$325.00**
U.K.:	**£150.00**

HN 2769A
Pearly Girl
Style Three
Designer: W. K. Harper
Height: 7 ½", 19.1 cm
Colour: Black, white and blue
Issued: 1989-1992
Varieties: HN 2769

U.S.:	**$250.00**
Can.:	**$325.00**
U.K.:	**£150.00**

HN 2770
New Companion
Designer: W. K. Harper
Height: 7 ¾", 19.7 cm
Colour: Purple, white
and black
Issued: 1982-1985

U.S.:	**$300.00**
Can.:	**$400.00**
U.K.:	**£175.00**

HN 2771
Charlie Chaplin
Designer: W. K. Harper
Height: 9", 22.9 cm
Colour: Grey
Issued: 1989 in a limited
edition of 5,000
Series: Entertainers
Comm.by: Lawleys By Post

U.S.:	**$375.00**
Can.:	**$525.00**
U.K.:	**£225.00**

HN 2772
Ritz Bell Boy
Designer: W. K. Harper
Height: 8", 20.3 cm
Colour: Black
Issued: 1989-1993

U.S.:	**$275.00**
Con.:	**$375.00**
U.K.:	**£175.00**

HN 2773
Robin Hood
Style One
Designer: W. K. Harper
Height: 7 ¾", 19.7 cm
Colour: Green
Issued: 1985-1990

U.S.:	**$300.00**
Can.:	**$400.00**
U.K.:	**£175.00**

HN 2774
Stan Laurel
Designer: W. K. Harper
Height: 9 ¼", 23.5 cm
Colour: Grey-black
Issued: 1990 in a limited edition of 9,500
Series: Entertainers
Comm.by: Lawleys By Post

U.S.:	**$475.00**
Can.:	**$675.00**
U.K.:	**£300.00**

HN 2775
Oliver Hardy
Designer: W. K. Harper
Height: 10", 25.4 cm
Colour: Black and grey
Issued: 1990 in a limited edition of 9,500
Series: Entertainers
Comm.by: Lawleys By Post

U.S.:	**$475.00**
Can.:	**$675.00**
U.K.:	**£300.00**

HN 2776
Carpet Seller
(Standing)
Style Two
Designer: W. K. Harper
Height: 9", 22.9 cm
Colour: Flambé
Issued: 1990-1995
Series: Flambé

U.S.:	**$600.00**
Can.:	**$775.00**
U.K.:	**£350.00**

HN 2777
Groucho Marx
Designer: W. K. Harper
Height: 9 ½", 24.1 cm
Colour: Black and grey
Issued: 1991 in a limited edition of 9,500
Series: Entertainers
Comm.by: Lawleys By Post

U.S.:	**$525.00**
Can.:	**$675.00**
U.K.:	**£300.00**

HN 2778
The Bobby
Designer: W. K. Harper
Height: 9", 22.9 cm
Colour: Black
Issued: 1992-1995

U.S.:	**$300.00**
Can.:	**$400.00**
U.K.:	**£175.00**

HN 2779
Private, 1st Georgia Regiment, 1777
Designer: E. J. Griffiths
Height: 11", 27.9 cm
Colour: Light brown
Issued: 1975 in a limited edition of 350
Series: Soldiers of the Revolution

U.S.:	**$1,500.00**
Can.:	**$2,000.00**
U.K.:	**£ 900.00**

HN 2780
Corporal, 1st New Hampshire Regiment, 1778
Designer: E. J. Griffiths
Height: 13", 33.0 cm
Colour: Green
Issued: 1975 in a limited edition of 350
Series: Soldiers of the Revolution

U.S.:	$1,500.00
Can.:	$2,000.00
U.K.:	£ 900.00

HN 2781
The Lifeguard
Designer: W. K. Harper
Height: 9 ½", 24.1 cm
Colour: Red, black and white
Issued: 1992-1995

U.S.:	$325.00
Can.:	$425.00
U.K.:	£175.00

HN 2782
The Blacksmith
Style One
Designer: W. K. Harper
Height: 9", 22.9 cm
Colour: Brown, white and grey
Issued: 1987-1991

U.S.:	$300.00
Can.:	$400.00
U.K.:	£175.00

HN 2783
Good Friends
Designer: W. K. Harper
Height: 9", 22.9 cm
Colour: Blue and brown
Issued: 1985-1990

U.S.:	$300.00
Can.:	$400.00
U.K.:	£175.00

HN 2784
The Guardsman
Designer: W. K. Harper
Height: 9 ¾", 24.8 cm
Colour: Red, black and white
Issued: 1992-1995

U.S.:	$325.00
Can.:	$425.00
U.K.:	£175.00

HN 2785 - 2787 not issued.

HN 2788
Marjorie
Designer: M. Davies
Height: 5 ¼", 13.3 cm
Colour: Pale blue
Issued: 1980-1984

U.S.:	$350.00
Can.:	$475.00
U.K.:	£225.00

HN 2789
Kate
Style One
Designer: M. Davies
Height: 7 ½", 19.1 cm
Colour: Flowered white dress
Issued: 1978-1987

U.S.:	$250.00
Can.:	$325.00
U.K.:	£150.00

HN 2790
June
Style Three
Designer: M. Davies
Height: 7 ¾", 19.7 cm
Colour: White and pink dress with roses
Issued: 1987-1987
Varieties: Also called 'Gillian' (Style Three) HN 3742
Series: Figure of the Month

U.S.:	$200.00
Can.:	$275.00
U.K.:	£125.00

HN 2791
Elaine
Style One
Designer: M. Davies
Height: 7 ½", 19.1 cm
Colour: Blue
Issued: 1980-2000
Varieties: HN 3307, 3741, 4130

U.S.:	**$325.00**
Can.:	**$475.00**
U.K.:	**£195.00**

HN 2792
Christine
Style Two
Designer: M. Davies
Height: 7 ½", 19.1 cm
Colour: Flowered blue and white dress
Issued: 1978-1994
Varieties: HN 3172

U.S.:	**$325.00**
Can.:	**$475.00**
U.K.:	**£195.00**

HN 2793
Clare
Designer: M. Davies
Height: 7 ½", 19.1 cm
Colour: Flowered lavender dress
Issued: 1980-1984

U.S.:	**$275.00**
Can.:	**$375.00**
U.K.:	**£175.00**

HN 2794
July
Style One
Designer: M. Davies
Height: 7 ¾", 19.7 cm
Colour: White dress; Forget-me-not flowers
Issued: 1987-1987
Varieties: Also called 'Gillian' (Style Three) HN 3742
Series: Figure of the Month

U.S.:	**$200.00**
Can.:	**$275.00**
U.K.:	**£125.00**

IIN 2795
French Horn
Designer: M. Davies
Height: 6", 15.2 cm
Colour: Purple and turquoise
Issued: 1976 in a limited edition of 750
Series: Lady Musicians

U.S.:	**$1,100.00**
Can.:	**$1,450.00**
U.K.:	**£ 650.00**

HN 2796
Hurdy Gurdy
Designer: M. Davies
Height: 6", 15.2 cm
Colour: Turquoise and white
Issued: 1975 in a limited edition of 750
Series: Lady Musicians

U.S.:	**$1,100.00**
Can.:	**$1,450.00**
U.K.:	**£ 650.00**

HN 2797
Viola d'Amore
Designer: M. Davies
Height: 6", 15.2 cm
Colour: Pale blue and yellow
Issued: 1976 in a limited edition of 750
Series: Lady Musicians

U.S.:	**$1,100.00**
Can.:	**$1,450.00**
U.K.:	**£ 650.00**

HN 2798
Dulcimer
Designer: M. Davies
Height: 6 ½", 16.5 cm
Colour: Lavender and cream
Issued: 1975 in a limited edition of 750
Series: Lady Musicians

U.S.:	**$1,100.00**
Can.:	**$1,450.00**
U.K.:	**£ 650.00**

HN 2799
Ruth
Style One
Designer: M. Davies
Height: 6", 15.2 cm
Colour: Green
Issued: 1976-1981
Series: Kate Greenaway

U.S.:	**$325.00**
Can.:	**$425.00**
U.K.:	**£195.00**

HN 2800
Carrie
Designer: M. Davies
Height: 6", 15.2 cm
Colour: Turquoise
Issued: 1976-1981
Series: Kate Greenaway

U.S.:	**$300.00**
Can.:	**$400.00**
U.K.:	**£180.00**

HN 2801
Lori
Designer: M. Davies
Height: 5 ¾", 14.6 cm
Colour: Yellow-cream
Issued: 1976-1987
Series: Kate Greenaway

U.S.:	**$300.00**
Can.:	**$400.00**
U.K.:	**£180.00**

HN 2802
Anna
Style One
Designer: M. Davies
Height: 5 ¾", 14.6 cm
Colour: Purple and white
Issued: 1976-1982
Series: Kate Greenaway

U.S.:	**$300.00**
Can.:	**$400.00**
U.K.:	**£180.00**

HN 2803
First Dance
Designer: M. Davies
Height: 7 ¼", 18.4 cm
Colour: Pale blue
Issued: 1977-1992
Varieties: Also called 'Samantha'
           (Style Two) HN 3304

U.S.:	**$250.00**
Can.:	**$325.00**
U.K.:	**£150.00**

HN 2804
Nicola
Designer: M. Davies
Height: 7", 17.8 cm
Colour: Red and lilac
Issued: 1987-1987
Varieties: HN 2839; also called
           'Tender Moment'
           (Style One) HN 3303
Series: M. Doulton Events

U.S.:	**$300.00**
Can.:	**$450.00**
U.K.:	**£200.00**

HN 2805
Rebecca
Style One
Designer: M. Davies
Height: 7 ¼", 18.4 cm
Colour: Pale blue and
           lavender
Issued: 1980-1996

U.S.:	**$500.00**
Can.:	**$650.00**
U.K.:	**£250.00**

HN 2806
Jane
Style Two
Designer: M. Davies
Height: 8", 20.3 cm
Colour: Yellow
Issued: 1982-1986

U.S.:	**$275.00**
Can.:	**$375.00**
U.K.:	**£175.00**

HN 2807
Stephanie
Style One
Designer: M. Davies
Height: 7 ¼", 18.4 cm
Colour: Gold
Issued: 1977-1982
Varieties: HN 2811

U.S.:	**$250.00**
Can.:	**$325.00**
U.K.:	**£150.00**

HN 2808
Balinese Dancer
Designer: M. Davies
Height: 8 ¾", 22.2 cm
Colour: Green and yellow
Issued: 1982 in a limited
           edition of 750
Series: Dancers of the World

U.S.:	**$ 900.00**
Can.:	**$1,200.00**
U.K.:	**£ 550.00**

HN 2809
North American Indian Dancer
Designer: M. Davies
Height: 8 ½", 21.6 cm
Colour: Yellow
Issued: 1982 in a limited
           edition of 750
Series: Dancers of the World

U.S.:	**$ 900.00**
Can.:	**$1,200.00**
U.K.:	**£ 550.00**

HN 2810
Solitude
Designer: M. Davies
Height: 5 ½", 14.0 cm
Colour: Cream, blue
           and orange
Issued: 1977-1983

U.S.:	**$450.00**
Can.:	**$625.00**
U.K.:	**£270.00**

HN 2811
Stephanie
Style One
Designer: M. Davies
Height: 7 ¼", 18.4 cm
Colour: Red and white
Issued: 1983-1994
Varieties: HN 2807

U.S.:	**$300.00**
Can.:	**$400.00**
U.K.:	**£175.00**

HN 2812 - 2813 not issued.

HN 2814
Eventide
Designer: W. K. Harper
Height: 7 ¾", 19.7 cm
Colour: Blue, white, red,
           yellow and green
Issued: 1977-1991

U.S.:	**$300.00**
Can.:	**$400.00**
U.K.:	**£175.00**

HN 2815
**Sergeant, 6th Maryland
Regiment, 1777**
Designer: E. J. Griffiths
Height: 13 ¾", 34.9 cm
Colour: Light grey
Issued: 1976 in a limited
           edition of 350
Series: Soldiers of the
           Revolution

U.S.:	**$1,500.00**
Can.:	**$1,950.00**
U.K.:	**£ 900.00**

HN 2816
Votes for Women
Designer: W. K. Harper
Height: 9 ¾", 24.7 cm
Colour: Gold and grey
Issued: 1978-1981

U.S.:	**$325.00**
Can.:	**$450.00**
U.K.:	**£200.00**

HN 2817 not issued.

HN 2818
Balloon Girl
Designer: W. K. Harper
Height: 6 ½", 16.5 cm
Colour: Green, white,
           grey and red
Issued: 1982-1997

U.S.:	**$375.00**
Can.:	**$500.00**
U.K.:	**£225.00**

HN 2819 - 2823 not issued.

HN 2824
Harmony
Style One
Designer: R. Jefferson
Height: 8", 20.3 cm
Colour: Grey
Issued: 1978-1984

U.S.:	**$325.00**
Can.:	**$475.00**
U.K.:	**£195.00**

HN 2825
Lady and the Unicorn
Designer: R. Jefferson
Height: 8 ¾", 22.2 cm
Colour: Blue, white and red
Issued: 1982 in a limited
           edition of 300
Series: Myths and Maidens

U.S.:	**$2,250.00**
Can.:	**$3,000.00**
U.K.:	**£1,350.00**

HN 2826
Leda and the Swan
Designer: R. Jefferson
Height: 9 ¾", 24.7 cm
Colour: Yellow, green,
           red and blue
Issued: 1983 in a limited
           edition of 300
Series: Myths and Maidens

U.S.:	**$2,250.00**
Can.:	**$3,000.00**
U.K.:	**£1,350.00**

HN 2827
Juno and the Peacock
Designer: R. Jefferson
Height: 11", 27.9 cm
Colour: Turquoise, lavender
           and gold
Issued: 1984 in a limited
           edition of 300
Series: Myths and Maidens

U.S.:	**$2,250.00**
Can.:	**$3,000.00**
U.K.:	**£1,350.00**

HN 2828
Europa and the Bull
Style Two
Designer: R. Jefferson
Height: 10 ½", 26.5 cm
Colour: Yellow, orange, white
           and lavender
Issued: 1985 in a limited
           edition of 300
Series: Myths and Maidens

U.S.:	**$2,250.00**
Can.:	**$3,000.00**
U.K.:	**£1,350.00**

HN 2829
Diana the Huntress
Designer: R. Jefferson
Height: 11 ¼", 28.6 cm
Colour: Green and gold
Issued: 1986 in a limited
           edition of 300
Series: Myths and Maidens

U.S.:	**$2,250.00**
Can.:	**$3,000.00**
U.K.:	**£1,350.00**

HN 2830
Indian Temple Dancer
Designer: M. Davies
Height: 9 ¼", 23.5 cm
Colour: Gold
Issued: 1977 in a limited
           edition of 750
Series: Dancers of the World

U.S.:	**$1,200.00**
Can.:	**$1,550.00**
U.K.:	**£ 725.00**

HN 2831
Spanish Flamenco Dancer
Designer: M. Davies
Height: 9 ½", 24.1 cm
Colour: Red and white
Issued: 1977 in a limited
edition of 750
Series: Dancers of the World

U.S.:	**$1,600.00**
Can.:	**$2,250.00**
U.K.:	**£1,000.00**

HN 2832
Fair Lady
Style One
Designer: M. Davies
Height: 7 ¼", 18.4 cm
Colour: Red and white
Issued: 1977-1996
Varieties: HN 2193, 2835; also
called 'Kay' HN 3340

U.S.:	**$250.00**
Can.:	**$325.00**
U.K.:	**£125.00**

HN 2833
Sophie
Style One
Designer: M. Davies
Height: 6", 15.2 cm
Colour: Red and grey
Issued: 1977-1987
Series: Kate Greenaway

U.S.:	**$275.00**
Can.:	**$350.00**
U.K.:	**£165.00**

HN 2834
Emma
Style One
Designer: M. Davies
Height: 5 ¾", 14.6 cm
Colour: Pink and white
Issued: 1977-1981
Series: Kate Greenaway

U.S.:	**$350.00**
Can.:	**$450.00**
U.K.:	**£215.00**

HN 2835
Fair Lady
Style One
Designer: M. Davies
Height: 7 ¼", 18.4 cm
Colour: Peach
Issued: 1977-1996
Varieties: HN 2193, 2832; also
called 'Kay' HN 3340

U.S.:	**$250.00**
Can.:	**$325.00**
U.K.:	**£125.00**

HN 2836
Polish Dancer
Designer: M. Davies
Height: 9 ½", 24.1 cm
Colour: Multicoloured
Issued: 1980 in a limited
edition of 750
Series: Dancers of the World

U.S.:	**$ 950.00**
Can.:	**$1,250.00**
U.K.:	**£ 575.00**

HN 2837
Awakening
Style Two
Designer: M. Davies
Height: 8 ½", 21.6 cm
Colour: Black
Issued: 1981-1997
Varieties: HN 2875
Series: Images

U.S.:	**$150.00**
Can.:	**$200.00**
U.K.:	**£ 90.00**

Also known in Flambé

HN 2838
Sympathy
Designer: M. Davies
Height: 11 ¾", 29.8 cm
Colour: Black
Issued: 1981-1986
Varieties: HN 2876
Series: Images

U.S.:	**$200.00**
Can.:	**$250.00**
U.K.:	**£125.00**

HN 2839
Nicola
Designer: M. Davies
Height: 7", 17.8 cm
Colour: Flowered lavender
          dress
Issued: 1978-1995
Varieties: HN 2804; also called
          'Tender Moment'
          HN 3303

U.S.:	**$325.00**
Can.:	**$450.00**
U.K.:	**£200.00**

HN 2840
Chinese Dancer
Designer: M. Davies
Height: 9", 22.9 cm
Colour: Red, green, purple
          and lavender
Issued: 1980 in a limited
          edition of 750
Series: Dancers of the World

U.S.:	**$ 900.00**
Can.:	**$1,200.00**
U.K.:	**£ 550.00**

HN 2841
Mother and Daughter
Style One
Designer: E. J. Griffiths
Height: 8 ½", 21.6 cm
Colour: White
Issued: 1981-1997
Varieties: HN 2843; also known
          in flambé
Series: Images

U.S.:	**$200.00**
Can.:	**$250.00**
U.K.:	**£120.00**

HN 2842
Innocence
Style One
Designer: E. J. Griffiths
Height: 7 ½", 19.1 cm
Colour: Red
Issued: 1979-1983

U.S.:	**$250.00**
Can.:	**$325.00**
U.K.:	**£150.00**

HN 2843
Mother and Daughter
Style One
Designer: E. J. Griffiths
Height: 8 ½", 21.6 cm
Colour: Black
Issued: 1981-1992
Varieties: HN 2841
Series: Images

U.S.:	**$200.00**
Can.:	**$250.00**
U.K.:	**£120.00**

Also known in flambé

HN 2844
Sergeant, Virginia 1st Regiment
Continental Light Dragoons,
1777
Designer: E. J. Griffiths
Height: 14 ¼", 36.1 cm
Colour: Brown and green
Issued: 1978 in a limited
          edition of 350
Series: Soldiers of the
          Revolution

U.S.:	**$5,000.00**
Can.:	**$7,000.00**
U.K.:	**£3,000.00**

HN 2845
Private, Connecticut Regiment,
1777
Designer: E. J. Griffiths
Height: 11 ¼", 28.5 cm
Colour: Brown and cream
Issued: 1978 in a limited
          edition of 350
Series: Soldiers of the
          Revolution

U.S.:	**$1,500.00**
Can.:	**$2,000.00**
U.K.:	**£ 900.00**

HN 2846
Private, Pennsylvania
Rifle Battalion, 1776
Designer: E. J. Griffiths
Height: 8", 20.3 cm
Colour: Grey
Issued: 1978 in a limited
          edition of 350
Series: Soldiers of the
          Revolution

U.S.:	**$1,500.00**
Can.:	**$2,000.00**
U.K.:	**£ 900.00**

HN 2847 - 2850 not issued.

HN 2851
Christmas Parcels
Style One
Designer: W. K. Harper
Height: 8 ¾", 22.2 cm
Colour: Black
Issued: 1978-1982

U.S.:	**$325.00**
Can.:	**$425.00**
U.K.:	**£195.00**

HN 2852 - 2854 not issued.

HN 2855
Embroidering
Designer: W. K. Harper
Height: 7 ¼", 18.4 cm
Colour: Grey
Issued: 1980-1990

U.S.:	**$350.00**
Can.:	**$450.00**
U.K.:	**£210.00**

HN 2856
St. George
Style Three
Designer: W. K. Harper
Height: 16", 40.6 cm
Colour: Cream and grey
Issued: 1978-1994

U.S.:	**$ 7,000.00**
Can.:	**$10,000.00**
U.K.:	**£ 4,500.00**

HN 2857
Covent Garden
Style Two
Designer: W. K. Harper
Height: 10", 25.4 cm
Colour: Pale blue and white
Issued: 1988-1990
Series: Reflections

U.S.:	**$250.00**
Can.:	**$325.00**
U.K.:	**£150.00**

IIN 2858
The Doctor
Style One
Designer: W. K. Harper
Height: 7 ½", 19.1 cm
Colour: Black and grey
Issued: 1979-1992

U.S.:	**$300.00**
Can.:	**$400.00**
U.K.:	**£175.00**

HN 2859
The Statesman
Designer: W. K. Harper
Height: 9", 22.9 cm
Colour: Black and grey
Issued: 1988-1990
Varieties: Also called 'Sir John
A. MacDonald'
HN 2860

U.S.:	**$225.00**
Can.:	**$325.00**
U.K.:	**£150.00**

HN 2860
Sir John A. MacDonald
Designer: W. K. Harper
Height: 9", 22.9 cm
Colour: Black and grey
Issued: 1987-1987
Varieties: Also called 'The
Statesman' HN 2859

U.S.:	**$275.00**
Can.:	**$375.00**
U.K.:	**£165.00**

NOTE ON CONDITION

Prices on the secondary market for Royal Doulton Figures, particularly the early HN numbers, have risen considerably over the years. As values rise, the condition and quality of these figurines takes on an increasingly important role.

The prices listed in *The Charlton Standard Catalogue of Royal Doulton Figurines* are for figures in mint condition.

Naturally, repaired or restored figures, no matter how professionally done, will sell at a discount. However the early figures, due to their rarity, may experience smaller discounts.

On Condition: For figures to command catalogue prices they must be in mint condition. This simply means that a figure will have no chips, scratches, hairline cracks, crazing, blemishes, or repairs. Any of which will remove the figure from the mint category.

On Quality: Some figures are better moulded, assembled or painted than others. High quality figures may command a premium over listed catalogue prices.

HN 2861
George Washington
at Prayer
Designer: L. Ispanky
Height: 12 ½", 31.7 cm
Colour: Blue and tan
Issued: 1977 in a limited
edition of 750

U.S.:	**$2,750.00**
Can.:	**$3,750.00**
U.K.:	**£1,650.00**

HN 2862
First Waltz
Designer: M. Davies
Height: 7 ¼", 18.4 cm
Colour: Red
Issued: 1979-1983

U.S.:	**$350.00**
Can.:	**$475.00**
U.K.:	**£210.00**

HN 2863
Lucy
Style One
Designer: M. Davies
Height: 6", 15.2 cm
Colour: Blue and white
Issued: 1980-1984
Series: Kate Greenaway

U.S.:	**$275.00**
Can.:	**$350.00**
U.K.:	**£165.00**

HN 2864
Tom
Designer: M. Davies
Height: 5 ¾", 14.6 cm
Colour: Blue and yellow
Issued: 1978-1981
Series: Kate Greenaway

U.S.:	**$350.00**
Can.:	**$450.00**
U.K.:	**£210.00**

HN 2865
Tess
Designer: M. Davies
Height: 5 ¾", 14.6 cm
Colour: Green
Issued: 1978-1983
Series: Kate Greenaway

U.S.:	**$275.00**
Can.:	**$350.00**
U.K.:	**£165.00**

HN 2866
Mexican Dancer
Designer: M. Davies
Height: 8 ¼", 21.0 cm
Colour: Gold and white
Issued: 1979 in a limited
edition of 750
Series: Dancers of the World

U.S.:	**$ 900.00**
Can.:	**$1,175.00**
U.K.:	**£ 525.00**

HN 2867
Kurdish Dancer
Designer: M. Davies
Height: 8 ¼", 21.0 cm
Colour: Blue
Issued: 1979 in a limited
edition of 750
Series: Dancers of the World

U.S.:	**$ 900.00**
Can.:	**$1,175.00**
U.K.:	**£ 525.00**

HN 2868
Cleopatra
Style One
Designer: M. Davies
Height: 7 ¼", 18.4 cm
Colour: White, blue and black
Issued: 1979 in a limited
edition of 750
Series: Les Femmes Fatales

U.S.:	**$1,850.00**
Can.:	**$2,500.00**
U.K.:	**£1,100.00**

HN 2869
Louise
Style One
Designer: M. Davies
Height: 6", 15.2 cm
Colour: Brown
Issued: 1979-1986
Series: Kate Greenaway

U.S.:	**$300.00**
Can.:	**$400.00**
U.K.:	**£175.00**

HN 2870
Beth
Style One
Designer: M. Davies
Height: 5 ¾", 14.6 cm
Colour: Pink and white
Issued: 1979-1983
Series: Kate Greenaway

U.S.:	**$425.00**
Can.:	**$550.00**
U.K.:	**£250.00**

HN 2871
Beat You To It
Designer: M. Davies
Height: 6 ½", 16.5 cm
Colour: Pink, gold and blue
Issued: 1980-1987

U.S.:	**$375.00**
Can.:	**$500.00**
U.K.:	**£225.00**

HN 2872
Young Master
Designer: M. Davies
Height: 7", 17.8 cm
Colour: Purple, grey and brown
Issued: 1980-1989

U.S.:	**$325.00**
Can.:	**$450.00**
U.K.:	**£200.00**

HN 2873
The Bride
Style Three
Designer: M. Davies
Height: 8", 20.3 cm
Colour: White with gold trim
Issued: 1980-1989

U.S.:	**$225.00**
Can.:	**$300.00**
U.K.:	**£135.00**

HN 2874
The Bridesmaid
Style Five
Designer: M. Davies
Height: 5 ¼", 13.3 cm
Colour: White with gold trim
Issued: 1980-1989

U.S.:	**$125.00**
Can.:	**$160.00**
U.K.:	**£ 75.00**

HN 2875
Awakening
Style Two
Designer: M. Davies
Height: 8 ½", 21.6 cm
Colour: White
Issued: 1981-1997
Varieties: HN 2837; also known in flambé
Series: Images

U.S.:	**$125.00**
Can.:	**$160.00**
U.K.:	**£ 75.00**

HN 2876
Sympathy
Designer: M. Davies
Height: 11 ¾", 29.8 cm
Colour: White
Issued: 1981-1986
Varieties: HN 2838
Series: Images

U.S.:	**$175.00**
Can.:	**$225.00**
U.K.:	**£100.00**

HN 2877
The Wizard
Style One
Designer: A. Maslankowski
Height: 9 ¾", 24.8 cm
Colour: Blue
Issued: 1979 to the present
Varieties: HN 3121, 4069

U.S.:	**N/I**
Can.:	**$590.00**
U.K.:	**£160.00**

HN 2878
Her Majesty
Queen Elizabeth II
Style Two
Designer: E. J. Griffiths
Height: 10 ½", 26.7 cm
Colour: Blue, red and cream
Issued: 1983 in a limited
edition of 2500

U.S.:	**$450.00**
Can.:	**$600.00**
U.K.:	**£275.00**

HN 2879
The Gamekeeper
Designer: E. J. Griffiths
Height: 7 ¼", 18.4 cm
Colour: Green, black and tan
Issued: 1984-1992

U.S.:	**$300.00**
Can.:	**$400.00**
U.K.:	**£175.00**

HN 2880
Monique
Designer: E. J. Griffiths
Height: 12 ½", 31.7 cm
Colour: Pale green
Issued: 1984-1984
Varieties: Colourways:
1. Pale blue;
2. Fawn
Also called 'Allure'
HN 3080
Series: Elegance (Series One)

U.S.:	**$450.00**
Can.:	**$600.00**
U.K.:	**£275.00**

HN 2881
Lord Olivier as Richard III
Designer: E. J. Griffiths
Height: 11 ½", 29.2 cm
Colour: Red, blue and black
Issued: 1985 in a limited
edition of 750

U.S.:	**$ 850.00**
Can.:	**$1,100.00**
U.K.:	**£ 500.00**

HN 2882
HM Queen Elizabeth
The Queen Mother
Style One
Designer: E. J. Griffiths
Height: 8", 20.3 cm
Colour: Pink
Issued: 1980 in a limited
edition of 1500

U.S.:	**$1,000.00**
Can.:	**$1,300.00**
U.K.:	**£ 600.00**

HN 2883
HRH The Prince of Wales
Style One
Designer: E. J. Griffiths
Height: 8", 20.3 cm
Colour: Purple, white and
black
Issued: 1981 in a limited
edition of 1500

U.S.:	**$750.00**
Can.:	**$975.00**
U.K.:	**£450.00**

HN 2884
HRH The Prince of Wales
Style Two
Designer: E. J. Griffiths
Height: 8", 20.3 cm
Colour: Red and black
Issued: 1981 in a limited
edition of 1500

U.S.:	**$750.00**
Can.:	**$975.00**
U.K.:	**£450.00**

HN 2885
Lady Diana Spencer
Designer: E. J. Griffiths
Height: 7 ¾", 19.7 cm
Colour: Blue and white
Issued: 1982 in a limited
edition of 1500

U.S.: $1,400.00
Can.: $1,800.00
U.K.: £ 800.00

HN 2886 not issued.

HN 2887
HRH The Princess of Wales
Designer: E. J. Griffiths
Height: 7 ¾", 19.7 cm
Colour: Cream
Issued: 1982 in a limited
edition of 1500

U.S.: $2,500.00
Can.: $3,250.00
U.K.: £1,500.00

HN 2888
His Holiness Pope John-Paul II
Designer: E. J. Griffiths
Height: 10", 25.4 cm
Colour: White
Issued: 1982-1992

U.S.: $300.00
Can.: $400.00
U.K.: £175.00

HN 2889
Captain Cook
Designer: W. K. Harper
Height: 8", 20.3 cm
Colour: Black and cream
Issued: 1980-1984
Series: Sea Characters

U.S.: $475.00
Can.: $625.00
U.K.: £275.00

HN 2890
The Clown
Designer: W. K. Harper
Height: 9", 22.9 cm
Colour: Gold and grey
Issued: 1979 to 1988

U.S.: $400.00
Can.: $525.00
U.K.: £240.00

HN 2891
The Newsvendor
Designer: W. K. Harper
Height: 8", 20.3 cm
Colour: Gold and grey
Issued: 1986 in a limited
edition of 2,500

U.S.: $300.00
Can.: $400.00
U.K.: £175.00

HN 2892
The Chief
Designer: W. K. Harper
Height: 7", 17.8 cm
Colour: Gold
Issued: 1979-1988

U.S.: $275.00
Can.: $375.00
U.K.: £175.00

HN 2893 not issued.

HN 2894
Balloon Clown
Designer: W. K. Harper
Height: 9 ¼", 23.5 cm
Colour: White and blue
Issued: 1986-1992

U.S.: $400.00
Can.: $525.00
U.K.: £240.00

HN 2895
Morning Ma'am
Designer: W. K. Harper
Height: 9", 23.5 cm
Colour: Pale blue
Issued: 1986-1989

U.S.:	**$250.00**
Can.:	**$325.00**
U.K.:	**£150.00**

HN 2896
Good Day Sir
Designer: W. K. Harper
Height: 8 ½", 21.6 cm
Colour: Purple
Issued: 1986-1989

U.S.:	**$250.00**
Can.:	**$325.00**
U.K.:	**£150.00**

HN 2897
Francoise
Designer: W. K. Harper
Height: 12 ½", 31.7 cm
Colour: Fawn
Issued: 1984-1984
Varieties: Colourways:
           1. Pale blue
           2. Pale green
Series: Elegance (Series One)

U.S.:	**$450.00**
Can.:	**$600.00**
U.K.:	**£275.00**

HN 2898
Ko-Ko
Style Two
Designer: W. K. Harper
Height: 11 ½", 29.2 cm
Colour: Yellow and blue
Issued: 1980-1985
Series: Gilbert and Sullivan

U.S.:	**$ 900.00**
Can.:	**$1,200.00**
U.K.:	**£ 550.00**

HN 2899
Yum-Yum
Style Two
Designer: W. K. Harper
Height: 10 ¾", 27.3 cm
Colour: Green and yellow
Issued: 1980-1985
Series: Gilbert and Sullivan

U.S.:	**$1,000.00**
Can.:	**$1,350.00**
U.K.:	**£ 600.00**

HN 2900
Ruth, The Pirate Maid
Designer: W. K. Harper
Height: 11 ¾", 29.8 cm
Colour: Brown and blue
Issued: 1981-1985
Series: Gilbert and Sullivan

U.S.:	**$ 900.00**
Can.:	**$1,200.00**
U.K.:	**£ 550.00**

HN 2901
The Pirate King
Designer: W. K. Harper
Height: 10", 25.4 cm
Colour: Blue and gold
Issued: 1981-1985
Series: Gilbert and Sullivan

U.S.:	**$ 900.00**
Can.:	**$1,200.00**
U.K.:	**£ 550.00**

HN 2902
Elsie Maynard
Style Two
Designer: W. K. Harper
Height: 12", 30.5 cm
Colour: Green and white
Issued: 1982-1985
Series: Gilbert and Sullivan

U.S.:	**$ 900.00**
Can.:	**$1,200.00**
U.K.:	**£ 550.00**

HN 2903
Colonel Fairfax
Designer: W. K. Harper
Height: 11 ½", 29.2 cm
Colour: Red and gold
Issued: 1982-1985
Series: Gilbert and Sullivan

U.S.:	**$1,100.00**
Can.:	**$1,500.00**
U.K.:	£ **650.00**

HN 2904 - 2905 not issued.

HN 2906
Paula
Designer: P. Parsons
Height: 7", 17.8 cm
Colour: Yellow with green trim
Issued: 1980-1986
Varieties: HN 3234

U.S.:	**$325.00**
Can.:	**$425.00**
U.K.:	£195.00

HN 2907
The Piper
Style One
Designer: M. Abberley
Height: 8", 20.3 cm
Colour: Green
Issued: 1980-1992

U.S.:	**$500.00**
Can.:	**$675.00**
U.K.:	£300.00

HN 2908
HMS Ajax
Designer: S. Keenan
Height: 9 ¾", 24.8 cm
Colour: Red, green and gold
Issued: 1980 in a limited
edition of 950
Series: Ships Figureheads

U.S.:	**$600.00**
Can.:	**$775.00**
U.K.:	£400.00

HN 2909
Benmore
Designer: S. Keenan
Height: 9 ¼", 23.5 cm
Colour: Blue, red, white
and gold
Issued: 1980 in a limited
edition of 950
Series: Ships Figureheads

U.S.:	**$600.00**
Can.:	**$775.00**
U.K.:	**£400.00**

HN 2910
Lalla Rookh
Designer: S. Keenan
Height: 9", 22.9 cm
Colour: Brown, green with
gold trim
Issued: 1981 in a limited
edition of 950
Series: Ships Figureheads

U.S.:	**$750.00**
Can.:	**$975.00**
U.K.:	**£450.00**

HN 2911
Gandalf
Designer: D. Lyttleton
Height: 7", 17.8 cm
Colour: Green and white
Issued: 1980-1984
Series: Middle Earth

U.S.:	**$375.00**
Can.:	**$550.00**
U.K.:	**£225.00**

Lord of the Rings Stand $2,500. U.S.F.

HN 2912
Frodo
Designer: D. Lyttleton
Height: 4 ½", 11.4 cm
Colour: Black and white
Issued: 1980-1984
Series: Middle Earth

U.S.:	**$200.00**
Can.:	**$300.00**
U.K.:	**£150.00**

HN 2913
Gollum
Designer: D. Lyttleton
Height: 3 ¼", 8.3 cm
Colour: Brown
Issued: 1980-1984
Series: Middle Earth

U.S.:	**$250.00**
Can.:	**$375.00**
U.K.:	**£175.00**

HN 2914
Bilbo
Designer: D. Lyttleton
Height: 4 ½", 11.4 cm
Colour: Brown
Issued: 1980-1984
Series: Middle Earth

U.S.:	**$200.00**
Can.:	**$300.00**
U.K.:	**£125.00**

HN 2915
Galadriel
Designer: D. Lyttleton
Height: 5 ½", 14.0 cm
Colour: White
Issued: 1981-1984
Series: Middle Earth

U.S.:	**$275.00**
Can.:	**$450.00**
U.K.:	**£150.00**

HN 2916
Aragorn
Designer: D. Lyttleton
Height: 6 ¼", 15.9 cm
Colour: Brown and green
Issued: 1981-1984
Series: Middle Earth

U.S.:	**$225.00**
Can.:	**$325.00**
U.K.:	**£150.00**

HN 2917
Legolas
Designer: D. Lyttleton
Height: 6 ¼", 15.9 cm
Colour: Cream and tan
Issued: 1981-1984
Series: Middle Earth

U.S.:	**$225.00**
Can.:	**$325.00**
U.K.:	**£150.00**

HN 2918
Boromir
Designer: D Lyttleton
Height: 6 ¾", 17.2 cm
Colour: Brown and green
Issued: 1981-1984
Series: Middle Earth

U.S.:	**$475.00**
Can.:	**$650.00**
U.K.:	**£300.00**

HN 2919
Rachel
Style One
Designer: P. Gee
Height: 7 ½", 19.1 cm
Colour: Gold and green
Issued: 1981-1984
Varieties: HN 2936

U.S.:	**$250.00**
Can.:	**$325.00**
U.K.:	**£150.00**

HN 2920
Yearning
Designer: P. Gee
Height: 11 ¾", 29.8 cm
Colour: White
Issued: 1982-1986
Varieties: HN 2921
Series: Images

U.S.:	**$175.00**
Can.:	**$225.00**
U.K.:	**£100.00**

HN 2921
Yearning
Designer: P. Gee
Height: 11 ¾", 29.8 cm
Colour: Black
Issued: 1982-1986
Varieties: HN 2920
Series: Images

U.S.:	$175.00
Can.:	$225.00
U.K.:	£100.00

HN 2922
Gimli
Designer: D. Lyttleton
Height: 5 ½", 14.0 cm
Colour: Brown and blue
Issued: 1981-1984
Series: Middle Earth

U.S.:	$275.00
Can.:	$450.00
U.K.:	£150.00

HN 2923
Barliman Butterbur
Designer: D. Lyttleton
Height: 5 ¼", 13.3 cm
Colour: Brown, tan and white
Issued: 1982-1984
Series: Middle Earth

U.S.:	$ 800.00
Can.:	$1,200.00
U.K.:	£ 500.00

HN 2924
Tom Bombadil
Designer: D. Lyttleton
Height: 5 ¾", 14.6 cm
Colour: Black and yellow
Issued: 1982-1984
Series: Middle Earth

U.S.:	$ 900.00
Can.:	$1,500.00
U.K.:	£ 600.00

HN 2925
Samwise
Designer: D. Lyttleton
Height: 4 ½", 11.4 cm
Colour: Black and brown
Issued: 1982-1984
Series: Middle Earth

U.S.:	$1,000.00
Can.:	$1,500.00
U.K.:	£ 650.00

HN 2926
Tom Sawyer
Designer: D. Lyttleton
Height: 5 ¼", 13.3 cm
Colour: Blue
Issued: 1982-1985
Series: Characters from
Children's Literature

U.S.:	$200.00
Can.:	$250.00
U.K.:	£125.00

HN 2927
Huckleberry Finn
Designer: D. Lyttleton
Height: 7", 17.8 cm
Colour: Tan and brown
Issued: 1982-1985
Series: Characters from
Children's Literature

U.S.:	$200.00
Can.:	$250.00
U.K.:	£125.00

HN 2928
Nelson
Designer: S. Keenan
Height: 8 ¾", 22.2 cm
Colour: Blue, gold and green
Issued: 1981 in a limited
edition of 950
Series: Ships Figureheads

U.S.:	$ 900.00
Can.:	$1,200.00
U.K.:	£ 550.00

HN 2929
Chieftain
Designer: S. Keenan
Height:　8 ¾", 22.2 cm
Colour:　Green and brown
Issued:　1982 in a limited
　　　　edition of 950
Series:　Ships Figureheads
U.S.:　**$1,350.00**
Can.:　**$1,750.00**
U.K.:　**£　800.00**

HN 2930
Pocahontas
Designer: S. Keenan
Height:　8", 20.3 cm
Colour:　White, red and gold
Issued:　1982 in a limited
　　　　edition of 950
Series:　Ships Figureheads
U.S.:　**$1,500.00**
Can.:　**$2,000.00**
U.K.:　**£　900.00**

HN 2931
Mary Queen of Scots
Style One
Designer: S. Keenan
Height:　9 ½", 24.1 cm
Colour:　Purple, red and white
Issued:　1983 in a limited
　　　　edition of 950
Series:　Ships Figureheads
U.S.:　**$2,000.00**
Can.:　**$2,750.00**
U.K.:　**£1,200.00**

HN 2932
Hibernia
Designer: S. Keenan
Height:　9 ½", 24.1 cm
Colour:　Black, white and gold
Issued:　1983 in a limited
　　　　edition of 950
Series:　Ships Figureheads
U.S.:　**$3,000.00**
Can.:　**$4,000.00**
U.K.:　**£1,750.00**

HN 2933
Kathleen
Style Two
Designer: S. Keenan
Height:　6 ½", 16.5 cm
Colour:　Orange, yellow
　　　　and green
Issued:　1983 Canada,
　　　　1984 Worldwide -1987
Varieties: HN 3100
U.S.:　**$350.00**
Can.:　**$475.00**
U.K.:　**£210.00**

HN 2934
Balloon Boy
Designer: P. Gee
Height:　7 ½", 19.1 cm
Colour:　Green and black
Issued:　1984-1998
U.S.:　**$375.00**
Can.:　**$475.00**
U.K.:　**£225.00**

HN 2935
Balloon Lady
Designer: P. Gee
Height:　8 ¼", 21.0 cm
Colour:　Purple, gold and white
Issued:　1984 to the present
U.S.:　**$245.00**
Can.:　**$550.00**
U.K.:　**£135.00**

HN 2936
Rachel
Style One
Designer: P. Gee
Height:　7 ½", 19.1 cm
Colour:　Red and cream
Issued:　1985-1997
Varieties: HN 2919
U.S.:　**$350.00**
Can.:　**$475.00**
U.K.:　**£200.00**

HN 2937
Gail
Style One
Designer: P. Gee
Height: 7 ½", 19.1 cm
Colour: Red and cream
Issued: 1986-1997

U.S.:   **$300.00**
Can.:   **$425.00**
U.K.:   **£175.00**

HN 2938
Isadora
Designer: P. Gee
Height: 8", 20.3 cm
Colour: Lavender
Issued: 1986-1992
Varieties: Also called 'Celeste'
          (Style Two) HN 3322

U.S.:   **$300.00**
Can.:   **$425.00**
U.K.:   **£175.00**

HN 2939
Donna
Designer: P. Gee
Height: 7 ¾", 19.7 cm
Colour: White
Issued: 1982-1994
Series: Vanity Fair Ladies

U.S.:   **$225.00**
Can.:   **$300.00**
U.K.:   **£135.00**

HN 2940
All Aboard
Designer: R. Tabbenor
Height: 9 ¼", 23.5 cm
Colour: Blue, cream and
          brown
Issued: 1982-1986
Series: Sea characters

U.S.:   **$375.00**
Can.:   **$500.00**
U.K.:   **£225.00**

HN 2941
Tom Brown
Designer: R. Tabbenor
Height: 6 ¾", 17.2 cm
Colour: Blue and cream
Issued: 1983-1985
Series: Characters from
          Children's Literature

U.S.:   **$175.00**
Can.:   **$225.00**
U.K.:   **£100.00**

HN 2942
Prized Possessions
Designer: R. Tabbenor
Height: 6 ½", 16.5 cm
Colour: Cream, purple
          and green
Issued: 1982-1982
Series: RDICC

U.S.:   **$600.00**
Can.:   **$800.00**
U.K.:   **£425.00**

HN 2943
The China Repairer
Designer: R. Tabbenor
Height: 6 ¾", 17.2 cm
Colour: Blue, white and tan
Issued: 1982 Canada,
          1983 Worldwide-1988

U.S.:   **$325.00**
Can.:   **$450.00**
U.K.:   **£200.00**

HN 2944
The Rag Doll Seller
Designer: R. Tabbenor
Height: 7", 17.8 cm
Colour: Green, lavender
          and white
Issued: 1983-1995

U.S.:   **$400.00**
Can.:   **$525.00**
U.K.:   **£240.00**

HN 2945
Pride and Joy
Style One
Designer: R. Tabbenor
Height: 7", 17.8 cm
Colour: Brown, gold and green
Issued: 1984-1984
Series: RDICC

U.S.:	**$300.00**
Can.:	**$450.00**
U.K.:	**£200.00**

HN 2946
Elizabeth
Style One
Designer: B. Franks
Height: 8", 20.3 cm
Colour: Green and yellow
Issued: 1982-1986

U.S.:	**$425.00**
Can.:	**$575.00**
U.K.:	**£250.00**

HN 2947 - 2951 not issued.

HN 2952
Susan
Style Two
Designer: P. Parsons
Height: 8 ½", 21.6 cm
Colour: Blue, black and pink
Issued: 1982-1993
Varieties: HN 3050

U.S.:	**$325.00**
Can.:	**$450.00**
U.K.:	**£200.00**

HN 2953
Sleepy Darling
Designer: P. Parsons
Height: 7 ¼", 18.4 cm
Colour: Pale blue and pink
Issued: 1981-1981
Series: RDICC

U.S.:	**$275.00**
Can.:	**$400.00**
U.K.:	**£175.00**

HN 2954
Samantha
Style One
Designer: P. Parsons
Height: 7", 17.8 cm
Colour: White
Issued: 1982-1984
Series: Vanity Fair Ladies

U.S.:	**$250.00**
Can.:	**$375.00**
U.K.:	**£165.00**

HN 2955
Nancy
Designer: P. Parsons
Height: 7 ½", 19.1 cm
Colour: White
Issued: 1982-1994
Series: Vanity Fair Ladies

U.S.:	**$275.00**
Can.:	**$350.00**
U.K.:	**£150.00**

HN 2956
Heather
Designer: P. Parsons
Height: 6", 15.2 cm
Colour: White
Issued: 1982-2000
Varieties: Also called 'Marie'
(Style Three) HN 3357
Series: Vanity Fair Ladies

U.S.:	**$225.00**
Can.:	**$300.00**
U.K.:	**£125.00**

HN 2957
Edith
Designer: P. Parsons
Height: 5 ¾", 14.6 cm
Colour: Green and white
Issued: 1982-1985
Series: Kate Greenaway

U.S.:	**$375.00**
Can.:	**$500.00**
U.K.:	**£225.00**

HN 2958
Amy
Style One
Designer: P. Parsons
Height: 6", 15.2 cm
Colour: White and blue
Issued: 1982-1987
Series: Kate Greenaway

U.S.:	**$275.00**
Can.:	**$375.00**
U.K.:	**£175.00**

HN 2959
Save Some For Me
Designer: P. Parsons
Height: 7 ¼", 18.4 cm
Colour: Blue and white
Issued: 1982-1985
Series: Childhood Days

U.S.:	**$250.00**
Can.:	**$325.00**
U.K.:	**£150.00**

HN 2960
Laura
Style One
Designer: P. Parsons
Height: 7 ¼", 18.4 cm
Colour: Pale blue and white,
          yellow flowers
Issued: 1982 Canada,
          1984 Worldwide -1994
Varieties: HN 3136

U.S.:	**$275.00**
Can.:	**$375.00**
U.K.:	**£175.00**

HN 2961
Carol
Designer: P. Parsons
Height: 7 ½", 19.1 cm
Colour: White
Issued: 1982-1995
Series: Vanity Fair Ladies

U.S.:	**$250.00**
Can.:	**$325.00**
U.K.:	**£150.00**

HN 2962
Barbara
Style Two
Designer: P. Parsons
Height: 8", 20.3 cm
Colour: White
Issued: 1982-1984
Series: Vanity Fair Ladies

U.S.:	**$275.00**
Can.:	**$375.00**
U.K.:	**£175.00**

HN 2963
It Won't Hurt
Designer: P. Parsons
Height: 7 ½", 19.1 cm
Colour: White, brown and blue
Issued: 1982-1985
Series: Childhood Days

U.S.:	**$250.00**
Can.:	**$325.00**
U.K.:	**£150.00**

HN 2964
Dressing Up
Style One
Designer: P. Parsons
Height: 7 ½", 19.1 cm
Colour: White and blue
Issued: 1982-1985
Series: Childhood Days

U.S.:	**$225.00**
Can.:	**$300.00**
U.K.:	**£135.00**

HN 2965
Pollyanna
Designer: P. Parsons
Height: 6 ½", 16.5 cm
Colour: White, grey and tan
Issued: 1982-1985
Series: Characters from
          Children's Literature

U.S.:	**$225.00**
Can.:	**$300.00**
U.K.:	**£135.00**

HN 2966
And So To Bed
Designer: P. Parsons
Height: 7 ½", 19.1 cm
Colour: Cream and gold
Issued: 1982-1985
Series: Childhood Days

U.S.:	**$275.00**
Can.:	**$375.00**
U.K.:	**£175.00**

HN 2967
Please Keep Still
Designer: P. Parsons
Height: 4 ½", 11.4 cm
Colour: Yellow and blue
Issued: 1982-1985
Series: Childhood Days

U.S.:	**$275.00**
Can.:	**$375.00**
U.K.:	**£175.00**

HN 2968
Juliet
Style One
Designer: P. Parsons
Height: 7", 17.8 cm
Colour: Blue and white
Issued: 1983-1984
Series: Ladies of Covent
             Garden
Comm.by: Amex

U.S.:	**$525.00**
Can.:	**$750.00**
U.K.:	**£325.00**

HN 2969
Kimberley
Style One
Designer: P. Parsons
Height: 8", 20.3 cm
Colour: Yellow and white
Issued: 1983-1984
Varieties: Also called 'Yours
             Forever' HN 3354
Series: Ladies of Covent
             Garden
Comm.by: Amex

U.S.:	**$525.00**
Can.:	**$750.00**
U.K.:	**£325.00**

HN 2970
And One For You
Designer: A. Hughes
Height: 6 ½", 16.5 cm
Colour: White and brown
Issued: 1982-1985
Series: Childhood Days

U.S.:	**$200.00**
Can.:	**$250.00**
U.K.:	**£125.00**

HN 2971
As Good As New
Designer: A. Hughes
Height: 6 ½", 16.5 cm
Colour: Blue, green and tan
Issued: 1982-1985
Series: Childhood Days

U.S.:	**$200.00**
Can.:	**$300.00**
U.K.:	**£150.00**

HN 2972
Little Lord Fauntleroy
Designer: A. Hughes
Height: 6 ¼", 15.9 cm
Colour: Blue and white
Issued: 1982-1985
Series: Characters from
           Children's Literature

U.S.:	**$200.00**
Can.:	**$250.00**
U.K.:	**£125.00**

HN 2973 not issued.

HN 2974
Carolyn
Style Two
Designer: A. Hughes
Height: 5 ½", 14.0 cm
Colour: Green
Issued: 1982 Canada,
           1984 Worldwide -1986

U.S.:	**$275.00**
Can.:	**$350.00**
U.K.:	**£175.00**

HN 2975
Heidi
Designer: A. Hughes
Height: 4 ½", 11.4 cm
Colour: Green and white
Issued: 1983-1985
Series: Characters from
            Children's Literature

U.S.:	**$225.00**
Can.:	**$300.00**
U.K.:	**£150.00**

HN 2976
I'm Nearly Ready
Designer: A. Hughes
Height: 7 ½", 19.1 cm
Colour: Black, white and brown
Issued: 1983 Canada,
            1984 Worldwide -1985
Series: Childhood Days

U.S.:	**$250.00**
Can.:	**$325.00**
U.K.:	**£150.00**

HN 2977
Magic Dragon
Designer: A. Hughes
Height: 4 ¾", 12.0 cm
Colour: Cream
Issued: 1983-1986
Series: Enchantment

U.S.:	**$225.00**
Can.:	**$325.00**
U.K.:	**£150.00**

HN 2978
The Magpie Ring
Designer: A. Hughes
Height: 8", 20.3 cm
Colour: Cream
Issued: 1983-1986
Series: Enchantment

U.S.:	**$225.00**
Can.:	**$325.00**
U.K.:	**£150.00**

HN 2979
Fairyspell
Designer: A. Hughes
Height: 5 ¼", 13.3 cm
Colour: Cream
Issued: 1983-1986
Series: Enchantment

U.S.:	**$225.00**
Can.:	**$325.00**
U.K.:	**£150.00**

HN 2980
Just One More
Designer: A. Hughes
Height: 7", 17.8 cm
Colour: Gold and blue
Issued: 1983 Canada,
            1984 Worldwide -1985
Series: Childhood Days

U.S.:	**$200.00**
Can.:	**$300.00**
U.K.:	**£150.00**

HN 2981
Stick 'em Up
Designer: A. Hughes
Height: 7", 17.8 cm
Colour: Blue and tan
Issued: 1983 Canada,
            1984 Worldwide -1985
Series: Childhood Days

U.S.:	**$225.00**
Can.:	**$300.00**
U.K.:	**£150.00**

HN 2982 - 2987 not issued.

HN 2988
The Auctioneer
Designer: R. Tabbenor
Height: 8 ½", 21.6 cm
Colour: Black, grey and
            brown
Issued: 1986-1986
Series: RDICC

U.S.:	**$300.00**
Can.:	**$425.00**
U.K.:	**£175.00**

HN 2989
The Genie
Designer: R. Tabbenor
Height: 9 ¾", 24.7 cm
Colour: Blue
Issued: 1983-1990
Varieties: HN 2999

U.S.:	$250.00
Can.:	$325.00
U.K.:	£150.00

HN 2990
Shepherdess
Style Three
Designer: R. Tabbenor
Height: 8", 20.3 cm
Colour: Pale blue, white
          and tan
Issued: 1987-1988
Series: Reflections

U.S.:	$250.00
Can.:	$325.00
U.K.:	£150.00

HN 2991
June
Style Four
Designer: R. Tabbenor
Height: 9", 22.9 cm
Colour: Lavender and red
Issued: 1988-1994

U.S.:	$300.00
Can.:	$425.00
U.K.:	£175.00

HN 2992
Golfer
Designer: R. Tabbenor
Height: 9 ½", 24.1 cm
Colour: Blue, white and
          pale brown
Issued: 1988-1991
Series: Reflections

U.S.:	$250.00
Can.:	$325.00
U.K.:	£150.00

HN 2993
Old Father Thames
Designer: R. Tabbenor
Height: 5 ¾", 14.6 cm
Colour: Cream with gold trim
Issued: 1988 in a limited
            edition of 500
Comm.by: Thames Water

U.S.:	$250.00
Can.:	$325.00
U.K.:	£150.00

HN 2994
Helen
Style Two
Designer: R. Tabbenor
Height: 5", 12.7 cm
Colour: White
Issued: 1985-1987
Series: Vanity Fair Children

U.S.:	$125.00
Can.:	$200.00
U.K.:	£ 75.00

HN 2995
Julie
Style One
Designer: R. Tabbenor
Height: 5", 12.7 cm
Colour: White
Issued: 1985-1995
Varieties: HN 3407
Series: Vanity Fair Children

U.S.:	$125.00
Can.:	$165.00
U.K.:	£ 75.00

HN 2996
Amanda
Designer: R. Tabbenor
Height: 5 ¼", 13.3 cm
Colour: White and pink
Issued: 1986-2000
Varieties: HN 3406, 3632, 3634,
           3635; Also called
           'Flower of the Month,
           Child'
Series: Vanity Fair Children

U.S.:	$125.00
Can.:	$200.00
U.K.:	£ 75.00

HN 2997
Chic
Designer: R. Tabbenor
Height: 13", 33.0 cm
Colour: Pale blue
Issued: 1987 N. America,
          1988 Worldwide -1990
Series: Reflections

U.S.:	**$350.00**
Can.:	**$450.00**
U.K.:	**£200.00**

HN 2998
Aperitif
Designer: P. Gee
Height: 12", 30.5 cm
Colour: Pale green
Issued: 1988-1988
Series: Reflections
Comm.by: Home Shopping
            Network, Florida

U.S.:	**$350.00**
Can.:	**$450.00**
U.K.:	**£200.00**

HN 2999
The Genie
Designer: R. Tabbenor
Height: 9 ¾", 24.7 cm
Colour: Red
Issued: 1990-1995
Varieties: HN 2989
Series: Flambé

U.S.:	**$475.00**
Can.:	**$600.00**
U.K.:	**£275.00**

HN 3000
Sweet Bouquet
Style One
Designer: R. Tabbenor
Height: 13", 33.0 cm
Colour: Blue and white
Issued: 1988-1988
Series: Reflections
Comm.by: Home Shopping
            Network, Florida

U.S.:	**$350.00**
Can.:	**$450.00**
U.K.:	**£200.00**

HN 3001
Danielle
Style Two
Designer: P. Gee
Height: 7", 17.8 cm
Colour: Pink and white
Issued: 1990-1995
Varieties: Also called 'Spring
           Song' HN 3446
Series: Vanity Fair Ladies

U.S.:	**$225.00**
Can.:	**$300.00**
U.K.:	**£135.00**

HN 3002
Marilyn
Designer: P. Gee
Height: 7 ¼", 18.4 cm
Colour: White dress
          with flowers
Issued: 1985 Canada,
          1986 Worldwide -1995

U.S.:	**$275.00**
Can.:	**$375.00**
U.K.:	**£165.00**

HN 3003
Lilian In Summer
Designer: P. Gee
Height: 8 ½", 21.6 cm
Colour: White, blue and pink
Issued: 1985
Series: The Seasons
            (Series Three)
Comm.by: Danbury Mint

U.S.:	**$450.00**
Can.:	**$600.00**
U.K.:	**£275.00**

HN 3004
Emily In Autumn
Designer: P. Gee
Height: 8", 20.3 cm
Colour: Yellow and white
Issued: 1986
Series: The Seasons
            (SeriesThree)
Comm.by: Danbury Mint

U.S.:	**$450.00**
Can.:	**$600.00**
U.K.:	**£275.00**

HN 3005
Sarah In Winter
Designer: P. Gee
Height: 8", 20.3 cm
Colour: Pale green and white
Issued: 1986
Series: The Seasons
            (SeriesThree)
Comm.by: Danbury Mint

U.S.:	$450.00
Can.:	$600.00
U.K.:	£275.00

HN 3006
Catherine In Spring
Designer: P. Gee
Height: 8 ½", 21.6 cm
Colour: Pink and white
Issued: 1985
Series: The Seasons
            (Series Three)
Comm.by: Danbury Mint

U.S.:	$450.00
Can.:	$600.00
U.K.:	£275.00

HN 3007
Mary, Countess Howe
Designer: P. Gee
Height: 9 ¼", 23.5 cm
Colour: Pink and blue
Issued: 1990 in a limited
            edition of 5,000
Series: Gainsborough
            Ladies

U.S.:	$550.00
Can.:	$725.00
U.K.:	£330.00

HN 3008
Sophia Charlotte, Lady Sheffield
Designer: P. Gee
Height: 10", 25.4 cm
Colour: Yellow and turquoise
Issued: 1990 in a limited
            edition of 5,000
Series: Gainsborough
            Ladies

U.S.:	$500.00
Can.:	$650.00
U.K.:	£300.00

HN 3009
Honourable Frances Duncombe
Designer: P. Gee
Height: 9 ¾", 24.7 cm
Colour: Blue and yellow
Issued: 1991 in a limited
            edition of 5,000
Series: Gainsborough
            Ladies

U.S.:	$575.00
Can.:	$750.00
U.K.:	£350.00

HN 3010
Isabella, Countess of Sefton
Designer: P. Gee
Height: 9 ¾", 24.7 cm
Colour: Yellow and black
Issued: 1991 in a limited
            edition of 5,000
Series: Gainsborough
            Ladies

U.S.:	$575.00
Can.:	$750.00
U.K.:	£350.00

HN 3011
My Best Friend
Designer: P. Gee
Height: 8", 20.3 cm
Colour: Pink
Issued: 1990-2000

U.S.:	$375.00
Can.:	$525.00
U.K.:	£225.00

HN 3012
Painting
Designer: P. Parsons
Height: 7 ½", 18.4 cm
Colour: Purple
Issued: 1987 in a limited
            edition of 750
Series: Gentle Arts

U.S.:	$1,300.00
Can.:	$1,800.00
U.K.:	£ 800.00

HN 3013
James
Designer: P. Parsons
Height: 6", 15.2 cm
Colour: White
Issued: 1983-1987
Series: Kate Greenaway

U.S.:	**$750.00**
Can.:	**$975.00**
U.K.:	**£450.00**

HN 3014
Nell
Designer: P. Parsons
Height: 4", 10.1 cm
Colour: White and pink
Issued: 1982-1987
Series: Kate Greenaway

U.S.:	**$325.00**
Can.:	**$425.00**
U.K.:	**£195.00**

HN 3015
Adornment
Designer: P. Parsons
Height: 7 ¼", 18.4 cm
Colour: Pink and lavender stripes
Issued: 1989 in a limited edition of 750
Series: Gentle Arts

U.S.:	**$1,300.00**
Can.:	**$1,800.00**
U.K.:	**£ 800.00**

HN 3016
The Graduate (female)
Style One
Designer: P. Parsons
Height: 8 ¾", 22.2 cm
Colour: Black, pink and yellow
Issued: 1984-1992

U.S.:	**$300.00**
Can.:	**$400.00**
U.K.:	**£175.00**

HN 3017
The Graduate (male)
Style One
Designer: P. Parsons
Height: 9 ¼", 23.5 cm
Colour: Black and grey
Issued: 1984-1992

U.S.:	**$300.00**
Can.:	**$400.00**
U.K.:	**£175.00**

HN 3018
Sisters
Designer: P. Parsons
Height: 8 ½", 21.6 cm
Colour: White
Issued: 1983 to the present
Varieties: HN 3019
Series: Images

U.S.:	**$125.00**
Can.:	**$225.00**
U.K.:	**£ 39.00**

HN 3019
Sisters
Designer: P. Parsons
Height: 8 ½", 21.6 cm
Colour: Black
Issued: 1983-1997
Varieties: HN 3018
Series: Images

U.S.:	**$150.00**
Can.:	**$200.00**
U.K.:	**£ 90.00**

HN 3020
Ellen
Style One
Designer: P. Parsons
Height: 3 ½", 8.9 cm
Colour: Blue and yellow
Issued: 1984-1987
Series: Kate Greenaway

U.S.:	**$750.00**
Can.:	**$950.00**
U.K.:	**£450.00**

HN 3021
Polly Put The Kettle On
Designer: P. Parsons
Height: 8", 20.3 cm
Colour: White and pink
Issued: 1984-1987
Series: Nursery Rhymes
           (Series Two)

U.S.:	**$225.00**
Can.:	**$350.00**
U.K.:	**£150.00**

HN 3022 - 3023 not issued.

HN 3024
April Shower
Designer: R. Jefferson
Height: 4 ¾", 12.0 cm
Colour: Cream
Issued: 1983-1986
Series: Enchantment

U.S.:	**$225.00**
Can.:	**$325.00**
U.K.:	**£175.00**

HN 3025
Rumpelstiltskin
Designer: R. Jefferson
Height: 8", 20.3 cm
Colour: Cream
Issued: 1983-1986
Series: Enchantment

U.S.:	**$250.00**
Can.:	**$325.00**
U.K.:	**£175.00**

HN 3026
Carefree
Designer: R. Jefferson
Height: 12 ¼", 31.1 cm
Colour: White
Issued: 1986-2001
Varieties: HN 3029
Series: Images

U.S.:	**$175.00**
Can.:	**$225.00**
U.K.:	**£100.00**

HN 3027
Windswept
Designer: R. Jefferson
Height: 12 ¾", 32.0 cm
Colour: Pale blue
Issued: 1985 N. America
           1987 Worldwide-1994
Series: Reflections

U.S.:	**$250.00**
Can.:	**$325.00**
U.K.:	**£150.00**

HN 3028
Panorama
Designer: R. Jefferson
Height: 12 ¾", 32.5 cm
Colour: Pale blue
Issued: 1985 N. America,
           1987 Worldwide-1988
Series: Reflections

U.S.:	**$200.00**
Can.:	**$250.00**
U.K.:	**£125.00**

HN 3029
Carefree
Designer: R. Jefferson
Height: 12 ¼", 31.1 cm
Colour: Black
Issued: 1986-1997
Varieties: HN 3026
Series: Images

U.S.:	**$200.00**
Can.:	**$250.00**
U.K.:	**£125.00**

HN 3030
Little Bo Peep
Designer: A. Hughes
Height: 8", 20.3 cm
Colour: White with blue trim
Issued: 1984-1987
Series: Nursery Rhymes
           (Series Two)

U.S.:	**$200.00**
Can.:	**$250.00**
U.K.:	**£125.00**

HN 3031
Wee Willie Winkie
Style Two
Designer: A. Hughes
Height: 7 ¾", 19.7 cm
Colour: White and blue
Issued: 1984-1987
Series: Nursery Rhymes
(Series Two)

U.S.:	**$250.00**
Can.:	**$325.00**
U.K.:	**£150.00**

HN 3032
Tom, Tom, the Piper's Son
Designer: A. Hughes
Height: 7", 17.8 cm
Colour: White, yellow
and pink
Issued: 1984-1987
Series: Nursery Rhymes
(Series Two)

U.S.:	**$200.00**
Can.:	**$250.00**
U.K.:	**£125.00**

HN 3033
Springtime
Style Two
Designer: A. Hughes
Height: 8", 20.3 cm
Colour: Yellow, cream
and green
Issued: 1983-1983
Series: 1. The Seasons
(Series Four)
2. RDICC

U.S.:	**$325.00**
Can.:	**$450.00**
U.K.:	**£200.00**

HN 3034
Little Jack Horner
Style Two
Designer: A. Hughes
Height: 7", 17.8 cm
Colour: White, yellow
and green
Issued: 1984-1987
Series: Nursery Rhymes
(Series Two)

U.S.:	**$200.00**
Can.:	**$250.00**
U.K.:	**£125.00**

HN 3035
Little Boy Blue
Style Two
Designer: A. Hughes
Height: 7 ¾", 19.7 cm
Colour: Blue and white
Issued: 1984-1987
Series: Nursery Rhymes
(Series Two)

U.S.:	**$200.00**
Can.:	**$250.00**
U.K.:	**£125.00**

HN 3036
Kerry
Designer: A. Hughes
Height: 5 ¼", 13.3 cm
Colour: White
Issued: 1986-1992
Varieties: HN 3461
Series: Vanity Fair Children

U.S.:	**$125.00**
Can.:	**$165.00**
U.K.:	**£ 75.00**

HN 3037
Miranda
Style Two
Designer: A. Hughes
Height: 8 ½", 21.5 cm
Colour: Cream, yellow
and purple
Issued: 1987-1990

U.S.:	**$300.00**
Can.:	**$425.00**
U.K.:	**£175.00**

HN 3038
Yvonne
Designer: A. Hughes
Height: 8 ½", 21.6 cm
Colour: Turquoise
Issued: 1987-1992

U.S.:	**$250.00**
Can.:	**$325.00**
U.K.:	**£150.00**

HN 3039
Reflection
Designer: A. Hughes
Height: 8", 20.3 cm
Colour: Pale blue, pale
brown and white
Issued: 1987-1991
Series: Reflections
U.S.: **$250.00**
Can.: **$325.00**
U.K.: **£150.00**

HN 3040
Flower Arranging
Designer: D. Brindley
Height: 7 ¼", 18.4 cm
Colour: Green, purple
and pink
Issued: 1988 in a limited
edition of 750
Series: Gentle Arts
U.S.: **$1,200.00**
Can.: **$1,550.00**
U.K.: **£ 725.00**

HN 3041
The Lawyer
Style One
Designer: P. Parsons
Height: 8 ¾", 22.2 cm
Colour: Grey and black
Issued: 1985-1995
U.S.: **$325.00**
Can.: **$450.00**
U.K.: **£200.00**

HN 3042
Gillian
(With shoulder straps)
Style Two
Designer: P. Parsons
Height: 8 ¼", 21.0 cm
Colour: Green
Issued: 1984-Unknown
Varieties: HN 3042A (without
shoulder straps)
Series: M. Doulton Events
U.S.: **$275.00**
Can.: **$400.00**
U.K.: **£175.00**

HN 3042A
Gillian
(Without shoulder straps)
Style Two
Designer: P. Parsons
Height: 8 ¼", 21.0 cm
Colour: Green
Issued: Unknown-1990
Varieties: HN 3042 (with
shoulder straps)
U.S.: **$200.00**
Can.: **$275.00**
U.K.: **£125.00**

HN 3043
Lynsey
Designer: P. Parsons
Height: 4 ¾", 12.0 cm
Colour: White
Issued: 1985-1995
Series: Vanity Fair Children
U.S.: **$125.00**
Can.: **$175.00**
U.K.: **£ 75.00**

HN 3044
Catherine
Style Two
Designer: P. Parsons
Height: 5", 12.7 cm
Colour: White with blue flowers
Issued: 1985-1996
Varieties: HN 3451
Series: Vanity Fair Children
U.S.: **$125.00**
Can.: **$175.00**
U.K.: **£ 75.00**

HN 3045
Demure
Designer: P. Parsons
Height: 12 ¾", 32.5 cm
Colour: Grey-blue and white
Issued: 1985 N. America,
1987 Worldwide -1988
Series: Reflections
U.S.: **$325.00**
Can.: **$475.00**
U.K.: **£200.00**

HN 3046
Debut
Style One
Designer: P. Parsons
Height: 12 ½", 32.0 cm
Colour: Pale blue ,
         white and green
Issued: 1985 N. America,
         1986 Worldwide -1989
Series: Reflections

U.S.:	**$325.00**
Can.:	**$425.00**
U.K.:	**£195.00**

HN 3047
Sharon
Style One
Designer: P. Parsons
Height: 5 ½", 14.0 cm
Colour: White and blue
Issued: 1984-1993
Varieties: HN 3455

U.S.:	**$150.00**
Can.:	**$200.00**
U.K.:	**£ 90.00**

HN 3048
Tapestry Weaving
Designer: P. Parsons
Height: 7 ½", 19.1 cm
Colour: Flowered pink dress
Issued: 1985 in a limited
         edition of 750
Series: Gentle Arts

U.S.:	**$1,500.00**
Can.:	**$2,000.00**
U.K.:	**£ 900.00**

HN 3049
Writing
Designer: P. Parsons
Height: 7 ¼", 18.4 cm
Colour: Flowered yellow dress
Issued: 1986 in a limited
         edition of 750
Series: Gentle Arts

U.S.:	**$1,400.00**
Can.:	**$2,000.00**
U.K.:	**£ 850.00**

HN 3050
Susan
Style Two
Designer: P. Parsons
Height: 8 ½", 21.6 cm
Colour: Pink and red
Issued: 1986-1995
Varieties: HN 2952

U.S.:	**$375.00**
Can.:	**$500.00**
U.K.:	**£225.00**

HN 3051
Country Girl
Style One
Designer: A. Hughes
Height: 7 ¾", 19.7 cm
Colour: Blue and white
Issued: 1987-1992
Series: Reflections

U.S.:	**$200.00**
Can.:	**$275.00**
U.K.:	**£120.00**

HN 3052
A Winter's Walk
Designer: A. Hughes
Height: 12 ¼", 31.1 cm
Colour: Pale blue and white
Issued: 1987 N. America,
         1988 Worldwide -1995
Series: Reflections

U.S.:	**$600.00**
Can.:	**$775.00**
U.K.:	**£350.00**

HN 3053
Martine
Designer: A. Hughes
Height: 13 ½", 34.3 cm
Colour: 1. Fawn
         2. Pale blue
         3. Pale green
Issued: 1984
Varieties: Reissued in 1985 as
         'Promenade' (Style
         Two), HN 3072
Series: Elegance (Series One)

U.S.:	**$600.00**
Can.:	**$775.00**
U.K.:	**£350.00**

HN 3054
Dominique
Designer: A. Hughes
Height: 14", 35.6 cm
Colour: Fawn
Issued: 1984-1984
Varieties: Colourways:
            1. Pale blue
            2. Pale green;
            Also called
            'Paradise' HN 3074
Series: Elegance (Series One)

U.S.:	**$ 475.00**
Can.:	**$ 600.00**
U.K.:	**£ 275.00**

Photograph
Not
Available

HN 3055
Claudine
Designer: A. Hughes
Height: 12", 30.5 cm
Colour: Fawn
Issued: 1984-1984
Varieties: Colourways:
            1. Pale blue
            2. Pale green
Series: Elegance (Series One)

U.S.:	**$ 475.00**
Can.:	**$ 600.00**
U.K.:	**£ 275.00**

HN 3056
Danielle
Style One
Designer: A. Hughes
Height: 12", 30.5 cm
Colour: Fawn
Issued: 1984-1984
Varieties: Colourways:
            1. Pale blue
            2. Pale green
Series: Elegance (Series One)

U.S.:	**$ 475.00**
Can.:	**$ 600.00**
U.K.:	**£ 275.00**

HN 3057
Sir Winston Churchill
Style One
Designer: A. Hughes
Height: 10 ½", 26.7 cm
Colour: White
Issued: 1985 to the present

U.S.:	**$ 360.00**
Can.:	**$ 465.00**
U.K.:	**£ 125.00**

HN 3058
Andrea
Style One
Designer: A. Hughes
Height: 5 ¼", 13.3 cm
Colour: Blue and white
Issued: 1985-1995
Series: Vanity Fair Children

U.S.:	**$125.00**
Can.:	**$165.00**
U.K.:	**£ 75.00**

HN 3059
Sophistication
Designer: A. Hughes
Height: 11 ½", 29.2 cm
Colour: Pale blue and white
Issued: 1987 N. America,
            1988 Worldwide-1990
Series: Reflections

U.S.:	**$300.00**
Can.:	**$400.00**
U.K.:	**£175.00**

HN 3060
Wintertime
Style One
Designer: A. Hughes
Height: 8 ½", 21.6 cm
Colour: Red and white
Issued: 1985-1985
Series: 1. The Seasons
               (Series Four)
            2. RDICC

U.S.:	**$300.00**
Can.:	**$400.00**
U.K.:	**£175.00**

NOTE ON CONDITION

Prices on the secondary market for Royal Doulton Figures, particularly the early HN numbers, have risen considerably over the years. As values rise, the condition and quality of these figurines takes on an increasingly important role.

The prices listed in *The Charlton Standard Catalogue of Royal Doulton Figurines* are for figures in mint condition.

Naturally, repaired or restored figures, no matter how professionally done, will sell at a discount. However the early figures, due to their rarity, may experience smaller discounts.

On Condition: For figures to command catalogue prices they must be in mint condition. This simply means that a figure will have no chips, scratches, hairline cracks, crazing, blemishes, or repairs. Any of which will remove the figure from the mint category.

On Quality: Some figures are better moulded, assembled or painted than others. High quality figures may command a premium over listed catalogue prices.

HN 3061
Hope
Style One
Designer: S. Mitchell
Height: 8 ¼", 21.0 cm
Colour: Pale blue
Issued: 1984 in a limited
edition of 9.500
Series: NSPCC Charity
Comm.by: Lawleys By Post

U.S.:	**$500.00**
Can.:	**$675.00**
U.K.:	**£300.00**

HN 3062 - 3065 not issued.

HN 3066
Printemps (Spring)
Designer: R. Jefferson
Height: 11 ¼", 28.6 cm
Colour: White, brown and
green
Issued: 1987 in a limited
edition of 300
Series: Les Saisons

U.S.:	**$1,450.00**
Can.:	**$2,000.00**
U.K.:	**£ 900.00**

HN 3067
Ete (Summer)
Designer: R. Jefferson
Height: 11 ¾", 29.8 cm
Colour: Yellow and green
Issued: 1989 in a limited
edition of 300
Series: Les Saisons

U.S.:	**$1,600.00**
Can.:	**$2,200.00**
U.K.:	**£ 950.00**

HN 3068
Automne (Autumn)
Designer: R. Jefferson
Height: 11 ½", 29.2 cm
Colour: Lavender and cream
Issued: 1986 in a limited
edition of 300
Series: Les Saisons

U.S.:	**$1,450.00**
Can.:	**$2,000.00**
U.K.:	**£ 900.00**

HN 3069
Hiver (Winter)
Designer: R. Jeffferson
Height: 11 ¾", 29.8 cm
Colour: White
Issued: 1988 in a limited
edition of 300
Series: Les Saisons

U.S.:	**$1,450.00**
Can.:	**$2,000.00**
U.K.:	**£ 900.00**

HN 3070
Cocktails
Designer: A. Hughes
Height: 11", 28.0 cm
Colour: Pale brown
Issued: 1985 N. America,
1987 Worldwide -1995
Series: Reflections

U.S.:	**$325.00**
Can.:	**$425.00**
U.K.:	**£200.00**

HN 3071
Flirtation
Designer: A. Hughes
Height: 10", 25.4 cm
Colour: Pale blue
Issued: 1985 N. America,
1987 Worldwide -1995
Series: Reflections

U.S.:	**$325.00**
Can.:	**$425.00**
U.K.:	**£200.00**

HN 3072
Promenade
Style Two
Designer: A. Hughes
Height: 13 ¼", 33.5 cm
Colour: Pale brown
Issued: 1985 N. America,
1987 Worldwide -1995
Varieties: Also called 'Martine'
HN 3053
Series: Reflections

U.S.:	**$600.00**
Can.:	**$775.00**
U.K.:	**£350.00**

HN 3073
Strolling
Style One
Designer: A. Hughes
Height: 13 ½", 34.3 cm
Colour: Pale green and white
Issued: 1985 N. America,
          1987 Worldwide -1995
Series: Reflections
  U.S.:   **$600.00**
  Can.:   **$775.00**
  U.K.:   **£350.00**

HN 3074
Paradise
Designer: A. Hughes
Height: 14", 35.5 cm
Colour: Pale brown
Issued: 1985 N. America,
          1987 Worldwide -1992
Varieties: Also called
          'Dominique' HN 3054
Series: Reflections
  U.S.:   **$375.00**
  Can.:   **$500.00**
  U.K.:   **£225.00**

HN 3075
Tango
Designer: A. Hughes
Height: 13", 33.0 cm
Colour: Pale blue and cream
Issued: 1985 N. America,
          1987 Worldwide -1992
Series: Reflections
  U.S.:   **$350.00**
  Can.:   **$450.00**
  U.K.:   **£200.00**

HN 3076
Bolero
Designer: A. Hughes
Height: 13 ½", 34.3 cm
Colour: Pale blue and pink
Issued: 1985 N. America,
          1987 Worldwide -1992
Series: Reflections
  U.S.:   **$350.00**
  Can.:   **$450.00**
  U.K.:   **£200.00**

HN 3077
Windflower
Style Four
Designer: A. Hughes
Height: 12 ¼", 31.1 cm
Colour: Pale blue
Issued: 1986 N. America,
          1987 Worldwide -1992
Series: Reflections
  U.S.:   **$300.00**
  Can.:   **$400.00**
  U.K.:   **£175.00**

HN 3078
Dancing Delight
Designer: A. Hughes
Height: 12 ¾", 32.0 cm
Colour: Pale brown
Issued: 1986 N. America,
          1987 Worldwide -1988
Series: Reflections
  U.S.:   **$350.00**
  Can.:   **$450.00**
  U.K.:   **£200.00**

HN 3079
Sleeping Beauty
Style One
Designer: A. Hughes
Height: 4 ½", 11.4 cm
Colour: Green and white
Issued: 1987-1989
  U.S.:   **$300.00**
  Can.:   **$400.00**
  U.K.:   **£175.00**

HN 3080
Allure
Designer: E. J. Griffiths
Height: 12 ½", 32.0 cm
Colour: Pale green
Issued: 1985 N. America
          1987 Worldwide-1988
Varieties: Also called 'Monique'
          HN 2880
Series: Reflections
  U.S.:   **$300.00**
  Can.:   **$400.00**
  U.K.:   **£175.00**

HN 3081 not issued.

HN 3082
Faith
Style One
Designer:	E. J. Griffiths
Height:	8 ½", 21.6 cm
Colour:	Pink
Issued:	1986 in a limited edition of 9,500
Series:	NSPCC Charity
Comm.by:	Lawleys By Post
U.S.:	**$250.00**
Can.:	**$350.00**
U.K.:	**£175.00**

HN 3083
Sheikh
Designer:	E. J. Griffiths
Height:	9 ¾", 24.7 cm
Colour:	White
Issued:	1987-1989
Series:	Reflections
U.S.:	**$250.00**
Can.:	**$325.00**
U.K.:	**£150.00**

HN 3084
Harvestime
Designer:	E. J. Griffiths
Height:	8", 20.3 cm
Colour:	Blue and blue-grey
Issued:	1988-1990
Series:	Reflections
U.S.:	**$250.00**
Can.:	**$325.00**
U.K.:	**£150.00**

HN 3085
Summer Rose
Style One
Designer:	E. J. Griffiths
Height:	8 ½", 21.6 cm
Colour:	Blue
Issued:	1987 N. America, 1988 Worldwide -1992
Series:	Reflections
U.S.:	**$250.00**
Can.:	**$325.00**
U.K.:	**£150.00**

HN 3086
The Duchess of York
Designer:	E. J. Griffiths
Height:	8 ¼", 21.0 cm
Colour:	Cream
Issued:	1986 in a limited edition of 1,500
Comm.by:	Lawleys By Post
U.S.:	**$ 900.00**
Can.:	**$1,200.00**
U.K.:	**£ 525.00**

HN 3087
Charity
Style One
Designer:	E. J. Griffiths
Height:	8 ½", 21.6 cm
Colour:	Yellow and purple
Issued:	1987 in a limited edition of 9,500
Series:	NSPCC Charity
Comm.by:	Lawleys By Post
U.S.:	**$500.00**
Can.:	**$675.00**
U.K.:	**£300.00**

HN 3088
Kate Hannigan
Designer:	E. J. Griffiths
Height:	9", 22.9 cm
Colour:	Light brown
Issued:	1989 in a limited edition of 9,500
Comm.by:	Lawleys By Post
U.S.:	**$450.00**
Can.:	**$600.00**
U.K.:	**£275.00**

HN 3089
Grace Darling
Designer:	E. J. Griffiths
Height:	9", 22.9 cm
Colour:	Blue, yellow and rose
Issued:	1987 in a limited edition of 9,500
Comm.by:	Lawleys By Post
U.S.:	**$350.00**
Can.:	**$450.00**
U.K.:	**£210.00**

HN 3090
Charisma
Designer: P. Parsons
Height: 12 ½", 31.7 cm
Colour: Pale blue, white
           and brown
Issued: 1986 N. America,
           1987 Worldwide -1990
Series: Reflections
U.S.:   **$275.00**
Can.:   **$350.00**
U.K.:   **£165.00**

HN 3091
Summer's Darling
Style One
Designer: P. Parsons
Height: 11 ½", 29.0 cm
Colour: Pale blue
Issued: 1986 N. America,
           1987 Worldwide -1995
Series: Reflections
U.S.:   **$300.00**
Can.:   **$400.00**
U.K.:   **£175.00**

HN 3092
Cherry Blossom
Designer: P. Parsons
Height: 12 ¾", 32.0 cm
Colour: Pale green and
           pale brown
Issued: 1986 N. America,
           1987 Worldwide -1989
Series: Reflections
U.S.:   **$300.00**
Can.:   **$400.00**
U.K.:   **£175.00**

HN 3093
Morning Glory
Designer: P. Parsons
Height: 13", 33.0 cm
Colour: Green and blue
Issued: 1986 N. America,
           1987 Worldwide-1989
Series: Reflections
U.S.:   **$275.00**
Can.:   **$350.00**
U.K.:   **£165.00**

HN 3094
Sweet Perfume
Designer: P. Parsons
Height: 13", 33.0 cm
Colour: Pale blue and white
Issued: 1986 N. America,
           1987 Worldwide-1995
Series: Reflections
U.S.:   **$275.00**
Can.:   **$350.00**
U.K.:   **£165.00**

HN 3095
Happy Birthday
Style One
Designer: P. Parsons
Height: 8 ½", 21.6 cm
Colour: Yellow and white
Issued: 1987-1994
Series: Special Occasions
U.S.:   **$275.00**
Can.:   **$350.00**
U.K.:   **£165.00**

HN 3096
Merry Christmas
Designer: P. Parsons
Height: 8 ½", 21.6 cm
Colour: Green and white
Issued: 1987-1992
Series: Special Occasions
U.S.:   **$300.00**
Can.:   **$400.00**
U.K.:   **£175.00**

HN 3097
Happy Anniversary
Style One
Designer: P. Parsons
Height: 6 ½", 16.5 cm
Colour: Purple and white
Issued: 1987-1993
Series: Special Occasions
U.S.:   **$275.00**
Can.:   **$350.00**
U.K.:   **£165.00**

HN 3098
Dorothy
Designer: P. Parsons
Height: 7", 17.8 cm
Colour: Grey
Issued: 1987-1990

U.S.: $450.00
Can.: $600.00
U.K.: £275.00

HN 3099
Queen Elizabeth I
Designer: P. Parsons
Height: 9", 22.9 cm
Colour: Red and gold
Issued: 1986 U.K.,
1987 Worldwide in a
limited edition of 5,000
Series: Queens of the Realm

U.S.: $ 750.00
Can.: $1,000.00
U.K.: £ 450.00

HN 3100
Kathleen
Style Two
Designer: S. Keenan
Height: 6 ½", 16.5 cm
Colour: Purple, cream
and pink
Issued: 1986-1986
Varieties: HN 2933
Series: M. Doulton Events

U.S.: $300.00
Can.: $425.00
U.K.: £175.00

HN 3101 - 3104 not issued.

HN 3105
The Love Letter
Style Two
Designer: R. Jefferson
Height: 12", 30.5 cm
Colour: Pale blue and
pale brown
Issued: 1986 N. America,
1987 Worldwide -1988
Series: Reflections

U.S.: $300.00
Can.: $400.00
U.K.: £175.00

HN 3106
Secret Moment
Designer: R. Jefferson
Height: 12 ¼", 31.1 cm
Colour: Pale blue, green
flowers
Issued: 1986 N. America,
1987 Worldwide-1988
Series: Reflections

U.S.: $275.00
Can.: $350.00
U.K.: £165.00

HN 3107
Daybreak
Style One
Designer: R. Jefferson
Height: 11 ¾", 29.8 cm
Colour: White, pale green
borders with yellow
flowers
Issued: 1986 N. America,
1987 Worldwide-1988
Series: Reflections

U.S.: $275.00
Can.: $350.00
U.K.: £165.00

HN 3108
Enchanting Evening
Designer: R. Jefferson
Height: 11 ¾", 29.8 cm
Colour: Pale pink
Issued: 1986 N. America,
1987 Worldwide -1992
Series: Reflections

U.S.: $300.00
Can.: $400.00
U.K.: £175.00

HN 3109
Pensive
Designer: R. Jefferson
Height: 13", 33.0 cm
Colour: White with yellow
flowers on skirt
Issued: 1986 N. America,
1987 Worldwide -1988
Series: Reflections

U.S.: $275.00
Can.: $350.00
U.K.: £165.00

HN 3110
Enigma
Designer: R. Jefferson
Height: 12 ¾", 32.0 cm
Colour: Cream
Issued: 1986 N. America,
           1987 Worldwide -1995
Series: Reflections

U.S.:	**$275.00**
Can.:	**$350.00**
U.K.:	**£165.00**

HN 3111
Robin Hood and Maid Marion
Designer: R. Jefferson
Height: 12 ¾", 33.0 cm
Colour: Blue, green and cream
Issued: 1994 in a limited
           edition of 150
Series: Great Lovers

U.S.:	**$2,500.00**
Can.:	**$3,250.00**
U.K.:	**£1,500.00**

HN 3112
Lancelot and Guinivere
Designer: R. Jefferson
Height: 12 ¾", 33.0 cm
Colour: Lilac, purple, cream,
           green and yellow
Issued: 1996 in a limited
           edition of 150
Series: Great Lovers

U.S.:	**$2,750.00**
Can.:	**$3,500.00**
U.K.:	**£1,650.00**

HN 3113
Romeo and Juliet
Style One
Designer: R. Jefferson
Height: 12", 30.5 cm
Colour: Lilac, purple, cream,
           yellow and green
Issued: 1993 in a limited
           edition of 150
Series: Great Lovers

U.S.:	**$2,500.00**
Can.:	**$3,250.00**
U.K.:	**£1,500.00**

HN 3114
Antony and Cleopatra
Designer: R. Jefferson
Height: 11 ¾", 29.8 cm
Colour: Pale blue and cream
Issued: 1995 in a limited
           edition of 150
Series: Great Lovers

U.S.:	**$2,750.00**
Can.:	**$3,500.00**
U.K.:	**£1,650.00**

HN 3115
Idle Hours
Designer: A. Maslankowski
Length: 12 ¼", 31.1 cm
Colour: Blue-white and
           pale green
Issued: 1986 N. America,
           1987 Worldwide -1988
Series: Reflections

U.S.:	**$300.00**
Can.:	**$400.00**
U.K.:	**£175.00**

HN 3116
Park Parade
Designer: A. Maslankowski
Height: 11 ¾", 29.8 cm
Colour: Pale green and
           pale blue
Issued: 1987 N. America,
           1988 Worldwide-1994
Series: Reflections

U.S.:	**$475.00**
Can.:	**$600.00**
U.K.:	**£275.00**

HN 3117
Indian Maiden
Designer: A. Maslankowski
Height: 12", 30.5 cm
Colour: Pale tan and pale blue
Issued: 1987-1990
Series: Reflections

U.S.:	**$325.00**
Can.:	**$450.00**
U.K.:	**£200.00**

HN Series

HN 1970
Milady
1941-1949

HN 1995
Olivia, Style One
1947-1951

HN 2058
Hermione
1950-1952

HN 2078
Elfreda
1951-1955

HN 2079
Damaris
1951-1952

HN 2112
Carolyn, Style One
1953-1965

HN Series

HN 2116
Ballerina, Style One
1953-1973

HN 2145
Wardrobe Mistress
1954-1967

HN 2149
Love Letter, Style One
1958-1976

HN 2166
The Bride, Style Two
1956-1976

HN Series

HN 2221
Nanny
1958-1991

HN 2255
Teatime
1972-1995

HN 2269
Leading Lady
1965-1976

HN 2276
Heart to Heart
1961-1971

HN 2337
Loretta
1966-1981

HN 2352
A Stich in Time
1966-1981

HN Series

HN 2430
Romance, Style Two
1972-1981

HN 2441
Pauline, Style Two
1983 Canada, 1984 Worldwide-1989

HN 2463
Olga
1972-1975

HN 2735
Young Love
1975-1990

HN 2749
Lizzie
1988-1991

HN 2810
Solitude
1977-1983

HN Series

HN 2855
Embroidering
1980-1990

HN 2858
The Doctor, Style One
1979-1992

HN 2862
First Waltz
1979-1983

HN 2871
Beat You To It
1980-1987

HN 2877
The Wizard, Style One
1979 to the present

HN 2919
Rachel, Style One
1981-1984

HN Series

HN 2933
Kathleen, Style Two
1983 Canada, 1984 Worldwide-1987

HN 2960
Laura, Style One
1982 Canada, 1984 Worldwide-1994

HN 2991
June, Style Four
1988-1994

HN 3168
Jemma
1988-1991

HN 3177
Harriet, Style One
1988-1991

HN 3180
Phyllis, Style Two
1988-1991

HN Series

HN 3253
Cheryl
1989-1994

HN 3315
Waiting For A Train
1991 in a limited edition of 9,500

HN 3355
Just For You, Style One
1992-1998

HN 3439
The Skater, Style Two
1992-1997

HN 3625
Anniversary
1994-1998

HN 3648
Sweet Sixteen, Style Two
1994-1998

HN Series

HN 3702
Le Bal
Collectors Club, 1995

HN 3756
Pamela, Style Three
Collectors Club, 1996

HN 3850
Jessica, Style Two
Figure of the Year 1997

HN 3857, **Sarah, Style Two**
1996 in a limited edition of 1,996,
Visitor Centre

HN 3864, **Kimberley, Style Two**
1997 in a limited edition of 2,000,
Visitor Centre

HN 3871
Susan, Style Three
Collectors Club, 1997

HN 3118
Lorraine
Style One
Designer: A. Maslankowski
Height: 7 ¾", 19.7 cm
Colour: Blue
Issued: 1988-1995

U.S.:	**$375.00**
Can.:	**$525.00**
U.K.:	**£225.00**

HN 3119
Partners
Designer: A. Maslankowski
Height: 6 ¾", 17.2 cm
Colour: Black, blue and grey
Issued: 1990-1992
Series: Clowns

U.S.:	**$375.00**
Can.:	**$500.00**
U.K.:	**£225.00**

HN 3120
Spring Walk
Designer: A. Maslankowski
Height: 13", 32.9 cm
Colour: Blue with white poodle
Issued: 1990-1992
Series: Reflections

U.S.:	**$600.00**
Can.:	**$775.00**
U.K.:	**£350.00**

HN 3121
Wizard
Style One
Designer: A. Maslankowski
Height: 10", 25.4 cm
Colour: Flambé
Issued: 1990-1995
Varieties: HN 2877, 4069
Series: Flambé

U.S.:	**$600.00**
Can.:	**$775.00**
U.K.:	**£350.00**

HN 3122
My First Pet
Designer: A. Maslankowski
Height: 4 ½", 11.4 cm
Colour: Blue and white
Issued: 1991-1997
Series: Vanity Fair Children

U.S.:	**$150.00**
Can.:	**$200.00**
U.K.:	**£ 85.00**

HN 3123
Sit
Designer: A. Maslankowski
Height: 4 ½", 11.4 cm
Colour: White and yellow
Issued: 1991-2000
Varieties: HN 3430
Series: Vanity Fair Children

U.S.:	**$150.00**
Can.:	**$200.00**
U.K.:	**£ 85.00**

HN 3124
Thinking of You
Style One
Designer: A. Maslankowski
Height: 6 ¾", 17.1 cm
Colour: White
Issued: 1991-2001
Varieties: HN 3490
Series: Sentiments

U.S.:	**$125.00**
Can.:	**$160.00**
U.K.:	**£ 70.00**

HN 3125
Queen Victoria
Style One
Designer: P. Parsons
Height: 8", 20.3 cm
Colour: Pink and white
Issued: 1987 U.K.,
1988 Worldwide in a
limited edition of 5,000
Series: Queens of the Realm

U.S.:	**$1,250.00**
Can.:	**$1,700.00**
U.K.:	**£ 750.00**

HN 3126
Storytime
Style One
Designer: P. Parsons
Height: 6", 15.2 cm
Colour: Pale blue
Issued: 1987-1992
Series: Reflections

U.S.:	**$200.00**
Can.:	**$275.00**
U.K.:	**£125.00**

HN 3127
Playmates
Designer: P. Parsons
Height: 8 ½", 21.6 cm
Colour: Pale blue, green
 and white
Issued: 1987-1992
Series: Reflections

U.S.:	**$200.00**
Can.:	**$275.00**
U.K.:	**£125.00**

HN 3128
Tomorrow's Dreams
Style One
Designer: P. Parsons
Height: 6 ½", 16.5 cm
Colour: White and green
Issued: 1987-1992
Series: Reflections

U.S.:	**$250.00**
Can.:	**$325.00**
U.K.:	**£150.00**

HN 3129
Thankful
Designer: P. Parsons
Height: 8 ½", 21.6 cm
Colour: White
Issued: 1987-1999
Varieties: HN 3135
Series: Images

U.S.:	**$125.00**
Can.:	**$160.00**
U.K.:	**£ 70.00**

HN 3130
Sisterly Love
Designer: P. Parsons
Height: 8 ½", 21.6 cm
Colour: Pale blue and white
Issued: 1987-1995
Series: Reflections

U.S.:	**$200.00**
Can.:	**$275.00**
U.K.:	**£125.00**

HN 3131 not issued.

HN 3132
Good Pals
Designer: P. Parsons
Height: 6 ¼", 15.9 cm
Colour: Pale blue and white
Issued: 1987-1992
Series: Reflections

U.S.:	**$200.00**
Can.:	**$275.00**
U.K.:	**£125.00**

HN 3133
Dreaming
Designer: P. Parsons
Height: 9", 22.9 cm
Colour: Pale pink
Issued: 1987-1995
Series: Reflections

U.S.:	**$225.00**
Can.:	**$300.00**
U.K.:	**£135.00**

HN 3134
Ballet Class
Style One
Designer: P. Parsons
Height: 6", 15.2 cm
Colour: White and tan
Issued: 1987 N. America,
 1988 Worldwide -1992
Series: Reflections

U.S.:	**$225.00**
Can.:	**$300.00**
U.K.:	**£135.00**

HN 3135
Thankful
Designer: P. Parsons
Height: 8 ½", 21.6 cm
Colour: Black
Issued: 1987-1994
Varieties: HN 3129
Series: Images

U.S.:	$175.00
Can.:	$225.00
U.K.:	£100.00

HN 3136
Laura
Style One
Designer: P. Parsons
Height: 7 ¼", 18.4 cm
Colour: Dark blue and white
Issued: 1988-1988
Varieties: HN 2960
Series: M. Doulton Events

U.S.:	$325.00
Con.:	$450.00
U.K.:	£200.00

HN 3137
Summertime
Style One
Designer: P. Parsons
Height: 8", 20.3 cm
Colour: White and blue
Issued: 1987-1987
Series: 1. The Seasons
(Series Four)
2. RDICC

U.S.:	$275.00
Can.:	$375.00
U.K.:	£165.00

HN 3138
Eastern Grace
Designer: P. Parsons
Height: 12", 30.5 cm
Colour: Cream
Issued: 1988-1989
Varieties: HN 3683
Series: Reflections

U.S.:	$325.00
Can.:	$425.00
U.K.:	£200.00

HN 3139
Free As The Wind
Designer: P. Parsons
Height: 9 ½", 24.1 cm
Colour: Pale blue
Issued: 1988 N. America,
1989 Worldwide -1995
Series: Reflections

U.S.:	$300.00
Can.:	$400.00
U.K.:	£175.00

HN 3140
Gaiety
Designer: P. Parsons
Height: 10 ¼", 26.0 cm
Colour: Pale green and
pale blue
Issued: 1988-1990
Series: Reflections

U.S.:	$300.00
Can.:	$400.00
U.K.:	£175.00

HN 3141
Queen Anne
Designer: P. Parsons
Height: 9", 22.9 cm
Colour: Green, red and white
Issued: 1988 in a limited
edition of 5,000
Series: Queens of the Realm
Comm.by: Lawleys By Post

U.S.:	$600.00
Can.:	$775.00
U.K.:	£350.00

HN 3142
Mary, Queen of Scots
Style Two
Designer: P. Parsons
Height: 9", 22.9 cm
Colour: Blue and purple
Issued: 1989 in a limited
edition of 5,000
Series: Queens of the Realm
Comm.by: Lawleys By Post

U.S.:	$1,000.00
Can.:	$1,300.00
U.K.:	£ 600.00

HN 3143
Rosemary
Style Two
Designer: P. Parsons
Height: 7 ½", 19.1 cm
Colour: White dress with
          pink flowers
Issued: 1988-1991

U.S.:	**$325.00**
Can.:	**$450.00**
U.K.:	**£195.00**

HN 3144
Florence Nightingale
Designer: P. Parsons
Height: 8 ¼", 21.0 cm
Colour: Red
Issued: 1988 in a limited
           edition of 5,000
Comm.by: Lawleys By Post

U.S.:	**$1,100.00**
Can.:	**$1,500.00**
U.K.:	**£ 650.00**

HN 3145
Rose Arbour
Designer: D. Brindley
Height: 12", 30.5 cm
Colour: Pale blue and white
Issued: 1987 N. America,
           1988 Worldwide -1990
Series: Reflections

U.S.:	**$275.00**
Can.:	**$350.00**
U.K.:	**£165.00**

HN 3146 - 3154 not issued.

HN 3155
Water Maiden
Designer: A. Hughes
Height: 12", 30.5 cm
Colour: Blue
Issued: 1987-1991
Series: Reflections

U.S.:	**$325.00**
Can.:	**$425.00**
U.K.:	**£195.00**

HN 3156
Bathing Beauty
Style One
Designer: A. Hughes
Height: 9 ¾", 24.7 cm
Colour: Pale grey
Issued: 1987-1989
Series: Reflections

U.S.:	**$525.00**
Can.:	**$675.00**
U.K.:	**£325.00**

HN 3157
Free Spirit
Style One
Designer: A. Hughes
Height: 10 ½", 26.5 cm
Colour: White
Issued: 1987-1992
Varieties: HN 3159
Series: Images

U.S.:	**$175.00**
Can.:	**$225.00**
U.K.:	**£100.00**

HN 3158 not issued.

HN 3159
Free Spirit
Style One
Designer: A. Hughes
Height: 10 ½", 26.5 cm
Colour: Black
Issued: 1987-1992
Varieties: HN 3157
Series: Images

U.S.:	**$200.00**
Can.:	**$250.00**
U.K.:	**£120.00**

HN 3160
Shepherd
Style Five
Designer: A. Hughes
Height: 8 ½", 21.6 cm
Colour: Grey-blue and black
Issued: 1988-1989
Series: Reflections

U.S.:	**$350.00**
Can.:	**$450.00**
U.K.:	**£200.00**

HN 3161
The Gardener
Designer: A. Hughes
Height: 8 ¼", 21.0 cm
Colour: Blue and pale brown
Issued: 1988-1991
Series: Reflection

U.S.: **$300.00**
Can.: **$400.00**
U.K.: **£175.00**

HN 3162
Breezy Day
Designer: A. Hughes
Height: 8 ½", 21.6 cm
Colour: Pale blue, pale
brown and white
Issued: 1988-1990
Series: Reflections

U.S.: **$250.00**
Can.: **$325.00**
U.K.: **£150.00**

HN 3163
Country Maid
Designer: A. Hughes
Height: 8 ¼", 21.0 cm
Colour: Blue, pink, white
and black
Issued: 1988-1991

U.S.: **$350.00**
Can.: **$450.00**
U.K.: **£200.00**

HN 3164
Farmer's Wife
Style Two
Designer: A. Hughes
Height: 8 ¾", 22.2 cm
Colour: Brown and blue
Issued: 1988-1991

U.S.: **$300.00**
Can.: **$400.00**
U.K.: **£175.00**

HN 3165
August
Style One
Designer: M. Davies
Height: 7 ¾", 19.7 cm
Colour: White and blue
dress, poppies
Issued: 1987-1987
Varieties: Also called 'Gillian'
(Style Three) HN 3742
Series: Figure of the Month

U.S.: **$200.00**
Can.: **$275.00**
U.K.: **£125.00**

HN 3166
September
Style One
Designer: M. Davies
Height: 7 ¾", 19.7 cm
Colour: White and yellow
dress, michaelmas
daisies
Issued: 1987-1987
Varieties: Also called 'Gillian'
(Style Three) HN 3742
Series: Figure of the Month

U.S.: **$200.00**
Can.: **$275.00**
U.K.: **£125.00**

HN 3167
Hazel
Style Two
Designer: M. Davies
Height: 8", 20.3 cm
Colour: Flowered white dress
Issued: 1988-1991

U.S.: **$350.00**
Can.: **$475.00**
U.K.: **£200.00**

HN 3168
Jemma
Designer: M. Davies
Height: 7 ¼", 18.4 cm
Colour: Red and blue
Issued: 1988-1991

U.S.: **$250.00**
Can.: **$325.00**
U.K.: **£150.00**

HN 3169
Jessica
Style One
Designer: M. Davies
Height: 7", 17.8 cm
Colour: White
Issued: 1988-1995
Varieties: HN 3497
Series: Vanity Fair Ladies

U.S.:	**$225.00**
Can.:	**$300.00**
U.K.:	**£135.00**

HN 3170
Caroline
Style One
Designer: M. Davies
Height: 7 ½", 19.1 cm
Colour: White dress with
blue flowers
Issued: 1988-1992
Varieties: Also called 'Winter
Welcome' HN 3611

U.S.:	**$250.00**
Can.:	**$325.00**
U.K.:	**£150.00**

HN 3171
Camille
Style Two
Designer: M. Davies
Height: 7 ½", 19.1 cm
Colour: Orange-yellow,
white and green
Issued: 1987
Varieties: 'Adéle' HN 2480;
'Margaret' (Style Two)
HN 2397, 3496
Comm.by: Marks and Spencer

U.S.:	**$325.00**
Can.:	**$425.00**
U.K.:	**£200.00**

HN 3172
Christine
Style Two
Designer: M. Davies
Height: 7 ½", 19.1 cm
Colour: Pink and white
Issued: 1987 in a limited
edition of 1,000
Varieties: HN 2792
Comm.by: Guild of Specialist
China and Glass
Retailers

U.S.:	**$375.00**
Can.:	**$500.00**
U.K.:	**£225.00**

HN 3173
Natalie
Style One
Designer: M. Davies
Height: 8", 20.3 cm
Colour: Yellow and white
Issued: 1988-1996
Varieties: HN 3498
Series: Vanity Fair Ladies

U.S.:	**$275.00**
Can.:	**$375.00**
U.K.:	**£165.00**

HN 3174
Southern Belle
Style Two
Designer: M. Davies
Remodeller: R. Tabbenor
Height: 4", 10.1 cm
Colour: Red and yellow
Issued: 1988-1997
Varieties: HN 3244
Series: Miniatures

U.S.:	**$200.00**
Can.:	**$250.00**
U.K.:	**£120.00**

HN 3175
Sweet Violets
Designer: D. V. Tootle
Height: 10 ¼", 26.0 cm
Colour: Pale blue and white
Issued: 1988-1989
Series: Reflections

U.S.:	**$250.00**
Can.:	**$325.00**
U.K.:	**£150.00**

HN 3176
Young Dreams
Designer: D. V. Tootle
Height: 6 ¼", 15.9 cm
Colour: Pink
Issued: 1988-1992

U.S.:	**$250.00**
Can.:	**$325.00**
U.K.:	**£150.00**

HN 3177
Harriet
Style One
Designer: D. V. Tootle
Height: 7 ¼", 18.4 cm
Colour: Pink
Issued: 1988-1991

U.S.:	**$400.00**
Can.:	**$550.00**
U.K.:	**£240.00**

HN 3178
Polly
Designer: D. V. Tootle
Height: 8", 20.3 cm
Colour: Green and lavender
Issued: 1988-1991

U.S.:	**$250.00**
Can.:	**$350.00**
U.K.:	**£150.00**

HN 3179
Eliza
Style Two
Designer: D. V. Tootle
Height: 7 ½", 19.1 cm
Colour: Red and lilac
Issued: 1988-1992

U.S.:	**$250.00**
Can.:	**$350.00**
U.K.:	**£150.00**

HN 3180
Phyllis
Style Two
Designer: D. V. Tootle
Height: 7 ¼", 18.4 cm
Colour: Red, white and purple
Issued: 1988-1991

U.S.:	**$350.00**
Can.:	**$450.00**
U.K.:	**£210.00**

HN 3181
Moondancer
Designer: D. V. Tootle
Height: 11 ¾", 29.8 cm
Colour: Blue, white and
pale green
Issued: 1988-1990
Series: Reflections

U.S.:	**$325.00**
Can.:	**$425.00**
U.K.:	**£195.00**

HN 3182
Stargazer
Designer: D. V. Tootle
Height: 10 ½", 26.7 cm
Colour: Blue and pale blue
Issued: 1988-1990
Series: Reflections

U.S.:	**$325.00**
Can.:	**$425.00**
U.K.:	**£195.00**

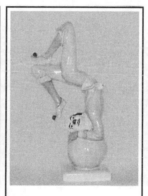

HN 3183
Tumbler
Designer: D. V. Tootle
Height: 9", 22.9 cm
Colour: Pink and yellow
Issued: 1989-1991
Varieties: Also called 'Tumbling'
HN 3283, 3289
Series: 1. Clowns
2. Reflections

U.S.:	**$400.00**
Can.:	**$525.00**
U.K.:	**£240.00**

HN 3184
Joy
Style One
Designer: D. V. Tootle
Height: 6 ¾", 17.2 cm
Colour: Blue and pink
Issued: 1988-1990
Series: Reflections

U.S.:	**$300.00**
Can.:	**$400.00**
U.K.:	**£175.00**

HN 3185
Traveller's Tale
Designer: E. J. Griffiths
Height: 9 ¼", 23.5 cm
Colour: Pale blue and
pale green
Issued: 1988-1989
Series: Reflections
- U.S.: $300.00
- Can.: $400.00
- U.K.: £175.00

HN 3186
Entranced
Designer: E. J. Griffiths
Height: 7 ¼", 18.4 cm
Colour: Green, white and tan
Issued: 1988-1989
Series: Reflections
- U.S.: $250.00
- Can.: $325.00
- U.K.: £150.00

HN 3187
Balloons
Designer: E. J. Griffiths
Height: 9 ¼", 23.5 cm
Colour: Pale blue
Issued: 1988-in a limited
edition of 1,000
Series: Reflections
Comm.by: Home Shopping
Network
- U.S.: $475.00
- Can.: $625.00
- U.K.: £275.00

HN 3188
Debutante
Style Two
Designer: E. J. Griffiths
Height: 12", 30.5 cm
Colour: Grey-pink
Issued: 1988 in a limited
edition of 1,000
Series: Reflections
Comm.by: Home Shopping
Network
- U.S.: $375.00
- Can.: $500.00
- U.K.: £225.00

HN 3189
HM Queen Elizabeth,
The Queen Mother
Style Two
Designer: E. J. Griffiths
Height: 8", 20.3 cm
Colour: Lavender, blue
and pink
Issued: 1990 in a limited
edition of 2,500
- U.S.: $ 775.00
- Can.: $1,000.00
- U.K.: £ 500.00

HN 3190
Old Ben
Designer: M. Nicholl
Height: 8 ½", 21.6 cm
Colour: Green, brown and
blue
Issued: 1990 in a limited
edition of 1,500
Comm.by: Newsvendors
Benevolent Society
- U.S.: $250.00
- Can.: $325.00
- U.K.: £150.00

HN 3191
Brothers
Designer: E. J. Griffiths
Height: 8 ¼", 21.0 cm
Colour: White
Issued: 1991 to the present
Series: Images
- U.S.: N/I
- Can.: $220.00
- U.K.: £ 39.00

HN 3192
Mantilla
Designer: E. J. Griffiths
Height: 11 ½", 29.2 cm
Colour: Red, black and white
Issued: 1992 in a limited
edition of 1992
Varieties: HN 2712
- U.S.: $450.00
- Can.: $600.00
- U.K.: £275.00

Issued to commemorate Expo 92
Seville, Spain
HN 3193 - 3194 not issued.

HN 3195
The Farmer
Style One
Designer: A. Hughes
Height: 9", 22.9 cm
Colour: Brown and white
Issued: 1988-1991

U.S.:	**$300.00**
Can.:	**$400.00**
U.K.:	**£175.00**

HN 3196
The Joker
Style One
Designer: A. Hughes
Height: 9 ¼", 23.5 cm
Colour: White and blue
Issued: 1988-1990
Varieties: Also called 'Tip-Toe';
           HN 3293
Series: 1. Clowns
           2. Reflections

U.S.:	**$375.00**
Can.:	**$500.00**
U.K.:	**£225.00**

HN 3197
Ballerina
Style Two
Designer: A. Hughes
Height: 14", 35.5 cm
Colour: White and beige
Issued: 1988 in a limited
           edition of 1,000
Series: Reflections
Comm.by: Home Shopping
           Network

U.S.:	**$400.00**
Can.:	**$525.00**
U.K.:	**£250.00**

HN 3198
Vanessa
Style Two
Designer: A. Hughes
Height: 8 ½", 21.6 cm
Colour: Green and black
Issued: 1989-1990

U.S.:	**$300.00**
Can.:	**$400.00**
U.K.:	**£175.00**

HN 3199
Maxine
Style One
Designer: A. Hughes
Height: 8 ½", 21.6 cm
Colour: Pink and purple
Issued: 1989-1990

U.S.:	**$300.00**
Can.:	**$400.00**
U.K.:	**£175.00**

HN 3200
Gloria
Style Two
Designer: A. Hughes
Height: 8 ¾", 22.2 cm
Colour: Pink
Issued: 1989-1990

U.S.:	**$300.00**
Can.:	**$400.00**
U.K.:	**£175.00**

HN 3201
Liberty
Style One
Designer: A. Hughes
Height: 8 ¼", 21.0 cm
Colour: White, blue and red
Issued: 1989-1990

U.S.:	**$300.00**
Can.:	**$400.00**
U.K.:	**£175.00**

HN 3202
The Boy Evacuee
Designer: A. Hughes
Height: 8 ½", 21.6 cm
Colour: Green and blue
Issued: 1989 in a limited
           edition of 9,500
Series: Children of the Blitz
Comm.by: Lawleys By Post

U.S.:	**$ 700.00**
Can.:	**$1,000.00**
U.K.:	**£ 450.00**

HN 3203
The Girl Evacuee
Designer:	A. Hughes
Height:	8", 20.3 cm
Colour:	Red, blue and brown
Issued:	1989 in a limited edition of 9,500
Series:	Children of the Blitz
Comm.by:	Lawleys By Post

U.S.:	$ 700.00
Can.:	$1,000.00
U.K.:	£ 450.00

HN 3204
Emily
Style One
Designer:	A. Hughes
Height:	8 ¼", 21.0 cm
Colour:	White and blue
Issued:	1989-1994
Series:	Vanity Fair Ladies

U.S.:	$225.00
Can.:	$300.00
U.K.:	£135.00

Exclusive to North America.

HN 3205
Veronica
Style Four
Designer:	A. Hughes
Height:	8", 20.3 cm
Colour:	White and pink
Issued:	1989-1992
Series:	Vanity Fair Ladies

U.S.:	$225.00
Can.:	$300.00
U.K.:	£135.00

HN 3206
Teresa
Style Two
Designer:	A. Hughes
Height:	7 ¾", 19.7 cm
Colour:	White with flowers
Issued:	1989-1992

U.S.:	$250.00
Can.:	$375.00
U.K.:	£150.00

HN 3207
Louise
Style Two
Designer:	A. Hughes
Height:	7 ½", 19.1 cm
Colour:	Red
Issued:	1990-1996

U.S.:	$300.00
Can.:	$425.00
U.K.:	£175.00

HN 3208
Emma
Style Two
Designer:	A. Hughes
Height:	4 ¼", 10.8 cm
Colour:	Red
Issued:	1990-1998
Series	Miniatures

U.S.:	$175.00
Can.:	$225.00
U.K.:	£100.00

HN 3209
Claire
Style One
Designer:	A. Hughes
Height:	8 ½", 21.6 cm
Colour:	Pink and with dress with flowers
Issued:	1990-1992

U.S.:	$225.00
Can.:	$300.00
U.K.:	£135.00

NOTE ON PRICING

Prices on the secondary market for Royal Doulton Figures, particularly the early HN numbers, have risen considerably over the years. As values rise, the condition and quality of these figurines takes on an increasingly important role.

The prices listed in *The Charlton Standard Catalogue of Royal Doulton Figurines* are for figures in mint condition.

Naturally, repaired or restored figures, no matter how professionally done, will sell at a discount. However the early figures, due to their rarity, may experience smaller discounts.

On Condition: For figures to command catalogue prices they must be in mint condition. This simply means that a figure will have no chips, scratches, hairline cracks, crazing, blemishes, or repairs. Any of which will remove the figure from the mint category.

On Quality: Some figures are better moulded, assembled or painted than others. High quality figures may command a premium over listed catalogue prices.

HN 3210
Christening Day
Designer: P. A. Northcroft
Height: 8 ½", 21.6 cm
Colour: White, baby's
　　　　shawl blue
Issued: 1988-1990
Varieties: HN 3211
Series: Special Occasions

U.S.:	**$200.00**
Can.:	**$250.00**
U.K.:	**£120.00**

HN 3211
Christening Day
Designer: P. A. Northcroft
Height: 8 ½", 21.6 cm
Colour: White, pink baby's
　　　　shawl
Issued: 1988-1990
Varieties: HN 3210
Series: Special Occasions

U.S.:	**$200.00**
Can.:	**$250.00**
U.K.:	**£120.00**

HN 3212
Christmas Morn
Style Two
Designer: M. Davies
Remodeller: R. Tabbenor
Height: 4", 10.1 cm
Colour: Red and white
Issued: 1988-1998
Varieties: HN 3245
Series: Miniatures

U.S.:	**$175.00**
Can.:	**$225.00**
U.K.:	**£100.00**

HN 3213
Kirsty
Style Two
Designer: M. Davies
Remodeller: P. Gee
Height: 3 ¾", 9.5 cm
Colour: Red
Issued: 1988-1997
Varieties: HN 3246, 3480,
　　　　3743
Series: Miniatures

U.S.:	**$150.00**
Can.:	**$200.00**
U.K.:	**£ 90.00**

HN 3214
Elaine
Style Two
Designer: M. Davies
Remodeller: P. Gee
Height: 4", 10.1 cm
Colour: Blue
Issued: 1988-1998
Varieties: HN 3247, 3900
Series: Miniatures

U.S.:	**$175.00**
Can.:	**$225.00**
U.K.:	**£100.00**

HN 3215
Ninette
Style Two
Designer: M. Davies
Remodeller: P. Gee
Height: 3 ½", 8.9 cm
Colour: Cream and lavender
Issued: 1988-1997
Varieties: HN 3248, 3901
Series: Miniatures

U.S.:	**$175.00**
Can.:	**$225.00**
U.K.:	**£100.00**

HN 3216
Fair Lady
Style Two
Designer: M. Davies
Remodeller: P. Gee
Height: 3 ¾", 9.5 cm
Colour: Lemon and blue
Issued: 1988-1995
Varieties: HN 3336
Series: Miniatures

U.S.:	**$175.00**
Can.:	**$225.00**
U.K.:	**£100.00**

HN 3217
Joan
Style Two
Designer: M. Davies
Height: 8", 20.3 cm
Colour: Yellow and green
Issued: 1988 in a limited
　　　　edition of 2,000
Varieties: Also called 'Adrienne'
　　　　HN 2152, 2304;
　　　　'Fiona' (Style Four),
　　　　HN 3748
Comm.by: Joan's Gift Shop,
　　　　Scotland

U.S.:	**$350.00**
Can.:	**$450.00**
U.K.:	**£200.00**

HN 3218
Sunday Best
Style Two
Designer: M. Davies
Remodeller: P. Gee
Height: 3 ¾", 9.5 cm
Colour: Green and blue
Issued: 1988-1993
Varieties: HN 3312
Series: Miniatures

U.S.:	$175.00
Can.:	$225.00
U.K.:	£100.00

HN 3219
Sara
Style Two
Designer: M. Davies
Remodeller: P. Gee
Height: 3 ¾", 9.5 cm
Colour: Pink and green
Issued: 1988-1998
Varieties: HN 3249
Series: Miniatures

U.S.:	$175.00
Can.:	$225.00
U.K.:	£100.00

HN 3220
Fragrance
Style Two
Designer: M. Davies
Remodeller: P. Gee
Height: 3 ¾", 9.5 cm
Colour: Gold
Issued: 1988-1992
Varieties: HN 3250
Series: Miniatures

U.S.:	$175.00
Can.:	$225.00
U.K.:	£100.00

HN 3221
Country Rose
Designer: M. Davies
Height: 8 ½", 21.6 cm
Colour: White dress,
            red flowers
Issued: 1989-2000
Varieties: Also called "Alyssa"
            HN 4132

U.S.:	$300.00
Can.:	$450.00
U.K.:	£175.00

HN 3222
Kelly
Style One
Designer: M. Davies
Height: 7 ½", 19.1 cm
Colour: White and blue
Issued: 1989
Varieties: HN 2478
Comm.by: Kay's Mail Order
            Catalogue

U.S.:	$300.00
Can.:	$450.00
U.K.:	$175.00

HN 3223
Pamela
Style Two
Designer: M. Davies
Height: 7", 17.8 cm
Colour: Blue and white
Issued: 1989-1989
Varieties: HN 2479
Series: M. Doulton Events

U.S.:	$275.00
Can.:	$425.00
U.K.:	£175.00

HN 3224 - 3227 not issued.

HN 3228
Devotion
Designer: P. Parsons
Height: 9 ½", 24.1 cm
Colour: Pale green
Issued: 1989-1995
Series: Reflections

U.S.:	$400.00
Can.:	$525.00
U.K.:	£250.00

HN 3229
The Geisha
Style Three
Designer: P. Parsons
Height: 9 ½", 24.1 cm
Colour: Flambé
Issued: 1989-1989
Series: 1. Flambé
          2. RDICC

U.S.:	$600.00
Can.:	$775.00
U.K.:	£350.00

HN 3230
HM Queen Elizabeth the Queen Mother as the Duchess of York
Designer: P. Parsons
Height· 9", 22.9 cm
Colour: Pale blue and pink
Issued: 1989 in a limited edition of 9,500
Comm.by: Lawleys By Post

U.S.:	**$ 750.00**
Can.:	**$1,000.00**
U.K.:	**£ 450.00**

HN 3231
Autumntime
Style One
Designer: P. Parsons
Height: 8", 20.3 cm
Colour: Golden brown
Issued: 1989-1989
Series: 1. The Seasons (Series Four)
2. RDICC

U.S.:	**$300.00**
Can.:	**$400.00**
U.K.:	**£175.00**

HN 3232
Anne Bolelyn
Designer: P. Parsons
Height: 8", 20.3 cm
Colour: Red and grey
Issued: 1990 in a limited edition of 9,500
Series: Six Wives of Henry VIII
Comm.by: Lawleys By Post

U.S.:	**$ 750.00**
Can.:	**$1,000.00**
U.K.:	**£ 450.00**

HN 3233
Catherine of Aragon
Designer: P. Parsons
Height: 6 ½", 16.5 cm
Colour: Green, blue and white
Issued· 1990 in a limited edition of 9,500
Series: Six Wives of Henry VIII
Comm.by: Lawleys By Post

U.S.:	**$ 750.00**
Can.:	**$1,000.00**
U.K.:	**£ 450.00**

HN 3234
Paula
Designer: P. Parsons
Height: 7", 17.8 cm
Colour: White and blue
Issued: 1990-1996
Varieties: HN 2906
Series: Vanity Fair Ladies

U.S.:	**$250.00**
Can.:	**$325.00**
U.K.:	**£150.00**

HN 3235
Mother and Child
Style One
Designer: P. Parsons
Height: 7 ½", 19.1 cm
Colour: White and blue
Issued: 1991-1993
Varieties: HN 3348, 3353

U.S.:	**$250.00**
Can.:	**$325.00**
U.K.:	**£150.00**

HN 3236
Falstaff
Style Three
Designer: C. J. Noke
Remodeller: R. Tabbenor
Height: 3 ¾", 9.5 cm
Colour: Brown, yellow and lavender
Issued: 1989-1990
Series: Miniatures

U.S.:	**$125.00**
Can.:	**$165.00**
U.K.:	**£ 75.00**

HN 3237 - 3243 not issued.

HN 3244
Southern Belle
Style Two
Designer: M. Davies
Remodeller: R. Tabbenor
Height: 4", 10.1 cm
Colour: Turquoise and gold
Issued: 1989-1996
Varieties: HN 3174
Series: 1. Miniatures
2. Signature
Comm.by: Lawleys By Post

U.S.:	**$250.00**
Can.:	**$325.00**
U.K.:	**£150.00**

HN 3245
Christmas Morn
Style Two
Designer: M. Davies
Remodeller: R. Tabbenor
Height: 3 ½", 8.9 cm
Colour: Green, blue and gold
Issued: 1991-1996
Varieties: HN 3212
Series: 1. Miniatures
             2. Signature
Comm.by: Lawleys By Post
U.S.:   **$250.00**
Can.:   **$325.00**
U.K.:   **£150.00**

HN 3246
Kirsty
Style Two
Designer: M. Davies
Remodeller: P. Gee
Height: 3 ¾", 9.5 cm
Colour: Purple, gold trim
Issued: 1989-1996
Varieties: HN 3213, 3480, 3743
Series: 1. Miniatures
             2. Signature
Comm.by: Lawleys By Post
U.S.:   **$250.00**
Can.:   **$325.00**
U.K.:   **£150.00**

HN 3247
Elaine
Style Two
Designer: M. Davies
Remodeller: P. Gee
Height: 4", 10.1 cm
Colour: Blue, gold trim
Issued: 1989-1996
Varieties: HN 3214, 3900
Series: 1. Miniatures
             2. Signature
Comm.by: Lawleys By Post
U.S.:   **$250.00**
Can.:   **$325.00**
U.K.:   **£150.00**

HN 3248
Ninette
Style Two
Designer: M. Davies
Remodeller: P. Gee
Height: 3 ½", 8.9 cm
Colour: Red, green and gold
Issued: 1989-1996
Varieties: HN 3215, 3901
Series: 1. Miniatures
             2. Signature
U.S.:   **$250.00**
Can.:   **$325.00**
U.K.:   **£150.00**

HN 3249
Sara
Style Two
Designer: M. Davies
Remodeller: P. Gee
Height: 3 ¾", 9.5 cm
Colour: Blue and pink,
             gold trim
Issued: 1989-1996
Varieties: HN 3219
Series: 1. Miniatures
             2. Signature
U.S.:   **$250.00**
Can.:   **$325.00**
U.K.:   **£150.00**

HN 3250
Fragrance
Style Two
Designer: M. Davies
Remodeller: P. Gee
Height: 3 ¾", 9.5 cm
Colour: Red, gold trim
Issued: 1989-1992
Varieties: HN 3220
Series: 1. Miniatures
             2. Signature
Comm.by: Lawleys By Post
U.S.:   **$250.00**
Can.:   **$325.00**
U.K.:   **£150.00**

HN 3251
May
Style One
Designer: D. V. Tootle
Height: 8", 20.3 cm
Colour: Blue, red and pink
Issued: 1989 in a limited
             edition of 2,000
Varieties: HN 2746
Comm.by: U.S.A. Direct Mail
             Service
U.S.:   **$300.00**
Can.:   **$425.00**
U.K.:   **£175.00**

HN 3252
Fiona
Style Three
Designer: D. V. Tootle
Height: 7", 17.8 cm
Colour: Red
Issued: 1989-1992
U.S.:   **$300.00**
Can.:   **$425.00**
U.K.:   **£175.00**

HN 3253
Cheryl
Designer: D. V. Tootle
Height: 7 ½", 19.1 cm
Colour: Red and white
Issued: 1989-1994

U.S.: $375.00
Can.: $525.00
U.K.: £225.00

HN 3254
Happy Anniversary
Style Two
Designer: D. V. Tootle
Height: 12", 30.5 cm
Colour: White
Issued: 1989 to the present
Series: Images

U.S.: $240.00
Can.: $345.00
U.K.: £110.00

HN 3255
Madeleine
Designer: D. V. Tootle
Height: 7 ½", 19.1 cm
Colour: Blue, pink and cream
Issued: 1989-1992

U.S.: $275.00
Can.: $375.00
U.K.: £165.00

HN 3256
**Queen Victoria and
Prince Albert**
Designer: D. V. Tootle
Height: 9 ¼", 20.3 cm
Colour: Yellow-pink, cream
and red
Issued: 1990 in a limited
edition of 2,500
Comm.by: Lawleys By Post

U.S.: $1,000.00
Can.: $1,300.00
U.K.: £ 600.00

HN 3257
Sophie
Style Two
Designer: D. V. Tootle
Height: 8", 20.3 cm
Colour: Blue and red
Issued: 1990-1992

U.S.: $325.00
Can.: $450.00
U.K.: £200.00

HN 3258
Dawn
Style Two
Designer: D. V. Tootle
Height: 8", 20.3 cm
Colour: Purple, red and white
Issued: 1990-1992

U.S.: $275.00
Can.: $425.00
U.K.: £175.00

HN 3259
Ann
Style Two
Designer: D. V. Tootle
Height: 8", 20.3 cm
Colour: Pink, green and blue
Issued: 1990-1996
Varieties: Also called 'Lauren'
(Style One) HN 3290

U.S.: $375.00
Can.: $525.00
U.K.: £225.00

HN 3260
Jane
Style Three
Designer: D. V. Tootles
Height: 7 ¾", 19.7 cm
Colour: Green, blue and
yellow
Issued: 1990-1993

U.S.: $325.00
Can.: $450.00
U.K.: £200.00

HN 3261
The Town Crier
Style Two
Designer: M. Davies
Remodeller: R. Tabbenor
Height: 4", 10.1 cm
Colour: Purple, green
                      and black
Issued: 1989-1991
Series: Miniatures

U.S.:	**$150.00**
Can.:	**$200.00**
U.K.:	**£ 90.00**

HN 3262
Good King Wenceslas
Style Two
Designer: M. Davies
Remodeller: R. Tabbenor
Height: 4", 10.1 cm
Colour: Black and purple
Issued: 1989-1992
Series: Miniatures

U.S.:	**$150.00**
Can.:	**$200.00**
U.K.:	**£ 90.00**

HN 3263
Beatrice
Designer: M. Davies
Height: 7", 17.8 cm
Colour: Blue flowered dress
Issued: 1989-1998
Varieties: HN 3631; also called
                'Kathryn' (Style One)
                HN 3413, 'Lucy' (Style
                Two) HN 3653,
                'Summer Serenade'
                HN 3610; 'Wildflower
                of the Month'

U.S.:	**$225.00**
Can.:	**$300.00**
U.K.:	**£120.00**

HN 3264
Alison
Designer: M. Davies
Height: 7 ½", 19.1 cm
Colour: White and pastel pink
Issued: 1989-1993
Varieties: HN 2336

U.S.:	**$225.00**
Can.:	**$300.00**
U.K.:	**£120.00**

HN 3265
Lisa
Style One
Designer: M. Davies
Height: 7 ½", 19.1 cm
Colour: White and rose
Issued: 1989-1995
Varieties: HN 2310, 2394

U.S.:	**$225.00**
Can.:	**$325.00**
U.K.:	**£125.00**

HN 3266
Diana
Style Two
Designer: M. Davies
Height: 8", 20.3 cm
Colour: Pink, blue and white
Issued: 1990-1990
Varieties: HN 2468
Series: M. Doulton Events

U.S.:	**$300.00**
Can.:	**$450.00**
U.K.:	**£200.00**

HN 3267
Salome
Style Two
Designer: M. Davies
Height: 9 ½", 24.1cm
Colour: Red, blue, lavender
                and green
Issued: 1990 in a limited
                edition of 1,000

U.S.:	**$1,100.00**
Can.:	**$1,500.00**
U.K.:	**£ 650.00**

HN 3268
Buttercup
Style Two
Designer: M. Davies
Remodeller: R. Tabbenor
Height: 4", 10.1 cm
Colour: Green
Issued: 1990-1998
Varieties   HN 3908
Series: Miniatures

U.S.:	**$175.00**
Can.:	**$225.00**
U.K.:	**£100.00**

HN 3269
Christine
Style Three
Designer:	M. Davies
Remodeller:	P. Gee
Height:	3 ¾", 9.5 cm
Colour:	Orange and pink
Issued:	1990-1994
Varieties:	HN 3337
Series:	Miniatures

U.S.:	**$175.00**
Can.:	**$225.00**
U.K.:	**£100.00**

HN 3270
Karen
Style Three
Designer:	M. Davies
Remodeller:	R. Tabbenor
Height:	4", 10.1 cm
Colour:	Red
Issued:	1990-1995
Varieties:	HN 3338, 3749
Series:	Miniatures

U.S.:	**$175.00**
Can.:	**$250.00**
U.K.:	**£125.00**

HN 3271
Guy Fawkes
Style Two
Designer:	C. J. Nokes
Remodeller:	P. Gee
Height:	4", 10.1 cm
Colour:	Red and black
Issued:	1989-1991
Series:	Miniatures

U.S.:	**$125.00**
Can.:	**$165.00**
U.K.:	**& 75.00**

HN 3272
Dick Turpin
Style One
Designer:	G. Tongue
Height:	12", 30.5 cm
Colour:	Brown and black
Issued:	1989 in a limited edition of 5,000
Comm.by:	Lawleys By Post

U.S.:	**$ 800.00**
Can.:	**$1,050.00**
U.K.:	**£ 475.00**

HN 3273
Annabel
Designer:	R. Tabbenor
Height:	6", 15.2 cm
Colour:	White and blue
Issued:	1989-1992

U.S.:	**$300.00**
Can.:	**$425.00**
U.K.:	**£175.00**

HN 3274
Over The Threshold
Designer:	R. Tabbenor
Height:	12", 30.5 cm
Colour:	White
Issued:	1989-1998
Series:	Images

U.S.:	**$225.00**
Can.:	**$300.00**
U.K.:	**£135.00**

HN 3275
Will He, Won't He
Designer:	R. Tabbenor
Height:	9", 22.9 cm
Colour:	Green
Issued:	1990-1994
Series:	Clowns

U.S.:	**$350.00**
Can.:	**$450.00**
U.K.:	**£200.00**

HN 3276
Teeing Off
Designer:	R. Tabbenor
Height:	9", 22.9 cm
Colour:	Yellow and green
Issued:	1990-1997

U.S.:	**$325.00**
Can.:	**$450.00**
U.K.:	**£200.00**

HN 3277
The Carpet Seller
(Seated)
Style Three
Designer: R. Tabbenor
Height: 7 ½", 19.0 cm
Colour: Red
Issued: 1990-1995
Series: Flambé

U.S.:	**$600.00**
Can.:	**$775.00**
U.K.:	**£350.00**

HN 3278
Lamp Seller
Designer: R. Tabbenor
Height: 9", 22.9 cm
Colour: Red
Issued: 1990-1995
Series: Flambé

U.S.:	**$700.00**
Can.:	**$900.00**
U.K.:	**£425.00**

HN 3279
Winning Put
Designer: R. Tabbenor
Height: 8", 20.3 cm
Colour: Blue and yellow
Issued: 1991-1995

U.S.:	**$300.00**
Can.:	**$400.00**
U.K.:	**£175.00**

HN 3280
Bridesmaid
Style Six
Designer: R. Tabbenor
Height: 8 ½", 21.6 cm
Colour: White
Issued: 1991-1999
Series: Images

U.S.:	**$125.00**
Can.:	**$165.00**
U.K.:	**£ 70.00**

HN 3281
Bride and Groom
Designer: R. Tabbenor
Height: 6 ¼", 15.9 cm
Colour: White
Issued: 1991-2000
Series: Images

U.S.:	**$125.00**
Can.:	**$165.00**
U.K.:	**£ 70.00**

HN 3282
First Steps
Style Two
Designer: R. Tabbenor
Height: 9 ½", 24.0 cm
Colour: White
Issued: 1991-2001
Series: Images

U.S.:	**$225.00**
Can.:	**$300.00**
U.K.:	**£125.00**

HN 3283
Tumbling
Designer: D. V. Tootle
Height: 8 ¾", 22.2 cm
Colour: White, yellow,
               blue and green
Issued: 1990-1994
Varieties: 3289; also called
               'Tumbler' HN 3183
Series: Clowns

U.S.:	**$425.00**
Can.:	**$550.00**
U.K.:	**£250.00**

HN 3284
The Bride
Style Four
Designer: D. V. Tootle
Height: 8 ¼", 21.0 cm
Colour: White
Issued: 1990-1997
Varieties: HN 3285

U.S.:	**$275.00**
Can.:	**$375.00**
U.K.:	**£165.00**

HN 3285
The Bride
Style Four
Designer: D. V. Tootle
Height: 8 ¼", 21.0 cm
Colour: Ivory
Issued: 1990-1996
Varieties: HN 3284

U.S.:	**$275.00**
Can.:	**$375.00**
U.K.:	**£165.00**

HN 3286
Alexandra
Style Two
Designer: D. V. Tootle
Height: 7 ¾", 19.7 cm
Colour: Yellow and peach
Issued: 1990-2000
Varieties: HN 3292

U.S.:	**$350.00**
Can.:	**$475.00**
U.K.:	**£200.00**

HN 3287
Harlequin
Style Two
Designer: D. V. Tootle
Height: 12 ½", 31.7 cm
Colour: Black, gold and yellow
Issued: 1993-1993
Varieties: HN 2737, 4058
Comm.by: Harrods

U.S.:	**$2,000.00**
Can.:	**$2,500.00**
U.K.:	**£1,200.00**

HN 3288
Columbine
Style Three
Designer: D. V. Tootle
Height: 12 ½", 31.7 cm
Colour: Red, yellow, black and gold
Issued: 1993-1993
Varieties: HN 2738, 4059
Comm.by: Harrods

U.S.:	**$2,000.00**
Can.:	**$2,500.00**
U.K.:	**£1,200.00**

HN 3289
Tumbling
Designer: D. V. Tootle
Height: 8 ¾", 22.2 cm
Colour: Pink and blue
Issued: 1991 in a limited edition of 2,500
Varieties: HN 3283; also called 'Tumbler' HN 3183
Series: Clowns
Comm.by: National Playing Fields Association

U.S.:	**$400.00**
Can.:	**$525.00**
U.K.:	**£250.00**

HN 3290
Lauren
Style One
Designer: D. V. Tootle
Height: 8", 20.3 cm
Colour: Mauve and yellow
Issued: 1992-1992
Varieties: Also called 'Ann' (Style Two), HN 3259
Comm.by: Great Universal Stores

U.S.:	**$400.00**
Can.:	**$525.00**
U.K.:	**£250.00**

HN 3291
Tracy
Designer: D.V. Toole
Height: 7 ½", 19.1 cm
Colour: White and pink
Issued: 1993-1999
Varieties: HN 2736

U.S.:	**$250.00**
Can.:	**$325.00**
U.K.:	**£150.00**

Exclusive t o U.S.A.

HN 3292
Alexandra
Style Two
Designer: D. V. Tootle
Height: 7 ¾", 19.7 cm
Colour: Pink and white
Issued: 1994-2002
Varieties: HN 3286

U.S.:	**$350.00**
Can.:	**$450.00**
U.K.:	**$200.00**

HN 3293
Tip-toe
Designer: A. Hughes
Height: 9", 22.9 cm
Colour: Black, white and yellow
Issued: 1990-1994
Varieties: Also called 'Joker' (Style One) HN 3196
Series: Clowns

U.S.:	**$400.00**
Can.:	**$525.00**
U.K.:	**£250.00**

HN 3294
Daddy's Joy
Designer: A. Hughes
Height: 8", 20.3 cm
Colour: Pink, yellow and white
Issued: 1990 in a limited edition of 12,500
Comm.by: Lawleys By Post

U.S.:	**$400.00**
Can.:	**$525.00**
U.K.:	**£250.00**

HN 3295
The Homecoming
Designer: A. Hughes
Height: 7", 17.8 cm
Colour: Blue, pink and green
Issued: 1990 in a limited edition of 9,500
Series: Children of the Blitz
Comm.by: Lawleys By Post

U.S.:	**$500.00**
Can.:	**$650.00**
U.K.:	**£300.00**

HN 3296
Fantasy
Designer: A. Hughes
Height: 12 ½", 31.7 cm
Colour: White
Issued: 1990-1992
Series: Reflections

U.S.:	**$600.00**
Can.:	**$750.00**
U.K.:	**£350.00**

HN 3297
Milestone
Designer: A. Hughes
Height: 7 ¼", 18.4 cm
Colour: Red and blue
Issued: 1990-1994

U.S.:	**$400.00**
Can.:	**$525.00**
U.K.:	**£250.00**

HN 3298
Hold Tight
Designer: A. Hughes
Height: 8 ½", 21.6 cm
Colour: Red, blue and green
Issued: 1990-1993

U.S.:	**$600.00**
Can.:	**$750.00**
U.K.:	**£350.00**

HN 3299
Welcome Home
Designer: A. Hughes
Height: 8 ½", 21.6 cm
Colour: Grey and turquoise
Issued: 1991 in a limited edition of 9,500
Series: Children of the Blitz
Comm.by: Lawleys By Post

U.S.:	**$500.00**
Can.:	**$650.00**
U.K.:	**£300.00**

HN 3300
Dressing Up
Style Two
Designer: A. Hughes
Height: 6 ¾", 17.5 cm
Colour: Yellow and blue
Issued: 1991 in a limited edition of 9,500
Comm.by: Lawleys By Post

U.S.:	**$400.00**
Can.:	**$525.00**
U.K.:	**£250.00**

HN 3301
Santa's Helper
Designer: A. Hughes
Height: 6 ½", 16.5 cm
Colour: Green, red and white
Issued: 1991-1995
Comm.by: Lawleys By Post

U.S.:	**$400.00**
Can.:	**$525.00**
U.K.:	**£250.00**

HN 3302
Please Sir
Designer: A. Hughes
Height: 8", 20.3 cm
Colour: Blue, grey and beige
Issued: 1992 in a limited
            edition of 7,500
Comm.by: Lawleys By Post
            'National Children's
            Home'

U.S.:	**$400.00**
Can.:	**$525.00**
U.K.:	**£250.00**

HN 3303
Tender Moment
Style One
Designer: M. Davies
Height: 7", 17.8 cm
Colour: Pink
Issued: 1990 1997
Varieties: Also called 'Nicola'
           HN 2804, 2839
Series: Vanity Fair Ladies

U.S.:	**$250.00**
Can.:	**$350.00**
U.K.:	**£150.00**

HN 3304
Samantha
Style Two
Designer: M. Davies
Height: 7 ½", 19.1 cm
Colour: White-green dress,
           flowered border
Issued: 1990-1996
Varieties: Also called 'First
           Dance' HN 2803

U.S.:	**$250.00**
Can.:	**$350.00**
U.K.:	**£150.00**

HN 3305
Kathy
Style Two
Designer: M. Davies
Height: 7 ¼", 18.4 cm
Colour: Blue-white dress,
           flowered border
Issued: 1990-1996
Varieties: Also called 'Lynne'
           (Style One) HN 2329,
           3740

U.S.:	**$275.00**
Can.:	**$400.00**
U.K.:	**£165.00**

HN 3306
Megan
Style One
Designer: M. Davies
Height: 7 ½", 19.0 cm
Colour: White and yellow
Issued: 1991-1994
Series: Vanity Fair Ladies

U.S.:	**$200.00**
Can.:	**$250.00**
U.K.:	**£125.00**

HN 3307
Elaine
Style One
Designer: M. Davies
Height: 7 ¼", 18.4 cm
Colour: Pink
Issued: 1990-2000
Varieties: HN 2791, 3741, 4130

U.S.:	**$325.00**
Can.:	**$450.00**
U.K.:	**£200.00**

HN 3308
Sara
Style One
Designer: M. Davies
Height: 7 ¾", 19.7 cm
Colour: Blue, pink and white
Issued: 1990-1996
Varieties: HN 2265

U.S.:	**$350.00**
Can.:	**$450.00**
U.K.:	**£200.00**

HN 3309
Summer Rose
Style Two
Designer: M. Davies
Height: 7 ½", 19.1 cm
Colour: White with
           pink flowers
Issued: 1991-1997
Varieties: Also called 'Denise'
           (Style Three) HN 2477

U.S.:	**$250.00**
Can.:	**$375.00**
U.K.:	**£150.00**

HN 3310
Diana
Style Three
Designer: M. Davies
Remodeller: D. Frith
Height: 4 ¼", 10.8 cm
Colour: Pale pink and blue
Issued: 1991-1995
Series: Miniatures

U.S.:	**$175.00**
Can.:	**$225.00**
U.K.:	**£100.00**

HN 3311
Fragrance
Style One
Designer: M. Davies
Height: 7 ¼", 18.4 cm
Colour: Red
Issued: 1991-1991
Varieties: HN 2334
Series: M. Doulton Events

U.S.:	**$275.00**
Can.:	**$375.00**
U.K.:	**£175.00**

HN 3312
Sunday Best
Style Two
Designer: M. Davies
Remodeller: P. Gee
Height: 3", 7.6 cm,
Colour: Green, blue, gold
Issued: 1991-1993
Varieties: HN 3218
Series: 1. Miniatures
            2. Signature
Comm.by: Lawleys By Post

U.S.:	**$250.00**
Can.:	**$350.00**
U.K.:	**£150.00**

HN 3313
Morning Breeze
Designer: P. Gee
Height: 8", 20.3 cm
Colour: Mottled blue
          and orange
Issued: 1990-1994

U.S.:	**$300.00**
Can.:	**$400.00**
U.K.:	**£175.00**

HN 3314
Confucius
Designer: P. Gee
Height: 9", 22.9 cm
Colour: Flambé
Issued: 1990-1995
Series: Flambé

U.S.:	**$600.00**
Can.:	**$775.00**
U.K.:	**£350.00**

HN 3315
Waiting For A Train
Designer: P. Gee
Height: 8 ½", 21.6 cm
Colour: Cashmere coat, black
          hat, 'biscuit' finish
Issued: 1991 in a limited
          edition of 9,500
Comm.by: Lawleys By Post

U.S.:	**$400.00**
Can.:	**$525.00**
U.K.:	**£250.00**

HN 3316
Amy
Style Two
Designer: P. Gee
Height: 8", 20.3 cm
Colour: Blue and rose
Issued: 1991-1991
Series: Figure of the Year

U.S.:	**$ 900.00**
Can.:	**$1,350.00**
U.K.:	**£ 600.00**

HN 3317
Countess of Harrington
Designer: P. Gee
Height: 9 ½", 24.3 cm
Colour: Pale green
Issued: 1992 in a limited
           edition of 5,000
Series: Reynolds Ladies

U.S.:	**$650.00**
Can.:	**$850.00**
U.K.:	**£400.00**

HN 3318
Lady Worsley
Designer: P. Gee
Height: 9 ½", 24.3 cm
Colour: Red, black and gold
Issued: 1991 in a limited
           edition of 5,000
Series: Reynolds Ladies

U.S.:	**$500.00**
Can.:	**$650.00**
U.K.:	**£300.00**

HN 3319
Mrs. Hugh Bonfoy
Designer: P. Gee
Height: 9 ½", 24.3 cm
Colour: Blue-pink
Issued: 1992 in a limited
           edition of 5,000
Series: Reynolds Ladies

U.S.:	**$500.00**
Can.:	**$650.00**
U.K.:	**£300.00**

HN 3320
Countess Spencer
Designer: P. Gee
Height: 9 ½", 24.3 cm
Colour: Red, blue and white
Issued: 1993 in a limited
           edition of 5,000
Series: Reynolds Ladies

U.S.:	**$500.00**
Can.:	**$650.00**
U.K.:	**£300.00**

HN 3321
Gail
Style Two
Designer: P. Gee
Height: 3 ¾", 9.5 cm
Colour: Red and white
Issued: 1992-1997
Series: Miniatures

U.S.:	**$175.00**
Can.:	**$225.00**
U.K.:	**£100.00**

HN 3322
Celeste
Style Two
Designer: P. Gee
Height: 8", 20.3 cm
Colour: Yellow
Issued: 1992-1992
Varieties: Also called 'Isadora'
            HN 2938
Comm.by: Great Universal
            Stores

U.S.:	**$325.00**
Can.:	**$425.00**
U.K.:	**£200.00**

HN 3323
June
Style Five
Designer: R. Tabbenor
Height: 5 ¼", 13.3 cm
Colour: White, pink flowers
Issued: 1990 to the present
Varieties: Also called 'Amanda'
            HN 2996, 3406, 3632,
            3634, 3635
Series: Flower of the Month,
            Child

U.S.:	**$ 36.95**
Can.:	**$128.50**
U.K.:	**N/I**

HN 3324
July
Style Two
Designer: R. Tabbenor
Height: 5 ¼", 13.3 cm
Colour: White, blue flowers
Issued: 1990 to the present
Varieties: Also called 'Amanda'
            HN 2996, 3406, 3632,
            3634, 3635
Series: Flower of the Month,
            Child

U.S.:	**$ 36.95**
Can.:	**$128.50**
U.K.:	**N/I**

HN 3325
August
Style Two
Designer: R. Tabbenor
Height: 5 ¼", 13.3 cm
Colour: White, purple flowers
Issued: 1990 to the present
Varieties: Also called 'Amanda'
HN 2996, 3406, 3632,
3634, 3635
Series: Flower of the Month,
Child

U.S.:	$ 36.95
Can.:	$128.50
U.K.:	N/I

HN 3326
September
Style Two
Designer: R. Tabbenor
Height: 5 ¼", 13.3 cm
Colour: White, lilac flowers
Issued: 1990 to the present
Varieties: Also called 'Amanda'
HN 2996, 3406, 3632,
3634, 3635
Series: Flower of the Month,
Child

U.S.:	$ 36.95
Can.:	$128.50
U.K.:	N/I

HN 3327
October
Style Two
Designer: R. Tabbenor
Height: 5 ¼", 13.3 cm
Colour: White, lilac/white flowers
Issued: 1990 to the present
Varieties: Also called 'Amanda'
HN 2996, 3406, 3632,
3634, 3635
Series: Flower of the Month,
Child

U.S.:	$ 36.95
Can.:	$128.50
U.K.:	N/I

HN 3328
November
Style Two
Designer: R. Tabbenor
Height: 5 ¼", 13.3 cm
Colour: White, lilac flowers
Issued: 1990 to the present
Varieties: Also called 'Amanda'
HN 2996, 3406, 3632,
3634, 3635
Series: Flower of the Month,
Child

U.S.:	$ 36.95
Can.:	$128.50
U.K.:	N/I

HN 3329
December
Style Two
Designer: R. Tabbenor
Height: 5 ¼", 13.3 cm
Colour: White, holly berries
Issued: 1990 to the present
Varieties: Also called 'Amanda'
HN 2996, 3406, 3632,
3634, 3635
Series: Flower of the Month,
Child

U.S.:	$ 36.95
Can.:	$128.50
U.K.:	N/I

HN 3330
January
Style Two
Designer: R. Tabbenor
Height: 5 ¼", 13.3 cm
Colour: White, yellow flowers
Issued: 1990 to the present
Varieties: Also called 'Amanda'
HN 2996, 3406, 3632,
3634, 3635
Series: Flower of the Month,
Child

U.S.:	$ 36.95
Can.:	$128.50
U.K.:	N/I

HN 3331
February
Style Two
Designer: R. Tabbenor
Height: 5 ¼", 13.3 cm
Colour: White, blue flowers
Issued: 1990 to the present
Varieties: Also called 'Amanda'
HN 2996, 3406, 3632,
3634, 3635
Series: Flower of the Month,
Child

U.S.:	$ 36.95
Can.:	$128.50
U.K.:	N/I

HN 3332
March
Style Two
Designer: R. Tabbenor
Height: 5 ¼", 13.3 cm
Colour: White, purple flowers
Issued: 1990 to the present
Varieties: Also called 'Amanda'
HN 2996, 3406, 3632,
3634, 3635
Series: Flower of the Month,
Child

U.S.:	$ 36.95
Can.:	$128.50
U.K.:	N/I

HN 3333
April
Style Two
Designer: R. Tabbenor
Height: 5 ¼", 13.3 cm
Colour: White, purple flowers
Issued: 1990 to the present
Varieties: Also called 'Amanda'
HN 2996, 3406, 3632,
3634, 3635
Series: Flower of the Month,
Child

U.S.:	$ 36.95
Can.:	$128.50
U.K.:	N/I

HN 3334
May
Style Three
Designer: R. Tabbenor
Height: 5 ¼", 13.3 cm
Colour: White with lily-of-
the-valley flowers
Issued: 1990 to the present
Varieties: Also called 'Amanda'
HN 2996, 3406, 3632,
3634, 3635
Series: Flower of the Month,
Child

U.S.:	$ 36.95
Can.:	$128.50
U.K.:	N/I

HN 3335
Jester
Style Three
Designer: C. J. Noke
Remodeller: R. Tabbenor
Height: 4", 10.1 cm
Colour: Brown and purple
Issued: 1990-1990
Series: 1. Miniatures
2. RDICC

U.S.:	$150.00
Can.:	$200.00
U.K.:	£ 90.00

HN 3336
Fair Lady
Style Two
Designer: M. Davies
Remodeller: P. Gee
Height: 3 ½", 8.9 cm
Colour: Red, purple, gold
Issued: 1991-1994
Varieties: HN 3216
Series: 1. Miniatures
2. Signature
Comm.by: Lawleys By Post

U.S.:	$250.00
Can.:	$350.00
U.K.:	£ 90.00

HN 3337
Christine
Style Three
Designer: M. Davies
Remodeller: P. Gee
Height: 3 ½", 8.9 cm
Colour: Yellow, black, gold
Issued: 1991-1994
Varieties: HN 3269
Series: 1. Miniatures
2. Signature
Comm.by: Lawleys By Post

U.S.:	$250.00
Can.:	$350.00
U.K.:	£150.00

HN 3338
Karen
Style Three
Designer: M. Davies
Remodeller: R. Tabbenor
Height: 3 ½", 8.9 cm
Colour: Purple, gold trim
Issued: 1991-1994
Varieties: HN 3270, 3749
Series: 1. Miniatures
2. Signature
Comm.by: Lawleys By Post

U.S.:	$250.00
Can.:	$350.00
U.K.:	£150.00

HN 3339
Olivia
Style Two
Designer: M. Davies
Height: 8", 20.3 cm
Colour: Red
Issued: 1992
Varieties: Also called 'Ninette'
(Style One) HN 2379,
3417
Comm.by: Great Universal
Stores

U.S.:	$375.00
Can.:	$525.00
U.K.:	£225.00

NOTE ON PRICING

As with all price guides, prices listed in this catalogue are suggested retail values. This is not a fixed price catalogue and figurines will be offered for sale at higher, lower, or catalogue prices, depending upon the supply-demand factors of the market place.

When our first edition was published in 1981 the Royal Doulton market was divided into three or four different geographical areas and pricing was based on each individual area.

In 2004 this is all changing, the global market place is coming to collectables. Our prices, while based on many different avenues that offer figurines for sale, are slowly turning into foreign exchange transactions between the former market areas. For now the collector is able to shop globally.

HN 3340
Kay
Designer: M. Davies
Height: 7 ¼", 18.4 cm
Colour: Dark blue and white
Issued: 1991
Varieties: Also called 'Fair
 Lady' (Style One)
 HN 2193, 2832,
 2835
Comm.by: Sears, Canada

U.S.:	**$250.00**
Can.:	**$375.00**
U.K.:	**£150.00**

HN 3341
January - Style Three
Designer: M. Davies
Height: 7 ½", 19.0 cm
Colour: White/blue, snowdrops
Issued: 1991-1991
Varieties: Also called 'Beatrice'
 HN 3263, 3631;
 'Kathryn' (Style One)
 HN 3413; 'Lucy'
 HN 3653; 'Summer
 Serenade' HN 3610
Series: Wildflower / Month

U.S.:	**$225.00**
Can.:	**$300.00**
U.K.:	**£135.00**

HN 3342
February - Style Three
Designer: M. Davies
Height: 7 ½", 19.0 cm
Colour: White/pink, anemones
Issued: 1991-1991
Varieties: 'Beatrice' HN 3263,
 3631; 'Kathryn'
 HN 3413; 'Lucy'
 HN 3653; 'Summer
 Serenade' HN 3610
Series: Wildflower / Month

U.S.:	**$225.00**
Can.:	**$300.00**
U.K.:	**£135.00**

HN 3343
March - Style Three
Designer: M. Davies
Height: 7 ½", 19.0 cm
Colour: White, violet flowers
Issued: 1991-1991
Varieties: 'Beatrice' HN 3263,
 3631; 'Kathryn'
 HN 3653; 'Lucy'
 HN 3653; 'Summer
 Serenade' HN 3610
Series: Wildflower / Month

U.S.:	**$225.00**
Can.:	**$300.00**
U.K.:	**£135.00**

HN 3344
April - Style Three
Designer: M. Davies
Height: 7 ½", 19.0 cm
Colour: White, primroses
Issued: 1991-1991
Varieties: 'Beatrice' HN 3263,
 3631; 'Kathryn'
 HN 3653; 'Lucy'
 HN 3653; 'Summer
 Serenade' HN 3610
Series: Wildflower / Month

U.S.:	**$225.00**
Can.:	**$300.00**
U.K.:	**£135.00**

HN 3345
May - Style Four
Designer: M. Davies
Height: 7 ½", 19.0 cm
Colour: White, lady's smock
Issued: 1991-1991
Varieties: 'Beatrice' HN 3263,
 'Kathryn' HN 3653;
 'Lucy' HN 3653; 3631;
 'Summer Serenade'
 HN 3610
Series: Wildflower / Month

U.S.:	**$225.00**
Can.:	**$300.00**
U.K.:	**£135.00**

HN 3346
June - Style Six
Designer: M. Davies
Height: 7 ½", 19.0 cm
Colour: White, briar roses
Issued: 1991-1991
Varieties: 'Beatrice' HN 3263,
 3631; 'Kathryn'
 HN 3653; 'Lucy'
 HN 3653; 'Summer
 Serenade' HN 3610
Series: Wildflower / Month

U.S.:	**$225.00**
Can.:	**$300.00**
U.K.:	**£135.00**

HN 3347
July - Style Three
Designer: M. Davies
Height: 7 ½", 19.0 cm
Colour: White, hare bells
Issued: 1991-1991
Varieties: 'Beatrice' HN 3263,
 3631; 'Kathryn'
 HN 3413; 'Lucy'
 HN 3653; 'Summer
 Serenade' HN 3610
Series: Wildflower / Month

U.S.:	**$225.00**
Can.:	**$300.00**
U.K.:	**£135.00**

HN 3348
Mother and Child
Style One
Designer: P. Parsons
Height: 7 ½", 19.0 cm
Colour: White and pink
Issued: 1991-1993
Varieties: HN 3235, 3353

U.S.:	$250.00
Can.:	$325.00
U.K.:	£150.00

HN 3349
Jane Seymour
Designer: P. Parsons
Height: 9", 22.9 cm
Colour: Orange and blue
Issued: 1991 in a limited
           edition of 9,500
Series: Six Wives of
           Henry VIII
Comm.by: Lawleys By Post

U.S.:	$ 850.00
Can.:	$1,100.00
U.K.:	£ 500.00

HN 3350
Henry VIII
Style Three
Designer: P. Parsons
Height: 9 ½", 24.0 cm
Colour: Gold-brown and red
Issued: 1991 in a limited
           edition of 1991
Comm.by: Lawleys By Post

U.S.:	$2,600.00
Can.:	$3,750.00
U.K.:	£1,500.00

HN 3351
Congratulations
Designer: P. Gee
Height: 11", 27.9 cm
Colour: White
Issued: 1991 to the present
Series: Images

U.S.:	N/I
Can.:	$345.00
U.K.:	£ 69.00

HN 3352 not issued.

HN 3353
Mother and Child
Style One
Designer: P. Parsons
Height: 7 ½", 19.0 cm
Colour: White
Issued: 1992-1999
Varieties: HN 3235, 3348
Series: Vanity Fair Series

U.S.:	$250.00
Can.:	$325.00
U.K.:	£150.00

HN 3354
Yours Forever
Designer: P. Parsons
Height: 8", 20.3 cm
Colour: Yellow and pink
Issued: 1992 Canada,
           1993 Worldwide-1997
Varieties: Also called 'Kimberley'
           (Style One) HN 2969
Series: Vanity Fair Ladies

U.S.:	$225.00
Can.:	$300.00
U.K.:	£135.00

HN 3355
Just For You
Style One
Designer: P. Parsons
Height: 8 ¼", 21 cm
Colour: White
Issued: 1992-1998
Series: Vanity Fair Ladies

U.S.:	$225.00
Can.:	$300.00
U.K.:	£135.00

HN 3356
Anne of Cleves
Designer: P. Parsons
Height: 6 ¼", 15.9 cm
Colour: Green and gold
Issued: 1991 in a limited
           edition of 9,500
Series: Six Wives of
           Henry VIII
Comm.by: Lawleys By Post

U.S.:	$1,000.00
Can.:	$1,300.00
U.K.:	£ 600.00

HN 3357
Marie
Style Three
Designer: P. Parson
Height: 6", 15.2 cm
Colour: Pink and yellow
Issued: 1992
Varieties: Also called 'Heather'
HN 2956
Comm.by: Great Universal
Stores

U.S.:	$275.00
Can.:	$375.00
U.K.:	£165.00

HN 3358
Loyal Friend
Designer: V. Annand
Height: 8 ¼", 20.9 cm
Colour: Pale green and white
Issued: 1991-1995

U.S.:	$450.00
Can.:	$600.00
U.K.:	£275.00

HN 3359
L'Ambitieuse
Designer: V. Annand
Height: 8 ¼", 20.9 cm
Colour: Rose and pale blue
Issued: 1991 in a limited
edition of 5,000
Series: RDICC

U.S.:	$450.00
Can.:	$600.00
U.K.:	£275.00

HN 3360
Katie
Style One
Designer: V. Annand
Height: 8 ¼", 21.0 cm
Colour: Yellow and pink
Issued: 1992-1997

U.S.:	$325.00
Can.:	$425.00
U.K.:	£200.00

HN 3361
First Steps
Style Three
Designer: V. Annand
Height: 5", 12.7 cm
Colour: Pink
Issued: 1992
Series: Little Cherubs
Comm.by: Lawleys By Post

U.S.:	$200.00
Can.:	$250.00
U.K.:	£120.00

HN 3362
Well Done
Designer: V. Annand
Height: 4", 10.1 cm
Colour: Pink
Issued: 1992
Series: Little Cherubs
Comm.by: Lawleys By Post

U.S.:	$200.00
Can.:	$250.00
U.K.:	£120.00

HN 3363
Peek a Boo
Designer: V. Annand
Height: 2 ½", 6.4 cm
Colour: Pink
Issued: 1992
Series: Little Cherubs
Comm.by: Lawleys By Post

U.S.:	$200.00
Can.:	$250.00
U.K.:	£120.00

HN 3364
What Fun
Designer: V. Annand
Height: 3 ¾", 9.5 cm
Colour: Pink
Issued: 1992
Series: Little Cherubs
Comm.by: Lawleys By Post

U.S.:	$200.00
Can.:	$250.00
U.K.:	£120.00

HN 3365
Patricia
Style Four
Designer: V. Annand
Height: 8 ½", 21.6 cm
Colour: Red and black
Issued: 1993-1993
Series: Figure of the Year

U.S.:	**$375.00**
Can.:	**$525.00**
U.K.:	**£225.00**

HN 3366
Wimbledon
Designer: V. Annand
Height: 7 ¾", 19.8 cm
Colour: Cream, pink and green
Issued: 1995 in a limited
edition of 5,000
Series: British Sporting
Heritage

U.S.:	**$650.00**
Can.:	**$850.00**
U.K.:	**£400.00**

HN 3367
Henley
Designer: V. Annand
Height: 8", 20.3 cm
Colour: Green and pink
Issued: 1993 in a limited
edition of 5,000
Series: British Sporting
Heritage

U.S.:	**$550.00**
Can.:	**$750.00**
U.K.:	**£325.00**

HN 3368
Alice
Style Two
Designer: N. Pedley
Height: 8 ¼", 21.0 cm
Colour: Light blue and pink
Issued: 1991-1996

U.S.:	**$350.00**
Can.:	**$450.00**
U.K.:	**£200.00**

HN 3369
Hannah
Style One
Designer: N. Pedley
Height: 8 ¼", 19.0 cm
Colour: Pale pink, yellow
and blue
Issued: 1991-1996
Varieties: HN 3655

U.S.:	**$350.00**
Can.:	**$450.00**
U.K.:	**£200.00**

HN 3370
Bunny's Bedtime
Designer: N. Pedley
Height: 6", 15.2 cm
Colour: Pale blue, pink ribbon
Issued: 1991 in a limited
edition of 9,500
Series: RDICC

U.S.:	**$350.00**
Can.:	**$550.00**
U.K.:	**£200.00**

HN 3371
Puppy Love
Designer: N. Pedley
Height: 7 ½", 19.0 cm
Colour: Yellow-orange
and brown
Issued: 1991 in a limited
edition of 9,500
Series: Age of Innocence

U.S.:	**$400.00**
Can.:	**$525.00**
U.K.:	**£250.00**

HN 3372
Making Friends
Designer: N. Pedley
Height: 5 ½", 14.0 cm
Colour: Pink-yellow and white
Issued: 1991 in a limited
edition of 9,500
Series: Age of Innocence

U.S.:	**$400.00**
Can.:	**$525.00**
U.K.:	**£250.00**

HN 3373
Feeding Time
Designer: N. Pedley
Height: 7", 17.8 cm
Colour: Yellow and white
Issued: 1991 in a limited
edition of 9,500
Series: Age of Innocence

U.S.:	**$400.00**
Can.:	**$525.00**
U.K.:	**£250.00**

HN 3374
Linda
Style Three
Designer: N. Pedley
Height: 8 ¼", 21.0 cm
Colour: Turquoise and white
Issued: 1990 Canada
1991 Worldwide -1995

U.S.:	**$375.00**
Can.:	**$475.00**
U.K.:	**£225.00**

HN 3375
Mary
Style Two
Designer: N. Pedley
Height: 8 ½", 21.6 cm
Colour: Blue and white
Issued: 1992-1992
Series: Figure of the Year

U.S.:	**$650.00**
Can.:	**$925.00**
U.K.:	**£400.00**

HN 3376
Single Red Rose
Designer: N. Pedley
Height: 8", 20.3 cm
Colour: Red
Issued: 1992-1995

U.S.:	**$300.00**
Can.:	**$425.00**
U.K.:	**£175.00**

HN 3377
First Outing
Designer: N. Pedley
Height: 7 ½", 19.0 cm
Colour: Peach and white
Issued: 1992 in a limited
edition of 9,500
Series: Age of Innocence

U.S.:	**$400.00**
Can.:	**$525.00**
U.K.:	**£250.00**

HN 3378
Summer's Day
Style Two
Designer: T. Potts
Height: 8 ½", 21.6 cm
Colour: Rose and white
Issued: 1991-1996

U.S.:	**$300.00**
Can.:	**$400.00**
U.K.:	**£175.00**

HN 3379
Kimberley
Style Two
Designer: T. Potts
Height: 8 ½", 21.6 cm
Colour: White and blue
Issued: 1992-1997
Varieties: HN 3382, 3864
Series: Vanity Fair Ladies

U.S.:	**$300.00**
Can.:	**$400.00**
U.K.:	**£175.00**

HN 3380
Sarah
Style One
Designer: T. Potts
Height: 8", 20.3 cm
Colour: Yellow and pink
Issued: 1993-1993
Series: M. Doulton Events

U.S.:	**$350.00**
Can.:	**$450.00**
U.K.:	**£200.00**

HN 3381
Maria
Designer: T. Potts
Height: 8", 20.3 cm
Colour: White and yellow
Issued: 1993-1999
Series: 1. Roadshow Events
           2. Vanity Fair Ladies

U.S.:	**$250.00**
Can.:	**$325.00**
U.K.:	**£150.00**

HN 3382
Kimberley
Style Two
Designer: T. Potts
Height: 8 ½", 21.6 cm
Colour: Yellow, pink and white
Issued: 1993-1996
Varieties: HN 3379, 3864

U.S.:	**$300.00**
Can.:	**$400.00**
U.K.:	**£175.00**

Exclusive to U.S.A.

HN 3383
Sally
Style Two
Designer: T. Potts
Height: 8 ¼", 21.0 cm
Colour: Red
Issued: 1995-1997
Varieties: HN 3851, 4160
Comm.by: Freemans

U.S.:	**$275.00**
Can.:	**$350.00**
U.K.:	**£150.00**

HN 3384
Sarah
Style Two
Designer: T. Potts
Height: 8", 20.3 cm
Colour: Red and pink
Issued: 1995-2000
Varieties: HN 3852, 3857

U.S.:	**$350.00**
Can.:	**$450.00**
U.K.:	**£200.00**

HN 3385 - 3387 not issued.

HN 3388
Forget Me Not
Style Two
Designer: A. Maslankowski
Height: 6", 15.2 cm
Colour: White
Issued: 1999-2002
Series: Sentiments

U.S.:	**$100.00**
Can.:	**$150.00**
U.K.:	**£ 60.00**

HN 3389
Loving You
Designer: A. Maslankowski
Height: 6 ¼", 15.8 cm
Colour: White
Issued: 1991 to the present
Series: Sentiments

U.S.:	**N/I**
Can.:	**$150.00**
U.K.:	**£ 42.00**

HN 3390
Thank You
Style Two
Designer: A. Maslankowski
Height: 6 ¼", 15.8 cm
Colour: White
Issued: 1991 to the present
Varieties: Also called 'Thank
           You Mother' HN 4251
Series: Sentiments

U.S.:	**N/I**
Can.:	**$150.00**
U.K.:	**£ 42.00**

HN 3391
Reward
Designer: A. Maslankowski
Height: 4 ½", 11.4 cm
Colour: White and pink
Issued: 1992-1996
Series: Vanity Fair Children

U.S.:	**$150.00**
Can.:	**$200.00**
U.K.:	**£ 90.00**

HN 3392
Christopher Columbus
Designer: A. Maslankowski
Height: 12", 30.5 cm
Colour: Green, brown and red
Issued: 1992 in a limited
          edition of 1,492

U.S.:	**$1,400.00**
Can.:	**$1,800.00**
U.K.:	**£ 800.00**

HN 3393
With Love
Designer: A. Maslankowski
Height: 6", 15.2 cm
Colour: White
Issued: 1992 to the present
Varieties: HN 3492
Series: Sentiments

U.S.:	**N/I**
Can.:	**$150.00**
U.K.:	**£ 42.00**

HN 3394
Sweet Dreams
Style Two
Designer: A. Maslankowski
Height: 6", 15.2 cm
Colour: White
Issued: 1992-1998
Series: Sentiments

U.S.:	**$100.00**
Can.:	**$150.00**
U.K.:	**£ 60.00**

HN 3395
Little Ballerina
Designer: A. Maslankowski
Height: 6", 15.2 cm
Colour: White; pink slippers
Issued: 1992 to the present
Varieties: HN 3431

U.S.:	**N/I**
Can.:	**$220.00**
U.K.:	**£ 50.00**

HN 3396
Buddies
Style Two
Designer: A. Maslankowski
Height: 4 ¼", 10.8 cm
Colour: Pink and beige
Issued: 1992-1996
Series: Vanity Fair Children

U.S.:	**$150.00**
Can.:	**$200.00**
U.K.:	**£ 90.00**

HN 3397
Let's Play
Designer: A. Maslankowski
Height: 4", 10.0 cm
Colour: Pale green and white
Issued: 1992-1996
Series: Vanity Fair Children

U.S.:	**$150.00**
Can.:	**$200.00**
U.K.:	**£ 90.00**

HN 3398
The Ace
Designer: R. Tabbenor
Height: 10", 25.4 cm
Colour: White
Issued: 1991-1995

U.S.:	**$250.00**
Can.:	**$325.00**
U.K.:	**£150.00**

HN 3399
Father Christmas
Designer: R. Tabbenor
Height: 9", 22.9 cm
Colour: Red and white
Issued: 1992-1999

U.S.:	**$350.00**
Can.:	**$475.00**
U.K.:	**£200.00**

HN 3400
God Bless You
Designer: R. Tabbenor
Height: 8", 20.3 cm
Colour: White
Issued: 1992 to the present
Series: Images
U.S.:	**N/I**
Can.:	**$160.00**
U.K.:	**£ 29.00**

HN 3401
Gardening Time
Designer: R. Tabbenor
Height: 5", 12.7 cm
Colour: Yellow, blue and green
Issued: 1992-1994
U.S.:	**$275.00**
Can.:	**$350.00**
U.K.:	**£160.00**

HN 3402
Samurai Warrior
Designer: R. Tabbenor
Height: 9", 22.7 cm
Colour: Red
Issued: 1992 in a limited
edition of 950
Series: Flambé
U.S.:	**$600.00**
Can.:	**$775.00**
U.K.:	**£350.00**

HN 3403
Lt. General Ulysses S. Grant
Designer: R. Tabbenor
Height: 11 ¾", 29.8 cm
Colour: Blue and brown
Issued: 1993 in a limited
edition of 5,000
U.S.:	**$1,300.00**
Can.:	**$1,800.00**
U.K.:	**£ 775.00**

HN 3404
General Robert E. Lee
Designer: R. Tabbenor
Height: 11 ½", 29.2 cm
Colour: Grey and brown
Issued: 1993 in a limited
edition of 5,000
U.S.:	**$1,300.00**
Can.:	**$1,800.00**
U.K.:	**£ 775.00**

HN 3405
Field Marshall Montgomery
Designer: R. Tabbenor
Height: 11 ¾", 29.2 cm
Colour: Browns
Issued: 1994 in a limited
edition of 1,944
U.S.:	**$1,250.00**
Can.:	**$1,800.00**
U.K.:	**£ 775.00**

HN 3406
Amanda
Designer: R. Tabbenor
Height: 5 ¼", 13.3 cm
Colour: White and pink
Issued: 1993-1999
Varieties: HN 2996, 3632,
3634, 3635; also
called Flower of
the Month, Child
Series: Vanity Fair Children
U.S.:	**$125.00**
Can.:	**$165.00**
U.K.:	**£ 75.00**

Exclusive to U.S.A.

HN 3407
Julie
Style One
Designer: R. Tabbenor
Height: 5", 12.7 cm
Colour: White and blue
Issued: 1993-1999
Varieties: HN 2995
U.S.:	**$125.00**
Can.:	**$165.00**
U.K.:	**£ 75.00**

Exclusive to U.S.A.

HN 3408
August
Style Three
Designer: M. Davies
Height: 7 ½", 19.1 cm
Colour: White, poppies
Issued: 1991-1991
Varieties: 'Beatrice' HN 3263,
          3631; 'Kathryn'
          HN 3413; 'Lucy'
          HN 3653; 'Summer
          Serenade' HN 3610
Series: Wildflower / Month

U.S.:	**$225.00**
Can.:	**$300.00**
U.K.:	**£125.00**

HN 3409
September
Style Three
Designer: M. Davies
Height: 7 ½", 19.1 cm
Colour: White, blue flowers
Issued: 1991-1991
Varieties: 'Beatrice' HN 3263,
          3631; 'Kathryn'
          HN 3413; 'Lucy'
          HN 3653; 'Summer
          Serenade' HN 3610
Series: Wildflower / Month

U.S.:	**$225.00**
Can.:	**$300.00**
U.K.:	**£125.00**

HN 3410
October
Style Three
Designer: M. Davies
Height: 7 ½", 19.1 cm
Colour: White, buttercups
Issued: 1991-1991
Varieties: 'Beatrice' HN 3263,
          3631; 'Kathryn'
          HN 3413; 'Lucy'
          HN 3653; 'Summer
          Serenade' HN 3610
Series: Wildflower / Month

U.S.:	**$225.00**
Can.:	**$300.00**
U.K.:	**£125.00**

HN 3411
November
Style Three
Designer: M. Davies
Height: 7 ½", 19.1 cm
Colour: White, pink flowers
Issued: 1991-1991
Varieties: 'Beatrice' HN 3263,
          3631; 'Kathryn'
          HN 3413; 'Lucy'
          HN 3653; 'Summer
          Serenade' HN 3610
Series: Wildflower / Month

U.S.:	**$225.00**
Can.:	**$300.00**
U.K.:	**£125.00**

HN 3412
December
Style Three
Designer: M. Davies
Height: 7 ½", 19.1 cm
Colour: White, Christmas roses
Issued: 1991-1991
Varieties: 'Beatrice' HN 3263,
          3631; 'Kathryn'
          HN 3413; 'Lucy'
          HN 3653; 'Summer
          Serenade' HN 3610
Series: Wildflower / Month

U.S.:	**$225.00**
Can.:	**$300.00**
U.K.:	**£125.00**

HN 3413
Kathryn
Style One
Designer: M. Davies
Height: 7", 17.8 cm
Colour: Blue and white
Issued: 1992-1992
Varieties: 'Beatrice' HN 3263,
          3631; 'Lucy' HN 3653;
          'Summer Serenade'
          HN 3610; Wildflower
          of the Month

U.S.:	**$225.00**
Can.:	**$300.00**
U.K.:	**£125.00**

HN 3414
Rebecca
Style Two
Designer: M. Davies
Remodeller: D. Frith
Height: 3 ½", 8.9 cm
Colour: Pale blue and pink
Issued: 1992-1997
Series: Miniatures

U.S.:	**$150.00**
Can.:	**$200.00**
U.K.:	**£ 90.00**

HN 3415
Janette
Designer: M. Davies
Height: 7 ½:, 19.1 cm
Colour: Blue and green
Issued: 1992-1992
Varieties: Also called 'Kirsty'
            (Style One) HN 2381
Comm.by: Great Universal
            Stores

U.S.:	**$350.00**
Can.:	**$450.00**
U.K.:	**£200.00**

HN 3416
Victoria
Style One
Designer: M. Davies
Height: 6 ½", 16.5 cm
Colour: Blue and rose
with gold trim
Issued: 1992-1992
Varieties: HN 2471
Series: Roadshow Events

U.S.:	**$450.00**
Can.:	**$575.00**
U.K.:	**£275.00**

HN 3417
Ninette
Style One
Designer: M. Davies
Height: 7 ½", 19.1 cm
Colour: Orange and green
dress, with gold trim
Issued: 1992-1992
Varieties: HN 2379; also called
'Olivia' (Style Two)
HN 3339
Series: Roadshow Events

U.S.:	**$450.00**
Can.:	**$575.00**
U.K.:	**£275.00**

HN 3418
Bedtime
Style Two
Designer: N. Pedley
Height: 7 ¼", 18.4 cm
Colour: Pink-yellow
Issued: 1992 in a limited
edition of 9,000
Comm.by: Lawleys By Post

U.S.:	**$275.00**
Can.:	**$350.00**
U.K.:	**£165.00**

HN 3419
Angela
Style Three
Designer: N. Pedley
Height: 8 ½", 21.6 cm
Colour: Blue, pink and white
Issued: 1992-1992
Series: M. Doulton Events

U.S.:	**$325.00**
Can.:	**$450.00**
U.K.:	**£200.00**

HN 3420
Ashley
Designer: N. Pedley
Height: 8", 20.3 cm
Colour: Lavender
Issued: 1992-1999
Series: Vanity Fair Ladies

U.S.:	**$250.00**
Can.:	**$325.00**
U.K.:	**£150.00**

HN 3421
Nicole
Style One
Designer: N. Pedley
Height: 7 ½", 19.1 cm
Colour: Pink and cream
Issued: 1993-1997
Varieties: HN 3686

U.S.:	**$250.00**
Can.:	**$375.00**
U.K.:	**£150.00**

HN 3422
Joanne
Style Two
Designer: N. Pedley
Height: 7 ½", 19.1 cm
Colour: White and pink dress
flowered border
Issued: 1993-1998
Varieties: Also called 'Annabelle'
HN 4090

U.S.:	**$275.00**
Can.:	**$400.00**
U.K.:	**£175.00**

HN 3423
Birthday Girl
Designer: N. Pedley
Height: 6", 15.2 cm
Colour: White
Issued: 1993-2000
Series: Vanity Fair Children

U.S.:	**$150.00**
Can.:	**$200.00**
U.K.:	**£ 95.00**

HN 3424
My First Figurine
Designer: N. Pedley
Height: 4 ¼", 10.8 cm
Colour: Red and pink
Issued: 1993-1998

U.S.:	**$150.00**
Can.:	**$225.00**
U.K.:	**£ 90.00**

HN 3425
Almost Grown
Designer: N. Pedley
Height: 4 ½", 11.4 cm
Colour: White and pale green
Issued: 1993-1997

U.S.:	**$125.00**
Can.:	**$175.00**
U.K.:	**£ 75.00**

HN 3426
Best Wishes
Style One
Designer: N. Pedley
Height: 6", 15.2 cm
Colour: Red and white
Issued: 1993-1995

U.S.:	**$225.00**
Can.:	**$300.00**
U.K.:	**£135.00**

HN 3427
Gift of Love
Designer: N. Pedley
Height: 7 ½", 19.1 cm
Colour: White, yellow and pink
Issued: 1993-2000
Series: Vanity Fair Ladies

U.S.:	**$225.00**
Can.:	**$325.00**
U.K.:	**£135.00**

HN 3428
Discovery
Designer: A. Munslow
Height: 12", 30.5 cm
Colour: Matte white
Issued: 1992-1992
Series: RDICC

U.S.:	**$200.00**
Can.:	**$250.00**
U.K.:	**£120.00**

HN 3429
Napoleon at Waterloo
Designer: A. Maslankowski
Height: 11 ½", 29.2 cm
Colour: Black, cream and
           green
Issued: 1992 in a limited
           edition of 1,500

U.S.:	**$1,600.00**
Can.:	**$2,250.00**
U.K.:	**£ 950.00**

HN 3430
Sit
Designer: A. Maslankowski
Height: 4 ½", 11.4 cm
Colour: Pink and white
Issued: 1992-1996
Varieties: HN 3123
Series: Vanity Fair Children

U.S.:	**$150.00**
Can.:	**$200.00**
U.K.:	**£ 90.00**

Exclusive to North America

HN 3431
Little Ballerina
Designer: A. Maslankowski
Height: 6", 15.2 cm
Colour: Pink
Issued: 1993 in a limited
           edition of 2,000
Varieties: HN 3395

U.S.:	**$150.00**
Can.:	**$200.00**
U.K.:	**£ 90.00**

Exclusive to North America

HN 3432
Duke of Wellington
Designer: A. Maslankowski
Height: 12", 30.5 cm
Colour: Dark blue and cream
Issued: 1993 in a limited
edition of 1,500

U.S.: $1,600.00
Can.: $2,250.00
U.K.: £ 950.00

HN 3433
Winston S. Churchill
Style Two
Designer: A. Maslankowski
Height: 12", 30.5 cm
Colour: Black and grey
Issued: 1993 in a limited
edition of 5,000

U.S.: $ 850.00
Can.: $1,100.00
U.K.: £ 500.00

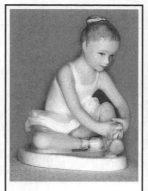

HN 3434
Ballet Shoes
Designer: A. Maslankowski
Height: 3 ¾", 9.5 cm
Colour: White
Issued: 1993-2001

U.S.: $150.00
Can.: $200.00
U.K.: £ 90.00

HN 3435
Daddy's Girl
Designer: A. Maslankowski
Height: 4 ½", 11.4 cm
Colour: Pink and white
Issued: 1993-1998
Series: Vanity Fair Children

U.S.: $150.00
Can.: $200.00
U.K.: £ 90.00

HN 3436
HM Queen Elizabeth II
Style Three
Designer: A. Maslankowski
Height: 8 ¼", 21.0 cm
Colour: Lilac and yellow
Issued: 1992 in a limited
edition of 2,500
Comm.by: Lawleys By Post

U.S.: $1,500.00
Can.: $2,250.00
U.K.: £ 900.00

HN 3437
Mary
Style Three
Designer: A. Maslankowski
Height: 3 ¼", 8.3 cm
Colour: White
Issued: 1993-1996
Varieties: HN 3485
Series: Holy Family

U.S.: $100.00
Can.: $150.00
U.K.: £ 60.00

Exclusive to North America

HN 3438
Joseph
Style One
Designer: A. Maslankowski
Height: 5 ¾", 14.6 cm
Colour: White
Issued: 1993-1996
Varieties: HN 3486
Series: Holy Family

U.S.: $100.00
Can.: $150.00
U.K.: £ 60.00

NOTE ON CONDITION
Prices on the secondary market for Royal Doulton Figures, particularly the early HN numbers, have risen considerably over the years. As values rise, the condition and quality of these figurines takes on an increasingly important role.

The prices listed in *The Charlton Standard Catalogue of Royal Doulton Figurines* are for figures in mint condition. Naturally, repaired or restored figures, no matter how professionally done, will sell at a discount. However the early figures, due to their rarity, may experience smaller discounts.

On Condition: For figures to command catalogue prices they must be in mint condition. This simply means that a figure will have no chips, scratches, hairline cracks, crazing, blemishes, or repairs. Any of which will remove the figure from the mint category.

On Quality: Some figures are better moulded, assembled or painted than others. High quality figures may command a premium over listed catalogue prices.

HN 3439
The Skater
Style Two
Designer: P. Gee
Height: 8", 20.3 cm
Colour: Red
Issued: 1992-1997

U.S.:	**$450.00**
Can.:	**$600.00**
U.K.:	**£250.00**

HN 3440
HM Queen Elizabeth II
Style Four
Designer: P. Gee
Height: 7 ½", 19.0 cm
Colour: Yellow and pink
Issued: 1992 in a limited
edition of 3,500

U.S.:	**$425.00**
Can.:	**$550.00**
U.K.:	**£250.00**

HN 3441
Barbara
Style Three
Designer: P. Gee
Height: 8", 20.3 cm
Colour: Pink and lavender
Issued: 1993 in a limited
edition of 9,500
Series: RDICC

U.S.:	**$550.00**
Can.:	**$775.00**
U.K.:	**£350.00**

HN 3442
Eliza Farren,
Countess of Derby
Designer: P. Gee
Height: 8 ¾", 22.2 cm
Colour: Pale blue, white
and beige
Issued: 1993 in a limited
edition of 5,000
Series: RDICC

U.S.:	**$350.00**
Can.:	**$475.00**
U.K.:	**£200.00**

HN 3443
Gift of Freedom
Designer: P. Gee
Height: 9 ¾", 24.8 cm
Colour: White
Issued: 1993 to the present
Series: Images

U.S.:	**N/I**
Can.:	**$245.00**
U.K.:	**£ 59.00**

HN 3444
Piper
Style Two
Designer: P. Gee
Height: 9 ¼", 23.4 cm
Colour: Black, red and green
Issued: 1993 in a limited
edition of 750
Comm.by: Site of the Green

U.S.:	**$475.00**
Can.:	**$600.00**
U.K.:	**£275.00**

HN 3445
Amy's Sister
Designer: P. Gee
Height: 8", 20.3 cm
Colour: Red, cream and blue
Issued: 1993-1996

U.S.:	**$250.00**
Can.:	**$325.00**
U.K.:	**£150.00**

HN 3446
Spring Song
Designer: P. Gee
Height: 7 ¼", 18.4 cm
Colour: Yellow and white
Issued: 1993-1996
Varieties: Also called 'Danielle'
(Style Two), HN 3001
Series: The Seasons
(Series Five)

U.S.:	**$175.00**
Can.:	**$225.00**
U.K.:	**£100.00**

HN 3447
Jennifer
Style Three
Designer: P. Gee
Height: 7 ¼", 18.4 cm
Colour: Deep pink
Issued: 1994-1994
Series: Figure of the Year

U.S.:	**$425.00**
Can.:	**$600.00**
U.K.:	**£275.00**

HN 3448
Charles Dickens
Designer: P. Gee
Height: 4", 10.1 cm
Colour: Black and grey
Issued: 1994 in a limited
edition of 1,500
Comm.by: Pascoe & Company

U.S.:	**$150.00**
Can.:	**$200.00**
U.K.:	**£ 90.00**

HN 3449
Catherine Howard
Designer: P. Parsons
Height: 8 ¼", 21.0 cm
Colour: Purple
Issued: 1992 in a limited
edition of 9,500
Series: Six Wives of
Henry VIII
Comm.by: Lawleys By Post

U.S.:	**$ 850.00**
Can.:	**$1,100.00**
U.K.:	**£ 500.00**

HN 3450
Catherine Parr
Designer: P. Parsons
Height: 6 ¼", 15.9 cm
Colour: Red
Issued: 1992 in a limited
edition of 9,500
Series: Six Wives of
Henry VIII
Comm.by: Lawleys By Post

U.S.:	**$ 850.00**
Can.:	**$1,100.00**
U.K.:	**£ 500.00**

HN 3451
Catherine
Style Two
Designer: P. Parsons
Height: 5", 12,7 cm
Colour: White and lemon
Issued: 1993-1999
Varieties: HN 3044

U.S.:	**$125.00**
Can.:	**$165.00**
U.K.:	**£ 75.00**

HN 3452
Our First Christmas
Designer: P. Parsons
Height: 11 ½", 29.2 cm
Colour: White
Issued: 1993-1998
Series: Images

U.S.:	**$175.00**
Can.:	**$225.00**
U.K.:	**£100.00**

HN 3453
Juliet
Style Two
Designer: P. Parsons
Height: 6", 15.2 cm
Colour: Red, pink and green
Issued: 1994 in a limited
edition of 5,000
Series: Shakespearean
Ladies
Comm.by: Lawleys By Post

U.S.:	**$500.00**
Can.:	**$650.00**
U.K.:	**£300.00**

HN 3454
Flowers For Mother
Designer: P. Parsons
Height: 5 ¾", 14.6 cm
Colour: White and pink
Issued: 1994-1997

U.S.:	**$150.00**
Can.:	**$200.00**
U.K.:	**£ 85.00**

Exclusive to U.S.A.

HN 3455
Sharon
Style One
Designer: P. Parsons
Height: 5 ½", 14.0 cm
Colour: White dress
with pink flowers
Issued: 1994-1999
Varieties: HN 3047

U.S.:	**$175.00**
Can.:	**$225.00**
U.K.:	**£100.00**

HN 3456
Grandpa's Story
Designer: P. Parsons
Height: 6", 15.2 cm
Colour: Green, blue and pink
Issued: 1994-2000

U.S.:	**$450.00**
Can.:	**$600.00**
U.K.:	**£275.00**

HN 3457
When I Was Young
Designer: P. Parsons
Height: 5 ½", 14.0 cm
Colour: Pink, green and purple
Issued: 1994-2000

U.S.:	**$450.00**
Can.:	**$600.00**
U.K.:	**£275.00**

HN 3458
Henry VIII
Style Four
Designer: P. Parsons
Height: 9 ¼", 23.5 cm
Colour: Browns, black
and white
Issued: 1994 in a limited
edition of 9,500
Comm.by: Lawleys By Post

U.S.:	**$ 850.00**
Can.:	**$1,100.00**
U.K.:	**£ 500.00**

HN 3459
King Charles
Designer: C. J. Noke and
H. Tittensor
Height: 16 ¾", 42.5 cm
Colour: Red, dark blue,
purple and white
Issued: 1992 in a limited
edition of 350
Varieties: HN 404, 2084

U.S.:	**$3,250.00**
Can.:	**$4,500.00**
U.K.:	**£1,950.00**

HN 3460
Brother and Sister
Designer: A. Hughes
Height: 8", 20.3 cm
Colour: White
Issued: 1993 to the present
Series: Images

U.S.:	**N/I**
Can.:	**$220.00**
U.K.:	**£ 39.00**

HN 3461
Kerry
Designer: A. Hughes
Height: 5 ¼", 13.3 cm
Colour: White and green
Issued: 1993-1999
Varieties: HN 3036

U.S.:	**$125.00**
Can.:	**$200.00**
U.K.:	**£ 75.00**

Exclusive to U.S.A.

HN 3462
Boy Scout
Designer: A. Hughes
Height: 7 ¾", 19.7 cm
Colour: Brown and black
Issued: 1994 in a limited
edition of 9,500
Comm.by: Lawleys By Post

U.S.:	**$450.00**
Can.:	**$600.00**
U.K.:	**£275.00**

HN 3463 - 3469 Animal and Bird
figures, except HN 3465 and 3469
not issued.

HN 3470
Croquet
Designer: V. Annand
Height: 8 ½", 21.6 cm
Colour: Red and blue
Issued: 1994 in a limited
edition of 5,000
Series: British Sporting
Heritage

U.S.: $600.00
Can.: $775.00
U.K.: £350.00

HN 3471
Ascot
Style Two
Designer: V. Annand
Height: 8 ½", 21.6 cm
Colour: Pink and purple
Issued: 1994 in a limited
edition of 5,000
Series: British Sporting
Heritage

U.S.: $600.00
Can.: $775.00
U.K.: £350.00

HN 3472
La Loge
Designer: V. Annand
Height: 8 ½", 21.6 cm
Colour: White and black
Issued: 1992 in a limited
edition of 7,500
Comm.by: Lawleys By Post

U.S.: $ 800.00
Can.: $1,050.00
U.K.: £ 475.00

HN 3473
Les Parapluies
Designer: V. Annand
Height: 8 ¼", 21.0 cm
Colour: Blue
Issued: 1993 in a limited
edition of 7,500
Comm.by: Lawleys By Post

U.S.: $ 900.00
Can.: $1,175.00
U.K.: £ 550.00

HN 3474
Lise
Designer: V. Annand
Height: 8 ½", 21.6 cm
Colour: Lavender and purple
Issued: 1994 in a limited
edition of 7,500
Comm.by: Lawleys By Post

U.S.: $600.00
Can.: $775.00
U.K.: £350.00

HN 3475
Marie Sisley
Designer: V. Annand
Height: 8 ½", 21.6 cm
Colour: Red, yellow and grey
Issued: 1994 in a limited
edition of 7,500
Comm.by: Lawleys By Post

U.S.: $750.00
Can.: $975.00
U.K.: £450.00

HN 3476
Bridesmaid
Style Seven
Designer: V. Annand
Height: 5 ½", 13.3 cm
Colour: Pink
Issued: 1994-1997
Varieties: Also called 'Flowergirl'
(Style One) HN 3479

U.S.: $175.00
Can.: $225.00
U.K.: £100.00

HN 3477
Springtime
Style Three
Designer: V. Annand
Height: 8", 20.3 cm
Colour: Pink and cream
Issued: 1993-1996
Series: The Seasons
(Series Six)

U.S.: $475.00
Can.: $600.00
U.K.: £275.00

HN 3478
Summertime
Style Two
Designer: V. Annand
Height: 8 ½", 21.6 cm
Colour: Lilac and green
Issued: 1994-1996
Series: The Seasons
          (Series Six)
U.S.:   **$400.00**
Can.:   **$525.00**
U.K.:   **£250.00**

HN 3479
Flowergirl
Style One
Designer: V. Annand
Height: 5", 12.7 cm
Colour: White and pink
Issued: 1994-1997
Varieties: Also called
          'Bridesmaid' (Style
          Seven) HN 3476
U.S.:   **$175.00**
Can.:   **$225.00**
U.K.:   **£100.00**

Exclusive to North America

HN 3480
Kirsty
Style Two
Designer: M. Davies
Remodeller: P. Gee
Height: 3 ¾", 9.5 cm
Colour: Blue
Issued: 1993-1997
Varieties: HN 3213, 3246, 3743
Series: Miniatures
U.S.:   **$150.00**
Can.:   **$200.00**
U.K.:   **£ 90.00**

Exclusive to Canada

HN 3481
Lavender Rose
Designer: M. Davies
Height: 6", 15.2 cm
Colour: White, pink flowers
Issued: 1993-1995
Varieties: 'Debbie' HN 2385,
          2400; 'Moonlight Rose'
          HN 3483; 'Old Country
          Roses' (Style One)
          HN 3482; 'Memory
          Lane' HN 3746;
          'Tranquility', HN 3747
U.S.:   **$125.00**
Can.:   **$200.00**
U.K.:   **£ 85.00**

HN 3482
Old Country Roses - Style One
Designer: M. Davies
Height: 6", 15.2 cm
Colour: White, red flowers
Issued: 1993-1995
Varieties: 'Debbie' HN 2385,
          2400; 'Lavender Rose'
          HN 3481; 'Moonlight
          Roses' HN 3483;
          'Memory Lane'
          HN 374;6 'Tranquillity'
          HN 3747
U.S.:   **$125.00**
Can.:   **$200.00**
U.K.:   **£ 85.00**

HN 3483
Moonlight Rose
Designer: M. Davies
Height: 6", 15.2 cm
Colour: White, blue flowers
Issued: 1993-1995
Varieties: Also called 'Debbie'
          HN 2385, 2400;
          'Lavender Rose' HN 3481;
          'Old Country Roses'
          (Style One) HN 3482;
          'Memory Lane' HN 3746
          'Tranquillity' HN 3747
U.S.:   **$125.00**
Can.:   **$200.00**
U.K.:   **£ 85.00**

HN 3484
Jesus
Designer: A. Maslankowski
Width: 2 ½", 6.4 cm
Colour: White
Issued: 1993-1996
Varieties: HN 3487
Series: Holy Family
U.S.:   **$75.00**
Can.:   **$95.00**
U.K.:   **£45.00**

Exclusive to North America

HN 3485
Mary
Style Three
Designer: A. Maslankowski
Height: 3 ¼", 8.3 cm
Colour: Blue and white
Issued: 1993-1996
Varieties: HN 3437
Series: Holy Family
U.S.:   **$100.00**
Can.:   **$150.00**
U.K.:   **£ 75.00**

Exclusive to North America

HN 3486
Joseph
Style One
Designer: A. Maslankowski
Height: 5 ¾", 14.6 cm
Colour: Brown and white
Issued: 1993-1996
Varieties: HN 3438
Series: Holy Family

U.S.:	$100.00
Can.:	$150.00
U.K.:	£ 75.00

Exclusive to North America

HN 3487
Jesus
Designer: A. Maslankowski
Width: 2 ½", 6.4 cm
Colour: White and brown
Issued: 1993-1996
Varieties: HN 3484
Series: Holy Family

U.S.:	$75.00
Can.:	$95.00
U.K.ı	£45.00

Exclusive to North America

HN 3488
Christmas Day
Designer: A. Maslankowski
Height: 6", 15.2 cm
Colour: White
Issued: 1993-1999
Varieties: HN 4062
Series: Sentiments

U.S.:	$125.00
Can.:	$160.00
U.K.:	£ 70.00

HN 3489
Vice Admiral Lord Nelson
Designer: A. Maslankowski
Height: 12 ½", 31.7 cm
Colour: Dark blue, gold
           and cream
Issued: 1993 in a limited
           edition of 950

U.S.:	$1,600.00
Can.:	$2,250.00
U.K.:	£ 900.00

HN 3490
Thinking of You
Style One
Designer: A. Maslankowski
Height: 6 ¾", 17.2 cm
Colour: White with pink sash
Issued: 1993-1993
Varieties: HN 3124
Series: 1. Roadshow Events
           2. Sentiments

U.S.:	$150.00
Can.:	$225.00
U.K.:	£ 90.00

HN 3491
Friendship
Designer: A. Maslankowski
Height: 6", 15.2 cm
Colour: White
Issued: 1994 to the present
Series: Sentiments

U.S.:	N/I
Can.:	$150.00
U.K.:	£ 42.00

HN 3492
With Love
Designer: A. Maslankowski
Height: 5 ¾", 14.6 cm
Colour: White dress and sash
Issued: 1994-1997
Varieties: HN 3393
Series: Sentiments

U.S.:	$100.00
Can.:	$150.00
U.K.:	£ 60.00

Exclusive to Canada

HN 3493
Christmas Parcels
Style Two
Designer: A. Maslankowski
Height: 6", 15.2 cm
Colour: White
Issued: 1994-1998
Varieties: HN 4063
Series: Sentiments

U.S.:	$100.00
Can.:	$150.00
U.K.:	£ 60.00

HN 3494
Tina
Designer:	M. Davies
Height:	7 ½", 19.1 cm
Colour:	Blue and white
Issued:	1993
Varieties:	Also called 'Maureen' (Style Three); HN 2481
Comm.by:	Great Universal Stores

U.S.:	**$175.00**
Can.:	**$225.00**
U.K.:	**£ 90.00**

HN 3495
Annette
Style Two
Designer:	M. Davies
Height:	8", 20.3 cm
Colour:	Pale green
Issued:	1993-1993
Varieties:	Also called 'Sandra' HN 2275, 2401

U.S.:	**$400.00**
Can.:	**$550.00**
U.K.:	**£225.00**

HN 3496
Margaret
Style Two
Designer:	M. Davies
Height:	7 ½", 19.1 cm
Colour:	White and green
Issued:	1993-1999
Varieties:	HN 2397; 'Adele' HN 2480; 'Camille' (Style Two) HN 3171

U.S.:	**$275.00**
Can.:	**$375.00**
U.K.:	**£165.00**

Exclusive to U.S.A.

HN 3497
Jessica
Style One
Designer:	M. Davies
Height:	7", 17.8 cm
Colour:	White and blue
Issued:	1993
Varieties:	HN 3169

U.S.:	**$225.00**
Can.:	**$300.00**
U.K.:	**£125.00**

Exclusive to North America.

HN 3498
Natalie
Style One
Designer:	M. Davies
Height:	8", 20.3 cm
Colour:	White and lemon
Issued:	1993-1999
Varieties:	HN 3173

U.S.:	**$250.00**
Can.:	**$325.00**
U.K.:	**£150.00**

Exclusive to U.S.A.

HN 3499
Top o' the Hill
Style Two
Designer:	L. Harradine
Remodeller:	P. Gee
Height:	3 ¾", 9.5 cm
Colour:	Red
Issued:	1993-1998
Varieties:	HN 2126
Series:	Miniatures

U.S.:	**$225.00**
Can.:	**$300.00**
U.K.:	**£135.00**

HN 3500 - 3552 Animal and Bird
figures, except HN 3537 not issued;
HN 3553 - 3599 not issued.

HN 3600
Dawn
Style Three
Designer:	N. Pedley
Height:	7 ½", 19.1 cm
Colour:	White and pink
Issued:	1993-1998
Series:	Vanity Fair Ladies

U.S.:	**$250.00**
Can.:	**$325.00**
U.K.:	**£150.00**

HN 3601
Helen
Style Three
Designer:	N. Pedley
Height:	8 ¼", 21.0 cm
Colour:	Blue and white
Issued:	1993-2002
Varieties:	HN 3687, 3763, 3886 Also called 'Miss Kay' HN 3659

U.S.:	**$300.00**
Can.:	**$400.00**
U.K.:	**£125.00**

HN 3602
Flowergirl
Style Two
Designer: N. Pedley
Height: 5 ¼", 13.3. cm
Colour: Pink and cream
Issued: 1993-1996

U.S.:	**$125.00**
Can.:	**$160.00**
U.K.:	**£ 75.00**

HN 3603
Sharon
Style Two
Designer: N. Pedley
Height: 8 ¾", 22.2 cm
Colour: Peach, cream
         and blue
Issued: 1994-1994
Series: M. Doulton Events

U.S.:	**$275.00**
Can.:	**$350.00**
U.K.:	**£165.00**

HN 3604
Diane
Designer: N. Pedley
Height: 8 ½", 21.6 cm
Colour: Pink and blue
Issued: 1994-1994
Series: RDICC

U.S.:	**$300.00**
Can.:	**$400.00**
U.K.:	**£175.00**

HN 3605
First Performance
Designer: N. Pedley
Height: 6", 15.2 cm
Colour: White and pink
Issued: 1994-1998

U.S.:	**$175.00**
Can.:	**$225.00**
U.K.:	**£100.00**

HN 3606
A Posy For You
Designer: N. Pedley
Height: 4 ¼", 10.8 cm
Colour: Blue and white
Issued: 1994-1997

U.S.:	**$150.00**
Can.:	**$200.00**
U.K.:	**£ 85.00**

HN 3607
Special Friend
Designer: N. Pedley
Height: 4 ¼", 10.8 cm
Colour: Blue and white
Issued: 1994-1998

U.S.:	**$150.00**
Can.:	**$200.00**
U.K.:	**£ 85.00**

HN 3608
Good Companion
Designer: N. Pedley
Height: 8 ½", 21.6 cm
Colour: Pink and white
Issued: 1994-1999
Series: Vanity Fair Ladies

U.S.:	**$250.00**
Can.:	**$325.00**
U.K.:	**£135.00**

HN 3609
Kathleen
Style Three
Designer: N. Pedley
Height: 8 ½", 21.6 cm
Colour: White and yellow
Issued: 1994-2000
Varieties: HN 3880; Also called
          'Brianna' HN 4126
Series: Vanity Fair Ladies

U.S.:	**$250.00**
Can.:	**$325.00**
U.K.:	**£135.00**

HN 3610
Summer Serenade
Designer: M. Davies
Height: 7", 17.8 cm
Colour: Blue and white
Issued: 1993-1996
Varieties: Also called 'Beatrice'
          HN 3263, 3631;
          'Kathryn' HN 3413;
          'Lucy' HN 3653;
          Wildflower / Month
Series: Seasons (Series Five)

U.S.:	$250.00
Can.:	$325.00
U.K.:	£135.00

HN 3611
Winter Welcome
Designer: M. Davies
Height: 7 ½", 19.1 cm
Colour: Rust and white
Issued: 1993-1996
Varieties: Also called 'Caroline'
          (Style One) HN 3170
Series: The Seasons
          (Series Five)

U.S.:	$250.00
Can.:	$325.00
U.K.:	£135.00

HN 3612
Autumn Attraction
Designer: M. Davies
Height: 6 ¾", 17.2 cm
Colour: Gold and white
Issued: 1993-1996
Varieties: Also called 'Michele'
          HN 2234
Series: The Seasons
          (Series Five)

U.S.:	$250.00
Can.:	$325.00
U.K.:	£135.00

HN 3613
Darling
Style Two
Designer: C. Vyse
Height: 5 ¼", 13.3 cm
Colour: Pale blue
Issued: 1993
Varieties: HN 1985

U.S.:	$150.00
Can.:	$200.00
U.K.:	£ 90.00

HN 3614 - 3616 not issued.

HN 3617
Monica
Style One
Designer: L. Harradine
Height: 4 ¼", 10.8 cm
Colour: Rose, lemon and white
Issued: 1993-1999
Varieties: HN 1458, 1459, 1467

U.S.:	$175.00
Can.:	$225.00
U.K.:	£ 90.00

HN 3618
Dinky Doo
Designer: L. Harradine
Height: 4 ½", 11.9 cm
Colour: White and blue
Issued: 1994-2002
Varieties: HN 1678, 2120

U.S.:	$125.00
Can.:	$160.00
U.K.:	£ 60.00

HN 3619 not issued.

HN 3620
Valerie
Style One
Designer: M. Davies
Height: 5 ¼", 13.3 cm
Colour: Blue, pink and white
Issued: 1994-1999
Varieties: HN 2107

U.S.:	$150.00
Can.:	$200.00
U.K.:	£ 80.00

HN 3621
Autumntime
Style Two
Designer: V. Annand
Height: 8 ¾", 22.2 cm
Colour: Turquoise and brown
Issued: 1994-1996
Series: The Seasons
          (Series Six)

U.S.:	$500.00
Can.:	$650.00
U.K.:	£300.00

HN 3622
Wintertime
Style Two
Designer: Valerie Annand
Height: 8 ½", 21.6 cm
Colour: Red, white and green
Issued: 1995-1996
Series: The Seasons
           (Series Six)

U.S.:	**$450.00**
Can.:	**$675.00**
U.K.:	**£275.00**

HN 3623
Lady Eaton
Designer: V. Annand
Height: 7 ½", 19.1 cm
Colour: Blue, white and yellow
Issued: 1994 in a limited
           edition of 2,500
Varieties: Also called 'Janice'
           (Style Two) HN 3624

U.S.:	**$600.00**
Can.:	**$775.00**
U.K.:	**£350.00**

HN 3624
Janice
Style Two
Designer: V. Annand
Height: 7 ½", 19.1 cm
Colour: Blue, pink, white
            and yellow
Issued: 1994-1997
Varieties: Also called 'Lady
            Eaton' HN 3623
Comm.by: Great Universal
            Stores

U.S.:	**$350.00**
Can.:	**$450.00**
U.K.:	**£200.00**

HN 3625
Anniversary
Designer: V. Annand
Height: 8 ¾", 22.2 cm
Colour: Blue, black and pink
Issued: 1994-1998

U.S.:	**$600.00**
Can.:	**$775.00**
U.K.:	**£375.00**

HN 3626
Lily
Style Two
Designer: V. Annand
Height: 9 ½", 24.0 cm
Colour: Mauve and yellow
Issued: 1995-1995
Series: 1. Lady Doulton 1995
           2. M. Doulton Events

U.S.:	**$350.00**
Can.:	**$450.00**
U.K.:	**£200.00**

HN 3627
England
Designer: V. Annand
Height: 8", 20.3 cm
Colour: Blue and pink
Issued   1996-1998
Series: Ladies of the
           British Isles

U.S.:	**$450.00**
Can.:	**$575.00**
U.K.:	**£275.00**

HN 3628
Ireland
Designer: V. Annand
Height: 7 ¾", 19.7 cm
Colour: Green and white
Issued: 1996-1998
Series: Ladies of the
           British Isles

U.S.:	**$600.00**
Can.:	**$775.00**
U.K.:	**£350.00**

HN 3629
Scotland
Designer: V. Annand
Height: 7 ¾", 19.7 cm
Colour: Green, white and
           pink
Issued: 1995-1998
Series::   Ladies of the
           British Isles

U.S.:	**$600.00**
Can.:	**$775.00**
U.K.:	**£350.00**

HN 3630
Wales
Designer: V. Annand
Height: 8 ½", 21.6 cm
Colour: Red, white and green
Issued: 1995-1998
Series: Ladies of the
           British Isles

U.S.:	**$700.00**
Can.:	**$900.00**
U.K.:	**£400.00**

HN 3631
Beatrice
Designer: M. Davies
Height: 7", 17.8 cm
Colour: White
Issued: 1994-1998
Varieties: HN 3263; also called
           'Kathryn' HN 3413;
           'Lucy' HN 3653;
           'Summer Serenade'
           HN 3610; Wildflower
           of the Month

U.S.:	**$250.00**
Can.:	**$325.00**
U.K.:	**£150.00**

HN 3632
Amanda
Designer: R. Tabbenor
Height: 5 ¼", 13.3 cm
Colour: White and pink
Issued: 1994-1996
Varieties: HN 2996, 3406,
           3634, 3635; also
           called 'Flower of the
           Month, Child'
Series: Vanity Fair Children

U.S.:	**$125.00**
Can.:	**$160.00**
U.K.:	**£ 70.00**

HN 3633
Shakespeare
Designer: R. Tabbenor
Height: 11 ¾", 29.8 cm
Colour: Browns and cream
Issued: 1994 in a limited
           edition of 1,564
Comm.by: Lawleys By Post

U.S.:	**$1,400.00**
Can.:	**$1,800.00**
U.K.:	**£ 800.00**

HN 3634
Amanda
Designer: R. Tabbenor
Height: 5 ¼", 13.3 cm
Colour: White and blue
Issued: 1995
Varieties: HN 2996, 3406,
3632,   3635; also called
           'Flower of The
           Month, Child'
Comm.by: Youngs, Canada

U.S.:	**$125.00**
Can.:	**$160.00**
U.K.:	**£ 75.00**

HN 3635
Amanda
Designer: R. Tabbenor
Height: 5 ¼", 13.3 cm
Colour: White and pink
Issued: 1995-1995
Series: R.D.I.C.C.
Varieties: HN 2996, 3406, 3632,
           3634; also called
           'Flower of The Month,
           Child'

U.S.:	**$125.00**
Can.:	**$160.00**
U.K.:	**£ 75.00**

HN 3636
Captain Hook
Designer: R. Tabbenor
Height: 9 ¼", 23.5 cm
Colour: Red, blue and brown
Issued: 1993-1996
Series: Character Sculptures

U.S.:	**$300.00**
Can.:	**$400.00**
U.K.:	**£150.00**

Resin

HN 3637
Dick Turpin
Style Two
Designer: R. Tabbenor
Height: 9", 22.9 cm
Colour: Brown, black, red
           and white
Issued: 1993-1996
Series: Character Sculptures

U.S.:	**$300.00**
Can.:	**$400.00**
U.K.:	**£150.00**

Resin

HN 3638
D'Artagnan
Style One
Designer: R. Tabbenor
Height: 9", 22.9 cm
Colour: Maroon, black, blue
          and brown
Issued: 1993-1996
Series: Character Sculptures

U.S.:	**$300.00**
Can.:	**$400.00**
U.K.:	**£150.00**

Resin

HN 3639
Sherlock Holmes
Designer: R. Tabbenor
Height: 7 ½", 19.1 cm
Colour: Brown and grey
Issued: 1995-1996
Series: Character Sculptures

U.S.:	**$300.00**
Can.:	**$400.00**
U.K.:	**£150.00**

Resin

HN 3640
W. G. Grace
Designer: R. Tabbenor
Height: 8", 20.3 cm
Colour: White, beige and red
Issued: 1995 in a limited
            edition of 9,500
Comm.by: Lawleys By Post

U.S.:	**$375.00**
Can.:	**$500.00**
U.K.:	**£225.00**

HN 3641
Robert Burns
Style Two
Designer: R. Tabbenor
Height: 7 ½", 19.1 cm
Colour: Green and brown
Issued: 1996-1998

U.S.:	**$550.00**
Can.:	**$700.00**
U.K.:	**£325.00**

HN 3642
The Moor
Designer: C.J. Noke
Height: 13 ½", 34.3 cm
Colour: Flambé
Issued: 1994-1995
Varieties: HN 1308, 1366, 1425,
           1657, 2082, 3926;
           also called 'An Arab'
           HN 33, 343, 378
Series: Flambé

U.S.:	**$3,000.00**
Can.:	**$3,750.00**
U.K.:	**£1,750.00**

HN 3643
Pauline
Style Three
Designer: N. Pedley
Height: 7 ¼", 18.4 cm
Colour: Red and white
Issued: 1994-1994
Varieties: HN 3656
Series: Roadshow Events

U.S.:	**$275.00**
Can.:	**$350.00**
U.K.:	**£150.00**

HN 3644
Deborah
Style Two
Designer: N. Pedley
Height: 7 ½", 19.1 cm
Colour: Yellow and white
Issued: 1995-1995
Series: Figure of the Year

U.S.:	**$325.00**
Can.:	**$450.00**
U.K.:	**£200.00**

HN 3645
Lindsay
Designer: N. Pedley
Height: 8", 20.3 cm
Colour: White, blue
          and cream
Issued: 1994-1998
Varieties: Also called 'Katie'
           (Style Two) HN 4123

U.S.:	**$275.00**
Can.:	**$375.00**
U.K.:	**£160.00**

HN 3646
Claire
Style Two
Designer: N. Pedley
Height: 8", 20.3 cm
Colour: White and blue
Issued: 1994-2000
Varieties: Also called 'Kaitlyn'
HN 4128; 'Molly'
HN 4091; 'Rosemary'
(Style Three)
HN 3691, 3698

U.S.:	**$250.00**
Can.:	**$350.00**
U.K.:	**£150.00**

HN 3647
Holly
Designer: N. Pedley
Height: 8", 20.3 cm
Colour: Green and red
Issued: 1994-2000

U.S.:	**$400.00**
Can.:	**$525.00**
U.K.:	**£225.00**

HN 3648
Sweet Sixteen
Style Two
Designer: N. Pedley
Height: 8", 20.3 cm
Colour: Dark pink and white
Issued: 1994-1998
Varieties: Also called 'Angela'
(Style Four) HN 3690;
'Kelly' (StyleTwo)
HN 3912

U.S.:	**$250.00**
Can.:	**$325.00**
U.K.:	**£150.00**

HN 3649
Hannah
Style Two
Designer: N. Pedley
Height: 4", 10.1 cm
Colour: Pink, yellow and blue
Issued: 1994-1998
Varieties: HN 3870
Series: Miniatures

U.S.:	**$175.00**
Can.:	**$225.00**
U.K.:	**£100.00**

HN 3650
Mother's Helper
Designer: N. Pedley
Height: 4 ½", 11.4 cm
Colour: White, pink
and yellow
Issued: 1994-2000

U.S.:	**$150.00**
Can.:	**$200.00**
U.K.:	**£ 85.00**

HN 3651
Hello Daddy
Designer: N. Pedley
Height: 5 ¾", 14.6 cm
Colour: White and green
Issued: 1994-2000

U.S.:	**$200.00**
Can.:	**$250.00**
U.K.:	**£110.00**

HN 3652
First Recital
Designer: N. Pedley
Height: 4 ½", 11.4 cm
Colour: Blue, pink and white
Issued: 1994-1996

U.S.:	**$150.00**
Can.:	**$200.00**
U.K.:	**£ 85.00**

HN 3653
Lucy
Style Two
Designer: M. Davies
Height: 7", 17.8 cm
Colour: White
Issued: 1994-1997
Varieties: 'Beatrice' HN 3263,
3631; 'Kathryn'
HN 3413; 'Lucy'
HN 3653; 'Summer
Serenade' HN 3610;
Wildflower / Month
Comm.by: Great Univ. Stores

U.S.:	**$250.00**
Can.:	**$325.00**
U.K.:	**£150.00**

HN 3654
Young Melody
Designer: N. Pedley
Height: 4 ¼", 10.8 cm
Colour: Yellow and white
Issued: 1994-1996

U.S.:	**$150.00**
Can.:	**$200.00**
U.K.:	**£ 80.00**

HN 3655
Hannah
Style One
Designer: N. Pedley
Height: 8 ¼", 19.0 cm
Colour: Blue
Issued: 1995-1995
Varieties: HN 3369

U.S.:	**$325.00**
Can.:	**$425.00**
U.K.:	**£180.00**

HN 3656
Pauline
Style Three
Designer: N. Pedley
Height: 7 ¼", 18.4 cm
Colour: Red and white
Issued: 1994-1994
Varieties: HN 3643
Comm.by: Littlewoods

U.S.:	**$275.00**
Can.:	**$375.00**
U.K.:	**£165.00**

HN 3657
Quiet, They're Sleeping
Designer: N. Pedley
Height: 5 ½", 14.0 cm
Colour: Blue, pink and white
Issued: 1994-1997
Comm.by: Lawleys By Post

U.S.:	**$225.00**
Can.:	**$300.00**
U.K.:	**£125.00**

HN 3658
Charlotte
Style Two
Designer: N. Pedley
Height: 8", 20.3 cm
Colour: Blue
Issued: 1995-1996
Comm.by: Littlewoods

U.S.:	**$275.00**
Can.:	**$375.00**
U.K.:	**£165.00**

HN 3659
Miss Kay
Designer: N. Pedley
Height: 8 ¼", 21.0 cm
Colour: Pink
Issued: 1994
Varieties: Also called 'Helen'
(Style Three),
HN 3601, 3687,
3763, 3886
Comm.by: Kay's Catalogue
Company

U.S.:	**$275.00**
Can.:	**$375.00**
U.K.:	**£165.00**

HN 3660
Happy Birthday
Style Two
Designer: N. Pedley
Height: 8", 20.3 cm
Colour: Green
Issued: 1995-1999

U.S.:	**$275.00**
Can.:	**$375.00**
U.K.:	**£165.00**

HN 3661
Gemma
Designer: N. Pedley
Height: 8", 20.3 cm
Colour: Green and pink
Issued: 1995-1998

U.S.:	**$250.00**
Can.:	**$350.00**
U.K.:	**£150.00**

HN 3662
Take Me Home
Designer:　N. Pedley
Height:　　8", 20.3 cm
Colour:　　White dress, pink roses
Issued:　　1995-1999

U.S.:	**$275.00**
Can.:	**$375.00**
U.K.:	**£165.00**

HN 3663
Special Treat
Designer:　N. Pedley
Height:　　6", 15.0 cm
Colour:　　Pink and white
Issued:　　1995-1997

U.S.:	**$175.00**
Can.:	**$225.00**
U.K.:	**£100.00**

HN 3664
Wistful
Style Two
Designer:　P. Gee
Height:　　12 ¼", 31.1 cm
Colour:　　White
Issued:　　1994-2002
Series:　　Images

U.S.:	**$175.00**
Can.:	**$250.00**
U.K.:	**£ 55.00**

HN 3665
Tomorrow's Dreams
Style Two
Designer:　P. Gee
Height:　　8 ½", 21.6 cm
Colour:　　White
Issued:　　1995 to the present
Series:　　Images

U.S.:	**N/I**
Can.:	**$170.00**
U.K.:	**£ 39.00**

HN 3666 - 3673 not issued.

HN 3674
Ophelia
Designer:　　P. Parsons
Height:　　　7", 17.8 cm
Colour:　　　Rose, yellow, white
Issued:　　　1995 in a limited
　　　　　　　edition of 5,000
Series:　　　Shakespearean
　　　　　　　Ladies
Comm.by:　　Lawleys By Post

U.S.:	**$500.00**
Can.:	**$650.00**
U.K.:	**£300.00**

HN 3675
Richard the Lionheart
Designer:　P. Parsons
Height:　　10", 25.4 cm
Colour:　　Grey and white
Issued:　　1995-2002

U.S.:	**$675.00**
Can.:	**$900.00**
U.K.:	**£325.00**

HN 3676
Desdemona
Designer:　　P. Parsons
Height:　　　9", 22.9 cm
Colour:　　　Blue, orange and
　　　　　　　white
Issued:　　　1995 in a limited
　　　　　　　edition of 5,000
Series:　　　Shakespearean
　　　　　　　Ladies
Comm.by:　　Lawleys By Post

U.S.:	**$500.00**
Can.:	**$650.00**
U.K.:	**£300.00**

HN 3677
Cinderella
Style One
Designer:　P. Parsons
Height:　　8", 20.3 cm
Colour:　　Blue and white
Issued:　　1995 in a limited
　　　　　　edition of 2,000
Series:　　The Disney Princess
　　　　　　Collection

U.S.:	**$425.00**
Can.:	**$600.00**
U.K.:	**£275.00**

HN 3678
Snow White
Designer: P. Parsons
Height: 8 ¼", 21.0 cm
Colour: Yellow, blue and red
Issued: 1995 in a limited
edition of 2,000
Series: The Disney Princess
Collection

U.S.:	$500.00
Can.:	$700.00
U.K.:	£325.00

HN 3679
Titania
Designer: P. Parsons
Height: 8 ¾", 22.2 cm
Colour: Rose-yellow and blue
Issued: 1995 in a limited
edition of 5,000
Series: Shakespearean
Ladies
Comm.by: Lawleys By Post

U.S.:	$600.00
Can.:	$775.00
U.K.:	£350.00

HN 3680
Lady Jane Grey
Designer: P. Parsons
Height: 8 ¼", 19.0 cm
Colour: Green and gold
Issued: 1995 in a limited
edition of 5,000
Series: Tudor Roses
Comm.by: Lawleys By Post

U.S.:	$ 950.00
Can.:	$1,250.00
U.K.:	£ 500.00

HN 3681
Joan of Arc
Designer: P. Parsons
Height: 10", 25.4 cm
Colour: Cream and blue
Issued: 1996-1998

U.S.:	$600.00
Can.:	$775.00
U.K.:	£350.00

HN 3682
Princess Elizabeth
Designer: P. Parsons
Height: 8 ½", 21.6 cm
Colour: Red and pink
Issued: 1996 in a limited
edition of 5,000
Series: Tudor Roses
Comm.by: Lawleys By Post

U.S.:	$ 800.00
Can.:	$1,000.00
U.K.:	£ 425.00

HN 3683
Eastern Grace
Designer: P. Parsons
Height: 12 ½", 31.7 cm
Colour: Flambé
Issued: 1995 in a limited
edition of 2,500
Varieties: HN 3138
Series: Flambé

U.S.:	$600.00
Can.:	$775.00
U.K.:	£350.00

HN 3684
What's The Matter?
Designer: N. Pedley
Height: 5 ½", 14.0 cm
Colour: Yellow and white
Issued: 1995-1998

U.S.:	$175.00
Can.:	$225.00
U.K.:	£100.00

HN 3685
Hometime
Designer: N. Pedley
Height: 6", 15.0 cm
Colour: White and blue
Issued: 1995-1997

U.S.:	$200.00
Can.:	$250.00
U.K.:	£120.00

HN 3686
Nicole
Style One
Designer: N. Pedley
Height: 7 ½", 19.1 cm
Colour: Pink and cream
Issued: 1995
Varieties: HN 3421
Comm.by: Birks, Canada

U.S.:	**$250.00**
Can.:	**$375.00**
U.K.:	**£150.00**

HN 3687
Helen
Style Three
Designer: N. Pedley
Height: 7 ½", 19.1 cm
Colour: Green
Issued: 1995-1996
Varieties: HN 3601, 3763,
             3886; also called
             'Miss Kay' HN 3659
Comm.by: Express Gifts

U.S.:	**$300.00**
Can.:	**$400.00**
U.K.:	**£150.00**

HN 3688
Emily
Style Two
Designer: N. Pedley
Height: 8 ¼", 21.0 cmm
Colour: Blue and yellow
Issued: 1995-1995
Series: RDICC

U.S.:	**$325.00**
Can.:	**$425.00**
U.K.:	**£200.00**

HN 3689
Jacqueline
Style Three
Designer: N. Pedley
Height: 8", 20.3 cm
Colour: White and green
Issued: 1995-1995
Series: Roadshow Events

U.S.:	**$250.00**
Can.:	**$325.00**
U.K.:	**£150.00**

HN 3690
Angela
Style Four
Designer: N. Pedley
Height: 8", 20.3 cm
Colour: Unknown
Issued: 1995-1997
Varieties: 'Kelly' (Style Two)
             HN 3912; 'Sweet
             Sixteen' (Style Two)
             HN 3648
Comm.by: Great Univ. Studios

U.S.:	**$250.00**
Can.:	**$325.00**
U.K.:	**£150.00**

HN 3691
Rosemary
Style Three
Designer: N. Pedley
Height: 8", 20.3 cm
Colour: Mauve and yellow
Issued: 1995 U.K.,
           1996 Canada-1997
Varieties: HN 3698; 'Claire'
           (Style Two) HN 3646;
           'Kaitlyn' HN 4128;
           'Molly' HN 4091

U.S.:	**$300.00**
Can.:	**$425.00**
U.K.:	**£175.00**

HN 3692
Old Country Roses
Style Two
Designer: N. Pedley
Height: 8", 20.3 cm
Colour: Red, white and
           yellow
Issued: 1995-1999

U.S.:	**$375.00**
Can.:	**$525.00**
U.K.:	**£225.00**

HN 3693
April
Style Four
Designer: N. Pedley
Height: 8", 20.3 cm
Colour: Green, yellow
           and white
Issued: 1995-1997

U.S.:	**$325.00**
Can.:	**$425.00**
U.K.:	**£200.00**

HN 3694
Caroline
Style Two
Designer: N. Pedley
Height: 8", 20.3 cm
Colour: Pink and yellow
Issued: 1995-1998

U.S.:	$300.00
Can.:	$425.00
U.K.:	£175.00

HN 3695
Storytime
Style Two
Designer: N. Pedley
Height: 4", 10.1 cm
Colour: White dress with
          red flowers
Issued: 1995-1998

U.S.:	$175.00
Can.:	$225.00
U.K.:	£ 90.00

HN 3696
Faithful Friend
Designer: N. Pedley
Height: 6", 15.0 cm
Colour: Rose-pink, yellow
          and white
Issued: 1995-1997

U.S.:	$175.00
Can.:	$225.00
U.K.:	£ 90.00

HN 3697
Home at Last
Designer: N. Pedley
Height: 5 ¾", 14.6 cm
Colour: Green and cream
Issued: 1995-1999

U.S.:	$175.00
Can.:	$225.00
U.K.:	£ 90.00

HN 3698
Rosemary
Style Three
Designer: N. Pedley
Height: 8", 20.3 cm
Colour: Mauve and yellow
Issued: 1995-1997
Varieties: HN 3691; 'Claire'
          (Style Two) HN 3646;
          'Kaitlyn' HN 4128;
          'Molly' HN 4091

U.S.:	$300.00
Can.:	$425.00
U.K.:	£175.00

HN 3699
Grace
Style Two
Designer: N. Pedley
Height: 8", 20.3 cm
Colour: Green
Issued: 1996-2001
Series: Vanity Fair Ladies

U.S.:	$300.00
Can.:	$400.00
U.K.:	£175.00

HN 3700
Forget-Me-Nots
Designer: V. Annand
Height: 9", 22.9 cm
Colour: Lavender
Issued: 1995-1998
Series: Flowers of Love

U.S.:	$475.00
Can.:	$600.00
U.K.:	£250.00

HN 3701
Camellias
Designer: V. Annand
Height: 8 ½", 21.6 cm
Colour: Pink
Issued: 1995-1998
Series: Flowers of Love

U.S.:	$475.00
Can.:	$600.00
U.K.:	£250.00

HN 3702
Le Bal
Designer: V. Annand
Height: 8 ½", 21.6 cm
Colour: Yellow and pink
Issued: 1995 in a limited
edition of 5,000
Series: RDICC

U.S.:	**$500.00**
Can.:	**$650.00**
U.K.:	**£275.00**

HN 3703
Belle
Style Three
Designer: V. Annand
Height: 8", 20.3 cm
Colour: Red and gold
Issued: 1996-1996
Series: Figure of the year

U.S.:	**$450.00**
Can.:	**$600.00**
U.K.:	**£250.00**

HN 3704
First Violin
Designer: V. Annand
Height: 9", 22.9 cm
Colour: Grey, yellow ribbon
Issued: 1995 in a limited
edition of 1,500
Series: Edwardian String
Quartet
Comm.by: Lawleys By Post

U.S.:	**$600.00**
Can.:	**$775.00**
U.K.:	**£350.00**

HN 3705
Second Violin
Designer: V. Annand
Height: 9", 22.9 cm
Colour: Grey, pink ribbon
Issued: 1995 in a limited
edition of 1,500
Series: Edwardian String
Quartet
Comm.by: Lawleys By Post

U.S.:	**$600.00**
Can.:	**$775.00**
U.K.:	**£350.00**

HN 3706
Viola
Designer: V. Annand
Height: 8 ¾", 22.2 cm
Colour: Grey, green ribbon
Issued: 1995 in a limited
edition of 1,500
Series: Edwardian String
Quartet
Comm.by: Lawleys By Post

U.S.:	**$600.00**
Can.:	**$775.00**
U.K.:	**£350.00**

HN 3707
Cello
Style Two
Designer: V. Annand
Height: 7", 17.8 cm
Colour: Grey, blue ribbon
Issued: 1995 in a limited
edition of 1,500
Series: Edwardian String
Quartet
Comm.by: Lawleys By Post

U.S.:	**$600.00**
Can.:	**$775.00**
U.K.:	**£350.00**

HN 3708
Katherine
Style Two
Designer: V. Annand
Height: 9", 22.9 cm
Colour: Peach
Issued: 1996-1996
Series: Lady Doulton, 1996

U.S.:	**$350.00**
Can.:	**$450.00**
U.K.:	**£200.00**

HN 3709
Rose
Style Two
Designer: V. Annand
Height: 8 ½", 21.6 cm
Colour: Peach and white
Issued: 1996-2000
Series: Flowers of Love

U.S.:	**$475.00**
Can.:	**$600.00**
U.K.:	**£250.00**

HN 3710
Primrose
Designer: V. Annand
Height: 9", 22.9 cm
Colour: Yellow and pink
Issued: 1996-1998
Series: Flowers of Love
  U.S.:   **$475.00**
  Can.:   **$600.00**
  U.K.:   **£250.00**

HN 3711
Jane
Style Four
Designer: V. Annand
Height: 9", 22.9 cm
Colour: White, green and red
Issued: 1997 in a limited
         edition of 1997
Series: Lady Doulton, 1997
  U.S.:   **$225.00**
  Can.:   **$350.00**
  U.K.:   **£135.00**

HN 3712
New Baby
Designer: V. Annand
Height: 2", 5.0 cm
Colour: White with pink
         highlights
Issued: 1997-2002
Varieties: HN 3713
Series: Name Your Own
  U.S.:   **$125.00**
  Can.:   **$170.00**
  U.K.:   **£ 75.00**

Metal plaque on base for engraved
name.

HN 3713
New Baby
Designer: V. Annand
Height: 2", 5.0 cm
Colour: White with blue
         highlights
Issued: 1997-2002
Varieties: HN 3712
Series: Name Your Own
  U.S.:   **$125.00**
  Can.:   **$170.00**
  U.K.:   **£ 75.00**

Metal plaque on base for engraved
name.

HN 3714
Emma
Style Three
Designer: V. Annand
Height: 8 ½", 21.6 cm
Colour: Red
Issued: 1997-2003
Varieties: Also called 'Madison'
         HN 4204
Series: In Vogue
  U.S.:   **$225.00**
  Can.:   **$300.00**
  U.K.:   **£100.00**

HN 3715
Sophie
Style Four
Designer: V. Annand
Height: 8 ¾", 22.2 cm
Colour: Green dress, yellow
         scarf and gloves
Issued: 1997-2001
Series: In Vogue
  U.S.:   **$250.00**
  Can.:   **$350.00**
  U.K.:   **£135.00**

HN 3716
Isabel
Style One
Designer: V. Annand
Height: 8 ½", 21.6 cm
Colour: Pale blue dress,
         pink scarf
Issued: 1997-2001
Series: Chelsea
  U.S.:   **$250.00**
  Can.:   **$350.00**
  U.K.:   **£150.00**

HN 3717
Olivia
Style Three
Designer: V. Annand
Height: 8 ¾", 22.2 cm
Colour: Pale blue
Issued: 1997-2002
Varieties" Also called 'Brittany'
         HN 4206
Series: Chelsea
  U.S.:   **$200.00**
  Can.:   **$275.00**
  U.K.:   **£100.00**

HN 3718
The Charge of the Light Brigade
Stsyle One
Designer: A. Maslankowski
Height: 17", 43.2 cm
Colour: Dark blue, brown
           and black
Issued: 1995 to the present
Series: Prestige

U.S.:	**$19,250.00**
Can.:	**$19,300.00**
U.K.:	**£10,500.00**

HN 3719
Long John Silver
Style Two
Designer: A. Maslankowski
Height: 8 ¾", 22.2 cm
Colour: Browns and yellow
Issued: 1993-1996
Series: Character Sculptures

U.S.:	**$300.00**
Can.:	**$400.00**
U.K.:	**£175.00**

Resin

HN 3720
Robin Hood
Style Two
Designer: A. Maslankowski
Height: 10 ½", 26.7 cm
Colour: Greens and browns
Issued: 1993-1996
Series: Character Sculptures

U.S.:	**$375.00**
Can.:	**$500.00**
U.K.:	**£225.00**

Resin

HN 3721
Pied Piper
Style Two
Designer: A. Maslankowski
Height: 8 ¾", 22.2 cm
Colour: Red, yellow and black
Issued: 1993-1996
Series: Character Sculptures

U.S.:	**$300.00**
Can.:	**$400.00**
U.K.:	**£175.00**

Resin

HN 3722
The Wizard
Style Two
Designer: A. Maslankowski
Height: 10", 25.4 cm
Colour: Blue
Issued: 1994-1996
Varieties: HN 3732
Series: Character Sculptures

U.S.:	**$350.00**
Can.:	**$450.00**
U.K.:	**£200.00**

Resin

HN 3723
Au Revoir
Style One
Designer: A. Maslankowski
Height: 7 ¾", 19.7 cm
Colour: Cream with gold trim
Issued: 1995-1998
Varieties: Also called 'Fond
           Farewell' HN 3815
Series: Elegance (Series Two)

U.S.:	**$225.00**
Can.:	**$300.00**
U.K.:	**£125.00**

HN 3724
Summer Breeze
Designer: A. Maslankowski
Height: 7 ¾", 19.7 cm
Colour: Cream with gold trim
Issued: 1995-1998
Varieties: Also called 'Moonlight
           Stroll' HN 3954
Series: Elegance (Series Two)

U.S.:	**$225.00**
Can.:	**$300.00**
U.K.:	**£125.00**

HN 3725
Spring Morning
Style Two
Designer: A. Maslankowski
Height: 7 ¾", 19.7 cm
Colour: Cream with gold trim
Issued: 1995-1998
Varieties: Also called 'Summer
           Scent' HN 3955
Series: Elegance (Series Two)

U.S.:	**$225.00**
Can.:	**$300.00**
U.K.:	**£125.00**

HN 3726
Dinnertime
Designer: A. Maslankowski
Height: 4 ½", 11.9 cm
Colour: White and green
Issued: 1995-1998
Series: Vanity Fair Children
U.S.:	**$125.00**
Can.:	**$200.00**
U.K.:	**£ 75.00**

HN 3727
Christmas Carols
Designer: A. Maslankowski
Height: 6", 15.0 cm
Colour: White
Issued: 1995-1999
Varieties: HN 4061
Series: Sentiments
U.S.:	**$125.00**
Can.:	**$165.00**
U.K.:	**£ 75.00**

HN 3728
Free Spirit
Style Two
Designer: A. Maslankowski
Height: 7 ½", 19.1 cm
Colour: Cream with gold trim
Issued: 1995-1998
Varieties: Also called 'Spring
           Serenade' HN 3956
Series: Elegance (Series Two)
U.S.:	**$225.00**
Can.:	**$300.00**
U.K.:	**£125.00**

HN 3729
Au Revoir
Style Two
Designer: A. Maslankowski
Height: 6 ½", 16.5 cm
Colour: White
Issued: 1996-1999
Series: Sentiments
U.S.:	**$125.00**
Can.:	**$165.00**
U.K.:	**£ 75.00**

HN 3730
Innocence
Style Two
Designer: A. Maslankowski
Height: 3 ½", 8.9 cm
Colour: Pink and white
Issued: 1996-2000
U.S.:	**$125.00**
Can.:	**$165.00**
U.K.:	**£ 70.00**

HN 3731
Ballet Class
Style Two
Designer: A. Maslankowski
Height: 6", 15.0 cm
Colour: White, yellow slippers
Issued: 1996-2003
Series: Images
U.S.:	**$ 95.00**
Can.:	**$220.00**
U.K.:	**£ 50.00**

HN 3732
The Wizard
Style Two
Designer: A. Maslankowski
Height: 10", 25.4 cm
Colour: Blue and orange
Issued: 1995-1996
Varieties: HN 3722
Series: Character Sculptures
Comm.by: Lawleys By Post
U.S.:	**$350.00**
Can.:	**$450.00**
U.K.:	**£200.00**

Resin

HN 3733
Christmas Angel
Designer: A. Maslankowski
Height: 5 ¾", 14.6 cm
Colour: White
Issued: 1996-1998
Varieties: HN 4060
Series: Sentiments
U.S.:	**$125.00**
Can.:	**$160.00**
U.K.:	**£ 75.00**

HN 3734
Top o' the Hill
Style Two
Designer: L. Harradine
Remodeller: P. Gee
Height: 3 ¾", 9.5 cm
Colour: Red, white, gold trim
Issued: 1995-1996
Varieties: HN 2126, 3499
Series: 1. Signature
                        2. Miniatures
Comm.by: Lawleys By Post

U.S.:	**$250.00**
Can.:	**$325.00**
U.K.:	**£150.00**

HN 3735
Victoria
Style Two
Designer: M. Davies
Remodeller: P. Gee
Height: 3 ½", 8.9 cm
Colour: Purple
Issued: 1995-1996
Varieties: HN 3744, 3909
Series: 1. Signature
                        2. Miniatures
Comm.by: Lawleys By Post

U.S.:	**$250.00**
Can.:	**$325.00**
U.K.:	**£150.00**

HN 3735A
Top o' the Hill
Style One
Designer: L. Harradine
Height: 7", 17.8 cm
Colour: Dark blue
Issued: 1997 in a limited
                        edition of 3,500
Varieties: HN 1833, 1834,
                        1849, 2127

U.S.:	**$400.00**
Can.:	**$525.00**
U.K.:	**£225.00**

HN 3736
Autumn Breezes
Style One
Designer: L. Harradine
Height: 7 ½", 19.1 cm
Colour: Blue and yellow
Issued: 1997-1998
Varieties: HN 1911,1913, 1934,
                    2131, 2147
Series: M. Doulton Events

U.S.:	**$375.00**
Can.:	**$475.00**
U.K.:	**£225.00**

HN 3737
Old Balloon Seller
Style One
Designer: L. Harradine
Height: 7 ½", 19.1 cm
Colour: Purple, blue, white,
                    yellow and green
Issued: 1999-1999
Varieties: HN 1315
Series: M. Doulton Events

U.S.:	**$375.00**
Can.:	**$475.00**
U.K.:	**£225.00**

Serial Numbered
HN 3738 - 3739 not issued.

HN 3740
Lynne
Style One
Designer: M. Davies
Height: 7", 17.8 cm
Colour: Multicoloured
                    with gold trim
Issued: 1995-1995
Varieties: HN 2329; also called
                    'Kathy' (Style Two)
                    HN 3305
Series: Roadshow Events

U.S.:	**$450.00**
Can.:	**$575.00**
U.K.:	**£250.00**

HN 3741
Elaine
Style One
Designer: M. Davies
Height: 7 ½", 19.1 cm
Colour: Red with gold trim
Issued: 1995-1995
Varieties: HN 2791, 3307, 4130
Series: Roadshow Events

U.S.:	**$450.00**
Can.:	**$575.00**
U.K.:	**£250.00**

HN 3742
Gillian
Style Three
Designer: M. Davies
Height: 7 ¾", 19.7 cm
Colour: White and pink
Issued: 1995-1997
Varieties: Also called Figure of
                        the Month
Comm.by: Great Universal
                        Studios

U.S.:	**$225.00**
Can.:	**$300.00**
U.K.:	**£125.00**

HN 3743
Kirsty
Style Two
Designer: M. Davies
Remodeller: P. Gee
Height: 3 ¾", 9.5 cm
Colour: Yellow
Issued: 1995
Varieties: HN 3213, 3246, 3480
Series: Miniatures
Comm.by: Great Universal
Studios

U.S.:	**$150.00**
Can.:	**$200.00**
U.K.:	**£ 75.00**

HN 3744
Victoria
Style Two
Designer: M. Davies
Remodeller: P. Gee
Height: 3 ½", 8.9 cm
Colour: Patterned pink dress
Issued: 1995-1998
Varieties: HN 3735, 3909
Series: Miniatures

U.S.:	**$175.00**
Can.:	**$225.00**
U.K.:	**£100.00**

HN 3745 not issued.

HN 3746
Memory Lane
Designer: M. Davies
Height: 5 ½", 14.0 cm
Colour: White with blue flowers
Issued: c.1996
Varieties: 'Debbie',HN 2385,
2400; 'Lavender Rose',
HN 3481; 'Moonlight
Roses', HN 3483; 'Old
Country Roses', (Style
One) HN 3842;
'Tranquillity' HN 3747

U.S.:	**$125.00**
Can.:	**$175.00**
U.K.:	**£ 75.00**

HN 3747
Tranquillity
Designer: M. Davies
Height: 5 ½", 14.0 cm
Colour: White with pink flowers
Issued: c.1996
Varieties: 'Debbie'; HN 2385,
2400; 'Lavender Rose'
HN 3481; 'Moonlight
Roses' HN 3483; 'Old
Country Roses', (Style
One) HN 3842;
'Memory Lane' HN 3746

U.S.:	**$125.00**
Can.:	**$175.00**
U.K.:	**£ 75.00**

HN 3748
Fiona
Style Four
Designer: M. Davies
Height: 7 ½", 19.1 cm
Colour: Lemon, tartan shawl
Issued: 1996-2002
Varieties: Adrienne HN 2152,
2304; Joan (Style
Two) HN 3217

U.S.:	**$225.00**
Can.:	**$300.00**
U.K.:	**£125.00**

HN 3749
Karen
Style Three
Designer: M. Davies
Remodeller: R. Tabbenor
Height: 4", 10.1 cm
Colour: White with gold trim
Issued: 1997
Varieties: HN 3270, 3338
Series: Miniatures

U.S.:	**$200.00**
Can.:	**$250.00**
U.K.:.:	**£120.00**

HN 3750
Gulliver
Designer: D. Biggs
Height: 8 ½", 21.6 cm
Colour: Blue, yellow,
green and red
Issued: 1995-1996
Series: Character Sculptures

U.S.:	**$300.00**
Can.:	**$400.00**
U.K.:	**£175.00**

Resin

HN 3751
Cyrano de Bergerac
Designer: D. Biggs
Height: 8 ½", 21.6 cm
Colour: Red, blue, black
and brown
Issued: 1995-1996
Series: Character Sculptures

U.S.:	**$300.00**
Can.:	**$400.00**
U.K.:	**£175.00**

Resin

HN 3752
Fagin
Style Two
Designer: A. Dobson
Height: 8 ½", 21.6 cm
Colour: Browns, black and
green
Issued: 1995-1996
Series: Character Sculptures

U.S.:	**$300.00**
Can.:	**$400.00**
U.K.:	**£175.00**

Resin
HN 3753 not issued.

HN 3754
For You
Designer: T. Potts
Height: 8 ½", 21.6 cm
Colour: Blue
Issued: 1996 to the present
Varieties: HN 3863
Series: Name Your Own

U.S.:	**N/I**
Can.:	**$315.00**
U.K.:	**£ 85.00**

Metal plaque on base for engraved
name.

HN 3755
Strolling
Style Two
Designer: T. Potts
Height: 8", 20.3 cm
Colour: Red and yellow
Issued: 1996-1999

U.S.:	**$275.00**
Can.:	**$375.00**
U.K.:	**£165.00**

HN 3756
Pamela
Style Three
Designer: T. Potts
Height: 8", 20.3 cm
Colour: Blue and pink
Issued: 1996-1996
Series: RDICC

U.S.:	**$300.00**
Can.:	**$400.00**
U.K.:	**£175.00**

HN 3757
Jean
Style Three
Designer: T. Potts
Height: 6 ¾", 17.2 cm
Colour: White and blue
Issued: 1996-1997
Varieties: HN 3862
Comm.by: Kay's Mail Order
Catalogue

U.S.:	**$200.00**
Can.:	**$250.00**
U.K.:	**£120.00**

HN 3758
Bride of the Year
Designer: T. Potts
Height: 8", 20.3 cm
Colour: White and peach
Issued: 1996
Varieties: Also called 'Wedding
Morn' (Style Two)
HN 3853
Comm.by: Kay's Mail Order
Catalogue

U.S.:	**$275.00**
Can.:	**$375.00**
U.K.:	**£175.00**

HN 3759
Stephanie
Style Two
Designer: T. Potts
Height: 8 ¼", 21.0 cm
Colour: Pink and lavender
Issued: 1996-1996
Series: Roadshow Events

U.S.:	**$200.00**
Can.:	**$250.00**
U.K.:	**$120.00**

HN 3760
Laura
Style Two
Designer: N. Pedley
Height: 8", 20.3 cm
Colour: White and blue
Issued: 1996-1999

U.S.:	**$225.00**
Can.:	**$300.00**
U.K.:	**£125.00**

HN 3761
Sleepyhead
Style Two
Designer: N. Pedley
Height: 4", 10.1 cm
Colour: White, green and brown
Issued: 1996-1998

U.S.:	$175.00
Can.:	$225.00
U.K.:	£ 90.00

HN 3762
Time For Bed
Designer: N. Pedley
Height: 5 ¼", 13.3 cm
Colour: Pink
Issued: 1996-1998

U.S.:	$175.00
Can.:	$225.00
U.K.:	£ 90.00

HN 3763
Helen
Style Three
Designer: N. Pedley
Height: 8 ¼", 21.0 cm
Colour: Pink
Issued: 1996
Varieties: HN 3601, 3687, 3886; also called 'Miss Kay' HN 3659
Comm.by: Sears, Canada

U.S.:	$250.00
Can.:	$325.00
U.K.:	£150.00

HN 3764
Welcome
Designer: N. Pedley
Height: 5 ¾", 14.6 cm
Colour: White
Issued: 1996-1996
Series: Club Membership Figure

U.S.:	$125.00
Can.:	$160.00
U.K.:	£ 75.00

HN 3765
Kate
Style Two
Designer: N. Pedley
Height: 8", 20.3 cm
Colour: Rose pink bodice, white flowered skirt
Issued: 1996
Varieties: HN 3882
Comm.by: Kay's Mail Order Catalogue

U.S.:	$250.00
Can.:	$325.00
U.K.:	£150.00

HN 3766
Anita
Designer: N. Pedley
Height: 8", 20.3 cm
Colour: White, green and yellow
Issued: 1996
Comm.by: Kay's Mail Order Catalogue

U.S.:	$200.00
Can.:	$250.00
U.K.:	£120.00

HN 3767
Christine
Style Four
Designer: N. Pedley
Height: 8", 20.3 cm
Colour: Blue
Issued: 1996-1998

U.S.:	$300.00
Can.:	$425.00
U.K.:	£175.00

HN 3768
Off to School
Designer: N. Pedley
Height: 5 ¼", 13.3 cm
Colour: Navy and grey
Issued: 1996-1998

U.S.:	$225.00
Can.:	$300.00
U.K.:	£125.00

HN 3769
Winter's Day
Designer: N. Pedley
Height: 7 ¾", 19.7 cm
Colour: Red and white
Issued: 1996-1997
Series: RDICC

U.S.:	**$325.00**
Can.:	**$425.00**
U.K.:	**£200.00**

HN 3770
Sir Francis Drake
Designer: D. Biggs
Height: 8 ½", 21.6 cm
Colour: Red, yellow, brown
and green
Issued: 1996-1996
Series: Character Sculptures

U.S.:	**$300.00**
Can.:	**$400.00**
U.K.:	**£175.00**

Resin
HN 3771 - 3779 not issued.

HN 3780
The Bowls Player
Designer: J. Jones
Height: 6", 15.0 cm
Colour: Yellow, white
and green
Issued: 1996-1996
Series: Character Sculptures

U.S.:	**$300.00**
Can.:	**$400.00**
U.K.:	**£175.00**

Resin
HN 3781 - 3784 not issued.

HN 3785
Bill Sikes
Designer: A. Dobson
Height: 9", 22.9 cm
Colour: Brown
Issued: 1996-1996
Series: Character Sculptures

U.S.:	**$300.00**
Can.:	**$400.00**
U.K.:	**£175.00**

Resin

HN 3786
Oliver Twist and
The Artful Dodger
Designer: A. Dobson
Height: 8", 20.3 cm
Colour: Browns, blue
and black
Issued: 1996-1996
Series: Character Sculptures

U.S.:	**$350.00**
Can.:	**$450.00**
U.K.:	**£200.00**

Resin
HN 3787 - 3789 not issued.

HN 3790
Sophie
Style Three
Designer: A. Maslankowski
Height: 9 ½", 24.1 cm
Colour: Cream and green
Issued: 1996-1997
Varieties: HN 3791, 3792, 3793
Series: Charleston

U.S.:	**$225.00**
Can.:	**$300.00**
U.K.:	**£125.00**

HN 3791
Sophie
Style Three
Designer: A. Maslankowski
Height: 9 ½", 24.1 cm
Colour: Cream and blue
Issued: 1996-1997
Varieties: HN 3790, 3792, 3793
Series: Charleston

U.S.:	**$225.00**
Can.:	**$300.00**
U.K.:	**£125.00**

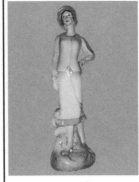

HN 3792
Sophie
Style Three
Designer: A. Maslankowski
Height: 9 ½", 24.1 cm
Colour: Cream and pink
Issued: 1996-1997
Varieties: HN 3790, 3791, 3793
Series: Charleston

U.S.:	**$225.00**
Can.:	**$300.00**
U.K.:	**£125.00**

HN 3793
Sophie
Style Three
Designer: A. Maslankowski
Height: 9 ½", 24.1 cm
Colour: Ivory and gold
Issued: 1996-1997
Varieties: HN 3790, 3791, 3792
Series: Charleston

U.S.:	**$225.00**
Can.:	**$300.00**
U.K.:	**£125.00**

HN 3794
Harriet
Style Two
Designer: A. Maslankowski
Height: 9 ¼", 23.5 cm
Colour: Cream and green
Issued: 1996-1997
Varieties: HN 3795, 3796, 3797
Series: Charleston

U.S.:	**$325.00**
Can.:	**$400.00**
U.K.:	**£150.00**

HN 3795
Harriet
Style Two
Designer: A. Maslankowski
Height: 9 ¼", 23.5 cm
Colour: Cream and blue
Issued: 1996-1997
Varieties: HN 3794, 3796, 3797
Series: Charleston

U.S.:	**$325.00**
Can.:	**$400.00**
U.K.:	**£150.00**

HN 3796
Harriet
Style Two
Designer: A. Maslankowski
Height: 9 ¼", 23.5 cm
Colour: Cream and pink
Issued: 1996-1997
Varieties: HN 3794, 3795, 3797
Series: Charleston

U.S.:	**$325.00**
Can.:	**$400.00**
U.K.:	**£150.00**

HN 3797
Harriet
Style Two
Designer: A. Maslankowski
Height: 9 ¼", 23.5 cm
Colour: Cream, ivory and gold
Issued: 1996-1997
Varieties: HN 3794, 3795, 3796
Series: Charleston

U.S.:	**$325.00**
Can.:	**$400.00**
U.K.:	**£150.00**

HN 3798
Eliza
Style Three
Designer: A. Maslankowski
Height: 9 ½", 24.1 cm
Colour: Cream and green
Issued: 1996-1997
Varieties: HN 3799, 3800, 3801
Series: Charleston

U.S.:	**$250.00**
Can.:	**$325.00**
U.K.:	**£125.00**

HN 3799
Eliza
Style Three
Designer: A. Maslankowski
Height: 9 ½", 24.1 cm
Colour: Cream and blue
Issued: 1996-1997
Varieties: HN 3798, 3800, 3801
Series: Charleston

U.S.:	**$250.00**
Can.:	**$325.00**
U.K.:	**£125.00**

HN 3800
Eliza
Style Three
Designer: A. Maslankowski
Height: 9 ½", 24.1 cm
Colour: Cream and pink
Issued: 1996-1997
Varieties: HN 3798, 3799, 3801
Series: Charleston

U.S.:	**$250.00**
Can.:	**$325.00**
U.K.:	**£125.00**

HN 3801
Eliza
Style Three
Designer: A. Maslankowski
Height: 9 ½", 24.1 cm
Colour: Ivory and gold
Issued: 1996-1997
Varieties: HN 3798, 3799, 3800
Series: Charleston

U.S.:	$250.00
Can.:	$325.00
U.K.:	£125.00

HN 3802
Daisy
Style Two
Designer: A. Maslankowski
Height: 9 ¼", 23.5 cm
Colour: Cream and green
Issued: 1996-1997
Varieties: HN 3803, 3804, 3805
Series: Charleston

U.S.:	$325.00
Can.:	$400.00
U.K.:	£150.00

HN 3803
Daisy
Style Two
Designer: A. Maslankowski
Height: 9 ¼", 23.5 cm
Colour: Cream and blue
Issued: 1996-1997
Varieties: HN 3802, 3804, 3805
Series: Charleston

U.S.:	$325.00
Can.:	$400.00
U.K.:	£150.00

HN 3804
Daisy
Style Two
Designer: A. Maslankowski
Height: 9 ¼", 23.5 cm
Colour: Cream and pink
Issued: 1996-1997
Varieties: HN 3802, 3803, 3805
Series: Charleston

U.S.:	$325.00
Can.:	$400.00
U.K.:	£150.00

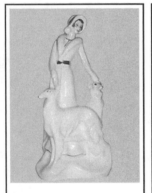

HN 3805
Daisy
Style Two
Designer: A. Maslankowski
Height: 9 ¼", 23.5 cm
Colour: Ivory and gold
Issued: 1996-1997
Varieties: HN 3802, 3803, 3804
Series: Charleston

U.S.:	$325.00
Can.:	$400.00
U.K.:	£150.00

HN 3806
Emily
Style Three
Designer: A. Maslankowski
Height: 9", 22.9 cm
Colour: Cream and green
Issued: 1996-1997
Varieties: HN 3807, 3808, 3809
Series: Charleston

U.S.:	$300.00
Can.:	$325.00
U.K.:	£125.00

HN 3807
Emily
Style Three
Designer: A. Maslankowski
Height: 9", 22.9 cm
Colour: Cream and blue
Issued: 1996-1997
Varieties: HN 3806, 3808, 3809
Series: Charleston

U.S.:	$300.00
Can.:	$325.00
U.K.:	£125.00

HN 3808
Emily
Style Three
Designer: A. Maslankowski
Height: 9", 22.9 cm
Colour: Cream and pink
Issued: 1996-1997
Varieties: HN 3806, 3807, 3809
Series: Charleston

U.S.:	$300.00
Can.:	$325.00
U.K.:	£125.00

HN 3809
Emily
Style Three
Designer: A. Maslankowski
Height: 9", 22.9 cm
Colour: Ivory and gold
Issued: 1996-1997
Varieties: HN 3806. 3807, 3808
Series: Charleston

U.S.:	**$300.00**
Can.:	**$325.00**
U.K.:	**£125.00**

HN 3810
Charlotte
Style Three
Designer: A. Maslankowski
Height: 9 ¼", 23.5 cm
Colour: Cream and green
Issued: 1996-1997
Varieties: HN 3811, 3812, 3813
Series: Charleston

U.S.:	**$400.00**
Can.:	**$500.00**
U.K.:	**£195.00**

HN 3811
Charlotte
Style Three
Designer: A. Maslankowski
Height: 9 ¼", 23.5 cm
Colour: Cream and blue
Issued: 1996-1997
Varieties: HN 3810, 3812, 3813
Series: Charleston

U.S.:	**$400.00**
Can.:	**$500.00**
U.K.:	**£195.00**

HN 3812
Charlotte
Style Three
Designer: A. Maslankowski
Height: 9 ¼", 23.5 cm
Colour: Cream and pink
Issued: 1996-1997
Varieties: HN 3810, 3811, 3813
Series: Charleston

U.S.:	**$400.00**
Can.:	**$500.00**
U.K.:	**£195.00**

HN 3813
Charlotte
Style Three
Designer: A. Maslankowski
Height: 9 ¼", 23.5 cm
Colour: Ivory and gold
Issued: 1996-1997
Varieties: HN 3810, 3811, 3812
Series: Charleston

U.S.:	**$400.00**
Can.:	**$500.00**
U.K.:	**£195.00**

HN 3814
The Cricketer
Style One
Designer: A. Maslankowski
Height: 8 ¼", 21.0 cm
Colour: White
Issued: 1996-1996

U.S.:	**$250.00**
Can.:	**$325.00**
U.K.:	**£150.00**

HN 3815
Fond Farewell
Designer: A. Maslankowski
Height: 8", 20.3 cm,
Colour: Red
Issued: 1997-1999
Varieties: Also called 'Au Revoir'
(Style One) HN 3723

U.S.:	**$325.00**
Can.:	**$425.00**
U.K.:	**£195.00**

HN 3816
Ellen
Style Two
Designer: A. Maslankowski
Height: 8 ¾", 22.2 cm
Colour: Blue
Issued: 1997-1997
Varieties: HN 3819
Series: Charleston

U.S.:	**$225.00**
Can.:	**$300.00**
U.K.:	**£110.00**

HN 3817 - 3818 not issued.

HN 3819
Ellen
Style Two
Designer: A. Maslankowski
Height: 8 ¾", 22.2 cm
Colour: Ivory with gold highlights
Issued: 1997-1997
Varieties: HN 3816
Series: Charleston

U.S.:	**$225.00**
Can.:	**$300.00**
U.K.:	**£110.00**

HN 3820
Lillie Langtry
Designer: D. V. Tootle
Height: 8 ¾", 22.2 cm
Colour: Pink
Issued: 1996 in a limited edition of 5,000
Series: Victorian and Edwardian actresses
Comm.by: Lawleys By Post

U.S.:	**$550.00**
Can.:	**$700.00**
U.K.:	**£250.00**

HN 3821
Alfred The Great
Designer: D. V. Tootle
Height: 9 ¼", 23.5 cm
Colour: Gold, red and green
Issued: 1996-1997

U.S.:	**$600.00**
Can.:	**$750.00**
U.K.:	**£300.00**

HN 3822
James I
(1603-1625)
Designer: D. V. Tootle
Height: 9", 22.9 cm
Colour: Red, grey, gold trim
Issued: 1996 in a limited edition of 1,500
Series: Stuart Kings
Comm.by: Lawleys By Post

U.S.:	**$ 850.00**
Can.:	**$1,000.00**
U.K.:	**£ 450.00**

HN 3823 not issued.

HN 3824
Charles I
(1625-1649)
Designer: Douglas Tootle
Height: 10", 25.4 cm
Colour: Green and white
Issued: 1997 in a limited edition of 1,500
Series: Stuart Kings
Comm.by: Lawleys By Post

U.S.:	**$1,200.00**
Can.:	**$1,000.00**
U.K.:	**£ 450.00**

HN 3825
Charles II
(1660-1685)
Designer: D.V. Tootle
Height: 9", 22.9 cm
Colour: Purple and beige
Issued: 1996 in a limited edition of 1,500
Series: Stuart Kings
Comm.by: Lawleys By Post

U.S.:	**$ 850.00**
Can.:	**$1,000.00**
U.K.:	**£ 425.00**

HN 3826
Ellen Terry
Designer: D.V. Tootle
Height: 9", 22.9 cm
Colour: Blue and yellow
Issued: 1996 in a limited edition of 5,000
Series: Victorian and Edwardian Actresses
Comm.by: Lawleys By Post

U.S.:	**$600.00**
Can.:	**$750.00**
U.K.:	**£300.00**

HN 3827
The Performance
Designer: D.V. Tootle
Height: 10 ¼", 26.0 cm
Colour: White
Issued: 1997-2001
Series: Images

U.S.:	**$275.00**
Can.:	**$425.00**
U.K.:	**£175.00**

HN 3828
The Ballerina
Style Three
Designer: D.V. Tootle
Height: 5 ½", 14.0 cm
Colour: White
Issued: 1997-2001
Series: Images

U.S.:	**$150.00**
Can.:	**$200.00**
U.K.:	**£ 85.00**

HN 3829
Happy Birthday
Style Three
Designer: D.V. Tootle
Height: 7 ½", 19.1 cm
Colour: White
Issued: 1997-2002
Series: Images

U.S.:	**$125.00**
Can.:	**$200.00**
U.K.:	**£ 60.00**

HN 3830
Belle
Style Four
Designer: P. Parsons
Height: 8", 20.3 cm
Colour: Yellow
Issued: 1996 in a limited
           edition of 2,000
Series: The Disney Princess
           Collection

U.S.:	**$400.00**
Can.:	**$600.00**
U.K.:	**£250.00**

HN 3831
Ariel
Designer: P. Parsons
Height: 8 ¼", 21.0 cm
Colour: White
Issued: 1996 in a limited
           edition of 2,000
Series: The Disney Princess
           Collection

U.S.:	**$400.00**
Can.:	**$600.00**
U.K.:	**£250.00**

HN 3832
Jasmine
Style Two
Designer: P. Parsons
Height: 7 ½", 19.1 cm
Colour: Lilac dress
Issued: 1996 in a limited
           edition of 2,000
Series: The Disney Princess
           Collection

U.S.:	**$400.00**
Can.:	**$600.00**
U.K.:	**£250.00**

HN 3833
Aurora
Designer: P. Parsons
Height: 7 ½", 19.1 cm
Colour: Blue dress
Issued: 1996 in a limited
           edition of 2,000
Series: The Disney Princess
           Collection

U.S.:	**$250.00**
Can.:	**$375.00**
U.K.:	**£150.00**

HN 3834
Mary Tudor
Designer: P. Parsons
Height: 6 ¼", 15.9 cm
Colour: Purple and peach-
            yellow dress
Issued: 1997 in a limited
            edition of 5,000
Series: Tudor Roses
Comm.by: Lawleys By Post

U.S.:	**$800.00**
Can.:	**$975.00**
U.K.:	**£350.00**

HN 3835
Scheherazade
Designer: P. Parsons
Height: 10 ½", 26.7 cm
Colour: Red and green
Issued: 1996 in a limited
            edition of 1,500
Series: Fabled Beauties
Comm.by: Lawleys By Post

U.S.:	**$700.00**
Can.:	**$875.00**
U.K.:	**£375.00**

HN 3836
Queen Elizabeth II and
The Duke of Edinburgh
Designer: P. Parsons
Height: 9 ¼", 23.5 cm
Colour: White wedding dress,
            navy naval uniform
Issued: 1997 in a limited
            edition of 750

U.S.:	$ 800.00
Can.:	$1,000.00
U.K.:	£ 475.00

Issued to celebrate their golden
wedding anniversary.
HN 3837 not issued.

HN 3838
Margaret Tudor
Designer: P. Parsons
Height: 6 ½", 16.5 cm
Colour: Green and gold dress
Issued: 1997 in a limited
            edition of 5,000
Series: Tudor Roses
Comm.by: Lawleys By Post

U.S.:	$ 850.00
Can.:	$1,000.00
U.K.:	£ 375.00

HN 3839
Cruella De Vil
Designer: P. Parsons
Height: 8", 20.3 cm
Colour: Black dress, white
           coat
Issued: 1997 in a limited
           edition of 2,000
Series: Disney Villains

U.S.:	$400.00
Can.:	$600.00
U.K.:	£250.00

HN 3840
Maleficent
Designer: P. Parsons
Height: 8", 20.3 cm
Colour: Black and purple
Issued: 1997 in a limited
           edition of 2,000
Series: Disney Villains

U.S.:	$400.00
Can.:	$600.00
U.K.:	£250.00

HN 3841
Rapunzel
Designer: P. Parsons
Height: 10", 25.4 cm
Colour: Purple and yellow
Issued: 1998 in a limited
            edition of 1,500
Series: Fabled Beauties
Comm.by: Lawleys By Post

U.S.:	$600.00
Can.:	$750.00
U.K.:	£350.00

HN 3842
Jane Eyre
Designer: P. Parsons
Height: 8 ¼", 21.0 cm
Colour: Blue dress with pale
            blue collar, white dog
            with black patches
Issued: 1997 in a limited
            edition of 3,500
Series: Literary Heroines
Comm.by: Lawleys by Post

U.S.:	$600.00
Can.:	$750.00
U.K.:	£300.00

HN 3843
Emma
Style Four
Designer: P. Parsons
Height: 8 ¼", 21.0 cm
Colour: Light yellow dress
            and hat, red bows
Issued: 1997 in a limited
            edition of 3,500
Series: Literary Heroines
Comm.by: Lawleys By Post

U.S.:	$450.00
Can.:	$600.00
U.K.:	£250.00

HN 3844
Nefertiti
Designer: P. Parsons
Height: 10 ½", 26.7 cm
Colour: Cream
Issued: 1998 in a limited
            edition of 950
Series: Egyptian Queens
Comm.by: Lawleys By Post

U.S.:	$700.00
Can.:	$900.00
U.K.:	£400.00

HN 3845
Elizabeth Bennet
Designer: P. Parsons
Height: 8 ¾", 22.2 cm
Colour: Browns
Issued: 1998 in a limited
              edition of 3,500
Series: Literary Heroines
Comm.by: Lawleys By Post

   U.S.:   **$500.00**
   Can.:   **$650.00**
   U.K.:   £260.00

HN 3846
Tess of the D'Urbervilles
Designer: P. Parsons
Height: 8 ¼", 21.0 cm
Colour: Tan, cream and white
Issued: 1998 in a limited
              edition of 3,500
Series: Literary Heroines
Comm.by: Lawleys By Post

   U.S.:   **$475.00**
   Can.:   **$600.00**
   U.K.:   £250.00

HN 3847
The Queen
Designer: P. Parsons
Height: 8 ¾", 22.2 cm
Colour: Black, white, purple,
              red and yellow
Issued: 1998 in a limited
              edition of 2,000
Series: Disney Villains

   U.S.:   **$325.00**
   Can.:   **$475.00**
   U.K.:   £200.00

HN 3848
The Witch
Style One
Designer: P. Parsons
Height: 7", 17.8 cm
Colour: Black and white
Issued: 1998 in a limited
              edition of 2,000
Series: Disney Villains

   U.S.:   **$325.00**
   Can.:   **$475.00**
   U.K.:   £200.00

HN 3849
Moll Flanders
Designer: P. Parsons
Height: 8½", 21.5 cm
Colour: Red, cream and white
Issued: 1999 in a limited
              edition of 3,500
Series: Literary Heroines

   U.S.:   **$475.00**
   Can.:   **$600.00**
   U.K.:   **£250.00**

HN 3850
Jessica
Style Two
Designer: N. Pedley
Height: 8", 20.3 cm
Colour: Light purple dress
Issued: 1997-1997
Series: Figure of the year

   U.S.:   **$275.00**
   Can.:   **$375.00**
   U.K.:   **£150.00**

HN 3851
Sally
Style Two
Designer: T. Potts
Height: 8 ¼", 21.0 cm
Colour: Blue
Issued: 1996-1998
Varieties: HN 3383, 4160

   U.S.:   **$275.00**
   Can.:   **$375.00**
   U.K.:   **£150.00**

HN 3852
Sarah
Style Two
Designer: T. Potts
Height: 8", 20.3 cm
Colour: Green
Issued: 1996-1999
Varieties: HN 3384, 3857

   U.S.:   **$300.00**
   Can.:   **$400.00**
   U.K.:   **£175.00**

HN 3853
Wedding Morn
Style Two
Designer: T. Potts
Height: 8", 20.3 cm
Colour: Ivory, gold highlights
Issued: 1996-1999
Varieties: Also called 'Bride of the Year' HN 3758

U.S.: $300.00
Can.: $450.00
U.K.: £200.00

HN 3854
Amy
Style Three
Designer: T. Potts
Height: 8", 20.3 cm
Colour: Pink
Issued: 1996-1999

U.S.: $275.00
Can.: $425.00
U.K.: £150.00

HN 3855
Lambing Time
Style Two
Designer: T. Potts
Height: 8", 20.3 cm
Colour: Ivory, gold highlights
Issued: 1996-1998
Series: Elegance (Series Two)

U.S.: $225.00
Can.: $300.00
U.K.: £100.00

HN 3856
Country Girl
Style Two
Designer: T. Potts
Height: 8", 20.3 cm
Colour: Ivory, gold highlights
Issued: 1996-1998
Series: Elegance (Series Two)

U.S.: $225.00
Can.: $300.00
U.K.: £100.00

HN 3857
Sarah
Style Two
Designer: T. Potts
Height: 8", 20.3 cm
Colour: Pink
Issued: 1996 in a limited edition of 1,996
Varieties: HN 3384, 3852
Series: Visitor Centre

U.S.: $350.00
Can.: $450.00
U.K.: £200.00

To commemorate the opening of the Royal Doulton Visitors Centre

HN 3858
Lucy
Style Three
Designer: T. Potts
Height: 8 ½", 21.6 cm
Colour: Pale pink and white dress, white cat with black patches
Issued: 1997-1999

U.S.: $300.00
Can.: $375.00
U.K.: £150.00

HN 3859
Sweet Bouquet
Style Two
Designer: T. Potts
Height: 8", 20.3 cm
Colour: Ivory, gold highlights
Issued: 1997 in a special edition of 250
Series: Elegance (Series Two)

U.S.: $225.00
Can.: $300.00
U.K.: £125.00

HN 3860
Morning Walk
Designer: T. Potts
Height: 8", 20.3 cm
Colour: Ivory, gold highlights
Issued: 1997-1998
Series: Elegance (Series Two)

U.S.: $325.00
Can.: $300.00
U.K.: £125.00

HN 3861
Centre Stage
Designer: T. Potts
Height: 8", 20.3 cm
Colour: Blue
Issued: 1996
Varieties: 'Courtney' HN 3869
Comm.by: Great Universal
Stores

U.S.:	**$225.00**
Can.:	**$275.00**
U.K.:	**£110.00**

HN 3862
Jean
Style Three
Designer: T. Potts
Height: 6 ¾", 17.2 cm
Colour: White and blue
Issued: 1997 in a special
edition of 350
Varieties: HN 3757
Comm.by: Seaway China

U.S.:	**$225.00**
Can.:	**$300.00**
U.K.:	**£125.00**

HN 3863
For You
Designer: T. Potts
Height: 8", 20.3 cm
Colour: Pink
Issued: 1997-1999
Varieties: HN 3754
Series: Name Your Own

U.S.:	**$200.00**
Can.:	**$250.00**
U.K.:	**£100.00**

Metal plaque on base for engraved
name.

HN 3864
Kimberley
Style Two
Designer: T. Potts
Height: 8 ½", 21.6 cm
Colour: White, pink and light
yellow dress, brown
and white cat
Issued: 1997 in a limited
edition of 2,000
Varieties: HN 3379, 3382
Series: Visitor Centre

U.S.:	**$325.00**
Can.:	**$425.00**
U.K.:	**£175.00**

HN 3865
Anna of the Five Towns
Designer: T. Potts
Height: 8", 20.3 cm
Colour: Dark and light brown
dress and hat
Issued: 1997-1998
Series: 1. Arnold Bennett
2. Visitor Centre

U.S.:	**$275.00**
Can.:	**$375.00**
U.K.:	**£150.00**

HN 3866
Bon Voyage
Designer: T. Potts
Height: 9", 22.9 cm
Colour: Pink and white dress
Issued: 1998-2001

U.S.:	**$275.00**
Can.:	**$375.00**
U.K.:	**£150.00**

HN 3867
The Countess of Chell
Designer: T. Potts
Height: 8 ½", 21.6 cm
Colour: Pale pink dress
with gold highlights
Issued: 1998-1998
Series: 1. Arnold Bennett
2. Visitor Centre

U.S.:	**$250.00**
Can.:	**$300.00**
U.K.:	**£100.00**

HN 3868
Danielle
Style Three
Designer: T. Potts
Height: 8 ¾", 22.2 cm
Colour: Orange
Issued: 1998
Comm.by: Great Universal
Stores

U.S.:	**$250.00**
Can.:	**$300.00**
U.K.:	**£100.00**

HN 3869
Courtney
Designer: N. Pedley
Height: 8", 20.3 cm
Colour: Blue
Issued: 1999 in a special
edition of 250
Varieties: Also called 'Centre
Stage' HN 3861
Comm.by: Seaway China
U.S.: **$225.00**
Can.: **$275.00**
U.K.: **£110.00**

HN 3870
Hannah
Style Two
Designer: N. Pedley
Height: 4", 10.1 cm
Colour: Red dress, pink
ruffles, gold trim
Issued: 1995-1996
Varieties: HN 3649
Series: 1. Signature
2. Miniatures
U.S.: **$225.00**
Can.: **$300.00**
U.K.: **£125.00**

HN 3871
Susan
Style Three
Designer: N. Pedley
Height: 8", 20.3 cm
Colour: Rose pink and
white dress
Issued: 1997-1997
Series: RDICC
U.S.: **$300.00**
Can.: **$400.00**
U.K.: **£165.00**

HN 3872
Lauren
Style Two
Designer: N. Pedley
Height: 9", 22.9 cm
Colour: Cream dress, pink
and yellow sash
Issued: 1997-1997
Series: Roadshow Events
U.S.: **$250.00**
Can.: **$325.00**
U.K.: **£125.00**

HN 3873 - 3874 not issued.

HN 3875
Joy
Style Two
Designer: N. Pedley
Height: 5 ¼", 13.3 cm
Colour: White dress
Issued: 1997-1997
Series: Club Membership
Figure
U.S.: **$125.00**
Can.: **$150.00**
U.K.: **£ 65.00**

HN 3876
Kitty
Style Two
Designer: N. Pedley
Height: 4 ½", 11.9 cm
Colour: White and blue dress,
ginger and white cat
Issued: 1997-2000
U.S.: **$150.00**
Can.: **$200.00**
U.K.: **£ 75.00**

HN 3877
On The Beach
Designer: N. Pedley
Height: 3 ½", 8.9 cm
Colour: Pink dress, yellow
ribbons and pail
Issued: 1997-1999
U.S.: **$175.00**
Can.: **$225.00**
U.K.: **£ 95.00**

HN 3878
Julie
Style Two
Designer: N. Pedley
Height: 8", 20.3 cm
Colour: Pink and white
Issued: 1997-2001
U.S.: **$225.00**
Can.: **$300.00**
U.K.: **£110.00**

HN 3879
Linda
Style Four
Designer:	N. Pedley
Height:	8", 20.3 cm
Colour:	Yellow
Issued:	1997
Comm.by:	Great Universal Stores
U.S.:	**$250.00**
Can.:	**$325.00**
U.K.:	**£125.00**

HN 3880
Kathleen
Style Three
Designer:	N. Pedley
Height:	8 ½", 21.6 cm
Colour:	Pink
Issued:	1997
Varieties:	HN 3609; also called 'Brianna' HN 4126
Comm.by:	Great Universal Stores
U.S.:	**$225.00**
Can.:	**$300.00**
U.K.:	**£110.00**

HN 3881 not issued.

HN 3882
Kate
Style Two
Designer:	N. Pedley
Height:	8", 20.3 cm
Colour:	Rose pink jacket, flowered white skirt
Issued:	1997
Varieties:	HN 3765
Comm.by:	Pascoe & Company
U.S.:	**$250.00**
Can.:	**$325.00**
U.K.:	**£150.00**

HN 3883
Chloe
Style Three
Designer:	N. Pedley
Height:	8" 20.3 cm
Colour:	Lemon
Issued:	1997-1998
Varieties:	HN 3914; also called 'Amber' HN 4125
Comm.by:	Index Catalogue Co.
U.S.:	**$200.00**
Can.:	**$350.00**
U.K.:	**£115.00**

HN 3884 not issued.

HN 3885
Melissa
Style Two
Designer:	N. Pedley
Height:	8 ¼", 21.0 cm
Colour:	Purple dress, cream hat
Issued:	1997-1999
U.S.:	**$225.00**
Can.:	**$375.00**
U.K.:	**£115.00**

HN 3886
Helen
Style Three
Designer:	N. Pedley
Height:	8", 20.3 cm
Colour:	Red and cream
Issued:	1997-1999
Varieties:	HN 3601, 3687, 3763; also called 'Miss Kay' HN 3659
U.S.:	**$325.00**
Can.:	**$450.00**
U.K.:	**£185.00**

HN 3887
Megan
Style Two
Designer:	N. Pedley
Height:	8", 20.3 cm
Colour:	White and light blue
Issued:	1997-2000
Varieties:	Also called 'Jasmine' (Style Three) HN 4127; 'Millie' HN 4212
Series:	Vanity Fair Ladies
U.S.:	**$200.00**
Can.:	**$250.00**
U.K.:	**£115.00**

HN 3888
Louise
Style Three
Designer:	N. Pedley
Height:	8", 20.3 cm
Colour:	White dress with flowered border
Issued:	1997-2000
U.S.:	**$225.00**
Can.:	**$300.00**
U.K.:	**£115.00**

HN 3889
Flowers For You
Designer: N. Pedley
Height: 5 ¾", 14.5 cm
Colour: Yellow dress
Issued: 1997-1999

U.S.:	**$125.00**
Can.:	**$175.00**
U.K.:	**£ 75.00**

HN 3890
Geoffrey Boycott
Designer: R. Tabbenor
Height: 9 ½", 24.0 cm
Colour: White
Issued: 1996 in a limited
edition of 8,114
Comm.by: Lawleys By Post

U.S.:	**$300.00**
Can.:	**$400.00**
U.K.:	**£115.00**

HN 3891
Sir Henry Doulton
Designer: R. Tabbenor
Height: 8 ¾", 22.2 cm
Colour: Grey suit, black
overcoat, hat and
umbrella
Issued: 1997 in a limited
edition of 1,997

U.S.:	**$400.00**
Can.:	**$600.00**
U.K.:	**£250.00**

HN 3892 - 3899 Animal and Birds
figures, except HN 3892, 3897 and
3899 not issued.

HN 3900
Elaine
Style Two
Designer: M. Davies
Remodeller: P. Gee
Height: 4", 10.1 cm
Colour: White and gold
Issued: 1997
Varieties: HN 3214, 3247
Series: Miniatures
Comm.by: Great Universal
Stores

U.S.:	**$150.00**
Can.:	**$200.00**
U.K.:	**£ 75.00**

HN 3901
Ninette
Style Two
Designer: M. Davies
Remodeller: P. Gee
Height: 3 ½", 8.9 cm
Colour: Yellow and white
Issued: 1997
Varieties: HN 3215, 3248
Series: Miniatures
Comm.by: Index Catalogue Co.

U.S.:	**$150.00**
Can.:	**$200.00**
U.K.:	**£ 75.00**

HN 3902
Lily
Style Three
Designer: M. Davies
Height: 7 ¾", 19.7 cm
Colour: Light and dark
green dress
Issued: 1998-1998
Series: Peggy Davies
Collection

U.S.:	**$250.00**
Can.:	**$350.00**
U.K.:	**£125.00**

HN 3903
Mary
Style Four
Designer: M. Davies
Height: 7", 17.8 cm
Colour: Red and pink dress
Issued: 1998-1998
Series: Peggy Davies
Collection

U.S.:	**$250.00**
Can.:	**$350.00**
U.K.:	**£125.00**

HN 3904
Valerie
Style Two
Designer: M. Davies
Height: 7 ¾", 19.7 cm
Colour: Blue and pink dress
Issued: 1998-1998
Series: Peggy Davies
Collection

U.S.:	**$250.00**
Can.:	**$350.00**
U.K.:	**£150.00**

HN 3905
Christine
Style Five
Designer: M. Davies
Height: 7 ½", 19.1 cm
Colour: White flowered dress,
             pink overskirt
Issued: 1998-1998
Series: Peggy Davies
             Collection
U.S.:	$250.00
Can.:	$350.00
U.K.:	£150.00

HN 3906
Eleanor
Style One
Designer: M. Davies
Height: 8", 20.3 cm
Colour: Pink and yellow dress
Issued: 1998-1998
Series: Peggy Davies
             Collection
U.S.:	$250.00
Can.:	$350.00
U.K.:	£150.00

HN 3907
Patricia
Style Five
Designer: M. Davies
Height: 7 ¾", 19.7 cm
Colour: Peach, yellow and
             white dress
Issued: 1998-1998
Series: Peggy Davies
             Collection
U.S.:	$250.00
Can.:	$350.00
U.K.:	£150.00

HN 3908
Buttercup
Style Two
Designer: M. Davies
Remodeller: P. Gee
Height: 3 ½", 8.9 cm
Colour: Pink
Issued: 1998
Varieties: HN 3268
Series: Miniatures
Comm.by: Great Universal
                Stores
U.S.:	$150.00
Can.:	$200.00
U.K.:	£ 75.00

HN 3909
Victoria
Style Two
Designer: M. Davies
Remodeller: P. Gee
Height: 3 ½", 8.9 cm
Colour: Pale blue
Issued: 1998
Varieties: HN 3735, 3744
Series: Miniatures
Comm.by: Index Catalogue Co.
U.S.:	$125.00
Can.:	$175.00
U.K.:	£ 70.00

HN 3910 not issued.

HN 3911
First Prize
Designer: N. Pedley
Height: 5 ¼", 13.3 cm
Colour: White shirt, brown
             jodhpurs, black hat,
             dark blue coat
Issued: 1997-1999
U.S.:	$175.00
Can.:	$250.00
U.K.:	£110.00

HN 3912
Kelly
Style Two
Designer: N. Pedley
Height: 8", 20.3 cm
Colour: Pink
Issued: 1997-1998
Varieties: Also called 'Angela'
             (Style Four) HN 3690;
             'Sweet Sixteen'
             (Style Two) HN 3648
Comm.by: Home Shopping
U.S.:	$200.00
Can.:	$250.00
U.K.:	£115.00

HN 3913
First Bloom
Designer: N. Pedley
Height: 8", 20.3 cm
Colour: Royal blue
Issued: 1997-1997
Varieties: Also called 'Mackenzie'
             HN 4109
Series: Roadshow Events
U.S.:	$225.00
Can.:	$300.00
U.K.:	£115.00

HN 3914
Chloe
Style Three
Designer: N. Pedley
Height: 8", 20.3 cm
Colour: Pink
Issued: 1997-2002
Varieties: HN 3883; also called
"Amber" HN 4125

U.S.: $275.00
Can.: $375.00
U.K.: £150.00

Exclusive to Canada

HN 3915
Colleen
Designer: N. Pedley
Height: 8", 20.3 cm
Colour: White and pale
yellow dress
Issued: 1997-2002

U.S.: $275.00
Can.: $375.00
U.K.: £150.00

Exclusive to Canada

HN 3916
Spring Posy
Designer: N. Pedley
Height: 8 ¾", 22.2 cm
Colour: Dark and light
green dress
Issued: 1997
Series: The Seasons
(Series Seven)
Comm.by: Guild of Specialist
China and Glass
Retailers

U.S.: $225.00
Can.: $300.00
U.K.: £135.00

HN 3917
Summer Blooms
Style One
Designer: N. Pedley
Height: 8 ¾", 22.2 cm
Colour: Light blue dress
Issued: 1997
Series: The Seasons
(Series Seven)
Comm.by: Guild of Specialist
China and Glass
Retailers

U.S.: $225.00
Can.: $300.00
U.K.: £135.00

HN 3918
Autumn Flowers
Designer: N. Pedley
Height: 8 ½", 21.5 cm
Colour: Red and yellow dress
Issued: 1997
Series: The Seasons
(Series Seven)
Comm.by: Guild of Specialist
China and Glass
Retailers

U.S.: $225.00
Can.: $300.00
U.K.: £135.00

HN 3919
Winter Bouquet
Designer: N. Pedley
Height: 8 ¾", 22.2 cm
Colour: Red dress
Issued: 1997
Series: The Seasons
(Series Seven)
Comm.by: Guild of Specialist
China and Glass
Retailers

U.S.: $250.00
Can.: $300.00
U.K.: £135.00

HN 3920
Jack Point
Designer: C. J. Noke
Height: 17", 43.2 cm
Colour: Blue, gold and red
Issued: 1996 in a limited
edition of 250
Varieties: HN 85, 91, 99, 2080,
3925

U.S.: $4,000.00
Can.: $5,000.00
U.K.: £2,500.00

HN 3921
Princess Badoura
Style One
Designer: H. Tittensor, Harry
E. Stanton and
F. Van Allen Phillips
Height: 20", 50.8 cm
Colour: Blue, gold and red
Issued: 1996-1999
Varieties: HN 2081
Series: Prestige

U.S.: $20,000.00
Can.: $26,000.00
U.K.: £12,000.00

HN 3922
A Jester (Parian)
Style One
Designer: C. J. Noke
Height: 10 ½", 26.7 cm
Colour: Pink, green and gold
Issued: 1997 limited to 950
Varieties: HN 45, 71, 71A,
              320, 367, 412, 426,
              446, 552, 616, 627,
              1295, 1702, 2016
Comm.by: Lawleys By Post

U.S.:	$550.00
Can.:	$700.00
U.K.:	£300.00

HN 3923 not issued.

HN 3924
Lady Jester (Parian)
Style Three
Designer: W. K. Harper
Height: 9 ½", 24.0 cm
Colour: Green and pink
Issued: 1998 in a limited
              edition of 950
Comm.by: Lawleys By Post

U.S.:	$550.00
Can.:	$700.00
U.K.:	£300.00

HN 3925
Jack Point
Designer: C. J. Noke
Height: 16 ¼", 41.2 cm
Colour: Purple, green and
              lavender
Issued: 1998 in a limited
              edition of 85
Varieties: HN 85, 91, 99, 2080,
              3920

U.S.:	$4,500.00
Can.:	$6,000.00
U.K.:	£3,000.00

HN 3926
The Moor
Designer: C. J. Noke
Height: 17 ½", 44.0 cm
Colour: Black and purple
Issued: 1999 in a limited
              edition of 99
Varieties: HN 1308, 1366, 1425
              1657, 2082, 3642;
              also called 'An Arab'
              HN 33, 343, 378
Series: RDICC

U.S.:	$4,000.00
Can.:	$6,000.00
U.K.:	£3,000.00

HN 3927 - 3929 not issued.

HN 3930
Constance
Style Two
Designer: A. Maslankowski
Height: 8 ¾", 22.2 cm
Colour: Blue
Issued: 1997-1997
Varieties: HN 3933
Series: Charleston

U.S.:	$250.00
Can.:	$325.00
U.K.:	£125.00

HN 3933
Constance
Style Two
Designer: A. Maslankowski
Height: 8 ¾", 22.2 cm
Colour: Ivory, gold highlights
Issued: 1997-1997
Varieties: HN 3930
Series: Charleston

U.S.:	$250.00
Can.:	$325.00
U.K.:	£125.00

HN 3934
Across the Miles
Designer: A. Maslankowski
Height: 4", 10.1 cm
Colour: White
Issued: 1997-1999
Series: Sentiments

U.S.:	$ 85.00
Can.:	$150.00
U.K.:	£ 65.00

HN 3935
Best Friends
Style One
Designer: A. Maslankowski
Height: 3", 7.6 cm
Colour: White shirt, blue
              trousers, black and
              white dog
Issued: 1997-1999

U.S.:	$125.00
Can.:	$225.00
U.K.:	£ 75.00

HN 3931 - 3932 not issued.

HN 3936
Goose Girl
Style Three
Designer: A. Maslankowski
Height: 11", 27.9 cm
Colour: White
Issued: 1997-1998
Series: Images
   U.S.:   **$150.00**
   Can.:   **$200.00**
   U.K.:   **£ 60.00**

HN 3937 not issued.

HN 3938
Mother and Child
Style Two
Designer: A. Maslankowski
Height: 11 ½", 29.2 cm
Colour: White
Issued: 1997 to the present
Series: Images
   U.S.:   **$140.00**
   Can.:   **$245.00**
   U.K.:   **£ 49.00**

HN 3939 not issued.

HN 3940
Angel
Designer: A. Maslankowski
Height: 11 ½", 29.2 cm
Colour: White
Issued: 1997-1999
Series: Images
   U.S.:   **$150.00**
   Can.:   **$200.00**
   U.K.:   **£ 85.00**

HN 3941 not issued.

HN 3942
Graduation (female)
Designer: A. Maslankowski
Height: 11 ½", 29.2 cm
Colour: White
Issued: 1997-2002
Series: Images
   U.S.:   **$150.00**
   Can.:   **$250.00**
   U.K.:   **£100.00**

HN 3943 not issued.

HN 3944
HM Queen Elizabeth
The Queen Mother
Style Three
Designer: A. Maslankowski
Height: 10 ½", 26.7 cm
Colour: Light purple suit and
             hat
Issued: 1997 in a limited
             edition of 5,000
Comm.by: Lawleys By Post
   U.S.:   **$500.00**
   Can.:   **$675.00**
   U.K.:   **£300.00**

HN 3945
Millie
Style One
Designer: A. Maslankowski
Height: 8 ¾", 22.2 cm
Colour: Green
Issued: 1997-1997
Varieties: HN 3946
Series: Charleston
   U.S.:   **$300.00**
   Can.:   **$400.00**
   U.K.:   **£150.00**

HN 3946
Millie
Style One
Designer: A. Maslankowski
Height: 8 ¾", 22.2 cm
Colour: Ivory, gold highlights
Issued: 1997-1997
Varieties: HN3945
Series: Charleston
   U.S.:   **$300.00**
   Can.:   **$400.00**
   U.K.:   **£150.00**

HN 3947
Henry V at Agincourt
Designer: A. Maslankowski
Height: 20", 50.8 cm
Colour: Blue, grey, red and
             gold
Issued: 1997 to the present
Series: Prestige
   U.S.:   **$18,300.00**
   Can.:   **$31,800.00**
   U.K.:   **£11,500.00**

HN 3948
Loving Thoughts
Style One
Designer: A. Maslankowski
Height: 6 ¼", 15.9 cm
Colour: White
Issued: 1997-1999
Series: Sentiments
U.S.:	**$125.00**
Can.:	**$160.00**
U.K.:	**£ 60.00**

HN 3949
Forever Yours
Style One
Designer: A. Maslankowski
Height: 3 ¾", 9.5 cm
Colour: White
Issued: 1998-2001
Series: Sentiments
U.S.:	**$125.00**
Can.:	**$160.00**
U.K.:	**£ 60.00**

HN 3950
Star Performer
Designer: A. Maslankowski
Height: 4", 10.1 cm
Colour: White, pink slippers
Issued: 1997-2003
Series: Images
U.S.:	**$ 95.00**
Can.:	**$200.00**
U.K.:	**£ 50.00**

HN 3951
Stage Struck
Designer: A. Maslankowski
Height: 3 ¾", 9.5 cm
Colour: White, blue slippers
Issued: 1997-2003
Series: Images
U.S.:	**$ 95.00**
Can.:	**$200.00**
U.K.:	**£ 50.00**

HN 3952
The Messiah
Designer: A. Maslankowski
Height: 11", 27.9 cm
Colour: White
Issued: 1997-1999
Series: Images
U.S.:	**$200.00**
Can.:	**$250.00**
U.K.:	**£110.00**

HN 3953
Christmas Lantern
Designer: A. Maslankowski
Height: 6", 15.0 cm
Colour: White
Issued: 1997-1998
Series: Sentiments
U.S.:	**$125.00**
Can.:	**$150.00**
U.K.:	**£ 60.00**

HN 3954
Moonlight Stroll
Designer: A. Maslankowski
Height: 7 ¾", 19.7 cm
Colour: Deep blue dress, flowered cream scarf and hat
Issued: 1997-1999
Varieties: Also called 'Summer Breeze' HN 3724
U.S.:	**$300.00**
Can.:	**$425.00**
U.K.:	**£175.00**

HN 3955
Summer Scent
Designer: A. Maslankowski
Height: 7 ¾", 19.7 cm
Colour: Pink and cream dress, blue scarf
Issued: 1997-1999
Varieties: Also called 'Spring Morning' (Style Two) HN 3725
U.S.:	**$275.00**
Can.:	**$375.00**
U.K.:	**£150.00**

HN 3956
Spring Serenade
Designer: A. Maslankowski
Height: 7 ½", 19.1 cm
Colour: Green dress,
           flowered cream scarf
Issued: 1997-1999
Varieties: Also called 'Free Spirit'
           (Style Two) HN 3728

U.S.:	$275.00
Can.:	$400.00
U.K.:	£175.00

HN 3957
Eleanor of Aquitaine
(1122-1204)
Designer: A. Maslankowski
Height: 9", 22.9 cm
Colour: Blue, gold and brown
Issued: 1997 in a limited
           edition of 5,000
Series: Plantagenet Queens
Comm.by: Lawleys By Post

U.S.:	$600.00
Can.:	$750.00
U.K.:	£300.00

HN 3958
Country Girl
Style Three
Designer: A. Maslankowski
Height: 10 ¾", 27.8 cm
Colour: White
Issued: 1998-1999
Series: Images

U.S.:	$150.00
Can.:	$225.00
U.K.:	£ 85.00

HN 3959
The Graduate (male)
Style Two
Designer: A. Maslankowski
Height: 11 ½", 29.2 cm
Colour: White
Issued: 1998-2001
Series: Images

U.S.:	$150.00
Can.:	$200.00
U.K.:	£ 75.00

HN 3960 - 3969 not issued.

HN 3970
Flower of Love
Designer: J. Bromley
Height: 7 ¼", 18.4 cm
Colour: Red
Issued: 1996-1997
Varieties: HN 2460; also called
           'Fleur' HN 2368, 2369

U.S.:	$350.00
Can.:	$450.00
U.K.:	£175.00

HN 3971
Best Wishes
Style Two
Designer: J. Bromley
Height: 8 ¾", 22.2 cm
Colour: Deep green
Issued: 1998 to the present
Varieties: Also called 'Kate'
           (Style Three) HN 4233;
           'Forever Yours' (Style
           Two), HN 4501
Series: Name Your Own

U.S.:	$220.00
Can.:	$425.00
U.K.:	£125.00

Metal plaque on base for engraved name.

HN 3972
Sweet Lilac
Designer: J. Bromley
Height: 8 ¾", 22.2 cm
Colour: Lilac bodice with white
           frill and mauve panel
           with cream floral skirt
Issued: 2000-2000
Series: RDICC

U.S.:	$325.00
Can.:	$450.00
U.K.:	£200.00

HN 3973 - 3974 not issued.

HN 3975
Lauren
Style Three
Designer: D. Hughes
Height: 9", 23.0 cm
Colour: Rose-pink dress
Issued: 1999-1999
Series: Figure of the Year

U.S.:	$275.00
Can.:	$375.00
U.K.:	£150.00

HN 3976
Rachel
Style Two
Designer: D. Hughes
Height: 8 ¼", 21.0 cm
Colour: Lilac, pink and cream
Issued: 2000-2000
Series: Figure of the Year

U.S.:	**$250.00**
Can.:	**$350.00**
U.K.:	**£135.00**

HN 3977
Melissa
Style Three
Deisgner: D. Hughes
Height: 8 ½", 22.2 cm
Colour: Blue
Issued: 2001-2001
Series: Figure of the Year

U.S.:	**$225.00**
Can.:	**$350.00**
U.K.:	**£135.00**

HN 3978
Sarah
Style Three
Designer: D. Hughes
Height: 8 ¼", 21.0 cm
Colour: Dark green
Issued: 2002-2002
Series: Figure of thc Year

U.S.:	**$225.00**
Can.:	**$350.00**
U.K.:	**£135.00**

HN 3979 - 3990 not issued.

HN 3991
Cinderella
Style Two
Modeller: J. Bromley
Height: 10", 25.4 cm
Colour: 1. Pink
2. Blue
Issued: 1. 1997 ltd. ed. 2,950
2. 2000 ltd. ed. 2,000
Series: 1. Fairytale Princesses
Comm.by: Compton/Woodhouse

U.S.:	**$450.00**
Can.:	**$600.00**
U.K.:	**£250.00**

HN 3992
Ellen
Style Three
Designer: J. Bromley
Height: 8 ¼", 21.0 cm
Colour: Rose pink dress, beige hat
Issued: 1997-1997
Series: Lady of the Year
Comm.by: Compton/Woodhouse

U.S.:	**$275.00**
Can.:	**$375.00**
U.K.:	**£150.00**

HN 3993
Carmen
Style Three
Designer: M. Halson
Height: 9 ½", 24.0 cm
Colour: Red dress, black shawl, gold highlights
Issued: 1997 in a limited edition of 12,500
Comm.by: Compton/Woodhouse

U.S.:	**$400.00**
Can.:	**$525.00**
U.K.:	**£225.00**

HN 3994
Red Red Rose
Designer: R. Hughes
Modeller: J. Bromley
Height: 9", 22.9 cm
Colour: Pink dress, gold highlights
Issued: 1997 in a limited edition of 12,500
Series: Language of Love
Comm.by: Compton/Woodhouse

U.S.:	**$350.00**
Can.:	**$450.00**
U.K.:	**£195.00**

HN 3995
Sophie
Style Five
Designer: J. Bromley
Height: 8 ¼", 21.0 cm
Colour: Pink dress, gold highlights
Issued: 1998-1998
Series: Lady of the Year
Comm.by: Compton/Woodhouse

U.S.:	**$275.00**
Can.:	**$375.00**
U.K.:	**£150.00**

HN 3996
Miss Violet
Designer: M. Evans
Height: 5 ½", 14.0 cm
Colour: Dark and light purple
Issued: 1998 in a limited
               edition of 12,500
Series: Pretty Maids
Comm.by: Compton/Woodhouse

U.S.:	**$200.00**
Can.:	**$250.00**
U.K.:	**£100.00**

HN 3997
Miss Maisie
Designer: M. Evans
Height: 5 ½", 14.0 cm
Colour: Green, blue and pink
Issued: 1998 in a limited
               edition of 12,500
Series: Pretty Maids
Comm.by: Compton/Woodhouse

U.S.:	**$200.00**
Can.:	**$250.00**
U.K.:	**£100.00**

HN 3998
Miss Tilly
Designer: M. Evans
Height: 5 ½", 14.0 cm
Colour: Pink and green
Issued: 1998 in a limited
               edition of 12,500
Series: Pretty Maids
Comm.by: Compton/Woodhouse

U.S.:	**$200.00**
Can.:	**$250.00**
U.K.:	**£100.00**

HN 3999
Shall I Compare Thee To A
Summer's Day
Designer: J. Bromley
Height: 9", 22.9 cm
Colour: White dress, blue
               bows, gold highlights
Issued: 1998 in a limited
               edition of 12,500
Series: Language of Love
Comm.by: Compton/Woodhouse

U.S.:	**$350.00**
Can.:	**$450.00**
U.K.:	**£195.00**

HN 4000
Sleeping Beauty
Style Two
Designer: S. Curzon
Modeller: J. Bromley
Height: 7 ½", 19.1 cm
Colour: White, gold highlights
Issued: 1998 in a limited
               edition of 4,950
Series: Fairytale Princesses
Comm.by: Compton/Woodhouse

U.S.:	**$350.00**
Can.:	**$500.00**
U.K.:	**£250.00**

HN 4001
My True Love
Designer: J. Bromley
Height: 9", 22.9 cm
Colour: White dress with pink
               flowers; dark red
               bodice
Issued: 1999 in a limited
               edition of 12,500
Comm.by: Compton/Woodhouse

U.S.:	**$350.00**
Can.:	**$450.00**
U.K.:	**£175.00**

HN 4002 not issued.

HN 4003
Alice
Style Four
Designer: J. Bromley
Height: 8 ¾, 22.2 cm
Colour: Red and yellow
Issued: 1999-1999
Series: Lady of the Year
Comm.by: Compton/Woodhouse

U.S.:	**$275.00**
Can.:	**$375.00**
U.K.:	**£160.00**

HN 4004 - 4014 not issued.

HN 4015
Eleanor
Style Two
Designer: J. Bromley
Height: 9", 22.9 cm
Colour: Green dress, cream
               shawl and hat
Issued: 2001-2001
Series: Lady of the Year
Comm.by: Compton/Woodhouse

U.S.:	**$275.00**
Can.:	**$375.00**
U.K.:	**£170.00**

HN 4016
A Love So Tender
Designer: M. Halson
Height: Unknown
Colour: White
Issued: 2001 in a limited
            edition of 7,500
Series: Images
U.S.: $250.00
Can.: $375.00
U.K.:   £100.00

HN 4017
Ellie
Style Two
Designer: J. Bromley
Height: 8 ¾", 22.2 cm
Colour: Dark and light
            purple
Issued: 2003-2003
Series: Lady of the Year
Comm. by: Compton/Woodhouse
U.S.: $350.00
Can.: $450.00
U.K.:   £195.00

HN 4018 - 4020 not issued.

HN 4021
Amen
Designer: D. V. Tootle
Height: 4 ¼", 10.8 cm
Colour: White
Issued: 1997 to the present
Series: Images
U.S.:   N/I
Can.: $140.00
U.K.:   £ 29.00

HN 4022
William III (1650-1702)
Designer: D. V. Tootle
Height: 10 ¼", 26.0 cm
Colour: White, red, beige
Issued: 1998 in a limited
            edition of 1,500
Series: Stuart Kings
Comm.by: Lawleys By Post
U.S.: $1,200.00
Can.: $1,500.00
U.K.:   £ 625.00

HN 4023
Sarah Bernhardt
Designer: D. V. Tootle
Height: 9", 22.9 cm
Colour: Green dress, flowered
            cream scarf and fan
Issued: 1998 in a limited
            edition of 5,000
Series: Victorian and
            Edwardian Actresses
Comm.by: Lawleys By Post
U.S.: $450.00
Can.: $600.00
U.K.:   £250.00

HN 4024
Prima Ballerina
Designer: D. V. Tootle
Height: 8 ¼", 21.0 cm
Colour: White
Issued: 1998-2000
Series: Images
U.S.: $150.00
Can.: $200.00
U.K.:   £ 85.00

HN 4025
The Dance
Style One
Designer: D. V. Tootle
Height: 7", 17.8 cm
Colour: White
Issued: 1998-2002
Series: Images
U.S.: $150.00
Can.: $200.00
U.K.:   £ 85.00

HN 4026
Best Friends
Style Two
Designer: D. V. Tootle
Height: 7", 17.8 cm
Colour: White
Issued: 1998-1998
Series: Images Figure of
            the Year
U.S.: $150.00
Can.: $200.00
U.K.:   £ 85.00

HN 4027
The Ballet Dancer
Designer: D. V. Tootle
Height: 9 ¼", 23.5 cm
Colour: White
Issued: 1998-2000
Series: Images
  U.S.: **$150.00**
  Can.: **$200.00**
  U.K.: **£ 85.00**

HN 4028
Ballet Lesson
Designer: D. V. Tootle
Height: 5", 13.0 cm
Colour: White
Issued: 1998-2001
Series: Images
  U.S.: **$125.00**
  Can.: **$150.00**
  U.K.: **£ 60.00**

HN 4029 not issued.

HN 4030
Leap-Frog
Designer: D. V. Tootle
Height: 8 ½", 21.5 cm
Colour: White
Issued: 1999-2001
Series: Images
  U.S.: **$125.00**
  Can.: **$175.00**
  U.K.: **£ 75.00**

HN 4031
Carol Singer (Boy)
Designer: D. V. Tootle
Height: 6", 15.2 cm
Colour: White
Issued: 1999 in a limited
        edition of 6,000
Series: 1. Christmas Choir
           Collection
        2. Images
  U.S.: **$75.00**
  Can.: **$95.00**
  U.K.: **£40.00**

HN 4032
Carol Singer (Girl)
Designer: D. V. Tootle
Height: 5", 12.0 cm
Colour: White
Issued: 1999 in a limited
        edition of 6,000
Series: 1. Christmas Choir
           Collection
        2. Images
  U.S.: **$75.00**
  Can.: **$95.00**
  U.K.: **£40.00**

HN 4033
The Promise
Designer: D. V. Tootle
Height: 6 ¼", 16.0 cm
Colour: White
Issued: 1999-1999
Series: Images of the Year
  U.S.: **$175.00**
  Can.: **$225.00**
  U.K.: **£100.00**

HN 4034
Mary and Jesus
Designer: D. V. Tootle
Height: Unknown
Colour: White
Issued: 1999 in a limited
        edition of 2,000
Series: 1. Images: The
           Christmas Story
        2. Millennium
  U.S.: **$300.00**
  Can.: **$450.00**
  U.K.: **£200.00 set price**

Note: 10 items sold as set

HN 4035
Joseph
Style Two
Designer: D. V. Tootle
Height: Unknown
Colour: White
Issued: 1999 in a limited
        edition of 2,000
Series: 1. Images: The
           Christmas Story
        2. Millennium
  U.S.: **$300.00**
  Can.: **$450.00**
  U.K.: **£200.00 set price**

Note: 10 items sold as set.

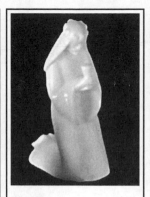

HN 4036
Balthazar
Designer: D. V. Tootle
Height: Unknown
Colour: White
Issued: 1999 in a limited
edition of 2,000
Series: 1. Images: The
Christmas Story
2. Millennium

U.S.:	$300.00
Can.:	$450.00
U.K.:	£200.00 set price

Note: 10 items sold as set

HN 4037
Melchior
Designer: D. V. Tootle
Height: Unknown
Colour: White
Issued: 1999 in a limited
edition of 2,000
Series: 1. Images: The
Christmas Story
2. Millennium

U.S.:	$300.00
Can.:	$450.00
U.K.:	£200.00 set price

Note: 10 items sold as set

HN 4038
Caspar
Designer: D. V. Tootle
Heieght: Unknown
Colour: White
Issued: 1999 in a limited
edition of 2,000
Series: 1. Images: The
Christmas Story
2. Millennium

U.S.:	$300.00
Can.:	$450.00
U.K.:	£200.00 set price

Note: 10 items sold as set

HN 4039
Boy Shepherd
Designer: D. V. Tootle
Height: Unknown
Colour: White
Issued: 1999 in a limited
edition of 2,000
Series: 1. Images: The
Christmas Story
2. Millennium

U.S.:	$300.00
Can.:	$450.00
U.K.:	£200.00 set price

Note: 10 items sold as set

HN 4040
Kathryn
Style Two
Designer: V. Annand
Height: 8 ½", 21.6 cm
Colour: Light yellow dress
Issued: 1997-2003
Varieties: Also called 'Alexis'
HN 4205
Series: Chelsea

U.S.:	$200.00
Can.:	$300.00
U.K.:	£ 85.00

HN 4041
Rebecca
Style Three
Designer: V. Annand
Height: 9", 22.9 cm
Colour: Blue dress,
yellow ribbons
Issued: 1998-1998
Series: Figure of the Year

U.S.:	$300.00
Can.:	$400.00
U.K.:	£175.00

HN 4042
Janet
Style Four
Designer: V. Annand
Height: 9", 22.9 cm
Colour: Rose pink and white
Issued: 1998-1998
Series: RDICC

U.S.:	$300.00
Can.:	$450.00
U.K.:	£195.00

HN 4043
Samantha
Style Three
Designer: V. Annand
Height: 8 ¼", 21.0 cm
Colour: Blue and white
Issued: 1998-1998
Series: Roadshow Events

U.S.:	$275.00
Can.:	$350.00
U.K.:	£150.00

HN 4044
Abigail
Designer: V. Annand
Height: 8 ¼", 21.0 cm
Colour: Light blue and
            cream dress
Issued: 1998-2001
Series: In Vogue

U.S.:   **$200.00**
Can.:   **$250.00**
U.K.:   **£115.00**

HN 4045
Blossomtime
Designer: V. Annand
Height: 8", 20.3 cm
Colour: Pink
Issued: 1998-1998
Series: Annabelle Doulton
            Collection
Comm.by: Lawleys By Post

U.S.:   **$ 750.00**
Can.:   **$1,000.00**
U.K.:   **£ 500.00**

HN 4046
Ellie
Style One
Designer: V. Annand
Height: 8 ¼", 21.0 cm
Colour: Pale pink dress with
            lemon scarf
Issued: 1998-2001
Varieties: Also called 'Allison'
            HN 4207
Series: Chelsea

U.S.:   **$200.00**
Can.:   **$250.00**
U.K.:   **£115.00**

HN 4047
Georgina
Style Two
Designer: V. Annand
Height: 8 ¼", 21.0 cm
Colour: Peach dress
Issued: 1998-2001
Series: Chelsea

U.S.:   **$200.00**
Can.:   **$250.00**
U.K.:   **£115.00**

HN 4048
Natalie
Style Two
Designer: V. Annand
Height: 8 ¼", 21.0 cm
Colour: Pink and cream dress;
            blue purse
Issued: 1999-2001
Series: In Vogue

U.S.:   **$250.00**
Can.:   **$325.00**
U.K.:   **£125.00**

HN 4049
Jessica
Style Three
Designer: V. Annand
Height: 8 ½", 21.6 cm
Colour: Yellow dress with
            peach shading
Issued: 1999-2001
Series: In Vogue

U.S.:   **$250.00**
Can.:   **$325.00**
U.K.:   **£125.00**

HN 4050
Hannah
Style Three
Designer: V. Annand
Height: 8 ¾", 22.2 cm
Colour: Blue and pink
Issued: 1998 in a special
            edition of 250
Varieties: HN 4051, 4052
Comm.by: Hadleigh

U.S.:   **$275.00**
Can.:   **$350.00**
U.K.:   **£150.00**

Note: HN 4050, 4051, 4053 - only
         variation is backstamp.

HN 4051
Hannah
Style Three
Designer: V. Annand
Height: 8 ¾", 22.2 cm
Colour: Blue and pink
Issued: 1998 in a special
            edition of 250
Varieties: HN 4050, 4052
Comm.by: Collectibles

U.S.:   **$275.00**
Can.:   **$350.00**
U.K.:   **£150.00**

Note: HN 4050, 4051, 4053 - only
         variation is backstamp.

HN 4052
Hannah
Style three
Designer: V. Annand
Height: 8 ½", 21.6 cm
Colour: Blue and pink
Issued: 1999-2000
Varieties: HN 4050, 4051

U.S.:	**$275.00**
Can.:	**$350.00**
U.K.:	**£150.00**

Note: HN 4050, 4051, 4052 - only variation is backstamp.

HN 4053
Joy
Style Three
Designer: V. Annand
Height: 8", 20.0 cm
Colour: Pink and white
Issued: 1999-2000
Varieties: HN 4054

U.S.:	**$275.00**
Can.:	**$350.00**
U.K.:	**£150.00**

HN 4054
Joy
Style Three
Designer: V. Annand
Height: 8", 20.0 cm
Colour: Red
Issued: 1999-2000
Varieties: HN 4053

U.S.:	**$275.00**
Can.:	**$350.00**
U.K.:	**£150.00**

HN 4055
Kneeling Shepherd
Designer: D. V. Tootle
Height: Unknown
Colour: White
Issued: 1999 in a limited edition of 2,000
Series: 1. Images: The Christmas Story
　　　　2. Millennium

U.S.:	**$300.00**
Can.:	**$450.00**
U.K.:	**£200.00 set price**

Note: 10 items sold as set.

HN 4056
Standing Shepherd
Designer: D. V. Tootle
Height: Unknown
Colour: White
Issued: 1999 in a limited edition of 2,000
Series: 1. Images: The Christmas Story
　　　　2. Millennium

U.S.:	**$300.00**
Can.:	**$450.00**
U.K.:	**£200.00 set price**

Note: 10 items sold as set

HN 4057
Romeo and Juliet
Style Two
Designer: D. V. Tootle
Height: 12", 30.5 cm
Colour: White and pink
Issued: 1999 in a limited edition of 300
Series: Prestige

U.S.:	**$3,000.00**
Can.:	**$4,500.00**
U.K.:	**£1,500.00**

HN 4058
Harlequin
Style Two
Designer: D. V. Tootle
Height: 12 ½", 31.7 cm
Colour: Multicoloured pastels
Issued: 1999 in a limited ediiton of 200
Variations: HN 2737, 3287
Series: 1. Millennium
　　　　2. Prestige
Comm. by: Lawleys By Post

U.S.:	**$2,000.00**
Can.:	**$2,750.00**
U.K.:	**£1,500.00**

HN 4059
Columbine
Style Three
Designer: D. V. Tootle
Height: 12 ½", 31.7 cm
Colour: Flowered pink dress
Issued: 1999 in a limited edition of 200
Varieties: HN2738, 3288
Series: 1. Millennium
　　　　2. Prestige
Comm. by: Lawleys By Post

U.S.:	**$2,000.00**
Can.:	**$2,750.00**
U.K.:	**£1,500.00**

HN 4060
Christmas Angel
Designer: A. Maslankowski
Height: 5 ¾", 14.6 cm
Colour: White
Issued: 1997-1998
Varieties: HN 3733
Series: Sentiments

U.S.:	**$125.00**
Can.:	**$165.00**
U.K.:	**£ 65.00**

Gold backstamp edition for Canada

HN 4061
Christmas Carols
Designer: A. Maslankowski
Height: 6", 15.0 cm
Colour: White
Issued: 1997-1998
Varieties: HN 3727
Series: Sentiments

U.S.:	**$125.00**
Can.:	**$165.00**
U.K.:	**£ 65.00**

Gold backstamp edition for Canada

HN 4062
Christmas Day
Designer: A. Maslankowski
Height: 6", 15.2 cm
Colour: White
Issued: 1997-1998
Varieties: HN 3488
Series: Sentiments

U.S.:	**$125.00**
Can.:	**$165.00**
U.K.:	**£ 65.00**

Gold backstamp edition for Canada

HN 4063
Christmas Parcels
Style Two
Designer: A. Maslankowski
Height: 6", 15.2 cm
Colour: White
Issued: 1997-1998
Varieties: HN 3493
Series: Sentiments

U.S.:	**$125.00**
Can.:	**$165.00**
U.K.:	**£ 65.00**

Gold backstamp edition for Canada

HN 4064
The Kiss (boy)
Designer: A. Maslankowski
Height: 6 ¼", 15.9 cm
Colour: White
Issued: 1998-2003
Series: Images

U.S.:	**$ 65.00**
Can.:	**$140.00**
U.K.:	**£ 35.00**

HN 4065
The Kiss (girl)
Designer: A. Maslankowski
Height: 6", 15.0 cm
Colour: White
Issued: 1998-2003
Series: Images

U.S.:	**$ 65.00**
Can.:	**$140.00**
U.K.:	**£ 35.00**

HN 4066
Philippa of Hainault
(1314-1369)
Style Two
Designer: A. Maslankowski
Height: 7", 17.8 cm
Colour: Red and green
Issued: 1998 in a limited
        edition of 5,000
Series: Plantagenet Queens
Comm.by: Lawleys By Post

U.S.:	**$500.00**
Can.:	**$650.00**
U.K.:	**£250.00**

HN 4067
Christmas Garland
Designer: A. Maslankowski
Height: 6", 15.0 cm
Colour: White
Issued: 1998-2000
Series: Sentiments

U.S.:	**$125.00**
Can.:	**$165.00**
U.K.:	**£ 65.00**

HN 4068
Happy Anniversary
Style Three
Designer: A. Maslankowski
Height: 5 ¾", 14.5 cm
Colour: White
Issued: 1998 to the present
Series: Sentiments

U.S.:	N/I
Can.:	$150.00
U.K.:	£ 42.00

HN 4069
Wizard (Parian)
Style One
Designer: A. Maslankowski
Height: 10", 25.4 cm
Colour: Green and pink
Issued: 1998 in a limited
          edition of 1,500
Varieties: HN 2877, 3121
Comm.by: Lawleys By Post

U.S.:	$400.00
Can.:	$525.00
U.K.:	£225.00

HN 4070
Good Luck
Designer: A. Maslankowski
Height: 6", 15.0 cm
Colour: White
Issued: 1999 to the present
Series: Sentiments

U.S.:	N/I
Can.:	$150.00
U.K.:	£ 42.00

HN 4071
Heathcliff and Cathy
Designer: A. Maslankowski
Height: 12 ½", 31.5 cm
Colour: Blue, cream, green
          and brown
Issued: 1999 in a limited
          edition of 750
Series: Literary Loves

U.S.:	$1,500.00
Can.:	$2,000.00
U.K.:	£ 800.00

HN 4072 not issued.

IIN 4073
Margaret of Anjou
(1430-1482)
Style Two
Designer: A. Maslankowski
Height: 7 ½", 19.1 cm
Colour: Purple and white
Issued: 1998 in a limited
           edition of 5,000
Series: Plantagenet Queens
Comm.by: Lawleys By Post

U.S.:	$500.00
Can.:	$650.00
U.K.:	£250.00

HN 4074
Sophia Dorothea
(1666-1726)
Designer: A. Maslankowski
Height: 9 ½", 24.0 cm
Colour: Red, pink and white
Issued: 1998 in a limited
           edition of 2,500
Series: Georgian Queens
Comm.by: Lawleys By Post

U.S.:	$400.00
Can.:	$525.00
U.K.:	£225.00

HN 4075 not issued.

HN 4076
Missing You
Designer: A. Maslankowski
Height: 6", 15.5 cm
Colour: White
Issued: 1999 - 2001
Series: Sentiments

U.S.:	$100.00
Can.:	$150.00
U.K.:	£ 50.00

HN 4077
Kindred Spirits
Designer: A. Maslankowski
Height: 6", 15.5 cm
Colour: White
Issued: 2000-2000
Series: Image of the Year

U.S.:	$150.00
Can.:	$225.00
U.K.:	£ 85.00

HN 4078
Aurora, Goddess of the Dawn
Designer: A. Maslankowski
Height: 18", 45.0 cm
Colour: White Parian body;
           gold base
Issued: 1999 in a limited
           edition of 250
Series: The Immortals and
           Aurora

U.S.:	**$2,500.00**
Can.:	**$3,250.00**
U.K.:	**£1,500.00**

HN 4079
Hebe, Handmaiden to the Gods
Designer: A. Maslankowski
Height: 14", 35.0 cm
Colour: White Parian body;
           gold base
Issued: 1999 in a limited
           edition of 250
Series: The Immortals and
           Aurora

U.S.:	**$1,200.00**
Can.:	**$1,500.00**
U.K.:	**£ 700.00**

HN 4080
Ceres, Goddess of Plenty
Designer: A. Maslankowski
Height: 14", 35.0 cm
Colour: White Parian body;
           gold base
Issued: 1999 in a limited
           edition of 250
Series: The Immortals and
           Aurora

U.S.:	**$1,200.00**
Can.:	**$1,500.00**
U.K.:	**£ 700.00**

HN 4081
Artemis, Goddess of the Hunt
Designer: A. Maslankowski
Height: 14", 35.0 cm
Colour: White Parian body;
           gold base
Issued: 1999 in a limited
           edition of 250
Series: The Immortals and
           Aurora

U.S.:	**$1,200.00**
Can.:	**$1,500.00**
U.K.:	**£ 700.00**

HN 4082
Erato, The Parnassian Muse
Designer: A. Maslankowski
Height: 14", 35.0 cm
Colour: White Parian body;
           gold base
Issued: 1999 in a limited
           edition of 250
Series: The Immortals and
           Aurora

U.S.:	**$1,450.00**
Can.:	**$2,000.00**
U.K.:	**£ 750.00**

HN 4083
Wisdom
Style One
Designer: A. Maslankowski
Height: Unknown
Colour: White
Issued: 1999-2001
Series: Sentiments
Comm.By.   Great Universal
           Stores

U.S.:	**$100.00**
Can.:	**$150.00**
U.K.:	**£ 50.00**

HN 4084
Noel
Designer: A. Maslankowski
Height: 6", 15.2 cm
Colour: White
Issued: 1999-1999
Series: Christmas Sentiments

U.S.:	**$125.00**
Can.:	**$165.00**
U.K.:	**$ 65.00**

HN 4085
Remembering You
Designer: A. Maslankowski
Height: 6", 15.5 cm
Colour: White
Issued: 2000-2002
Series: Sentiments

U.S.:	**$100.00**
Can.:	**$150.00**
U.K.:	**£ 50.00**

Exclusive to Canada

HN 4086
H.M. Queen Elizabeth
The Queen Mother
Style Four
Designer: A. Maslankowski
Height: 9", 22.9 cm
Colour: Pale blue
Issued: 2000 in a limited
edition of 2,000

U.S.:	$500.00
Can.:	$650.00
U.K.:	£250.00

HN 4087 Bird figure.

HN 4088
Storytime (Boy)
Designer: A. Maslankowski
Length: 4", 10.4 cm
Colour: White
Issued: 2000-2003
Series: Images

U.S.:	$100.00
Can.:	$130.00
U.K.:	£ 35.00

HN 4089
Storytime (Girl)
Designer: A. Maslankowski
Height: 4 ¼", 11.0 cm
Colour: White
Issued: 2000 to the present
Series: Images

U.S.:	N/I
Can.:	$130.00
U.K.:	£ 35.00

HN 4090
Annabelle
Designer: N. Pedley
Height: 7 ½", 19.1 cm
Colour: Pink dress with
flowered border
Issued: 1998 in a special
edition of 2,500
Varieties: Also called Joanne
(Style Two) HN 3422

U.S.:	$275.00
Can.:	$375.00
U.K.:	$175.00

Exclusive to QVC, U.S.A.

HN 4091
Molly
Designer: N. Pedley
Height: 8", 20.3 cm
Colour: Red and yellow dress
Issued: 1997-2003
Varieties: Also called Claire
(Style Two) HN 3646;
Kaitlyn HN 4128;
Rosemary (Style
Three) HN 3691,
3698
Comm.by: Debenhams

U.S.:	$225.00
Can.:	$300.00
U.K.:	£125.00

HN 4092
Charlotte
Style Four
Designer: N. Pedley
Height: 8 ½", 21.6 cm
Colour: Blue and white
Issued: 1998-2002
Varieties: HN 4303

U.S.:	$225.00
Can.:	$325.00
U.K.:	£125.00

HN 4093
Emily
Style Four
Designer: N. Pedley
Height: 8 ¼", 21.0 cm
Colour: Green and white
Issued: 1998 to the present

U.S.:	$205.00
Can.:	$385.00
U.K.:	£105.00

HN 4094
Rosie
Designer: N. Pedley
Height: 8", 20.3 cm
Colour: Rose pink
Issued: 1998 to the present

U.S.:	$205.00
Can.:	$385.00
U.K.:	£110.00

HN 4095
Anna
Style Two
Designer: N. Pedley
Height: 6 ¾", 17.2 cm
Colour: White and pink dress
Issued: 1998-2000
Series: Vanity Fair Ladies

U.S.:	$200.00
Can.:	$300.00
U.K.:	£110.00

HN 4096
Harmony
Style Two
Designer: N. Pedley
Height: 5 ¾", 14.6 cm
Colour: White
Issued: 1998-1998
Series: Club Membership
           Figure

U.S.:	$100.00
Can.:	$150.00
U.K.:	£ 50.00

HN 4097
Hope
Style Two
Designer: N. Pedley
Height: 8 ½", 21.6 cm
Colour: Pink
Issued: 1998-1999
Series: Charity (Breast Cancer)

U.S.:	$325.00
Can.:	$450.00
U.K.:	£200.00

HN 4098
Suzanne
Style One
Designer: N. Pedley
Height: 8 ½", 21.6 cm
Colour: Lilac
Issued: 1998-2001
Series: Vanity Fair Ladies

U.S.:	$250.00
Can.:	$350.00
U.K.:	£125.00

HN 4099
Ruth
Style Two
Designer: N. Pedley
Height: 8", 20.3 cm
Colour: Rose pink
Issued: 1998-2001

U.S.:	$225.00
Can.:	$300.00
U.K.:	£115.00

HN 4100
Special Occasion
Designer: N. Pedley
Height: 8¼", 21.0 cm
Colour: Red and yellow
Issued: 1998-2002

U.S.:	$300.00
Can.:	$425.00
U.K.:	£170.00

HN 4101
Kirsten
Designer: N. Pedley
Height: 8", 20.3 cm
Colour: Blue
Issued: 1998-2000
Series: Vanity Fair Ladies

U.S.:	$225.00
Can.:	$275.00
U.K.:	£110.00

HN 4102
Pride and Joy
Style Two
Designer: N. Pedley
Height: 4 ½", 11.9 cm
Colour: White shirt, light blue
           overalls, red hat,
           black and white ball
Issued: 1998 to the present
Series: Name Your Own

U.S.:	N/I
Can.:	$235.00
U.K.:	£ 65.00

Metal plaque on base for engraved
name.

HN 4103
Sugar and Spice
Designer: N. Pedley
Height: 4 ¼", 10.8 cm
Colour: Pink dress, brown
teddy bear
Issued: 1998-2003
Series: Name Your Own

U.S.:	$115.00
Can.:	$235.00
U.K.:	£ 65.00

Metal plaque on base for engraved name.
HN 4104 - 4108 not issued.

HN 4109
Mackenzie
Designer: N. Pedley
Height: 8", 20.3 cm
Colour: Blue
Issued: 1998 in a special
edition of 350
Varieties: Also called 'First
Bloom' HN 3913
Comm.by: Seaway China

U.S.:	$225.00
Can.:	$300.00
U.K.:	£115.00

HN 4110
Jane
Style Five
Designer: N. Pedley
Height: 8¼", 21.0 cm
Colour: Pink
Issued: 1998
Comm.by: Great Universal
Stores

U.S.:	$200.00
Can.:	$250.00
U.K.:	£100.00

HN 4111
Alice
Style Three
Designer: N. Pedley
Height: 8 ¼", 21.0 cm
Colour: Pink and white
Issued: 1998-2001
Comm.by: Index Mail Order
Catalogue

U.S.:	$200.00
Can.:	$250.00
U.K.:	£100.00

HN 4112
Nicole
Style Two
Designer: N. Pedley
Height: 8", 20.0 cm
Colour: Red, cream and green
Issued: 1999-1999
Series: RDICC

U.S.:	$400.00
Can.:	$525.00
U.K.:	£225.00

HN 4113
Sweet Poetry
Designer: N. Pedley
Height: 8", 20.0 cm
Colour: Lilac and pink
Issued: 1999-2002

U.S.:	$325.00
Can.:	$400.00
U.K.:	£175.00

HN 4114
Mary
Style Five
Designer: N. Pedley
Height: 8 ½", 21.5 cm
Colour: Red and lilac
Issued: 1999-2002

U.S.:	$275.00
Can.:	$400.00
U.K.:	£150.00

HN 4115
Brenda
Designer: N. Pedley
Height: 8 ½", 21.5 cm
Colour: White dress with
pink shading
Issued: 1999-2003
Series: Vanity Fair Ladies

U.S.:	$250.00
Can.:	$325.00
U.K.:	£150.00

Exclusive to Canada

HN 4116
Barbara
Style Four
Designer: N. Pedley
Height: 8 ¼", 21.0 cm
Colour: White and pale green
dress; pink purse and
ribbon
Issued: 1999-2003
Series: Vanity Fair Ladies

U.S.:	**$250.00**
Can.:	**$325.00**
U.K.:	**£150.00**

Exclusive to Canada

HN 4117
Melody
Style Two
Designer: N. Pedley
Height: 5 ½", 14.0 cm
Colour: White and blue
Issued: 1999-1999
Series: Club Membership
Figure

U.S.:	**$125.00**
Can.:	**$165.00**
U.K.:	**£ 75.00**

HN 4118
Special Gift
Designer: N. Pedley
Height: 5 ½", 14.0 cm
Colour: White dress; pink sash
Issued: 1999-1999
Varieties: HN 4129

U.S.:	**$125.00**
Can.:	**$165.00**
U.K.:	**£ 75.00**

Exclusive to Canada
HN 4119 - 4122 not issued.

HN 4123
Katie
Style Two
Designer: N. Pedley
Height: 8", 20.3 cm
Colour: Blue and white
Issued: 1998-2002
Varieties: Also called 'Lindsay'
HN 3645
Comm.by: Debenhams

U.S.:	**$250.00**
Can.:	**$325.00**
U.K.:	**£115.00**

HN 4124
Julia
Style Two
Designer: N. Pedley
Height: 8", 20.3 cm
Colour: Pink
Issued: 1999-1999
Series: M. Doulton Events

U.S.:	**$200.00**
Can.:	**$250.00**
U.K.:	**£115.00**

HN 4125
Amber
Designer: N. Pedley
Height: 8", 20.3 cm
Colour: White dress with
yellow shading
Issued: 1999-2003
Varieties: Also called 'Chloe'
(Style Three)
HN 3883, 3914

U.S.:	**$200.00**
Can.:	**$250.00**
U.K.:	**£100.00**

Exclusive to U.S.A

HN 4126
Brianna
Designer: N. Pedley
Height: 8 ½", 21.6 cm
Colour: White dress with
dark green accents
Issued: 1999-2003
Varieties: Also called 'Kathleen'
(Style Three)
HN 3609, 3880

U.S.:	**$200.00**
Can.:	**$250.00**
U.K.:	**£100.00**

Exclusive to U.S.A

HN 4127
Jasmine
Style Three
Designer: N. Pedley
Height: 8", 20.3 cm
Colour: White and pink
Issued: 1999-2003
Varieties: Also called 'Megan'
(Style Two) HN 3887;
Millie (Style Two)
HN 4212

U.S.:	**$200.00**
Can.:	**$250.00**
U.K.:	**£100.00**

Exclusive to U.S.A

HN 4128
Kaitlyn
Designer: N. Pedley
Height: 8", 20.3 cm
Colour: White and peach
Issued: 1999-2003
Varieties: Also called 'Claire'
           (Style Two) HN 3646;
           'Molly' HN 4091;
           'Rosemary' (Style
           Three) HN 3691, 3698
   U.S.:   **$200.00**
   Can.:   **$250.00**
   U.K.:   **£100.00**

Exclusive to U.S.A

HN 4129
Special Gift
Designer: N. Pedley
Height: 5 ½" 14.0 cm
Colour: Peach
Issued: 1999-2000
Varieties: HN 4118
Series: Visitor Centre
   U.S.:   **$125.00**
   Can.:   **$175.00**
   U.K.:   **£ 65.00**

HN 4130
Elaine
Style One
Designer: M. Davies
Height: 7 ¼", 18.4 cm
Colour: Red
Issued: 1998 in a limited
           edition of 2,500
Varieties: HN 2791, 3307,
           3741
Comm.by: Great Universal
           Stores
   U.S.:   **$300.00**
   Can.:   **$400.00**
   U.K.:   **£165.00**

HN 4131
Elyse
Designer: M. Davies
Height: 5 ¾", 14.6 cm
Colour: Rose-pink
Issued: 1998 in a limited
           edition of 2,500
Varieties: HN 2429, 2474
Comm.by: Great Universal
           Stores
   U.S.:   **$300.00**
   Can.:   **$400.00**
   U.K.:   **£165.00**

HN 4132
Alyssa
Designer: M. Davies
Height: 8 ½", 21.6 cm
Colour: White and pale blue
Issued: 1999-2003
Varieties: Also called 'Country
           Rose' HN 3221
   U.S.:   **$200.00**
   Can.:   **$250.00**
   U.K.:   **£100.00**

Exclusive to U.S.A.
HN 4133 - 4139 not issued.

HN 4140
Darling
Style One
Designer: C. Vyse
Remodeller: W. K. Harper
Height: 7 ¾", 19.5 cm
Colour: Pale blue
Issued: 1998 in a limited
            edition of 1,913
Varieties: HN 1, 1319, 1371,
            1372
Comm.by: Lawleys By Post
   U.S.:   **$200.00**
   Can.:   **$250.00**
   U.K.:   **£100.00**

HN 4141
The Mask
Style Two
Designer: L. Harradine
Modeller: W. K. Harper
Height: 9 ½", 24.0 cm
Colour: Blue, black and pink
Issued: 1999 in a limited
           edition of 1,500
Comm.by: Lawleys By Post
   U.S.:   **$400.00**
   Can.:   **$525.00**
   U.K.:   **£225.00**

HN 4142 - 4150 not issued.

HN 4151
Faith
Style Two
Designer: N. Pedley
Height: 8 ¼", 21.0 cm
Colour: Pale blue and
           dusky pink
Issued: 1999-2000
Series: Charity (Breast Cancer)
   U.S.:   **$275.00**
   Can.:   **$375.00**
   U.K.:   **£150.00**

HN 4152
Madeline
Designer: N. Pedley
Height: 8 ¼", 21.0 cm
Colour: Yellow and white
Issued: 1999-2003

U.S.:	**$225.00**
Can.:	**$450.00**
U.K.:	**£115.00**

HN 4153
Marianne
Style Two
Designer: N. Pedley
Height: 8 ¼", 21.0 cm
Colour: Red and white
Issued: 1999-2002
Varieties: Also called 'Jayne'
(Style One) HN 4210

U.S.:	**$275.00**
Can.:	**$400.00**
U.K.:	**£150.00**

HN 4154
Natasha
Designer: N. Pedley
Height: 8 ¼", 21.0 cm
Colour: Yellow and white
Issued: 1999-2001

U.S.:	**$475.00**
Can.:	**$600.00**
U.K.:	**£250.00**

HN 4155
Lynne
Style Two
Designer: N. Pedley
Height: 8 ¼", 21.0 cm
Colour: Rose and pale pink
Issued: 1999-2002

U.S.:	**$250.00**
Can.:	**$400.00**
U.K.:	**£125.00**

HN 4156
Beth
Style Two
Designer: N. Pedley
Height: 8 ¼", 21.0 cm
Colour: Lilac
Issued: 1999-2002
Varieties: Also called 'Lydia'
(Style Two) HN 4211

U.S.:	**$250.00**
Can.:	**$400.00**
U.K.:	**£125.00**

HN 4157
Kelly
Style Three
Designer: N. Pedley
Height: 8 ¼", 21.0 cm
Colour: Green and white
Issued: 1999 to the present

U.S.:	**$215.00**
Can.:	**$425.00**
U.K.:	**£110.00**

HN 4158
Michelle
Designer: N. Pedley
Height: 8 ¼", 21.0 cm
Colour: Blue and white
Issued: 1999-2002

U.S.:	**$225.00**
Can.:	**$350.00**
U.K.:	**£110.00**

HN 4159 not issued.

HN 4160
Sally
Style Two
Designer: T. Potts
Height: 8 ¼", 21.0 cm
Colour: Rose pink jacket,
turquoise skirt
Issued: 1998 in a limited
edition of 1,500
Varieties: HN 3383, 3851
Series: Visitor Centre

U.S.:	**$300.00**
Can.:	**$425.00**
U.K.:	**£150.00**

HN 4161
The Open Road
Designer: T. Potts
Height: 9", 23.0 cm
Colour: Pink
Issued: 1999-2001

U.S.:	**$325.00**
Can.:	**$425.00**
U.K.:	**£175.00**

HN 4162
Clara Hamps
Designer: T. Potts
Height: 8 ½", 21.5 cm
Colour: Blue and white
Issued: 1999-2001
Series: 1. Arnold Bennett
        2. Visitor Centre

U.S.:	**$325.00**
Can.:	**$450.00**
U.K.:	**£175.00**

HN 4163
Ecstasy
Deisgner: T. Potts
Height: 17", 43.2 cm
Colour: Fleshtone; brown
        and gold
Issued: 1999 in a limited
        edition of 500
Series: Art Deco

U.S.:	**$1,400.00**
Can.:	**$1,800.00**
U.K.:	**£ 800.00**

HN 4164
Destiny
Designer: T. Potts
Height: 19", 48.0 cm
Colour: Fleshtone; brown
        and gold
Issued: 1999 in a limited
        edition of 500
Series: Art Deco

U.S.:	**$1,400.00**
Can.:	**$1,800.00**
U.K.:	**£ 800.00**

HN 4165
Optimism
Designer: T. Potts
Height: 16", 40.6 cm
Colour: Fleshtone, brown
        and gold
Issued: 1999 in a limited
        edition of 500
Series: Art Deco

U.S.:	**$1,400.00**
Can.:	**$1,800.00**
U.K.:	**£ 800.00**

HN 4166
Wisdom
Style Two
Designer: T. Potts
Height: 19", 48.0 cm
Colour: Fleshtone, brown
        and gold
Issued: 1999 in a limited
        edition of 500
Series: Art Deco

U.S.:	**$1,400.00**
Can.:	**$1,800.00**
U.K.:	**£ 800.00**

HN 4167
Sophia Baines
Designer: T. Potts
Height: 8", 20.3 cm
Colour: Blue and white
Issued: 2000-2001
Series: 1. Arnold Bennett
        2. Visitor Centre

U.S.:	**$375.00**
Can.:	**$450.00**
U.K.:	**£175.00**

HN 4168
Gladys
Second Version
Designer: L. Harradine
Remodeller: T. Potts
Height: 4 ¼", 11.0 cm
Colour: Sage green
Issued: 2000 in a limited
        edition of 2,000
Comm.by: Lawleys By Post

U.S.:	**$225.00**
Can.:	**$300.00**
U.K.:	**£125.00**

HN 4169
Vera
Second Version
Designer: L. Harradine
Remodeller: T. Potts
Height: 4 ¼", 11.0 cm
Colour: Pink and white
Issued: 2000 in a limited
              edition of 2,000
Comm.by: Lawleys By Post
U.S.:   **$225.00**
Can.:   **$300.00**
U.K.:   **£125.00**

HN 4170 - 4173 Animal figures.

HN 4174
The Land of Nod
Second Version
Designer: H. Tittensor
Remodeller: R. Tabbenor
Height: 7 ¾, 19.7 cm
Colour: Pale blue nightgown;
              white and tan owl;
              tan base
Issued: 2000 in a limited
              edition of 2,500
Comm.by: Lawleys By Post
U.S.:   **$250.00**
Can.:   **$325.00**
U.K.:   **£125.00**

HN 4175
Santa Claus
Style Two
Designer: R. Tabbenor
Height: 9 ½", 24.0 cm
Colour: Red and white suit;
            black belt and boots
Issued: 2000-2003
U.S.:   **$350.00**
Can.:   **$650.00**
U.K.:   **£180.00**

HN 4176 - 4178 Animal figures.

HN 4179
Princess Badoura
Style Two
Designer: R, Tabbenor
Height: 7 ½", 19.1 cm
Colour: Pink, brown, red,
            blue and grey
Issued: 2001 In a limited
            edition of 500
U.S.:   **$1,000.00**
Can.:   **$1,500.00**
U.K.:   **£ 600.00**

HN 4180 - 4189 not issued, except
HN 4181, 4182 and 4184 Animal
figures.

HN 4190
Ankhesenamun
Designer: P. Parsons
Height: 10 ½", 26.7 cm
Colour: Green
Issued: 1998 in a limited
             edition of 950
Series: Egyptian Queens
Comm.by: Lawleys By Post
U.S.:   **$ 775.00**
Can.:   **$1,000.00**
U.K.:   **£ 425.00**

HN 4191
Hatshepsut
Designer: P. Parsons
Height: 10 ½", 26.7 cm
Colour: Cream, blue, brown,
             rust and gold
Issued: 1999 in a limited
             edition of 950
Series: Egyptian Queens
Comm.by: Lawleys By Post
U.S.:   **$ 775.00**
Can.:   **$1,000.00**
U.K.:   **£ 425.00**

HN 4192
Tender Moment
Style Two
Designer: P. Parsons
Height: 12", 31.5 cm
Colour: Lilac and cream
Issued: 1999-2003
Series: Impressions
U.S.:   **$250.00**
Can.:   **$465.00**
U.K.:   **£130.00**

HN 4193
Sweet Dreams
Style Three
Designer: P. Parsons
Height: 12", 30.5 cm
Colour: Yellow and cream
Issued: 1999-2002
Series: Impressions
U.S.:   **$300.00**
Can.:   **$425.00**
U.K.:   **£150.00**

HN 4194
Summer Blooms
Style Two
Designer: P. Parsons
Height: 13", 33.0 cm
Colour: Lilac, cream, green and tan
Issued: 1999-2003
Series: Impressions
- **U.S.:** **$250.00**
- **Can.:** **$465.00**
- **U.K.:** **£130.00**

Variation exists with arms in a more downward position.

HN 4195
Summer Fragrance
Designer: P. Parsons
Height: 12", 30.5 cm
Colour: Pink, cream and green
Issued: 1999-2000
Series: Impressions
- **U.S.:** **$300.00**
- **Can.:** **$450.00**
- **U.K.:** **£175.00**

HN 4196
Daybreak
Style Two
Designer: P. Parsons
Height: 13", 33.0 cm
Colour: Blue and cream
Issued: 1999-2003
Series: Impressions
- **U.S.:** **$250.00**
- **Can.:** **$465.00**
- **U.K.:** **£130.00**

HN 4197
Secret Thoughts
Style Two
Designer: P. Parsons
Height: 13", 32.5 cm
Colour: Pink and cream
Issued: 1999-2003
Series: Impressions
- **U.S.:** **$250.00**
- **Can.:** **$465.00**
- **U.K.:** **£130.00**

HN 4198
Sunset
Designer: P. Parsons
Height: 7", 17.8 cm
Colour: Blue and cream
Issued: 2000-2003
Series: Impressions
- **U.S.:** **$250.00**
- **Can.:** **$465.00**
- **U.K.:** **£130.00**

HN 4199
Sunrise
Designer: P. Parsons
Height: 7", 17.8 cm
Colour: Yellow
Issued: 2000-2003
Series: Impressions
- **U.S.:** **$250.00**
- **Can.:** **$465.00**
- **U.K.:** **£130.00**

HN 4200
Scarlett O'Hara
Designer: V. Annand
Height: 9", 22.9 cm
Colour: Dark green overdress, green-gold underskirt
Issued: 1999-2000
Series: Classic Movies
- **U.S.:** **$500.00**
- **Can.:** **$650.00**
- **U.K.:** **£275.00**

Serial numbered edition.

HN 4201A
Chloe
Style Four
Designer: J. Bromley
Height: 8 ½", 21.6 cm
Colour: Pink and cream
Issued: 2000 in a limited edition of 2000
Series: Millennium Lady of the Year
Comm.by: Compton/Woodhouse
- **U.S.:** **$300.00**
- **Can.:** **$375.00**
- **U.K.:** **£150.00**

HN 4201B
Millennium Celebration
Designer: V. Annand
Height: 8 ¼", 21.0 cm
Colour: Turquoise and
             yellow
Issued: 1999-2001
Varieties: HN 4321, 4325
Comm.by: Great Universal
             Store

U.S.:   **$225.00**
Can.:   **$275.00**
U.K.:   **£125.00**

HN 4202
Joanne
Style Three
Designer: V. Annand
Height: 9", 22.9 cm
Colour: Mint green dress
Issued: 2000-2002
Series: In Vogue

U.S.:   **$250.00**
Can.:   **$375.00**
U.K.:   **£125.00**

HN 4203
Rebecca
Style Four
Designer: V. Annand
Height: 9", 22.9 cm
Colour: Pale pink skirt,
             red flowers on
             cream bodice
Issued: 2000-2002
Series: In Vogue

U.S.:   **$250.00**
Can.:   **$375.00**
U.K.:   **£125.00**

HN 4204
Madison
Designer: V. Annand
Height: 8 ½", 21.6 cm
Colour: Pale green
Issued: 2000-2003
Varieties: Also called 'Emma'
             (Style Three) HN 3714

U.S.:   **$200.00**
Can.:   **$250.00**
U.K.:   **£110.00**

Exclusive to U.S.A.

HN 4205
Alexis
Designer: V. Annand
Height: 8 ½", 21.6 cm
Colour: Pale yellow
Issued: 2000-2003
Varieties: Also called 'Kathryn'
             (Style Two) HN 4040

U.S.:   **$200.00**
Can.:   **$250.00**
U.K.:   **£110.00**

Exclusive to U.S.A.

HN 4206
Brittany
Designer: V. Annand
Height: 8 ¾", 22.2 cm
Colour: Pale pink dress
Issued: 2000-2003
Varieties: Also called 'Olivia'
             (Style Three) HN 3717

U.S.:   **$200.00**
Can.:   **$250.00**
U.K.:   **£110.00**

Exclusive to U.S.A.

HN 4207
Allison
Designer: V. Annand
Height: 8 ¼", 21.0 cm
Colour: Pale blue dress
Issued: 2000-2003
Varieties: Also called 'Ellie'
             HN 4046

U.S.:   **$200.00**
Can.:   **$250.00**
U.K.:   **£110.00**

Exclusive to U.S.A.

HN 4208
Zoe
Designer: V. Annand
Height: 8 ¼", 21.0 cm
Colour: Lilac
Issued: 2000-2003
Series: Chelsea

U.S.:   **$200.00**
Can.:   **$350.00**
U.K.:   **£100.00**

HN 4209
Melinda
Designer: V. Annand
Height: 8 ¼", 21.0 cm
Colour: Peach
Issued: 2000-2002
Series: Chelsea

U.S.:	**$225.00**
Can.:	**$325.00**
U.K.:	**£115.00**

HN 4210
Jayne
Style One
Designer: N. Pedley
Height: 8¼", 21.0 cm
Colour: Pale blue and yellow
Issued: 1999-2001
Varieties: 'Marianne'
          (Style Two) HN 4153
Comm.by: Great Universal
          Store

U.S.:	**$250.00**
Can.:	**$325.00**
U.K.:	**£135.00**

HN 4211
Lydia
Style Two
Designer: N. Pedley
Height: 8 ¼", 21.0 cm
Colour: Red
Issued: 1999-2001
Varieties: Also called 'Beth'
          (Style Two) HN 4156
Comm.by: Great Universal
          Store

U.S.:	**$250.00**
Can.:	**$325.00**
U.K.:	**£135.00**

HN 4212
Millie
Style Two
Designer: N. Pedley
Height: 8", 20.3 cm
Colour: Pink and white
Issued: 1999
Varieties: Also known as
          'Jasmine' HN 4127;
          'Megan' HN 3887
Comm.by: Debenham

U.S.:	**$200.00**
Can.:	**$250.00**
U.K.:	**£110.00**

HN 4213
With All My Love
Designer: N. Pedley
Height: 5", 12.7 cm
Colour: White and blue
Issued: 2000 in a limited
          edition of 2,500
Varieties: HN 4241

U.S.:	**$200.00**
Can.:	**$250.00**
U.K.:	**£100.00**

Exclusive to Canada

HN 4214
Christmas Day 1999
Designer: N. Pedley
Height: 8", 20.3 cm
Colour: Red dress and hat;
          ivory jacket; ermine
          trim and muff
Issued: 1999-1999
Series: Christmas Figures

U.S.:	**$325.00**
Can.:	**$475.00**
U.K.:	**£200.00**

HN 4215
Happy Birthday 2000
Designer: N. Pedley
Height: 8 ¾", 22.0 cm
Colour: Pink
Issued: 2000-2000
Series: Happy Birthday

U.S.:	**$200.00**
Can.:	**$300.00**
U.K.:	**£100.00**

HN 4216
Wedding Celebration
Designer: N. Pedley
Height: 8 ¾", 22.0 cm
Colour: Ivory dress with
          pale pink panel;
          pink flowers
Issued: 2000-2002
Varieties: HN 4229
Series: Name Your Own

U.S.:	**$200.00**
Can.:	**$300.00**
U.K.:	**£110.00**

Metal plaque on base for engraved name.
HN 4217 - 4219 not issued.

HN 4220
Camilla
Style Two
Designer: N. Pedley
Height: 8 ½", 21.5 cm
Colour: Pink dress with
           white trim
Issued: 2000-2002
U.S.:   **$235.00**
Can.:   **$400.00**
U.K.:   **£130.00**

HN 4221
Susannah
Designer: N. Pedley
Height: 8", 20.3 cm
Colour: Cream cardigan;
           cream skirt decorated
           with gold flowers
Issued: 2000-2003
Series: Vanity Fair
U.S.:   **$225.00**
Can.:   **$425.00**
U.K.:   **£115.00**

HN 4222
Fair Maid
Designer: N. Pedley
Height: 8", 21.0 cm
Colour: Blue and lemon
Issued: 2000-2002
Series: Country Maids
U.S.:   **$225.00**
Can.:   **$375.00**
U.K.:   **£125.00**

HN 4223
Josephine
Designer: N. Pedley
Height: 8 ½", 21.5 cm
Colour: Blue and white
Issued: 2000-2003
Varieties: Also called 'Caroline'
           (Style three) HN 4395
Series: Vanity Fair
U.S.:   **$175.00**
Can.:   **$335.00**
U.K.:   **£100.00**

HN 4224 not issued.

HN 4225
Summer Duet
Designer: N. Pedley
Height: 6", 15.0
Colour: Ivory and gold
Issued: 1999 in a limited
           edition of 1,500
Series: Ivory and Gold
Comm.by: Lawleys By Post
U.S.:   **$150.00**
Can.:   **$200.00**
U.K.:   **£ 75.00**

HN 4226
After the Rain
Designer: N. Pedley
Height: 6", 15.0
Colour: Ivory and gold
Issued: 1999 in a limited
           edition of 1,500
Series: Ivory and Gold
Comm.by: Lawleys By Post
U.S.:   **$150.00**
Can.:   **$200.00**
U.K.:   **£ 75.00**

HN 4227
Off to the Pond
Designer: N. Pedley
Height: 6", 15.0
Colour: Ivory and gold
Issued: 1999 in a limited
           edition of 1,500
Series: Ivory and Gold
Comm.by: Lawleys By Post
U.S.:   **$150.00**
Can.:   **$200.00**
U.K.:   **£ 75.00**

HN 4228
Helping Mother
Designer: N. Pedley
Height: 6", 15.0
Colour: Ivory and gold
Issued: 1999 in a limited
           edition of 1,500
Series: Ivory and Gold
Comm.by: Lawleys By Post
U.S.:   **$150.00**
Can.:   **$200.00**
U.K.:   **£ 75.00**

HN 4229
Wedding Celebration
Designer: N. Pedley
Height: 8 ¾", 22.0 cm
Colour: White with pink
         highlights
Issued: 2000-2002
Varieties: HN 4216
Series: Name Your Own

U.S.:	**$225.00**
Can.:	**$350.00**
U.K.:	**£135.00**

HN 4230
Susan
Style Four
Designer: J. Bromley
Height: 8 ½", 21.6 cm
Colour: Yellow and pink
Issued: 2000-2000
Series: M. Doulton Events

U.S.:	**$300.00**
Can.:	**$400.00**
U.K.:	**£175.00**

Serial numbered.

HN 4231
Ellen
Style Four
Designer: J. Bromley
Height: 8 ½", 21.6 cm
Colour: Red dress; pink
         shawl with red
         flowers
Issued: 2000-2002

U.S.:	**$300.00**
Can.:	**$475.00**
U.K.:	**£175.00**

HN 4232
Specially For You
Designer: J. Bromley
Height: 8 ½", 21.6 cm
Colour: Green jacket; mauve
         skirt and bonnet;
         ermine trim and muff
Issued: 2000 to the present

U.S.:	**$335.00**
Can.:	**$595.00**
U.K.:	**£175.00**

HN 4233
Kate
Style Three
Designer: J. Bromley
Height: 8 ½", 21.6 cm
Colour: Dusky rose
Issued: 2000-2000
Varieties: 'Best Wishes'
          HN 3971; 'Forever
          Yours' HN 4501
Series: Charity figure 2000
Comm.by: Compton/Woodhouse

U.S.:	**$275.00**
Can.:	**$375.00**
U.K.:	**£150.00**

Brass plaque on base for engraving.

HN 4234
Special Celebration
Designer: J. Bromley
Height: 8 ¾", 22.2 cm
Colour: Purple and cream
Issued: 2001 to the present

U.S.:	**$335.00**
Can.:	**$695.00**
U.K.:	**£195.00**

HN 4235
Belle
Style Five
Designer: J. Bromley
Height: 8 ½", 21.6 cm
Colour: Purple with ermine
         trim
Issued: 2001 to the present

U.S.:	**$360.00**
Can.:	**$695.00**
U.K.:	**£195.00**

HN 4236
Just For You
Style Two
Designer: J. Bromley
Height: 8 ¾", 22.2 cm
Colour: Deep pink
Issued: 2002 to the present

U.S.:	**$315.00**
Can.:	**$595.00**
U.K.:	**£175.00**

HN 4237
Georgina
Style Three
Designer: J. Bromley
Height: 9 ¼", 23.5 cm
Colour: Pink and white
Issued: 2002-2002
Series: Lady of the Year
Comm.by.   Compton/Woodhouse

U.S.:	**$250.00**
Can.:	**$375.00**
U.K.:	**£150.00**

HN 4238
Francesca
Designer: D. Hughes
Height: 8 ½", 21.5 cm
Colour: Red
Issued: 2001 in a limited
               edition of 2,500
Comm.by.   Home Shopping Ltd.

U.S.:	**$250.00**
Can.:	**$375.00**
U.K.:	**£150.00**

HN 4239 not issued.

HN 4240
Flower of Scotland
Designer: N. Pedley
Height: 9", 22.9 cm
Colour: Blue and white dress,
               pale green plaid shawl
Issued: 2000-2003

U.S.:	**$225.00**
Can.:	**$425.00**
U.K.:	**£115.00**

HN 4241
With All My Love
Designer: N. Pedley
Height: 5", 12.7 cm
Colour: White and pink
Issued: 2000-2001
Varieties: HN 4213
Series: Visitor Centre

U.S.:	**$125.00**
Can.:	**$150.00**
U.K.:	**£ 60.00**

HN 4242
Christmas Day 2000
Designer: N. Pedley
Height: 8 ¼", 21.0 cm
Colour: Dark green dress; red
          jacket trimmed with
          ermine; ermine muff;
          green hat
Issued: 2000-2000
Series: Christmas Day

U.S.:	**$250.00**
Can.:	**$375.00**
U.K.:	**£150.00**

HN 4243
Charity
Style Two
Designer: N. Pedley
Height: 8 ¼", 21.0 cm
Colour: Pink
Issued: 2000-2001
Series: Charity
          Breast Cancer

U.S.:	**$275.00**
Can.:	**$375.00**
U.K.:	**£150.00**

HN 4244
The Bather
Style One, Second Version
Designer: L. Harradine
Remodeller: N. Pedley
Height: 7 ¼", 18.4 cm
Colour: Royal blue robe
Issued: 2000 in a limited
             edition of 2,000
Series: Bathers

U.S.:	**$500.00**
Can.:	**$675.00**
U.K.:	**£275.00**

HN 4245
The Sunshine Girl
Second Version
Designer: L.Harradine
Remodeller: N. Pedley
Height: 4 ½", 11.5 cm
Colour: Green, red and white
Issued: 2000 in a limited
             edition of 2,000
Series: Bathers

U.S.:	**$500.00**
Can.:	**$675.00**
U.K.:	**£275.00**

HN 4246
The Swimmer
Second Version
Designer: L. Harradine
Remodeller: N. Pedley
Height: 7 ¼", 18.4 cm
Colour: Dark blue, red
             and black
Issued: 2000 in a limited
             edition of 2,000
Series: Bathers

U.S.:	**$500.00**
Can.:	**$675.00**
U.K.:	**£275.00**

HN 4247
Lido Lady
Second Version
Designer: L. Harradine
Remodeller: N. Pedley
Height: 6 ¾", 17.2 cm
Colour: Pink
Issued: 2000-2001
Series: 1. Bathers
             2. RDICC

U.S.:	**$300.00**
Can.:	**$450.00**
U.K.:	**£200.00**

HN 4248
Jennifer
Style Four
Designer: N. Pedley
Height: 8 ¼", 21.0 cm
Colour: Yellow
Issued: 2000 to the present

U.S.:	**$235.00**
Can.:	**$450.00**
U.K.:	**£120.00**

HN 4249
Dairy Maid
Designer: N. Pedley
Height: 8 ¼", 21.0 cm
Colour: Lemon, white and pink
Issued: 2000-2002
Series: Country Maids

U.S.:	**$225.00**
Can.:	**$400.00**
U.K.:	**£135.00**

HN 4250
Greetings
Designer: A. Maslankowski
Height: 5 ¾", 14.6 cm
Colour: White and yellow
Issued: 2000-2000
Series: 1. Club Membership
             Gift
          2. Sentiments

U.S.:	**$100.00**
Can.:	**$150.00**
U.K.:	**$ 50.00**

HN 4251
Thank You Mother
Designer: A. Maslankowski
Height: 6 ¼", 15.8 cm
Colour: White with violet sash
Issued: 2000-2003
Varieties: Also called 'Thank You'
            (Style Two) HN 3390
Series: Sentiments

U.S.:	**$125.00**
Can.:	**$185.00**
U.K.:	**£ 75.00**

HN 4252
The Sorcerer
Designer: A. Maslankowski
Height: 9 ¼", 23.5 cm
Colour: Purple, red, white,
          gold and yellow
Issued: 2000-2002
Series: Mystical Figures

U.S.:	**$500.00**
Can.:	**$750.00**
U.K.:	**£300.00**

HN 4253
The Sorceress
Designer: A. Maslankowski
Height: 9 ½", 24.0 cm
Colour: Purple, red, yellow
          and gold
Issued: 2000-2002
Series: Mystical Figures

U.S.:	**$400.00**
Can.:	**$525.00**
U.K.:	**£225.00**

Exclusive to Canada

HN 4254
Many Happy Returns
Designer: A. Maslankowski
Height: 5 ¾", 14.6 cm
Colour: White
Issued: 2000 to the present
Series: Sentiments

U.S.:	N/I
Can.:	$150.00
U.K.:	£ 42.00

HN 4255
Happy Christmas
Designer: A. Maslankowski
Height: 6 ¼", 15.9 cm
Colour: White
Issued: 2000-2003
Series: Sentiments

U.S.:	$ 85.00
Can.:	$120.00
U.K.:	£ 45.00

HN 4256
Carol Singer with Lantern
Designer: D. V. Tootle
Height: 6 ¼", 15.9 cm
Colour: White
Issued: 2000 in a limited
          edition of 6,000
Series: 1. Images
          2. Christmas Choir
             Collection

U.S.:	$75.00
Can.:	$95.00
U.K.:	£40.00

HN 4257
Special Friends
Designer: A. Maslankowski
Height: 6 ¾", 17.2 cm
Colour: White
Issued: 2001-2001
Series: Image of the Year

U.S.:	$175.00
Can.:	$250.00
U.K.:	£100.00

HN 4258
Embrace
Designer: A. Maslankowski
Height: 6", 15.0 cm
Colour: White
Issued: 2001-2001
Series: Club Membership
          Figure

U.S.:	$ 95.00
Can.:	$150.00
U.K.:	£ 50.00

HN 4259 not issued.

HN 4260
Henrietta-Maria
(Wife of Charles I)
Style Two
Designer: P. Parsons
Height: 9", 22.9 cm
Colour: Red, yellow, white
            and blue
Issued: 2000 in a limited
            edition of 2,500
Series: Stuart Queens
Comm.by: Doulton Direct

U.S.:	$500.00
Can.:	$650.00
U.K.:	£275.00

HN 4261
Tender Greetings
Designer: P. Parsons
Height: 11", 27.9 cm
Colour: Mint green overdress;
          cream underskirt with
          floral design
Issued: 2000-2002
Series: Impressions

U.S.:	$265.00
Can.:	$450.00
U.K.:	£160.00

HN 4262
In Loving Arms
Designer: P. Parsons
Height: 12", 30.5 cm
Colour: Pink overdress;
          cream underskirt
Issued: 2000-2002
Series: Impressions

U.S.:	$265.00
Can.:	$450.00
U.K.:	£160.00

HN 4263
Edward VI
Designer: P. Parsons
Height: 8 ¼", 21.0 cm
Colour: Red, cream, black,
            gold and brown
Issued: 2000 in a limited
            edition of 5,000
Comm.by: Lawleys By Post

U.S.:	**$650.00**
Can.:	**$850.00**
U.K.:	**£350.00**

HN 4264
Cleopatra
Style Two
Designer: P. Parsons
Height: 10", 25.4 cm
Colour: Pale blue, turquoise,
            yellow, light brown
            and red
Issued: 2001 In a limited
            edition of 950
Series: Egyptian Queens
Comm.by: Doulton-Direct

U.S.:	**$ 775.00**
Can.:	**$1,100.00**
U.K.:	**£ 425.00**

HN 4265
Cherished Memories
Designer: P. Parsons
Height: 12 ¾", 32.4 cm
Colour: Pale yellow
Issued: 2001-2002
Series: 1. ICC
            2. Impressions

U.S.:	**$300.00**
Can.:	**$400.00**
U.K.:	**£150.00**

HN 4266
Anne of Denmark
(Wife of James 1)
Designer: P. Parsons
Height: 9", 23.0 cm
Colour: Green, white and red
Issued: 2001 In a limited
            edition of 2,500
Series: Stuart Queens
Comm.by: Doulton-Direct

U.S.:	**$650.00**
Can.:	**$850.00**
U.K.:	**£350.00**

HN 4267
Catherine of Braganza
(Wife of Charles II)
Designer: P. Parsons
Height: 9", 23.0 cm
Colour: Orange and white
            dress, brown chair,
            green cushion
Issued: 2001 In a limited
            edition of 2,500
Series: Stuart Queens
Comm.by: Doulton-Direct

U.S.:	**$650.00**
Can.:	**$850.00**
U.K.:	**£350.00**

HN 4268 - 4269 not issued.

HN 4270
Spring
Style Five
Designer: M. King
Height: 8 ½", 21.6 cm
Colour: Yellow and white
Issued: 2000 in a limited
            edition of 2,000
Series: The Seasons
            (Series Eight)
Comm.by: Compton/Woodhouse

U.S.:	**$375.00**
Can.:	**$450.00**
U.K.:	**£175.00**

HN 4271
Summer
Style Three
Designer: M. King
Height: 8 ½", 21.6 cm
Colour: Blue, yellow and white
Issued: 2000 in a limited
            edition of 2,000
Series: The Seasons
            (Series Eight)
Comm.by: Compton/Woodhouse

U.S.:	**$375.00**
Can.:	**$450.00**
U.K.:	**£175.00**

HN 4272
Autumn
Style Three
Designer: M. King
Height: 8 ½", 21.6 cm
Colour: Purple
Issued: 2000 in a limited
            edition of 2,000
Series: The Seasons
            (Series Eight)
Comm.by: Compton/Woodhouse

U.S.:	**$375.00**
Can.:	**$450.00**
U.K.:	**£175.00**

HN 4273
Winter
Style Three
Designer: M. King
Height: 8 ½", 21.6 cm
Colour: Red
Issued: 2000 in a limited
               edition of 2,000
Series: The Seasons
               (Series Eight)
Comm.by: Compton/Woodhouse

U.S.:	**$375.00**
Can.:	**$450.00**
U.K.:	**£175.00**

HN 4274 - 4279 not issued.

HN 4280
Love Everlasting
Designer: A. Hughes
Height: 6 ½", 16.5 cm
Colour: White
Issued: 2000 to the present
Series: Images

U.S.:	**$ 90.00**
Can.:	**$175.00**
U.K.:	**£ 39.00**

HN 4281
Debut
Style Two
Designer: A. Hughes
Height: 9", 22.9 cm
Colour: White
Issued: 2000 in a limited
               edition of 2,000
Series: Images
Comm.by: Lawleys By Post

U.S.:	**$125.00**
Can.:	**$165.00**
U.K.:	**£ 60.00**

HN 4282
Encore
Style Two
Designer: A. Hughes
Height: 9", 22.9 cm
Colour: White
Issued: 2000 in a limited
               edition of 2,000
Series: Images
Comm.by: Lawleys By Post

U.S.:	**$125.00**
Can.:	**$165.00**
U.K.:	**£ 60.00**

HN 4283
Trumpet Player
Designer: A. Hughes
Height: 9 ½", 24.0 cm
Colour: White
Issued: 2000 in a limited
               edition of 1,500
Series: The Age of Jazz
Comm.by: Lawleys By Post

U.S.:	**$125.00**
Can.:	**$165.00**
U.K.:	**£ 60.00**

HN 4284
Saxophone Player
Designer: A. Hughes
Height: 9 ½", 24.0 cm
Colour: White
Issued: 2000 in a limited
               edition of 1,500
Series: The Age of Jazz
Comm.by: Lawleys By Post

U.S.:	**$125.00**
Can.:	**$165.00**
U.K.:	**£ 60.00**

HN 4285
The Age of Swing
Designer: A. Hughes
Height: 8", 20.3 cm
Colour: White
Issued: 2000 in a limited
               edition of 1,500
Comm.by: Lawleys By Post

U.S.:	**$125.00**
Can.:	**$175.00**
U.K.:	**£ 75.00**

HN 4286
Doctor
Style Two
Designer: A. Hughes
Height: 9 ¼", 23.5 cm
Colour: Brown suit, black
            waistcoat and bag
Issued: 2001-2002

U.S.:	**$395.00**
Can.:	**$600.00**
U.K.:	**£220.00**

HN 4287
Nurse
Designer: A. Hughes
Height: 8 ½", 21.6 cm
Colour: White, blue and red
         uniform
Issued: 2001 to the present
  U.S.:   **$395.00**
  Can.:   **$695.00**
  U.K.:   **£220.00**

HN 4288 not issued.

HN 4289
Lawyer
Style Two
Designer: A. Hughes
Height: 8 ¾", 22.2 cm
Colour: Black robes, white
         collar, red book
         brown stand
Issued: 2001-2003
  U.S.:   **$330.00**
  Can.:   **$650.00**
  U.K.:   **£175.00**

HN 4290
Carol Singer (Brother)
Designer: D. V. Tootle
Height: 6 ¼", 15.9 cm
Colour: White
Issued: 2000 in a limited
         edition of 6,000
Series: 1. Christmas Choir
         2. Images
  U.S.:   **$75.00**
  Can.:   **$95.00**
  U.K.:   **£40.00**

HN 4291
Carol Singer (Sister)
Designer: D. V. Tootle
Height: 6 ¼", 15.9 cm
Colour: White
Issued: 2000 in a limited
         edition of 6,000
Series: 1. Christmas Choir
         2. Images
  U.S.:   **$75.00**
  Can.:   **$95.00**
  U.K.:   **£40.00**

HN 4292 - 4299 not issued.

HN 4300
Bells Across the Valley
Designer: N. Pedley
Height: 8 ½", 21.5 cm
Colour: Lilac
Issued: 1999 to the present
  U.S.:   **$275.00**
  Can.:   **$475.00**
  U.K.:   **£150.00**

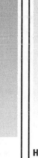

HN 4301
Lorraine
Style Two
Designer: N. Pedley
Height: 8 ¼", 21.0 cm
Colour: Cream jacket,
         aqua skirt and hat
Issued: 2000 to the present
  U.S.:   **$185.00**
  Can.:   **$350.00**
  U.K.:   **£ 95.00**

HN 4302
Sweet Music
Designer: N. Pedley
Height: 8 ½", 21.6 cm
Colour: Pink and white
Issued: 2001 to the present
  U.S.:   **$195.00**
  Can.:   **$385.00**
  U.K.:   **£110.00**

HN 4303
Charlotte
Style Four
Designer: N. Pedley
Height: 8 ½", 21.6 cm
Colour: Green and white
Issued: 2000-2001
Varieties: HN 4092
Comm.by: Great Universal
          Store
  U.S.:   **$175.00**
  Can.:   **$250.00**
  U.K.:   **£125.00**

HN 4304
Catherine
Style Three
Designer: N. Pedley
Height: 8 ½", 21.5 cm
Colour: White and pale blue
Issued: 2001 to the present

U.S.:	N/I
Can.:	$425.00
U.K.:	£115.00

HN 4305
Milk Maid
Style Three
Designer: N. Pedley
Height: 8", 20.3 cm
Colour: Soft mint green, cream,
            white and pale pink
Issued: 2001-2002
Series: Country Maids

U.S.:	$225.00
Can.:	$375.00
U.K.:	£120.00

HN 4306
Congratulations To You
Designer: N. Pedley
Height: 8", 20.3 cm
Colour: Lilac
Issued: 2000 to the present
Series: Name Your Own

U.S.:	N/I
Can.:	$450.00
U.K.:	£130.00

Metal plaque on base for engraved name.

HN 4307
Christine
Style Six
Designer: N. Pedley
Height: 8 ½", 21.0 cm
Colour: Red dress, yellow hat
Issued: 2001-2001
Series: M. Doulton Events

U.S.:	$250.00
Can.:	$375.00
U.K.:	£150.00

HN 4308
Happy Birthday 2001
Designer: N. Pedley
Height: 8", 21.0 cm
Colour: Light green
Issued: 2001-2001
Series: Happy Birthday

U.S.:	$175.00
Can.:	$225.00
U.K.:	£100.00

HN 4309
Jacqueline
Style Four
Designer: N. Pedley
Height: 8 ½", 21.6 cm
Colour: Cherry blossom
            pink and yellow
Issued: 2001-2001
Series: ICC

U.S.:	$250.00
Can.:	$375.00
U.K.:	£170.00

HN 4310
Janet
Style Five
Designer: N. Pedley
Height: 8", 20.3 cm
Colour: Pale blue
Issued: 2001-2002

U.S.:	$225.00
Can.:	$375.00
U.K.:	£125.00

HN 4311
Margaret
Style Three
Designer: N. Pedley
Height: 8 ½", 21.6 cm
Colour: Pink and white
Issued: 2001 to the present
Series: Vanity Fair

U.S.:	$175.00
Can.:	$335.00
U.K.:	£100.00

HN 4312
Pretty As A Picture
Designer: N. Pedley
Height: 5 ¾", 14.6 cm
Colour: White dress with pale pink trim
Issued: 2001 to the present
Series: Name Your Own
U.S.: $ 95.00
Can.: $235.00
U.K.: £ 55.00

HN 4313
For Your Special Day
Designer: N. Pedley
Height: 6", 15.2 cm
Colour: Lemon-white
Issued: 2001-2003
Varieties: Also called 'Sweet Delight' HN 4398
U.S.: $100.00
Can.: $150.00
U.K.: £ 60.00

Exclusive to Canada

HN 4314
New Dawn
Designer: N. Pedley
Height: 8 ½", 21.0 cm
Colour: Lilac and pink
Issued: 2001-2002
Series: Charity (Breast Cancer)
U.S.: $235.00
Can.: $350.00
U.K.: £130.00

Seven models of "New Dawn" were painted in different colourways and auctioned with the proceeds going to breast cancer research.

HN 4315
Christmas Day 2001
Designer: N. Pedley
Height: 8 ¾", 22.2 cm
Colour: Dark green dress and hat, red cape, all trimmed with ermine
Issued: 2001-2001
Series: Christmas Figures
U.S.: $225.00
Can.: $350.00
U.K.: £125.00

HN 4316
Maid of the Meadow
Designer: N. Pedley
Height: 8 ½", 21.0 cm
Colour: Tan, white and yellow
Issued: 2001-2002
Series: Country Maids
U.S.: $225.00
Can.: $375.00
U.K.: £125.00

HN 4317
Gentle Breeze
Designer: N. Pedley
Height: 8 ½", 21.6 cm
Colour: Pink, red and white
Issued: 2001-2002
U.S.: $245.00
Can.: $400.00
U.K.: £150.00

HN 4318
Loving Thoughts
Style Two
Designer: N. Pedley
Height: 8", 20.3 cm
Colour: Green dress, tan hat
Issued: 2001 to the present
U.S.: $225.00
Can.: $450.00
U.K.: £130.00

HN 4319
Sweetheart
Designer: N. Pedley
Height: 8", 20.3 cm
Colour: Pink
Issued: 2001 to the present
U.S.: $245.00
Can.: $425.00
U.K.: £125.00

HN 4320
Claudia
Designer: V. Annand
Height: 8 ¼", 21.0 cm
Colour: Pale blue
Issued: 2000-2002
Varieties: Also called 'Amelia'
           HN 4327
Series: In Vogue
U.S.: $200.00
Can.: $375.00
U.K.:   £130.00

HN 4321
Millennium Celebration
Designer: V. Annand
Height: 8 ¼", 21.0 cm
Colour: Turquoise and yellow
Issued: 2000
Varieites: HN 4201B, 4325
U.S.: $175.00
Can.: $275.00
U.K.:   £125.00

Australian backstamp

HN 4322
Becky
Style Two
Designer: V. Annand
Height: 8 ¾", 22.2 cm
Colour: Pale lilac
Issued: 2001 to the present
Series: Chelsea
Varieties: Also called 'Annabel
           Vision in Red' HN 4493
U.S.: $175.00
Can.: $350.00
U.K.:   £100.00

HN 4323
Katie
Style Three
Designer: V. Annand
Height: 8", 20.5 cm
Colour: Blue
Issued: 2001 to the present
Series: Chelsea
U.S.: $175.00
Can.: $350.00
U.K.:   £ 99.00

HN 4324
The Bride
Style Five
Designer: V. Annand
Height: 8 ½", 21.5 cm
Colour: White and pink
Issued: 2000-2003
Series: In Vogue
U.S.: $200.00
Can.: $390.00
U.K.:   £105.00

HN 4325
Millennium Celebration
Designer: V. Annand
Height: 8 ¼", 21.0 cm
Colour: Turquoise and yellow
Issued: 2000-2000
Varieties: HN 4201B, 4321
U.S.: $175.00
Can.: $275.00
U.K.:   £125.00

Canadian backstamp

HN 4326
Bethany
Designer: V. Annand
Height: 8 ¾", 22.2 cm
Colour: Yellow and white
Issued: 2001-2003
Series: Chelsea
U.S.: $200.00
Can.: $350.00
U.K.:   £ 90.00

HN 4327
Amelia
Designer: V. Annand
Height: 8 ½", 21.5 cm
Colour: Black with silver trim
Issued: 2002-2003
Varieties: Also called 'Claudia'
           HN 4320
Series: In Vogue
U.S.: $195.00
Can.: $425.00
U.K.:   £120.00

HN 4328
Applause
Designer: V. Annand
Height: 8 ½", 21.5 cm
Colour: Yellow, white, burnt orange edging
Issued: 2002-2002
Series: ICC

U.S.:	$270.00
Can.:	$400.00
U.K.:	£150.00

HN 4329
Finishing Touch
Designer: V. Annand
Height: 9", 22.5 cm
Colour: White skirt, dark blue bodice
Issued: 2002 to the present
Series: In Vogue

U.S.:	$195.00
Can.:	$425.00
U.K.:	£120.00

HN 4330 - 4349 not issued.

HN 4350
Christmas Eve
Designer: A. Maslankowski
Height: 5 ¾", 14.6 cm
Colour: White
Issued: 2000-2002
Series: Sentiments

U.S.:	$125.00
Can.:	$150.00
U.K.:	£ 75.00

Exclusive to Canada

HN 4351
Sweetheart (Boy)
Designer: A. Maslankowski
Height: 6", 15.0 cm
Colour: White
Issued: 2000-2003
Series: Images

U.S.:	$ 75.00
Can.:	$140.00
U.K.:	£ 30.00

HN 4352
Sweetheart (Girl)
Designer: A. Maslankowski
Height: 6 ½", 16.5 cm
Colour: White
Issued: 2000-2003
Series: Images

U.S.:	$ 75.00
Can.:	$140.00
U.K.:	£ 30.00

HN 4353
Liberty
Style Two
Designer: A. Maslankowski
Height: 10 ¼", 26 cm
Colour: Fleshtones and brown
Issued: 2000 in a limited edition of 1,500
Comm.by: Lawleys By Post

U.S.:	$250.00
Can.:	$325.00
U.K.:	£125.00

HN 4354
Felicity
Designer: A. Maslankowski
Height: 10 ¼", 26.0 cm
Colour: Fleshtones and brown
Issued: 2000 in a limited edition of 1,500
Comm.by: Lawleys By Post

U.S.:	$250,00
Can.:	$325.00
U.K.:	£125.00

HN 4355 not issued.

HN 4356
Sister and Brother
Designer: A. Maslankowski
Height: 7 ½", 19.0 cm
Colour: White
Issued: 2001 to the present
Series: Images

U.S.:	N/I
Can.:	$190.00
U.K.:	£ 39.00

HN 4357
Perfect Pose
Designer: A. Maslankowski
Height: 6 ¼", 15.9 cm
Colour: White
Issued: 2001-2003
Series: Images
  U.S.:   **$ 70.00**
  Can.:   **$140.00**
  U.K.:   **£ 30.00**

HN 4358
First Lesson
Designer: A. Maslankowski
Height: 6 ¼", 15.9 cm
Colour: White
Issued: 2001-2003
Series: Images
  U.S.:   **$ 70.00**
  Can.:   **$140.00**
  U.K.:   **£ 30.00**

HN 4359 not issued.

HN 4360
Arnold Bennett
Designer: T. Potts
Height: 8 ½", 21.6 cm
Colour: Dark grey suit, brown
              waistcoat, white shirt,
              black shoes
Issued: 2001
Series: 1. Arnold Bennett
              2. Visitor Centre
  U.S.:   **$275.00**
  Can.:   **$400.00**
  U.K.:   **£175.00**

HN 4361
Land Girl
Designer: T. Potts
Height: 8 ¾", 22.2 cm
Colour: Tan pants, black shirt
              and boots, yellow
              collar, brown basket
Issued: 2001 In a limited
              edition of 2,500
Series: Nostalgia
Comm.by.: Doulton-Direct
  U.S.:   **$350.00**
  Can.:   **$450.00**
  U.K.:   **£175.00**

HN 4362
Moonlight Gaze
Designer: T. Potts
Height: 8", 20.5 cm
Colour: Blue
Issued: 2002-2002
Series: Lady of the Year
Comm.by: Doulton-Direct
  U.S.:   **$250.00**
  Can.:   **$375.00**
  U.K.:   **£175.00**

HN 4363
Farewell Daddy
Designer: T. Potts
Height: 10 ½", 26.7 cm
Colour: Khaki
Issued: 2002 in a limited
              edition of 2,500
Series: Nostalgia
Comm.by: Doulton-Direct
  U.S.:   **$400.00**
  Can.:   **$500.00**
  U.K.:   **£250.00**

HN 4364
Women's Land Army
Designer: T. Potts
Height: 8 ¾", 22.2 cm
Colour: Green and brown
Issued: 2002 in a limited
              edition of 2,500
Series: Nostalgia
Comm.by: Doulton-Direct
  U.S.:   **$400.00**
  Can.:   **$500.00**
  U.K.:   **£250.00**

HN 4365 not issued.

HN 4366
The Batsman
Designer: T. Potts
Height: 8 ¾", 22.2 cm
Colour: Cream, yellow, green,
              light and dark blue
Issued: 2003 in a limited
              edition of 2,500
Comm.by: Doulton-Direct
  U.S.:   **$300.00**
  Can.:   **$400.00**
  U.K.:   **£175.00**

HN 4367 - 4369 not issued.

HN 4370
Skating
Designer: A. Maslankowski
Height: 6 ¼", 15.9 cm
Colour: White
Issued: 2001-2001
Series: Sentiments

U.S.: $150.00
Can.: $200.00
U.K.: £ 85.00

Exclusive to Canada

HN 4371
St. George
Style Four
Designer: A. Maslankowski
Height: 17", 43.2 cm
Colour: Charcoal, white, red and yellow
Issued: 2001 in a limited edition of 50
Series: Prestige

U.S.: $17,950.00
Can.: $25,000.00
U.K.: £10,000.00

HN 4372
HM Queen Elizabeth II
Style Five
Designer: A. Maslankowski
Height: 8 ½", 21.0 cm
Colour: White with gold trim
Issued: 2001 in a limited edition of 1,500

U.S.: $500.00
Can.: $700.00
U.K.: £275.00

HN 4373
Bridesmaid
Style Eight
Designer: A. Maslankowski
Height: 6 ½", 16.5 cm
Colour: White
Issued: 2001 to the present
Series: Images

U.S.: $ 65.00
Can.: $120.00
U.K.: £ 29.00

HN 4374
Pageboy
Designer: A. Maslankowski
Height: 6 ¼", 16.0 cm
Colour: White
Issued: 2001-2002
Series: Images

U.S.: $ 75.00
Can.: $100.00
U.K.: £ 45.00

HN 4375
Independence
Designer: A. Maslankowski
Height: 9 ", 22.9 cm
Colour: White
Issued: 2002-2002
Series: 1. Images
2. Save the Children Charity

U.S.: $150.00
Can.: $250.00
U.K.: £ 80.00

HN 4376
Surprise
Designer: A. Maslankowski
Height: 7 ¼", 18.5 cm
Colour: White
Issued: 2001-2002
Series: Images

U.S.: $ 65.00
Can.: $125.00
U.K.: £ 45.00

HN 4377
Keep In Touch
Designer: A. Maslankowski
Height: 7", 17.8 cm
Colour: White
Issued: 2002-2002
Series: Image of the Year

U.S.: $135.00
Can.: $200.00
U.K.: £ 75.00

HN 4378
Prayers
Designer: A. Maslankowski
Height: 6", 15.0 cm
Colour: White
Issued: 2002 to the present
Series: Images

U.S.:	$ 62.50
Can.:	$120.00
U.K.:	£ 29.00

HN 4379
Wedding Vows
Styel Two
Designer: A. Maslankowski
Height: 10 ¼", 26.0 cm
Colour: White
Issued: 2002 to the present
Series: Images

U.S.:	N/I
Can.:	$245.00
U.K.:	£ 59.00

HN 4380
From This Day Forward
Designer: N. Lee
Height: 10", 25.4 cm
Colour: White
Issued: 2000
Series: Images
Comm.by.: Compton/Woodhouse

U.S.:	$150.00
Can.:	$225.00
U.K.:	£100.00

HN 4381 - 4389 not issued.

HN 4390
Julia
Style Three
Designer: N. Pedley
Height: 8 ½", 21.6 cm
Colour: Lavender and peach
Issued: 2001-2002

U.S.:	$235.00
Can.:	$400.00
U.K.:	£140.00

HN 4391
Anna
Stsyle Three
Designer: N. Pedley
Height: 8 ¼", 21.0 cm
Colour: Pale blue and white
Issued: 2001 to the present
Series: Vanity Fair

U.S.:	$175.00
Can.:	$335.00
U.K.:	£ 90.00

HN 4392
My Love
Style Two
Designer: N. Pedley
Height: 8 ¼", 21.0 cm
Colour: Red
Issued: 2001 to the present
Series: Name Your Own

U.S.:	$235.00
Can.:	$425.00
U.K.:	£120.00

HN 4393
Happy Birthday 2002
Designer: N. Pedley
Height: 8 ¼", 21.0 cm
Colour: Pale blue
Issued: 2002-2002
Series: Happy Birthday

U.S.:	$175.00
Can.:	$300.00
U.K.:	£100.00

HN 4394 not issued.

HN 4395
Caroline
Style Three
Designer: N. Pedley
Height: 8 ¼", 21.0 cm
Colour: Yellow
Issued: 2001
Varieties: Also called
           'Josephine' HN 4223
Comm.by.: Great Universal
           Store

U.S.:	$175.00
Can.:	$250.00
U.K.:	£100.00

HN 4396
Serenity
Designer: N. Pedley
Height: 8 ¼", 21.0 cm
Colour: Dark blue bodice,
pale blue skirt
Issued: 2001-2003
U.S.: **$200.00**
Can.: **$425.00**
U.K.: **£115.00**

HN 4397
Thoughts For You
Designer: N. Pedley
Height: 8 ¼", 21.0 cm
Colour: Blue, white and
yellow
Issued: 2001
Series: Name Your Own
Comm.by.: Great Universal
Store
U.S.: **$175.00**
Can.: **$250.00**
U.K.: **£100.00**

HN 4398
Sweet Delight
Designer: N. Pedley
Height: 6", 15.2 cm
Colour: Pink
Issued: 2001 to the present
Varieties: Also called 'For Your
Special Day' HN 4313
Series: Visitor Centre
U.S.: **N/I**
Can.: **N/I**
U.K.: **£48.00**

HN 4399
Bathing Beauty
Style Two
Designer: N. Pedley
Height: 7 ¼", 18.5 cm
Colour: Flesh tones, dark blue
and yellow towel
Issued: 2001 in a limited
edition of 1,000
Series: Leslie Harradine
Tribute
Varieties: HN 4599
U.S.: **$275.00**
Can.: **$400.00**
U.K.: **£150.00**

HN 4400
Brighton Belle
Designer: N. Pedley
Height: 7", 17.8 cm
Colour: Flesh tones, pink
bathing suit
Issued: 2001 in a limited
edition of 1,000
Series: Leslie Harradine
Tribute
Varieties: HN 4600
U.S.: **$275.00**
Can.: **$400.00**
U.K.: **£150.00**

HN 4401
Summer's Darling
Style Two
Designer: N. Pedley
Height: 4 ¼", 10.8 cm
Colour: Flesh tones, dark
green robe
Issued: 2001 in a limited
edition of 1,000
Series: Leslie Harradine
Tribute
Varieties: HN 4601
U.S.: **$275.00**
Can.: **$400.00**
U.K.: **£150.00**

HN 4402
Taking The Waters
Designer: N. Pedley
Height: 6 ¼", 16.0 cm
Colour: Flesh tones, purple
bathing suit
Issued: 2001 in a limited
edition of 1,000
Series: Leslie Harradine
Tribute
Varieties: HN 4602
U.S.: **$275.00**
Can.: **$400.00**
U.K.: **£150.00**

HN 4403
Samantha
Style Four
Designer: N. Pedley
Height: 8 ½", 21.6 cm
Colour: Pale pink
Issued: 2002 to the present
U.S.: **$195.00**
Can.: **$425.00**
U.K.: **£120.00**

HN 4404
Gillian
Style Four
Designer: N. Pedley
Height: 8 ¼", 21.0 cm
Colour: Green, white and yellow
Issued: 2002-2003
Varieties: Also called 'Christine', (Style seven) HN 4526

U.S.:	**$200.00**
Can.:	**$425.00**
U.K.:	**£115.00**

HN 4405
Angela
Style Five
Designer: N. Pedley
Height: 8", 20.5 cm
Colour: White and pale green
Issued: 2002-2003

U.S.:	**$200.00**
Can.:	**$425.00**
U.K.:	**£115.00**

HN 4406
Summer Stroll
Designer: N. Pedley
Height: 8 ¼", 21.0 cm
Colour: White, yellow and pink
Issued: 2002 to the present

U.S.:	**$195.00**
Can.:	**$425.00**
U.K.:	**£115.00**

HN 4407
Hannah
Style Four
Designer: N. Pedley
Height: 8 ¼", 21.0 cm
Colour: Blue, yellow and white
Issued: 2002 to the present

U.S.:	**$195.00**
Can.:	**$425.00**
U.K.:	**£120.00**

HN 4408
Scarlett
Designer: N. Pedley
Height: 8 ½", 20.5 cm
Colour: Red
Issued: 2002 to the present

U.S.:	**$295.00**
Can.:	**$540.00**
U.K.:	**£165.00**

HN 4409
Perfect Gift
Designer: N. Pedley
Height: 8", 20.3 cm
Colour: Pale pink
Issued: 2002 to the present
Series: Name Your Own

U.S.:	**$195.00**
Can.:	**$425.00**
U.K.:	**£120.00**

HN 4410
Policeman
Designer: A. Hughes
Height: 8 ¾", 22.2 cm
Colour: Dark blue uniform
Issued: 2001-2003

U.S.:	**$330.00**
Can.:	**$650.00**
U.K.:	**£175.00**

HN 4411
Fireman
Designer: A. Hughes
Height: 8", 20.0 cm
Colour: Dark blue uniform, yellow helmet
Issued: 2002 - 2003

U.S.:	**$350.00**
Can.:	**$650.00**
U.K.:	**£195.00**

Childhood Days

HN 2959
Save Some For Me
1982-1985

HN 2964
Dressing Up
1982-1985

HN 2967
Please Keep Still
1982-1985

HN 2970
And One For You
1982-1985

HN 2971
As Good As New
1982-1985

HN 2976
I'm Nearly Ready
1983 Canada,
1984 Worldwide-1985

HN 2980
Just One More
1983 Canada,
1984 Worldwide-1985

HN 2981
Stick 'em Up
1983 Canada,
1984 Worldwide-1985

Les Femmes Fatales

HN 2328
Queen of Sheba
1982 in a limited edition of 750

HN 2342
Lucrezia Borgia
1985 in a limited edition of 750

HN 2387
Helen of Troy
1981 in a limited edition of 750

HN 2391
T'zu-hsi, Empress Dowager
1983 in a limited edition of 750

HN 2466
Eve
1984 in a limited edition of 750

HN 2868
Cleopatra, Style One
1979 in a limited edition of 750

Character Sculptures

HN 3636
Captain Hook
1993-1996

HN 3637
Dick Turpin
1993-1996

HN 3638
D'Artagnan, Style One
1993-1996

HN 3639
Sherlock Holmes
1995-1996

HN 3750
Gulliver
1995-1996

HN 3751
Cyrano de Bergerac
1995-1996

HN 3785
Bill Sikes
1996-1996

HN 3786
**Oliver Twist and
The Artful Dodger**, 1996-1996

Classique Series

CL 3982
Susanne
1997-1998

CL 3984
Faye
1997-2002

CL 3986
Felicity
1997-1999

CL 3988
Penelope
1997-1999

CL 3990
From This Day Forth
1997-1999

CL 3991
Christina
1998-2001

CL 3995
Kate
1998-2000

In Vogue

HN 4551
Daniella
2003-current

HN 4500
Nadine, Style two
2003-current

HN 4550
Mikaela
2003-current

HN 4499
Alana
2003-current

Ladies of the Year
(Compton & Woodhouse)

HN 4015
Eleanor, Style Two
Lady of the Year 2001

HN 4017
Ellie, Style Two
Lady of the Year 2003

HN 4539
Megan, Style Three
Lady of the Year 2004

Nostalgia

HN 4498
Women's Royal Navy Service
2003 in a limited edition of 2,500

HN 4554
Women's Auxiliary Air Force
2003 in a limited edition of 2,500

HN 4495
Auxiliary Territorial Service
2002 in a limited edition of 2,500

HN 4555
Air Raid Precaution Warden
2003 in a limited edition of 2,500

HN 4494
Home Guard
2002 in a limited edition of 2,500

HN 4364
Women's Land Army
2002 in a limited edition of 2,500

HN 4475
Queen Victoria, Style Two
2003 in a limited edition of 950

HN 4363
Farewell Daddy
2002 in a limited edition of 2,500

HN 4476
H.M. Elizabeth II, Style Six
2003 in a limited edition of 2,000

Charity Figures – Breast Cancer Research

HN 4097
Hope, Style Two
1998-1999

HN 4151
Faith
1999-2000

HN 4243
Charity, Style Two
2000-2001

HN 4314
New Dawn
2001-2002

HN 4451
Spring Morning, Style Three
2002-2003

HN 4529
Love of Life
2003-2004

HN 4412
Judge
Style Two
Designer: A. Hughes
Height: 7", 17.5 cm
Colour: Red and white robes,
brown chair
Issued: 2002 to the present

U.S.:	**$395.00**
Can.:	**$695.00**
U.K.:	**£195.00**

HN 4413
Sleepyhead
Style Three
Designer: A. Hughes
Height: 6", 15.0 cm
Colour: White
Issued: 2002 to the present
Series: Images

U.S.:	**$ 62.50**
Can.:	**$120.00**
U.K.:	**£ 29.00**

HN 4414
Athos
Designer: A. Hughes
Height: 8 ¾", 22.2 cm
Colour: Black, white and
cream
Issued: 2001 In a limited
edition of 950
Comm.by.: Doulton-Direct

U.S.:	**$425.00**
Can.:	**$600.00**
U.K.:	**£275.00**

HN 4415
Aramis
Designer: A. Hughes
Height: 9 ¼", 23.0 cm
Colour: Dark navy and white
Issued: 2001 In a limited
edition of 950
Comm.by.: Doulton-Direct

U.S.:	**$425.00**
Can.:	**$600.00**
U.K.:	**£275.00**

HN 4416
Porthos
Designer: A. Hughes
Height: 9 ½", 24.0 cm
Colour: Browns, white and
black
Issued: 2001 In a limited
edition of 950
Comm.by.: Doulton-Direct

U.S.:	**$425.00**
Can.:	**$600.00**
U.K.:	**£275.00**

HN 4417
D'Artagnan
Style Two
Designer: A. Hughes
Height: 8 ¾", 22.5 cm
Colour: Browns and white
Issued: 2001 In a limited
edition of 950
Comm.by.: Doulton-Direct

U.S.:	**$425.00**
Can.:	**$600.00**
U.K.:	**£275.00**

HN 4418
Railway Sleeper
Designer: T. Potts
Height: 7", 17.5 cm
Colour: Brown uniform with
green shading, black
hat and trunk
Issued: 2001 In a limited
edition of 2,500
Series: Nostalgia
Comm.by.: Doulton-Direct

U.S.:	**$600.00**
Can.:	**$775.00**
U.K.:	**£250.00**

HN 4419 not issued.

HN 4420
Prince Albert, Duke of York
(Wedding Day)
Designer: V. Annand
Height: 9", 22.5 cm
Colour: Dark blueuniform,
gold trim
Issued: 2002 in a limited
edition of 1,000

U.S.:	**$ 715.00**
Can.:	**$1,350.00**
U.K.:	**£ 400.00 pair**

Sold as a pair with HN 4421

HN 4421
Elizabeth Bowes-Lyon
(Wedding Day)
Designer: V. Annand
Height: 8 ¼", 21.0 cm
Colour: White
Issued: 2002 in a limited
           edition of 1,000

U.S.:	$ 715.00
Can.:	$1,350.00
U.K.:	£ 400.00 pair

Sold as pair with HN 4420

HN 4422
Christmas Day 2002
Designer: V. Annand
Height: 8 ¼", 21.0 cm
Colour: Green, cream, white
           and red
Issued: 2002-2002
Series: Christmas Figures

U.S.:	$275.00
Can.:	$475.00
U.K.:	£150.00

HN 4423
Jenny
Designer: V. Annand
Height: 8", 20.3 cm
Colour: Lilac
Issued: 2002 to the present
Varieties: Also called 'Alexandra'
           (Style Three) HN 4557
Series: Chelsea

U.S.:	$160.00
Can.:	$350.00
U.K.:	£ 90.00

HN 4424
Antique Dealer
Designer: V. Annand
Height: 6 ¾", 17 cm
Colour: Dark grey, light
           and dark brown
Issued: 2002 to the present

U.S.:	$350.00
Can.:	$695.00
U.K.:	£195.00

HN 4425 not issued.

HN 4426
Elizabeth
Style Three
Designer: J. Bromley
Height: 8 ¼", 21.0 cm
Colour: Peach
Issued: 2003-2003
Series: Figure of the Year

U.S.:	$215.00
Can.:	$410.00
U.K.:	£120.00

HN 4427
Baby's First Christmas
Designer: V. Annand
Height: 4", 10.1 cm
Colour: White, green and red
Issued: 2002-2003

U.S.:	$130.00
Can.:	$170.00
U.K.:	£ 45.00

HN 4428
Here A Little Child I Stand
Second Version
Designer: V. Annand
Height: 4 ¾", 12.2 cm
Colour: Blue-grey, flesh tones
            dark green and pink
            base
Issued: 2002 in a limited
            edition of 1,000
Series: Leslie Harradine Tribute

U.S.:	$250.00
Can.:	$300.00
U.K.:	£100.00

HN 4429
Do You Wonder Where
The Fairies Are
Second Version
Designer: V. Annand
Height: 4 ¾", 12.2 cm
Colour: Blue-grey pants,
            flesh tones, yellow,
            green base
Issued: 2002 in a limited
            edition of 1,000
Series: Leslie Harradine Tribute

U.S.:	$250.00
Can.:	$300.00
U.K.:	£100.00

HN 4430
Special Moments
Designer: C. Froud
Height: 9", 22.9 cm
Colour: Pink and white
Issued: 2002 to the present

U.S.:	**$235.00**
Can.:	**$425.00**
U.K.:	**£130.00**

HN 4431
Jasmine
Style Four
Designer: C. Froud
Height: 8", 20 cm
Colour: Red
Issued: 2002 to the present

U.S.:	**$275.00**
Can.:	**$540.00**
U.K.:	**£155.00**

HN 4432 - 4439 not issued;
HN 4440 - 4441 Animal Figures.

HN 4442
Cherish
Designer: A. Maslankowski
Height: 6", 15.0 cm
Colour: White
Issued: 2002-2002
Series: 1. Club Membership
Figure
2. Sentiments

U.S.:	**$50.00**
Can.:	**$75.00**
U.K.:	**£30.00**

HN 4443
Happy Holidays
Designer: A. Maslankowski
Height: 6 ¼", 15.5 cm
Colour: White
Issued: 2002-2003
Series: Sentiments

U.S.:	**$100.00**
Can.:	**$150.00**
U.K.:	**£ 60.00**

Exclusive to Canada

HN 4444
Witch
Style Two
Designer: A. Maslankowski
Height: 10", 25.4 cm
Colour: Dark red, dark blue
and black
Issued: 2002-2003

U.S.:	**$350.00**
Can.:	**$695.00**
U.K.:	**£220.00**

HN 4445
Charmed
Designer: A. Maslankowski
Height: 5 ½", 14.0 cm
Colour: White
Issued: 2003-2003
Series: 1. Club Membership
Figure
2. Sentiments

U.S.:	**$50.00**
Can.:	**$75.00**
U.K.:	**£30.00**

HN 4446
Gift of Friendship
Designer: A. Maslankowski
Height: 5 ½", 14.0 cm
Colour: White
Issued: 2003-2003
Series: Images of the Year

U.S.:	**$100.00**
Can.:	**$200.00**
U.K.:	**£ 60.00**

HN 4447
Christmas Dreams
Designer: A. Maslankowski
Height: 6", 15.0 cm
Colour: White
Issued: 2002-2003
Series: Images

U.S.:	**$100.00**
Can.:	**$160.00**
U.K.:	**£ 30.00**

HN 4448
Father and Son
Designer: A. Maslankowski
Height: 8 ¾", 22.2 cm
Colour: White
Issued: 2002-2003
Series: Images

U.S.:	**$200.00**
Can.:	**$370.00**
U.K.:	**£ 70.00**

HN 4449
A Gift For You
Designer: A. Maslankowski
Height: 6", 15 cm
Colour: White
Issued: 2002 to the present
Series: Images

U.S.:	**N/I**
Can.:	**$140.00**
U.K.:	**£ 29.00**

HN 4450
Linda
Style Five
Designer: N. Pedley
Height: 8 ¼", 21.0 cm
Colour: Light and dark blue
Issued: 2002-2002
Series: M. Doulton Events

U.S.:	**$300.00**
Can.:	**$400.00**
U.K.:	**£150.00**

HN 4451
Spring Morning
Style Three
Designer: N. Pedley
Height: 8", 20.0 cm
Colour: White and green
Issued: 2002-2003
Series: Charity (Breast Cancer)

U.S.:	**$275.00**
Can.:	**$350.00**
U.K.:	**£130.00**

HN 4452
Suzanne
Style Two
Designer: N. Pedley
Height: 8 ¼", 21.0 cm
Colour: Yellow
Issued: 2002

U.S.:	**$300.00**
Can.:	**$400.00**
U.K.:	**£150.00**

Exclusive to U.K. Mail Order and
Canada

HN 4453
Pride of Scotland
Designer: N. Pedley
Height: 8 ¼", 21.0 cm
Colour: White, mauve,
           purple and blue
Issued: 2002 to the present
Varieties: HN 4310 Janet (Style
           Five)

U.S.:	**$210.00**
Can.:	**$425.00**
U.K.:	**£120.00**

HN 4454
From The Heart
Designer: N. Pedley
Height: 5 ¾", 14.6 cm
Colour: Pale blue
Issued: 2002-2002

U.S.:	**$125.00**
Can.:	**$150.00**
U.K.:	**£ 70.00**

Exclusive to Canada
  HN 4455 not issued.

HN 4456
Chloe
Style Five
Designer: N. Pedley
Height: 8", 20.0 cm
Colour: White with green
           bodice
Issued: 2002 to the present

U.S.:	**$175.00**
Can.:	**$385.00**
U.K.:	**£100.00**

HN 4457
Georgia
Designer: N. Pedley
Height: 8", 20.0 cm
Colour: Yellow
Issued: 2002 to the present

U.S.:	**$195.00**
Can.:	**$425.00**
U.K.:	**£110.00**

HN 4458
Isabel
Style Two
Designer: N. Pedley
Height: 8 ¼", 21.0 cm
Colour: Light and dark blue
Issued: 2002 to the present

U.S.:	**$195.00**
Can.:	**$425.00**
U.K.:	**£120.00**

HN 4459
Lucy
Style Four
Designer: N. Pedley
Height: 8", 20.0 cm
Colour: Lilac and white
Issued: 2002 to the present

U.S.:	**$195.00**
Can.:	**$425.00**
U.K.:	**£115.00**

HN 4460 not Issued.

HN 4461
Stephanie
Style Three
Designer: N. Pedley
Height: 8", 20.0 cm
Colour: Pale green, white
with yellow fan
Issued: 2002 to the present

U.S.:	**$195.00**
Can.:	**$425.00**
U.K.:	**£115.00**

HN 4462 not Issued.

HN 4463
Eleanor
Style Three
Designer: N. Pedley
Height: 8 ¼", 21.0 cm
Colour: Green
Issued: 2003-2003
Series: M. Doulton Events

U.S.:	**$225.00**
Can.:	**$395.00**
U.K.:	**£130.00**

HN 4464
Happy Birthday 2003
Designer: N. Pedley
Height: 8 ¼", 21.0 cm
Colour: Yellow and lilac
Issued: 2003-2003
Series: Happy Birthday

U.S.:	**$175.00**
Can.:	**$370.00**
U.K.:	**£100.00**

HN 4465
Lights Out
Style Two
Designer: N. Pedley
Height: 6 ¼", 15.9 cm
Colour: Pale blue and white
pyjamas
Issued: 2003-2003
Series: ICC

U.S.:	**$175.00**
Can.:	**$225.00**
U.K.:	**£ 90.00**

HN 4466
The Recital
Designer: N. Pedley
Height: 8 ¼", 21.0 cm
Colour: Purple dress; cream
shawl
Issued: 2003-2003
Series: ICC

U.S.:	**$300.00**
Can.:	**$400.00**
U.K.:	**£165.00**

HN 4467
Katrina
Style Two
Designer: N. Pedley
Height: 8", 20.0 cm
Colour: White and yellow
Issued: 2002 to the present
Series: Vanity Fair Ladies

U.S.:	**$175.00**
Can.:	**$350.00**
U.K.:	**£ 95.00**

HN 4468
Deborah
Style Three
Designer: N. Pedley
Height: 8 ¼', 21.0 cm
Colour: Light and dark blue
Issued: 2002 to the present

U.S.:	**$195.00**
Can.:	**$425.00**
U.K.:	**£110.00**

HN 4469
Spirit of Scotland
Designer: N. Pedley
Height: 8 ¼", 21.0 cm
Colour: Lilac
Issued: 2003 to the present

U.S.:	**$215.00**
Can.:	**N/I**
U.K.:	**£120.00**

Exclusive to Scotland 2003.

HN 4470
For Someone Special
Designer: N. Pedley
Height: 5 ½", 14.0 cm
Colour: Pale blue and white
Issued: 2003-2003

U.S.:	**$115.00**
Can.:	**$150.00**
U.K.:	**£ 70.00**

Canadian exclusive.
HN 4471 - 4473 not issued.

HN 4474
Queen Mary II
(Wife of William of Orange)
Designer: P. Parsons
Height: 8 ¾", 22.2 cm
Colour: Pale blue and purple dress, red and gold tablecloth
Issued: 2002 in a limited edition of 2,500
Series: Stuart Queens
Comm.by: Doulton-Direct

U.S.:	**$600.00**
Can.:	**$750.00**
U.K.:	**£325.00**

HN 4475
Queen Victoria
Style Two
Designer: P. Parsons
Height: 5 ½", 14.0 cm
Colour: Purple, pink and white
Issued: 2003 in a limited edition of 950
Comm.by: Doulton-Direct

U.S.:	**$475.00**
Can.:	**$600.00**
U.K.:	**£275.00**

HN 4476
H.M. Queen Elizabeth II
Style Six
Designer: P. Parsons
Height: 7 ¾", 19.7 cm
Colour: White dress with gold accessories, purple robe, purple and white crown
Issued: 2003 in a limited edition of 2,000
Comm.by: Doulton-Direct

U.S.:	**$475.00**
Can.:	**N/I**
U.K.:	**£275.00**

HN 4477 - 4480 not issued.

HN 4481
Alexander the Great
Designer: A. Maslankowski
Height: 18 ¼", 46.0 cm
Colour: Mauve toga, black horse, tiger skin
Issued: 2002 In a limited edition of 50
Series: Prestige

U.S.:	**$17,950.00**
Can.:	**$30,000.00**
U.K.:	**£12,000.00**

HN 4482
Clever Boy
Designer: A. Maslankowski
Height: 6 ¼", 16.0 cm
Colour: White
Issued: 2003 to the present
Series: Images

U.S.:	**N/I**
Can.:	**$140.00**
U.K.:	**£ 29.00**

HN 4483
Clever Girl
Designer: A. Maslankowski
Height: 6 ¼", 16.0 cm
Colour: White
Issued: 2003 to the present
Series: Images

U.S.:	**N/I**
Can.:	**$140.00**
U.K.:	**£ 29.00**

HN4484
Father and Daughter
Designer: A. Maslankowski
Height: 8 ¼", 21.0 cm
Colour: White
Issued: 2003 to the present
Series: Images

U.S.:	**N/I**
Can.:	**$245.00**
U.K.:	**£ 75.00**

HN 4485
Unity
Designer: A. Maslankowski
Height: 6 ¾", 17.2 cm
Colour: White
Issued: 2003-2003
Series: 1. Images
           2. Save the Children
              Charity

U.S.:	**$175.00**
Can.:	**$225.00**
U.K.:	**£120.00**

HN 4486
Charge of the Light Brigade
Style Two
Designer: A. Maslankowski
Height: 8", 20.3 cm
Colour: Blues, grey, brown
           and green
Issued: 2002 in a limited
           edition of 500
Series: Prestige

U.S.:	**$1,600.00**
Can.:	**$2,700.00**
U.K.:	**£ 900.00**

HN 4487
Farmer
Style Two
Designer: A. Hughes
Height: 8 ¼", 21.0 cm
Colour: Brown, white and
           black
Issued: 2003 to the present

U.S.:	**$345.00**
Can.:	**$695.00**
U.K.:	**£195.00**

HN 4488
Blacksmith
Style Two
Designer: T. Potts
Height: 8 ¾", 22.2 cm
Colour: White, grey and
           dark brown
Issued: 2003 to the present

U.S.:	**$345.00**
Can.:	**$695.00**
U.K.:	**£195.00**

HN 4489 - 4490 not issued.

HN 4491
Little Child So Rare And Sweet
Style Three
Designer: V. Annand
Height: 4 ¾", 12.1 cm
Colour: Pink, mottled pink
           and purple base
Issued: 2002 in a limited
           editin of 1,000
Series: Leslie Harradine
           Tribute
Comm.by: Doulton-Direct

U.S.:	**$250.00**
Can.:	**$300.00**
U.K.:	**£100.00**

HN 4492
Dancing Eyes and Sunny Hair
Style Two
Designer: V. Annand
Height: 4 ¾", 12.1 cm
Colour: Pale green
Issued: 2002 in a limited
             edition of 1,000
Series: Leslie Harradine
             Tribute
Comm.by: Doulton-Direct

U.S.:	**$250.00**
Can.:	**$300.00**
U.K.:	**£100.00**

HN 4493
Annabel Vision in Red
Designer: V. Annand
Height: 8 ¼", 21.0 cm
Colour: Red
Issued: 2003 to the present
Series: Chelsea
Varieties: Also called 'Becky'
             HN 4322

U.S.:	**N/I**
Can.:	**$425.00**
U.K.:	**N/I**

Exclusive to Canada

HN 4494
Home Guard
Designer: V. Annand
Height: 8 ¾", 22.2 cm
Colour: Khaki
Issued: 2002 in a limited
             edition of 2,500
Series: Nostalgia
Comm.by: Doulton-Direct

U.S.:	**N/I**
Can.:	**N/I**
U.K.:	**£195.00**

HN 4495
Auxiliary Territorial Service
Designer: V. Annand
Height: 8 ¾", 22.2 cm
Colour: Khaki
Issued: 2002 in a limited
             edition of 2,500
Series: Nostalgia
Comm.by: Doulton-Direct

U.S.:	**N/I**
Can.:	**N/I**
U.K.:	**£195.00**

HN 4496
Taylor
Designer: V. Annand
Height: 8 ¼", 21.0 cm
Colour: Blue and lemon
Issued: 2003 to the present
Series: In Vogue

U.S.:	**$210.00**
Can.:	**$425.00**
U.K.:	**£120.00**

HN 4497
Helen of Troy
Style Two
Designer: V. Annand
Height: 9 ¾", 24.7 cm
Colour: White, pink, green,
             yellow and beige
Issued: 2002 in a limited
             edition of 950
Series: Greek Mythology
Comm.by: Doulton-Direct

U.S.:	**$500.00**
Can.:	**$650.00**
U.K.:	**£275.00**

HN 4498
Women's Royal Navy Service
Designer: V. Annand
Height: 9", 22.9 cm
Colour: Navy uniform, brown
             bags
Issued: 2003 in a limited
             edition of 2,500
Series: Nostalgia
Comm.by: Doulton-Direct

U.S.:	**N/I**
Can.:	**N/I**
U.K.:	**£195.00**

HN 4499
Alana
Designer: V. Annand
Height: 8 ½", 21.5 cm
Colour: Black
Issued: 2003 to the present
Series: In Vogue

U.S.:	**$165.00**
Can.:	**$325.00**
U.K.:	**£ 95.00**

HN 4500
Nadine
Style Two
Designer: V. Annand
Height: 8 ½", 21.5 cm
Colour: Black
Issued: 2003 to the present
Series: In Vogue

U.S.: **$165.00**
Can.: **$325.00**
U.K.: **£ 95.00**

HN 4501
Forever Yours
Style Two
Designer: J. Bromley
Height: 8 ¾", 22.2 cm
Colour: Pink
Issued: 2002-2003
Varieties: Also called 'Best
Wishes' (Style Two)
HN 3971; 'Kate' (Style
Three) HN 4233

U.S.: **$350.00**
Can.: **$425.00**
U.K.: **£125.00**

Canadian and U.K. Catalogue
HN 4502 - 4509 not issued.

HN 4510
The Pilot Skipper
Designer: Unknown
Height: 6 ¾", 17.2 cm
Colour: Brown, grey, white
and yellow
Issued: 2002
Comm.by: Pilot Insurance

U.S.: **$300.00**
Can.: **$450.00**
U.K.: **£195.00**

HN 4511
Fisherman
Designer: M. Alcock
Height: 7", 17.8 cm
Colour: Brown and grey with
green base
Issued: 2003 to the present

U.S.: **$325.00**
Can.: **N/I**
U.K.: **£185.00**

HN 4512 4515 not issued;
HN 4516 - 4517 Animal figures.

HN 4517
Footballer
Designer: M. Alcock
Height: 8 ¼", 21.0 cm
Colour: White
Issued: 2004 to the present
Series: Images

U.S.: **N/I**
Can.: **N/I**
U.K.: **£54.00**

HN 4518
Cricketer
Style Two
Designer: M. Alcock
Height: 8 ¼", 21.0 cm
Colour: White
Issued: 2004 to the present
Series: Images

U.S.: **N/I**
Can.: **N/I**
U.K.: **£49.00**

HN 4519
Hockey Player
Designer: M. Alcock
Height: 8 ¼", 21.0 cm
Colour: White
Issued: 2004 to the present
Series: Images

U.S.: **N/I**
Can.: **N/I**
U.K.: **£29.00**

HN 4520
April
Style Five
Designer: N. Pedley
Height: 8 ½", 21.6 cm
Colour: Pink and white
Issued: 2003 to the present

U.S.: **$235.00**
Can.: **$450.00**
U.K.: **£135.00**

HN 4521
Ruby
Style Two
Designer: N. Pedley
Height: 8 ¼", 21.0 cm
Colour: Red
Issued: 2003 to the present

U.S.:	$225.00
Can.:	$480.00
U.K.:	£130.00

HN 4522
Anne Marie
Designer: N. Pedley
Height: 8 ¼", 21.0 cm
Colour: Pale green and white
Issued: 2003 to the present

U.S.:	$225.00
Can.:	$385.00
U.K.:	£110.00

HN 4523
Faye
Designer: N. Pedley
Height: 8 ½", 21.6 cm
Colour: Pale green, white and grey
Issued: 2003 to the present

U.S.:	$175.00
Can.:	$425.00
U.K.:	£100.00

HN 4524
Jayne
Style Two
Designer: N. Pedley
Height: 8", 20.3 cm
Colour: Pink and white
Issued: 2003 to the present
Series: Vanity Fair

U.S.:	$165.00
Can.:	$350.00
U.K.:	£ 95.00

HN 4525
Lisa
Style Two
Designer: N. Pedley
Height: 8 ¼", 21.0 cm
Colour: Lemon and white
Issued: 2003 to the present

U.S.:	$185.00
Can.:	$385.00
U.K.:	£ 95.00

HN 4526
Christine
Style Seven
Designer: N. Pedley
Height: 8 ¼", 21.0 cm
Colour: Dark and light blue, white
Issued: 2003-2003
Varieties: Also called 'Gillian' (Style Four) HN 4404
Comm.by: G.U.S.

U.S.:	$200.00
Can.:	$275.00
U.K.:	£115.00

HN 4527
Nicole
Style Three
Designer: N. Pedley
Height: 8 ¼", 21.0 cm
Colour: Purple and pink
Issued: 2003 to the present

U.S.:	$260.00
Can.:	$525.00
U..K.:	£150.00

HN 4528
Happy Birthday 2004
Designer: N. Pedley
Height: 8 ¼", 21.0 cm
Colour: Yellow
Issued: 2004-2004
Series: Happy Birthday

U.S.:	$175.00
Can.:	N/A
U.K.:	£100.00

HN 4529
Love of Life
Designer: N. Pedley
Height: 8 ¾", 22.2 cm
Colour: Pink and white
Issued: 2003-2004
Series: Charity (Breast Cancer)

U.S.:	**$225.00**
Can.:	**$350.00**
U.K.:	**£130.00**

HN 4530
Moonlight Serenade
Designer: J. Bromley
Height: 8 ¾", 22.2 cm
Colour: Blue and white
Issued: 2003 to the present

U.S.:	**$260.00**
Can.:	**$625.00**
U.K.:	**£150.00**

HN 4531
Message of Love
Designer: J. Bromley
Height: 9 ¼", 23.5 cm
Colour: Mauve and white
Issued: 2003 to the present

U.S.:	**$310.00**
Can.:	**$695.00**
U.K.:	**£175.00**

HN 4532
Susan
Style Five
Designer: J. Bromley
Height: 9", 23.0 cm
Colour: Dark and light blue and white
Issued: 2004-2004
Series: Figure of the Year

U.S.:	**$215.00**
Can.:	**N/A**
U.K.:	**£100.00**

HN 4533
Beautiful Blossom
Designer: J. Bromley
Height: 8 ¾", 22.2 cm
Colour: Lilac
Issued: 2003 to the present

U.S.:	**$260.00**
Can.:	**$525.00**
U.K.:	**£150.00**

HN 4538
A Winter's Morn
Designer: J. Bromley
Height: 8 ¾", 22.2 cm
Colour: Red coat; white dress, ermine hat and muff, gold highlights
Issued: 2004
Varieties: HN 4622
Comm.by: Compton/Woodhouse

U.S.:	**N/I**
Can.:	**N/I**
U.K.:	**£165.00**

HN 4539
Megan
Style Three
Designer: J. Bromley
Height: 8 ¾", 22.2 cm
Colour: Purple and lilac dress with white trim
Issued: 2004-2004
Series: Lady of the Year
Comm.by: Compton/Woodhouse

U.S.:	**Prices not**
Can.:	**available**
U.K.:	**at press time**

HN 4540
Merlin
Designer: S. Ridge
Height: 9 ¾", 24.7 cm
Colour: Green, yellow, brown and grey
Issued: 2003 in a limited edition of 950
Comm.by: Doulton-Direct

U.S.:	**N/I**
Can.:	**N/I**
U.K.:	**£250.00**

HN 4534 - 4537 not issued.

HN 4541
King Arthur
Designer: S. Ridge
Height: 9", 22.9 cm
Colour: Light brown, blue, light and dark grey and brown
Issued: 2003 in a limited edition of 950
Comm.by: Doulton-Direct

U.S.: N/I
Can.: N/I
U.K.: £295.00

HN 4542
Graduate Female
Style Two
Designer: S. Ridge
Height: 8", 20.3 cm
Colour: White
Issued: 2004 to the present
Series: Images

U.S.: N/I
Can.: N/I
U.K.: £39.00

HN 4543
Graduate Male
Style Three
Designer: S. Ridge
Height: 8", 20.3 cm
Colour: White
Issued: 2004 to the present
Series: Images

U.S.: N/I
Can.: N/I
U.K.: £39.00

HN 4544 - 4549 not issued.

HN 4550
Mikaela
Designer: V. Annand
Height: 8 ½", 21.6 cm
Colour: Black
Issued: 2003 to the present
Series: In Vogue

U.S.: $165.00
Can.: $325.00
U.K.: £ 95.00

HN 4551
Daniella
Designer: V. Annand
Height: 8 ½", 21.5 cm
Colour: Black
Issued: 2003 to the present
Series: In Vogue

U.S.: $165.00
Can.: $325.00
U.K.: £ 95.00

HN 4552
Christmas Day 2003
Designer: V. Annand
Height: 8 ¾", 22.2 cm
Colour: Red and white
Issued: 2003-2003
Series: Christmas Figures

U.S.: $375.00
Can.: $560.00
U.K.: £150.00

HN 4553
The Dance
Style Two
Designer: V. Annand
Height: 8 ¾", 22.2 cm
Colour: Pale blue, pale pink and white
Issued: 2004
Series: ICC

U.S.: Prices not
Can.: available
U.K.: at press time

HN 4554
Women's Auxiliary Air Force
Designer: V. Annand
Height: 8 ¼", 21.0 cm
Colour: Navy uniform; brown, grey and black
Issued: 2003 in a limited edition of 2,500
Series: Nostalgia
Comm.by: Doulton-Direct

U.S.: N/I
Can.: N/I
U.K.: £195.00

HN 4555
Air Raid Precaution Warden
Designer: V. Annand
Height: 5 ½", 14.0 cm
Colour: Green jacket; grey
             trousers, hat and
             base; brown seat
             and bag
Issued: 2003 in a limited
             edition of 2,500
Series: Nostalgia
Comm.by: Doulton-Direct

U.S.:   N/I
Can.:   N/I
U.K.   £195.00

HN 4556
Hayley
Designer: V. Annand
Height: 8 ½", 21.5 cm
Colour: Pale green and pink
Issued: 2003 to the present
Series: Chelsea Collection

U.S.:   **$215.00**
Can.:   **$425.00**
U.K.:   **£125.00**

HN 4557
Alexandra
Style Three
Designer: V. Annand
Height: 8", 20.3 cm
Colour: Blue
Issued: 2003
Varieties: Also called 'Jenny'
            HN 4423
Comm.by: G.U.S.

U.S.:   N/I
Can.:   N/I
U.K.:   £115.00

HN 4558
Christmas Day 2004
Designer: V. Annand
Height: 8 ¼", 21.0 cm
Colour: Burgundy and white
Issued: 2004-2004
Series: Christmas Day

U.S.:   **Prices not**
Can.:   **available**
U.K.:   **at press time**

HN 4559 not issued.

HN 4560
The Secret
Designer: A. Maslankowski
Height: 6 ¼", 15.9 cm
Colour: White
Issued: 2004-2004
Series: Image of the Year

U.S.:   N/I
Can.:   N/I
U.K.:   £59.00

HN 4561
Hercules
Designer: A. Maslankowski
Height: 16 ¼", 41.2 cm
Colour: Light brown, brown,
           flesh tones, white,
           grey base
Issued: 2003 in a limited
           edition of 50
Series: Prestige

U.S.:   N/I
Can.:   N/I
U.K.:   **£10,000.00**

HN 4562
Mother and Daughter
Style Two
Designer: A. Maslankowski
Height: 7 ½", 19.1 cm
Colour: White
Issued: 2003 to the present
Series: Images

U.S.:   N/I
Can.:   N/I
U.K.:   **£65.00**

HN 4563
Studious Boy
Designer: A. Maslankowski
Height: 3 ¼", 8.3 cm
Colour: White
Issued: 2003 to the present
Series: Images

U.S.:   N/I
Can.:   **$130.00**
U.K.:   **£ 39.00**

HN 4564
Studious Girl
Designer: A. Maslankowski
Height: 3 ¼", 8.3 cm
Colour: White
Issued: 2003 to the present
Series: Images

U.S.:	**N/I**
Can.:	**$130.00**
U.K.:	**£ 39.00**

HN 4565
Hope
Style Three
Designer: A. Maslankowski
Height: 6", 15.2 cm
Colour: White with ermine trim
Issued: 2003-2003
Series: Holiday Collection

U.S.:	**$100.00**
Can.:	**$150.00**
U.K.:	**£ 60.00**

Exclusive to Canada

HN 4566
Matador and Bull
Style Two
Designer: A. Maslankowski
Height: 7", 17.8 cm
Colour: Black, yellow, pink and gold
Issued: 2004 in a limited edition of 250

U.S.:	**$875.00**
Can.:	**N/A**
U.K.:	**N/A**

HN 4567
Harmony
Style Three
Designer: A. Maslankowski
Height: 7 ¼", 18.4 cm
Colour: White
Issued: 2004-2004
Series: 1. Images
2. Save The Children Charity

U.S.:	**N/I**
Can.:	**N/I**
U.K.:	**£99.00**

HN 4568 - 4569 not issued.

HN 4570
Lifeboat Man
Style Two
Designer: A. Hughes
Height: 9", 22.9 cm
Colour: Yellow and brown
Issued: 2003 to the present

U.S.:	**$325.00**
Can.:	**$695.00**
U.K.:	**£185.00**

HN 4571 - 4579 not issued.

HN 4580
Irish Charm
Designer: N. Pedley
Height: 8 ½", 21.6 cm
Colour: Green and white
Issued: 2004 to the present

U.S.:	**N/I**
Can.:	**N/I**
U.K.:	**£130.00**

Exclusive to Ireland for 2004.

HN 4581
Rose
Style Three
Designer: N. Pedley
Height: 8 ¼", 21.o cm
Colour: Pale yellow, orange trim
Issued: 2004-2004
Series: M. Doulton Event

U.S.:	**$225.00**
Can.:	**N/A**
U.K.:	**£130.00**

HN 4582
Sweet Memories
Designer: N. Pedley
Height: 8 ¼", 21.0 cm
Colour: Pink
Issued: 2003 to the present

U.S.:	**$210.00**
Can.:	**N/I**
U.K.:	**£120.00**

HN 4583
Jessica
Style Four
Designer: N. Pedley
Height: 8 ½", 21.6 cm
Colour: Red and white
Issued: 2003 to the present

U.S.:	**$260.00**
Can.:	**$525.00**
U.K.:	**£150.00**

HN 4584
Andrea
Style Two
Designer; N. Pedley
Height: 8 ¼", 21.0 cm
Colour: Green
Issued: 2003 to the present

U.S.:	**$210.00**
Can.:	**N/I**
U.K.:	**£120.00**

HN 4585
Thinking of You
Style Two
Designer: N. Pedley
Height: 8 ½", 21.6 cm
Colour: Pale yellow
Issued: 2003 to the present
Series: Name Your Own

U.S.:	**$210.00**
Can.:	**$425.00**
U.K.:	**£120.00**

HN 4586
Springtime
Style Four
Designer: N. Pedley
Height: 6", 15.0 cm
Colour: Pink
Issued: 2004-2004
Series: Club Membership
Figure

U.S.:	**Membership**
Can.:	**Figure**
U.K.:	

HN 4587 - 4598 not issued.

HN 4599
Bathing Beauty
Designer: N. Pedley
Height: 7 ¼", 18.5 cm
Colour: Flesh tones, red towel
Issued: 2003 in a limited
edition of 200
Varieties: HN 4399
Series: Leslie Harradine
Tribute
Comm.by: Sinclairs

U.S.:	**N/I**
Can.:	**N/I**
U.K.:	**£100.00**

HN 4600
Brighton Belle
Designer: N. Pedley
Height: 7", 17.8 cm
Colour: Flesh tones, yellow
bathing suit
Issued: 2003 in a limited
edition of 200
Varieties: HN 4400
Series: Leslie Harradine
Tribute
Comm.by: Sinclairs

U.S.:	**N/I**
Can.:	**N/I**
U.K.:	**£100.00**

HN 4601
Summer's Darling
Designer: N. Pedley
Height: 4 ¼", 10.8 cm
Colour: Flesh tones, Purple
towel
Issued: 2003 in a limited
edition of 200
Varieties: HN 4401
Series: Leslie Harradine
Tribute
Comm.by: Sinclairs

U.S.:	**N/I**
Can.:	**N/I**
U.K.:	**£100.00**

HN 4602
Taking the Waters
Designer: N. Pedley
Height: 6 ¼", 16.0 cm
Colour: Flesh tones, black
bathing suit
Issued: 2003 in a limited
edition of 200
Varieties: HN 4402
Series: Leslie Harradine
Tribute
Comm.by: Sinclairs

U.S.:	**N/I**
Can.:	**N/I**
U.K.:	**£100.00**

HN 4603
Dawn
Style Four
Designer: N. Pedley
Height: 8 ¼", 21.0 cm
Colour: Pink and white
Issued: 2004 to the present

U.S.:	**$195.00**
Can.:	**N/A**
U.K.:	**£110.00**

HN 4604
Happy Anniversary
Style Four
Designer: N. Pedley
Height: 8 ¼", 21.0 cm
Colour: Pale blue skirt;
silver bodice; dark
blue sleeves
Issued: 2004 to the present
Varieties: HN 4605, 4606

U.S.:	**$275.00**
Can.:	**N/A**
U.K.:	**£150.00**

HN 4605
Happy Anniversary
Style Four
Designer: N. Pedley
Height: 8 ¼", 21.0 cm
Colour: Pale green skirt;
white bodice; dark
green sleeves
Issued: 2004 to the present
Varieties: HN 4604, 4606

U.S.:	**N/A**
Can.:	**N/A**
U.K.:	**£150.00**

HN 4606
Happy Anniversary
Style Four
Designer: N. Pedley
Height: 8 ¼", 21.0 cm
Colour: White dress; red
bodice; pink sleeves
Issued: 2004 to the present
Varieties: HN 4604, 4605

U.S.:	**N/A**
Can.:	**N/A**
U.K.:	**£150.00**

HN 4607
Magical Moments
Designer: N. Pedley
Height: 5 ¾", 14.6 cm
Colour: Pink
Issued: 2004 to the present

U.S.:	**Prices**
Can.:	**not available**
U.K.:	**at press time**

Exclusive to Canada.

HN 4608
Heart of Scotland
Designer: N. Pedley
Height: 8", 20.3 cm
Colour: Dark green dress;
red tartan scarf
Issued: 2004 to the present

U.S.:	**N/I**
Can.:	**N/I**
U.K.:	**£120.00**

Exclusive to Scotland for 2004.
General release 2005.
HN 4609 not issued.

HN 4610
Daybreak
Style Three
Designer: N. Welch
Height: 8 ¼", 21.0 cm
Colour: White dress
Issued: 2004 to the present

U.S.:	**N/A**
Can.:	**N/A**
U.K.:	**£110.00**

HN 4611
Moonlight
Designer: N. Welch
Height: 8 ¼", 21.0 cm
Colour: Pale blue-grey dress
Issued: 2004 to the present

U.S.:	**N/A**
Can.:	**N/A**
U.K.:	**£110.00**

HN 4612 - 4619 not issued.

HN 4620
Sophie
Style Six
Designer: J. Bromley
Height: 8 ¼", 21.0 cm
Colour: Dark blue
Issued: 2004 to the present

U.S.:	N/A
Can.:	N/A
U.K.:	£165.00

HN 4621
True Love
Designer: J. Bromley
Height: 8 ¼", 21.0 cm
Colour: Purple and gold dress,
          grey shawl
Issued: 2004 to the present

U.S.:	$295.00
Can.:	N/I
U.K.:	£165.00

HN 4622
A Winter's Morn
Designer: J. Bromley
Height: 8 ¾", 22.2 cm
Colour: White
Issued: 2004
Varieties: HN 4538
Comm.by: Compton/Woodhouse

U.S.:	N/I
Can.:	N/I
U.K.:	£99.00

HN 4623 - 4629 not issued;
HN 4630 - 4631 Animal figures;
HN 4632 - 4634 not issued

HN 4635
Bowler
Designer: T. Potts
Height: 8 ¾", 22.2 cm
Colour: White; flesh tones,
          green base
Issued: 2003 in a limited
          edition of 2,500
Comm.by: Doulton-Direct

U.S.:	N/I
Can.:	N/I
U.K.:	£150.00

Hercules HN 4561

ART IS LIFE SERIES

AIL1
Kiss
Designer: A. Maslankowski
Height: 14 ¾, 37.5 cm
Colour: White Parian
Issued: 2000 in a limited
           edition of 950
Series: Art Is Life

U.S.:	**$325.00**
Can.:	**$475.00**
U.K.:	**£200.00**

AIL2
Love
Designer: A. Maslankowski
Height: 11 ¼, 28.5 cm
Colour: White Parian
Issued: 2000 in a limited
           edition of 950
Series: Art Is Life

U.S.:	**$325.00**
Can.:	**$475.00**
U.K.:	**£200.00**

AIL6
Girl Stretching
Designer: A. Maslankowski
Height: 11 ¼", 28.5 cm
Colour: White Parian
Issued: 2000 in a limited
           edition of 2,000
Series: Art Is Life

U.S.:	**$275.00**
Can.:	**$425.00**
U.K.:	**£175.00**

AIL7
Girl With Pony Tail
Designer: A. Maslankowski
Height: 10 ¾, 27.9 cm
Colour: White Parian
Issued: 2000 in a limited
           edition of 2,000
Series: Art Is Life

U.S.:	**$275.00**
Can.:	**$425.00**
U.K.:	**£175.00**

AIL8
Girl on Rock
Designer: A. Maslankowski
Height: 9", 22.9 cm
Colour: White Parian
Issued: 2000 in a limited
           edition of 2,000
Series: Art Is Life

U.S.:	**$250.00**
Can.:	**$375.00**
U.K.:	**£150.00**

AIL9
Ballerina
Designer: A. Maslankowski
Height: 12", 30.5 cm
Colour: White Parian
Issued: 2000 in a limited
           edition of 1,250
Series: Art Is Life

U.S.:	**$325.00**
Can.:	**$475.00**
U.K.:	**£200.00**

AIL10
Ballet Dancer
Designer: A. Maslankowski
Height: 14", 35.5 cm
Colour: White Parian
Issued: 2000 in a limited
           edition of 1,250
Series: Art Is Life

U.S.:	**$325.00**
Can.:	**$475.00**
U.K.:	**£200.00**

CLASSIQUE SERIES

CL 3980
Isobel
Designer: T. Potts
Height: 10 ½", 26.7 cm
Colour: Yellow and blue
Issued: 1997-1999
Varieties: Also called 'Annabel'
CL 3981

U.S.:	**$175.00**
Can.:	**$250.00**
U.K.:	**£100.00**

CL 3981
Annabel
Designer: T. Potts
Height: 10 ½", 26.7 cm
Colour: Black and yellow
Issued: 1997-2001
Varieties: Also called 'Isobel'
CL 3980

U.S.:	**$175.00**
Can.:	**$250.00**
U.K.:	**£100.00**

CL 3982
Susanne
Designer: T. Potts
Height: 10 ½", 26.7 cm
Colour: Yellow dress and hat,
peach scarf
Issued: 1997-1998
Varieties: Also called 'Lucinda'
CL 3983

U.S.:	**$175.00**
Can.:	**$250.00**
U.K.:	**£100.00**

CL 3983
Lucinda
Designer: T. Potts
Height: 10 ½", 26.7 cm
Colour: Green skirt and hat,
beige blouse
Issued: 1997-2001
Varieties: Also called 'Susanne'
CL 3982

U.S.:	**$175.00**
Can.:	**$250.00**
U.K.:	**£100.00**

CL 3984
Faye
Designer: T. Potts
Height: 10 ½", 26.7 cm
Colour: Green flowered dress
Issued: 1997-2002
Varieties: Also called 'Stephanie'
CL 3985

U.S.:	**$175.00**
Can.:	**$250.00**
U.K.:	**£100.00**

CL 3985
Stephanie
Designer: T. Potts
Height: 10 ½", 26.7 cm
Colour: Rose pink with gold
highlights
Issued: 1997-2001
Varieties: Also called 'Faye'
CL 3984

U.S.:	**$175.00**
Can.:	**$250.00**
U.K.:	**£100.00**

CL 3986
Felicity
Designer: T. Potts
Height: 10 ½", 26.7 cm
Colour: Light brown, rose
and yellow
Issued: 1997-1999
Varieties: Also called 'Bethany'
CL 3987; CL 4103

U.S.:	**$175.00**
Can.:	**$250.00**
U.K.:	**£100.00**

CL 3987
Bethany
Designer: T. Potts
Height: 10 ½", 26.7 cm
Colour: Yellow flowered dress
Issued: 1997-1998
Varieties: Also called 'Felicity'
CL 3986; CL 4103

U.S.:	**$175.00**
Can.:	**$250.00**
U.K.:	**£100.00**

CL 3988
Penelope
Designer: T. Potts
Height: 10 ½", 26.7 cm
Colour: Pink with gold highlights
Issued: 1997-1999
Varieties: Also called 'Vanessa' CL 3989

U.S.: $175.00
Can.: $250.00
U.K.: £100.00

CL 3989
Vanessa
Designer: T. Potts
Height: 10 ½", 26.7 cm
Colour: White and brown
Issued: 1997-2001
Varieties: Also called 'Penelope' CL 3988

U.S.: $175.00
Can.: $250.00
U.K.: £100.00

CL 3990
From This Day Forth
Designer: T. Potts
Height: 10 ½", 26.7 cm
Colour: White dress
Issued: 1997-1999

U.S.: $175.00
Can.: $250.00
U.K.: £100.00

CL 3991
Christina
Designer: T. Potts
Height: 11 ¼", 28.5 cm
Colour: Pink and cream
Issued: 1998-2001
Varieties: Also called 'Theresa' CL 3992

U.S.: $175.00
Can.: $250.00
U.K.: £100.00

CL 3992
Theresa
Designer: T. Potts
Height: 11 ¼", 28.5 cm
Colour: Yellow and blue
Issued: 1998-2000
Varieties: Also called 'Christina' CL 3991

U.S.: $175.00
Can.: $250.00
U.K.: £100.00

CL 3993
Julia
Designer: T. Potts
Height: 11", 27.9 cm
Colour: Pink dress and pearls
Issued: 1998-2001
Varieties: Also called 'Chloe' CL 4017; 'Helena' CL 3994

U.S.: $175.00
Can.: $250.00
U.K.: £100.00

CL 3994
Helena
Designer: T. Potts
Height: 11", 27.9 cm
Colour: Peach lustre dress and pearls
Issued: 1998-2001
Varieties: Also called 'Chloe' CL 4017; 'Julia' CL 3993;

U.S.: $175.00
Can.: $200.00
U.K.: £100.00

CL 3995
Kate
Designer: T. Potts
Height: 11", 27.9 cm
Colour: Green and pink
Issued: 1998-2000
Varieties: Also called 'Naomi' CL 3996

U.S.: $225.00
Can.: $325.00
U.K.: £125.00

CL 3996
Naomi
Designer: T. Potts
Height: 11", 27.9 cm
Colour: Cream and pink
Issued: 1998-2001
Varieties: Also called 'Kate'
         CL 3995

U.S.:	**$225.00**
Can.:	**$325.00**
U.K.:	**£125.00**

CL 3997
Lorna
Designer: T. Potts
Height: 10 ½", 26.7 cm
Colour: Pink and brown
Issued: 1998-1999
Varieties: Also called 'Harriet'
         CL 3998

U.S.:	**$175.00**
Can.:	**$250.00**
U.K.:	**£100.00**

CL 3998
Harriet
Designer: T. Potts
Height: 10 ½", 26.7 cm
Colour: Green and brown
Issued: 1998-2001
Varieties: Also called 'Lorne'
         CL 3997

U.S.:	**$175.00**
Can.:	**$250.00**
U.K.:	**£100.00**

CL 3999
Virginia
Designer: T. Potts
Height: 10 ½", 26.7 cm
Colour: Blue dress
Issued: 1998-1999
Varieties: Also called 'Nicola'
         CL 4000

U.S.:	**$175.00**
Can.:	**$250.00**
U.K.:	**£100.00**

CL 4000
Nicola
Designer: T. Potts
Height: 10 ½", 26.7 cm
Colour: Gold dress
Issued: 1998-2000
Varieties: Also called 'Virginia'
         CL 3999

U.S.:	**$175.00**
Can.:	**$250.00**
U.K.:	**£100.00**

CL 4001
Frances
Designer: T. Potts
Height: 8 ½", 21.6 cm
Colour: Pale pink and yellow
Issued: 1998-1999
Varieties: Also called 'Eve'
         CL 4002

U.S.:	**$175.00**
Can.:	**$250.00**
Ster:	**£100.00**

CL 4002
Eve
Designer: T. Potts
Height: 8 ½", 21.6 cm
Colour: Green
Issued: 1998-2001
Varieties: Also called 'Frances'
         CL 4001

U.S.:	**$175.00**
Can.:	**$250.00**
U.K.:	**£100.00**

CL 4003
To Love and To Cherish
Designer: T. Potts
Height: 11 ½", 29.2 cm
Colour: Cream
Issued: 1999-2001

U.S.:	**$175.00**
Can.:	**$250.00**
U.K.:	**£100.00**

CL 4004
Simone
Designer: T. Potts
Height: 11 ½", 29.2 cm
Colour: Rose-pink dress;
          lemon collar; light
          and dark brown coat
Issued: 1999-2001

U.S.:   **$175.00**
Can.:   **$250.00**
U.K.:   **£100.00**

CL 4005
Bernadette
Designer: T. Potts
Height: 11", 27.9 cm
Colour: Orange flowers on
          white dress; white
          coat; light grey cuffs
          and collar
Issued: 1999-2001

U.S.:   **$225.00**
Can.:   **$325.00**
U.K.:   **£125.00**

CL 4006
Tanya
Designer: T. Potts
Height: 11", 27.9 cm
Colour: Red dress and
          shoes; white gloves
Issued: 1999-2001

U.S.:   **$175.00**
Can.:   **$250.00**
U.K.:   **£100.00**

CL 4007
Anyone For Tennis ?
Designer: T. Potts
Height: 10", 25.4 cm
Colour: White and lilac
Issued: 1999-2001

U.S.:   **$175.00**
Can.:   **$250.00**
U.K.:   **£100.00**

CL 4008
To The Fairway
Designer: T. Potts
Height: 10", 25.4 cm
Colour: Green skirt with red,
          yellow and blue
          check; yellow jumper;
          blue coat; red golf bag
Issued: 1999-2001

U.S.:   **$225.00**
Can.:   **$325.00**
U.K.:   **£125.00**

CL 4009
Elizabeth
Designer: T. Potts
Height: 10", 25.4 cm
Colour: Blue
Issued: 2000-2002

U.S.:   **$175.00**
Can.:   **$250.00**
U.K.:   **£100.00**

Serial numbered

CL 4010
Philippa
Designer: T. Potts
Height: 10", 25.4 cm
Colour: Silver grey dress;
          grey shoes; white cat
Issued: 2000-2002

U.S.:   **$175.00**
Can.:   **$250.00**
U.K.:   **£100.00**

CL 4011
Celebration
Designer: T. Potts
Height: 10", 25.4 cm
Colour: Silver and gold gown;
          white gloves
Issued: 2000-2002

U.S.:   **$175.00**
Can.:   **$250.00**
U.K.:   **£100.00**

CL 4012
Gabrielle
Designer: T. Potts
Height: 10", 25.4 cm
Colour: Mottled purple top
and scarf; peach
trousers
Issued: 2000-2001
  U.S.: **$175.00**
  Can.: **$250.00**
  U.K.: **£100.00**

CL 4013
Taking the Reins
Designer: T. Potts
Height: 11 ½", 28.5 cm
Colour: Lilic blouse with
purple bow, beige
trousers, black and
brown boots and hat
Issued: 2001-2002
  U.S.: **$175.00**
  Can.: **$250.00**
  U.K.: **£100.00**

CL 4014
At the Races
Designer: T. Potts
Height: 11 ¾", 29.8 cm
Colour: Pale pink
Issued: 2001-2002
  U.S.: **$175.00**
  Can.: **$250.00**
  U.K.: **£100.00**

CL 4016
Victoria
Designer: T. Potts
Height: 11 ¼", 28.5 cm
Colour: Blue dress with
gold trim; light
brown dogs
Issued: 2001-2002
  U.S.: **$225.00**
  Can.: **$325.00**
  U.K.: **£125.00**

CL 4017
Chloe
Designer: T. Potts
Height: 10 ¾", 27.8 cm
Colour: Black, silver, white
and grey
Issued: 2001-2002
Varieties: Also called 'Helena'
CL 3994; 'Julia'
CL 3993
Comm.by: Compton/Woodhouse
  U.S.: **$175.00**
  Can.: **$250.00**
  U.K.: **£100.00**

CL 4103
Felicity
Designer: T. Potts
Height: 10 ½", 26.7 cm
Colour: Bronze
Issued: c.2000
Varieties: CL 3986; Also called
'Bethany' CL 3987
  U.S.: **$175.00**
  Can.: **$250.00**
  U.K.: **£110.00**

M SERIES

M 1
Victorian Lady
Style Two
Designer: L. Harradine
Height: 3 ¾", 9.5 cm
Colour: Pink and green
Issued: 1932-1945
Varieties: M 2, 25

U.S.:	**$675.00**
Can.:	**$900.00**
U.K.:	**£375.00**

M 2
Victorian Lady
Style Two
Designer: L. Harradine
Height: 3 ¾", 9.5 cm
Colour: Lavender and green
Issued: 1932-1945
Varieties: M 1, 25

U.S.:	**$550.00**
Can.:	**$725.00**
U.K.:	**£300.00**

M 3
Paisley Shawl
Style Two
Designer: L. Harradine
Height: 4", 10.1 cm
Colour: Lavender
Issued: 1932-1938
Varieties: M 4, 26

U.S.:	**$625.00**
Can.:	**$850.00**
U.K.:	**£350.00**

M 4
Paisley Shawl
Style Two
Designer: L. Harradine
Height: 4", 10.1 cm
Colour: Purple and green
Issued: 1932-1945
Varieties: M 3, 26

U.S.:	**$425.00**
Can.:	**$550.00**
U.K.:	**£250.00**

M 5
Sweet Anne
Style Two
Designer: L. Harradine
Height: 4", 10.1 cm
Colour: Lavender and green
Issued: 1932-1945
Varieties: HN 6, 27

U.S.:	**$475.00**
Can.:	**$625.00**
U.K.:	**£275.00**

M 6
Sweet Anne
Style Two
Designer: L. Harradine
Height: 4", 10.1 cm
Colour: Blue
Issued: 1932-1945
Varieties: HN 5, 27

U.S.:	**$475.00**
Can.:	**$625.00**
U.K.:	**£275.00**

M 7
Patricia
Style Two
Designer: L. Harradine
Height: 4", 10.1 cm
Colour: Pink and green
Issued: 1932-1945
Varieties: HN 8, 28

U.S.:	**$625.00**
Can.:	**$850.00**
U.K.:	**£350.00**

M 8
Patricia
Style Two
Designer: L. Harradine
Height: 4", 10.1 cm
Colour: Orange and yellow
Issued: 1932-1938
Varieties: HN 7, 28

U.S.:	**$625.00**
Can.:	**$850.00**
U.K.:	**£350.00**

M 9
Chloe
Style Two
Designer: L. Harradine
Height: 2 ¾", 7.0 cm
Colour: Pink
Issued: 1932-1945
Varieties: HN 10, 29

U.S.: **$550.00**
Can.: **$725.00**
U.K.: **£325.00**

M 10
Chloe
Style Two
Designer: L. Harradine
Height: 2 ¾", 7.0 cm
Colour: Lavender
Issued: 1932-1945
Varieties: HN 9, 29

U.S.: **$550.00**
Can.: **$725.00**
U.K.: **£325.00**

M 11
Bridesmaid
Style Two
Designer: L. Harradine
Height: 3 ¾", 9.5 cm
Colour: Pink and lavender
Issued: 1932-1938
Varieties: M 12, 30

U.S.: **$600.00**
Can.: **$800.00**
U.K.: **£325.00**

M 12
Bridesmaid
Style Two
Designer: L. Harradine
Height: 3 ¾", 9.5 cm
Colour: Yellow and lavender
Issued: 1932-1945
Varieties: M 11, 30

U.S.: **$450.00**
Can.: **$600.00**
U.K.: **£275.00**

M 13
Priscilla
Style Two
Designer: L. Harradine
Height: 4", 10.1 cm
Colour: Green and yellow
Issued: 1932-1938
Varieties: M 14, 24

U.S.: **$ 750.00**
Can.: **$1,000.00**
U.K.: **£ 400.00**

M 14
Priscilla
Style Two
Designer: L. Harradine
Height: 4", 10.1 cm
Colour: Lavender and pink
Issued: 1932-1945
Varieties: M 13, 24

U.S.: **$ 750.00**
Can.: **$1,000.00**
U.K.: **£ 400.00**

M 15
Pantalettes
Style Two
Designer: L. Harradine
Height: 3 ¾", 9.5 cm
Colour: Lavender
Issued: 1932-1945
Varieties: M 16, 31

U.S.: **$625.00**
Can.: **$850.00**
U.K.: **£350.00**

M 16
Pantalettes
Style Two
Designer: L. Harradine
Height: 3 ¾", 9.5 cm
Colour: Pink
Issued: 1932-1945
Varieties: M 15, 31

U.S.: **$625.00**
Can.: **$850.00**
U.K.: **£350.00**

M 17
Shepherd
Style Two
Designer: Unknown
Height: 3 ¾", 9.5 cm
Colour: Purple, pink
         and green
Issued: 1932-1938
Varieties: HN 709, M 19

U.S.: **$3,500.00**
Can.: **$4,500.00**
U.K.: **£2,000.00**

M 18
Shepherdess
Style One
Designer: Unknown
Height: 3 ½", 8.9 cm
Colour: Green and lavender
Issued: 1932-1938
Varieties: HN 708, M 20

U.S.: **$3,500.00**
Can.: **$4,500.00**
U.K.: **£2,000.00**

M 19
Shepherd
Style Two
Designer: Unknown
Height: 3 ¾", 9.5 cm
Colour: Purple, green
         and brown
Issued: 1932-1938
Varieties: HN 709, M 17

U.S.: **$3,500.00**
Can.: **$4,500.00**
U.K.: **£2,000.00**

M 20
Shepherdess
Style One
Designer: Unknown
Height: 3 ¾", 9.5 cm
Colour: Yellow
Issued: 1932-1938
Varieties: HN 708, M 18

U.S.: **$3,500.00**
Can.: **$4,500.00**
U.K.: **£2,000.00**

M 21
Polly Peachum
Style Three
Designer: L. Harradine
Height: 2 ¼", 5.7 cm
Colour: Pink
Issued: 1932-1945
Varieties: HN 698, 699, 757,
         758, 759, 760, 761,
         762, M 22, 23

U.S.: **$ 850.00**
Can.: **$1,100.00**
U.K.: **£ 450.00**

M 22
Polly Peachum
Style Three
Designer: L. Harradine
Height: 2 ¼", 5.7 cm
Colour: Red and blue
Issued: 1932-1938
Varieties: HN 698, 699, 757,
         758, 759, 760, 761,
         762, M 21, 23

U.S.: **$1,500.00**
Can.: **$2,000.00**
U.K.: **£ 850.00**

M 23
Polly Peachum
Style Three
Designer: L. Harradine
Height: 2 ¼", 5.7 cm
Colour: Purple, pink
         and white
Issued: 1932-1938
Varieties: HN 698, 699, 757,
         758, 759, 760, 761,
         762, M 21, 22

U.S.: **$1,500.00**
Can.: **$2,000.00**
U.K.: **£ 850.00**

M 24
Priscilla
Style Two
Designer: L. Harradine
Height: 3 ¾", 9.5 cm
Colour: Red
Issued: 1932-1945
Varieties: M 13, 14

U.S.: **$600.00**
Can.: **$775.00**
U.K.: **£325.00**

M 25
Victorian Lady
Style Two
Designer: L. Harradine
Height: 3 ¾", 9.5 cm
Colour: Lavender and pink
Issued: 1932-1945
Varieties: M 1, 2

U.S.:	**$600.00**
Can.:	**$775.00**
U.K.:	**£325.00**

M 26
Paisley Shawl
Style Two
Designer: L. Harradine
Height: 3 ¾", 9.5 cm
Colour: Green
Issued: 1932-1945
Varieties: M 3, 4

U.S.:	**$625.00**
Can.:	**$800.00**
U.K.:	**£350.00**

M 27
Sweet Anne
Style Two
Designer: L. Harradine
Height: 4", 10.1 cm
Colour: Red, blue and yellow
Issued: 1932-1945
Varieties: M 5, 6

U.S.:	**$600.00**
Can.:	**$775.00**
U.K.:	**£325.00**

M 28
Patricia
Style Two
Designer: L. Harradine
Height: 4", 10.1 cm
Colour: Lavender
Issued: 1932-1945
Varieties: M 7, 8

U.S.:	**$625.00**
Can.:	**$800.00**
U.K.:	**£350.00**

M 29
Chloe
Style Two
Designer: L. Harradine
Height: 2 ¾", 7.0 cm
Colour: Pink and yellow
Issued: 1932-1945
Varieties: M 9, 10

U.S.:	**$650.00**
Can.:	**$875.00**
U.K.:	**£350.00**

M 30
Bridesmaid
Style Two
Designer: L. Harradine
Height: 3 ¾", 9.5 cm
Colour: Pink and lavender
Issued: 1932-1945
Varieties: M 11, 12

U.S.:	**$600.00**
Can.:	**$775.00**
U.K.:	**£325.00**

M 31
Pantalettes
Style Two
Designer: L. Harradine
Height: 4", 10.1 cm
Colour: Green and blue
Issued: 1932-1945
Varieties: M 15, 16

U.S.:	**$725.00**
Can.:	**$950.00**
U.K.:	**£400.00**

M 32
Rosamund
Style Three
Designer: L. Harradine
Height: 4 ¼", 10.8 cm
Colour: Yellow
Issued: 1932-1945
Varieties: M 33

U.S.:	**$1,200.00**
Can.:	**$1,500.00**
U.K.:	**£ 675.00**

M 33
Rosamund
Style Three
Designer: L. Harradine
Height: 4", 10.1 cm
Colour: Red
Issued: 1932-1945
Varieties: M 32

U.S.:	**$1,100.00**
Can.:	**$1,500.00**
U.K.:	**£ 600.00**

M 34
Denise
Style One
Designer: L. Harradine
Height: 4 ½", 11.4 cm
Colour: Green, red and blue
Issued: 1933-1945
Varieties: M 35

U.S.:	**$1,350.00**
Can.:	**$1,750.00**
U.K.:	**£ 700.00**

M 35
Denise
Style One
Designer: L. Harradine
Height: 4 ½", 11.4 cm
Colour: Blue and pink
Issued: 1933-1945
Varieties: M 34

U.S.:	**$1,500.00**
Can.:	**$2,000.00**
U.K.:	**£ 850.00**

M 36
Norma
Designer: L. Harradine
Height: 4 ½", 11.4 cm
Colour: Red and green
Issued: 1933-1945
Varieties: M 37

U.S.:	**$1,400.00**
Can.:	**$1,750.00**
U.K.:	**£ 750.00**

M 37
Norma
Designer: L. Harradine
Height: 4 ½", 11.4 cm
Colour: Blue, red
           and white
Issued: 1933-1945
Varieties: M 36

U.S.:	**$1,600.00**
Can.:	**$2,000.00**
U.K.:	**£ 900.00**

M 38
Robin
Designer: L. Harradine
Height: 2 ½", 6.4 cm
Colour: Pink and lavender
Issued: 1933-1945
Varieties: M 39

U.S.:	**$ 875.00**
Can.:	**$1,150.00**
U.K.:	**£ 500.00**

M 39
Robin
Designer: L. Harradine
Height: 2 ½", 6.4 cm
Colour: Blue and green
Issued: 1933-1945
Varieties: M 38

U.S.:	**$ 875.00**
Can.:	**$1,150.00**
U.K.:	**£ 500.00**

M 40
Erminie
Designer: L. Harradine
Height: 4", 10.1 cm
Colour: White and pink
Issued: 1933-1945

U.S.:	**$1,100.00**
Can.:	**$1,500.00**
U.K.:	**£ 625.00**

M 41
Mr. Pickwick
Style One
Designer: L. Harradine
Height: 4", 10.1 cm
Colour: Yellow and black
Issued: 1932-1983
Varieties: HN 529
Series: Dickens (Series One)

U.S.:	**$100.00**
Can.:	**$150.00**
U.K.:	**£ 65.00**

■

M 42
Mr. Micawber
Style One
Designer: L. Harradine
Height: 4", 10.1 cm
Colour: Yellow and black
Issued: 1932-1983
Varieties: HN 532
Series: Dickens (Series One)

U.S.:	**$100.00**
Can.:	**$150.00**
U.K.:	**£ 65.00**

Prices are based on bone china
bodies for Dickens (Series One).

M 43
Pecksniff
Style One
Designer: L. Harradine
Height: 4 ¼", 10.8 cm
Colour: Black
Issued: 1932-1982
Varieties: HN 535
Series: Dickens (Series One)

U.S.:	**$100.00**
Can.:	**$150.00**
U.K.:	**£ 65.00**

M 44
Fat Boy
Style One
Designer: L. Harradine
Height: 4 ¼", 10.8 cm
Colour: Blue and white
Issued: 1932-1983
Varieties: HN 530
Series: Dickens (Series One)

U.S.:	**$100.00**
Can.:	**$150.00**
U.K.:	**£ 65.00**

M 45
Uriah Heep
Style One
Designer: L. Harradine
Height: 4", 10.1 cm
Colour: Black
Issued: 1932-1983
Varieties: HN 545
Series: Dickens (Series One)

U.S.:	**$100.00**
Can.:	**$150.00**
U.K.:	**£ 65.00**

M 46
Sairey Gamp
Style One
Designer: L. Harradine
Height: 4", 10.1 cm
Colour: Green
Issued: 1932-1983
Varieties: HN 533
Series: Dickens (Series One)

U.S.:	**$100.00**
Can.:	**$150.00**
U.K.:	**£ 65.00**

M 47
Tony Weller
Style Two
Designer: L. Harradine
Height: 4", 10.1 cm
Colour: Green, black,
         red and yellow
Issued: 1932-1981
Varieties: HN 544
Series: Dickens (Series One)

U.S.:	**$100.00**
Can.:	**$150.00**
U.K.:	**£ 65.00**

M 48
Sam Weller
Designer: L. Harradine
Height: 4", 10.1 cm
Colour: Yellow and
         brown
Issued: 1932-1981
Varieties: HN 531
Series: Dickens (Series One)

U.S.:	**$100.00**
Can.:	**$150.00**
U.K.:	**£ 65.00**

M 49
Fagin
Style One
Designer: L. Harradine
Height: 4", 10.1 cm
Colour: Brown
Issued: 1932-1983
Varieties: HN 534
Series: Dickens (Series One)
  U.S.:   **$100.00**
  Can.:   **$150.00**
  U.K.:   **£ 65.00**

M 50
Stiggins
Designer: L. Harradine
Height: 4", 10.1 cm
Colour: Black
Issued: 1932-1981
Varieties: HN 536
Series: Dickens (Series One)
  U.S.:   **$100.00**
  Can.:   **$150.00**
  U.K.:   **£ 65.00**

M 51
Little Nell
Designer: L. Harradine
Height: 4 ¼", 10.8 cm
Colour: Pink
Issued: 1932-1983
Varieties: HN 540
Series: Dickens (Series One)
  U.S.:   **$100.00**
  Can.:   **$150.00**
  U.K.:   **£ 65.00**

M 52
Alfred Jingle
Designer: L. Harradine
Height: 3 ¾", 9.5 cm
Colour: Black and white
Issued: 1932-1981
Varieties: HN 541
Series: Dickens (Series One)
  U.S.:   **$100.00**
  Can.:   **$150.00**
  U.K.:   **£ 65.00**

M 53
Buz Fuz
Designer: L. Harradine
Height: 4", 10.1 cm
Colour: Black and red
Issued: 1932-1983
Varieties: HN 538
Series: Dickens (Series One)
  U.S.:   **$100.00**
  Can.:   **$150.00**
  U.K.:   **£ 65.00**

M 54
Bill Sykes
Designer: L. Harradine
Height: 4 ¼", 10.8 cm
Colour: Black and brown
Issued: 1932-1981
Varieties: HN 537
Series: Dickens (Series One)
  U.S.:   **$100.00**
  Can.:   **$150.00**
  U.K.:   **£ 65.00**

M 55
Artful Dodger
Designer: L. Harradine
Height: 4 ¼", 10.8 cm
Colour: Black and brown
Issued: 1932-1983
Varieties: HN 546
Series: Dickens (Series One)
  U.S.:   **$100.00**
  Can.:   **$150.00**
  U.K.:   **£ 65.00**

M 56
Tiny Tim
Designer: L. Harradine
Height: 3 ¾", 9.5 cm
Colour: Black and brown
Issued: 1932-1983
Varieties: HN 539
Series: Dickens (Series One)
  U.S.:   **$100.00**
  Can.:   **$150.00**
  U.K.:   **£ 65.00**

*

M 64
Veronica
Style Two
Designer: L. Harradine
Height: 4 ½", 10.8 cm
Colour: Pink
Issued: 1934-1949
Varieties: M 70

U.S.:	$1,100.00
Can.:	$1,500.00
U.K.:	£ 600.00

M 65
June
Style Two
Designer: L. Harradine
Height: 4 ¼", 10.8 cm
Colour: Pink and lavender
Issued: 1935-1949
Varieties: M 71

U.S.:	$1,000.00
Can.:	$1,500.00
U.K.:	£ 600.00

M 66
Monica
Style Two
Designer: L. Harradine
Height: 3", 7.6 cm
Colour: Blue and pink
Issued: 1935-1949
Varieties: M 72

U.S.:	$1,200.00
Can.:	$1,600.00
U.K.:	£ 675.00

M 67
Dainty May
Style Two
Designer: L. Harradine
Height: 4", 10.1 cm
Colour: Turquoise and pink
Issued: 1935-1949
Varieties: M 73

U.S.:	$1,200.00
Can.:	$1,600.00
U.K.:	£ 675.00

M 68
Mirabel
Style Two
Designer: L. Harradine
Height: 4", 10.1 cm
Colour: Pink and green
Issued: 1936-1949
Varieties: M 74

U.S.:	$1,000.00
Can.:	$1,500.00
U.K.:	£ 600.00

M 69
Janet
Style Two
Designer: L. Harradine
Height: 4", 10.1 cm
Colour: Blue and white
Issued: 1936-1949
Varieties: M 75

U.S.:	$ 900.00
Can.:	$1,250.00
U.K.:	£ 450.00

M 70
Veronica
Style Two
Designer: L. Harradine
Height: 4 ¼", 10.8 cm
Colour: Green
Issued: 1936-1949
Varieties: M 64

U.S.:	$1,400.00
Can.:	$1,850.00
U.K.:	£ 775.00

M 71
June
Style Two
Designer: L. Harradine
Height: 4 ¼", 10.8 cm
Colour: Lavender and green
Issued: 1936-1949
Varieties: M 65

U.S.:	$1,350.00
Can.:	$1,750.00
U.K.:	£ 725.00

M 72
Monica
Style Two
Designer: L. Harradine
Height: 3", 7.6 cm
Colour: Blue and white
Issued: 1936-1949
Varieties: M 66

U.S.: $1,400.00
Can.: $1,800.00
U.K.: £ 775.00

M 73
Dainty May
Style Two
Designer: L. Harradine
Height: 4", 10.1 cm
Colour: Pink and turquoise
Issued: 1936-1949
Varieties: M 67

U.S.: $1,400.00
Can.: $1,800.00
U.K.: £ 775.00

M 74
Mirabel
Style Two
Designer: L. Harradine
Height: 4", 10.1 cm
Colour: Turquoise and red
Issued: 1936-1949
Varieties: M 68

U.S.: $1,200.00
Can.: $1,600.00
U.K.: £ 650.00

M 75
Janet
Style Two
Designer: L. Harradine
Height: 4", 10.1 cm
Colour: Purple
Issued: 1936-1949
Varieties: M 69

U.S.: $1,000.00
Can.: $1,500.00
U.K.: £ 600.00

M 76
Bumble
Designer: L. Harradine
Height: 4", 10.1 cm
Colour: Green and red
Issued: 1939-1982
Series: Dickens (Series One)

U.S.: $100.00
Can.: $150.00
U.K.: £ 65.00

M 77
Captain Cuttle
Designer: L. Harradine
Height: 4", 10.1 cm
Colour: Yellow and black
Issued: 1939-1982
Series: Dickens (Series One)

U.S.: $100.00
Can.: $150.00
U.K.: £ 65.00

M 78
Windflower
Style Three
Designer: L. Harradine
Height: 4", 10.1 cm
Colour: Red and pink
Issued: 1939-1949
Varieties: M 79

U.S.: $1,400.00
Can.: $2,000.00
U.K.: £ 750.00

M 79
Windflower
Style Three
Designer: L. Harradine
Height: 4", 10.1 cm
Colour: Blue and green
Issued: 1939-1949
Varieties: M 78

U.S.: $1,400.00
Can.: $2,000.00
U.K.: £ 750.00

M 80
Goody Two Shoes
Style Two
Designer: L. Harradine
Height: 4", 10.1 cm
Colour: Pink and blue
Issued: 1939-1949
Varieties: M 81

U.S.:	**$1,350.00**
Can.:	**$1,750.00**
U.K.:	**£ 800.00**

M 81
Goody Two Shoes
Style Two
Designer: L. Harradine
Height: 4", 10.1 cm
Colour: Lavender and pink
Issued: 1939-1949
Varieties: M 80

U.S.:	**$1,350.00**
Can.:	**$1,750.00**
U.K.:	**£ 800.00**

M 82
Bo-Peep
Style Three
Designer: L. Harradine
Height: 4", 10.1 cm
Colour: Pink
Issued: 1939-1949
Varieties: M 83

U.S.:	**$1,500.00**
Can.:	**$2,000.00**
U.K.:	**£ 750.00**

M 83
Bo-Peep
Style Three
Designer: L. Harradine
Height: 4", 10.1 cm
Colour: Purple
Issued: 1939-1949
Varieties: M 82

U.S.:	**$1,500.00**
Can.:	**$2,000.00**
U.K.:	**£ 750.00**

M 84
Maureen
Style Two
Designer: L. Harradine
Height: 4", 10.1 cm
Colour: Pink
Issued: 1939-1949
Varieties: M 85

U.S.:	**$1,350.00**
Can.:	**$1,750.00**
U.K.:	**£ 750.00**

M 85
Maureen
Style Two
Designer: L. Harradine
Height: 4", 10.1 cm
Colour: Purple
Issued: 1939-1949
Varieties: M 84

U.S.:	**$1,350.00**
Can.:	**$1,750.00**
U.K.:	**£ 750.00**

M 86
Mrs. Bardell
Designer: L. Harradine
Height: 4 ¼", 10.8 cm
Colour: Green
Issued: 1949-1982
Series: Dickens (Series One)

U.S.:	**$100.00**
Can.:	**$150.00**
U.K.:	**£ 65.00**

M 87
Scrooge
Designer: L. Harradine
Height: 4", 10.1 cm
Colour: Brown
Issued: 1949-1982
Series: Dickens (Series One)

U.S.:	**$100.00**
Can.:	**$150.00**
U.K.:	**£ 65.00**

M 88
David Copperfield
Designer: L. Harradine
Height: 4 ¼", 10.8 cm
Colour: Black and tan
Issued: 1949-1983
Series: Dickens (Series One)

U.S.:	**$100.00**
Can.:	**$150.00**
U.K.:	**£ 65.00**

M 89
Oliver Twist
Designer: L. Harradine
Height: 4 ¼", 10.8 cm
Colour: Black and tan
Issued: 1949-1983
Series: Dickens (Series One)

U.S.:	**$100.00**
Can.:	**$150.00**
U.K.:	**£ 65.00**

M 90
Dick Swiveller
Designer: L. Harradine
Height: 4 ¼", 10.8 cm
Colour: Black and tan
Issued: 1949-1981
Series: Dickens (Series One)

U.S.:	**$100.00**
Can.:	**$150.00**
U.K.:	**£ 65.00**

M 91
Trotty Veck
Designer: L. Harradine
Height: 4 ¼", 10.8 cm
Colour: Black and brown
Issued: 1949-1982
Series: Dickens (Series One)

U.S.:	**$100.00**
Can.:	**$150.00**
U.K.:	**£ 65.00**

M 200
Christine
Style Eight
Designer: M. Davies
Remodeller: Unknown
Height: 2", 5.0 cm
Colour: White, pink, pale blue
             and yelllow
Issued: 2004 to the present
Series: Miniatures

U.S.:	**N/I**
Can.:	**N/I**
U.K.:	**£15.00**

M 201
Elaine
Style Three
Designer: M. Davies
Remodeller: Unknown
Height: 2", 5.0 cm
Colour: Blue and white
Issued: 2004 to the present
Series: Miniatures

U.S.:	**N/I**
Can.:	**N/I**
U.K.:	**£15.00**

M 202
Elizabeth
Style Four
Designer: B. Franks
Remodeller: Unknown
Height: 2", 5.0 cm
Colour: White, yellow and
             green
Issued: 2004 to the present
Series: Miniatures

U.S.:	**N/I**
Can.:	**N/I**
U.K.:	**£15.00**

M 203
Jane
Style Six
Designer: D. V. Tootles
Remodeller: Unknown
Height: 2", 5.0 cm
Colour: Blue-green, blue,
             white and yellow
Issued: 2004 to the present
Series: Miniatures

U.S.:	**N/I**
Can.:	**N/I**
U.K.:	**£15.00**

M 204
Karen
Style Four
Designer: M. Davies
Remodeller: Unknown
Height: 2", 5.0 cm
Colour: Red, white and black
Issued: 2004 to the present
Series: Miniatures

U.S.:	N/I
Can.:	N/I
U.K.:	£15.00

M 205
Margaret
Style Four
Designer: M. Davies
Remodeller: Unknown
Height: 2", 5.0 cm
Colour: White dress; pale
                     blue sash
Issued: 2004 to the present
Series: Miniatures

U.S.:	N/I
Can.:	N/I
U.K.:	£15.00

M 206
Ninette
Style Three
Designer: M. Davies
Remodeller: Unknown
Height: 2", 5.0 cm
Colour: Yellow dress; white
                     ruffles; pink shading
Issued: 2004 to the present
Series: Miniatures

U.S.:	N/I
Can.:	N/I
U.K.:	£15.00

M 207
Rachel
Style Three
Designer: P. Gee
Remodeller: Unknown
Height: 2", 5.0 cm
Colour: Red cloak with white
                     trim; pale lemon dress
Issued: 2004 to the present
Series: Miniatures

U.S.:	N/I
Can.:	N/I
U.K.:	£15.00

M 208
Susan
Style Six
Designer: P. Parsons
Remodeller: Unknown
Height: 2", 5.0 cm
Colour: White, pink and black
Issued: 2004 to the present
Series: Miniatures

U.S.:	N/I
Can.:	N/I
U.K.:	£15.00

M 209
Victoria
Style Three
Designer: M. Davies
Remodeller: Unknown
Height: 2", 5.0 cm
Colour: Red, pink and white
Issued: 2004 to the present
Series: Miniatures

U.S.:	N/I
Can.:	N/I
U.K.:	£15.00

Matador and Bull, Style Two HN 4566

COLLECTING BY TYPE OR SERIES

SWEET AND TWENTIES

Deauville	HN 2344
Monte Carlo	HN 2332

TEENAGERS

Columbine (Style Two)	HN 2185
Faraway	HN 2133
Harlequin (Style One)	HN 2186
Melody (Style One)	HN 2202
Sea Sprite (Style Two)	HN 2191
Sweet Sixteen (Style One)	HN 2231
Teenager	HN 2203
Wood Nymph	HN 2192

TUDOR ROSES

Lady Jane Grey	HN 3680
Margaret Tudor	HN 3838
Mary Tudor	HN 3834
Princess Elizabeth	HN 3682

VANITY FAIR CHILDREN

Amanda	HN 2996, 3406, 3632
Andrea	HN 3058
Birthday Girl	HN 3423
Buddies (Style Two)	HN 3396
Catherine (Style Two)	HN 3044
Daddy's Girl	HN 3435
Dinnertime	HN 3726
Helen (Style Two)	HN 2994
Julie (Style One)	HN 2995
Kerry	HN 3036
Let's Play	HN 3397
Lynsey	HN 3043
My First Pet	HN 3122
Reward	HN 3391
Sit	HN 3123, 3430

VANITY FAIR LADIES

Angela (Style Two)	HN 2389
Ann (Style One)	HN 2739
Anna (Style Two)	HN 4095
Anna (Style Three)	HN 4391
Ashley	HN 3420
Barbara (Style Four)	HN 4116
Barbara (Style Two)	HN 2962
Brenda	HN 4115
Carol	HN 2961
Danielle (Style Two)	HN 3001
Dawn (Style Three)	HN 3600
Denise (Style Three)	HN 2477
Donna	HN 2939
Emily (Style One)	HN 3204
Flower of Love	HN 2460
Gift of Love	HN 3427
Good Companion	HN 3608
Grace (Style Two)	HN 3699
Heather	HN 2956
Jayne	HN 4524
Jean (Style Two)	HN 2710
Jessica (Style One)	HN 3169
Joanne (Style One)	HN 2373
Josephine	HN 4223
Just For You	HN 3355
Kathleen (Style Three)	HN 3609
Katrina (Style Two)	HN 4467
Kimberley (Style Two)	HN 3379
Kirsten	HN 4101
Linda (Style Two)	HN 2758
Margaret (Style Two)	HN 2397
Maria	HN 3381
Margaret (Style Three)	HN 4311
Mary (Style One)	HN 2374
Maureen (Style Three)	HN 2481
Megan (Style One)	HN 3306
Megan (Style Two)	HN 3887
Mother and Child (Style One)	HN 3353
Nancy	HN 2955
Natalie (Style One)	HN 3173
Pamela (Style Two)	HN 2479
Patricia (Style Three)	HN 2715

Paula	HN 3234
Samantha (Style One)	HN 2954
Susannah	HN 4221
Suzanne (Style One)	HN 4098
Tender Moment	HN 3303
Tracy	HN 2736
Veronica (Style Four)	HN 3205
Yours Forever	HN 3354

VICTORIAN AND EDWARDIAN ACTRESSES

Ellen Terry	HN 3826
Lillie Langtry	HN 3820
Sarah Bernhardt	HN 4023

VISITOR CENTRE

Anna of the Five Towns	HN 3865
Arnold Bennett	HN 4360
Clara Hamps	HN 4162
Countess of Chell	HN 3867
Kimberley (Style Two)	HN 3864
Sally (Style Two)	HN 4160
Sarah (Style Two)	HN 3857
Sophia Baines	HN 4167
Special Gift	HN 4129
Sweet Delight	HN 4398
With All My Love	HN 4241

WILDFLOWER OF THE MONTH

January (Style Three)	HN 3341
February (Style Three)	HN 3342
March (Style Three)	HN 3343
April (Style Three)	HN 3344
May (Style Four)	HN 3345
June (Style Six)	HN 3346
July (Style Three)	HN 3347
August (Style Three)	HN 3408
September (Style Three)	HN 3409
October (Style Three)	HN 3410
November (Style Three)	HN 3411
December (Style Three)	HN 3412

ALPHABETICAL INDEX

U

V

W

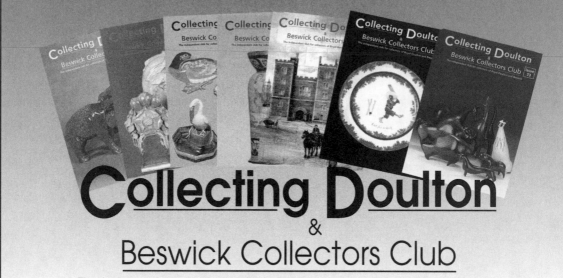

Collecting Doulton

&

Beswick Collectors Club

The independent magazine for collectors of Royal Doulton and Beswick

If you are a collector of Doulton or Beswick you cannot afford to be without this lively, authoritative and completely independent publication.

If you are a previous subscriber to Collecting Doulton, you may not know how much the magazine has improved over the past few months.

Published six times a year, Collecting Doulton contains articles by leading experts on the wide range of Doulton and Beswick ceramics, including:

- Latest auction results
- Your questions answered
- Collectors' profiles
- Free wants and for sale small ads
- Histories of artists, designers and wares
- Events diary
- News from around the world
- Book reviews

Amongst the subjects regularly covered are Lambeth wares, seriesware, figurines, character jugs, Bunnykins, Burslem wares, Doulton and Beswick animals, commemorative wares, advertising wares, new discoveries, rarities, Beatrix Potter etc etc... *Subscribe today*

Website: www.collectingdoulton.com • Email: barryjhill@hotmail.com

-------------------------- *Please photocopy and mail* -------------------------

I wish to subscribe to Collecting Doulton magazine.
I enclose my cheque made out to Collecting Doulton Marketing for £21(UK) or £36 (overseas) for six issues.
Please start my subscription from issue No............/the current issue.
Mr/Mrs/Miss/Ms/Dr   First Name..
Surname ....
Address..
....Town ....
Country ....Postcode ....
email ....
Please send to: Collecting Doulton Marketing, PO Box 310, Richmond, Surrey TW10 7FU England

485

LOUIS TAYLOR
FINE ART AUCTIONEERS & VALUERS

EST 1877

Four Major Doulton-Beswick Auctions in 2004:

- March 8th and 9th
- June 14th and 15th
- September 8th and 9th
- December 13th and 14th

Competitive Comission Rates

Negligée, HN 1228
Sold June 2003 for £3600

Windmills Lady, HN 1400
Sold Dec. 2000 for £5200

LOUIS TAYLOR
FINE ART AUCTIONEERS & VALUERS

Tel: 01782 214111
Fax: 01782 215283

Britannia House, 10 Town Road, Hanley, Stoke-on Trent, Staffordshire, England, ST1 2QG

We Buy & Sell:

✧ **FIGURINES**   ✧ **BUNNYKINS**
✧ **CHARACTER JUGS**   ✧ **BEATRIX POTTER**

STAMPS 'N' STUFF™

8190 Hickman Road, Des Moines
IA, USA 50325•4405

Tel: 515•331•4307 • Fax: 515•331•4957
US & Canada: 800•999•5964

E-mail: jbkoepp@msn.com
www.stampsnstuff.com

WRITE FOR A FREE PRICE LIST

486

'Rabbitting On'

BUNNYKINS NEWSLETTER
~by Leah Selig~

A quarterly publication on Bunnykins information & up-to-date details about Bunnykins Figurines, China Paraphernalia

Subscription Rate for one year
Australia $22.00 U.K. £10.00
U.S.A. & Canada $20.00 U.S. funds

ELEVENTH SERIES BEGINS ON THE 1ST OF AUGUST 2003

'Rabbitting On'
2 Harper Street
Marrylands 2160
New South Wales, Australia
Overseas Phone/Fax: 612 9 637 2410
Australia Phone/Fax: 02 9 637 2410
email: rabbittingon@yahoo.com.au

search4doulton.com
Royal Doulton, Beswick & Royal Crown Derby

Thousands of visitors to date
• Private & Trade Sales •
• Dealer Listings •
• Free Message Board •

Buying current production figurines or character jugs?

Let us quote you for your next purchase. Worldwide delivery from the UK. Visit our website for more information or telephone us with your enquiry if you prefer.

Within the UK **0117-904-9994**
From outside the UK **+44-117-904-9994**

www.search4doulton.com

Precious Memories

Fine China, Gifts & Collectibles Inc.
World's Number One Royal Doulton Website
www.doultonfigurines.com

Figurines • Jugs • Tableware
Discontinued, Current, Prestige, Flambé and Limited Edition Figurines

**Royal Doulton • Lladró • Coalport
Wedgwood • Royal Worcester • Snowman
Bunnykins • Brambly Hedge • Beatrix Potter
Royal Crown Derby • Beswick
Dept. 56 • Harmony Kingdom**

❖ Insurance Replacement Service ❖
❖ Guaranteed Safe Delivery Service Worldwide ❖
❖ If requested, free gift wrapping ❖

We also buy Royal Doulton and collectibles, pay the best price • No collection too big or too small

Visit our showroom
89 Trans-Canada Highway, Charlottetown, PEI C1E 1E8 Canada • 1633 Mountain Road, Moncton, NB E1G 1A5 Canada
Phone: 902-368-1212; 506-388-1112; 1-800-463-5200 • Fax: 902-368-7321
email: sales@doultonfigurines.com

BESWICK QUARTERLY

The Newsletter for Beswick Collectors by Beswick Collectors

Featuring photographs (including a colour cover photo), columns, articles, up-to-date information on the whole Beswick range, and For Sale and Wanted ads.
Mailed on or about the first of February, May, August and November

For subscription and advertising rates check out our website
http://members.tripod.com/~BeswickQuarterly/
email: beswickquarterly@yahoo.com

Phone: (631) 589-9027 in U.S.A.
Beswick Quarterly
Laura J. Rock-Smith
Dept. BQCP
10 Holmes Court
Sayville, NY 11782-2408 U.S.A.

the site of the green

R.R. #1 Dundas, Ontario, L9H 5E1
(Highway #5, $^1/_2$ mile east of Peter's Corner)

Specializing in Royal Doulton Discontinued Figurines & Character Jugs

Visit our website at
www.siteofthegreen.com

Order by phone, mail, fax or online

1-800-263-4730
(toll free in US & Canada)
Phone: (905) 627-1304
Fax: (905) 627-0511
email: sales@siteofthegreen.com

Join our mailing list to receive monthly newsletter & Royal Doulton Quarterly lists

MARNALEA ANTIQUES

The ROYAL DOULTON Figurine Specialist
Serving Collectors since 1974

Discontinued Figurines • Jugs • Bunnykins
Animals • Beatrix Potter • Series Ware
Flambé • Royal Crown Derby • Worcester

Mailing list available • Full Inventory List On-line:
Web site: www.marnalea.com • email: doulton@marnalea.com

51 Main Street North, Box 152, Campbellville
Ontario, Canada L0P 1B0
Toll Free: 1-866-885-9024
Tel: (905) 854-0287 Fax: (905) 854-3117

488

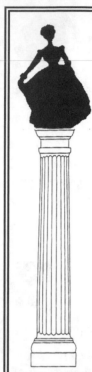

Pirie's Fine Gifts

We buy and sell fine collectibles

❖ **Royal Doulton**
❖ **Royal Crown Derby**
❖ **Beswick**
❖ **Beatrix Potter**
❖ **Brambly Hedge**
❖ **Hummel/Goebel**
❖ **Coalport**
❖ **Waterford**

Tel.: (905) 332-9801
Website: www.bvx.ca/pirie/
email: pirie@spectranet.ca
Burlington, Ontario
Canada

My Daughters' Doultons

Authorized Dealer for Royal Doulton
M. I. Hummel & Melody in Motion

**WE SPECIALIZE IN DISCONTINUED FIGURINES
& INSURANCE REPLACEMENTS**
Worldwide Mail Order Service
Gift Certificates Available

Enquiries: 519-456-5544
Store: 519-485-2101 or 1-877-MDDOULT
(toll-free in Canada & USA)
Fax: 519-485-2103 or 1-866-485-2103
(toll-free in Canada & USA)

Web: www.mddoultons.on.ca
Email: mddoultons@mddoultons.on.ca
(store open by appointment, Mon-Sat)
583546 Hamilton Rd., Ingersoll, ON N5C 3J7 Canada

Colonial House of Collectibles

ROYAL DOULTON IS OUR SPECIALTY!
WE BUY • WE SELL • WE APPRAISE

Colonial House Features the Largest Selection of Current and Discontinued Items in Old and New Royal Doulton

Colonial House of Collectibles
182 Front Street
Berea, OH 44017
Tel.: (440) 826-4169 or
(800) 344-9299
Fax: (440) 826-0839
Web Site: www.e-colonialhouse.com
email: yworrey@aol.com

Mail Order is our Business...

Monday to Saturday
10 am to 5 pm
or by appointment

➙ ADVERTISING WARE
➙ BOYER
➙ ANIMALS
➙ BEATRIX POTTER
➙ BESWICK
➙ BRAMBLY HEDGE
➙ BUNNYKINS
➙ CHARACTER & TOBY JUGS
➙ FLAMBÉ
➙ FIGURINES
➙ MINTON
➙ ROYAL CROWN DERBY
➙ SERIES WARE
➙ STONEWARE
SEND US YOUR WANTS

Dorothy's Doultons
&
Collectables

Specializing in current and discontinued
Royal Doulton figurines, toby and character jugs
Royal Doulton and Beswick Animals, Beatrix Potter
Brambly Hedge, Bunnykins, Hummel
Lladro, Nao, Paragon, Coalport and Royal Crown Derby

Come visit us in our new store location at:

2374 Main Street
Box 87, Lambeth Station
London, Ontario N6P 1P9

Wednesday to Saturday
10:00am to 5:00pm
or by appointment

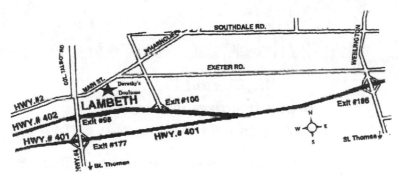

Tel.: (519) 652-8444 • **Fax:** (519) 652-8411
Toll Free: 1-888-652-8367
email: dorothy@dorothysdoultons.ca

Visit us on the web:
www.dorothysdoultons.ca

490

BUYING & SELLING

Royal Doulton Figurines

*Royal
Doulton
Figurines
Character Jugs
Toby Jugs
Animals*

*Discontinued
& Current*

*Discontinued
Beswick
Figurines & Animals*

*Retired
Swarovski
Silver Crystal
Annuals & Figures*

**We fill want lists
Dealer inquiries welcomed
Call us and let s make a deal!**

For the past eleven years Marcus & Company has been travelling across Canada buying collections from St. Johns to Victoria. If you are looking to sell - we are looking to buy. We are Canadas leading buyer of Royal Doulton Figurines. We buy entire collections or inventories, both current and discontinued, regardless of size.

Marcus & Company Estate Buyers Inc.

**#6-1131 Gorham Street, Newmarket, Ontario, Canada L3Y 5G9
• By Appointment Only •
Tel: (905)895-5005 • Fax: (905)895-2585
Toll Free: 1-800-689-7308 • email: marcusandco@rogers.com**

THE
ROYAL DOULTON
COMPANY

INTERNATIONAL COLLECTORS CLUB

If you do not *belong* you cannot *receive*:

✧ Your Choice of a Fully Coloured Figure: Springtime (HN4586) or Ankhesenamun (DB295)
✧ Exclusive Offers Available only to Members
✧ The *Gallery* Magazine Issued Quarterly for Royal Doulton Collectors
✧ Free Historical Enquiry Service
✧ Free Admission to the Visitor Centre with your Membership Card

Springtime
HN4586
Complimentary gift

Ankhesenamun
DB295
Complimentary gift

JOIN THE CLUB

2004 ANNUAL MEMBERSHIP
You may visit a shop opposite
or our website at: www.royaldoulton.com

Royal Doulton Shops

ROYAL DOULTON SHOPS – CANADA

Calgary
Market Mall
C2 - 3625 Shaganappi Trail
NW, Calgary, AB
T3A 0E2

Cookstown
Cookstown Manufactures
Outlet, RR1, Cookstown,
ON L0L 1L0

Dartmouth
Micmac Mall, 21 Micmac
Dartmouth, NS B3A 4K7

Edmonton
West Edmonton Mall
8882 - 170th Street
Edmonton, AB T5T 3J7

Fredericton
Regent Mall
1381 Regent Street,
Fredericton, NB E3C 1A2

London
White Oaks Mall
1105 Wellington Road
London, ON N6E 1V4

Markham
Markville Shopping Centre
5000 Highway #7
Markham, ON
L3R 4M9

Pickering
Pickering Town Centre
1355 Kingston Road
Pickering, ON L1V 1B8

Surrey
Guildford Town Centre
Surrey, BC V3R 7C1

Toronto
Fairview Mall
1800 Sheppard Avenue East
Willowdale, ON M2J 5A7

Waterloo
St. Jacobs Factory Outlet
Mall, 25 Benjamin Road
Waterloo, ON N2V 2G8

Winnipeg
Polo Park Shopping Centre
1485 Portage Ave.
Winnipeg, MA R3G 0W4

ROYAL DOULTON SHOPS – UNITED STATES

Birch Run
Prime Outlets - Birch Run
12240 S. Beyer Rd., Suite E80
Birch Run, MI 48415

Burlington
Prime Outlets – Burlington
288 Fashion Way, Store #5
Burlington, WA 98233

Cabazon
Dester Hills Premium Outlets
48650 Seminole Dr.
Building C, Suite 152
Cabazon, CA 92230

Calhoun
Prime Outlets - Colhoun
455 Belwood Rd., Suite 20
Calhoun, GA 30701

Camarillo
Camarillo Premium Outlets
740 Ventura Blvd., Suite 530
Camarillo, CA 93010

Central Valley
Woodbury Common
Premium Outlets
161 Marigold Court
Central Valley, NY 10917

Conroe
Prime Outlets – Conroe
1111 League Line Rd.
Suite 112
Conroe, TX 77303

Dawsonville
North Georgia
Premium Outlets
800 Highway 400
Suite 250
Dawsonville, GA 30534

Ellenton
Gulf Coast Factory Stores
5501 Factory Shops Blvd.
Ellenton Fl 34222

Estero
Miromar Outlets
10801 Corkscrew Rd.
Suite 366, Estero, Fl
33928

Flemington
Liberty Village
Premium Outlets
34 Liberty Village
Flemington, NJ
08822

Gilroy
Premium Outlets – Gilroy
681 Leavesley Road
Suite B290, Gilroy CA 95020

Grove City
Prime Outlets at Grove City
1911 Leesburg-Grove City Rd.
Suite 210, P.O. Box 1014
Grove City, PA 16127

Jeffersonville
Ohio Factory Shops
8150 Factory Shops Blvd.
Jeffersonville, OH 43128

Kittery
Kittery Outlet Center
Route 1
Kittery, ME 03904-2505

Las Vegas
Belz Factory Outlet World
7400 Las Vegas Blvd. South
Suite 244
Las Vegas, NV 89123

Pigeon Forge
Belz Factory Outlet
2655 Teaster Lane, Suite 26
Pigeon Forge, TN 37683

Prince William
Potomac Mills
2700 Potomac Mills Circle
Suite 976
Prince William, VA
22192

San Marcos
Tanger Factory Outlet Centre
4015 Interstate 35 South
Suite 402
San Marcos, TX
78666

St. Augustine
Belz Factory Outlet World
500 Belz Outlet Blvd
Suite 80
St. Augustine, Fl 32084

Tannersville
The Crossings Outlet Center
1000 Rte 611, Suite A-23
Tannersville, PA 18372

Vacaville
Factory Stores at Vacaville
336 Nut Tree Rd.
Vacaville CA
95687

ROYAL DOULTON | Visit our website at:
www.royaldoulton.com

Royal Doulton Shops

FACTORY SHOPS AND OUTLETS IN UK

Bridgend
Factory Outlet, Unit 66
Welsh Designer Outlet Village
Bridgend Shropshire
CF32 9SU

Burslem
Factory Shop, Nile Street
Burslem, Stoke-on-Trent
Staffordshire, ST6 2AJ

Colne
Factory Outlet
Boundary Mill Stores
Burnley Road
Colne, Lancashire
BB8 8LS

Dover
Factory Outlet, De Bradelei Wharf
Cambridge Road, Dover, Kent
CT17 9BY

Ellesmere Port
Factory Outlet, Unit 106
Cheshire Oaks, Kinsey Road
Ellesmere Port, Cheshire
L65 9LA

Fenton
Factory Shop
Distribution Centre
Victoria Road, Fenton
Stoke-on-Trent, Staffordshire
ST4 2PJ

Longton
Factory Shop, Regent Works
Lawley Street, Longton
Stoke-on-Trent, Staffordshire
ST3 1LZ

Stoke
Doulton & Company Outlet
Forge Lane, Etruria
Stoke-on-Trent, Staffordshire
ST1 5NN

Stourbridge
Factory Shop, Crystal Glass Centre
Churton House, Audnam
Stourbridge, West Midlands
DY8 4AJ

STORES IN UK

Blackpool
Lawleys, Unit 37
Houndshill Shopping Centre
Fylde, Blackpool, Lancashire
FY1 4HU

Carlisle
Lawleys
63 Castle Street, Carlisle
Cumbria, CA3 8SL

Chelmsford
Lawleys, 42 High Chelmer
Chelmsford, Essex
CM1 1XU

Derby
Lawleys
Edwards, 71 St. Peters Street
Derby, Derbyshire, DE1 2AB

Dudley
Doulton & Company, Unit 52
Merry Hill, Brierley Hill, Dudley
West Midlands, DY5 1SR

Eastbourne
Lawleys
220 Terminus Road
Eastbourne, East Sussex
BN21 3DF

Hereford
Lawleys, 19-21 Maylords Street
Maylord Shopping Centre
Hereford, Herefordshire
HR1 2DS

Peterborough
Lawleys, 7 Bridge Street
Peterborough, Cambridgeshire
PE1 1HJ

Reading
Lawleys
21 Queen Victoria Street
Reading, Berkshire, RG1 1SY

ROYAL DOULTON | Visit our website at:
www.royaldoulton.com

494

Potteries Specialist Auctions

271 Waterloo Road, Cobridge, Stoke-on-Trent, ST6 3HR, England
Tel.: 01782 286 622 • Fax: 01782 201 518

HN1348
Sunshine Girl
Realized
£7200

- The UK's leading provincial Auction House specialising in Royal Doulton, Beswick and 20th Century British Pottery.
- We hold many world record prices in our salesroom for Royal Doulton and Beswick collectables
- We require single items to complete collections
- Excellent commission rates on request
- Free collection of large quantities of lots
- Fast payout and Fully insured
- Free verbal and email estimates
- Why not take advantage of our services

Interested in Selling?

- ◆ Our auctions are fully catalogued and illustrated
- ◆ On line catalogues are available on our website
- ◆ We ship worldwide
- ◆ Contact Martyn Bullock for further enquiries at enquiries@potteriesauctions.com

www.potteriesauctions.com

Open Monday - Saturday, 9am - 5.30pm

•Royal Doulton Character and Pretty Ladies Figurines are on display plus a huge selection of Bunnykins, Storybook, Flambé and Series Ware items.

• Over fifty display cabinets filled with Royal Doulton, Beswick, Moorcroft, Wedgwood, Minton, Wade, Coalport, Royal Worcester, Charlotte Rhead, Clarice Cliff, Carltonware, Paragon, Pendelfin, Royal Crown Derby and lots more...

• Figurines, Animals, Birds, Vases, Character & Toby Jugs, Limited and Special Editions, Rare and Discontinued.

**271 Waterloo Road
Cobridge
Stoke-on-Trent
Staffordshire
England
ST6 3HR
Tel.: 01782 201 455
Fax: 01782 201 518
email: sales@potteriesantiquecentre.com
website: www.potteriesantiquecentre.com**

Over 8,000 items to purchase today on our website!

www.potteriesantiquecentre.com

Specialists in Worldwide Mail Order

Computer "Wants" Service for that hard to find piece

We purchase single items and complete collections

Open Monday - Saturday 9am - 5:30pm

496

www.seawaychina.com

Seaway China

The Figurine Specialists

We carry a complete line of current and discontinued Royal Doulton figures and specialize in locating rare pieces.

Call for your FREE Color Catalog!

International: (305) 668-7765
Toll Free: (800) 968-2424
Toll Free Fax: (800) 968-9005

866-DOULTON

*Contact us TOLL-FREE
24 hours a day!*

We Ship Worldwide

We buy Royal Doulton

Seaway China — A Whitley Collection Company
7340 SW 48th Street, Suite 105, Miami, FL 33155

WHITLEY

COLLECTION

SPECIALIZING IN UNIQUE AND UNUSUAL ROYAL DOULTON

An extensive collection of Figures,
Character and Toby Jugs, Storybook Figures,
Animals, Series Ware, Flambé, Kingsware
and one-of-a-kind items.

WE BUY ROYAL DOULTON

Gregg Whittecar and Arron Rimpley
Experts in Royal Doulton

We Ship Worldwide

7340 SW 48th Street, Suite 105, Miami, FL 33155
Phone: (305) 668-5858   Fax: (305) 668-7980

Toll Free: (888)562-4463

E-mail: info@whitleycollection.com   Website: www.whitleycollection.com

PASCOE AND COMPANY

World's largest Royal Doulton specialist

Collectible Royal Doulton Figurines always in stock

HN 3232, Anne Boleyn

HN 3350, King Henry VIII

HN 3233, Catherine of Aragon

We also buy Royal Doulton and pay *the highest* prices

Shop online at
www.pascoeandcompany.com
Check out our upcoming shows

PASCOE AND COMPAN

575 SW 22nd Avenue, Miami, FL 33

Tel.: (305) 643-2550 Fax: (305) 643-

E-mail: sales@pascoeandcompany.

Call for details (In US and Canada

1-800-872-0195